ATHENS

the collected traveler

ΕΛΛΑΣ Λ. 10

Also in the series by Barrie Kerper

CENTRAL ITALY

The Collected Traveler

PARIS

The Collected Traveler

PROVENCE

The Collected Traveler

MOROCCO

The Collected Traveler

VENICE

The Collected Traveler

NORTHERN SPAIN

The Collected Traveler

SOUTHWEST FRANCE

The Collected Traveler

ATHENS

the collected traveler

Selected by Barrie Kerper
New York

First Edition

Library of Congress Cataloging-in-Publication Data is available upon request

ISBN 1-4000-5005-7

Design by Lynne Amft

Cover photos: Adam Crowley/Photodisc/Getty Images; Michael Storrings/Photodisc/Getty Images (border)

Because many of the essays that appear in this book were originally published some years ago, prices, hours, and contact information may have changed, and Fodor's cannot accept responsibility for facts that are outdated or for inadvertent errors or omissions. So always confirm information when it matters, especially if you're making a detour to visit a specific place.

Special Sales

This book is available for special discounts for bulk purchases for sales promotions or premiums. Special editions, including personalized covers, excerpts of existing books, and corporate imprints, can be created in large quantities for special needs. For more information, write to Special Markets/Premium Sales, 1745 Broadway, MD 6-2, New York, New York 10019, or e-mail specialmarkets@randomhouse.com. Inquiries for Canada should be directed to your local Canadian bookseller or sent to Random House of Canada, Ltd., Marketing Department, 2775 Matheson Boulevard East, Mississauga, Ontario L4W 4P7. Inquiries from the United Kingdom should be sent to Fodor's Travel Publications, 20 Vauxhall Bridge Road, London SW1V 2SA, England.

PRINTED IN THE UNITED STATES OF AMERICA

10 9 8 7 6 5 4 3 2 1

dedication

Once again, for my mother, Phyllis, who always believed my boxes of files held something of value, and who still cherishes the trip she took to Greece with my dear father, Peter. Though they missed the first day of their guided tour (they overslept and didn't wake up until the afternoon of the following day), they nonetheless were awed by the sight of the Acropolis and thoroughly succumbed to the Greek way of life.

The author (right) with friends at Katikies on Santorini.

acknowledgments

I extend an enormous thank you to my editor, Paul Eisenberg, who I suspect never imagined this book would prove to be so challenging and whose patience for the finer points of Nescafé, *raki,* and *kouloures* was severely tried. His ability to edit succinctly but sensitively was, and is, greatly appreciated. Additionally, a Herculean effort was made by other talented colleagues in the extended Fodor's family, including Stacy Berenbaum, Karen Cure, Nina Freeman, Denise DeGennaro, Fabrizio LaRocca, Jean McCall, David Naggar, Linda Schmidt, Bob Shields, Andrew Stanley, Rong Qian, and Katie Ziga. I am extremely grateful for the assistance of two hardworking and smart interns, Alexia Christodoulides and Rachel Goldman, who willingly researched and verified hundreds of facts and figures, identified potential sales channels for all the books in *The Collected Traveler* series, and approached every assignment with the kind of enthusiasm that will earn them well deserved respect in their future endeavors. *Efharisto* to Amalia Cosmetatou at the Alexander S. Onassis Public Benefit Foundation USA, Grace Firogenis and Fay Georgousis at the Greek National Tourist Office in New York, and to Matt Barrett, George Kokkotos, and the staff of the St. George Lycabettus hotel. Sincere thanks to each of the individual writers, agents, and permissions representatives for various publishers and periodicals without whose cooperation there would be nothing to publish. Special thanks to travelers and friends Wendy Lamb, Arlene Lasagna, and Amy Myer, my fellow members of the Katikies Fan Club. I am deeply grateful to Chip Gibson, my wonderful boss who has all the best qualities of a Greek god. Finally, thanks to my husband, Jeffrey, and our daughter, Alyssa, who was, after all, given a Greek name ("logical one").

contents

The Peloponnese

The Greek Table

Good Things, Favorite Places

Introduction

"A traveler without knowledge is a bird without wings."
—Sa'di, *Gulistan* (1258)

Some years ago my husband and I fulfilled a dream we'd had since we first met: we put all our belongings in storage and traveled around the countries bordering the Mediterranean Sea for a year. In preparation for this journey, I did what I always do in advance of a trip, which is to consult my home archives, a library of books and periodicals. I have been an obsessive clipper since I was very young, and by the time I was preparing for this extended journey, I had amassed an enormous number of articles from periodicals on various countries of the world. After a year of reading and organizing all this material, I then created a package of articles and notes for each destination and mailed them ahead to friends we'd be staying with as well as appropriate American Express offices—although we had no schedule to speak of, we knew we would spend no fewer than six weeks in each place.

My husband wasted no time informing me that my research efforts were perhaps a bit over the top. He shares my passion for travel (my mother-in-law told me that when he was little he would announce to the family exactly how many months, weeks, days, hours, minutes, and seconds it was before the annual summer vacation) but not necessarily for clipping (he has accused me of being too much like the anal-retentive fisherman in an old *Saturday Night*

Live skit, the one where the guy neatly puts his bait, extra line, snacks, hand towels, et cetera, into individual sandwich bags. In my defense, I'm not quite that bad (although I am guilty of trying to improve upon pocket organizers, and I do have a wooden rack for drying rinsed plastic bags in my kitchen).

While we were traveling that year, we would occasionally meet other Americans, and I was continually amazed at how ill prepared some of them were. Information, in so many different forms, is in such abundance in the twenty-first century that it was nearly inconceivable to me that people had not taken advantage of the resources available to them. Some didn't even seem to be having a very good time; they appeared to be ignorant of various customs and observances and were generally unimpressed with their experiences because they had missed the significance of what they were seeing and doing. Therefore I was surprised again when some of these same people—and they were of varying ages with varying wallet sizes—were genuinely interested in my little packages of notes and articles. Some even offered to pay me for them, and I began to think that my collected research would perhaps appeal to other travelers. I also began to realize that my packages were of interest not only to people like me—who enjoy reading and planning for a trip—but also to those who have done little or no planning, as well as to the most well-intentioned people who are overwhelmed by the details of organizing a trip or haven't had the time to put it all together. Later, friends and colleagues told me they really appreciated the packages I prepared for them, and somewhere along the line I was being referred to as a "modern-day hunter-gatherer," a sort of "one-stop information source." Each book in *The Collected Traveler* provides resources and information to travelers—people I define as inquisitive, individualistic, and indefatigable in their eagerness to explore—or informs them of where they may look further to find it.

While there is much to be said for a freewheeling approach to travel—I am not an advocate of sticking to rigid schedules—I do believe that, as with most things in life, what you get out of a trip is equal only to what you put into it. James Pope-Hennessy, in his wonderful book *Aspects of Provence*, notes that "if one is to get best value out of places visited, some skeletal knowledge of their history is necessary. . . . Sight-seeing is by no means the only object of a journey, but it is as unintelligent as it is lazy not to equip ourselves to understand the sights we see." Distinguished military historian Stephen Ambrose, before his passing in 2002, reminded us in his last work, entitled *To America*, that "it is through history that we learn who we are and how we got that way, why and how we changed, why the good sometimes prevailed and sometimes did not." He also noted that "the last five letters of the word 'history' tell us that it is an account of the past that is about people and what they did, which is what makes it the most fascinating of subjects." I feel that learning about a place is part of the excitement of travel, and I wouldn't dream of venturing anywhere without first poring over a mountain of maps, books, and periodicals. I include cookbooks in my reading (some cookbooks reveal much historical detail as well as prepare you for the food and drink you will most likely encounter), and I also like to watch movies before I leave that have something to do with where I'm going. Additionally, I buy a blank journal and begin filling it with all sorts of notes, reminders, and entire passages from books I'm not bringing along. In other words, I completely immerse myself in my destination before I leave. It's the most enjoyable homework assignment I could ever give myself.

Every destination, new or familiar, merits some attention. I don't endorse the extreme—you don't want to spend all your time in the hotel room reading books—but it most definitely pays to know before you go. Even if you've traveled to southern Greece before, for pleasure, you still have to do some planning to get there;

and if you've traveled there on business, you have to keep up with what's happening in the cities and towns where you meet clients. So the way I see it, you might as well read and learn a little more. The reward for your efforts is that you'll acquire a deeper understanding and appreciation of the place and the people who live there, and not surprisingly, you'll have more fun.

"Every land has its own special rhythm, and unless the traveler takes the time to learn the rhythm, he or she will remain an outsider there always."
—Juliette de Bairacli Levy, English writer

Occasionally I meet people who are more interested in how many countries I've visited than in those I might know well or particularly like. If *well-traveled* is defined only by the number of places one has been, then I suppose I'm not. But I feel I *really know* and have *really seen* the places I've visited, which is how *I* define *well-traveled*. I travel to see how people live in other parts of the world—not to check countries off a list—and doing that requires immediately adapting to the local pace and rhythm and (hopefully) sticking around for more than a few days. Certainly any place you decide is worthy of your time and effort is worthy of more than a day, but you don't always need an indefinite period of time to immerse yourself in the local culture or establish a routine that allows for getting to know the merchants and residents of your adopted neighborhood. Alain de Botton, in *The Art of Travel*, notes that John Ruskin, from an early age, "was unusually alive to the smallest features of the visual world." Ruskin was apparently distressed by how seldom people noticed the small details of everyday life. "He deplored the blindness and haste of modern tourists, especially those who prided themselves on covering Europe in a week by train (a service first offered by Thomas Cook in 1862): 'No changing of place at a hundred miles an hour will make us one whit stronger, happier, or wiser. There was always more in the world than men could see, walked they ever so slowly; they will see it no better for going fast. The really precious things are thought and sight, not pace."

One of the fastest ways to adjust to daily life in Greece, wherever you are, is to abandon whatever schedule you observe at home and eat when the Greeks eat. Mealtimes in Greece are generally well established, even if it isn't always obvious to foreigners what those times are. I'll address eating hours in more detail in the *Practical Information* section, but generally speaking, if you have not bought provisions for a picnic or found a place to eat by two o'clock, you will find many restaurants full (or the day's specials completely finished) and shops closed. Likewise, dinner is not typically served at 6, an hour that is entirely too early for anyone in a Mediterranean country to contemplate eating a meal. Adjust your schedule and you'll be on Greek time, doing things when the Greeks do them, eliminating possible disappointment and frustration. I personally prefer this Mediterranean timetable—I grew up in a family that ate dinner later—and I believe that a big meal in the middle of the day, in combination with an evening stroll, is healthier than one at the end of the day. I find nowadays that when my husband and I receive an invitation for dinner for an hour before 8:00 P.M., I am crestfallen, and the date looms ahead like a dreaded task. I would add here that it is rewarding to rise rather early. Vacation travelers who like to sleep late may not want to roll out of bed a bit earlier, but if you sleep in every day, you will most definitely miss much of the local rhythm. By 10:00 A.M. in Greece—and in any Mediterranean country—much has already happened, and besides, you can always look forward to a delicious afternoon nap. "This early morning animation," Lawrence Durrell noted in *The Greek Islands,* "is somehow the tempo at which Greece lives; you rise each morning to a new day, a new world, which has to be created from scratch. Each day is a brilliant improvisation with full orchestra—the light on the sea, the foliage, the stabbing cypresses, the silver spindrift olives."

About fifteen years ago the former Paris bureau chief for *The New York Times*, John Vinocur, wrote a piece for the travel section entitled "Discovering the Hidden Paris." The French, he noted, have a word, *dépaysement*, that is not easily translated into English but that he translated as "the feeling of not being assaulted by the familiarity of things, a change in surroundings where there is no immediate point of reference." He went on to quote a French journalist who once said that "Americans don't travel to be *dépaysés*, but to find a home away from home." This is unfortunate but too often true. These tourists can travel around the world if they desire, but their unwillingness to adapt ensures they will never really leave home. I am of like mind with Paul Bowles, who noted in *Their Heads Are Green, Their Hands Are Blue*, "Each time I go to a place I have not seen before, I hope it will be as different as possible from the places I already know. I assume it is natural for a traveler to seek diversity, and that it is the human element which makes him most aware of difference. If people and their manner of living were alike everywhere, there would not be much point in moving from one place to another."

Similar to the *dépaysés*-phobic are those who endorse "adventure travel," words that make me cringe as they seem to imply that unless one partakes of kayaking, mountain climbing, biking, rock climbing, or some other physical endeavor, a travel experience is somehow invalid or unadventurous. *All* travel is an adventure, and unless "adventure travel" allows one plenty of time to adapt to the local rhythm, the so-called adventure is really just a physically strenuous—if memorable—outdoor achievement. Occasionally I hear a description of a biking excursion, for example, in which the participants spent the majority of each day the same way: making biking the priority instead of working biking into the local cadence of daily life. When I ask if they joined the locals for a morning Nescafé or an evening ouzo, shopped at the outdoor market, or people-watched in a village square, the answer is invariably no. They may have had an amazing bike trip, but they did not get to know Greece—one has to get off the bike a bit more often for that sort of knowledge—and if a biking experience alone was what they were seeking, they certainly didn't need to fly to Greece: there are plenty of challenging and beautiful places to bike in North America.

I believe that every place in the world offers *something* of interest. In her magnificent book *Black Lamb, Grey Falcon*, Rebecca West recounted how in the 1930s she passed through Skopje (now in the Former Yugoslav Republic of Macedonia) by train twice, without stopping, because friends had told her the town wasn't worth visiting. A third time through she did stop, and she met two wonderful people who became lasting friends. "Now, when I go through a town of which I know nothing," she wrote, "a town which appears to be a wasteland of uniform streets wholly without quality, I look on it in wonder and hope, since it may hold a Mehmed, a Militsa." I too have been richly rewarded by pausing in places (Skopje included) that at first appeared quite limiting. While the world today truly is more accessible than in the past—and therefore feels smaller—I do not believe it is more homogenous. Those who think Europe, or Greece, isn't exotic enough are simply mistaken. Perhaps it's been a while since they were there; perhaps they've never been at all. Things *are* different in Greece, as Durrell noted: "The nagging question, 'In what way does Greece differ from Italy or Spain?' will answer itself. The light! One hears the word everywhere *'to phos'* and can recognize its pedigree—among other derivatives is our English word 'phosphorescent,' which summons up at once the dancing magnesium-flare quality of the sunlight blazing on a white wall."

"Travel is fatal to prejudice, bigotry, and narrow-mindedness."

—Mark Twain

"The world is a book, and those who do not travel read only a page."

—Saint Augustine

I am assuming that, if you've read this far, something has compelled you to pick up this book, and that you feel travel is an essential part of life. I would add to Mark Twain's quote one by Benjamin Disraeli (1804–81): "Travel teaches toleration." People who travel with an open mind and are receptive to the ways of others cannot help but return with more tolerance for people and situations at home, at work, and in their cities and communities. James Ferguson, a nineteenth-century Scottish architect, observed this perfectly when he wrote, "Travel is more than a visitor seeing sights; it is the profound changing—the deep and permanent changing—of that visitor's perspective of the world, and of his own place in it." I find that travel also ensures I will not be quite the same person I was before I left. After a trip I typically have a lot of renewed energy and bring new perspectives to my job. At home I ask myself how I can incorporate attributes or traits I observed into my own life and share them with my husband and daughter. I am eager to explore my own hometown more fully (when was the last time you visited your local historical society, or the best-known tourist site in your part of the country?), and in appreciation of the great kindnesses shown to me by people from other nations, I always go out of my way to help tourists who are visiting New York City by giving directions, explaining the subway, or sharing the name of a favorite museum or place to eat.

The anthologies in the *Collected Traveler* series offer a record of people's achievements and shortcomings. It may be a lofty goal to expect that they might also offer an opportunity for us to measure our own deeds and flaws as Americans, and realize that despite cultural differences between us and our hosts—in *any* country where we happen to be guests—we have much more in common than not. It is a sincere goal, however, one that I hope readers and travelers will embrace. Bruce Northam, author of a wonderful little book, *Globetrotter Dogma,* perhaps puts it best of all: "Remember, we are all one. Find out for yourself what a miraculous world we live in, contrary to media portrayals . . . as the global village shrinks, we become increasingly aware of our interdependence. Because we all play a part, however small, in the interlocking of cultures, our new objectives should include having firsthand interactions with the staggering beauty and diversity of our planet."

About This Series

The *Collected Traveler* editions are not guidebooks in the traditional sense, but they are books that guide readers to other sources: each edition is really the first book you should turn to when planning a trip. If you think of the individual volumes as a sort of planning package, you've got the right idea. If you enjoy acquiring knowledge about where you're going—whether you plan to travel independently or with a like-minded tour organization—this series is for you. If you're looking for a guide that simply informs you of exact prices, hours, and highlights, you probably won't be interested in the depth this book offers. (That is not meant to offend, merely to say you've got the wrong book.)

A few words about me may also help you determine if this series is for you. I travel somewhat frugally, less out of necessity than because I choose to. I respect money and its value, and I'm not convinced that spending $600 a night on a hotel room, for example, would represent a good value or would make for a better trip. I've been to some of the world's finest hotels, mostly to visit friends who are staying there or to have a drink in the hotel bar. With a few notable exceptions, the majority of these places seem to me all alike, conforming to a code of sameness and predictability. Nothing about them is particularly Greek, French, Moroccan, Italian, Spanish, or Turkish—you could be *anywhere*. The cheapest of the cheap accommodations don't represent good value, either. I look for places to stay that are usually old, possibly historic, with lots of charm and character. I do not mind if my room is small; I do not necessarily need a television, telephone, or hair dryer; and I most definitely do not care for an American-style buffet breakfast, which is hardly what the locals eat. I also prefer to make my own plans, send my own letters and faxes, place telephone calls, and arrange transportation. It's not that I think I can do it better than a professional agent (whose expertise I admire); rather, I enjoy it and learn a lot in the process. Finally, lest you think I do not appreciate elegance, I think you'll quickly ascertain that I do indeed enjoy many of life's little luxuries, when I perceive them to be of good value to me.

This series promotes the practice of staying longer within a smaller area. Susan Allen Toth refers to this approach in one of her many wonderful books, *England as You Like It*, in which she subscribes to the "thumbprint theory of travel": she spends at least a week in one spot no larger than her thumbprint covers on a large-scale map of England. Excursions are encouraged, she explains, as long as they're about an hour's drive away. As I have discovered in my own travels, a week in one place, even a spot no bigger than my thumbprint, is rarely long enough to see and enjoy it all.

The Collected Traveler focuses on one corner of the world, the countries bordering the Mediterranean Sea. I find the Mediterranean endlessly fascinating: the sea itself is the world's largest, the region is one of the world's ancient crossroads, and as it stretches from Asia to the Atlantic, it is one of the most culturally diverse regions on the planet. As Paul Theroux noted in his excellent book, *The Pillars of Hercules,* "The Mediterranean, this simple almost tideless sea, the size of thirty Lake Superiors, had everything: prosperity, poverty, tourism, terrorism, several wars in progress, ethnic strife, fascists, pollution, drift nets, private islands owned by billionaires, Gypsies, seventeen countries, fifty languages, oil drilling platforms, sponge fishermen, religious fanatics, drug smuggling, fine art, and warfare. It had Christians, Muslims, Jews; it had the Druzes, who are a strange farrago of all three religions; it had heathens, Zoroastrians and Copts and Baha'is."

The great explorers in the service of Spain and Portugal departed from Mediterranean ports to discover much of the rest of the world, as Carlos Fuentes has noted in *his* excellent book, *The Buried Mirror:* "The facts remained that the Mare Nostrum, the Mediterranean, had been to all effects and purposes an Islamic lake for nearly eight hundred years, and that European expansion was severely hindered by such mastery. To find a way out, a way around, a way toward the Orient became a European obsession. It began in the Venetian republic, with Marco Polo's opening of overland trade routes to China. But soon the rise of a new Muslim power, the Ottoman Empire, once more threatened the Mediterranean; the Ottomans captured Greece and the Balkans and forced Europe and its rising merchant class to look elsewhere." And look elsewhere they did: Prince Henry of Portugal, who became known as Henry the Navigator, arranged the sailing expeditions to Madeira, the Azores, Senegal, and the Cape of Good Hope, and Vasco da Gama added India to these ports of call. "This sea," writes Lisa Lovatt-Smith in *Mediterranean Living,* "whose shores have hosted the main currents in civilization, creates its own homogenous culture, endlessly absorbing newcomers and their ideas . . . and is the one I consider my own." I too consider this sea my own, even though I live thousands of miles away from it. Plenty of other travelers obviously feel the same way, as Nancy Harmon Jenkins confirms in *The*

Essential Mediterranean: "The Mediterranean is the Number One tourist destination in the world. In some especially popular coastal environments, like much of the Mediterranean Spain, along with Aegean Turkey and many of the Greek islands, local populations quadruple during July and August."

With the exception of my *Morocco* edition, this series focuses on individual cities and regions rather than on entire countries, as readers who are not new to *The Collected Traveler* already know. While this book covers southern Greece, I am mindful that all corners of Greece are members of three communities—European, Balkan, and Mediterranean. I have tried to reflect this wider sense of community throughout the book, especially in the bibliography in the *Kiosque—Points of View* section. When I first contemplated an edition on Greece, I was most attentive to the very wise words of writer Patrick Leigh Fermor: "All of Greece is absorbing and rewarding. There is hardly a rock or a stream without a battle or a myth, a miracle or a peasant anecdote or a superstition; and talk and incident, nearly all of it odd or memorable, thicken round the traveller's path at every step." Therefore, I knew I would have to divide the nation into two parts. When I mentioned to this to a young woman who was helping me at the Greek National Tourist Organization office in New York, she looked dismayed. Pointing to a large map of Greece that hung on the wall, she tried to dissuade me from doing so, intently explaining that to serve the country properly, four books would be necessary. Hers is a European view, and it is one I share; but I also know that North Americans do not travel the same way Europeans do, and it is doubtful I would ever be able to convince my editor that a book devoted exclusively to the Peloponnese and another focusing solely on the Aegean Islands would fare well in the marketplace. Greece is somewhat deceiving: it's a big country, and getting around always takes longer than you predict. It's also different enough from north to south to warrant two individual editions. On my first visit I traveled from north to south but stayed for ten weeks. This particular thumbprint is a bit bigger than I traditionally promote, but it can manageably be seen in one trip (though it would, of course, be ideal if one allowed about three weeks). And you certainly won't receive a demerit from me if you head west of Athens to Delphi, one of the most spiritual and beautiful spots I've ever visited.

Each section of this book contains a selection of articles from various periodicals and an annotated bibliography relevant to its theme. The articles and books were chosen from my own files and home library, which I've maintained for over two decades. (I often feel I am the living embodiment of a comment that Samuel Johnson made in 1775, that "a man will turn over half a library to make one book.") The selected writings reflect the culture, politics, history, current social issues, religion, cuisine, and arts of the people you'll be visiting. They also represent the observations and opinions of a wide variety of novelists, travel writers, and journalists. These writers are typically authorities on Greece, or a particular part of Greece, or both; they either live there (as permanent or part-time residents) or visit there often, for business or pleasure. I've included numerous older articles (even though some of the specific information regarding prices, hours, and the like is no longer accurate) because they were particularly well written, thought-provoking, or unique in some way, and because the authors' views stand as a valuable record of a certain time in history. Often, even with the passage of many years, you may share the same emotions and opinions of the writer, and equally as often, *plus ça change, plus c'est la même chose*. I have many, many more articles in my files than I am able to reprint here. Though there are a few pieces whose absence I very much regret, I believe the anthology you're holding is very good.

A word about the food and restaurant section, *The Greek Table*: I have great respect for restaurant reviewers, and though their work may seem glamorous—it sometimes is—it is also very hard. It's an all-consuming, full-time job, and that is why I urge you to consult the very good cookbooks listed in the bibliography, as well as guidebooks. Restaurant (and hotel) reviewers are, for the most part, professionals who have dined in hundreds of eating establishments (and spent hundreds of nights in hotels). They are far more capable of assessing the qualities and flaws of a place than I am. I have selected a few articles that give you a feel for eating out in this part of Greece, alert you to some things to look for in selecting a truly worthwhile place versus a mediocre one, and highlight dishes that are not commonplace in North America.

The annotated bibliographies in this book represent my favorite aspect of this series. One reason I do not include excerpts from books is that I am not convinced an excerpt will always lead a reader to the book in question, and I think good books deserve to be read in their entirety. Art critic John Russell wrote an essay in 1962 entitled "Pleasure in Reading," in which he stated, "Not for us today's selections, readers, digests, and anthologizings: only the Complete Edition will do." Years later, in 1986, he noted in the foreword to *John Pope-Hennessy: A Bibliography,* that "bibliographies make dull reading, some people say, but I have never found them so. They remind us, they prompt us, and they correct us. They double and treble as history, as biography, and as a freshet of surprises. They reveal the public self, the private self, and the buried self of the person commemorated. How should we not enjoy them, and be grateful to the devoted student who has done the compiling?" The section of a nonfiction book I always turn to first is the bibliography. There, I learn something about the author who has done the compiling as well as about other notable books I know I will want to read.

Reading about travel in the days before transatlantic flights, I always marvel at the number of steamer trunks and pieces of baggage that people were accustomed to taking. If it were me traveling then, however, my bags would be filled with books, not clothes. Robert Eisner, in his wonderful book, *Travelers to an Antique Land*, informs us of some book-packing habits of famous globetrotters: "Evelyn Waugh was victim of that too-common tendency to lug along those tomes one feels guilty about not having read— Spengler's *Decline of the West*, Pope's early verse, that sort of thing—with which one returns, cursing them as a dead weight in the bottom of the suitcase. On his second trip to Greece, Byron brought the complete nineteen-volume edition of Swift. In contrast, Norman Douglas's habit was never to take along more than one book, but few would find such Epicurean restraint appealing. Aldous Huxley, in *Along the Road,* recommends old, out-of-date guidebooks and a volume of the encyclopedia; Peter Levi once read most of the traveling edition of the Britannica while hiding out in an Athens flat from the Junta's secret police, and recommends S for general reading." For his part, Eisner made up his own lists of packable books, one of which specified "a paperback dictionary, a guidebook, a book for fun (either an old friend or something light but elegant), a play of Shakespeare, a book of poetry, a large masterpiece, and perhaps a work of science or politics, or if taste requires, the Bible or Book of Common Prayer or Bhagavad Gita." He admits he has never managed to keep to this list, and his bags have always been too book-heavy. Although I travel light and seldom check bags, I have been known to fill an entire suitcase with books, secure in the knowledge that I could have them all with me for the duration of my trip.

I thought I had a decent home library of books about Greece until I started to poke around the library stacks and bookstores. Thousands of books have been published about various aspects of ancient and contemporary Greece, more than those for any other place I've discussed in this series. Much to my disappointment, there are undoubtedly books with which I'm unfamiliar and that therefore do not appear here. I would be grateful to hear from you if a favorite of yours is missing. If some of the bibliographies seem long, they are—there are an awful lot of really good books out there! I'm not suggesting you read them *all,* but I do hope you will not be content with just one. I have identified some books as essential, but I sincerely believe that *all* the books I've mentioned are important, helpful, well written, or all three.

I have not hesitated to list out-of-print titles because some excellent books are declared out of print (and deserve to be returned to print!) and because many, many out-of-print books can be found through libraries, online searches, booksellers, and individuals who specialize in them. Since I believe the companion reading you bring along should be related in some way to where you're going, the books listed in *Good Things, Favorite Places* are novels, poetry, drama, and other works of fiction with characters or settings in Greece or that include aspects of Greece and the Greeks.

Together the articles and suggested books ought to lead you on and off the beaten path and provide a reality check of sorts. Will you learn of some nontouristy things to see and do? Yes. Will you learn more about the better-known aspects of Greece? Yes. The Parthenon, ouzo, an Aegean beach, wild oregano, Nafplio, a *tyropita,* herds of goats, and the theater at Epidaurus are all equally representative of the region. Seeing them *all* is what makes for a memorable visit, and no one, by the way, should make you feel guilty for wanting to see some famous sites. They have become famous for a reason: they are really something to see, the Acropolis and the Parthenon included. Canon number eighty-four in Bruce Northam's *Globetrotter Dogma* is "The Good Old Days Are Now,"; destinations are not ruined even though they may have been more "real" however many years ago: "'Tis a haughty condescension to insist that because a place has changed or lost its innocence it's not worth visiting; change requalifies a destination. Your first time is your first time; virgin turf simply is. The moment you commit to a trip, there begins the search for adventure."

Readers will have no trouble finding other travel titles on southern Greece that offer plenty of noncontroversial viewpoints. This is my attempt at presenting a more balanced picture. Ultimately, this book, and the others in this series, attempt to pull together different points of view—-some of them critical—-that add up to a balanced portrayal of the region. The book you have in your hands is the compendium of information that I wish I'd had between two covers years ago. I admit it isn't the "perfect" book; for that, I envision a waterproof jacket, pockets inside the front and back covers, pages and pages of accompanying maps, lots of blank pages for notes, a bookmark, and mileage and size conversion charts . . . in other words, something so encyclopedic—in both weight and size—that positively no one, my editor assures me, would want to carry it, let alone read it. I think I envisioned such a large volume because I believe that to really get to know a place, to truly understand it in a nonsuperficial way, one must either live there or travel there again and again. Grasping Greece can take nothing short of a lifetime of studying and traveling. I do not pretend to have completely grasped it now, many years and many trips later; nor do I pretend to have completely grasped the other Mediterranean destinations featured in *The Collected Traveler*; but I am trying, by continuously reading, collecting, and traveling. And I presume readers like you are, too. All of this said, I believe this edition will prove helpful in enhancing your anticipation of your upcoming journey; your enjoyment of your trip while it's happening; and your remembrance of it when you're back home.

It is not difficult to convey how very beautiful, wonderful, and unique southern Greece is; but perhaps less obvious is the sense of a tremendous accumulated weight of tradition among the Greeks themselves. Seeing only sites, and not the people who created them, leaves the visitor with only half the insight and knowledge of a particular place. Richard Stoneman, in his interesting book *A Literary Companion to Travel in Greece,* notes that this almost suffocating link with tradition is well expressed in a poem by George Seferis: "I woke with this marble head in my hands; / it exhausts my elbows and I don't know where to put it down . . . / so our life became one and it will be very difficult for it to separate again." Stoneman observes that "since the liberation, the Greek intelligentsia have struggled with that weight of tradition, overvaluing it . . . or strenuously ignoring it. . . Those Greek writers who have achieved the widest reputation are those who have to some extent reconciled these conflicting forces, so that myth, literature, and the present form a true whole." Additionally, "it would be wrong to approach the country as a museum, a shrine to a dead civilization," as Nicholas Gage, in *Greece: Land of Light,* wisely reminds us. "Those who come to worship the ancient Greeks and gaze only at their temples miss the dynamic, creative civilization of today." Patrick Leigh Fermor, in his excellent book *Roumeli* (a companion volume of sorts to *Mani,* which focuses on northern Greece), explores this idea best in a passage in which a local man rails against the ancient Greeks. The man tells Fermor he comes from Smyrna, an ancient Greek city certainly, and that he may be more Greek than the Greeks in Athens: "Who cares? Greece is an idea, that's the thing! That's what keeps us together—that, and the language and the country and the Church—not that I like priests particularly, but we owe them a lot. And those old Greeks, our celebrated ancestors, are a nuisance and I'll tell you why. They haunt us. We can never be as great as they were, nobody can. They make us feel guilty. We can't do anything, people think, because of a few old books and temples and lumps of marble. And clever foreigners who know all about the ancients come here expecting to be surrounded by apollos and gentlemen in helmets and laurel leaves, and what do they see? Me: a small dark fat man with a moustache and eyes like boot buttons!" He laughed good-naturedly. "To hell with them! Give me the men of the War of Independence, who chucked out the Turks, give me Averoff, who presented us with a battleship out of his own pocket, give me Venizelos, who saved us all and turned Greece into a proper country. What's wrong with them?"

The Greeks are not chauvinistic about their language. They fully understand that Greek is spoken in only a small corner of the world, and they do not expect foreigners to learn it. As a foreigner, however, you are immediately of interest, and Greeks love few things more than conversation (especially conversation about politics). They therefore do expect you to communicate and respond to their inquiries, about where you come from, your family, your job, and even your income (this is not considered impolite). They also expect you to ask *them* questions, about their country, the climate, their own families, and where the neighborhood's best taverna and *kafeneion* are. In a short time you will find that you have made a fast friend. "Make the effort," notes travel writer Victor Walker, "and you have turned the key to understanding Greece without even leaving your hotel. To open the door and slip through, you have to move about a little in the country itself. Do not just see Athens and the main town of your chosen island but, at least in passing, visit the bustling little provincial cities; observe the industries as well as the antiquities, and go to where the grapes grow, as well as where the wine is drunk."

I hope after reading this edition, and traveling to southern Greece, you too will realize that, as Nicholas Gage observed, "to know Greece well, Henry Miller once suggested, would take more than a lifetime, but to fall in love with it takes only an instant."

Kalo taxidi!

Practical Information

"You neither need nor could hope to pick up the deaf-and-dumb language of Greece in the course of a short visit, but there are two gestures which it is advisable to know if you want to avoid misunderstandings. Most Greeks are by now aware that the foreigner's raised right hand to signify 'no, thank you,' 'please don't,' or 'that's enough' is not to be confused with the almost identical Greek 'sign of the five' that means, in its most polite interpretation, 'damn your eyes!' But in the villages it could still occasion a moment of frigid misapprehension. If you really do intend to 'give him five,' named for the four fingers and thumb that stab in the direction of the face, all you need do is reverse the direction of the gesture for refusal from defensively backward to aggressively forward. You have then administered the worst possible insult that can be offered without use of words; obviously this should be done sparingly and after due consideration. The gesture you should not misinterpret is the blown kiss. The head jerks back, the lips open with a sometimes audible pop, and you have been informed that the answer is no, there isn't any, or he's not interested. You have neither been insulted nor made the recipient of an improper proposal."

—Victor Walker, travel writer
and newspaper journalist

A-Z Practical Information

Accommodations

In his wonderful book *Siren Feasts*, Andrew Dalby notes that in Greece and Turkey, before the increase in European-style traveling in the late nineteenth century, the usual inn (*xenodokheion* in Greek and *han* in Turkish) "seemed to foreign travellers more in the nature of a hostel, and a very down-at-heel one. . . . The American Nicholas Biddle, shortly after 1800, summarised the situation that had held, for those with introductions, for two thousand years and more: 'there being no taverns in Greece you are always lodged in the houses of individuals.'" As little as five years ago it could still be said that there were only a handful of unique, quality places to stay in all of Greece, but this situation changed almost overnight, and while generally speaking the list of fabulous accommodations is still a bit short, there are now outstanding, memorable places to stay, especially in Athens and the Aegean islands. Over the years I have stayed in campgrounds, rooms in private homes, inexpensive hotels, bed and breakfast accommodations, and hotels I consider a splurge—$200 a night—and never once was a room less than spotlessly clean. (Even some of the campgrounds were quite fancy.)

I don't recommend that you show up anywhere without a reservation—unless it's the off season or you're traveling for an extended period of time—because in Greece, especially in the summer months and during the upcoming 2004 Summer Olympic Games, you stand an excellent chance of not finding anything available. Traveling without reservations has a certain appeal, and I am sympathetic to it, but to those who prefer to travel without them, I would recommend reserving at least for the first night or two of your journey. You may underestimate how tired you will be upon arrival, and the last thing you'll want to do is search for a place to stay. Having a known base from which to embark on your spontaneous itinerary is welcome indeed. Especially during August—when nearly all Europeans are on vacation, and especially on or around August 15, *dekapende Augustou,* when Greeks make every effort to visit their home village or island—it is never advisable to arrive without reservations. In the islands in the off season, almost every inn or hotel is closed for renovations, painting, and general clean-up—this is the only time of year when proprietors can ready their establishments for the busy seasons ahead.

Just like France, Italy, and Spain, Greece has a number of wonderful, charming places to stay with only a dozen rooms, sometimes fewer; they have deservedly received some publicity and fill up fast, even in the so-named "shoulder" seasons. Most of us have a limited number of precious vacation days, and searching for a place to stay can be a most time-consuming and frustrating experience—certainly not what you came to Greece to do. A frequent business traveler to Athens stands a better chance of obtaining a last-minute room due to his or her longstanding relationship with a particular hotel or innkeeper. The frequent pleasure traveler, too, may be able to score a room at a time of year when lodgings are fully booked. But the rest of us have to plan a bit more in advance and will probably want to carefully select the places we'll call home for a few days or longer—unless you've bought a special rail pass and are traveling from city to city, in which case you probably don't have a carved-in-stone itinerary and are going from youth hostel to youth hostel. If you do arrive without reservations, the Greek tourist office staff will assist you as best they can in securing accommodations. In my experience the staff at even the smallest tourist office in the smallest village in Greece is happy to assist people in finding a place to stay, even if it's a room in the house of a neighbor. They may not place telephone calls for you or make reservations, but they will tell you what choices are available, give directions, and generally help in any way they're able.

You might argue that the choice of lodging isn't important, since you won't be spending much time in your room anyway; but I disagree with this notion. Meeting the owners of a family-run hotel or inn, getting to know the front desk clerk at a posh property, or simply returning to a nicely kept room for an afternoon siesta are all part of a memorable and enjoyable trip. I see no reason *not* to devote some time to researching where you will stay—the only problem may be narrowing your choices in certain areas because of the many great lodgings. North America, of course, has some wonderful and wonderfully expensive places to stay, as well as a growing number of bed and breakfasts. But it also has an overabundance of inexpensive places overpriced for what they are because they are devoid of character. In these "plastic places," all the furnishings are plastic, acrylic, or, my favorite, "wood product." Sometimes a continental breakfast is included in the price, which typically consists of a previously frozen bagel or something resembling a muffin, and dreadful coffee with nondairy creamer. Breakfast in Greece may be nothing more than the standard Greek coffee or Nescafé and *kouloures* (sesame-studded rings of dough), or something more substantial with an assortment of breads, jams, honey, yogurt, fresh-squeezed orange juice, coffee or tea; but at least the *kouloures* and the breads are either homemade or fresh from the corner bakery. What we *don't* have in North America (or at least in the States) that Greece *does* is a great number of moderately priced, simple, but well-cared-for places that are charming and reasonable. By moderately priced, I mean costing $50 to $150 a night, though I have stayed in Greek places that were $25 to $60 a night and were exceptional in terms of the room furnishings (quality pieces, sometimes antiques) and the quality of the welcome. All of this is to say that your wallet doesn't have to be opened very wide to sleep in Greece, and especially in parts of the Peloponnese, accommodations can be very affordable, even for the budget traveler. Additionally, the variety of lodgings in Greece allows travelers to experience different types of lodgings in one trip. I always try to include a mix of places on my visits, reserving a city hotel, a bed and breakfast, a country inn, and a fancy splurge, and I encourage you to experiment, too. I sometimes plan my itinerary around a special inn or hotel where I want to stay, feeling it is nearly equal in importance to a particular village or historic site that I am keen on visiting.

Greece has an official rating system for lodging establishments, but it would be a mistake to depend on it solely: often the only amenity standing between a three-star place and a four-star may be a swimming pool, a bigger bathtub, a hair dryer, or a ceiling fan. Currently, the system is based on letters—ranging from L for luxury to E for economy class—rather than stars, as in other countries, though this may change. You may, in your research and travels, discover places that are not classified and therefore have no rating. A zero rating means either that the tourist office has deemed the establishment unworthy of even one star or that the owners of the lodging have not requested to be reviewed. I have stayed in a number of places with no rating—throughout Greece and elsewhere around the Mediterranean—and they were all perfectly fine and clean, some quite deserving of at least one or two stars. The booklets published by the regional tourist offices in Greece tend to be nothing more than listings, useful only for obtaining contact information, determining what amenities are offered, and learning how each establishment is rated; rarely do they provide any subjective descriptions of a place. It's far better to consult a guidebook and read the descriptions so you'll know exactly what you're getting.

Here are some general notes on different types of accommodations you'll find in Greece:

Bed and breakfast accommodations may be simple or fancy, based either in private homes or small inns. B&Bs operating out of private homes are relatively new to Greece and until recently were viewed as rather quirky quarters existing solely as a way for farmers and other country people to earn extra money. But as was perhaps inevitable after Greece joined the European Union, the country began to open up more, and the idea of taking paying guests into one's home seemed less threatening and less odd. Rates are generally inexpensive and can sometimes be a bargain. If your hosts speak English (and most of them speak at least a little), they'll suggest local restaurants, cafés, hikes, shops, and sights to see, and they may even cook you a delicious meal, with ingredients straight from the garden or henhouse. B&Bs are often great for families—Greeks love fussing over children, and many places have suites or large rooms with a kitchenette.

Camping can be a viable option for those who have a car and preferably a lot of time, and there are plenty of campgrounds in both the cities and small towns of Attica and the Peloponnese. (Don't count on there being campgrounds on all the islands.) The thing to understand about the European concept of camping is that it is about as far from the American concept as possible. Europeans do not go camping to seek a wilderness experience, and their campgrounds are designed without much privacy in mind. Campgrounds in Greece offer amenities ranging from hot water showers or solar showers, facilities for washing clothes and dishes, electrical outlets, and flush toilets to tiled bathrooms with heat, swimming pools, cafés, bars, restaurants, telephones, televisions, discos, and general stores. Some of the more basic campgrounds make up for their lack of amenities with stunning scenery. If you find yourself at a Greek campground during the summer, you may notice that entire families—many Greek-American—have literally moved in (having reserved their spaces many months in advance) and that they return every year to spend time with their friends, the way we might return every year to a ski cabin or a house at the beach. It's quite an entertaining and lively spectacle. I have camped fairly extensively in Greece, and except in the north, every site had a swimming pool or access to the Aegean. Off-site camping is seriously prohibited in Greece due to the very great and real danger of fire.

If you plan to camp for even a few nights, I recommend that you join Family Campers and RVers (FCRV). Annual membership (valid for one year from the time you join) is $25. FCRV is a member of the Fédération Internationale de Camping et de Caravanning (FICC), and is the only organization in America authorized to issue the International Camping Carnet—like a camping passport—for camping in Europe. Only FCRV members are eligible to buy the carnet—it cannot be purchased separately. The carnet is $10—you pay it concurrently with your FCRV membership fee—and it is valid for one year. Since many FICC member campgrounds in Europe are privately owned, the carnet provides entry to these member-only campsites. A carnet offers you priority status and occasionally discounts. An additional benefit is that instead of keeping your passport overnight—which hotels and campgrounds are often required to do—the campground staff keeps only your carnet. One FICC membership is good for the entire family: parents and all children under eighteen. To receive an application and information, contact the organization at 4804 Transit Road, Building 2, Depew NY 14043; 800-245-9755 or 716-668-6242; www.fcrv.org.

An outstanding mail-order catalog (and retail store) for a most thorough selection of camping gear and accoutrements—including travel and biking accessories, cookware, and lots of items for kids—is Campmor. I have been a customer at some major outdoors stores in North America, but I don't think any of them are as complete as the Campor emporium. Contact information: 28 Parkway, P.O. Box 700-Q, Saddle River NJ 07458; 888-CAMPMOR; www.campmor.com (for the catalog); 810 Route 17 North, Paramus NJ; 201-445-5000 (for the store).

For complete information about camping in Greece, you should consult the annual *Camping in Greece* brochure published by the Panhellenic Camping Association and the Hellenic Chamber of Hotels (available at the Greek Tourist Office). This helpful booklet lists sites and their amenities, gas stations, shipping companies, caravan and camper spare parts and service outlets, touring clubs, and museums and archaeological sites.

Home exchange might be an appealing option for you: I've read wildly enthusiastic reports from people who've swapped apartments/houses, and it's usually always an economical alternative. Some services to contact include:

HomeExchange.com (a Web-only company based in Santa Barbara), www.home exchange.com

Homelink International, P.O. Box 47747, Tampa FL 33647; 800-638-3841 or 813-975-9825; fax: 813-910-8144; www.homelink.org

Intervac, Box 12066, S-291, 12 Kristianstad, Sweden (world headquarters); 30 Corte San Fernando, Tiburon CA 94920 (U.S. address); 800-756-HOME; www.intervacus.com

Seniors Home Exchange (limited to members over age fifty), www.seniorshomeexchange.com

Trading Homes International, P.O. Box 787, Hermosa Beach CA 90254; 800-877-TRADE; fax: 310-798-3865; www.trading-homes.com

~Consumer Reports Travel Letter presented a special report on home exchange in its November 2001 issue, which noted that the number-one complaint filed by home exchangers is cleanliness. Obviously, different people interpret "clean" in different ways (males and females do, too), so this is something to keep in mind when making arrangements. To obtain a copy of the report, send $5 to CRTL, 101 Truman Avenue, Yonkers NY 10703-1057.

Hotels *are where most of us stay when we travel. As I mentioned earlier, recommendations for hotels in general guidebooks are usually reliable, but even better are books exclusively about hotels. (These are not great in number for Greece, which reduces your research time.) As with guidebooks, the right hotel book for you is the one whose author shares a sensibility or philosophy with you. In the same way that you put your trust in the author of a guidebook, put that same faith in the author of a hotel guide. Once you've selected the book you like, trust the author's recommendations, make your decisions, and move on to the next stage of your planning. ~The Greek Hotel Reservation Center is a service that represents more than seven thousand hotels in Greece. A fee is charged, but if you prefer that someone else do the work, this agency has "all Greek hotels under one umbrella." Contact information: 17220 Newhope Street, Suite 227, Fountain Valley CA 92708; 800-736-5717; fax: 714-641-0303.*

Monasteries and convents *are a singular (and budget) accommodation choice. I have seen no book exclusively devoted to monastery lodgings in Greece, but guidebooks usually have a few listings, and the North American Greek tourist offices can provide you with information on lodgings of this sort. (It is not required you be Christian to stay at a monastery, by the way.) You should know, however, that staying at a convent is not the same as staying in a hotel, and you should not expect great comfort or a lot of amenities. (Few monasteries have a television or a private telephone, for example.) Rather, you'll find simple, immaculately clean quarters, solitude, possibly a meal or two (though you need to eat when the resident monks or nuns eat), little English spoken, possibly a curfew, possibly single-sex accommodations (some convents admit only men, others only women) . . . and a wholly unique and untouristy experience.*

Renting an apartment or villa *might be a suitable choice depending on how long you'll be in Greece and the number of people you'll be traveling with. While I very much like staying in inns and hotels, I also like renting because it forces you to take an active part in the culture rather than catch a mere glimpse of it. It's a quick way to feel a part of the local routine—you have daily chores to accomplish just like everyone else (except that I would hardly call going to pick up provisions at the local market a chore). Though your tasks are mixed in with lots of little pleasures, sight-seeing, and trips, you often avoid the too-much-to-do rut. What to eat suddenly looms as the most important question of the day, the same question that all the local families are trying to answer. A list of organizations that arrange short- and long-term rentals would fill a small book, and it is not my intention to provide a comprehensive listing. Rather, here are a few sources with properties in Greece that have either come highly recommended or with which I have had a positive experience:*

Barclay International Group, 3 School Street, Glen Cove NY 11542; 800-845-6636 or 516-759-5100; fax: -609-0000; www.barclayweb.com
Rentvillas.com (an Internet company based in the United States), 700 East Main Street, Ventura CA 93001; 800-726-6702 or 805-641-1650; fax: -641-1630; www.rentvillas.com

A new and welcome resource for those interested in self-catered accommodations is *Countryside Vacations*, a newsletter published five times a year for people who travel either a lot or a little. The first issue of *CV* appeared in the spring of 2002, and I think the editor and her staff have hit upon a very good idea. Each issue has tips and trip profiles from travelers who've rented previously, as well as reports on various destinations within four European countries, reviews of particular cottages or villas, and a profile of a rental agency. This newsletter is a great addition to resources now available to renter-travelers, and I would personally not confirm any plans until I browsed it. An annual subscription is $59. Contact information: *Countryside Vacations*, P.O. Box 975, Melrose MA 02176; 888-505-8800; 781-979-9394; fax: -979-9395; www.countryside-vacations.com. ~When renting a property, don't forget to ask thorough questions and read the fine print. Some questions to ask include: "Is there air conditioning?" (air conditioning is more common than it used to be in Greece, but it is definitely not widespread. If the place has none, ask if there's cross-ventilation or a ceiling fan), "How is the water pressure?" "Is hot water available at all times?" "Are children or pets welcome?" "Is there a crib for a young child?" "What is the charge for use of the telephone?" "Are toilet paper, sheets, and blankets provided?" "Is there a coffee maker, and are coffee filters provided?" "Is there a corkscrew in the kitchen?" "Is there a mosquito coil?" (screens are rare in windows in Mediterranean countries, and if you spy a mosquito coil— either the kind you light with a match or the kind that plugs into the wall—that is your clue that pesky bugs will be about after the sun goes down, and you'll be happy to have the protection), "Is construction going on nearby?," and "How far is the food market?" (some of the most appealing houses in the country are in rather rural areas, so keep in mind that you may be some distance from a main road).

~Note the following advice from Homebase Abroad, which arranges rentals exclusively in Italy: "Renting abroad is an adventure, no matter the level of house you're considering. If the myriad differences between an Italian [or Greek] home and your home, between the Italian [or Greek] lifestyle and your lifestyle are unwelcome, you might have to conclude this is not the right trip for you and your group."

Traditional settlements are a relatively new accommodations option, created by the Greek National Tourist Office, and I think they're wonderful. They are old buildings of architectural and historical merit that have been renovated and converted into tourist accommodations. They're not inexpensive, and are by no means luxurious, but the expense is worth every euro. I've so far been unable to find a complete listing of traditional settlements, but some are recommended in guidebooks. Santorini, Chios, Cephalonia, Psara, Makrynitsa, Vizitsa, Zagorohoria, and Areopoli are some areas of Greece chosen for settlements.

Youth hostels are one of the most popular choices for those seeking budget accommodations (and if it's been a while since your salad days, keep in mind that hostels are not just for the under-thirty crowd). I would go back in a minute to my summer of vagabonding around Europe, meeting young people from all over the world, and feeling that my life was one endless possibility. I now prefer to share a room with my husband rather than five twentysomethings, but hostelling remains a fun and exciting experience. Younger budget travelers need no convincing that it is the way to go, and older budget travelers should remember that some hostels do have individual rooms, reserved mostly for couples or small families. But do compare costs, as sometimes hostel rates are the same as rates for a room in a real (albeit inexpensive) hotel, where you can reserve in advance and comfortably keep your luggage. You must pack up your luggage every day when hostelling, and you can't make a reservation. Additionally, most hostels have an 11:00 P.M. curfew. Petty theft—of the T-shirts-stolen-off-the-clothesline variety—seems to be more prevalent than it once was, and it would be wise to sleep and shower with your money belt close at hand. Hostels involve no age limits or advance bookings, but many require membership in Hostelling International (HI), whose national headquarters are at 733 Fifteenth Street N.W., Suite 840, Washington DC 20005; 202-783-6161; fax: -6171; www.hiayh.org. An HI membership card is free for anyone up to his or her eighteenth birthday. Annual fees are $25 for anyone over eighteen and $15 for anyone fifty-five or over. HI also publishes several guidebooks, one of which is *Europe and the Mediterranean*, priced at $13.95. If you would like to visit an HI council affiliate, HI staff can provide the address and phone number for the one nearest you.

Addresses

Like other Europeans, Greeks use a format for street addresses that is different than what is common in North America. If you are searching for a residential or business address, note that the number *follows* the name of the street, such as Koumbari 1. But if an address is on a *plateia* (square) or avenue, the number appears *before* the name.

Airfares and Airlines

We all know that not everyone pays the same price for seats on an airplane. One reason is that seats do not hold the same value at all times of the year, month, or even day of the week. Not long ago I was researching some fares to Paris for a long weekend. One of my calls produced a particularly helpful representative who proceeded to detail all available fares for the entire month of September. There were approximately fifteen different prices—based on a seemingly endless number of variables—within that month alone. The best way, therefore, to get the best deal that accommodates your needs is to check a variety of sources and be flexible. Flexibility is, and has always been, the key to low-cost travel, so be prepared to slightly alter the dates of your planned trip to take advantage of cheaper airline seats.

If you think all the best deals are to be found on the Internet, you're mistaken: airlines, consolidators, and other discounters offer plenty of good fares over the telephone and through advertisements. In order to know with certainty that you've got a good deal, you need to comparison-shop, which requires checking more than one source. Many people have cornered me over the years and asked for my "secret" to finding a cheap airfare. The answer is that there is no "secret," only diligent research. Price isn't the only factor in planning a trip, and if a supposedly cheap fare is only offered only at times that are inconvenient for me, then it isn't cheap at all, it's outside the realm of possibility, and therefore is worthless. If there is a secret to finding the best fare, it is this: on any day of the week the lowest fares can be found *equally* among websites, wholesalers, airlines, charters, tour operators, travel agents, and sky auctions. No website can claim to offer the best choice for all travelers, and you don't know who's offering what until you inquire.

I like flying a country's own airline whenever possible, and Greece's official airline is Olympic Airways, founded in 1957 by the late Aristotle Onassis, the modern Greek shipping industry's answer to King Midas. Olympic is truly the little airline that could: its fleet is relatively small but covers a lot of ground, touching down at eighty-three airports on five continents. It's still the most reliable airline within Greece, and flies to airports on some of the larger islands. With one of the newest airports in Europe—the brand, spanking new Eleftherios Venizelos terminal—as its home base in Athens, and Thessaloniki as its secondary hub, Olympic's out to wow the visitor. The airline has been owned by the Greek government since 1975, and has had some financial troubles and some uneven service; but on the eve of the Olympics, the airline seems poised to meet the challenges of a changing marketplace and stiff competition. Olympic is trying hard to meet passenger demand for the Summer Olympics and plans to increase the number of flights, improve its customer service, and offer more competitive pricing. If you fly Olympic on the transatlantic leg of your journey, the airline will reward you by charging very little for in-country flights. Although Olympic's fares are usually among the highest available, its off-season fares are among the lowest, and it offers some unbeatable packages and deals throughout the year. Like other airlines, Olympic has specially priced Internet-only fares that are discounted from promotional fares, and it's worth it to browse its website (www.olympic.com) periodically to check on airfare specials as well as special packages. At this writing Delta is the only other carrier that flies nonstop to Athens, so if you're determined to compare schedules and fares, it won't take you very long. I encourage you to consider what Olympic is offering when you make your flight plans.

The travel section of *The New York Times* (my local daily newspaper) is a good source for researching airfares. I scan the ads of all the area agencies and often find the same low fares offered by one or two particular airlines. The airlines are almost always smaller foreign lines currently trying to expand their business in the United States. (I once flew on Pakistan International Air to Paris; the PIA flight was destined for Karachi but stopped in Paris en route.) Remember to consider alternative airports in your area, not just the obvious major hubs. For example, I always find different fares when I compare flights departing from Newark, New Jersey, and JFK on Long Island. If you're already in Greece and want to fly somewhere else within Europe, check with Europe by Air (888-387-2479; www.europebyair.com; typically these fares are lower than those offered by other European carriers.

Alcohol

I recently ran across a great essay entitled "The Tourist's Manual" by Evelyn Waugh, in which he argues that "when all is said and done, perhaps the most valuable commodity for the tourist, whether he is cruising along the French Riviera in a yacht or ploughing through unmapped areas of virgin forest, is alcohol. It is the universal language, the Esperanto, through which contact can be made with people of the most remote sympathies; it passes agreeably the leaden hours of waiting for trains and boats and mail; it gently obliterates one's rage at inefficient subordinates and soothes one's own exhaustion and irritation; it renders one oblivious to mosquitoes, calms one's apprehensions of being lost or catching fever; it gives glamour to the empty, steaming nights of the tropics. With a glass in his hand, the tourist can gaze out on the streets of Tangier, teeming with English governesses and retired colonels, and happily imagine himself a Marco Polo." It brought a smile to my face because I remembered fondly the evening ritual of drinking ouzo that my husband and I adopted while we were in Greece. I never fancied myself a Marco Polo exactly, but I was about as happy as any human being is allowed to be.

Alexander the Great

As you read books on Greece, you will of course come across thousands of references to Alexander, the most famous Greek of all. Just one worth repeating here is found in *Dinner with Persephone* by Patricia Storace: "You know that in Greece you must never use the past tense when you are speaking of Alexander the Great, although you also know that he is dead." A few worthwhile books to read include: *Alexander the Great: Man of Action, Man of Spirit* (Discoveries series, Harry Abrams), which like each volume in this series was originally published in France and is pocket-sized, quite substantive, and lavishly illustrated; and *Alexander the Great: Son of the Gods* (by Alan Fildes and Joann Fletcher, Duncan Baird Publishers, 2002), a beautifully produced volume published with the J. Paul Getty Museum in Los Angeles; the text reflects the latest archaeological research and the most up-to-date scholarly conclusions, and it includes more than 150 gorgeous illustrations.

Amphorae

Amphorae are earthenware jugs that constituted the first containers used for the transport of commercial goods by boat, and you'll see a lot of them in Greek museums. (I have had a special affection for them since I prepared a final report on their history for an archaeology class in college.) The word *amphora* is, of course, Greek. Though the shape of amphorae changed over time, they generally had a narrow mouth, a tall neck, an oval body, symmetrical handles, and a pointed base. Amphorae were often filled with wine or olive oil and were stored on the boats lying down. In addition to holding wine and oil, they also proved to be excellent vessels for holding beer, milk, butter, honey, meat, poultry, fish, cheese, grains, legumes, fruits, spices, filberts, almonds, walnuts, sugar, kohl, and gum arabic. The stoppers were made of clay, wood, or cork. The contents of some amphorae remain remarkably well preserved. In January 2003 the remains of a 2,400-year-old ship were discovered at the bottom of the Black Sea, laden with amphorae, one of which held the bones of a six- or seven-foot-long freshwater catfish that had been dried and cut into steaks. Scientists presume the ship was sailing from a Black Sea colony to the Greek mainland. It is the oldest shipwreck ever found in the Black Sea and is a testament to its role as a vibrant crossroads of ancient commerce. Additionally, the Kyrenia Castle and Shipwreck Museum (a lovely, well-maintained, and extremely interesting museum in northern Cyprus) is home to the oldest trading ship known to us with her cargo. The ship sank 300 years before the birth of Christ, and in 1967, the University Museum of Pennsylvania directed a team to survey the coast. More than four hundred amphorae, mostly made in Rhodes, were the main cargo. Additionally, the team also uncovered jars of perfectly preserved almonds, nine thousand in all!

Archaeology

It's difficult to travel very far in Greece, especially on some of the islands and on the Peloponnese, without encountering an archaeological dig or an excavated site, and in fact these digs and sites are among the major reasons many people visit Greece. Your visits to some of them will be much more rewarding if you read about them before you arrive, especially if you have not visited ancient sites (such as Pompeii, Herculaneum, or the Roman Forum) before and are wondering why people make such a fuss over ruined marble columns and rocks. The best source that really conveys the thrill of archaeological discovery is *Gods, Graves and Scholars: The Story of Archeology* (by C. W. Ceram, Alfred A. Knopf, 1951). Though this extremely interesting book also discusses Mayan temples, the ruins at Pompeii, the Pyramids and tombs in Egypt, and sites in the kingdoms of Sumer, Assyria, and Babylonia, its chapters on Mycenae, Troy, Tiryns, and the Palace of Knossos on Crete remain, I think, the best introduction to the discovery of these Greek tombs. Ceram writes of the nineteenth-century archaeologist Heinrich Schliemann, "Now comes a fairy tale, the story of the poor boy who at the age of seven dreamed of finding a city [Troy], and who thirty-nine years later went forth, sought, and found not only the city but also treasure such as the world had not seen since the loot of the conquistadors. This fairy tale is the life of Heinrich Schliemann, one of the most astounding personalities not only among archaeologists but among all men to whom any science has ever been indebted." This book was on a required reading list in my freshman archaeology class, but it's not a textbook; it's an engrossing read, with a thirty-two-page insert of black-and-white photos.

Art and Architecture

Kate Simon, in her incomparable *Italy: The Places In Between,* reminded readers that a little learning can be a pleasant thing; "above all, it helps to turn the pages of a few art and architecture books to become reacquainted with names other than those of the luminous giants." Though she was obviously referring to Italy, the reference is easily applied to Greece, and I cannot emphasize enough how much more rewarding your visit will be if you brush up on (or introduce yourself to) the great artworks of ancient Greece that you'll encounter in museums and at historic sites. Following is a thorough list of books that will serve you well. I have not, as in previous editions, elaborated upon each title. This is a departure for me, and not one I'm particularly happy about, but the body of work on Greek art and architecture is enormous, more so even than works on Italy or France, and certain authors have dozens of specialized books to their credit, all of them worthy. I am uncomfortable with recommending a staggering number of titles just for the sake of compiling a list; rather, what follows is a necessarily brief selection of titles, some for more serious art enthusiasts than others. I admit that many are what I personally refer to as "essential," so I recommend that you take your time compiling the books you want to read and look at as many of these as you can find—I'm betting you'll find that many will appeal, and that you'll identify at least half a dozen you, too, will deem essential.

GENERAL ART REFERENCE

Angels A to Z: A Who's Who of the Heavenly Host (by Matthew Bunson, Three Rivers Press, 1996).

From Abacus to Zeus: A Handbook of Art History (by James Smith Pierce, Prentice-Hall, 1977).

Gods and Heroes in Art (by Lucia Impelluso, J. Paul Getty Museum, 2002).

Greatest Works of Art of Western Civilization (by Thomas Hoving, Artisan, 1997).

History of Art (by H. W. Janson and Anthony F. Janson, 6th rev. ed., Harry N. Abrams, 2001).

The Illustrated Age of Fable: The Classic Retelling of Greek and Roman Myths Accompanied by the World's Greatest Paintings (by Thomas Bulfinch, Stewart, Tabori and Chang, 1998).

The Museum Companion: Understanding Western Art (by Marcus Lodwick, Harry N. Abrams, 2003).

The Oxford Companion to Christian Art and Architecture: The Key to Western Art's Most Potent Symbolism (by Peter and Linda Murray, Oxford University Press, 1998).

The Story of Art (by E. H. Gombrich, 16th ed., Phaidon Press, 1995).

Who's Who in the Bible (by Peter Calvocoressi, Penguin Books, 1987).

Ancient Greece: The Famous Monuments, Past and Present (no author indicated, Muses Publishers, Vision S.R.L., Rome, 1997). A word about this publication is helpful: I hear often from visitors to Greece that they were bored, after a while, at seeing ancient sites on their own, without a good guide and without much interpretive material. This book brings those sites to life with acetate pages that you view on top of a current photograph of the site. It's remarkable to see the sites in this way, and I really think it's essential for everyone but the most academic scholar. All the sites featured in this paperback volume are in southern Greece, so it's a worthwhile book to purchase and bring along. Though published in Italy, I bought my copy in the bookstore at The Metropolitan Museum of Art in New York.

Architecture and City Planning (by Ioanna Phoca and Panos Valavanis, Kedros Publishers, Athens, 1999). This volume, and the same authors' *Greek Pottery*, I bought in Greece, so I feel I should note that they are both editions in the excellent Rediscovering Ancient Greece paperback series, which introduces the general reader to the ancient Greek world through the medium of its vast wealth of material remains, be they objects of everyday use or masterpieces of art. In this volume the authors attempt to bring the ruins back to life and show what the buildings' original functions were, and they've succeeded admirably. I bought this set in the archaeology museum in Nafplio, and I think it's the best one I've seen for nonspecialists.

Greece and Rome (1987). The Metropolitan Museum of Art's classical collections are among the most comprehensive and representative in North America, and this book is one in a very good series that represents the scope of the museum's holdings while selectively presenting the very finest objects from each of its curatorial departments. The books have been described as being "more detailed than a museum guide and broader in scope than the museum's scholarly publications." Though this book also covers Rome, its coverage of Greek art is thorough.

Greek Art (by Nigel Spivey, Phaidon, 1997).

Greek Pottery: A Culture Captured in Clay (by Ioanna Phoca and Panos Valavanis, Kedros Publishers, Athens, 1992).

Mosaics of the Greek and Roman World (by Katherine M. D. Dunbadin, Cambridge University Press, 1999).

The Oxford History of Classical Art (by John Boardman, Oxford University Press, 1993).

The Oxford Illustrated History of Greece and the Hellenistic World (by John Boardman, Jasper Griffin, and Oswyn Murray, 1986). Try to find the hardcover edition of this title, as the smaller paperback includes only an eight-page insert of black-and-white illustrations.

Disarmed: The Story of the Venus de Milo (by Gregory Curtis, Alfred A. Knopf, 2003). This is one of those hard-to-describe books that, once begun, is nearly impossible to put down, so I thought it required more than a cursory listing. Though it is indeed the story of what is arguably the most famous sculpture in the world (discovered on the Aegean island of Milos in 1820 and part of the permanent collection of the Louvre in Paris since 1821), it is also of particular relevance here as the author reveals the European obsession with Hellenic ideals and art in the nineteenth century. As Curtis notes, "Classical Greece did not seem distant to a European in the 1820s. Instead, it was a vital heritage that had recently been revived, a force that had to be understood because it was so much a part of the times." Herculaneum and Pompeii had been rediscovered in 1738 and 1748, and in 1755, Johann Joachim Winckelmann's *Reflections on the Imitation of Greek Painting and Sculpture*, in which he stated that "Good taste, which is becoming more prevalent throughout the world, had its origins under the skies of Greece," changed European taste, art, and thinking forever. In Paris in the 1760s, Curtis informs us that a worldly observer noted, ". . . The interior and exterior decoration of buildings, furniture, fabrics, jewelry of all kinds, everything in Paris is *à la grecque*." Curtis not only relates the story of the Venus but includes chapters on the role of sculptors ("There was such a thing as art in the ancient world, but there wasn't really such a thing as an artist in the modern sense. A sculptor might be considered more elevated than a sandal maker, say, but he was still a tradesman and part of that social group"), sexuality, and women in ancient Greece. And Curtis reminds us of the relevance of the Venus in more modern times: Cézanne, Magritte, and Dalí all created works based on her image; Jim Dine cast the Venus as massive bronzes that stand today on Avenue of the Americas in midtown Manhattan (I walk by them every day!); in 1966 a Mercedes ad for its Class E sedan featured the statue, and French retailer Darty used her in a 1980s ad campaign; the poster for Robert Altman's film *Nashville* has the Venus in a cowboy hat and dark glasses; and there are numerous cartoons: my favorite is one of a Greek sculptor in his workshop with the Venus de Milo, and he complains to a friend, "I just can't do arms." Curtis concludes with the observation that though the French wanted the glory of the Venus to reflect onto them, French propaganda is not the reason why the Venus has fascinated artists for generations or why great numbers of tourists come to the Louvre every day to see her. They come "because the statue is beautiful in a way that even an untrained eye immediately understands. Its classicism is the source of that instant recognition. Ever since Winckelmann brought Greek art back into our culture, we have thought of Greek idealized nude sculpture as both the beginning of Western art and an achievement that has not been surpassed in the two and a half millennia since."

Athens Festival

The Athens Festival, held each year from mid-June to August, is the city's major annual event and may be the most popular festival in all of Greece. It certainly gets my vote, presenting classical music concerts, dance performances, and performances of ancient Greek drama at the Theater of Herodes Atticus on the Acropolis. If you've ever seen the theater on your way up or down the Acropolis, you know what I mean when I say that this is a ticket worth obtaining no matter *what's* being performed. The Greek dramas are performed in modern Greek, but who cares if you don't understand a word? Needless to say, tickets sell out quickly. You may purchase them at the festival box office in the arcade at Stadiou 4, Syntagma Square, but I would first inquire at the tourist office about the best way to secure tickets well in advance. There are other wonderful, outdoor festivals elsewhere—in Athens at the Lycabettus Theater and at the Hill of the Pnyx, and at Epidaurus, to name a few—but nothing compares with the Athens Festival.

B

Balkan Wars

Contemporary conflicts in the region known as the Balkans (including Greece, Romania, Bulgaria, and all parts of the former Yugoslavia) do not involve Greece as directly as the first Balkan Wars, of 1912–13. Briefly, these rather short wars were fought for the possession of the European territories of the Ottoman Empire. The Treaty of London ended the First Balkan War on May 30, 1913, and Turkey ceded all possessions in Europe to the allies west of a line from Enos on the Aegean Sea to Midia on the Black Sea, with the exception of Albania (this is when the Great Powers began to draw the lines of a new Albanian state). Turkish sovereignty over Crete was withdrawn and the island was united with Greece, and the Aegean islands that Greece occupied were given to the Great Powers. The creation of Albania left Serbia with no direct access to the sea, so she demanded a greater share of Macedonia from Bulgaria. This request was not received well, and Bulgaria attacked Serbia in June 1913, but was then attacked by Romania, Greece, and Turkey, effectively the Second Balkan War. Bulgaria lost territory to all her enemies by the Treaty of Bucharest in August 1913, and according to *The Columbia Encyclopedia* (sixth edition, 2001), the Balkan Wars "prepared the way for World War I by satisfying some of the aspirations of Serbia and thereby giving a great impetus to the Serbian desire to annex parts of Austria-Hungary; by alarming Austria and stiffening Austrian resolution to crush Serbia; and by giving causes of dissatisfaction to Bulgaria and Turkey." Three outstanding books to read and learn more about these initial wars as well as more recent troubles are *The Balkans: Nationalism, War and the Great Powers, 1804–1999* (Misha Glenny, Penguin,

2001); *The Balkan Wars: Conquest, Revolution, and Retribution from the Ottoman Era to the Twentieth Century and Beyond* (André Gerolymatos, Basic Books, 2003); and *The Balkans: A Short History* (Mark Mazower, Modern Library Chronicles, 2000; at 240 pages, the best choice for those who don't want a lengthy volume).

Bargaining

Bargaining has long been an accepted way of conducting business in the Levant (eastern Mediterranean), and though not *all* goods and services in Greece may be bargained for, you may find yourself in a number of situations where bargaining is acceptable. I believe that nearly every item or service is negotiable to some degree, so it is worthwhile to be aware of the basics of bargaining and how rewarding it can be for both buyer and seller. Bargaining makes many North American visitors uncomfortable, but mainly because they have never taken the time to understand and appreciate the art of bargaining, and they have some of the most backward and wrong opinions, usually stemming from the fear that they're being taken to the cleaners. It's important to *appreciate* bargaining: it's fun, interesting, and revealing of national character. It isn't something you do in a hurry, though, and it's not an antagonistic game of Stratego—it does incorporate strategy, but it isn't about territory being conquered or battleships sunk, it's about goods or services on offer that you do or do not have to purchase.

As in my *Morocco* edition, however, I caution readers against placing too much emphasis on the deal itself. There are few absolutes in the art of bargaining—each merchant is different, and the particulars of each transaction are different, and you will not be awarded a medal at the end of your visit for driving hard bargains, especially if you accumulate things you don't really want. More important than any of my tips that follow is that you *do not lose sight of the fact that what you want is something that appeals to you in some special way, and that you bargained for it in the accepted manner.* Does it really matter, at the end of the day, that you *might* have gotten it for 20 or 50 euros less? If you end up with a purchase that you love and every time you look at it or wear it you have a warm feeling about your trip to Greece, it definitely does not matter what you paid for it. There is a difference between savvy bargaining and obsessive bargaining, and I don't know about you, but when I'm on vacation, obsessing about mercantile matters is the equivalent of postponing joy.

~Politeness goes a long way. Vendors appreciate being treated with respect, and don't at all mind answering questions from interested browsers. Strike up a conversation while you're looking at the wares; ask about the vendor's family, share pictures of yours, or ask for a recommendation of a good local restaurant. Establishing a rapport also shows that you are reasonable, and that you are willing to make a purchase at the right (reasonable) price. ~You'll always get the best price if you pay with cash, and in fact many vendors in Greece accept only cash. I prepare an assortment of paper euros and coins in advance so that, if necessary, I can pull them out and indicate that it's all I have. It doesn't seem right to bargain hard for something, agree to buy it for 50 euros, then pay for it with a 1,000-euro note. ~The last time I was in Greece, many shopkeepers were amenable to offering my two friends and I one advantageous price for the quantity of items that we were purchasing together, and they bettered the price further if we paid in cash. Also, they often threw in an additional item at no extra charge. ~If you're interested in buying antiques—or making large purchases of any kind—it would be worthwhile to read the *Know Before You Go* brochure from the U.S. Customs Service. Write for a free copy (1300 Pennsylvania Avenue N.W., Washington, DC 20229), or view it online at www.customs.ustreas.gov.

Beaches

Greeks "study and describe the characters of beaches with the nuance of wine connoisseurs talking vintages," according to Patricia Storace. There are beaches aplenty in southern Greece, and a few favorites that immediately come to mind are Mavra Volia on Chios; Kardamíli on the Peloponnese; and Mátala on Crete. This last, I understand, has become too popular for its own good, but when I was there in the month of October, it was gloriously memorable.

Biking

Biking is not quite as popular in Greece as hiking, probably due to the terrain, but you'll find information about local biking routes in most guidebooks as well as at the tourist offices in North America and in Greece. Cycling enthusiasts should inquire directly with the airline they're flying with about rules and regulations for carrying on bicycles, and if you want to take a bike to an island, inquire at the tourist office about what regulations the ferryboat may require. The majority of biking books I've paged through tend to focus on longer, multiday bike trips, as opposed to shorter circuits of a day or a few hours. As I touched upon in the introduction, I'm not at all impressed by travelers who spend every day of their visit to Greece, or anywhere, on a bike; in fact, they are rightly referred to not as travelers but as bikers. Therefore I'm a bit skeptical about tour operators that arrange biking trips that don't allow for at least part of each day—or better, several days— off the bike completely. Some of these companies are very committed to international understanding and immersing the participants in Greek culture, so I must embrace them as I share these views; yet my hope is that they will allow for more time off the bike in future trips. If you feel this is important too, select a company that is more flexible about being off the bike, or consider adding a few extra days to your journey to do some exploring without a two-wheeled vehicle.

Boats and Ferries

Much of Greece is water (there are about 100,000 miles of coastline alone), and it is said that a Greek is never more than a day's walk from the sight of the ocean. As Nicholas Gage writes in *Greece: Land of Light*, "from a glass of water to the village well to the sea, water has dictated the quality of Greek life throughout history. . . . It was by sea that the first inhabitants came and by sea that the island dwellers left home to seek their fortunes because the land could not support them. Greek mariners, from the Argonauts to the ship owners of today, succeeded so well that there are now half as many Greeks living outside the country as the ten million still here." It's likely, therefore, that you will spend at least one portion of your trip on a boat of one type or another. One of the easiest ways, in fact, to get to Greece from mainland Europe is to take the overnight ferry from Italy. Several companies operate service from Venice, Ancona, Bari, and Brindisi to ports on the western coast of Greece, stopping at Igoumenítsa, Corfu, and Patras. Most, if not all, companies transport cars and RVs. If you're traveling with an InterRail or Eurail pass, two companies do not charge (beyond about $15 in port taxes) for space outdoors on the deck of the ship—check the details on your rail pass. Sleeping on deck—at least in the summer months, and when it's not raining—is cheap and fun, and looking up at all those stars over all that water is quite moving. If you don't prefer the equivalent of camping, you may also sleep inside in an airplane-style seat or in a private cruise-ship-style cabin; prices vary accordingly. Once you're in Greece, island-hopping is a fantastic way to see what life is like outside the cities.

Some important facts to remember about boat and ferry travel: ~Schedules vary throughout the year, with many more departures in summer than in winter. In the off season there may be only one boat a week to certain islands. ~Some ferry companies operate runs among the islands, rather than departing from the mainland, and are not listed in guidebooks, but locals will be happy to point you in the right direction for timetables, tickets, and the like. ~No matter what season of the year you'll be visiting Greece, check the schedules in advance to get an approximate idea of the sailing frequencies (*approximate* being the key word, as schedules are famously changeable, depending as they do upon the weather). Greek tourist offices always stock copies of the *Domestic Sea Lines* brochure, updated monthly, and the Hellenic Tourism Organization publishes the *Maritime Transport and Communications* brochure that lists the companies traveling between Italy and Greece and the major companies that serve the islands. But I recommend that you also check the website www.greekferries.gr as your departure date approaches, since this site seems to be updated more frequently. Additionally, all the local tourist offices on the islands post up-to-date schedules, and the staffs are well versed in the details of ferry travel. ~Several types of service are available, including large ferryboats that carry both people and vehicles; high-speed catamarans; and hydrofoils, referred to as Flying Dolphins. The faster the service, the more expensive the fare, but you may deem the extra expense worth it to satisfy your itinerary. ~Depending on where you're going, be prepared to wake up at dawn, since many boats leave very early; take the same precaution on your return. ~Don't ever plan a tight schedule if you can at all avoid it. Stuff happens, and Murphy's Law is alive and well in Greece. A number of famous winds thrive in the Aegean, notably the *maistros* (an Ionian Sea wind that blows along the east coast of the Peloponnese), the Sirocco (a very hot south wind also common in Italy), and the *meltemi* (the most famous wind, predominating from July until late September). These winds, which are depicted in ancient works of art, affect travelers because boats won't sail if it's deemed too windy, and sometimes a sailing is delayed a few hours or even days. Additionally, believe it or not, smaller boats break down and sailings are canceled until the problem is repaired. This really did happen to me once in late February, when I tried to sail to the island of Kéa. First the boat was broken, but after it was repaired, it was too windy, the sailing was delayed, and I never made it to the island.

Buses

The only occasion I have ever ridden a bus in Greece was to travel from Nafplio to Epidaurus and back again. Otherwise, I have always opted against the bus, first because I prefer train travel, and second because there is George, the most famous taxi driver in Greece (more about him in the Taxis entry). Friends and colleagues who relate tales of bus travel to me all emphasize that short trips are fine on a bus, but long-distance journeys are almost unbearable. If your budget is very tight and you have no choice but to get around by bus, refer to some good guidebooks for more detailed information. Within most city and town centers in Greece it is seldom necessary to ride a bus, as most of what visitors will want to see and do is concentrated in a rather small area, and they can usually walk from neighborhood to neighborhood without public transport.

Though I have little first-hand experience with buses in Greece, here are a few universal bus truths valid throughout Greece that are worth remembering: ~If you're making a round-trip journey, purchase your tickets for both legs at the same time; smaller villages may have only one ticket outlet, which may very well be closed at the time of your departure (you may also occasionally buy your tickets on the bus). ~The schedules serving smaller villages are meant to accommodate local residents, not tourists, so the timetables coincide with the villagers' needs. You may find, for example, that in order to visit a particular village, you have to catch an early morning bus, then have only a few hours to see the village, because the return bus departs only once more; or you may have to make arrangements to spend the night, because the return bus departs early the next morning. ~Departure times are honored in Greece, but just as with the proper hour to eat meals (see the Eating Out entry), the right moment to show up for a bus is equally mystifying. About fifteen minutes before my scheduled trip to Epidaurus, my friends and I walked across the street to a bakery to buy some provisions for lunch. We placed our order and periodically kept our eye on the bus, to see if people were boarding. Every time we checked, not a soul was in sight, including the driver. It took about twelve or thir-teen minutes for our lunch to be wrapped up and paid for, so at approximately three minutes before departure, we began walking back across the street to the bus. Within that span of, say, one minute, passengers suddenly materialized, and by the exact departure time, the bus was nearly full.

Byzantium and Byzantine History

For a thorough understanding of Greece and Greek history, as well as a complete itinerary, a visit to Istanbul and the Aegean coast of Turkey would be most desirable. But including those areas in this edition of *The Collected Traveler* would simply make it too large, so I will explore Istanbul, and other parts of Turkey, in upcoming editions. Readers young and old are probably familiar with a song—originally a hit in the 1950s, I believe—about Istanbul once being Constantinople. (The band They Might Be Giants recorded it about ten years ago.) The Roman emperor Constantine, in A.D. 330, moved his capital from Rome to an old Greek city on the Bosporus called Byzantion. Constantine, you may recall, was the first emperor to convert to Christianity, and Byzantion was renamed Constantinople in his honor. Constantinople thus became the capital of the Eastern Roman Empire (Byzantium) and remained the center of that empire for more than a thousand years. For some time after the founding of Constantinople there were two Roman empires, the eastern and the western, both symbolized by a two-headed eagle. After the Western Roman Empire began to fall apart in the fifth century, Byzantium thrived and grew to include parts of southern and eastern Europe, northern Africa, and the Near East. Administratively, the empire was Roman, but its language and culture were Greek. Nicholas Gage, in *Greece: Land of Light*, sums up succinctly the most visible achievement of the Byzantine Empire, notably its domed churches, "usually plain on the outside but encrusted inside with frescoes, mosaics, highly stylized murals, and icons, shimmering with gold and the colors of jewels. The church's plain exterior was meant to represent the daily world, but the interior, gleaming with saints and angels and dominated by the all-seeing face of Christ the Pantocrator gazing down from the dome, represented the ideal or spiritual universe. Although Byzantine artists were influenced by the artistic traditions of ancient Greece, their focus was spiritual and mystical, resulting in flat, two-dimensional figures designed on abstract patterns to emphasize their holiness. The usually anonymous artist was required by the Church to follow very specific formulas when portraying holy figures. Icons were and are considered sacred. Each iconographer who painted a holy figure had to follow the design and colors of his predecessors as closely as possible. Even today Orthodox Christians believe that an icon is a kind of window between earth and heaven through which the inhabitants have chosen to reveal themselves." The eastern and western Christian churches parted ways in 1054 and developed in different directions, the Eastern church becoming more mystical. On May 29, 1453—a Tuesday, still a day of the week on which Greeks will not marry or plan any major life event—Constantinople fell to the Turks and became Istanbul. The Patriarch of the Eastern Orthodox Church, the spiritual leader of approximately 300 million Orthodox Christians around the world, remains in Istanbul. If you have never set foot in an Eastern Orthodox church, you may find the experience, as I did, wholly different from that of walking into a Catholic church. It seems to me much more solemn, more sacred, and darker, with lots of lit candles and the smell of incense always heavy in the air.

There are many, many books on Byzantium, but the following are some that I consider very good, if not among the best on the subject (but I'm always looking for more, so if you have a favorite you feel I've overlooked, please write and let me know): *Alexiad* (by Anna Comnena, Penguin Classics, 1979); *Byzantium: The Early Centuries* (by John Julius Norwich, Alfred A. Knopf, 1989); *A Short History of Byzantium*, also by Norwich, Alfred A. Knopf, 1997); *The Fall of Constantinople: 1453* (by Sir Steven Runciman, Cambridge University Press, 1990); *Fourteen Byzantine Rulers* (by Michael Psellus, Penguin Classics, 1979); and *The Secret History* (by Procopius, Penguin Classics, 1982).

C

Car Rental

You will find repeated references to the supposed danger of renting a car in Greece in every guidebook you read. Traffic accident reports are followed religiously in Greece, a country celebrated for its high-risk driving. A very helpful woman at the Greek National Tourist Organization office in New York urged me, in fact, to make sure I cautioned readers against renting a car—so I've just done so. But in the interest of full disclosure, my husband and I did drive a car, albeit one we had bought—all over the Greek mainland, north and south, and on the island of Corfu, for ten weeks, and we concluded that Greece was only slightly more difficult to drive in than the other Mediterranean countries we had visited. We both believe that, generally speaking, if you do any driving in a major North American city, or drive a lot for business, you simply will not find driving in Greece to be dangerous. Of greater concern is your desire to occasionally traverse a badly maintained road, which could lead to a flat tire or worse, and the expense of taking a car on a ferry. We were grateful to have our own car because the flexibility was so appealing and many corners of the Peloponnese, for example, are best explored with a car. If you're still undecided, perhaps a good compromise is to rent one for a portion of your trip, perhaps for a day trip outside of Athens. And note that, unlike in other

Mediterranean countries, you *do* need an International Driver's License in Greece. I think this is somewhat of a scam, albeit on a small scale as the license is only about ten dollars, but it is a mild annoyance and not worth a fuss.

If you're entering Greece with a car—rented, leased, or owned—make sure you know how old it is, as the issue of foreign cars in Greece is actually quite a serious one. My husband and I bought our used Talbot in Amsterdam, as we had been told (correctly) that the Netherlands was a hassle-free country in which to buy a car. (It took us a grand total of fifteen minutes at the post office to complete the transaction.) We had also been told (incorrectly) that Greece was a great country in which to sell a foreign car because Greece has few, if any, of its own cars and people would pay a high price for a foreign car. All was well until we stopped for a few nights at a great campsite, Gritsa 66, in northern Greece, where a friendly Dutch fellow told us we would *never* be able to sell our car in Greece because it was beyond the age limit—apparently one can get a handsome price indeed for a foreign car, as long as it is no more than six years old; ours, of course, was seven. For the details about the rest of our odyssey, I refer you to the letters my husband sent home to his parents:

Escape from Athens, Part 1

Dear Mom and Dad,

I'm sitting here on the upper deck of a huge ferry, sailing from Athens to our destination of Sífnos, a little island in the western Aegean. The ship is crowded . . . backpackers are sprawled on the deck in their sleeping bags, some with their boom boxes cranking out music indistinguishable above the hum of the engines. I've just come up top here for some air, the view, and to take a few minutes to write this letter. Barrie is down below, in the nonsmoking section equipped with airplane-style seats (albeit slightly roomier and more comfortable). Let me bring you up to date on the car saga. As you recall, we bought the car in Holland nearly five months ago, used and cheap, figuring we'd drive it all over creation and sell it here in Greece, then travel by boat or bus or train or whatever. Well, we overlooked one small detail. When we drove across the border from Macedonia to Greece, the customs guys stamped my passport (in Greek of course) and noted the make, model, and license plate of my car. Now, I am unable to leave the country *without* the car. We've heard horror stories: one Dutch woman abandoned her car, reported it stolen, tried to leave the country, and is still in a Greek jail somewhere. We've tried to sell it, but the law is no car more than six years old can be sold here. Of course, ours is seven years old. We tried to put it on someone else's passport, under the theory that as long as *someone* drives it out of the country, the authorities will accept that. But we've had no luck finding a taker, even assuming that's legal. So we finally got to Athens, still with the albatross around our necks, and tried to figure out how to get out of here. Our first hotel in Athens had no A/C . . . *huge* problem. Between the heat (97 degrees) and the smog, A/C is a must. Two days later we switched hotels and are breathing easier. We then made our first foray to the port of Piraeus, looking for a way to ship some of our gear home, since we would need to be traveling light once the car was gone. Lightening up is an issue, though. Barrie can't seem to bring herself to trade or give away or throw away anything . . . empty ouzo bottles, rocks, books, shells, you name it, she keeps it. I would prefer to travel very light, wash our clothes daily, and be unburdened. But the rock and shell collection would inevitably weigh me down, so what's the use? Anyway, after going from one shipping company to another, we finally opted for air freight, and hopefully some kind family member can go to the airport to retrieve our duffel bag. Back in Athens, bumming out about the car, Barrie approached some guy in the pharmacy, in the shampoo aisle, and casually asked him if he wanted to buy a car. Honestly. And he said yes. This man, Sudanese by birth, agreed to pay us $200 American for our car (quite a letdown after we were told we could get $7,000 if our car was legal). Mr. Sudan, as he will ever after be known, advised me that he still needed to take his driving test, news that didn't seem important at the moment. However, after driving him home to get the cash, he then asked to give the car a test drive. It was then I realized Mr. Sudan had never driven a car in his life, had no idea how to operate a clutch or manual transmission, and it was my responsibility to teach him from the passenger seat while ensuring none of us got killed. It seems the "stay on the pavement" concept was a bit too much for him to grasp. Luckily, there wasn't another car for miles around. In any event, we survived that ordeal, and then arranged to meet Mr. Sudan's friend, an émigré from Libya who escaped from Qaddafi. The aptly dubbed Mr. Libya ran some sort of export business out of Athens, knew cars, understood Greek bureaucracy, and was basically in charge of the smooth transfer of ownership of our vehicle. Ha!! Here's what happened:

Mr. Sudan, Mr. Libya, Barrie, and I went to the Greek customs authority, in an attempt to remove the car from my passport and transfer it to Mr. Sudan's. Then we would board the ship to Sífnos, and be free and clear. Well, after much arguing, screaming, cajoling, and irritation, we have been finally told that the *only* way we can get the car off our passport is agree to ship the car out of the country. Mr. Libya has agreed to load the car onto a Libyan freighter, but the boat sails once a month and it

doesn't arrive for five more days, so off we went to Sífnos, with the understanding that we needed to return to Piraeus for the transfer. Did I mention the Greek (and I believe all Levantine) manner of saying no? They
don't shake their heads from side to side like we do. They raise their eyebrows and jerk their head upward at the same time. If they want to be
emphatic, they simultaneously make a clicking noise with their tongue on
the roof of their mouth. Took me a while to figure this out. But imagine
me standing there, watching Mr. Libya and Mr. Midlevel Power-Hungry
Greek customs bureaucrat going at it toe to toe, basically screaming in
each other's faces (apparently this is normal for conducting business
around here) with the argument punctuated with these emphatic clicking
tongue noises and eyebrows shooting upwards. Like I said, at the end of
the day, we decided to leave the car, go to Sífnos for a few days, and
return to deal with the car for good.

Escape from Athens part 2

Relaxing in our room on the island of Chios, Greek territory, but
within sight of the Turkish coast, savoring the taste of freedom. The
dreaded car is on the Libyan freighter, the Libyans and Sudanese turned
out to be great guys, my passport is legal for exit to Turkey, and I have
$200 cash in my pocket. We spent a nice few days on Sífnos, enjoying the
sun and retsina (Barrie has acquired a taste for the wretched stuff; I am
less enamored). Our ferry from Sífnos back to Piraeus was delayed by the
first rainfall in six months, so we had to hole up in a local bar drinking
ouzo and making friends till 2:00 A.M. Boarded the ship, slept on the floor
of the lounge area (with everyone else) and arrived at 8:00 A.M. One phone
call and two *tyropites* later, Mr. Libya and Mr. Sudan arrived with our car
and we drove to the customs house. Time was slipping away, the
freighter was scheduled to leave at noon, and had our boat from Sífnos
been later, or this transaction taken longer, we would have been stuck for
another month with the car. Fortunately, the gods were smiling on us. The
car was inspected, and sealed up in front of the freighter. We avoided the
glares of the Libyan sailors, and when Mr. Libya asked what the Grateful
Dead stickers on the car signified, we told him they were for good luck!
We headed back to the customs house for the final paperwork, and it only
took us four hours to get things in order . . . passport altered, stamped,
written upon (all in Greek of course), validated, dated, etc., etc. Then off
to the tourist police to sign a document verifying that the car had been
sold legally. Sent away to have the document retyped in Greek. More
screaming, near fisticuffs between the tourist police and Mr. Libya, though

it is becoming increasingly clear that this is the norm for communicating with the authorities. Finally, finally, everything signed, and legal, we bid farewell to these two very helpful and sincere guys, eat a massive lunch in the sun, and board our ship for Chios. Turkey, here we come.

Castro and Chora

These words refer to the hilltop village of an island, usually a Cycladic island. The hilltop village is usually the main town on the island, where in medieval times the villagers had a chance of protecting themselves against piracy and invasion. The town is usually called a *chora* or *chorio* (which simply mean "village"), but if it is fortified, then it's referred to as a *castro* (or *kastro*, "castle"). The town or village at the port is referred to as a *skala*, "steps," referring to the many that are often required to ascend before reaching the *chora*. Nowadays the *skala* is often the more significant part of the island.

Cats and Dogs

Especially on the islands, visitors to Greece may notice rather quickly that there are an awful lot of stray cats and dogs roaming around. Cats especially seem to be everywhere in Greece. They keep the rodent count down, but there are far too many of them; yet the cost to have them spayed is prohibitive, so owners allow their female cats to continue to reproduce. Cats mostly hover for extra scraps of food at your table at outdoor tavernas, but dogs may actually follow you down streets and alleys, testing the patience of even serious animal lovers. I believe the dogs are essentially harmless, if annoying, but I wouldn't want to anger one (a hungry dog, after all, isn't a happy dog). I read recently that a nationwide effort to solve the problem in time for the Summer Olympics is underway, though I think a goal like this will take considerably more time to achieve.

Children

The Greeks extend a warm welcome to children, and include them in nearly every event or gathering, which is why—as in most other Mediterranean countries—young children stay up late at night, even at restaurants (it's also why there isn't a tradition of babysitting). Do not be surprised if it's ten, eleven, or twelve o'clock—yes, midnight—and there are lots of kids running around. I've never seen the children looking unhappy or tired, and it seems to make sense in a country with a tradition of an afternoon siesta.

A few months before my daughter was born, I was feeling anxious that my life as a mother was going to drastically alter my ability to travel. My colleague and friend, Bruce H., helped me snap out of this funk by pointing out that my husband and I would have to travel *differently* than we did before but we would indeed still travel, because we love it. As Bruce is both a parent and world traveler, he advised us not to overthink the situation, because then we would find a million reasons *not* to travel. The way I see it, parents can make the decision never to go anywhere and deprive both children and adults of a priceless experience, or they can plan an itinerary with kids in mind and take off on a new journey. I believe that children have as much to teach us as we do them, especially when traveling—their curiosity and imagination make even familiar destinations seem new.

When I first began working on this series, I could not find country-specific books devoted to traveling with children. Happily, this situation is changing, and publishers have rightly recognized this as a publishing niche to be filled (though there still is not one available for Greece). Parents can, however, find many useful tips and words of advice in many guidebooks and books addressing traveling with children in general (and if you want to read a *really* ambitious account, read *One Year Off: Leaving it All Behind for a Round-the-World Journey with Our Children,* David Elliott Cohen, Simon & Schuster, 1999; and yes, the family of five visited Patras, Olympia, Athens, and Mykonos). Additionally, some good tips can be gathered from a few websites: www.merck.com/disease/travel; www.mylifeguard-forhealth.com; and www.travelwithyourkids.com. Among some of the best words of advice I've discovered from these sources are "above all, don't let a bad moment become a bad day, and don't let a bad day become a bad week" and "decide how much of the trip is going to be FOR the kids and how much will be WITH the kids, though keep in mind that any trip will include a dose of each." And from my friend Katie W., whose one-year-old son projectile vomited over dozens of people in an airport shuttle, "There are just some things you can't prepare for, and some situations when you really need a sense of humor" (I especially tried to keep that one in mind when my three-year-old daughter threw up three times on a flight from Bordeaux to Paris). Following are some general traveling with children tips that have worked for me you may want to try: *If you really enjoy activities such as dining out in fine restaurants or hiking, it makes sense to plan a trip with other adults who also have children. This way, two adults can have some time to themselves—perhaps a day-long hike or a leisurely lunch at nice restaurant—while the other two watch the kids. Taking turns throughout the trip ensures that the adults will feel they had some relaxing, kid-free time to pursue interests they rarely enjoy as well as quality time with the kids. Traveling with grandparents helps in this regard, too. *Build excitement in advance of the trip by involving children in the planning, showing them maps and books and talking about the things you'll see and do. *Read some appropriate books in advance, or save a few for the airplane. A few suggestions, for both toddlers and young adults, are *Ancient Greece: History in Stone* (Philip Wilkinson, Silver Dolphin Books, San Diego, 2001; includes a miniature replica of the Parthenon); *The Children's Homer: The Adventures of Odysseus and the Tale of Troy* (Padraic Colum, illustrated by Willy Pogany, Aladdin paperbacks, original copyright 1918, renewed 1946; recommended for children age ten and up); *The Cod's Tale* (Mark Kurlansky, illustrated by S. D. Schindler, Putnam Publishing Group, 2001; though not exclusively about Greece, Kurlansky brilliantly conceived a book for children based on his wonderful book for adults, *Cod: A Biography of the Fish That Changed the World*, Walker Publishing Company, 1997); *The Courtesan's Daughter* (Priscilla Galloway, Delacorte, 2002; a novel based during the time of ancient Athens); *Island Summer* (Catherine Stock, Lothrop, Lee & Shepard Books,1999; about summer life on the island of Sífnos); *The Odyssey: A Retelling for Young Readers* (Adrian Mitchell, illustrated by Stuart Robertson, DK Classics, 2000; I'm not embarrassed to add that this hardcover volume is great for adults too—as the classics have not been required in many public and private schools for some time, there are plenty of otherwise literate adults who have never read this most classic Greek saga, and while I of course endorse the outstanding "adult" versions of The Odyssey, I see nothing wrong with reading an elementary version such as this, especially if the alternative is to read nothing of *The Odyssey* at all); *The Trojan Horse: How the Greeks Won the War* (Emily Little, Step Into Reading/Random House; for children reading chapters); *Greek Gazette* (Usborne Publishing, 1997), for older readers, is a funny paperback presented in the style of a daily newspaper—some of the stories are entitled '101 Things to Do with Cheese and Olives,' 'Archimedes Splash Smash,' 'The Oracle Speaks—Live From Delphi,' and 'The Trojan War—"Too Much Horseplay" says General'; in the same vein is *The Greek News* (Candlewick Press, Cambridge, Massachusetts), which is in a series of other History News books—the edition I saw featured the headline, 'Alexander Victorious'; *a few titles that are not specifically related to Greece but that I love for their underlying message of learning about other people and celebrating the world's diversity are *And to Think That We Thought That We'd Never Be Friends* (Mary Ann Hoberman, illustrated by Kevin Hawkes, Dell Dragonfly Books, 2003) and *People* (Peter Spier, Doubleday, 1980; I think this book should be required reading for every American). *Lastly, though these are not books, the Greek Coins set created by Winter Reproductions Ltd is a great little diversion for kids. The package includes four coins, made of zinc alloy (containing no lead), that are reproductions of actual, ancient Greek coins. *Select an overnight flight, if possible. Kids are used to going to sleep at night, so you don't upset their schedule as drastically. *Bring along some "surprises" for the flight over. I started a pile of new books, games, and activities about a month before our departure and kept them hidden from my daughter so that she would see them for the first time on the plane. Two of the greatest books I've seen for literally hours of blissful busyness are *Best Travel Activity Book Ever!* (Rand McNally, for ages four to eight) and *The Most Incredible, Outrageous, Packed-to-the-Gills, Bulging-at-the-Seams Sticker Book You've Ever Seen* (Klutz Press, for ages four and up, and winner of a Parents' Choice Award; Klutz, by the way, is my most favorite publisher of unique, fun activity packages for children. Klutz celebrated its 25th anniversary in 2002, and it offers dozens of items that are great for traveling. Good bookstores carry the full line of Klutz products, but interested parents may also want to view its website, www.klutz.com). *For older kids, buy an inexpensive disposable camera and let them take their own pictures. *For kids of all ages, buy a blank journal and help them create a record of the trip (the photos they take will go nicely in here). *Wherever you arrive first in Greece—probably Athens—find a souvenir stand and buy one of those floaty pens—you know, the kind where the Acropolis floats back and forth—or some other kind of nifty pen so kids can use it to write in their journals. *When you arrive at an art museum, first buy some postcards (this is not an original idea, but I've expanded upon it). If you have more than one child, tell the kids that whoever finds the most paintings/works of art or particular works of sculpture or art first, wins a special prize (you must decide this in advance; it could be ice cream, a spoon sweet, or a trinket in the Plaka—whatever your budget allows—but make sure it's something they will want to compete for); if you have one child, tell him or her to find all the artworks—there is no race—to receive a special prize. The last time I tried this was actually not in Greece but Italy. I asked my daughter, Alyssa, to select five postcards from the racks in front of the Accademia in Venice, which she did with enthusiasm. Then, once we were inside, we came upon a mini version of the bookstore about a quarter of the way through the galleries, and I saw a wooden box of colored pencils. I bought the pencils (which she loved) and she then colored on the reverse sides of the postcards. This activity enabled me to walk slowly around every room in the museum. I saw everything in a leisurely fashion, and she never once asked if we could leave. *Strollers are both a blessing and a curse when traveling: on the one hand, when your child needs to take a nap, he or she will fall asleep quite easily in the stroller; on the other, sometimes naptime is precisely when you've reached a spot where you are forced to wake him or her. You may want to consider changing course at some point in your trip. After a few days of leaving the hotel early in the morning and not returning until late in the evening, I decided to plan our days differently, making sure we left early in the morning with not too great a distance to go—so Alyssa could walk—and returning to the hotel in time for lunch and a siesta. In the mid-afternoon, we would set out again, occasionally with, but mostly without, the stroller, making the days less physically exhausting for me and more fun for her. *Finally, for anyone who may still be wondering about the benefits of traveling with the kids, quickly find a copy of this wonderful, creative, and inspiring book: *Storybook Travels: From Eloise's New York to Harry Potter's London, Visits to 30 of the Best-Loved Landmarks in Children's Literature* (Colleen Dunn Bates and Susan Latempa, Three Rivers Press, 2002). This book will motivate anyone to help children make a connection between the books they've read (or books you suspect they may like) and the actual cities or regions of the world where they take place. As the authors note, "These actual places, so vividly imagined by young readers and so fondly remembered by adults, can become the scenes of real-life adventures. Great stories transport the reader, in his or her imagination, to another place. So why not go there for real?" Some of the books selected include *The Adventures of Pinocchio*, *And Now Miguel, A Bear Called Paddington, From the Mixed-Up Files of Mrs. Basil E. Frankweiler, Island of the Blue Dolphins, The Tale of Peter Rabbit*, and *The Watsons Go to Birmingham*. No books with Greek locales are featured, and the authors don't stray outside of North America and Europe (hopefully they will expand upon this and explore Asia, Africa, and South America); nonetheless, this is one of the most fabulous books I've run across in years. *Also worth noting is a letter to the editor I read recently in the travel section of *The New York Times*. The writer stated she felt that the author of a previously published essay underestimated the impact of a five-year-old child's first trip to Europe. She emphasized that twenty years after *her* first trip to Italy, she became an art student, earned her master's degree in art history, and worked as a museum curator. My personal experiences in traveling with children have taught me that one should never underestimate how much children will absorb and retain, and what will inspire and enthuse them.

Clothing

In general I pack light, and unless I have plans to be at fancy places, I pack double-duty items (stuff that can go from daytime to evening) in low-key colors that also mix and match so I can wear garments more than once. I also tend to bring items that aren't my favorites, figuring that if someone does snatch my suitcase or rummage through my hotel room, at least I won't lose the things I love the most. Appearance counts for a lot with the Greeks, and they—like other Europeans—tend to dress up a bit more than Americans. Greeks remain conservative, especially in smaller towns and villages, when it comes to visiting religious houses of worship. You will earn respect and goodwill by refraining from wearing sleeveless shirts, short skirts, and shorts away from the beaches, no matter how hot it is. You may find this odd in a country where topless sunbathing is permitted on the beaches, but make no mistake about it: Dressing inappropriately around town and in church is frowned upon, even in a bigger city like Athens, where some level of respect is expected in sacred establishments.

While blue jeans are as popular in Greece as anywhere, I recommend that you reserve them for casual daytime wear and the most casual places at night (though it does make a difference if you dress them up by also wearing nice shoes, a blazer or nice jacket, a button-down shirt, or a classic sweater or blouse). For men, a suit and tie is necessary only at the finest restaurants and venues, and even at many fine establishments diners wear *nice* clothes but not finery. Polo shirts and khakis are always appropriate during the day and at most places at night. Shorts and T-shirts are popular on beaches and on the islands, though longer shorts are met with more approval than short ones. Although comfortable shoes are of the utmost importance, I never, ever bring sneakers, and I positively forbid my husband to bring them. *You* might not ever bring them again either once you realize that they scream "American." Opt instead for walking shoes and sandals.

Coffee

I have not included a separate entry for coffee in my previous books, but I feel it's applicable for this one. Readers who, like me, feel that a day without coffee is like a day without sunshine, should be forewarned that coffee as you're probably used to drinking it every day is not readily available in Greece, anywhere. Aside from the few Italian *caffès*, which serve the full range of Italian-style espresso drinks, every other establishment where coffee is available serves instant Nescafé. It may come cold, in which case it is better known as a frappé, with ice and water or with milk added (you have to ask for milk)—or, you may ask for traditional Greek coffee, thick hot coffee with grounds at the bottom of the cup (also known outside of Greece as Turkish coffee). I have grown to not only *prefer* Greek coffee but very much *like* it, and my brass *briki* sits on my stovetop for weekend use. Early on during my first visit to Greece I learned how to order an *hellenico metrio* (a medium sweet Greek coffee) and, even now, years later, when I order one, it is instantly assumed that I speak Greek. There are apparently thirty-six different shades of sweetness to a Greek coffee, but the three major varieties are *variglyko* (which is heavy and sweet), *glykivastro* (sweet and boiled), and *metrio* (medium sweet). Though I do not typically add sugar to my coffee here in the States, I find Greek coffee undrinkable without it. A glass of cold water is always served with Greek coffee, and one does not, of course, drink the grounds left at the bottom of the cup—they are for reading, like tea leaves.

Cooking Schools

Greek food is easy to prepare—if sometimes labor-intensive—and learning how to do so in a class can make it that much more enjoyable. Although Greece doesn't offer the sheer volume of cooking classes of, say, France or Italy, the choices are still plentiful and mouthwatering. The best single source for cooking schools in Greece—and the entire world—is the *Shaw Guide to Cooking Schools: Cooking Schools, Courses, Vacations, Apprenticeships, and Wine Instruction Throughout the World* (ShawGuides, New York, updated annually). It lists both internationally famous programs and lesser-known classes, and interested food lovers can view updates to the guide at its website, www.cookforfun.shawguides.com. Among the better-known programs in southern Greece are those offered by Cuisine International (www.cuisineinternational.com); cookbook author Diane Kochilas (who offers weeklong classes every year on the island of Ikaria, where she lives with her husband (http://cuisineinternational.com/index2.html?/greece/glorious/); cookbook author Rosemary Barron, who offers short cooking vacations on the islands of Thíra and Zákinthos (www.rosemarybarronsgreece.com/); and Zante Feast, which offers hands-on classes on Zákinthos (www.zante-feast.org).

Customs
There seems to be a lot of confusion—not only on the part of travelers but of customs agents too—over what items can and cannot be brought into the United States from Greece. The rules are not as confusing as they may seem, but sometimes neither customs staff nor travelers are up to date on what they are. Some examples of what's legal and what's not include: olive oil yes, olives no (unless they're vacuum-packed); fruit jams and preserves yes, fresh fruit no; hard cheeses yes, soft runny cheeses no; commercially canned meat yes (if the inspector can determine that the meat was cooked in the can after it was sealed), fresh and dried meats and meat products no; nuts yes, chestnuts and acorns no; coffee yes, but roasted beans only; dried spices yes, but not curry leaves; fresh and dried flowers yes, but not eucalyptus or any variety with roots. If you think all this is unnecessary bother, remember that it was quite likely a tourist who carried in the wormy fruit that brought the Mediterranean fruit fly to California in 1979. Fighting this pest cost more than $100 million. For more details, call the U.S. Department of Agriculture's Animal and Plant Health Inspection Service at 301-734-8645 or go to its website, www.aphis.usda.gov. By calling 866-SAFGUARD, you may listen to a recording of information for travelers.

Cyclades
The Cyclades are a group of islands in the Aegean Sea that are so called because they form, more or less, a circle (*cyclos* in Greek) around the island of Delos. *Cycladic* is also the name given to one of the Mediterranean's most important prehistoric civilizations, which thrived from 3000 to 1000 B.C. Geologists attribute the peculiar form of the Cyclades to a succession of geological upheavals—earthquakes, volcanic eruptions, movements of the earth's crust—that resulted in the submergence of large chunks of land; many believe that one such stretch of land was the lost continent of Atlantis. According to the curatorial staff of the Metropolitan Museum of Art in New York, the Cyclades are rich in marble, emery, and obsidian, a volcanic glass. As in much of southern Greece, life in the Cyclades is today a mixture of medieval and modern. British travel writer Ernle Branford, in 1998, noted that a book entitled *The Cyclades,* written by Theodore Bent in 1884, remains the best book ever written about the islands. The life Bent saw "has not altogether vanished, nor has the poverty which went with it. Tourism has brought prosperity to the fringes, and some money is beginning to seep through to the inland villages, but the life of the islanders is hard and their ways simple."

Cyprus

The absence of pieces about Cyprus in this edition is not meant to indicate that the island isn't worthy or historically important. Cyprus is wonderful and very much worth the plane or boat trip there. But I was firm in my desire for a piece that presented both the Greek *and* the Turkish sides of the island, and I simply do not have one in my files. This entry will provide some background information as well as resources and tips for readers who are considering adding Cyprus to their itineraries.

In the interest of full disclosure, I confess that I have not yet been to Greek-controlled Cyprus. It's not that I didn't want to, but I was already on the Turkish-controlled northern side of the island, and to get to the Greek side I would have had to retrace my path back to Rhodes and buy a ticket on a Greek boat headed for Greek Cyprus, all of which amounted to a considerable amount of time and additional funds. At that time the Turks thoughtfully stamped a loose sheet of paper that I kept in my passport, because if my passport itself had actually been stamped, I would not have been readmitted into Greece. I cannot, therefore, speak knowledgeably about the different sides of the island, but I can confirm that the Turkish side was beautiful, and I understand that the Greek side is at least equally as appealing. I was most fortunate, while working on this book, to have as an intern Alexia Christodoulides, who has contributed the following profile of Greek Cyprus:

Diesel fumes make me nostalgic for Cyprus. When I was growing up, many cars and trucks in Cyprus ran on diesel, and the smell as we'd overtake some truck on an unpaved single-lane road leading to the beach has stayed with me. Just the word *diesel* conjures up memories of the hot sun on my arm in the backseat of a relative's car, the red dust we'd kick up in our wake, the blue of the sky not softened by humidity, the truck driver's hand waving out the window to signal to us that it was safe to overtake him. I'm remembering the late 1970s and early 1980s when I recall this, since by now almost nobody drives anything anymore that runs on diesel. New cars are just as much of a status symbol in Cyprus as they are elsewhere, and Cyprus's flying leap into the twenty-first century has necessitated their purchase. The island is far removed from how I remember it from my childhood; and only ghosts of the island Lawrence Durrell wrote about in *Bitter Lemons* remain.

I was born in America, shortly after the 1974 Turkish invasion of Cyprus, to a Cypriot father and an American mother. My family's village, Kythrea, fell to the Turks; I've never been there because it's on the north side of the Green Line that denotes the farthest advance of the Turkish troops, physically dividing the island. But I'm aware of the gaping sense of loss that haunts my relatives, whether they lived in Kythrea at the time or had already moved to the capital, Nicosia (Lefkosia). "Our house was the biggest in the village," my aunt likes to tell me; whether it's really true, I can't say because I've never seen the house or the village. What I have seen, though, are the solemn, baby-faced Greek-Cypriot troops guarding the sandbag-and-oil-barrel stations along the Green Line, the blue-and-white-striped guard booths with the stern pictogram warning not to take photos. Their presence reminds me that this line is really a scar, much like the Berlin Wall was a scar, walling in and walling out the tension. The partition of the island, by now, is like the phantom limb of an amputee, aching or itching but not there to be soothed or scratched. Life on the south side of the island has continued, busily, prosperously, but that doesn't mean nobody notices the absence of the north side. Nobody knows how long it will last, but the Turkish government has recently authorized the opening of several checkpoints along the Green Line, which prompted a weird sort of tourism as Greek Cypriots rushed to visit homes they haven't seen in decades.

"Isn't Cyprus a war zone?" a new acquaintance asked me. When I think of Cyprus I think of the perfume of frankincense in churches, the taste of Papaphilipou strawberry ice cream or the souvlaki from the restaurant near my aunt's house, the blocks of designer shops, and long, warm evenings at the houses of relatives, watching the conversation politely with a half-smile frozen on my face because I don't speak Greek. The tension of the conflict is palpable to me because it affects my family (indeed, almost all Cypriot families, Greek or Turkish) personally, but the fighting is finished except in diplomatic circles. It's hard to even imagine it when you're eating some of Cyprus's incomparable french fries or learning to bone fried red mullet in the taverna at Fig Tree Bay (when I was little there was no development at all in the bay, other than the aforementioned taverna—just soft sand, crystal-clear water, the huge fig tree, and the scent of food on the breeze).

In another scene from another visit, my Aunt Olvia threw her hands up in disgust. "They eat their dinner out of a box!" she said, distressed. She was talking about my cousin Nicos and his wife Agni, who sometimes get take-out food from local restaurants instead of calling her to arrange their lunches and dinners for the week. Nicos refers to her services as "Chez Olvia." He's a good cook, but neither he nor his wife really has the time. Many of the usual American corporate food heavyweights (KFC, TGI Friday's, McDonald's, etc.) have franchises in Cyprus and still have the lure of the new and unusual. This weird modernity, this take-out convenience, worries Olvia because it's alien to her. Olvia grew up in a time when restaurants were for special occasions, and home cooking was a competitive sport among women. Olvia is doubly preoccupied because the box-diners are raising their children on this stuff instead of on made-from-scratch Cypriot food, and maybe it means the kids will grow up less Cypriot.

Cyprus has been conquered or colonized by just about every major maritime power in history. There is a theory that the Vikings must have passed through Cyprus because Danish Hardanger embroidery very closely resembles Cypriot Lefkara lace (one of which was chosen by Leonardo da Vinci to adorn the altar of the Duomo in Milan). The Cyprus Handicraft Center in Nicosia shows and sells some examples of Lefkara lace and other crafts, and is a good yardstick to measure quality and price elsewhere (www.kypros.org/Cyprus/Folk/laces.html). If you have access to a car, the drive through the mountains up to Lefkara, where the lace is made by widows dressed in black, is pretty spectacular and makes for a decent escape from the summer heat; and if you're a racing buff, you might be interested to know that the Cyprus Rally runs through this area every summer (www.cyprusaa.org).

One of the best aspects of a desert climate is that monuments don't suffer as much from the elements as in other climates. Cyprus has its fair share of archaeological sites, from the well-preserved mosaics near Paphos to the ancient city of Kourion just west of Limassol, and is home to three UNESCO World Heritage sites. Some of the ancient amphitheaters are still used for theatrical productions: the Kourion amphitheater usually hosts classical productions, Theatro Ena in Nicosia produces plays in Greek, and the Cyprus Tourist Organisation lists a slew of other cultural venues (13 East Fortieth Street, New York NY 10019; 212-683-5280; fax: -5282; www.visit-cyprus.org.cy/ctoweb).

For any reading needs you might have, there are foreign-language bookstores in the cities, usually in or near the main square or on the main shopping street. In Nicosia there's a good international newspaper and magazine selection in Eleftheria Square; and books on just about anything and everything pertaining to Cyprus are available at MAM (Konstantinou Palaiologou Avenue 19, 22.75.35.36, http://mam.cy.net).

Cyprus has been divided since 1974, though Greek Cypriots' demands for *énosis* ("union," the political unification of Cyprus and the Greek "mother country," which you might see spray-painted in places) were first raised in the 1950s. Rather than provide a recitation of the events leading up to the partition, I refer you to *Bitter Lemons* (by Lawrence Durrell, Faber and Faber, 1958), the very best, must-read book about Cyprus that you should make every effort to find (it's inexplicably out of print) and among the most balanced books, on any subject, I've ever encountered. Durrell stated that it was not a political book but rather a study of the moods and atmospheres of Cyprus during the years 1953 to 1956. "Circumstances," he wrote, "gave me several unique angles of vision on Cyprus life and affairs, for I did a number of different jobs while I was there, and even served as an official of the Cyprus Government for the last two years of my stay in the island. Thus I can claim to have seen the unfolding of the Cyprus tragedy both from the village tavern and from Government House. I have tried to illustrate it through my characters and evaluate it in terms of individuals rather than policies, for I wanted to keep the book free from the smaller contempts, in the hope that it would be readable long after the current misunderstandings have been resolved as they must be sooner or later." In addition to this account, *Hostage to History: Cyprus From the Ottomans to Kissinger* (by Christopher Hitchens, Verso, 1997) is another excellent, more recent book that reads like a political thriller. Lastly, a third very good book, also balanced but with maps, color photos, and some practical information for visitors, is *Cyprus* (by Klaus Gallas, Odyssey, London, 1999; distributed in the United States by Seven Hills Book Distributors).

D

Dates

As in many other countries around the world, dates in Greece are written with the day first, followed by the month and then the year, as in 9 September 1959. If you're having trouble adjusting, try thinking of a date as consisting of units of measure, going from the smallest (the individual day) to the largest (the year)—it may be easier to remember that way. If you buy airline, bus, ferryboat, or train tickets in Greece, be absolutely certain you are purchasing them for the correct day, as the date will be printed in the order of day, month, year (and arrival and departure times will be given using the military clock, such as 1300 hours or 1500 hours).

Dodecanese

The Dodecanese—often referred to as the twelve islands—are grouped along the western coast of Asia Minor (Turkey) in the Aegean. They were also referred to by the Turks as 'The Privileged Islands,' according to Ernle Branford, because they enjoyed special privileges and tax exemptions granted them in the sixteenth century by Suleiman the Magnificent. These privileges were retained until 1908, and upon learning they would be removed, the inhabitants of the islands united in protest. Italy took advantage of this situation during war with Turkey in 1911–12, which ended with Italy occupying the islands, though with a promise they would eventually be returned to Greece. At the Treaty of Sèvres, however, after World War I, Italy was awarded the Dodecanese for her participation in the Allied victory, and the islands were not formally united with Greece until 1948, when Italy had been on the losing side of World War II. There is a bit of confusion over exactly which islands are in the Dodecanese group, because fifteen islands were claimed by the Italians in 1912 and then given to Greece in 1948. It's a minor quibble, though; the important thing to note is that they are quite distinctive from their Cycladic neighbors.

E

Eating Out

As the authors of *World Food: Greece* note, "Wherever you go in Greece you might not find lodging, accurate clocks, punctual flights, or a good cup of tea, but by Zeus you will find sustenance!" Greece offers a variety of unique eating and drinking establishments, and though the features that distinguish a restaurant from a *kafeneion*, for example, are usually clear, it's important to recognize the differences, and know what you should—or should not—expect from each place. As travel writer Sandra Gustafson has reminded readers over the years in her many books, "when ordering, remember where you are and stay within the limits of the chef's abilities. Do not expect gourmet fare in a self-service restaurant, and do not go to a proper restaurant and order only a small salad and glass of wine." Greece being the warm-weather country it is, most of the year there are some establishments that are open to the sky. I'm not referring to sidewalk cafés but rather to places that sprouted up between walls (the roofs having caved in as a result of age, earthquake, or wartime bombing) or in long-deserted lots. I love these places and feel they're rather exotic, in the same way I love hotel lobbies without walls in the Caribbean.

Following is a list of all the eating establishments you may encounter in Greece, and just as I recommend that you try different types of accommodations, I encourage you to try different places at mealtimes:

Bar: Bars as we know them in North America are more recent newcomers to Greece. A country with the traditions of the *kafeneion* and *ouzeria* (below) really had no need for yet another drinking establishment. But with the explosion of tourism, especially to the Greek islands, beginning in the 1960s, bars as we know them became more common. Like bars in other European or Mediterranean countries, Greek bars offer a wide selection of alcoholic beverages, as well as sodas and a few other nonalcoholic choices, and some bars serve light snacks and nibbles, such as olives or nuts. I tend to prefer a *kafeneion* or *ouzeria* to one of these more newfangled bars, but that's mostly because very loud pop music of some variety or another is often blasting from a bar.

Estiatorio: An *estiatorio* is a restaurant, which in Greece is sometimes hard to differentiate from a taverna (below). In theory, a restaurant is *supposed* to be different from a taverna, both in terms of the menu and the physical surroundings, and sometimes it is. But other times the only difference between the two is the type of covering on the tables: paper for a taverna, cloth for an *estiatorio*. Seriously.

Often the very same dishes offered in a taverna are also offered in an *estiatorio*, but for double the price. Restaurants that truly offer something different—this is sometimes referred to as modern Greek cuisine—are generally quite delicious and are, justly, more expensive than a taverna. A restaurant specializing in foreign cuisine (anything non-Greek) is also always referred to as an *estiatorio*. I have never eaten at one of these, as I prefer to remain loyal to my host country's cuisine, but I have read that foreign restaurants (except perhaps Italian) are almost universally bad and rarely worth the money.

Fastfundadhiko: This looks a bit like what it is: a fast-food joint. In *Taste of the Aegean*, Andy Harris notes that hamburgers hit Athens in 1969, when the Royale opened in the neighborhood of Glyfada, and today they are available at every snack bar in the city: "After the *tyropita* and *loukanopita* (sausage roll) they are probably the most popular street food." Two popular fast-food chains you may see are Everest and Goody's. I have never set foot in either one. 'Nuff said.

Furnos: A *furnos* is a Greek pie shop, but by pie, I mean the savory pies that Greeks love, *tyropita* (cheese) and *spanakopita* (spinach). Pie shops are just about everywhere in Greece and are perhaps more common than souvlaki stalls. Again to quote from *World Food: Greece*, "You can't get away from them. . . . In every city in Greece at any time of day or night you'll see people walking down the street eating pies." I'm a big fan of both the cheese and the spinach varieties, and I've been known to have one or the other for breakfast, with a *hellenico metrio* (Greek coffee, medium sweet; see the Coffee entry).

Kafeneion: As its name implies, a *kafeneion,* one of the oldest establishments in Greece, was the original coffee shop. Yes, patrons can get coffee here, but nowadays a *kafeneion* may also serve other beverages as well as food, some of it quite good. A *kafeneion* is really the Greek equivalent of a bar (or a café in France), so if you're ever simply looking for a place to sit down and have a drink and you can't find an establishment called "bar," just walk into a *kafeneion* instead—the smallest village, even every neighborhood, has at least one, "even if it's no more than a gaggle of chairs beneath the plane tree in the village square," according to Nicholas Gage. As another travel writer has observed, "As in many Mediterranean countries, café life has always played a large role in shaping the people's and the country's destinies. In many of the city-centre cafes of Athens contracts are drafted, debts contracted and settled, dowries discussed, important new contracts made and plots to overthrow the government hatched."

Kafeteria: The *k* establishes this as a Greek version of a cafeteria. While I probably would not seek out a cafeteria in the States, I've been to a number in Athens and have had some memorable light dishes and snacks, which is what they're for, as opposed to full-course meals. Like a cafeteria in the States, you pay for your food and sit down at a communal table.

Kreperi: The *k* makes it Greek, but it's a creperie nonetheless, serving both savory and sweet crepes all day and into the night. Some of these crepe establishments are simple stalls, while others have tables, a full bar, and music.

Mezethopoleion: This is a general *meze* place, as the name suggests, where you'll find an array of *mezéthes* and a full bar (see the entry for Mezéthes).

Ouzerí or *ouzeria*: As you'll read in the Greek Table section, a number of *ouzeríes* offer full meals and have become quite renowned for their cooking; but their original existence was as a place to drink ouzo. According to *World Food: Greece, ouzeríes* "are tavernas in all but name and have lost their link with the past. And of course tavernas now sell ouzo . . . the cosy, convivial and homely *ouzerí*, a snug place to spend a mildly boozy evening of song and stories is disappearing." While I lament this change, I have had some outstanding meals in some *ouzeríes* and would never fault the owners for providing such excellent cuisine; thankfully, there are still a few remaining traditional *ouzeríes* that you can visit (particularly one in Athens that I recommend in the Good Things, Favorite Places section). Many *ouzeríes* now also offer wine, beer, and brandy.

Paradhosiaki psarotaverna: This is a taverna specializing in seafood, typically fish as opposed to shellfish. These establishments are not very common outside of coastal communities but are definitely good places to seek out if you like fresh fish simply prepared.

Souvlatzidhiko: Souvlaki stalls are everywhere throughout Greece but are especially ubiquitous in large cities, especially Athens. They are very simple operations—resembling street vendors more than proper establishments—and are meant to provide quick nourishment for people on the run. Carved, spit-roasted pork (sometimes chicken) is stuffed into a pita with salad and *tzatziki,* and the patron typically stands right there and eats it or walks away with it. Souvlaki is quite tasty and filling, the perfect nourishment for a day with an especially busy schedule.

Taverna: A taverna is usually much more casual than a restaurant, but all the traditional Greek dishes with which you're familiar appear on taverna menus. Often, in smaller villages and towns, neighbors provide some of the home-cooked dishes offered in the local taverna, and just as often you'll be invited into the kitchen to select what you want. Alcoholic beverages are also served in a taverna, and some patrons (mostly men) ignore the food entirely and arrive only to imbibe.

Tsipouradiko: *Tsipouro* is Greek eau-de-vie (though I've never had one that is as refined as in France) and seems to be interchangeable with *raki*, a strong liquor also popular in more-refined form in Turkey. A *tsipouradiko* typically offers a better selection of ouzo and *raki* than wine, naturally, and it doesn't have as substantial a menu as an *ouzeria* or *mezethopoleion*.

Zaharoplasteio: This unusual-sounding place is a bakery where you can either buy something to take away or sit down at a table and enjoy a treat with a cup of coffee.

In addition to these places, where one mostly sits down, Greece has a number of specialty food retail shops, handy for picnics or boat or train trips. Shops are named for their specialty, with the suffix -*poleion* (meaning "a place that sells") added to the name. Even if you can't pronounce them, you'll at least recognize their names and know what their proprietors are selling:

Alantozythopoleion: a delicatessen, and my favorite tongue twister.
Allantopoleion: a sausage shop.
Artopoleion: a bakery, also known as a *fourno* (oven), mostly for bread.
Galaktopoleion: a milk and dairy shop.
Ichthyopoleion: a fish market, also known as a *psaropoleion*.
Kreopoleion: a meat store.
Lahanopoleion: a vegetable shop.
Oinopoleion: a wine shop.
Oporopoleion: a fruit purveyor.
Tyropoleion: a cheese shop.
Zacharopoleion: a bakery for sweets and pastries, like a French patisserie.

Vilma Liacouras Chantiles, in *The Food of Greece,* notes that in her travels around Greece she has discovered some variations on these standard names, none of which astonished her more than the discovery of a *kafegalaktozacharoplasteion*, which is, in Greek, two letters longer than the entire Greek alphabet!

Following are some tips to keep in mind about eating in Greece: ~Breakfast typically consists of a cup of Greek coffee or Nescafé and a *kouloura,* a doughy, not very sweet, ring rolled in sesame seeds. For readers who've been to Turkey, a *kouloura* will remind you of *simit*. Italian coffee shops seem to be very popular (probably because younger Greeks, who are better traveled than their parents, have moved beyond Greek coffee and prefer cappuccino and other Italian coffee drinks with milk) and offer a wider range of breakfast breads. If this is not enough breakfast for you, you can *always* find a *tyropita* an hour or two later, or a piece of fruit from an outdoor market or corner grocery, or you can sit down at a *kafeteria* and grab a quick snack. Make sure you do find yourself something because lunch is not generally served until about 2:00 P.M. "And," according to *World Food: Greece*, "you'll not have the experience of having struggled up the Acropolis, looked out upon the stunning view, and thought only of eggs and bacon." ~About lunch: precise times for both the lunch and dinner service can be vexing in Greece. My husband and I were once at an upscale campground near Epidaurus, and at 1:15 we walked over to the campground restaurant to inquire what time lunch would be served. The host said 1:30, so we decided to wait and linger just in front of the entrance. At 1:25 it did not at all appear that the restaurant was ready to open, and no one else, not a single person, was waiting with us, so we decided to walk down to the beach and come back. At exactly 1:40 we returned, and the restaurant was completely full. The host told us that he was so sorry, but there was not a single table available, and as the restaurant was of the open-air variety, we could clearly see that it was packed. Our fellow campers—all Greeks, by the way—somehow knew, in the span of fifteen minutes, precisely when to descend upon the restaurant. This is my most extreme example of a vexing mealtime in Greece, but it wasn't my only one. Regarding lunch, however, one thing you can count on is that it is not served at noon or 12:30 and rarely at 1:00 either. It remains the biggest meal of the day, just as in other Mediterranean countries, and it can last, especially in the summer months, as long as two or three hours. "Their [the Greeks'] world will revolve around food and each other," to quote again from *World Food: Greece*. "They will eat and drink and talk and laugh. Life will happen in Greece when all are at the table." Dinner, accordingly, is not eaten until about 10:00 P.M. or later and is typically lighter and less substantial than lunch. My husband and I have nursed many a bottle of ouzo, and eaten platefuls of *mezéthes*, waiting for a taverna to officially open for dinner. We've sometimes been the first to arrive, at 10:00, and then have practically finished eating our meal before a single other person walked in the door. The most important piece of advice about dinner in Greece is that you can never arrive too late.

~ Haute cuisine is not prevalent in Greece, but there are a handful of fine world-class restaurants that are very much worth frequenting (and that require advance reservations). To my mind, this level of fine dining is not simply a dining experience: it's an elaborate stage production of the highest caliber. True, it's very expensive, even in Greece, but properly executed, the experience is sublime and unforgettable and worth every euro. When considering the price of haute cuisine, remember that it is extremely labor-intensive and typically requires enormously expensive ingredients. Also, you do not have to wait for a table because you effectively "buy" a table for the afternoon or evening. Economically speaking, Greek restaurants are completely different from American restaurants, which concentrate on turning over as many tables as possible during mealtimes. Finally, prices on Greek menus include tax and tip, both of which add up to a hefty sum. ~As in most other European countries, the price of food and drink in Greece varies depending on where you sit at a bar or a restaurant. If you opt for a table, you can also expect to remain there for as long as you like. A waiter may ask you to settle a bill if he or she is going off duty, but no one will come along and request that you leave: it simply isn't done. ~Don't let the words *tourist menu* or *fixed price special* necessarily turn you away from a potentially good meal. Just like the *menu turistico* in Italy or the *prix fixe* meal in France, a set meal in Greece is sometimes a good value, often consisting of three preselected courses and nearly always including a carafe or half bottle of wine and coffee or tea. The day's specials are generally prepared with fresh, seasonal ingredients or are specialties of the chef. ~Don't expect credit cards to be universally accepted at bars and small restaurants and cafés. Some bars and smaller establishments will accept them, but counting on it, arriving with no euros in your pocket, could prove a mistake. Nearly every large establishment accepts credit, however, as do those few holding Michelin stars. ~Not very many restaurants set aside a separate section for nonsmokers (and in those that do, the policy is probably not honored). But as a nonsmoker, I have never been at a bar or restaurant in Greece where the smoking particularly bothered me or made me feel like I had to leave. ~Just as in Spain, France, and Italy, most restaurants in Greece close one day of the week; some also close either for lunch or dinner on a particular day of the week (often on weekends), and most close for an annual vacation (usually in the summer). Be sure to check before you set out. ~A good quote to bear in mind from time to time is the following by food writer, cookbook author, editor of *Saveur*, and one of my favorite foodies, Colman Andrews: "I believe, above all, that we ought to learn to dine, or even just sit down and eat, not with fear or with the feeling that we're doing something bad, but with the happiness born of appetite and anticipation—with, if possible, sheer, ravenous joy." (Andrews penned that line for his book *Everything on the Table: Plain Talk About Food and Wine*, Bantam, 1992, a good read, with recipes.) I think he has the right idea about approaching food in general, but his words are especially accurate when applied to how the Greeks, and all Mediterranean peoples really, approach their meals. ~As far as vegetarian dining is concerned, I highly recommend that you give up personal dietary restrictions (unless of course they are health concerns) in favor of getting a taste of the culture you are experiencing. If you are served a regional dish that contains meat, my opinion would be to defer to local custom and experience life in the region you are visiting. But if you insist upon sticking to a vegetarian diet, rather than be a pain in the neck at restaurants with five minutes' worth of pesky questions (almost all of which will have answers you won't like and that you could have predicted), get to know an organization called the Happy Cow's Global Guide to Vegetarian Restaurants and Health Food Stores, which offers information on vegetarian dining throughout the world. Visit its website, www.happycow.org, for resources specific to Greece.

Efharisto

Also transliterated as *evharisto* or *efcharisto*, *efharisto* may be the most important Greek word for you to know, as it means "thank you." A good way to remember it is as "F. Harry Stow." The *h* is correctly pronounced as a guttural *ch*, as in the word *chora,* but you will be understood if you utter it as a soft *h*. To say its use is much appreciated is an understatement.

Evil Eye

Belief in the evil eye is the most common superstition in Greece. Even the Greek Orthodox Church believes in it, referring to it as *vaskania*. Greece is not, of course, the only country in the world with a tradition of the evil eye (it is especially prevalent in the countries of the Levant, including Israel), but within Europe it may be the country where the belief is the most widespread and immediately apparent (see also the entry for Spitting). Blue charms with an eye painted on them are sold at every vendor, shop, market, and tourist shop. Even before you leave Venizelos airport to head into Athens, you will probably spot a great number of them. The charms are made mostly of glass or plastic and are available in dozens of different forms, including beads and wall hangings, on goat bells, and charms on bracelets or necklaces. The belief is that to ward off the evil eye, you should wear the charm, and blue is the color that wards off the evil of the eye. Blue-eyed people are thought to be exceptional carriers of evil, so if a blue-eyed person pays you a compliment, beware: disaster could befall you at any moment. I am not an especially superstitious person (though in recent years I have become more so), but over the years I have amassed a small collection of evil eyes simply because I like them—some of them are quite beautiful. Evil eyes also make great souvenirs, for children and adults.

F

Fairs, Festivals, and Holidays

In her wonderful book *Foods of Greece*, Aglaia Kremezi notes that "our customs and traditions, based on the Greek Orthodox religion, are very often a continuation of ancient Greek rites and pagan rituals. The official church festivals are closely related to the different agricultural or maritime tasks of the early Greeks; indeed, many Christian saints assumed the role Olympian gods occupied in antiquity. For example, Saint Nicholas is the protector of sailors, as Poseidon was for our ancestors. In the Greek Orthodox religion, fasting always precedes an important religious feast, and each festivity has its own foods, which are not necessarily the same in all parts of the country." Besides food, particular customs and traditions also vary from village to village and island to island. I have not included every fair and festival in southern Greece here, as it would fill pages and pages, and many of them are unique to only one region or island. Readers who need more detailed information should consult guidebooks and the Greek National Tourist Organization (Olympic Tower, 645 Fifth Avenue, 9th Fl., New York, NY 10022; 212-421-5777; fax: 212-826-6940; www.greektourism.com) the staff will help you get in touch with smaller local offices if necessary. I do think it's important, however, for travelers to be aware of major holidays that are celebrated all over Greece, and these are briefly outlined below. You may be interested in attending one (or more), or you may prefer to avoid them. Either way, remember that hotel rooms and restaurant reservations are typically hard to come by at these popular times, and if a holiday falls on a Thursday or a Tuesday, Greeks like to bridge the holiday by also taking off on Friday or Monday. This is extremely useful to keep in mind as stores and businesses may also be closed for all or part of the time, and the plumber you need to fix the pipes at the villa you've rented may be unavailable. The calendar below begins with the most important holiday of the year:

Easter: Usually March or April; Greek Orthodox Easter is celebrated on the first Sunday following the full moon after the spring equinox, and always following Passover.
Holy Week.
May 1: In addition to honoring workers, May Day celebrates Mother Nature, flowers, and the first fruits.
Saints Constantine and Helen: May 21. This holiday commemorates Saint Constantine and his mother, Saint Helen, as well as the last Byzantine emperor, Constantine Paleologos.
Assumption of the Virgin Mary: August 15. Assumption is the most important festival in the Greek islands.
Saint Nicholas's Day: December 6
Epiphany: January 6. The Day of the Light is an important religious holiday.
Ai Yianniou: January 7 is the date of Saint John the Baptist's Day.
Saint Dominikis's Day: January 8. This holiday honors a female saint who is the protector of midwives.
Carnival: Three weeks and four Sundays in late winter/early spring, always before Greek Easter. According to Kremezi, "Carnival, complete with disguises and mad parties, is not a religious festival but a collection of folk traditions that have their roots in the ancient celebrations for Dionysus, the god of wine."
First Day of Lent: This is the first of the 40 days preceding Easter, a public holiday in Greece and is also known as *Kathari Deftera,* or Clean Monday, when women clean all their pots and pans to remove all traces of animal fat.
Forty Days of Lent: No marriages, engagements, or any other family celebrations are permitted during Lent, except for March 25, the feast of the Annunciation and also Greek Independence Day.
Saint George's Day: April 23; customarily celebrated on Easter Monday. Kremezi reminds us that "Because nearly half of Greek families celebrate one member's name day on Saint George's Day, there are more banquets, roasted meats, and sweets offered to the relatives and friends who come to visit." Kremezi concludes by writing that "Some of these traditional celebrations have lost their importance in the last few years, because they tend to be forgotten by the second-generation descendants of the villagers who moved to the big cities. There are also many traditional popular feasts that have become soulless tourist attractions, the ritual repeated just for the sake of foreign tourists. This, I think, is worse than forget-

ting the tradition altogether. But in remote villages and islands, you can still find men and women who follow their ancestral customs with unbroken respect."

Film

You'll read often that the quality of the light in Greece is unique and legendary. It also wreaks havoc on film and light meters, so if you plan to capture some of this light, be sure to pack some extra rolls of film to allow for lots of experimentation. To quote again from Nicholas Gage in *Greece: Land of Light*, the light of Greece "tolerates no half-tones, no secrets." Read up on shooting pictures in bright, intense light!

Flora and Fauna

There are almost six thousand species of native flowers in Greece, and the country is practically bursting at the seams with wildflowers in particular—of the 200 species of wild orchid in Europe, about half grow in Greece; and Crete alone boasts 120 unique species of wildflowers. Crete is also home to the endangered kri-kri goat, the last of the island's fauna to walk across the vanished land bridge from Asia (you can still see the kri-kri in the little zoo in Chania). Unfortunately, many of the guides to Greek flora and fauna—including those on wildflowers—are out of print or hard to find in North America. Bookstores in Athens may stock some of these worthy titles: *Wildflowers of Greece* (by G. Sfikas, Efstathiadis, 1993); *Wildflowers of Crete* (by G. Sfikas, Efstathiadis, 1992); *Greek Wild Flowers and Plant Lore in Ancient Greece* (by Hellmut Baumann, W. Stearn, and Eldwyth Ruth Stearn, A&C Black Publishers, 1993); and *Flowers of Greece and the Aegean* (by Anthony Julian Huxley, William Taylor, Trafalgar Square, 1990).

Foundation for Hellenic Culture

In a narrow red-brick building squeezed unobtrusively between Bergdorf-Goodman and Brasserie 8 1/2 on Fifty-seventh Street near Fifth Avenue, the New York City branch of the Foundation for Hellenic Culture is easy to overlook but shouldn't be missed. Established in 1992 in Athens, the foundation also has branches in Alexandria, Berlin, and Odessa, as well as representatives in London, Paris, and Rabat. It promotes Greek language and culture throughout the world by organizing events, publishing Greek books, and exhibiting Greek artworks. Each branch has a library providing newspapers, books, videos, CDs, and other information about Greek life and society. The foundation also organizes regular film screenings and an annual film festival; it offers frequent seminars, lectures, and readings by prominent Greek scholars and authors. The Alexandria, Berlin, and Odessa branches offer Greek language classes at all levels; the New York branch can point you to Greek classes elsewhere in the city. Contact information: 7 West Fifty-seventh Street, Suite 1, New York, NY 10019; 212-308-6908; fax: -0919; www.foundationhellenicculture.com.

G

Greek Gastronomy

There are two names to note in the history of Greek gastronomy. The first is Athenaeus, a Greek writer and gourmet who lived during the second century A.D. Athenaeus authored the world's oldest surviving work of gastronomy, *The Deipnosophists*, which has been translated as The Learned Banquet, Banquet of the Wise, Sophists at Dinner, and Banquet of the Sophists. (Note that it is not to be confused with the world's oldest surviving cookbook, *De Re Coquinaria* by the first-century Roman Apicius.) According to the Loeb Classical Library (see the entry on this authoritative resource), Athenaeus's work tells about a dinner party at a scholar's house to which guests brought texts for reading and discussion. "The work is enjoyable in itself and of great value as a treasury of quotations from works now lost. The reader also learns much about Greek, Persian, Roman, and Sicilian cuisine; the music and entertainments that ornamented banquets; and the intellectual talk that was the heart of Greek conviviality." The Loeb Classical Library, by the way, offers *The Deipnosophists,* translated by Charles Burton Gulick, as a set of seven volumes.

The second, more modern, name in Greek gastronomy is Nicholas Tselementes, who trained as a chef and, in the 1920s, decided it was up to him to educate his countrymen and bring them into modern times by teaching them to eat like the French. According to *World Food: Greece*, Tselementes published a cookbook in which he asserted that "The spices used in the Byzantine kitchen were naïve, even barbaric. He taught them to make sauces on the French model, with chemical precision. He urged the use of butter, and less olive oil. He systematically denuded two thousand years of Greek cookery of its Greekness. He was apparently blissfully unaware that it was the Greeks who taught the Italians, who taught the French, who taught so many others how to cook. His influence is so widely felt that, in Greece, a *tselementes* is slang for a cookbook! City Greeks are still recovering. You will see many of them slavishly imitating foreign cooks because they think that's what's sophisticated. A tug of war is in the souls and bellies of many a Greek between the eastern past and the western future. But go to the islands. Go to the mountains. Go to the villages. There Athenaeus still dwells."

Though most guidebooks don't address it in depth, there is quite a controversy over how much influence the Turks had on Greek culinary history, including most of the foods we think of as being typically—and solely—Greek. Clifford Wright, in his monumental work *A Mediterranean Feast,* has written a most interesting essay on this topic, entitled 'Whither and Whence the Greeks,' parts of which I have excerpted below:

"Among the mountain peoples of the Mediterranean, those of the Greek peninsula and its archipelago are salient. Could Greek cuisine be the font of all contemporary Mediterrean cuisine? We know that some of the earliest written references to cuisine in the Mediterranean are Greek. But some scholars point out that the Greeks of today have not an ounce of classical Greek blood and are in fact a mixture of Albanians, Slavs, and Turks. This is certainly overstating the case, but there is an element of truth. Even so, the story is more complicated than Greek food writers have admitted. A look at the contemporary food of Greece is enlightening. At first glance it appears indebted entirely to Turkish food; and, in fact, many of the names of Greek dishes attest to this. But we should remember that culinary influence flows two ways. This two-way flow is complicated by the fact that when Turkish tribes expanded their control over Anatolia in the twelfth and thirteenth centuries, leading to the establishment of the Seljuk and, later, the Ottoman empires, the population was hugely Greek. Before the arrival of these Turkic tribes from Central Asia, Anatolia was part of the Greek Byzantine Empire. Many of these Greeks converted to Islam. Today scholars are not sure of the extent to which a Byzantine Greek cultural substratum influenced the nomadic Turks moving into Anatolia. There are other influences on Greek cuisine, too, such as Italian. When we think of the contemporary tension between Greece and Turkey, we sometimes forget that the Greeks once hated the Venetians far more than they did the Turks. The Italian influence shows up clearly in many dishes from Ionian islands, and the Turkish influence is felt in the Dodecanese archipelago in the form of pilaf and in the use of spices and seeds such as cumin and sesame seeds. I've been told of other culinary traces, such as spit-roasting on Crete, a method that is said not to have existed before its introduction by Albanians.

As any of the latest naval standoffs between Turks and Greeks in the Aegean shows, the Greeks are not much amenable to the idea that their food might be indebted to Turkish cooking. It is commonplace for Greek food writers to introduce Greek cuisine as one "shaped through over three thousand years of history." The sumptuous feasts described by Homer or Plato and menus from Athenaeus— all this will be described as part of the Greek culinary heritage. Sometimes it can get rather silly, such as the comment of one writer that "When you start your day with rolls and coffee, you are following an ancient Greek custom." One Greek writer went so far as to state that Greek cuisine is twenty-five centuries old and is the ur-cuisine that the Turks, Italians, and other Europeans borrowed from, not the other way around. Nicolas Tselementes was a noted Greek food authority who claimed the Greeks influenced western European foods via Rome; he traced the ancestry of such dishes as *keftedes*, dolmades, moussaka, and *yuvarelakia* to ancient Greek preparations that subsequently became masked behind Turkish and

European names. He also said that bouillabaisse was an off-spring of the Greek *kakaviá*.

The Greek food writers are right about one thing: Greece is the source of an original European cuisine, just as it is the source of Western philosophy. The Hellenist influence on the Mediterranean is no doubt a powerful and important one and should not be underestimated. But whether it is the only font of Mediterranean cuisine is another matter. Greek culinary nationalism has hindered any reasoned debate and research on this question of the degree to which the Greek people preserved and maintained the classical heritage through twenty-five hundred years, including Roman occupation, barbarian invasions, and five hundred years of occupation by the Turks, not to mention interference and occupation by Venetians, Genoese, and Catalans. They ignore the fact that the majority population of peninsular Greece in the Middle Ages was Slav. They also underemphasize the importance of the Byzantine Empire, the Greek successor state to the Roman Empire in the East.

. . . Unfortunately, there are no comparative historical studies of Greek and Turkish food by disinterested third-party scholars, although at least one Greek scholar believes his countrymen claim too much ownership. In any case, all claims regarding the heritage of Greek food must be taken with a grain of salt, for Greek culinary history still awaits its Maxime Rodinson, the French historian who treated culinary history with objective scholarship. As the scholar of medieval Hellenism, Speros Vryonia Jr. warned: "In matters of cuisine the conquerors undoubtedly absorbed some items from the conquered, but the problem is again obscured by a similarity in Byzantine and Islamic cuisine which probably existed before the appearance of the Turks." For my part, I am convinced of the possibility that contemporary Greek food, when it is not directly taken from the Turks or Italians, has its roots more properly in Greek Byzantium than it does in the classical era.

The history of Greek food is as complicated as Greek history. Listening today, one would think that the boundary between Greek and Turkish is true and clear—but it isn't, for although Greece was part of the Ottoman Empire for a long time, the Greeks themselves sometimes benefited from a pax turcica. In the Middle Ages, the Greek peasants of Anatolia rose up against the towns where their Greek landlords lived, converted to Islam, and welcomed the Turkish nomads arriving from the East. Remember, too, that the Greeks helped the Turkish expedition against Crete in the seventeenth century because they hated the Venetians. Before the Turks, Greece was under the scourge of the Catalans, who took Athens in 1311 and set up their own dynasty, not to mention the Florentines in the late fourteenth and early fifteenth centuries.

. . . The rivalry between the Houses of Anjou and Aragon over the island of Sicily affected Greek history of the late thirteenth century more than any other cause. Once peace came to Sicily, the Catalan auxiliaries of Aragon sought their mercenary adventure in Greece, wreaking havoc on the Greeks and the Frankish rulers of the Levant. The Catalans ruled Attica and Boetia for seventy-five years, until Athens was taken by Nerio Acciaiuoli, a member of a famous Florentine banking and arms manufacturing family in 1388 and the Greeks subjugated. The position of the Greeks during this time is reflected in Catalan, Sicilian, and Florentine documents where, when concerned with Greece, the Greeks remain nameless. For a hundred years Greece was dominated by this conflict, only to fall to the Ottoman Turks in short order. By the late fourteenth and early fifteenth centuries, there was an upsurge in Greek ethnic awareness that sustained the Greeks as a people through four centuries of Turkish rule. This spirit was fostered and guided by the Greek Orthodox Church. Whatever exists in the way of a unique Greek cuisine more than likely derives from the efforts of the Orthodox church in sustaining Greek Byzantine culture, rather than from the classical period, and was influenced by mountain Greeks who were not so easily subjugated by occupying powers."

Joyce Goldstein, in *Mediterranean: The Beautiful Cookbook*, observes that "Like other subject peoples, the Greeks enjoyed a broad measure of cultural autonomy under Ottoman rule, and no comparable body of loan words can be found in any other sector of Greek vocabulary . . . the traffic was in any event not all one way. The safest conclusion to draw on this contentious aspect of Greco-Turkish relations is that both peoples made their varying contributions to a culinary synthesis that came to perfection during the centuries of Ottoman rule."

Greek Travel Pages

This directory, available both in book form and online, is the bible for transportation schedules all over Greece. You can find the book at tourist offices and travel agents that specialize in trips to Greece, or you can view the website to find what you're looking for (www.gtp.gr). A number of other travel-related listings are also featured, but its real purpose is domestic transportation within Greece—everything from airplanes to yachts. For over twenty-five years, GTP has been the only monthly tourism guide, in English, that has established itself as an invaluable source of information for travel and tourism professionals.

H

Health

Staying healthy while traveling in Greece should not be a challenge, but things do happen. One of the main causes, I suspect, is the drinking water. Though I have drunk water from the tap in Greece and read that it is fine, most of the time I drink bottled water. ~Yogurt, which is exceptionally delicious in Greece and is available everywhere, is a great addition to your daily diet and is known to help in preventing traveler's diarrhea. ~If you need to make a trip to a pharmacy (*farmakio*), you'll find it quite busy (Greeks famously live up to one of their words, *hypochondriac*), and Greek pharmacists are legally authorized to dispense many drugs that in the States would require a prescription from a doctor. Pharmacies are typically closed evenings and Saturday mornings, but just as in Spain, France, and Italy, all of them post a monthly schedule on the door indicating the pharmacists who have night and weekend duty.

Hellas

Hellas is the Greek word for Greece, *Hellene* is a noun for Greek, and *Hellenic* refers to the ancient Greeks or their language, culture, thought, etc. from the eighth century B.C. to the death of Alexander the Great in 323 B.C. It's interesting to note, however, that the Greeks, when they living under Ottoman rule, referred to themselves as *Romaioi*—inhabitants of the Roman empire. According to Mark Mazower in *The Balkans*, this term had replaced the older *Hellenes*, which had come to mean "pagan."

Herodotus

The man who Cicero described as the 'Father of History' deserves his own entry here. Though some historians believe Herodotus occasionally stretched the truth a bit in his reporting in *The Histories*, he is nonetheless the most significant historian of all time. There are numerous editions of *The Histories*, but I am partial to the Everyman's Library volume, translated by George Rawlinson. In this handsome hardcover we are reminded that for more than a hundred generations, Herodotus' prose has "drawn readers into his panoramic vision of the war between the Greek city-states and the great empire to the east. And in the generosity of his spirit, in the instinctive empiricism that took him searching over much of the known world for information, in the care he took with sources and historical evidence, in his freedom from intolerance and prejudice, he virtually defined the rational, humane spirit that is the enduring legacy of Greek civilization." Some readers may be interested to delve into a great Herodotus website, www.herodotuswebsite.co.uk, maintained by a British enthusiast named John (I was unable, in my brief visit, to ascertain his last name). The site is quite commendable, with a great section of maps of the ancient world, a glossary, related links, bibliography, essays, commentaries, timescale, etc. I was visitor number 14,785 when I logged on, so apparently there is a community of Herodotus fans.

Hiking

There are lots of opportunities for hiking in southern Greece. The Peloponnese is perhaps the most obvious choice, but there are also some great hiking trails on the islands, notably Crete and Rhodes. Ramblers and serious hikers will be rewarded, whether for day hikes or longer treks. An important difference between hiking in the United States and Greece (and in Europe and the Mediterranean basin generally) is that hiking is generally not considered a wilderness experience the way we know and expect it to be in North America. In Canada and the United States wide open spaces and undeveloped land are of significant importance, but in Greece the land has been much more cultivated and deforested. Therefore, most of what you walk on is a well-worn *route*, not a leisurely hiking trail. The routes were not created at random but often connect old paths that have existed for hundreds of years. There are very few places in Europe—now or ever—where you can backpack into a completely isolated area and not encounter roads, people, or towns.

The best source for organizing a hiking trip is Trekking Hellas, the leading outdoors tour operator in Greece, which has ten offices around the country. On the Peloponnese it offers a number of single-day excursions as well as weekend trips and longer excursions. On the Aegean islands it offers a trekking trip through the Cyclades and a nine-day/eight-night journey on Crete. Several writers highly recommended Trekking Hellas and have praised the company's guides in particular. Contact information: Filellinon 7, 105-57 Athens; 210.331.0323; fax: 323.4548; www.trekking.gr.

Honey

Greek honey is legendary, and if you've never tasted any, don't miss the opportunity to do so while in Greece. According to Andrew Dalby in his fascinating *Siren Feasts*, the domestication of bees in Greece may have come relatively late: "They were kept in Egypt in the late third millennium B.C., but the first identified beehive of Greece comes from Akrotiri, destroyed by the eruption of Thera (Thíra) in 1628 B.C. The find reported by Doumas is over a thousand years older than the earliest evidence of bee domestication in Greece previously known."

Hours

As I mentioned in the Introduction, you should as quickly as possible embrace a daily schedule that allows for a rather early rising, an afternoon siesta, and dinner no earlier than 8:00 or 9:00 (and even then, you'll be the only patrons in a place). Nearly everyone participates in the evening *volta* ("stroll"—see the Volta entry) before sitting down to dinner. Generally, the majority of shops, businesses, and government offices are open by 8:00 or 8:30 A.M. They close for lunch sometime between 1:00 and 2:00. Shops typically open again at 5:00 or 5:30 and remain open until about 8:00 or 8:30, while banks and post offices operate on a different schedule. Banks are open until 1:30 or 2:00 and do not open again except in some large cities and towns, where they might be open from 3:30 to 6:30. They are not typically open on Saturdays, though in large cities and towns banks may be open Saturday mornings only. Post offices generally open by 7:30 in the morning and close for the day at 2:00. In major cities they are open until about 8:00 P.M., and some also open from 7:30 to 2:00 on Saturdays. Supermarkets and department stores are generally continuously open, from 8:00 to 8:00, though they are typically closed on Sundays.

Greek cookbook author Vilma Liacouras Chantiles notes that this Greek, and Mediterranean, way of life seems to create two days in one. "Schools and government support the rest period. For example, the *dimosia* (public schools), which open at 8:00 A.M., close for the day at 1:00 P.M., so that youngsters may go home for the main meal and rest period. Construction work must stop: Greek people feel imposed upon if their nap is interrupted by disturbing sounds . . . after the family meal, children as well as adults must 'rest.' They must be quiet even if they do not sleep. 'Why do we have to rest?' our youngsters ask. It is through this pattern, we try to explain to them, that the Greek family stays closely knit; it is the reason that Greek people can stay up longer and need less sleep at night, and possibly can wait longer between meals—all so very different from American habits and life."

I

Ikonostasi

Ikonostasi (to which the word *icon* is related) are religious shrines that are found all over Greece. I have seen more little roadside shrines in Greece than in any other Mediterranean country, nearly as many as I encountered in Thailand. Some are quite elaborate, some are quite simple, all are quite moving.

The Iliad *and* The Odyssey

Typically, I mention works of fiction in the *Good Things, Favorite Places* section of my books. I make an exception here because there is still debate over whether these singular poems by Homer (often referred to as the world's first travel writer) are fiction or non-fiction, and *The Iliad* and *The Odyssey* are among the world's literary masterpieces (*The Iliad* has been referred to as the "world's greatest war story"; *The Odyssey* as "literature's grandest evocation of everyman's journey through life"). You'll find dozens of translations—spend some time selecting one you think suits your reading interest—though I recommend the pair of volumes translated by Robert Fagles (both published by Viking in hardcover). I cast my votes for Fagles because, as his publisher has noted, his translations "delight both the classicist and the public at large." And an indispensable and wonderful companion/guide is *Homeric Moments: Clues to Delight in Reading* The Odyssey *and*

The Iliad (Eva T. H. Brann, Paul Dry Books, 2002). I could go on for pages casting off superlatives about this phenomenal—yes, phenomenal—book, but perhaps it's best to simply urge you to search for a copy in a good bookstore or your library and begin your journey in the wine-colored sea.

Immigration History Research Center

The IHRC, located on the campus of The University of Minnesota, is an out-standing resource that I only learned of when I was working on this book. Its mission is to collect, preserve, and make available archival and published resources documenting immigration and ethnicity on a national scope. Materials are particularly rich for ethnic groups that originated in eastern, central, and southern Europe and the Near East—those who came to America during the Great Migration that gained momentum in the 1880s and peaked in the first decades of the twentieth century. The IHRC's Greek American collection is extensive and contains a variety of archival and published material documenting Greek settlement and activity throughout the U.S. The cornerstone of the collection is the large—thirty-three linear feet—body of personal and professional papers compiled by the leading historian of Greek immigration, Theodore Saloutos. The Saloutos collection is complemented by other archival sources, including records of the U.S. Department of State, 1910–29, concerning political relations between the United States and Greece. Additionally, the IHRC holds more than 400 books and pamphlets written by, for, and about Greek Americans. The IHRC website—http://www1.umn.edu/ihrc.com—is one you can easily lose yourself in, and the links—including one for genealogy—are great.

Islands

Islands make up one-fifth of the land area of Greece, and collectively they represent enormous tourist dollars, being the destination of many tourists. What I propose to travelers who are trying to form an island itinerary is to select islands that are different from one another and that are in different island groups. For example, I think it is worthwhile to visit one of the home islands of the Saronic Gulf, add on at least one Cycladic island, and then select an island farther away, such as one in the Dodecanese group, or Crete.

J

Jewish History in Greece

Greece was home to a Jewish community before the beginning of the Roman Diaspora in A.D. 71, earlier than any other European country, and travelers' accounts trace it back even farther, to the third century B.C. The Jews who settled in Greece during the third century built synagogues on Delos, in the Agora of ancient Athens, and on the island of Aegina; they were known as Romaniotes. Until the fifteenth century they made up the majority of the Jewish population of Greece, and at the end of that century, many thousands of Sephardic Jews, expelled from the Iberian Peninsula, settled in the Ottoman Empire, especially in Constantinople, Smyrna, Rhodes, and Thessaloníki. Between 1832 and 1913 the Jewish community of Greece rose in number from 10,000 to 100,000. Despite the interfaith civil and spiritual national resistance to the Nazi expulsions during 1943 and 1944, approximately 87 percent of Greece's Jewish population was annihilated. Only 10 percent of the entire community survived. Thessaloníki's Jewish community holds the dubious record for the highest percentage decimated of any Jewish community in Europe. Postwar emigration further reduced the size of the community, and today only about 5,000 Jews makes their home in Greece, specifically in Athens, Thessaloníki, Larissa, Ioánnina, Volos, Tríkala, Khalkī, Corfu, and Rhodes.

A good book to consult for further information on sites, monuments, synagogues, cemeteries, and restaurants is *A Travel Guide to Jewish Europe* (by Ben Frank, Pelican Publishing, Gretna, La.). For some excellent historical companion reading, consider *Balkan Ghosts* (by Robert Kaplan, St. Martin's Press, 1993), which includes a section entitled "Greece: Western Mistress, Eastern Bride." Its first chapter—"Farewell to Salonika"—focuses on the large Jewish community of Thessaloníki (Salonika), the second largest city in Greece. In fact, the history of Salonika is said to be the history of Judaism in Greece. Also worthy is *Salonika: A Family Cookbook* (by Esin Eden and Nicholas Stavroulakis, Talos Press, Athens, 1997). This little cookbook conveys much about the history of Greek Judaism in general, and as there are not many sources at all on the subject, I am pleased to include it here.

K

Kali orexi!

This *k* word is the phrase for "good appetite."

Kalokairi

Another good word to know, meaning "good time," as well as "summer." You may never hear anyone use it, but it's such a happy-sounding word, I had to include it.

Kalimera

Extremely useful and polite, this word means "good morning." Two other essential *k* words are *kalispera* ("good evening") and *kalinichta* ("good night").

Karagiozi

This is Greek shadow puppet theater, and if you've never seen the puppets or a performance, make an effort to secure tickets. Though the tradition may, in fact, have derived from the Ottomans (shhh!), in Greece the shows are of course very Greek (there is even a weekly show on television). The puppets themselves are often made of painted leather and are beautiful. The performances are not just for children, and though they're in Greek, it doesn't matter: it's great fun to watch everyone else laugh, and you may even be able to follow a little bit of the thread yourself. (Some themes are universal, after all.)

Kefi

Kefi is an essential Greek word to know and translates as a zest for life as only the Greeks can express it, or as Nicholas Gage writes in *Greek Light, kefi* is "an enthusiasm that can make a man rise from the table in a taverna or nightclub and begin to dance by himself, driven by the plaintive melodies of the bouzouki or clarinet." Kefi is perhaps best expressed in *Zorba the Greek,* but you may, if you frequent the kind of clubs that are not generally for tourists, experience *kefi* firsthand.

L

Language

In Greece, as Patricia Storace has noted in her wonderful book *Dinner with Persephone*, "where every enterprise that involves language—publishing, entertainment, journalism, tourism—is dependent on the roughly nine million people who speak Greek, knowing one or more foreign languages is a professional necessity." Storace also wonders "how it affects people here to have to add the learning of languages to other everyday necessities, and I wonder how it affects native English speakers to be in possession of the current lingua franca, a status once held by Latin, and before that, by Greek. Being able to rely on the dominance of English may affect English speakers' ability to approach and imagine other cultures—as if they were rich children, who have inherited such an enormous trust fund that they can choose whether or not to go to work." Storace also noticed, in Athens, a plethora of advertisements for English language classes, as well as others. While this might give one the impression that English is widely spoken, in fact it isn't quite true, at least in my experience. On my most recent visit all the staff members at my hotel in Athens spoke English in varying degrees, but some taxi drivers could not speak a word; neither did some kiosk vendors, shop sales staff, and café employees. This proved to be true outside Athens as well. But many more Greeks speak English than did so five to ten years ago, which I believe is somewhat due to Greece's membership in the European Union as well as the selection of Athens as the site of the 2004 Summer Olympic Games.

It really is true, as it's emphasized in the film *My Big Fat Greek Wedding*, that so very many of our English words come from the Greek. Though it may seem like an outdated language today, Greek was, for quite some time, widely spoken and highly regarded. Norman Cantor, in his fine book *Antiquity: The Civilization of the Ancient World* (HarperCollins, 2003), reminds us that "The Greeks picked up a written alphabet (much superior to the Egyptian and Iraqi form of writing) from another sea people, the Phoenicians (centered in Lebanon and what today is Tunis). By 350 B.C., written and spoken Greek became the international commercial and intellectual language of the Mediterranean. For nine months out of a year, the Mediterranean Sea was actively traversed by Greek ships carrying goods from one end to the other." Mark Mazower, in *The Balkans,* notes that Greek was the ruling language during the Byzantine period, and as the language of the Gospels, Christian culture and classical learning through Ottoman times as well, attracted ambitious young Vlach or Slav men—just as Venetian, German and later French would do as well. As late as the 1860s, according to the memoirs of one Ottoman official, Greek was still known to "all Romanians of distinction" and used in preference to Turkish when Ottoman and Romanian notables met. Jewish communities that dated back to classical times acquired Greek as their vernacular tongue.

Even more than in France, a few polite words of Greek will win you a huge smile, grateful appreciation, a surprised expression, or all three. I've already mentioned the key words of *efharisto, kalimera, kalispera,* and *kalinichta*; a few others—*parakalo* and *yia sas*—have separate entries as well. It is useful to try to memorize as much of the ancient Greek alphabet as you can, especially for reading street signs, bus destinations, and shop signs. Now is your chance to say "It's Greek to me" and really mean it! It's important to remember that the various spellings of Greek words you will encounter in travel guides and other books is due to the difficulty, if not impossibility, of transliteration from the Greek alphabet to the Latin (English). As I was informed by Harry Avery, a classics professor at the University of Pittsburgh, the issue of transliteration "has been a long-standing headache." As with Hebrew, Arabic, and Cyrillic, there is more than one way to transliterate a word into English, and therefore the English spelling of a word in one book will rarely match the spelling in another (I once read that the word *chanukah* may be spelled 125 different ways). Total consistency may be a will-of-the-wisp, but my editor and I have tried to maintain some form of consistency in this book (by the way, professor Avery recommends the *Modern Greek-English Dictionary* by J. T. Pring, Oxford University Press, as a respected source in this matter). Some basic pointers: 'f' and hard 'c' do not exist in Greek (though they do appear on transliterated road signs and maps), but their equivalents, 'ph' and 'k' exist in both alphabets. 'Ch' (pronounced as in the Scottish word 'loch') is used in the words *chora*, the island of Chios, and the Cretan town Chania. 'Y' exists in Greek as the letter upsilon, and appears in the place names Syros, Pyrgos, and Hydra. However, in words like *Ágios* and *Agía*, the 'y' sound is employed instead of the 'g' with which we're familiar. Additionally, there is a feminine form for surnames. Generally, you convert a man's name ending in *–as* or *–is* into that of his wife or daughter by dropping the final letter: Dimas to Dima, Kapsis to Kapsi; if the name ends in *–os*, you convert with an *–ou* and shift the stress one syllable: Papa*do*poulos to Papa*do*pou*lou. If you'd like to enroll in Greek language classes, a few options to consider include the Athens Centre (Archimidous 48, Athens 11636; www. athenscentre.gr); Study Abroad in Greece (International Center for Hellenic and Mediterranean Studies, Vassileos Constantinou 2, 11635 Athens); and College Year in Athens, P.O. Box 309890, Cambridge MA 02139; www.cyathens.org. College Year in Athens is more than forty years old, and in addition to language, it offers a full program of other classes, including Greek and Byzantine art and architecture; history; poetry and modern Greek literature; philosophy; and politics and society.

Finally, though the Greeks themselves are gregarious talkers and avid debaters, they rarely shout. In fact, if you're walking around or eating in a restaurant and you hear loud voices, they will invariably be American. It is more the custom to converse in a regular tone, if somewhat excitedly, than to speak loudly. Bruce Northam, in *Globetrotter Dogma* that I cannot stop enthusing about, created a list of six American impulses to avoid if you do not wish to be viewed as unsavory: "High-fiving everyone; wearing high-top sneakers and a baseball cap backward; talking incessantly, volume set on loud. Observation: There are *two* North American languages: English and louder; defending American football players against charges that they're overpadded, compared to helmetless, and possibly toothless, rugby players; giving an enthusiastic thumbs-up, accompanied by a light-headed grin; prefixing your sentences with 'yo' and 'like.' Responding with 'totally' and 'definitely!' Then high-fiving again."

Lepanto

The Battle of Lepanto, in 1571, is a hugely significant conflict in Mediterranean—especially Greek, Spanish, Venetian, and Turkish—history (readers who have visited Vatican City may remember that in the impressive *Galleria delle Carte Geografiche*, the covered peristyle that connects the old Vatican palace to the Belvedere, there is an enormous wall painting of the Battle of Lepanto). The site of this naval battle was outside the narrows in the Gulf of Patras, overlooked by the castle of Lepanto (at the time, in fact, the gulf was known as the Gulf of Lepanto). The fleet that set out to fight the Turks was primarily Spanish, and had strong papal and Venetian contingents. The Christians were victorious—and the victory reasserted Spanish supremacy in the Mediterranean—and was celebrated with much fanfare in Europe. However, Sir Charles Petrie, in his work *Philip II of Spain* (1963), noted that "The battle of Lepanto did not break the back of Ottoman naval power, it did not recover Cyprus, and it did not lead to the policing of the Mediterranean by Spain. Though a tactical victory of the first order, because of the dissolution of the [Holy] League strategically it left the Sultan the victor. But morally it was decisive, for by lifting the pall of terror which had shrouded eastern and central Europe since 1453, it blazoned throughout Christendom the startling fact that the Turk was no longer invincible. Hence onward to the battle of Zenta, in 1697, when Eugene, Prince of Savoy, drove in rout the army of Sultan Mustafa II into the river Theiss, and thereby finally exorcised the Turkish threat to Europe. Though there were to be many ups and downs, never was the full prestige of Suleyman the Magnificent to be revived. His reign marks the summit of Turkish power, and it was the day of Lepanto which broke the charm upon which it rested." More recently (2000), historian Bernard Lewis, in *A Middle East Mosaic,* notes that Lepanto made very little difference to the real balance of power in southeastern Europe and the Mediterranean. "The Turkish armies remained dominant on land; the Turkish fleets were swiftly rebuilt. When the sultan expressed concern about the cost, his grand vizier replied: "The might of our empire is such that if we wished to equip the entire fleet with silver anchors, silken rigging and satin sails, we could do it."

Sir Charles Petrie has noted that "both Philip and Don John have been subject to criticism, chiefly civilian, for not having followed up the victory of Lepanto by an immediate attack upon Constantinople, which, according to the critics, would inevitably have been followed by the overthrow of the Ottoman Empire. The blame is usually placed upon the shoulders of the king either on the grounds of his habitual procrastination or of his jealousy of his brother." Two excellent accounts of Lepanto are found in *Decisive Battles of the Western World,* volume I, by J. F. C. Fuller (see bibliography in The Kiosk section) and my *Northern Spain* edition ('Victory at Sea, 1571: Lepanto,' by Oliver Warner).

Loeb Classical Library

It is a rare thing indeed when the story of a library is as peripatetic as that of one of its most famous texts, but that's the case of the Loeb Classical Library. Originally founded in 1911 by banker and philanthropist James Loeb, the idea for the Library was to make Greek and Latin texts accessible to everyone. Loeb contacted several publishers about his idea and was told in no uncertain terms that the idea was unmarketable, until finally William Heinemann agreed to publish the first twenty volumes in the series. Business went smoothly in the early years. Upon Loeb's death in 1933, the Library was bequeathed to his alma mater, Harvard University, which then appointed Harvard University Press to publish it (with Heinemann still overseeing manufacturing, and distribution outside America, an arrangement that lasted until 1989, through Heinemann's sale several times over). The books were manufactured in England and published simultaneously in America, a process that proved problematic during World War II, when it was difficult to import the books across U-boat patrolled waters, and the stock in the warehouses was destroyed twice by air attacks. Since 1989 Harvard University Press has had sole responsibility for the Library, which, like Odysseus returning home to Attica and Penelope, can stop wandering for a while.

The collection—plays, philosophical and political texts, poetry, histories, speeches, and letters—is printed with the original text and its English translation on facing pages. The Library's goal is to provide the most accurate, faithful translations possible. Loeb books are sold at major bookstore chains, at many university bookstores, and in some independent bookshops.

M

Macedonia

When, in 1991, this southern region of the former Yugoslavia declared itself independent and intent on calling itself by the name of the region—home of Alexander the Great—that included a large swath of northern Greece and southern Bulgaria as well, thousands of Greeks protested, and the Greek government threatened to withdraw from the European Community if the name (and the flag, which uses the Alexandrian star) was allowed to stand. The Former Yugoslav Republic of Macedonia (FYROM) is the name the two communities eventually compromised on, but many Greeks still call the republic by the name of its capital, Ta Skópia (Skopje). Greeks are offended by what they see as co-opting a piece of their cultural identity, certainly, but considering the instability of the Balkan region in the past fifteen years they also see the claim to this particular name as a threat of larger ambitions. As Senator Christopher Dodd wrote in a May 1992 letter to *The New York Times*, "When Marshal Tito established the so-called 'People's Republic of Macedonia' as part of Yugoslavia, he did so with the thought in mind of annexing as well the adjoining Macedonian provinces of Greece and Bulgaria. . . . Although he failed in his efforts to annex Greek Macedonia, he obviously left a legacy of suspicion about Yugoslav intentions." The Macedonian argument is that after the Greek civil war (1946–49), Greeks were a minority in the region. Those who sided with the Athens government against the Communists were rewarded with the property from thousands of Greeks—and Slavs—who fled the area known as Macedonia. The Greek constitution guarantees the right of return, or at least compensation for their property, to ethnic Greeks; but the Slavs have no such rights under the constitution, and they feel wronged. According to one travel writer, the ongoing argument for legitimacy hinges mostly on "whether the ancient Macedonian kings were pure-bred Hellenes (the Greek position), Hellenized barbarians (the neutral conclusion) or proto-Slavs (the Macedonian claim)." You are bound to see bumper stickers or graffiti claiming that "Macedonia was, is and always will be Greek and only Greek!" Stay tuned—I think this will be an issue to watch in the twenty-first century.

Magna Graecia

The phrase *Magna Graecia* refers to the ancient colonial cities and settlements of Greece in southern Italy. The authors of *Hellas,* Keith Branigan and Michael Vickers, note that between approximately 750 and 550 B.C. colonists from Corinth, Mégara, Euboea, Rhodes, Crete, and elsewhere made their way westward to make their fortunes. The reasons why so many should have left Greece in this way are complex. There were the landless poor, of course, but there were also the landless rich—younger sons with no hope of an inheritance at home, but who wished to possess their own estates. There were also merchants attracted by the hope of trade; indeed, the earliest settlements in the west seem to have been trading posts, although later on some clearly derived most of their wealth from agriculture." An outstanding—and quite authoritative—book to read is *The Greek World: Art and Civilization in Magna Graecia and Sicily* (edited by Giovanni Pugliese Carratelli, Rizzoli, 1996; published on the occasion of the exhibition "The Western Greeks," held at the Palazzo Grassi, Venice, March–December 1996).

Maps

Though I employ a variety of maps for driving, hiking, and walking around cities, I always prefer, and like to recommend, the maps of other countries. Like France, Italy, and Spain, Greece has one company, Road Editions, that with the assistance of the Hellenic Army Geographical Service publishes a series of excellent maps for driving and hiking. These are not, to my knowledge, sold outside Greece, but they are easily found in shops throughout Greece and at the Road Editions bookshop in Athens (odos Ippokratous 39; 01.361.3242). It's a good idea, mainly for Athens, to look at a map of the city and acquaint yourself with the layout and get to know the names of the major thoroughfares, which in Athens include Vassilíssis Sofías, Athinás, Ermou, Stadiou, Amalias, Vassileos Konstantinou, Alexandras, and Dionissiou Areopagitou, which runs along the south side of the Acropolis and is also the first street to be redesigned as a broad, pedestrian-only avenue that will be part of a vast network of streets reserved exclusively for pedestrians linking the major archeological sites of Athens. Memorize also the names and locations of neighborhoods as well as the major *plateias* (squares), which include Omonia, Syntagma, Kolokotroni, Exarchia, and Karaisaki. Note that as in a number of other countries, the names of streets and squares typically appear with the first word in lowercase letters—unless it is the name of a person. Note, too, the key words for street (*dromos*) and avenue (*leoforos*).

Markets

Among my best memories of every place I've been are the visits to local markets, especially outdoor extravaganzas with dozens and dozens of vendors. I have sampled some of the most delicious culinary specialties of my life at markets, bought lasting treasures that are not what anyone would call priceless but that mean a heck of a lot to me, captured some of the friendliest, most generous people on film, and have simply had hours of pure joy. Novelist Gloria Nagy, writing for *National Geographic Traveler,* says a market is the portal through which she enters a new place. "The food of a place," she writes, "holds its biography, sensibility, personality, and prosperity (or lack thereof)." She is obviously referring to food markets with that statement, but when she writes that "a city market is like Cliff Notes; it educates quickly," she is referring to *any* type of market. I too am most fond of food markets, but I've also thoroughly enjoyed browsing plenty of flea markets. Athens has legendary markets of both kinds, and the food markets of Crete and Rhodes are also wonderful. Again to borrow a phrase from Nagy, "Markets are maps of sorts, full of tastes, sniffs, sounds, and surprises. They force you to engage, to risk being foolish, to make mistakes, to talk to strangers without a common language, to be shocked." So don a pair of your most comfortable shoes and a camera, take your time walking around, remember to stop for something to eat or drink so your stomach (or companion) doesn't grumble, and enjoy soaking up the atmosphere while searching for a unique souvenir.

Mediterranean Diet

There is much to be said in defense of the Mediterranean Diet—I am convinced that a large part of why I have had consistently good annual health exams over the years is because I observe this healthful regime. In 1993 the Harvard School of Public Health and the Oldways Preservation and Exchange Trust (see my entry for this organization) sponsored a landmark international conference on the diet. The conference revealed a developing consensus "that the traditional diet of people in the Mediterranean is a major factor in their *generally* good health profiles, their *generally* long lives, their *general* lack of chronic and debilitating diseases." To this day, Greeks have a heart disease rate that's 90 percent lower than that of Americans. Deborah Krasner, in her excellent book *The Flavors of Olive Oil,* reminds us that the Oldways Mediterranean diet pyramid it is different from the USDA food pyramid, "particularly in regard to the consumption of dairy products (there is a lower consumption in the Mediterranean) as well as the consumption of olive oil. It's important to note that it is an accurate representation of the kind of diet eaten not only in Crete in the 1950s, but throughout the Mediterranean to some degree even to this day. Unlike the USDA pyramid, it was not devised under the influence of food industry lobbyists."

Nancy Harmon Jenkins (or Med Guru, as I refer to her and some of her food writing colleagues) believes that the Mediterranean way of eating is the result of Mediterranean history and an integral part of Mediterranean culture. She offers perhaps the best overall summation of the Mediterranean Diet: "I like to describe it as a way of thinking about food. Tunisians or Turks, Cypriots or Spaniards, rich people or poor, country folk or city dwellers, Mediterranean people are on the whole conscious of food in a way that most people, certainly most Americans, are not. I think it's because of this that what they eat is, on the whole, delicious—nourishing to the body because it's wholesome and to the soul because it tastes so very good. I don't mean to suggest an obsession with food. Rather, it seems to me that in the countries of the Mediterranean there exists a deep-seated and largely unspoken consensus that eating is one of the most important things we humans do in our lives . . . in Mediterranean countries there's a real sense of eating as a social act, a way of communicating, of expressing solidarity and relationship. Gathering around the table, literally breaking bread together, is both a symbol of communion and an act of communion in and of itself. And so from a very early age—probably, if it could be measured, from infancy—children absorb the cultural message that it's important to *pay attention*, to *be aware*, almost in a Zen way, of what food is, where it comes from, and how it gets to be the way it is when it comes into our lives." I believe that if more people in North America embraced the Mediterranean way of eating, or at least adopted a diet based on fresh foods and cut out the processed stuff, far fewer of them would have to diet in the first place. For anyone who has a significant amount of weight to lose, the Mediterranean diet may not be the best initial program to follow, as weight loss may not occur quickly enough to maintain confidence and commitment; but once progress has been made, I think the diet is the clear choice for a healthy, lifelong change.

Megali Ithea

Translated as the "Great Idea," the *Megali Ithea* is the concept of incorporating all the territories inhabited by Greeks and restoring Greek power on both sides of the Aegean (picture Greece as it was at the time of the old Byzantine Empire), a concept that Greece pursued relentlessly in the late nineteenth century and the first two decades of the twentieth. The *Megali Ithea* has been referred to by one writer as "a dream that started and ended badly but nevertheless gave Greece its present borders"; Patricia Storace, in *Dinner with Persephone*, refers to it as "the dream of a Greece as it had momentarily been under Alexander, the idea that so many Greeks died for in the twenties. . . . It was never an idea, though, but a dream, beyond the reach of thought." Leading up to the final confrontation, the Balkan Wars of 1912 and 1913 restored to Greece Thessaloníki, most of central and western Macedonia, Ioánnina, and south Epirus. Together with Crete, which had united with Greece in 1908, and the eastern Aegean islands, Greece emerged from the Balkan Wars with its surface area and population almost doubled. After World War I the Treaty of Sèvres (France) liquidated the Ottoman Empire and virtually abolished Turkish sovereignty. Smyrna (İzmir) and its environs were placed under Greek administration, pending a plebiscite to determine its permanent status. Turkey ceded parts of eastern Thrace as well as some Aegean islands to Greece. The treaty was accepted by the government of Sultan Mohammed VI but was rejected by the rival nationalist government of Kemal Atatürk. Some historians have written that the result of Sèvres was a foretaste, on a small scale, of what would later occur in Germany because of the Treaty of Versailles: too much was demanded of Turkey for having fought on the losing side in World War I. The final campaign of the *Megali Ithea* was the Greek-Turkish War of 1922, which led that same year to the Asia Minor disaster (the banishment of Greek communities from the area), and the sack of Smyrna and massacre of its inhabitants. The Treaty of Lausanne (Switzerland) in 1923 returned eastern Thrace and several Aegean islands to Turkey, which recovered full sovereign rights over all its territory. A separate agreement between Greece and Turkey provided for a compulsory exchange of minorities, what I call the great human migration: Greek Christians living in Turkey returned to Greece, and Turks living in Greece returned to Turkey. (According to Esin Eden and Nicholas Stavroulakis in *Salonika: A Family Cookbook*, "Ethnic Turkish Christians were allowed to remain in Turkey while Greek ethnic Christians were obliged to leave.") Eden and Stavroulakis also note, about the migration, that "Nationalism in its modern and apparently successful Balkan form had finally supplanted the strange and tolerant world of the Ottomans. Under the Ottomans all of the subjects of the Sultan, whether Muslim, Christian, or Jew, had been Ottoman. After the Izmir disaster, and the exchange of populations, religious identity became the equivalent of ethnic identity, though with peculiar contradictions. For instance, it was well known that the Cretan Muslims who arrived in Istanbul in great numbers and almost depleted the urban centers of Crete, were Cretan to the core and not Turks."

Mezéthes

Mezéthes is the plural of *meze,* referring to the small snacks or more substantial dishes that are meant to accompany drinks. Rosemary Barron, in *Meze: Small Bites, Big Flavors*, notes that "An approximate translation of the word is 'appetizers,' a wholly inadequate term to express the variety, vitality, and sensual pleasure of the *meze* table, or its integral place in the national culture. *Mezes* are the embodiment of a living, continuing tradition; in them, modern Greeks experience and savor the flavors, textures, and ingredients that excited and intrigued their forebears in the ancient classical world." I am an enormous fan of *mezéthes*, just as I am a big fan of Spanish tapas, probably the closest equivalent in the Mediterranean. No matter where I've traveled in Greece, I have rarely, if ever, been served a drink in the evening (for me, this was usually ouzo) without some sort of accompaniment, even if it was only a small bowl of olives, sliced cucumbers, or dried chickpeas. I consider this practice to be exceptionally civilized. As Barron notes, "The ancients discovered, no doubt through bitter experience, that drinking on an empty stomach was bad news and that alcohol's less-pleasing effects could be avoided or reduced by the simple expedient of eating morsels of food while drinking." Or as cleverly stated by the authors of *World Food: Greece*, "The Greek tippler must be the Greek nibbler, lest he become a Greek tragedy." Diane Kochilas, in *Meze*, clarifies the definition even further: "*Meze* culture is not akin to Spanish tapas or to French hors d'oeuvres or to Italian antipasti. *Mezéthes* are not appetizers, and never immediately precede a main meal. Greeks have appetizers, too. They call them *orektika*. *Mezéthes* are different. The words *meze, mezze, maza, meza* mean middle, as in middle of the day or between lunch and dinner. *Mezéthes* are almost always meant to play second fiddle to the drink at hand."

Missolonghi

Missolonghi (known today as Mesolóngion) is a town on the north shore of the Corinthian Gulf that was a major battle site in the War of Independence (1821–29). According to Robert Eisner in *Travelers to an Antique Land*, Missolonghi was "chosen as a rallying-point by the Philhellenes and Greek chieftains because of its situation in a lagoon too shallow to allow the sudden approach of a Turkish fleet." It is also the death-place of Lord Byron "and consequently hallowed ground for Greeks and philhellenic travelers alike."

Money

The most important advice I impart to travelers about money is that they should travel is with a combination of local cash, American Express traveler's checks (other types are not universally accepted), and credit cards. If you have all three, you will *never* have a problem. (In Greece you should not rely on wide acceptance of credit cards, especially in the smaller villages and towns.) How you divide this up depends on how long you'll be traveling and on what day of the week you arrive—banks, which offer the best exchange rate, aren't generally open on the weekends and aren't open all day during the week. If you rely solely on your ATM card and you encounter a problem, you can't fix it until Monday, when the banks reopen. Overseas ATMs may also limit the number of daily transactions you can make, as well as place a ceiling on the total amount you can withdraw; there are very often long lines at cash machines at airports, and cash machines are sometimes out of order, or out of cash: it was in Greece that I had the admittedly unusual experience of going to a large bank only to find a posted sign stating that the bank was closed because it had *run out of money*!? Money pointers to note: *Make sure your password is compatible with Greek ATMs (if you have too many digits, you'll have to change it) and if, like me, you have memorized your password as a series of letters rather than numbers, write down the numerical equivalent before you leave. Most

European cash machines do not display letters, and even if they did, they do not always appear in the same sequence as we know it in the U.S. Besides the obvious problem of not being able to retrieve any cash, there is further reason for concern if you do not remember your password: the ATM machine will simply eat your card. This happened to me twice in France, and it was a big pain in the neck. I did not know that ATM machines only allow customers to try three, sometimes only two, combinations before the card is confiscated. If this happens to you on a Friday afternoon at about 5:00 (as it did for me, the first time), needless to say, your weekend plans may very well be ruined (mine weren't, but only because I pounded on the glass door of the bank like a mad woman and a rather scared gentleman was essentially forced to open the door). *Refrain from wearing one of those ubiquitous waist bags, or, as my friend, Carl, says, "Make our country proud and don't wear one of those fanny packs!" A tourist + fanny pack = magnet for pickpockets. Keep large bills, credit cards and your passport hidden from view in a money belt worn under your clothes, in a pouch that hangs from your neck, or in an interior coat or blazer pocket. My husband has had great success with a money belt worn around his leg, underneath his pants. This obviously won't work with shorts, but it's quite a good solution for long pants. Also, the Socaroo tube sock is another good alternative: it's a cotton sock meant for joggers that also happens to be great for travelers as it holds cash and credit cards in a small, two-by-three-inch pocket. A pair of socks is about $5, and readers may view the website (www.socaroo.com) or call 310-559-4011 for more information. *Finally, keep in mind that making change is problematic in Greece. Shopkeepers and vendors, even in museum stores, rarely have sufficient paper bills and coins to make change if you pay with a large bill. Make an effort to carry an assortment of paper euro denominations and keep all your coins—you will definitely use them. And don't take personally the frown or the obvious scowl that shopkeepers sometimes display if you have no choice but to pay with a big bill— remember that they are just as frustrated as you are at their inability to make change. They *want* to give you the proper change, and it's embarrassing for them to be in a position where they simply cannot; time will improve the situation—it was not long ago that the Italians couldn't make change, either.

Movies

Robert Eisner, in *Travelers to an Antique Land,* writes that "Myself, every time I go to Greece I swear it's for the last time. But I have only to see a silly movie set on some island, like *High Season,* in which Irene Pappas plays a *ya-ya* (grandma) who walks like an *evzone* (palace guardsman) . . . and immediately I start planning a return." Plan a meal from one or more of the cookbooks mentioned in the *Greek Table* bibliography, and invite some friends and family over for dinner and a movie. A few suggestions (besides *High Season*) include *My Big Fat Greek Wedding, Zorba the Greek, Summer Lovers, For Your Eyes Only*, and *Never on Sunday*. And while you're cooking, get in the mood by listening to some appropriate music: *A Mediterranean Odyssey: Athens to Andalucia* (Putumayo World Music), *All the Best From Greece* (Madacy Records), *Greek Songs, Dances, and Rembétiko* (Easydisc), *Soul of Greece* (Alshire), *Zorba's Dance: The Best From Greece* (Madacy), *The Best of Bouzouki* (Koch Records), and *Classic Greek Film Music* (Silva America).

Museums and Monuments

Opening and closing hours for museums in Greece follow the same general pattern as in other Mediterranean countries. The very first thing you must do upon arriving in Athens is go to the tourist office nearest you and pick up a copy of the museums and monuments schedule. This invaluable schedule, usually three pages long, lists the opening hours and admission fees at all archaeological sites, museums, galleries, and monasteries in Athens, Piraeus, and the suburbs. It is the *only* accurate schedule of its kind in existence, and you must obtain one or your trip will be a disaster. Really. The hours and days of the week that sites are open defies logic sometimes; a few are open by appointment only, while others are closed for renovations. You can consult the website (www.culture.gr) in advance, but I would not count on the site being as accurately maintained as the hard copy.

The Metropolitan Museum of Art in New York City recently launched an extraordinary program that deserves an enormous amount of praise: the Timeline of Art History (www.metmuseum.org/toah), which at this writing recounts art history from its inception to the year 1800 A.D., but the timeline will continue to grow in scope and depth, eventually spanning art history to the present day. The museum's Greek, Cypriot, and Byzantine departments are outstanding, and the Met has also compiled a wonderful package of resource materials for teachers entitled *Greek Art: From Prehistoric to Classical*. The kit includes lesson plans, slides, posters, and texts for use in the classroom; it also encompasses key aspects of fifth-century-B.C. Greek life, including myth and religion; ideas about death and the afterlife; philosophy and science; music; poetry; sports; the symposium, and warfare. I mention it here not only for educators but also for readers who would like a basic but thorough foundation in Greek art.

An ongoing project of mine for this series is to compile a list of North American museums that hold notable collections of Mediterranean art, historical artifacts and documents, and other related *objets* that readers may view in advance of their trip (and hopefully continue their interest in when they return). It's all a part of immersing oneself, I believe, in one's destination. I'd be grateful to hear from you if you'd like to share the specifics of a museum with a strong collection of Greek vases, sculpture, painting, drawings, literature, letters, or decorative arts.

Music

Greece has a long tradition of music. Take a look at urns, figurines, and friezes from classical times, and you'll see depictions of musicians or musical instruments (lutes, lyres, *piktis* or pipes, and various string and percussion instruments). But where a generation or two ago many young people wanted to hear only foreign singers like the Rolling Stones, today's young Greeks are engineering a resurgence in the popularity of Greek music. The most famous style of Greek music involves the ubiquitous mandolinlike bouzouki. Bouzouki music is often very sad because, as Robert Kaplan notes in *Balkan Ghosts,* "For the Greeks it is meant to evoke memories of the loss of Byzantium, Hagia Sophia, and Smyrna." The bouzouki's plaintive sound, the frequent use of minor chords, and the chugging rhythm of many bouzouki songs have all made the music an easy target for mockery—there is a Monty Python "Cheese Shop" sketch in which the normally mild-mannered John Cleese loses his temper after five minutes of listening to a bouzouki band. What is often overlooked in such Western silliness is the much-maligned bouzouki's role in a much darker genre, *rembétika,* which has its roots in Asia Minor in the late nineteenth and early twentieth centuries. The Greek-Turkish War of 1922 made refugees of the ethnic Greeks living in the region (which is part of modern-day Turkey). They brought to mainland Greece, particularly the port cities, their particular style of music, which is often characterized as the Greek equivalent of the blues, or possibly a predecessor of the high-rolling, fast-living ethos of gangsta rap. Many of the songs deal with themes of hashish, drug addiction, prostitution, gambling, fighting, and erotic love. *Rembétika's* period of greatest popularity was between the two world wars, but later artists have staged a revival of the sound (if not the lifestyle and the gritty lyrics). The acknowledged master of the genre is Markos Vamvakaris, whose collected songs are available on *Bouzouki Pioneer 1932–1940* (Rounder Records), but Georgos Dalaras, more than anyone else, has been responsible for the reawakened interest in *rembétika.* His double album, '50 Chronia Rembetiko,' sold more than 100,000 copies, and his concerts still fill venues to capacity (besides *rembétika,* Dalaras has recorded more than forty albums of popular Greek music and has been described as a 'musical phenomenon' and a 'undisputed ambassador of song,' though he remains relatively unknown outside of Greece).

Opera is in a different category, as it usually is. Towering above all other divas everywhere is Maria Callas, whose body of work is immense. It would be pointless to include a discography here, but delving into Callas's work is a warm and wonderful introduction to the soul of Greece, as her devoted fans already know, and if you think you don't like opera or are decidedly not a fan, you might want to give it one more try with Callas. If you're not sure where to begin, let an expert guide you: Fred Plotkin, the author of an excellent pair of books that every fan of *The Collected Traveler* should have, *Classical Music 101: A Complete Guide to*

Learning and Loving Classical Music (2002) and *Opera 101: A Complete Guide to Learning and Loving Opera* (1994), both published by Hyperion. In his opera book he recommends particular Callas performances, and as someone who has religiously followed his advice, I can report that I have not once been disappointed, and I don't think you will be either. (Plotkin's opera book is particularly helpful for visitors to Greece, as he includes an appendix of opera houses around the world, including those in Greece.) Fans and soon-to-be-admirers of Callas may want to devour (as I did) two great books: *Greek Fire: The Story of Maria Callas and Aristotle Onassis* (by Nicholas Gage, Alfred A. Knopf, 2000) and *Maria Callas Remembered* (by Nadia Stancioff, DaCapo Press, 2000). Gage, in *Greek Fire,* presents what he feels is a more accurate account than those previously published of the passionate but tragic relationship between Callas and Onassis, and it's a well-researched, balanced, and compelling read. Finally, *Maria Callas: A Musical Biography* (Robert Levine, Black Dog & Leventhal, 2003) is a fabulous book and CD package (two CDs, recorded by EMI, are included featuring thirty major performances). This is not a biography but a unique interplay of text and music—one may listen to the arias while following the text—and Levine also provides photographs, a discography, chronology, and complete performance history. He reminds us that Callas continues to change the way people listen to opera. "To this day, when opera lovers and other singers discuss the way opera is perceived and what is expected of a singer, they often refer to B.C. and A.C.—Before and After Callas. One has only to hear her to understand why."

Mythology

Like paging through books of art and architecture history, it is to the traveler's benefit to reacquaint oneself with Greek mythology. Books devoted to Greek mythology are almost as numerous as those on Greek art, but a few very worthy volumes are:

D'Aulaire's Book of Greek Myths (Ingri D'Aulaire and Paul Parin D'Aulaire, Doubleday, 1962, hardcover; Yearling, 1992, paperback; note that even though the D'Aulaires are an author/illustrator team for children's books, this is an excellent book for adults, too).
Gods and Heroes of Ancient Greece (Gustav Schwab, translated from the German text and its Greek sources by Olga Marx and Ernst Morwitz, Pantheon, 1946, renewed 1974; paperback but a bit heavy for bringing along).
Greek Gods and Heroes (Robert Graves, Laurel Leaf , 1960; a slender paperback that fits easily in a handbag or blazer pocket).
Mythology (Edith Hamilton, Little, Brown and Company, 1940, hardcover; New American Library, 1969, paperback; also a small paperback good for bringing along).

The Gods of Greece (Arianna Huffington, paintings by Francoise Gilot, Atlantic Monthly Press, 1993; a retelling of the myths that illustrates how the events surrounding the gods correspond to modern realities).

N

November 17

Authorities are slowly rounding up members of Greece's most famous leftist terrorist organization, November 17, in response to worries that attacks, or fear of attacks, would mar the 2004 Summer Olympics in Athens. The group was formed after (and takes its name from the date of) the November 17, 1973, student uprising at Athens Polytechnic University protesting the military junta that was then in power in Greece. The Greek army brought in tanks and crushed the protest; at least 20 students were killed. In its lifespan November 17 has killed upward of twenty-five victims, mainly American and British officials and Greek public figures. Its agenda is fairly straightforwardly anti-Western: it opposes Greek participation in NATO and the EU, rejects American military bases in Greece, and wants to kick the Turkish military out of Cyprus. During the group's history, seemingly everyone in Greece with access to the press has speculated on who its members might be, where they get their money, and how they've managed to evade arrest for decades. The group's cell system—similar to Al Qaeda's—has made them embarrassingly difficult for Greek police to track down and capture, but the arrest of the first few members of the group in 2002 caught the interest of newspaper readers around the world.

O

Ohi Day

October 28, a major national holiday in Greece, commemorates the moment in 1940 when Metaxas said no—*ohi*—to Mussolini's demand that the Greek-Albanian border be opened to Italian troops. As Lawrence Durrell noted, "A word had been uttered, a single small word for which the whole of Europe had waited and waited in vain. It was the word 'no' (*ohi*) and Greece had uttered it on behalf of all of us at a time when the so-called great powers were all cringing, fawning and trying to temporize in the face of the Hitlerian menace. With that small word Greece found her soul, and Europe found its example. A small, almost unarmed nation, internally self-divided, once more decided to defy the Persian hordes as it had done in the past. I think we were filled with a secret relief that at last the word had been uttered, for it brought us the certain knowledge that now, however long the war took, and however many of us did not return from it, it would finally be won."

Oldways Preservation and Exchange Trust

Oldways (www.oldwayspt.org), a nonprofit educational organization founded in 1990, deserves wider recognition and is one for which we should be grateful. The brainchild of K. Dun Gifford (whom Julia Child appointed chairman of the American Institute of Wine and Food in 1988), it promotes specific alternatives to the unhealthful foods characteristically eaten in industrialized countries, and it is a "think tank and brain trust" rooted in equal parts of science; good, clean food; and tradition. Of particular relevance to Greece is the recently established European Center for Mediterranean Diet Studies on the island of Chios, a partnership between Oldways, ENA-Chios (the development agency for the Chios prefect) and SEVE (Export Association of Northern Greece) Additionally, Oldways sponsors a number of important initiatives, including tours for food lovers. Allow me to go out on a limb here and share one of the most valuable tips in this book: Oldways tours are something special. I receive a staggering number of brochures and catalogs from a great number of tour operators, some of which I very much respect and admire, but none offer anything quite like an Oldways trip. The combination of outstanding seminars, cooking demonstrations, guided historical tours to museums, monuments, and markets (all by noted specialists in their field), roundtable discussions, winery tours and tastings, meals focusing on local cuisine, and a nice amount of free time is unmatched by other companies. In past years, Oldways has sponsored tours to the North Aegean, Crete, and Pórto Carrás in Greece.

Oliviers & Co.

Oliviers & Co. (www.oliviers-co.com) is a network of shops with a theme tailor-made for *The Collected Traveler*: olive oils and related products from around the Mediterranean. Founder Olivier (whose name appropriately means "olive tree" in French) Baussan created this wonderful concept in the early 1990s, with each store offering extra-virgin, first-cold-pressed oils from a variety of regions of Provence, Greece, North Africa, Spain, Italy, and Israel. In addition to straightforward olive oils, the stores sell herbal and citrus-infused oils, vinegars, olive oil soap, pottery, olive wood spoons, condiments, empty bottles and flasks, and *scourtins* (round, woven disks used in olive harvesting, which also make great placemats!). If you're interested in sampling Greek olive oil before you leave (or after you return), Oliviers & Co. sells bottles of the Peloponnese brand Manitnea & Avia in two sizes and may also have Cretan olive oil in stock. Oliviers & Co. stores in North America are in New York City, Boston, Los Angeles, San Francisco, and Seattle.

Olympic Games

Modern sportsmanship owes its existence, in part, to the ancient Greeks—and to the Greeks of the late nineteenth century who decided to revive the ancient Olympic

Games. Homer mentions earlier similar competitions in the *Iliad*, but the Olympics owe their name to both the location and the gods the games honored. This famous sporting extravaganza—which centered mainly on footraces and honored the god Zeus—was held for the first time in Olympia, in the western Peloponnese, in 776 B.C. The games were held regularly every four years until the decline of ancient Greece and were not revived as an international competition until 1896, when Athens had the honor of hosting the first modern Olympic Games. The games in antiquity consisted of events such as boxing, javelin and discus throwing, jumping, running, wrestling, equestrian events, the pentathlon, and pankration (a sort of cross between wrestling and boxing). Depending on what your definition of *official* is, the 2004 Summer Olympics will be either the second or the third time Athens has hosted the Games—the city held a competition in 1906 that the International Olympic Committee does not recognize, but people did compete. Today the Olympics are stirring up controversy in Athens: residents of areas near Olympic venue construction haven't always been thrilled with plans to change their neighborhoods; and the site for the rowing events is being disputed, since it will disrupt a natural wetland and infringe on the historic site of the Battle of Marathon. At this writing construction is so far behind schedule that the IOC has threatened to take the Games away from Athens, and mere months before the official start of the Games, there is a worrisome hotel bed shortage, leading to inventive solutions such as putting up hotel guests on cruise ships anchored in Piraeus harbor. Despite the chaos, however, I believe the Greeks will prevail—they're determined to do so, to show the world that they truly are the inheritors of the Olympic spirit. When I was last in Athens, practically everything was under construction, all in preparation for the Games. The new airport and metro system are to be admired, and many, many residents are bursting with pride.

The 2004 Summer Olympic Games (www.athens2004.com) are being held from August 13 to 29 Their mascots, Athena and Phevos, inspired by an ancient Greek doll from the seventh century B.C., are now emblazoned on T-shirts, towels, keychains, and the like all over the country. At first, I found the characters rather odd looking, but they grew on me, and now I'm fond of the puffy figures. A great book, filled with photographs, is *The Ancient Olympic Games* by Judith Swaddling (published by the University of Texas Press in conjunction with the trustees of the British Museum), which has a foreword by Anne, the Princess Royal. The Greek tourist office and the Athens Games' Organizing Committee also have useful information.

Alexander S. Onassis Public Benefit Foundation
Since only a few American cities have nonstop flights to Athens, chances are you'll have to change planes and possibly stay the night somewhere along the way. If it's in New York, then I'd suggest you visit the Alexander S. Onassis Public Benefit

Foundation (www.onassisusa.org), an excellent place to start immersing yourself in Hellenic culture even before you leave the United States. (The original Onassis Foundation is in Athens, should you not pass through New York City.) Aristotle Onassis provided, in his handwritten will, for the creation of the foundation, named after his only son who died in an airplane crash in 1973. The American branch promotes Greek culture; the Greek branch offers grants and scholarships and has contributed money to social welfare projects in countries around the Mediterranean and the world. While perhaps best remembered for his shipping empire and for being Mister Jacqueline Bouvier Kennedy, Aristotle Onassis also founded Greece's national airline, Olympic Airways, in 1957. It makes sense, then, that the foundation headquarters should be in the Olympic Tower, which looms above St. Patrick's Cathedral on Fifth Avenue in midtown Manhattan.

Opa

Opa! is a common one-word expression that you may hear often in Greece. It is used in two different ways. The form you're most likely to hear is when a child falls down or otherwise gets a boo-boo; the parents will say *Opa!* in a singsong voice to indicate "It's okay, you just had a little fall, don't worry." The other form is expressed at nightclubs when a singer or a patron is in a state of *kefi*. Onlookers, instead of clapping, will say *Opa!* in the way we might say *Encore!* to commend a performer.

P.

Packing

Most people who travel, be it for business or for pleasure, view packing as a stressful chore. It doesn't have to be. Some tips that work for me and might for you too: ~Select clothing that isn't prone to wrinkling, like cotton and wool knits. When I *am* concerned about limiting wrinkles, I lay out a large plastic dry cleaning bag, place the garment on top of it, place *another* bag on top of that, and fold the item up between the two bags—the key is that the plastic must be layered in with the clothing, otherwise it doesn't really work. ~If I'm packing items with buttons, I button them up before I fold them; the same with zippers and snaps. ~If I'm carrying a bag with more than one separate compartment, I use one of them for shoes; otherwise I put shoes at the bottom (or back) of the bag opposite the handle so they'll remain there while I'm carrying the bag. ~Transfer shampoo and lotions to travel-size plastic bottles, which can be purchased at pharmacies—and then put them inside a Ziploc bag to prevent leaks. ~Don't skimp on underwear—it's lightweight and takes up next to no room in your bag; it's never a mistake to have more than you think you need. ~Belts can be either rolled up and stuffed into shoes or fastened together along the inside edge of your suitcase. ~Ties should be rolled, not folded, and also stuffed into shoes or pockets. ~Some handy things to bring along that are often overlooked: a pocket flashlight, for looking into ill-lit corners of Byzantine churches, reading in bed at night (the lights are often not bright enough), or if you're staying at a hotel where the bathroom is down the hall, for navigating the dark hallway at night (the light is often on a timer and always runs out before you've made it to the end of the hall); binoculars, for looking up at architectural details; a small travel umbrella; a penknife/corkscrew; plastic shoes—known in the United States as jellies—for campground showers and rocky beaches; an empty, lightweight duffel bag, which you can fold up and pack and then use as a carry-on bag for gifts and breakable items on the way home; a plastic bag big enough for a wet swimsuit; copies of any current prescriptions in case you need to have a medicine refilled; photocopies of your passport and airline tickets (which should also be left with someone at home).

Pantocrator

Pantocrator is the all-seeing Christ the Pantocrator, images of which appear in the domes and on the walls of Byzantine churches in Greece. (Notable ones in southern Greece are in Athens and Mistra. Mary McCarthy, in her wonderful book *Venice Observed*, perceptively noted that "the Byzantine mode, in Venice, lost something of its theological awesomeness. The stern, solemn figure of the Pantocrator who dominates the Greek churches with his frowning brows and upraised hand does not appear in St. Mark's in His arresting majesty. In a Greek church, you feel that the eye of God is on you from the moment you step in the door; you are utterly encompassed by this all-embracing gaze, which in peasant chapels is often represented by an eye over the door. The fixity of this divine gaze is not punitive; it merely calls you to attention and reminds you of the eternal Law of the universe arching over time and circumstance."

Parakalo

A most worthy word to know, and quite lovely to pronounce: *parakalo* means "please," "don't mention it," "you're welcome," and "a pleasure!"

Passatempo

This lovely Greek (and Italian) word means "passing the time." Rosemary Barron says that for Greeks, the best way to *passatempo* "is to chat with friends over a glass of ouzo, tsipouro, or wine." Indeed.

Períptero

The *períptero* is a ubiquitous and brilliant invention of modern Greek life. Reportedly, the idea for this "best-equipped kiosk in the world" (according to travel writer Dana Facaros) came about after the Second World War as a way to provide war veterans with work. A *períptero* sells just about everything: aspirin, bottled water, phone cards, a wide range of Greek and foreign periodicals, shampoo, stamps, postcards, small toys and games for children, film, cigarettes, candy, deodorant, and condoms . . . name almost anything, and a *períptero* has it, and conveniently, a *períptero* can be found on almost every street corner in Athens as well as in every port town on the islands. As Facaros writes, "You'll wonder how you ever survived before *perípteros* and the treasures they contain."

Philhellenes

The most notable philhellenes (non-Greeks who admire Greece and everything Greek) were all British—Lord Byron, Percy Bysshe Shelley, and Oscar Wilde—but Byron is arguably the most notable; he is, after all, included in the pantheon of Greece's heroes and statesmen in the Benaki Museum in Athens. You'll come across references to him in every Greek guidebook, but for those wishing to read more about his patriotic fervor for Greece, Benita Eisler's *Byron: Child of Passion, Fool of Fame* (Alfred A. Knopf, 1999) is an excellent biography. Byron's ill-fated journey to Missolonghi (see my entry for this city) and his subsequent death there are recounted in the final chapters of Eisler's book. (Byron did not die in battle, as many people assume; rather, it seems he caught a plague that was circulating in Missolonghi, and after a few days of fever and chills—and being bled by leeches— he passed away.) Eisler provides the text carved on his tombstone in England: "In the vault beneath where many of his ancestors and his mother are buried, lie the remains of GEORGE GORDON NOEL BYRON, Lord Byron, of Rochdale in the county of Lancaster, the author of Childe Harold's Pilgrimage. He was born in London on the 22nd of January 1788. He died at Missolonghi, in western Greece, on the 19th of April 1824, engaged in the glorious attempt to restore that country to her ancient freedom and renown."

Polis

Polis is the Greek word for "city," the most notable city being Istanbul (whose name is a corruption of *eis teen polis,* "in the city"). Even today when a Greek speaks of "the *polis,"* he is probably referring to Constantinople, believing that there is no other city in the world without the need of a proper name. According to Jacob Burckhardt, in *The Greeks and Greek Civilization,* the *polis* "was the definitive Greek form of the State; it was a small independent state controlling a certain area of land in which scarcely another fortified position and certainly no secondary independent citizenship were tolerated. This state was never thought of as having come into being gradually, but always suddenly, as the result of a momentary and deliberate decision. The Greek imagination was full of such instantaneous foundings of cities, and as from the beginning nothing happened of itself, the whole life of the *polis* was governed by necessity." Interestingly, Burckhardt also relates that before the Greeks, the Phoenicians had founded *poleis*, city-states with constitutions. "It is now generally acknowledged that in very many respects Phoenician culture penetrated Greek life at an early stage, and it is possible that Thebes was originally a Phoenician city in what came to be Boeotian territory. In any case the Greeks must have been aware of the Phoenician coastal cities and their colonies."

Philoxenía

Literally, this word means "hospitality" and refers to the biblical Abraham being hospitable to the three angels.

Politeness

While the Greeks may not be as formal as the French in the forms of *politesse*, they are well versed in daily etiquette, and I find it so refreshing, frankly, after much-too-casual American ways. It is expected, therefore, that a visitor will greet a shop owner and staff when walking into a store, say good-bye upon departing, and simply display good manners all around. Many shop owners, even more than they want to make a sale, want to engage in English conversation for practice, know where you are from, and learn how you like Greece.

S

Santorini Volcano

An article that appeared in the 'Science Times' section of *The New York Times* (October 21, 2003) revealed that scientist now believe that the eruption of the Thera (Santorini) volcano more than three thousand years ago was far worse than the 1883 Krakatoa eruption, which killed more than 36,000 people. According to the writer, William J. Broad, scientists also believe that "The blast's cultural repercussions were equally large, rippling across the eastern Mediterranean for decades, even centuries." Scientists are still studying how the distant effects of the eruption slowly led to the decline of Crete's Minoan civilization, and they know that by 1450 B.C., Mycenaean invaders from mainland Greece took control of Crete, effectively ending the Minoan era. Two archaeologists, Dr. Jan Driessen and Dr. Colin Macdonald, observed in a scholarly article that the volcano's destructiveness "culminated in Crete being absorbed to a greater or lesser extent into the Mycenaean, and therefore, the Greek world."

The Seven Wonders of the Ancient World

Though there are only seven wonders, most people, when quizzed, can name only one or two. In case you're curious, the list of the seven wonders was originally compiled sometime around the second century B.C., and the first reference to the idea was found in *The Histories* by Herodotus as long ago as the fifth century B.C. Chief Librarian of the Alexandria Library, Callimachus of Cyrene (305 B.C.–240 B.C.), wrote a document entitled 'A Collection of Wonders Around the World,' but all we know of this is its title as it was destroyed with the Alexandria Library. The final list was compiled during the Middle Ages, and includes the seven most impressive monuments of the ancient world, some of which barely survived to the Middle Ages. Of the seven, four were in the Greek world: the Great Pyramid of Giza; the Hanging Gardens of Babylon; the Statue of Zeus at Olympia; the Temple of Artemis at Ephesus; the Mausoleum at Halicarnassus; the Colossus of Rhodes; and the Lighthouse of Alexandria.

Siesta

The afternoon siesta is major facet of life in Greece and throughout the Mediterranean. It has been noted that Greece is a quieter country from three to five in the afternoon than in the middle of the night, and it is considered legitimate to call the police if anyone is disturbing the peace of an afternoon. And making a telephone call to a house during the siesta is the very definition of bad manners. I find it a healthy habit, just like the *volta* (evening walk), and I like that it forces people to slow down. Though, as in Italy and Spain, more businesses these days are staying open (in particular the shipping offices in Piraeus), the siesta is a time-honored custom. If you smirk at it, according to one travel writer, "you will be reminded— all Greeks know this—that 'Churchill won the war while sleeping in the afternoon.'"

Spitting

If you've seen the movie *My Big Fat Greek Wedding,* you know that Greeks spit to ward off the evil eye. (See also my entry for Evil Eye.) It's a very old superstition mostly practiced in more rural areas, and Greeks believe that if you hear someone speaking about some sort of misfortune, you should spit three times on your own person; in this way you ward off the evil that may come to you. Additionally, it's common to spit so that you don't give the evil eye to yourself and jinx some endeavor. Greek fishermen sometimes spit in their nets before lowering them into the sea to ward off evil and catch a lot of fish, while students may spit onto a report before turning it in so that any bad spirits are sent away.

Spoon Sweets

Throughout Greece, and in other countries of the Levant as well, spoon sweets— intensely flavored, syrupy preserves—have long been a symbol of hospitality.

Known as *glyká*, Greek spoon sweets are offered in several flavors throughout the year. Most are flavored with fruit—grapefruit, cherry, plum, apricot, fig, quince, and grape. Other flavors include walnut, raisin, rose petal, pistachio, and bergamot (one I haven't yet tried). Spoon sweets are absolutely delicious and are one of the most classic Greek culinary items. Making them is not difficult, but you do need to allow the fruit (or other flavor) to macerate with sugar overnight, so they are not a last-minute thought, and the number of Greek women who still devote the time to making them is dwindling. Try at least one at some point during your visit, or buy some and bring them home. If you're ambitious to make them yourself, you'll find recipes in some of the cookbooks in the *Greek Table* bibliography.

Staring

Patricia Storace notes that "It is very hard to get used to, but there is no social prohibition against frank, assessing, concentrated staring, and my first pervasive sensation in Greece is of those eyes—the stares of the coffee-drinking shopkeepers, the gazing icons, the tin and glass eyes dangling from key chains and rearview mirrors and hung over doors as protection against harm from living eyes." I was glad I had read this before my last visit to Greece, because even before my friends and I arrived there, we had what must be one of the most intense staring experiences on record. My friend Arlene actually recorded it in her journal while we were in the airport lounge: "I must make mention of the first wacky character of our trip, dubbed 'staring cell phone lady.' This black-clad elderly woman is a nut job. Her cell phone rings and rings. At first she seems oblivious. The annoyed and confused stares of passersby prompt her to open the phone and hold it to her ear, but remarkably, she lets it continue to ring while pacing around the waiting room. This happens repeatedly, until finally one man can no longer stand it so he walks over to her, takes the phone out of her hand, presses the 'talk' button, and hands it back to her . . . and voila! She is actually conversing (in Greek) with whomever it is that's been trying to reach her. Just our luck that this lady ends up sitting next to us on the plane, along with her eight-hundred-year-old acquaintance, also completely clad in black, and she proceeds to stare intently at the three of us, never once dropping her gaze, even when the meal was served, for *nine hours* . . . all the while clutching that damn cell phone."

Stendhal Syndrome

Named for the sick, physical feeling that afflicted French novelist Stendhal after he visited Santa Croce in Florence, this syndrome is synonymous with being completely overwhelmed by your surroundings (my translation: seeing and doing way too much). Though it happened to Stendhal in Florence, it can just as easily happen anywhere, and visitors who arrive in Greece with too long a list of must-sees are prime candidates. Even a relatively less traveled place—with not nearly as many attractions as Florence—may cause the overly ambitious to expire. My advice: organize your days, factor in how long it takes to get from place to place, and see what you want to see. There will be no quiz.

The Sun

There is nothing quite like a warm, sunny day in the Aegean to make you want to shed your clothes and don a swimsuit (or not—naturalists will find plenty of nude beaches in Greece; check guidebooks for specific recommendations). The famous light in Greece, which has been praised by so many writers, is of course only possible with the sun, which is responsible for so many picture-postcard-perfect days in Greece. It is also extremely strong, and can easily throw even veteran sun worshippers for a loop.

Readers of my *Provence* edition may recall that I mentioned Parsol 1789, the most effective UVA shield in American sunscreens. However, in an article in *Vogue* by writer Sarah Brown ('Made in the Shade,' June 2003), it was revealed that Parsol pales in comparison to Mexoryl SX, a UVA-absorbing ingredient that's been in most European sunscreens since its introduction about ten years in France by L'Oréal. A New York City dermatologist interviewed for the article said she sends her patients to Europe and Canada for sun protection, because, "There's nothing on the American market that adequately protects you from the sun." As I write this, Mexoryl has not yet been approved by the FDA, a process that Brown describes as painstaking and that can take up to five years and cost up to thirty million dollars. She discovered, however, that at least one European product—Anthélios XL SPF 60+—was available at a few upscale New York apothecaries, including Zitomer (969 Madison Avenue, (888) 219-2888; www.zitomer.com; curious readers may also want to browse the website of feelbest.com, Canada's largest online health and beauty aids site, with a specific link to Anthélios products: www.feelbest.com/anthelios.cfm).

Even if you will not be partaking in sunbathing at the beach or other outdoor pursuits, bring some protective lotion—of any kind—and use it, liberally. Most people don't realize that they don't use enough lotion (an eight-ounce bottle is good for eight applications) and that it's important to apply lotion before you go out in the sun. (As an example, if a person who normally burns in eight minutes applies SPF 10 before going in the sun, he or she will be able to stay in the sun for eighty minutes (eight x ten) and be protected. Putting lotion on five minutes *after* being in the sun uses up 5/8 of the time before being burned, thus 3/8 of the normal protection time before burning is left. As (3/8) (80) is thirty, a person has thirty minutes before burning.) Some doctors recommend applying sunscreen even if you're just running errands around town; this would apply to sight-seeing and visiting outdoor markets as well. Women who wear makeup should consider selecting a brand with

UV (ultraviolet) protection, and *everyone* should note that by not using protective lotion you are exposing your skin to a lot of irreversible damage. Melanoma cases have more than doubled since 1973, and the mortality rate has risen "a staggering forty-two percent," according to Brown in her *Vogue* piece. Also, overexposure to the sun is dangerous to your eyes, with the potential of causing the development of cataracts (moisturizing eye sticks are great to apply around your eyes, and also work on ears and the tip of your nose). In addition to applying lotion, be mindful of the benefits of a good hat and sunglasses. A few companies specialize in UV-proof clothing, including shirts and serious hats that even cover the back of your neck. My friend Wendy L. took a few of these items to Greece last August, and though she said she sometimes felt conspicuously overdressed, she was really glad she had them (one company to contact is Sun Precautions: www.sunprecautions.com). Though it will never be possible to achieve complete sun protection, remember: there is no such thing as a healthy tan.

T

Tavli

After *komboloï* (worry beads), the second most common visual memory of Greece is probably men playing *tavli*, very similar to backgammon. In almost every *kafeneion,* in every town of every size, you will see men playing *tavli*. It is believed to be one of the oldest games in existence, dating back almost five thousand years to the time of the ancient Egyptians. Just as in backgammon, opponents try to move their fifteen pieces off the board first. The game we know today as backgammon was refined in England in the seventeenth century, and one significant innovation of the twentieth century was the addition of the doubling cube, in the 1920s, which was not introduced in *tavli*. If you're a fast backgammon player and want to feel a part of the *kafeneion,* invite yourself to play a game and buy a round of drinks for the onlookers—there are few experiences more Greek.

Taxis

Taxis in Greece are among the least expensive in Europe and are employed by visitors often, not only for reaching destinations in and around Athens but also for touring around the Peloponnese and farther afield. You should always make sure the meter is turned on or, if the driver claims the meter is broken, negotiate a rate in advance, and remember that there are legal surcharges for luggage and airport pick-ups or drop-offs. ~Taxis are allowed to enter Athens on any day of the week, but on certain days of the week regular vehicular traffic is limited to the city center. This effort to reduce congestion is enforced by permitting even and odd numbered license plates to enter on alternate days. But some taxi drivers have more than one car, not all of them licensed for official use, so do not be surprised if your driver takes you first to his house (outside of the city center), then switches cars, to head into the city center in the "right" taxicab.

Among the most valuable tips I share in this book is this one: contact George Kokkotos, known in many circles as "the most famous taxi driver of Greece." Employing George is like giving yourself a present—he is extremely reliable, is willing to work with any itinerary, and is among the kindest, most generous human beings I've ever met—and in one fell swoop you will have eliminated any headaches in your trip planning. George will meet you at the airport, take you to the port for a departing boat, be your personal tour guide, and become your friend. He may be reached in Athens at 210.96.37.030; mobile: 093.22.05.887; fax: 210.96.37.029; greektaxi@aol.com; www.greecetravel.com/taxi.

Telephones

Remember that Greece is seven hours ahead of Eastern Standard Time, eight ahead of Central Time, nine ahead of Mountain Time, and 10 hours ahead of Pacific Standard Time. To call Greece from the United States., dial 011 + 30 + local number (011 is the overseas line, 30 is the country code for Greece, and the local number includes the appropriate city code). Note that in October 2002 the Ellinikós Orghanismós Telepikinonion (EOT) changed the digit sequence of all telephone numbers: the first 0 of a number was changed to a 2 for standard phones and to a 6 for mobile phones, so if you're using a guidebook that's a few years old, adjust the numbers when telephoning or sending a fax.

A *telekarta* (phone card) is what the vast majority of people use to make local and overseas calls—it's definitely the cheapest option for calling North American numbers directly, and you can also connect with North American operators. A *telekarta* is available in two denominations and can be purchased at *períptera* and hotels and at some *kafeneia,* travel agents, and shops. The only catch is that you can't get reimbursed for unused units on the card, so try to purchase the *telekarta* in the denomination you're sure you'll use. ~I won't elaborate on my feelings about cell phone abuse here, but at least the Greeks have the excuse that their public telephone system was, until very recently, rather unreliable. If you feel you really must have your own cell phone, check with your service provider first to ensure the phone is programmed to be compatible. Renting a compatible cellular phone may be a better, though not inexpensive, option.

Terrorism

Western Europe is home to about fifteen million Muslim immigrants, and while the majority is opposed to terrorism, its large presence does provide a convenient cover for terrorist cells as well as a recruiting ground. New groups that are moving into Europe have apparently been well trained in hopping from country to country in the border-free European Union, and they are mostly self-financed through common criminal activities like credit card fraud, making it difficult if not impossible for the authorities to follow their money trail. In one recent article, a French anti-terrorism expert is quoted as saying that a new threat now comes from the Caucasus; another official said, "Chechnya is just three hours away. This is not just a Russian problem. It's going to be more global."

Francine Prose, in the last-page essay that is one of my favorite features of *The New York Times* travel section, has written what I think are the sanest reflections on terrorism. She reminds us that "Travel alters and expands our perspective. By showing us that life really is different in other places, it provides a reality check against which we can measure the misperceptions and even prejudices we may have developed at home," and she concludes that "The events of September 11 have—or should have—turned us not just into patriotic Americans, but into citizens of the world. And we owe it to ourselves, and to our fellow citizens, to go out and see for ourselves this fragile, damaged and brave new world that, like it or not, we've come to inhabit." (Prose's essay appeared in the *Times* on September 8, 2002.)

~I compile books like this because I have a deep respect for the people, the culture, and the religion of the particular place I'm visiting, and I assume that you share this respect. Like a *Condé Nast Traveler* reader who wrote a letter to the editor to say she believed that "Every American who travels abroad is a bridge for peace," I believe we are all, in a small way, promoting international understanding by reading about other places and traveling to them. On days when the newspaper makes the world seem like a particularly nasty place, I remember that my friend Lindsay M. sent me the following lines from Shakespeare's *The Tempest* at eight o'clock on the morning of September 11, 2002, a year after the attacks: "How beautious mankind is! / O brave new world / That has such people in't!"

Theft

Whether of the pickpocket variety or something more serious, theft can happen anywhere, in the finest neighborhood, on a bus, in a park, on a street corner. Do not wear a waist pack, which is nothing but a neon magnet for thieves. A lot of incidents could easily have been avoided. In 1998 a lengthy piece in the travel section of the *Philadelphia Inquirer* described about a husband and wife traveling in France who had a pouch with all their valuables in it stolen. What made this story remarkable was that they were shocked the pouch was stolen. *I* was shocked that they had thought it a good idea to *strap their pouch under the driver's seat of their rental car*. This couple had apparently traveled all over Europe and North America every year for twelve years, so they weren't exactly novices. I think it's a miracle, however, that they hadn't been robbed earlier.

Some pointers: ~Rental cars are easily identified by their license plates and other markings that may not be obvious to you and me but that signify pay dirt to thieves.

Do not leave anything, anything at all, in a rental car, even if you're parking it in a secure garage. My husband and I never even put items in the trunk unless we're immediately getting in the car and driving away, as anyone watching us would know there's something of value there. Hatchback-type cars are good to rent because you can back into spots against walls or trees, making it impossible for thieves to open the trunk. ~Do not leave your passport, money, credit cards, important documents, or expensive camera equipment in your hotel room. (Yes, American passports are still very much a hot commodity.) The hotel safe? If the letters I read are any indication, leaving your belongings in a hotel safe—whether it is in your room or in the main office—is only slightly more reliable than leaving them out in plain view. Sometimes I hear that valuable jewelry was taken from a hotel safe, which I find baffling as there really is only one safe place for valuable jewelry: your home. No occasion, meeting, or celebration, no matter how important or festive, requires bringing valuable jewelry. *Leave it at home.* I happen to also find displaying such wealth offensive. ~Pickpockets employ a number of tactics to prey on unaware travelers. Even if you travel often, live in a big city, and think you're savvy, professional thieves can usually pick you out immediately—and they'll identify you as American if you're wearing the trademark sneakers and fanny pack. Beware the breastfeeding mother who begs you for money while her other children surround you looking for a way into your pockets; the arguing couple who make a scene while their accomplices work the crowd of onlookers; and the tap on your shoulder at the baggage security checkpoint—by the time you turn around, someone's made off with your bags after they've passed through the X-ray machine. Avoid anything at all that looks or feels like a set-up.

Tipping

Be prepared to tip by putting some small change in your pocket *in advance,* before you arrive at the hotel or leave for the theater. ~If you use the services of a concierge, it is considered appropriate to give a small amount per day, about five to ten dollars, for overall helpfulness and small tasks requested. For a one-time-only task like obtaining reservations or tickets, it's expected that you'll show your gratitude in a larger way, with about $50 or $100—or even more, depending on the task. If you use a concierge's services only once, it's customary to tip on the spot. To thank a concierge for several services performed during the course of a longer stay, tip on your last day. Should you want to enclose your tip in an envelope marked with the concierge's name, make sure you hand-deliver it, or it may get shared among *all* the hotel's concierges; a nice gift—such as fine candy—is also an appropriate thank-you. ~I am a firm believer in maintaining a proper balance with regard to tipping. Excellent service should be awarded sufficiently, and poor service should not, but excessive tipping is gross and should be avoided. Wild tipping upsets the balance and destroys the concept of service. I know people who swear by the power of a twenty-dollar (or hundred-dollar) bill, but I think this should be reserved only for dire situations.

Toilets and Toilet Paper

Greece has plenty of good flush toilets in most hotels, museums, and restaurants, but it has an equal number of abominable water closets. It also has a fair number of squat toilets, often referred to as Turkish toilets. If you have never encountered a squat toilet, have no fear: they are perfectly fine, and sometimes they are spotlessly clean. Sometimes a Turkish toilet will flush (look for a chain or a button to push), but note that when some toilets flush, they produce quite a wave, with the water coming up over the basin and potentially onto your feet. Guard against this possibility by not flushing until you're ready to step away, then flush as you simultaneously open the door of the stall. ~The thing to know about all toilets in Greece is that the stalls are rarely stocked with toilet paper, so never set out each day without some toilet paper in your pockets or handbag. Even if they are stocked, you *cannot always flush the paper down the toilet*. Greek plumbing is just not very advanced. ~You will usually see a bucket in the stall where you are to dispose of used tissue, and please don't disobey the little sign that tells you to do so, even if the English grammar is poor—travel writer Dana Facaros saw one that read, "the papers they please to throw in the basket." Clogged pipes are nothing short of a catastrophe in Greece. (Women travelers especially should take note of this if they are in Greece while menstruating.) ~It is not considered polite in Greece to use the toilet facility at a bar or café without also ordering something to eat or drink, and I admit that when I've violated this principle, I've always felt a little guilty, especially since the toilets are usually located at the back of the establishment and often down the stairs, so one can't slip in unnoticed. Therefore I typically plan on sitting down for a few minutes when I have to make a stop. ~I have always found good, soft, American-style toilet paper in the bathrooms at American Express offices.

Tourist (as in being one)

Whether you travel often for business or are making a trip for the first time, let's face it: we're all tourists, and there's nothing shameful about that fact. In a dated but wonderful book—*Five Cities: An Art Guide to Athens, Rome, Florence, Paris, and London* (Doubleday, 1964), author Blanche Brown offers a piece of great advice: "Do not be ashamed to be a tourist! There is a kind of traveler who feels that he has reached the apex of success when someone mistakes him for a native and asks him the way to the men's room . . . there is no stigma attached to sightseeing. Tourism is not a dishonorable occupation. If skiers are not ashamed of their skis and poles, if mountain climbers are not ashamed of their boots and picks, if underwater fiends are not ashamed of their swimsuits and snorkels, why should a sightseer be ashamed of his crepe soles and Baedeker? There is appropriate gear for certain human activities, including looking at art in foreign lands. Let those of us who participate in this activity wear our nylons proudly and carry our guidebooks boldly." Yes, it's true that you feel you are a real part of the daily grind when you blend in and are mistaken for a native; but since that's not likely to happen in Greece unless you speak Greek, it's far better to just get on with it and have a good time.

Tour Operators

I am suspicious of all-inclusive package tours, no matter what the price—the wonderful, boutique accommodations where I like to stay are *never* part of any packages that I hear about, and the meals are probably no better than cafeteria food, making the whole package a poor value indeed. And packages are *not* always cheaper than making the arrangements yourself. But some full-service tour companies offering trips to Greece are excellent and provide an unbeatable combination of experience, insider's knowledge, and savvy guides, a combination that is most definitely not found by searching the Web. While I prefer to travel independently, I recognize that organizing a trip requires a substantial amount of research and attention to detail, which some travelers do not always have the time or inclination to give (and for which they are willing to pay a great deal). ~Two tour operators offer an outstanding, enlightening experience.

For almost thirty years Archaeological Tours has focused on the historical, anthropological, and archaeological aspects of culturally significant areas of the world; inquire about the nineteen-day tour to Cyprus, Crete, and Santorini. Contact information: 271 Madison Avenue, Suite 904, New York NY 10016; 866-740-5130 or 212-986-3054; www.archaeologicaltrs.com.
Humanities Abroad deserves special recognition for its "Crete and Classical Greece: Where History and Myth Converge" trip and offers many history and geography lectures. Contact information: 11 Gloucester Street, #1, Boston MA 02115; 800-754-9991; www.humanitiesabroad.com.

Trains

The Greek train network is known as the Ellinikós Orghanismós Sidhrodhrómon (EOS, and even though it is slower than the equivalent bus, I prefer the train to the bus (see my Buses entry). In Greece, unlike in other countries, the train is cheaper than the bus. There is a really neat, rack-and-pinion line between Diakoftó and Kalávrita in the Peloponnese. Frustrating to me about the EOS is that schedules are only published annually, and they're in short supply, and changes of course occur, so the only reliable sources for schedule information are the EOS offices in Athens and Thessaloníki and the train stations in these two cities. ~First- and second-class services are available, as well as sleeper service between Athens and Thessaloníki. ~Just as in other countries, if you purchase your ticket on board, you're eligible for a hefty surcharge. ~The EOS doesn't offer quite the array of reduced-fare options (other than rail passes) that the Italian, French, and Spanish services do, but inquire anyway, as there may be one or more that will apply to your travels. ~For specific information about special rail passes and their benefits, contact Budget Europe Travel Service (2557 Meade Court, Ann Arbor MI 48105; 800-441-2387 or 734-668-0529; www.budgeteuropetravel.com) or Rail Europe Group (877-275-2887 in the United States; 800-361-RAIL in Canada; www.raileurope.com.

Turkey

As I noted in the Introduction, a truly extraordinary journey would be to see Greece and Turkey together. The following observation by Patricia Storace appears very near the end of her book *Dinner with Persephone*: "Turkey is veined with Greece as Greece is veined with Turkey. The keenness and beauty that is also a part of the dialogue between the Greeks and the Turks makes their mutual hatreds tragic not only for themselves, but for the world. I have never seen a city more dazzlingly situated than Istanbul, nor one with a keener sense of what domestic pleasure might be. The wooden villas along the Bosporus construct a relation between sea and garden that makes Venice seem myopic; their combination of the ingenious, the playful, and the comfortable is a vision of domestic beauty. They often have the *krokalia* pebble mosaic decoration that Greek villas do, and the beautifully detailed woodwork that I have seen in the houses in Greece in Epirus; I learn from my hostess that the finest carpenter in Istanbul at the end of the nineteenth century was a Greek named Antonis Politis. And these waterfront houses are themselves called *yialis,* from the Greek word for waterfront . . . in 1932, it was estimated that thirty-five percent of Turkish vocabulary was of Turkish origin, a percentage which changed drastically after the linguistic reforms decreed by Atatürk. I wonder sadly how much of the repressed vocabulary was Greek, feeling how much the Greek incorporation of Turkish vocabulary adds to the Greek language and sensibility, and thinking that the presence of its Greek vocabulary must be as valuable for Turkish."

V

Volta

The *volta* is the evening stroll, a very old and popular Mediterranean custom. (In Spain, France, and Morocco it is known as the *paseo,* while in Italy it is known as the *passegiata*.) It's a custom well suited to a hot climate and has historically served as a venue for young men and women to meet each other. *Everyone* turns out for this pre-dinner walk—grandparents, babies, teenagers, and toddlers, and both watchers and walkers are considered participants. The *volta* flows a bit better on straight stretches of cobblestone, macadam, marble, or whatever, but even in large cities like Athens, residents have adopted a neighborhood or a section of town for their walk. Sometimes elderly residents do not actually walk but gather on park benches and catch up on the day's news. It's a ritual not to be missed, and an essay in the wonderful book *The Walker Within* (by the editors of *Walker Magazine*) notes that "Were Americans to take up this custom, the rate of criminal violence would surely drop, for it's easier to gun down strangers than people with whom you've passed the time."

W

Weather

The warm weather months are undoubtedly the best time of year to visit Greece. Certainly it's nice to be in Athens in cooler temperatures and with fewer crowds, but most of the Aegean islands are at least 50 percent shut down in the off season, and if you want to swim in Homer's legendary wine dark sea, it really is too cold. I was surprised to learn recently that some people actually believe it's hot and sunny year round in Greece. It's cold enough to don coats, sweaters, hats, and gloves in the winter months, which is the rainy season. I've had occasion to be in Greece during the late summer months, early fall, and winter, and I'm happy to report that even in February there were plenty of bright, warm, sunny days mixed in with gray skies and fierce thunderstorms. Fall may be my favorite time of year (many places in the world are wonderful in the fall), but each season offers its own delights. Picking the "perfect" time of year is subjective, and you should go when you have the opportunity, and that will be your experience, your Greece. Peak season means higher prices and more people, but if you're determined to attend the Athens Festival in July, witness Easter celebrations in the spring, or visit Santorini in August, then the cost and the crowds don't matter (and I guarantee you'll have a fantastic trip).

Women

The history of women in ancient Greece is not a happy one, and even in modern times Greek women have not been treated particularly well or fairly. This seems to be changing, however, and younger generations of Greek women stand a much better chance than their older sisters or mothers of progressing in the career of their choice and of being perceived by their future husbands as a more equal partner.

Less common in Athens but still prevalent in the islands and in villages on the mainland is the tradition of women wearing certain scarves. Colored scarves are worn by women who are married; black scarves are worn only by women who have recently been widowed; and white scarves are worn by widows of long standing. A handful of good books to read include *Women in Greek Myth* (by Mary Lefkowitz, Johns Hopkins University Press, Baltimore, 1986); *Women's Life in Greece and Rome* (by Maureen B. Fant and Mary Lefkowitz, Johns Hopkins University Press, 1992); *Women in Ancient Greece* (by Sue Blundell, Harvard University Press, 1995); and *Making Silence Speak: Women's Voices in Greek Literature and Society* (by André Lardinois and Laura McClure, Princeton University Press, 2001).

X

Xeni

This word refers to foreigners (note its similarity to *xenophobia*), and it's interesting that the word for hotel is *xenodochion*—"container for strangers."

Xenitia

Xenitia, loosely defined and condensed, refers to the quality of being in a foreign place, somewhat like the phrase, 'stranger in a strange land.' I have often seen the word translated as 'homesick,' but that isn't quite right. *Xenitia* is a word that crops up often in the writings of Greek émigrés, and though they reflect often on their homeland, *xenitia* refers more to their feeling of being entirely foreign, being Greek, in a particular place. The word is a powerful one. Nicholas Gage, in *Greece: Land of Light,* noted that there is a saying: "The most painful experiences a Greek can know are to be an orphan, to be alone, to be in love, and to be away from Greece. And to be away from Greece is the worst of all." Patricia Storace relates that a friend once said to her, "I warn you of what the novelist Vassilikos says about Greece—that is the place where when you are here you long to leave, and the minute you leave, you yearn uncontrollably to come back. I know. When I am in Greece, I think about my month in France. And in France, the whole month, of Greece." Vilma Liacouras Chantiles, in *The Foods of Greece,* writes, "An emotional bond ties the expatriate to Greece, no matter how far he wanders. Greek ethos outwears hardship: it survives amid the ferment of new concepts and bustling modern economies. Greece maintains a strong hold on the child who has grown up in the motherland, even if his adult years are lived far to the west." And the authors (Suzanne Slesin, Stafford Cliff, Daniel Rozensztroch) of *Greek Style* write, "For many Greeks, there is nothing more important than the family. Although they are by nature voyagers and adventurers, merchants, ships' captains, and pirates, they sooner or later will all return home."

Yachting

Some adventures in life are once-in-a-lifetime experiences, unparalleled in every way. Yachting in Greece may be one of them. Not that *I've* ever been so fortunate, but if you have your own boat (or access to someone else's), you must set sail right away.

Two booklets on this topic are indispensable.

Yachting, published by the Hellenic Tourism Organization, has gorgeous, glossy photographs and outlines such basics as formalities for port entry and exit, chartering yachts in Greece, radio frequencies, and rules and prohibitions. Even if you weren't considering yachting, you might after you see the photos in *Yachting*. *Sailing the Greek Seas*, published by the GNTO, includes weather and navigation forecasts, coastal radio telephone stations, a complete list of marinas and their facilities, and harbor and canal dues.

Greece has between 9,000 and 15,000 miles of coastline, depending on whether the islands are included, and which ones. The actual number of Greek islands is a matter of dispute between Athens and Ankara, but at least 2,000 habitable islands are securely in Greece's hands—and thousands more are little more than rocky outcroppings with a spit of sand or a tiny natural harbor suitable for a quiet afternoon of swimming or sunbathing. On a private yacht you can reach coves and shoreline that DROPs (dreaded other people, a phrase I borrowed from Frank Booth, author of *The Independent Walker's Guide to France*) cannot.

Yia sas

Only in Greek, perhaps, is it not difficult to find a word to include under *y*. *Yia sas* is a good phrase to remember, as it may be used for "hello," "good-bye," or more commonly, "Cheers!" (which is also voiced as *yia mas*).

The Kiosque—
Points of View

"What a very ancient modern little country it is—for one can see the shadow of the ancients shining through the fabric of modern Greek life. The Romans for all their marvelous engineering could not help feeling that they were hollow copies of something better."
                                    —Lawrence Durrell, THE GREEK ISLANDS

Restoration
of the Parthenon Marbles

JENIFER NEILS

∽

editor's note

The story of Lord Elgin and the Elgin Marbles, as they have come to
be known, has been told and retold. In case you need a refresher on the
story, here is a brief retelling, in the words of Jenifer Neils in her excellent
book *The Parthenon Frieze*: "On July 31, 1801, a motley crew consisting of
an Italian landscape painter, a Tartar figure painter from central Asia, and
a hunchback draftsman from Naples, all under the direction of the
Reverend Philip Hunt, a thirty-year-old English clergyman, began the sys-
tematic removal from the Parthenon of its sculptural adornment—works of
art that had remained for more than 2,000 years in the position for which
they were carved. This team was carrying out its operations with the direct
permission of the Sultan of Turkey, Selim III, in the form of a *firman* (edict)
obtained by and on behalf of the British ambassador to the Sublime Port,
Thomas Bruce, seventh Earl of Elgin. In addition to the fifteen metopes
from the south side and all but two of the remaining pedimental figures
(which were believed incorrectly to be Roman), they took down approximately one-third of the north and south friezes. In order to lessen the excessive weight of these frieze blocks for ease in transport, their back halves
were sawed off. Having survived the 1687 explosion relatively intact, the
western end of the temple still retained its superstructure and so made
removal of the west frieze too difficult; most of it remained in place until
1993, when it was finally removed because of the devastating air pollution
in modern Athens." For more than two hundred years Lord Elgin's actions,
both on legal and ethical grounds, have been debated; the French even
coined a word, *elginisme,* to describe the plunder of cultural treasures in
general, and Thomas Hoving, former director of the Metropolitan Museum
of Art in New York, said in 1997 that "The controversy over whether these
magnificent stones should remain in London or be returned to the
Acropolis burns as consistently as any political issue of modern times." The
debate has never been as heated as it is right now, on the eve of the 2004
Summer Olympic Games in Athens.

In December 2002 the directors of eighteen major European and American museums issued a statement affirming their right to keep long-held antiquities that countries like Greece and Egypt have demanded be repatriated. The statement argued that objects acquired in the past should be "viewed in the light of different sensitivities and values, reflective of that earlier era," yet significantly the statement also recommended that each repatriation case be judged individually. The British Museum, home to the Elgin Marbles since 1817, was not one of the signatories. Neils notes in her book that in May 1997 a representative of a British organization called the Heritage Society stated that "It was not a feasible or sensible option" to return the marbles to Greece, as they form "an integral part of the museum's collection." What this official failed to acknowledge, by taking such a short, nationalistic view of history, is that they were an integral part of the buildings on the Acropolis for even longer. How does one weigh two centuries of ownership against twenty-two? The Italian government, shortly after the museum statement was issued, returned to Greece a small piece of the Parthenon frieze depicting the foot of the goddess Peitho, which had been in a museum in Palermo since the nineteenth century. Though I generally refrain from stating my opinions too strongly on controversial issues in my books—preferring that travelers read as much as they can and reach their own conclusions—I feel I must support Greece in its efforts to have the Marbles returned. I have visited the British Museum, a fine and outstanding institution that will, without doubt, remain so even without the Elgin Marbles in its collection.

The New Acropolis Museum, which is being constructed with a magnificent glass Parthenon Hall duplicating the space and orientation of the Parthenon on the Sacred Rock, will house for the first time ever all the surviving treasures of the Acropolis. I have seen only a model of this new museum, at the Onassis Cultural Center in New York, but I understand that the construction of a new museum has been a goal of the Greek state for more than two decades, and that visitors will have the opportunity to view the Acropolis treasures in historical sequence and grouped according to their original locations on the Rock in an exhibition space of 14,000 square meters.

DR. JENIFER NEILS is Ruth Coutler Heede Professor of Art History at Case Western Reserve University, where she has taught since 1980. A renowned scholar of Greek art and archaeology, she is the author of numerous books—including several museum exhibition catalogs—and an even greater number of articles that have appeared in scholarly publications around the world. Additionally, Neils has participated in archaeological excavations in Greece and Italy and has held academic appointments at the American School of Classical Studies at Athens.

Let me say from the outset that I speak not as a representative of any specific organization but as an art historian and scholar who has devoted most of her research toward a fuller understanding of ancient Athenian art and ideology. In the past, cases, most notably by Melina Mercouri, have been made for the restitution and/or the repatriation of the Parthenon Marbles, terms that imply the return of property to its deemed rightful owner. I will avoid these backward-looking arguments that rest on what I consider unprovable issues of ownership and will speak instead about *restoration* in both senses of the word: that is, to bring something back to its original state or condition, and to return or give back.

As a teacher and especially as author of a recent book on the Parthenon frieze, I have made a concerted effort to present this important monument to students in its entirety—which is not an easy task with a work of art that is 160 meters long and contains 378 human figures and 245 animals. Frustrated by slides that artificially chop up the flow of the procession, I included in my book a compact disc that allows one to view the entire frieze as if walking around the Parthenon in either direction. Also, I commissioned the first complete drawings of all four sides of the frieze for a foldout inserted in the book.

As useful as these aids are for understanding the frieze, they can never substitute for viewing the carved marble slabs in person. Whenever I am in London, I make a point of getting to the British Museum just before the ten o'clock opening time so I can go directly to the Duveen Gallery, where I have the Parthenon Marbles to myself (and two guards) for about ten minutes. I have done this many, many times and continue to feel overwhelmed by the experience each time. My first thought on seeing this spectacular monument is that it is perfect in this setting. Entry is free to anybody who will invest the time and effort, including even the blind, thanks to

Ian Jenkins's admirable project called Second Sight. Of course, this excellent accessibility could change if Her Majesty's government ever develops different priorities, but for now this is a real plus. The frieze is installed at eye level and is well lighted except on very dark days. The explanatory labels are exemplary. Altogether an impressive presentation is my first reaction.

My second thought, as I gaze at these accumulated fragments of the Parthenon sculptures, is how much more moving and educational it would be to see the entire ensemble together, an experience that has not been possible since the seventeenth century. The few commentators from earlier times whose writings are preserved were certainly overwhelmed by the sight of the Parthenon. Cyriac of Ancona, who visited the Acropolis in 1436, wrote of the Temple of Athena: "on the topmost citadel of the city . . . [it is] splendidly adorned with the noblest images (*preclaris imaginibus*) on all sides which you see superbly carved on both fronts, on the friezes on the walls, and on the epistyles (i.e., metopes)." In 1667 the Ottoman poet Evliya Chelebi stated, "In civilized countries no sanctuary exists to equal it. May its construction remain eternal until the completion of time." Tragically, as we all know, its construction did not remain eternal, as only twenty years later the Parthenon exploded, shattering many of its "noblest images."

These now fragmentary sculptures have been scattered, many far beyond their original home on the Acropolis. Because of Lord Elgin's enterprise, the bulk of them are currently housed in the British Museum. But not all of them. An important slab of the east frieze, along with a head of a horseman, are in the Louvre. A pair of heads of distinguished older men made it to Vienna, while a fragment with the head of a tray-bearer is in the Vatican. The National Museum of Denmark has the head of a centaur from south metope four. A small bit of the frieze with some horse hooves ended up in a marble pile on the Athenian Agora and so is now housed in the storerooms of the Stoa of Attalos. Such *membra disiecta*, like a foot of Artemis from the east frieze in Athens that now sits forlornly on the wall in the archaeological museum of Palermo, are simply trophies, virtually meaningless out of their original context.

Many scholars, and in particular the keepers of the British Museum, have labored tirelessly to reconstitute the Parthenon's sculptural ensemble. Up until the time of Duveen, casts were acquired of all the pieces in other museums, as well as those excavated in Athens, so the display in London could be as complete as possible. Although the casts were removed for the Duveen Gallery, this tradition has been carried on admirably in the Skulpturhalle in Basel, Switzerland, which functions as a scholarly laboratory with movable casts of all the Parthenon sculptures. But the British Museum decided in the 1930s that casts, good as they might be, are no substitute for the original sculptures. One recognizes this when visiting Basel or the display in the Acropolis Study Center. Casts cannot reproduce exactly the texture or color of Pentelic marble; nor can they capture accurately the subtleties of the carving, the tool marks, or the delicate details of hair, drapery, veins, and fingernails. Useful as they are for study purposes and for reconstituting the overall plan of the sculptural program, casts remain poor substitutes for the originals. For this reason neither the British Museum nor the Acropolis Museum will display them alongside original marble sculptures.

For connoisseurs of art there is no substitute for the original, and that original should be as complete as possible for a true understanding of the work of art. In the case of a Greek vase, for instance, it is tacitly understood that the owner of a smaller fragment will give, trade, or sell it to the owner of the larger piece so the whole can be reconstituted as near as possible to the original. In the case of the Ionic frieze of the Parthenon, the need to reassemble the disparate pieces is even more compelling, since they form parts of a programmatic sculpture in which each element is purposefully designed to reflect the prevailing ideology of classical Athens. The sculptural embellishment of the Parthenon was a unified concept that is impossible to visualize, much less understand, in its current sundered condition.

I often use the example of the Sistine Chapel Ceiling. If Michelangelo's masterpiece had been detached and broken up into dispersed pieces, we would want and need to see this fresco program reassembled so it could be understood and appreciated as it was conceived by a great artistic genius. The same holds for the Parthenon sculptures, as the masterpiece of Phidias. Here the case is even more compelling because his real masterworks in ancient Greek eyes—the chryselephantine statues of Athena in the Parthenon and the Zeus at Olympia—are gone forever. In both the Parthenon and the Sistine Chapel the artistic genius responsible for the design planned his conception for a specific building, worked out complex narratives, and accommodated these to predetermined spaces. The images were executed to be read as a meaningful whole. It is our responsibility as lovers and protectors of art to respect that original plan and honor the artist's creation to the extent possible. Every effort should be made to restore the monument to the creator's original design. Otherwise we will surely fail in our efforts to understand the artistic masterpieces of the past.

That said, what practically can be done to bring back to light or "restore" the original intention of Phidias? In the last chapter of my book I argued that because the Parthenon frieze was designed as an integral whole, its far-flung pieces should be reunited. In the new European Union, of which Britain and Greece are members, cooperative exchange of this nature not only should be possible but could become common practice. I believe, for instance, that the small marble heads and the severed limb fragments from the Temple of Zeus currently on display in the Louvre should go back to Olympia, where they would join the more complete metopes. In exchange Greece could, for instance, "restore" to France the lower legs of the Lyons *kore*. The Italians in general and the Museo Archeologico di Palermo in particular have recently shown the way and set an excellent example for others to follow by "restoring" the right foot to the beautiful image of Artemis from the Parthenon's east frieze, now in the Acropolis Museum. In return the Italians have received on long-term loan one of the two bronze helmets dedicated by Hieron, the tyrant of Syracuse, to Zeus at Olympia. Rather than diminishing Palermo or Olympia, such loans and exchanges enrich and enhance both institutions.

So much for the first definition of *restore*. As for the second definition, "to give back," there are many compelling moral reasons why the Parthenon Marbles should be restored to their original homeland. These reasons outweigh certain facts, namely: that the majority of the best preserved sculptures are currently in Britain, that the sculptures have been relatively well cared for in their current repository for two hundred years, and that the British heritage claims the sculptures since they were one of the catalysts for the rebirth of classicism in northern Europe.

Again as an art historian and former museum curator, I believe that one must seriously take into account both what is best for a particular work of art and what is optimum for the viewers of this art. One could invoke—and museums do—the principle of repose, which states that objects are best left where they are unless a compelling case is made to remove them. In spite of this principle, irreplaceable works of art are moved continually by museums for money-making blockbuster exhibitions. Sometimes little thought is given to what is best for the particular work of art and more consideration is given to the bottom line. Fortunately that is not the case here, but rather the opposite.

The display area for the Parthenon sculptures in the British Museum is now more than half a century old and no longer state of the art, whereas a newly constructed, specially designed museum is precisely what is best for the works of art at this point in time. The design of Bernard Tschumi is masterful and especially sensitive to the particular needs of exhibiting this sculptural program in its entirety. For the first time in two hundred years we would be able to view the frieze as it was intended, not from "outside in," so to speak. The frieze will also be not only in close conjunction with all of the other sculptures of the temple but in sight of the temple itself. And most important aesthetically, the natural, bright, clear light of the Mediterranean will illuminate this masterpiece more effectively than the cold, gray gloom of London, wonderful as that can be in its own way. The famous British sculptor Henry Moore wrote of this light: "The Greek light is, as everyone says, something you can't imagine till you've experienced it. In England half the light is, as it were, absorbed into the object, but in Greece the object seems to give off light as if it were lit up from inside itself."

The authorities of the British Museum and British scholars of Greek art, most recently Sir John Boardman, have argued that it is educational to see classical antiquities in proximity to the antiquities of other ancient civilizations, such as Egypt and Mesopotamia, and this is indeed a valid point. But an even stronger educational purpose is served by viewing the Parthenon sculpture in proximity to the archaic *korai,* equestrian statues, and votives reliefs that preceded and directly inspired it, and then in relation to the sculpture of the Acropolis, such as the caryatids, that it in turn influenced. One of the great learning experiences in Athens is to encounter firsthand the unfolding development of Greek sculpture as one walks though either the National Museum or that of the Acropolis. This ability to experience the development and continuity of Greek art at its source is, to my mind as a historian of Greek art, a stronger claim, and one that trumps the universal museum argument.

While I fervently support the claims of Greece to the most significant monument of its classical past, I also strongly defend the need for accessibility to this monument for all people. Currently one can enter the British Museum free of charge and have generous access to all of its holdings. I am sorry to say that this is sometimes not the case in Greece. Even I, a somewhat recognized scholar of Athenian art, was denied official permission to view the west frieze while researching my latest book. In the spirit of the EU and scholarly inquiry, I would advocate free admission and easy access for scholars and students to all antiquities. Only in this way can we do full justice to the great enterprise that took place in Athens in the fifth century B.C., what Pericles so presciently termed "an education to all of Greece."

Finally, perhaps the most compelling art historical reason for a return or restoring to Greece of the Parthenon sculptures is the rare opportunity it would present to know a work of art in a different context. The display in Britain, as good as it is, has now for two centuries shaped our understanding and reading of the Parthenon sculptures and the frieze in particular. By displaying it anew in a different and more complete context, we may be able to shed old preconceptions and gain new insights to this sculpture, which is after all one of the glories of art historical research. I for one welcome this opportunity, as it would give me the chance to test visually some of my theories about the arrangement of the figures of the frieze in space, something I can do at this point only on paper and with computer technology. Viewing the sculptures in a new light and a more complete configuration would inspire the next generation of scholars, students, artists, travelers, and museum visitors to see this complex monument we call the Parthenon as it was conceived and executed—that is, in its entirety.

The Byzantine Empire: Rome of the East

BY MERLE SEVERY

∽

editor's note

The Byzantine civilization, centered on Constantinople, was a star that shone brightly during Europe's Dark Ages. The empire preserved the heritage of Greece and Rome and spread Christianity across a vast realm. After eleven centuries, it finally splintered, its many accomplishments falling in the shadow of the Italian Renaissance and later movements.

In this brilliantly detailed, interpretive piece, Merle Severy takes an end-of-the-twentieth-century look at Byzantium's importance "as a buffer shielding medieval Europe from the empire-building Persians, Arabs, and Turks; as a bridge between ancient and modern times; as the creator and codifier of laws and religious, political, and social practices vibrant to this day." This essay, written in 1983, remains one of the most valued articles in my files, and whenever friends and colleagues tell me they are visiting Greece, Turkey, or northern Italy, I eagerly thrust it into their hands. It is one of the few pieces in which history is presented in a complete, wide-ranging circle. The various cities and towns highlighted in the essay would, together, make for an outstanding itinerary—only, of course, if one had about a month to do it.

MERLE SEVERY was on the staff of *National Geographic* for almost thirty-eight years, and was one of the few writers equally talented at taking photographs for the magazine.

On the twenty-ninth of May in 1453—6,961 years after the creation of the world, by Byzantine reckoning; 1,123 years and 18 days after Constantine the Great dedicated his new Christian Rome on the Bosporus—Constantinople fell to the Turks. With it fell the heart of the Byzantine Empire that once ruled from the Caucasus to the Atlantic, from the Crimea to Sinai, from the Danube to the Sahara.

Yet 1453, a pivot on which ages turn, was a beginning as well. Just as the double-headed eagle, symbol of Byzantium and its spiritual heir, imperial Russia, looks both east and west, forward and backward in time, so Byzantine ways of government, laws, religious concepts, and ceremonial splendor continue to move our lives today.

Much of our classical heritage was transmitted by Byzantium. Its art affected medieval and modern art. Byzantines taught us how to set a large dome over a quadrangular space, gave us patterns of diplomacy and ceremony—even introduced forks. (An eleventh-century Byzantine princess brought these in marriage to a doge of Venice, shocking guests, just as her cousin, wed to a German emperor, scandalized his court by taking baths and wearing silk.)

"City of the world's desire," hub of the medieval universe, Constantinople bestrode a superbly defensible peninsula and sheltered harbor, the Golden Horn, at the crossroads of Europe and Asia. Here in the legendary past Greek settlers named the place after their leader, Byzas. And Byzantium it also continued to be called, as well as the Eastern Roman Empire it ruled, until the Turks captured it in that fateful year, 1453, and later renamed it Istanbul.

To this day the city retains its fascination: the kaleidoscope of craft like water bugs on the Golden Horn, the cries of vendors in the labyrinthine covered bazaar, porters jackknifed under loads threading teeming alleys—the unpredictability of its life. Forget logic if you search a street address. Sit to sip tea by the seawall near Justinian's palace, and don't be surprised if a brown bear shags by with a gaggle of Gypsies.

Threading crowds of fervent Muslims boarding buses for the pilgrimage to Mecca, I entered Hagia Sophia, once the Church of the Holy Wisdom, Christendom's crowning glory. Fragmentary mosaics hint at the golden sheen that illumined the shrine. Light shafting through a corona of windows seems to levitate the giant ribbed dome. Let imagination fill the vast nave with worshipers, chanting clergy robed in brocade, incense swirling through a constellation of oil lamps toward that gilded dome suspended as if from heaven, and you will share Justinian's exultation. In 537 he beheld his masterwork complete: "Solomon, I have outdone thee!"

Constantine and Justinian—these two emperors, both born in Serbia, set Byzantium on the path to greatness. Constantine's Christianization of the Roman Empire in the fourth century is one of history's mightiest revolutions. He chose a persecuted minority sect—an illegal, subversive intruder into the Roman state—and made it the cornerstone of a world-shaking power: Christendom.

His sainted mother, Helena, in her old age made a pilgrimage to the Holy Land. There, with a rapidity and assurance that can only strike wonder in the modern archaeologist, legend has it she unearthed the True Cross, the lance, and the crown of thorns and identified, under a temple of Aphrodite, the tomb of Christ. Over it her thrilled son ordered buildings to "surpass the most magnificent monuments any city possesses"—a decade-long labor now incorporated in Jerusalem's Church of the Holy Sepulchre.

Constantine himself presided over some 250 bishops assembled at Nicaea for the first of seven ecumenical, or universal, councils that forged the Orthodox faith. They formulated the familiar Nicene Creed ("I believe in one God, the Father Almighty, maker of heaven and earth . . ."). Those opposing the council's decrees were branded heretics.

Constantine gave Byzantium its spiritual focus. Justinian in the sixth century gave it its greatest temporal sway. Reconquering lands once Roman, he magnified his empire by founding or rebuilding cities, monasteries, and seven hundred fortifications. In the Balkans, the Levant, Italy, from the Euphrates to the Pillars of Hercules, I found impressive works. In Algeria, Tunisia, and Libya I strolled cities roofless to the North African sky. Triumphal arches, amphitheaters, baths, and grids of stone-paved streets lined with shops and town houses bespoke Roman origins. Justinian's fortresses and churches placed them in the Byzantine world. Some stand alone in an empty countryside.

In the Algerian-Tunisian frontier city of Tebessa (Byzantine Theveste), life pulses at the crossroads of a fertile belt of towns shielded from the Sahara by a crescent of the Atlas Mountains. Burnoosed men and veiled women, donkeys, and vehicles stream through a sculptured, porticoed Byzantine gate. Children clamber on Byzantine walls in whose shade old men sit and watch the passing parade, and women gossip.

But none of Justinian's cities matched the splendor of his Constantinople.

Medieval visitors from the rural West, where Rome had shrunk to a cow town, were struck dumb by this resplendent metropolis, home to half a million, its harbor crowded with vessels, its markets filled with silks, spices, furs, precious stones, perfumed woods, carved ivory, gold and silver, and enameled jewelry. "One could not believe there was so rich a city in all the world," reported the crusader Villehardouin.

The first Rome, on the Tiber, did not fall in 476, as schoolbooks often say; it withered away. No emperor died on its walls when it was sacked by Visigoths in 410, or by Vandals from Carthage in 455; emperors had long resided elsewhere. From the third century the course of empire had set eastward.

The Dark Ages are dark only if you look at Western Europe, for long centuries a backwater: decaying towns, isolated manors, scattered monasteries, squabbling robber barons. In the East blazed the light of Byzantium, studded with cities such as Thessalonica, Antioch, and Alexandria, more cosmopolitan than any Western society before the modern age.

While Charlemagne could barely scrawl his name and only clerics had clerical skills, many Byzantine emperors were scholars. Even laymen knew their Homer as they knew their Psalms. While men in the West for centuries tested guilt by ordeal—picking up a red-hot iron (you were innocent if you didn't burn your hand)—Justinian set scholars to compiling his famous Corpus Juris Civilis, the foundation of Roman law in continental Europe today. Via the Code Napoléon, Byzantine precepts were transmitted to Latin America, Quebec Province, and Louisiana, where they still hold sway.

Though the empire became officially Greek in speech soon after Justinian's day, people of the East still considered themselves Romans. (Westerners they called Latins or Franks, when they weren't calling them barbarians.) Their Emperor of the Romans was the legitimate heir of Augustus Caesar. Down to 1453 theirs was *the* Roman Empire. But it was the old pagan Roman world Christianized and turned upside down, the kingdom of heaven on earth.

Such was the Byzantine worldview: a God-centered realm, universal and eternal, with the emperor as God's vice-regent surrounded by an imperial entourage that reflected the heavenly hierarchy of angels, prophets, and apostles. One God, one world, one emperor. Outside this cosmos was only ignorance and war, a fury of barbarians. The emperor had a divine mandate to propagate the true faith and bring them under his dominion.

Ceremony reinforced his role. His coronation procession moved through the Golden Gate along the Mese, the arcaded, shop-lined avenue leading through the Forum of Constantine and past the Hippodrome to the Augusteum, the main square with its gargantuan statue of Justinian on horseback gesturing eastward atop his pillar, and the Milion, the milestone where the routes of empire converged. Along the way a legitimate successor or victorious usurper transformed himself by a series of costume changes from a hero in gleaming armor to a robed personification of Christ. On Easter and at Christmas twelve courtiers symbolically gowned as the Apostles would accompany him in procession to worship in Hagia Sophia, the populace prostrating in adoration.

Ruling from his labyrinthine sacred palace, the emperor, crown and gown festooned with precious stones, invested his officials in silken robes and bestowed titles such as Excellency (used by ambassadors, governors, and Roman Catholic bishops today) and Magnificence (still used by rectors of German universities). Popes would adopt his tiara; England's monarchs, his orb and scepter; protocol officers, the order of precedence at imperial banquets.

The splendor of Byzantine ceremonial in rooms with doors of bronze and ceilings in gold and silver awed the foreigner, especially when a bit of mechanical wizardry was thrown in. Liudprand of Lombardy, on a diplomatic mission in 949, describes an imperial audience:

Golden lions guarding the throne "beat the ground with their tails and gave a dreadful roar with open mouth and quivering tongue." Bronze birds cried out from a gilded tree. "After I had three times made obeisance . . . with my face upon the ground, I lifted my head, and behold, the man whom just before I had seen sitting on a moderately elevated seat had now changed his raiment and was sitting at the level of the ceiling."

Beneath the glittering ritual we can perceive a prototype of today's bureaucratic state. A hierarchy of officials, including the custodian of the imperial inkstand, who readied the quill pen and red ink with which the emperor signed decrees, minutely supervised this "paradise of monopoly, privilege, and protectionism" that subordinated the individual's interest to the state's.

Constantinople organized its trades in tightly regulated guilds; controlled prices, wages, and rents; stockpiled wheat to offset poor harvests. Officials inspected shops; checked weights and measures, ledgers, quality of merchandise. Hoarders, smugglers, defrauders, counterfeiters, tax evaders faced severe punishment.

Unlike the West, trade or industry seldom bore a stigma. One empress distilled perfume in her palace bedroom. The emperor himself was the empire's leading merchant and manufacturer, with monopolies in minting, armaments, and Byzantium's renowned luxury articles. Justinian had founded its famed silk industry with silkworm eggs smuggled into Constantinople. (Hitherto the empire had paid a pound of gold for a pound of Chinese silk.) Special brocades from imperial looms and other "prohibited articles" not for sale abroad made prestigious gifts for foreign princes.

Import, export, sales, purchase taxes, and shop rents swelled the imperial coffers (Basil II left 200,000 pounds of gold)—this at a time when the West more often bartered than bought. Nor were interest-bearing loans condemned as sinful; in the West they were, and this put moneylending into the scorned hands of Jews. Justinian set an 8 percent ceiling on interest—12 percent on maritime loans because of increased risk. (The borrower did not have to repay if ship or cargo was lost to storm or pirate.) Insurance and credit services were developed. Banking was closely audited. The gold solidus, the coin introduced by Constantine and later called bezant for Byzantium, held its value for seven centuries—history's most stable currency.

In the spirit "if any would not work, neither should he eat," the indigent were put to work in state bakeries and market gardens. "Idleness leads to crime," noted Emperor Leo III. And drunkenness to disorder and sedition—so taverns closed at eight.

God's state would protect the working girl: a fine of two pounds of gold for anyone who corrupted a woman employed in the imperial textile factories. Incest, homicide, privately making or selling purple cloth (reserved for royalty alone), or teaching shipbuilding to enemies might bring decapitation, impalement, hanging—or drowning in a sack with a hog, a cock, a viper, and an ape. The grocer who gave false measure lost his hand. Arsonists were burned.

The Byzantines came to favor mutilation as a humane substitute for the death penalty; the tongueless or slit-nosed sinner had time to repent. Class distinctions in law were abolished. Judges were paid salaries from the treasury instead of taking money from litigants, "for gifts and offerings blind the eyes of the wise."

"Men . . . should not shamelessly trample upon one another," observed Leo VI, the Wise. Contractors had to replace faulty construction at their own cost. Housing codes forbade balconies less than ten feet from the facing house, storing noxious matter, or encroaching on a neighbor's light or sea view.

As solicitous for its subjects' welfare as it was in controlling their thoughts and deeds, the state provided much of the cradle-to-grave care expected by the Communist faithful today. Emperors and wealthy citizens vied in endowing hospitals, poorhouses, orphanages, homes for the blind or aged (where "the last days of man's earthly life might be peaceful, painless, and dignified"), homes for repentant prostitutes (some became saints), even a reformatory for fallen women aristocrats. Medical services included surgical and maternity wards, psychiatric clinics, and leprosariums. In contrast to the unwashed West, early Byzantium abounded in public baths. Street lighting made the nights safer.

A modern state in many ways. Passports were required for travel in frontier districts. Tourists can sympathize with Liudprand; he ran afoul of customs on his way out. From his baggage, officials confiscated prized cloths of purple silk.

Sunrise burnished the gold of autumn leaves in the Balkan Mountains. A horse plowed a Bulgarian field where peasant women bent to their toil. My photographic colleague and I stopped our camper to capture the scene.

A police car pulled up. A policeman and a political official checked and recorded our documents. The official ordered us to strip our cameras. With no explanation, no heed to our anguished protests, he ground the cassettes under his heel, pulled out the film, and cast in the dirt our color record of the region's Byzantine churches.

The incident came as an unpleasant reminder that a harbinger of Eastern Europe's police states was Byzantium, suspicious of foreigners and as chary about letting out information as it was avid in gaining it.

State visitors were shown what officials wanted them to see. En route to Constantinople a guard of honor kept them from deviating from the imperial post route. Assigned servants and interpreters learned as much as possible from the envoy's entourage. Also, merchants were kept under surveillance. No alien might trade or trespass beyond fairs held near the borders except in the presence of an official. In the capital the prefect assigned them separate compounds to curb spying—fur-clad Rus with drooping mustaches; unkempt Bulgars belted with iron chains; Khazars and Petchenegs from the steppes; merchants of Venice, Genoa, Pisa, Amalfi, Lombardy, and Catalonia. If one overstayed his three-month term, he was stripped of goods, whipped, and expelled.

How free was speech? How welcome criticism? One clue was the name of the imperial council: Silentium. The historian Procopius extolled Justinian's military and building campaigns—on the emperor's orders. He had to reserve his bitter personal opinions for a *Secret History*, "for neither could I elude the watchfulness of vast numbers of spies, nor escape a most cruel death, if I were found out." Only at chariot races and other events in the Hippodrome could the populace express discontent before the emperor. Factions among the 60,000 spectators sometimes exploded into riot. Justinian survived one attempted rebellion by drowning the Hippodrome in blood.

Behind the court's glittering facade lay perhaps "the most thoroughly base and despicable form that civilisation has yet assumed," fulminated a Victorian historian, William Lecky: "a monotonous story of the intrigues of priests, eunuchs, and women, of poisonings, of conspiracies, of uniform ingratitude, of perpetual fratricides."

Surrounded by would-be usurpers and assassins, no incompetent emperor remained God's vicar on earth very long. Of the eighty-eight emperors from Constantine I to XI, thirteen took to a monastery. Thirty others died violently—starved, poisoned, blinded, bludgeoned, strangled, stabbed, dismembered, decapitated. The skull of Nicephorus I ended up as a silver-lined goblet from which Khan Krum of the Bulgars toasted his boyars. The Empress Irene was so obsessed with retaining power that she had her son blinded and took his title of emperor. Even the sainted Constantine the Great had his eldest son slain and his wife suffocated in her bath.

Yet the empire, ringed with enemies, endured more than eleven hundred years. Behind the silken glove of its diplomacy lay the mailed fist of its navy, sophisticated defenses, and small but highly trained army, based on a battering wedge of armored cavalry and mounted archers.

Proudly continuing Rome's iron discipline, the Byzantines now defended the empire as "champions and saviours of Christendom." On campaign they rose and slept to a round of prayers. Parading a most sacred relic—the Virgin's robe—around Constantinople's walls was credited with saving the "city guarded by God" from Rus attack in the ninth century. The Emperor Heraclius's ultimate triumph was not in crushing the millennial enemy, Persia, near Nineveh. Rather it was in recovering the True Cross looted by the Persians and returning it in person to Jerusalem in 630.

What about that nasty reputation for duplicity and cowardice? The Byzantines weren't cowards. They neither romanticized war nor gloried in it as a sport. They studied it as a science and used it as a last resort if gold, flattery, and intrigue failed.

Fire beacons and flag towers gave distant early warning. Ten centuries before Florence Nightingale set up field hospitals in the Crimean War, Byzantine medics got a bonus for each man they brought alive off the field of battle.

The fortified Crimea was the empire's listening post for the steppes, that invasion corridor for Huns, Slavs, Khazars, Magyar hordes "howling like wolves," and Bulgars born of that wild marriage of "wandering Scythian witches to the demons of the sands of Turkestan." Information also came from distant ports, naval patrols, envoys, merchants, spies, defectors. ("Never turn away freeman or slave, by day or night," counseled a tenth-century officer.) Collating this intelligence, the Bureau of Barbarians—Constantinople's CIA—analyzed strengths and weaknesses of each nation, calculated the price of each prince, determined when to unleash a pretender to spark rebellion.

If fight they must, Byzantines bet on brains over brawn. Military manuals stressed mobility, scouting, surprise. Immobilize an invader by capturing his baggage, food, and mounts while grazing. Scorch the earth, block the springs. Don't join an action unless strategy, numbers, and odds are in your favor. "God ever loves to help men in dangers which are necessary, not in those they choose for themselves," explained Justinian's famed general, Belisarius.

If things got desperate, the Byzantines unmasked their ultimate weapon: Greek fire. Volatile petroleum, preheated under pressure, was projected through a flame-thrower, incinerating ships and crews. It even spread fire on the water, turning a foe's fleet into a raging inferno. This Byzantine A-bomb broke five years of naval assaults on Constantinople in the late seventh century and a year-long siege in the early eighth, changing history by stopping the Arabs at Europe's doorstep. And when, two centuries later, Rus flotillas swept into the Bosporus, Byzantines sent them reeling with "lightning from heaven," in the words of Prince Igor's defeated force.

I came to a place named Ohrid in today's Yugoslavia—a peaceful town, its red-tiled roofs shouldering down a peninsula to a Macedonian lake backed by the stern mountains of forbidden Albania. A fishermen's church stands on the promontory, high-cheekboned saints staring out of their halos with large black Byzantine eyes. Ohrid a thousand years ago was the capital of a Bulgarian empire whose Tsar Samuel had triumphed from the Black Sea to the Adriatic. But in Byzantine emperor Basil II, Samuel found his nemesis.

For decades their campaigns seesawed through the Balkans with ghastly carnage. Samuel, slippery as a Lake Ohrid eel, finally set a trap for Basil in a gorge along the upper Struma. Eluding it, Basil pinned Samuel's entire army there. Now he would teach the tsar a lesson in Byzantine revenge.

Descending at dusk from Samuel's citadel, which still crowns the peninsula at Ohrid, I joined the stream of parents, children, and lovers promenading in the main street. Dark eyes flashed, teasing in courtship; restless eyes scanned, recognized, questioned, eyes gazing boldly, eyes falling shyly.

A shudder shot through me when I thought of another procession. Basil blinded the 15,000 prisoners, sparing one in a hundred to lead the macabre march home.

Samuel watched in horror the return of his once proud army, eye sockets vacant, shuffling, stumbling, clutching one another, each hundred led by a one-eyed soldier. The sight killed him. And his empire too—swallowed by Byzantium. Basil the Bulgar-slayer was one name Bulgarians would not forget.

Awesome magnificence and diplomatic cunning, military might, terror—more effective than these were Byzantium's missionaries. The Orthodox faith forged unity out of a diversity of nations. It brought the Slavs into the Byzantine universe.

The "apostles of the Slavs," ninth-century Cyril and Methodius of Thessalonica, invented an alphabet in which the newly converted Slavs first learned to write. Their script, and the Greek-based Cyrillic that soon supplanted it, conveyed Byzantine liturgy and learning to the Balkans, then to Russia, molding their thoughts, giving them brotherhood in faith and a Slavonic literary language, the Latin of the East.

"Civilizing the Slavs was Byzantium's most enduring gift to the world," Harvard professor Ihor Ševčenko told me. Among the consequences, Kievan Russia emerged from pagan isolation to join the European political and cultural community. Byzantium was Russia's gateway to Europe.

In Kiev, Professor Andrei Bielecki told me how Vladimir, prince in that Mother of Russian Cities, shopped about for a religion for his people. He sampled the Hebrew, Latin, and Islamic faiths. Fond of women, he favored the Muslim promise after death of fulfillment of carnal desires. But alas, no wine. "Drinking is the joy of the Rus," a chronicle has him say.

So he sent emissaries to Constantinople. Inspired by the resplendent liturgy in Hagia Sophia, they "knew not whether we were in heaven or on earth. For on earth there is no such splendor. . . . We only know that God dwells there among men." Whereupon Vladimir had his people, on pain of the sword, baptized in the Dnieper.

Out of the wreckage of the Mongol empire, princes of Muscovy climbed to power, golden domes and crosses gleaming above the red-brick walls of their Kremlin. Cossacks, fur traders, missionaries spread across Siberia.

At Sitka, on snow-peaked Baranof Island in Alaska, the icons, incense, and chanting in onion-domed St. Michael's Cathedral serve as reminders that in the eighteenth century the faith of Byzantium came across the Bering Sea to its fourth continent: Russian America. Here I joined a Tlingit congregation worshiping with an Aleut priest—a ritual like that I had witnessed in Justinian's monastery of St. Catherine in Sinai.

"We change very little," Father Eugene Bourdukofsky said as he proudly showed me an icon, the Virgin of Sitka. "That is the essence of Orthodoxy, the true faith."

To change or not to change. Here was a key to understanding the chasm that divides the thought world of Byzantium—and eastern Europe—from the West. The West transformed itself through the Renaissance, Reformation, Enlightenment, and the rise of science into a dynamic society enshrining the individual and progress through free inquiry and experiment. The East, until the eighteenth century, remained essentially static. Byzantine thought sees its world not in process; it has arrived, its eternal order God-ordained.

The Byzantine mind transformed the classical Greek word *to innovate* into *to injure*. In a monarch, a penchant for innovation is disastrous, Procopius insisted, for where there is innovation, there is no security. In a subject, deviation is not only heresy but also a crime against the state. So threatening was change that ritual reforms in seventeenth-century Russia split the church. Old Believers endured unspeakable tortures and martyred themselves in mass suicide rather than make the sign of the cross with three fingers instead of two.

Ritual details widened the rift between Rome and Constantinople in the eleventh century. Until then East and West shared a common faith and heritage. The patriarchs of five Christian centers had helped shape this universal faith. Then in the seventh century the march of Islam engulfed three—Jerusalem, Antioch, and Alexandria.

Slavic invasions of the Balkans and Lombard conquests in Italy drove a wedge between the remaining two. Rome, deprived of imperial support, linked its fortunes to the rising Germanic West. Constantinople's contracting empire became increasingly Greek.

The break came in 1054, when Rome and Constantinople exchanged excommunications. The Latins had added *Filioque* to the Nicene Creed, making it read that the Holy Spirit proceeds from the Father *and the Son;* they also used unleavened rather than leavened bread in the Eucharist. Absurd that East and West should sunder over a phrase and a pinch of yeast? Not when eternal salvation seemed at stake.

This was the lesson of Byzantine monasticism: I saw men bend their necks to the yoke of obedience and, through self-denial and punctilious repetitions of ritual, follow unquestioningly an ordained path of salvation. For as Orthodoxy was central to Byzantium, monasticism, ever the conserver of traditions, is the living heart of Orthodoxy.

The face of that boy still haunts me. I saw him on the boat to Mount Athos—father and son come from Germany to see the Holy

Mountain. He was about thirteen, the same age as my son. We boarded at a Greek port at the base of the steep-walled peninsula that juts thirty-five miles into the northern Aegean. The motors revved up, and with a flurry of monks crossing themselves and murmuring "*Kyrie eleison*—Lord, have mercy," we were off for a United Nations of monastic communities—Greek, Russian, Bulgarian, Serbian—where no female has been allowed to set foot for a thousand years.

I saw the boy again when we debarked at Daphni. We crowded in, wall-to-wall black robes and black cylindrical hats, for the jolting bus ride up the mountainside to Kariai, headquarters village for the monastic republic, the world's oldest. Then as I trudged off to join the rounds of worship and work and share Spartan meals in half a dozen monasteries, the boy slipped from mind.

Stavroniketa, thrusting massive walls and crenellated keep above the sea, was a hive of purposeful piety. There the rhythmic beats of the *semantron* wakened me in the night. Noah had summoned the animals into the ark with such a resonant wooden plank and mallet, I had been told. Now it called the faithful into the spiritual ark, the church, to save them from the deluge of sin.

In Stavroniketa's church, under the brazen eagles of Byzantium agleam in chandelier coronas, I stood absorbed by the symphony of motion—monks bowing, prostrating themselves, making rounds to kiss the icons, lighting and snuffing candles, swinging the smoking censer, reading and singing antiphonally, raising voices in fervent prayer. The frescoed church itself mirrored the cosmos, martyrs and saints and angelic hosts rising in a scale of sanctity toward the symbolic vault of heaven where a stern Pantocrator, the almighty Christ, looks down disturbingly into the depth of one's soul.

To relax my limbs, I shifted position.

"Hisssssssssssss!"

I had clasped my hands improperly. As the hours wore on, if

anyone made a false move or kissed an icon in the wrong order, a hiss signaled instant correction.

Back in our guest cell near dawn, my cellmate, an American anthropologist, whispered, "Reminds me of the military. The Benedictines in France are the infantry; the Franciscans in Italy, the air force, free and easy. These Orthodox monks are the marines—a crack outfit of shock troops under a tough master sergeant. No sloppiness here."

As I topped a shoulder of the 6,670-foot Holy Mountain, wincing at each sharp penitential stone in the steep path, I found monks building a wall. A decade earlier dilapidated Philotheou Monastery had seven graybeards. I counted ten times that many monks, beards as black as their robes.

Father Nikon, the young *archontaris,* or guestmaster, radiated inner peace and joy as he offered me the ritual brandy, coffee, gummy sweet *loukoumi,* and water, then showed me to a neat guest room near a flower-lined balcony over the courtyard. "People come to us troubled," Father Nikon said. "A day or two in the monastery brings peace, and they leave refreshed."

On Athos, even meals are a continuation of worship. A bell clangs in the courtyard. The monks file in, stand silently at long tables until the abbot blesses the food. After a communal prayer, all sit, and eat swiftly under the eyes of frescoed saints lining the refectory walls while a monk at the lectern reads from a saint's life. A bell tinkles. He returns the book to its niche, kneels to kiss the abbot's hand, receives his blessing. Then all file out silently. After Vespers, the monastery gates swing shut and everyone turns in, soon to rise for the night's round of prayers, for the first hour of the Byzantine day begins with sunset.

"Lord Jesus Christ, have mercy on me." Pinpoints of lamplight in the cells silhouette monks in ceaseless prayers of repentance. Four hours of solitary prayer before the call to four hours of communal prayer. Bread and tea, a snatch of sleep, and then silent prayer continues as the monk goes about his daytime tasks, in the kitchen, garden, at manual labor.

One moonlit night at Dionysiou Monastery a howling wind rattled the window of my cell. Dawn disclosed gray clouds beetling the brow of the Holy Mountain, and the face of the sea furrowed in anger. Below, waves slammed over the landing. No mail boat today. To get to Gregoriou, next monastery along the coast, meant going by foot.

"It's a very dangerous path," cautioned Father Euthymios as we set out together. The gangling New York–born Vietnam veteran was coming from the "desert," hermitages farther out on the peninsula, where he paints icons. "Part of it is along a causeway swept by the sea." Then came an afterthought of small comfort: "Darius lost his fleet here in such a storm." Three hundred of the Persian king's ships and 20,000 men dashed on the rocks of Athos in 491 B.C.

Pausing on a crest, buffeted by a devil of a wind, Father Euthymios said, "I always fear this next stretch. It's along a cliff with a straight drop to the sea. But with God's grace we will make it." We did. And next day we again tempted fate.

The storm roared unabated. Winds clutched at us as we climbed and descended ravines, bone weary, wet through. Breakers roared as we leaped from rock to slippery rock at the base of sea cliffs. Too close.

If you must wait out an Athos storm, you will find no more dramatic haven than Simonopetra, high on a spur above the Aegean. It opens its dovecote of cells onto tiers of rickety balconies propped by aged beams. To walk along one eight hundred feet over the sea in a storm is an act of faith. Clutching the splintery rail, stepping over a gap in the floor planks, I looked down mesmerized at walls of water battering walls of rock.

Next day Simonopetra no longer shook. The wind had lost its howl; the sea was flattening its crests. No more dodging waves. I had been lucky. Not so that boy who looked like my son. As he leaped across the rocks, a wave swept him away before his father's eyes. When the boats ran again, they found his body and brought it in from the sea.

The year 1071 was a bad one for the Byzantines, East and West. At Manzikert, in the highlands of eastern Turkey, the multinational Byzantine Army, riven by dissensions and desertions and for once sloppy in reconnaissance, was annihilated by the invading Seljuk Turks it had marched east to destroy. Anatolia, breadbasket and prime recruiting ground for Byzantium, subsequently was stripped forever from Christendom, opening the way to later Ottoman invasions of Europe.

In Bari, port city in southeastern Italy, I saw blood on the pavement. Assassins had gunned down a political opponent, and grieving partisans marched around the stain in bitter memorial. Nine centuries earlier blood had flowed in the streets of Byzantine Bari, sacked by the Normans after a three-year siege. Five years after the Battle of Hastings in England, the Normans had conquered southern Italy.

The year 1204 was even worse. On April 13 Fourth Crusaders en route to Jerusalem committed what historian Sir Steven Runciman called "the greatest crime in history"—the Christian sack of Constantinople. Burning, pillaging, raping, the crusaders looted what they didn't destroy to enrich Venice, Paris, Turin, and other Western centers with "every choicest thing found upon the earth." (They even brought back *two* heads of John the Baptist, so rich was Constantinople in relics.)

When, after fifty-seven years, a Byzantine emperor once again reigned in Constantinople, the Universal Empire was but a large head on a shrunken body. The Venetians and Genoese had a stranglehold on its trade. Franks still held territory. Trebizond ruled an independent empire on the Black Sea. Byzantine princes had set up their own power centers in Greece. Byzantium was soon pressed between the Ottoman Turks and the Serbs.

Crossing the Dardanelles, the Turks first settled in Europe at Gallipoli in 1354. A year later, with Serbian power at its peak, Stephen Dushan, who had proclaimed himself emperor of Serbs and Greeks, made his bid for Constantinople. Death robbed him of a chance to sit on Byzantium's throne, but the Serbs never forgot the common Balkan dream of conquering Constantinople. Nor will they ever forget the collision three decades later with the Turks.

In the mists of morning rolling over brown-tilled earth at Kosovo in Yugoslavia, I peopled that "field of the blackbirds" with Turks and Serbs locked in battle. A physical defeat, it was yet a moral victory the Serbs celebrate to this day. Folk legend and epics extolling Serb bravery fed the fires of nationalism during the five centuries the Serbs suffered the Turkish yoke. Kosovo: June 28, 1389. How ironic that Archduke Franz Ferdinand of Austria chose June 28 of all days to make his entry into Sarajevo, where his assassination by a Serb patriot plunged the world into war in 1914.

As the Turkish shadow lengthened, Byzantine emperors traveled west to reconcile differences in an effort to secure military aid. Neither pope nor patriarch considered the rupture of 1054 final. Twice, union of the churches was proclaimed (only to founder on the reef of residual hatred for the crusaders' desecration of holy Constantinople in 1204). As for aid, the West dragged its feet. Venice arrested one emperor for debt.

On a spur of snow-crowned mountains walling Sparta's valley in the Peloponnese clings the Byzantine city of Mistra. Today its citadel, palace, red-roofed churches, and dwellings lie empty. Only a few nuns live in this once vibrant city, the renown of its scholars and artists outshining the empire's fading power. Here in 1449, where a double-headed eagle is carved in the cathedral's marble paving, the last Byzantine emperor was crowned.

With him as he journeyed north went a legend: Constantinople's last emperor would bear the same name as the first. His name? Constantine. And his mother, like the mother of Constantine the Great, was named Helena.

Acclaimed by the populace, tolerated by the indolent Sultan Murad II, he could settle, it seemed, for peaceful coexistence. Having failed in besieging Constantinople and succeeded in crushing a crusader army at Varna on the Black Sea, the sultan was content, in his sumptuous capital of Edirne (ancient Adrianople) in Thrace, to let Constantinople wither on the vine while he sported with his stable of stallions and his harem of hundreds of women.

Murad's death in 1451 changed that. His mantle fell to his eldest son, who began his reign typically by strangling his baby brother. Scarcely twenty, he burned to conquer Constantinople. As legend would have it, he bore the Prophet's name—Muhammad.

Mounting the walls of Constantine's city, I scanned the line of towers. The green of garden vegetables flooded moats that in 1453 had run red. An aged Turk tended a peaceful cemetery by walls where forty carts could not have carried away the Turks slain in a single assault, noted an eyewitness to the siege. Imagination restored these impressive ruins to the triple-tiered ramparts raised by fifth-century Emperor Theodosius II—13 miles around, studded with 192 towers to landward, 110 to seaward, and pierced by 50 gates. In my mind's eye I saw centuries of invaders—Huns, Avars, Persians, Arabs, Rus, Bulgars, Turks—pour out their blood in futile assaults.

Mehmed (Muhammad) II invested the city with the largest force it had yet faced: an estimated 100,000 troops deployed to landward, the Ottoman fleet massed offshore. Against this: a scant 8,000 to man the walls, and a few ships behind the chain across the Golden Horn.

Why so few defenders? Stripped of the lands that gave it food and fighters, Constantinople was a skeleton, and divided against itself. The West had finally promised help—but at a fearful price: submission of Byzantium's Holy Orthodox Church to the Church of Rome. The pope's emissary presided over a *Te Deum* in a nearly empty Hagia Sophia to sighs of dismay. "Better the Turkish turban than the Latin miter!" ran the popular sentiment. Still, they had the invincible walls. Optimists quoted the old saying: the city would stand until ships sailed over land, a manifest impossibility.

The thunder of Mehmed's attack on April 11, 1453, shook the invincibility of those walls. Ramparts shattered under the barrage of bronze cannon, the largest the world had ever seen. The smallest of the sultan's 67 guns fired a 200-pound stone shot. The biggest, three feet in bore, hurled a 1,200-pound ball. Sixty oxen were needed to draw it from Edirne, preceded by road and bridge builders and flanked by 10,000 cavalry. Fortunately for the defenders, the Basilica, as Mehmed called it, took so long to clean and load that it could fire only seven times a day.

Filling breaches in the ramparts by night, the defenders beat back assault after assault. Turkish sappers were countermined and slaughtered underground. When four ships made it through the Turkish gantlet into port, the furious sultan gave his admiral a hundred lashes.

Seven weeks: Still the city held. Advisers urged Mehmed to raise the siege.

Give up his dream? Never! The impetuous sultan would press the siege to victory.

If he could get a flotilla inside the Golden Horn, the Byzantines would have to thin out to defend that side too. His engineers built a log slipway over the hill between the Bosporus and the Golden Horn. Brute force—man and beast bending to the ropes—inched some seventy ships over the crest.

Dismaying sight! Descending to the Golden Horn, canvas bellying to the breeze, were "ships sailing over the land!"

It is May 28. For the last time the setting sun glints on the cross atop Hagia Sophia. This evening, as on all others, the tireless Constantine attends holy services and checks the guards on the walls, though his courtiers have begged him to flee. Day by day anxious eyes have scanned the horizon for relief that does not come. Now the city is one, the thin line of soldiers determined to sell their lives dearly.

For several evenings the Turkish lines have blazed from the Sea of Marmara to the Golden Horn, the din of trumpets, drums, shouts driving a deep wedge of terror into the night. Tonight, in sultry air, the lines fall ominously silent.

Two hours after midnight men on the wall hear a rustle: the Turks moving two thousand scaling ladders into the moat and up to the walls.

Flames roaring from cannon mouths signal the attack. Batteries concentrate on St. Romanos Gate. Here the emperor takes the point of greatest danger beside the Genoese captain, Giustiniani (Italian for Justinian), whose seven hundred men have fought valiantly.

Turkish archers, musketeers, slingers rain deadly fire on the parapets. Turks swarm up the ladders but are hurled back. Heavy infantry attack through breaches pounded by the cannon. Defenders repel them. Mehmed commits his elite Janissaries. Hand-to-hand battle seesaws. Then Turks discover a lightly guarded sally port in the moat. They pour through. "The Turk is in the city!" The emperor turns to meet the new threat. As night fades, he falls, hidden as bodies heap up around his.

Dawn reveals a lurid sight: streets crimson with blood as Turkish soldiers race through the city, slaughtering, sacking. Screams split the air as they drag women and children from hiding places in looted homes. They topple altars, seize golden chalices. They force open the massive bronze portals of Hagia Sophia and burst in upon the last Christian service ever held in Justinian's great church.

At midday Mehmed, whom history will call the Conqueror, rides into the city on his white horse. The chronicler Kritovoulos reports that the sultan shed tears of compassion: "What a city we have given over to plunder and destruction!"

It is Tuesday, May 29, 1453. Don't ever ask a Greek to embark on an important project on a Tuesday. That's the unlucky day his city fell to the Turk.

Catastrophically, the Byzantine Empire was no more. Zealots of Islam removed the cross from atop Hagia Sophia, and soon the muezzin's chant rang from minarets rising by the Bosporus. But Byzantium lived on.

Priding himself as a new Constantine sitting on the throne of the Caesars, Mehmed the Conqueror repopulated his new capital and restaffed its bureaucracy partly with Greeks and Serbs. In his court, influenced by Persian as well as Byzantine traditions, he became an aloof autocrat surrounded by elaborate ceremony.

The once migratory Ottomans, now based on Constantine's city, proceeded to conquer a mosaic of nations similar in extent to Justinian's empire. The Ottoman Empire let its Orthodox subjects keep their Christian religion and Greco-Roman laws—so long as they paid tribute, kept their churches inconspicuous so as not to offend Islamic eyes, and furnished levies for its armies and administration. This tithe in humans periodically took the strongest, most intelligent Christian Balkan boys, aged eight to fifteen, converted them to Islam, and drafted them into the elite army corps, the Janissaries, or trained them as court functionaries.

The conquerors emulated Hagia Sophia in their great single-domed shrines, such as Istanbul's Blue Mosque, built over and using materials from the Great Palace. Greeks became prominent in trade, seafaring, banking, and medicine; Greek and Serbian initially served alongside Turkish as the languages of the chancery; and the Turks, who had long used Byzantine currency in foreign exchange, minted their own gold coins two decades after the conquest.

"When we Turks came off the steppes, we were nomads with little culture," Dr. Nezih Firatli, then director of Istanbul's Museum of Archaeology, told me. "It was natural to adopt some Byzantine ways. Our forebears had no ovens for making bread—only portable iron griddles for unleavened flat cakes. Hence the Turkish word for oven comes from the Greek." The Turkish *han* replaced the Byzantine caravansary, and the famed Turkish bath, the Byzantine bath.

Daily life in Nicaea or Philadelphia (Turkish İznik and Alaşehir) only two generations ago differed little from Byzantine times. "Byzantine continuity is not a popular idea in Turkey," said Dr. Firatli, looking me squarely in the eye, "but it is the truth."

To create a modern Turkish state, Mustafa Kemal (Atatürk) turned his back on cosmopolitan Constantinople and made his capital at Ankara, in the heart of Anatolia (though, ironically, the national flag bore the crescent-and-star device first stamped on coins of ancient Greek Byzantium). In 1922, during an abortive Greek attempt to reconquer Ionia, considered a "cradle of the Hellenic civilization," came a violent break with the Byzantine past.

In that fateful year Atatürk's army hurled the invaders back into the sea amid the wreckage of three thousand years of Greek settlement in Asia Minor. This rout triggered a mass exodus from Turkey. A twenty-three-year-old correspondent for the *Toronto Daily Star*, Ernest Hemingway, described a silent, ghastly procession: "Twenty miles of carts . . . with exhausted, staggering men, women and children . . . walking blindly along in the rain" as the Christians of eastern Thrace jammed the roads toward Macedonia.

Near the Byzantine walls of Thessalonica, which threw back waves of medieval Slavs, nestles the Byzantine Church of St. David. Lamp flicker animated a beardless fifth-century mosaic Christ and caressed the deep-etched face of a woman. She told me of the tragic exchange of populations—one and a quarter million Greeks from Turkey, 400,000 Turks from Greece. Her gnarled hands clasped and unclasped, tears ran down her cheeks as she recalled her family's being wrenched, when she was fourteen, from their village near Ankara, and dying one by one of malaria in a refugee camp in a Macedonian swamp.

I had visited a village like hers near Konya (Byzantine Iconium) in Anatolia, its Greek Orthodox church padlocked, the screened women's balconies empty, the ornate *ikonostasis* gaping eyeless, stripped of icons.

I had climbed a spectacular mountain gorge behind walled Trebizond, the last Byzantine city to fall—in 1461, eight years after Constantinople. Ancient Trebizond, where Xenophon's 10,000 Greek soldiers exulted to reach the Black Sea. Fabled Trebizond, where caravans brought riches of Persia and China, and monarchs sought the beauty of its Byzantine princesses. Noonday Trebizond, where phalanxes of schoolchildren in black smocks pour out onto cobbled streets teeming with colorfully garbed women and tur-baned merchants hawking fish, hot chestnuts, and fruit.

Eight hundred feet over a foaming mountain stream I had climbed to a great monastery that seemed to cling to the towering rock wall by faith alone. Founded even before the age of Justinian, Soumela in the later Middle Ages was one of the richest monastic establishments in the East. I found it gutted, blackened by fire. Since 1923 no chant of Greek liturgy has sounded in that solitude, as it still does in the western mountains and valleys of Cyprus, where achingly empty Turkish villages tell of another more recent transfer of populations. These have lessened the danger from fifth columns but have done nothing to allay the hatred that has poisoned relations between Greek and Turk.

There on Cyprus I saw barbed wire and military checkpoints in the divided capital city of Nicosia, and white-painted UN tanks patrolling the advance lines of the Turkish Army, which had invaded in response to a Greek overthrow of the island republic. This 1974 coup brought to mind the *Megali Ithea*—the Great Idea—that fired the Greek imagination for generations: reconquest of Constantinople and the Byzantine Empire.

"For Greeks there is only one city. *The* City—Constantinople," the widow of a Greek Army officer told me in Thessalonica. "Even the Turkish name 'Istanbul' comes from the Greek *eis teen polis*—'in the city.'" Her sentiments echoed nineteenth-century patriots: "Our capital is Constantinople. Our national temple is Hagia Sophia, for nine hundred years the glory of Christendom. The Patriarch of Constantinople is our spiritual leader." In cherished legend a priest bearing the chalice, interrupted in the last liturgy in Hagia Sophia, will emerge to complete the service when the shrine is again Christian.

The Greek dream, however, collided with Balkan dreams of imperial glory. The sultan fanned endemic hatreds by classing all his Orthodox subjects—whether Serb or Bulgar, Greek or Albanian or

Romanian—as the *Rum Milleti,* the Roman people, and putting them under the civil as well as ecclesiastical control of the Greek Patriarch of Constantinople. Patriarchs adopted the eagle symbol, ceremonies, dress, and functions of a Byzantine emperor and set their Greek bishops to hellenizing the proud Balkan peoples.

In the 1820s Greece rose against the Ottoman overlord; in 1830 it was the first Balkan nation to break free. But many more Greeks lived outside the new kingdom than in it. With *énosis*—union—with Greece the battle cry, the modern map of Greece was assembled piece by piece, escalating the hatred of her neighbors, who watched with cannibal eyes and devoured one another in two Balkan Wars.

Then Sarajevo . . . 1914. Today it is a market city tucked amid the stern Bosnian mountains of Yugoslavia, where minarets of nearly eighty mosques thrust like rockets above Orthodox and Catholic churches, and men in fezzes and women in veils and baggy trousers thread a booth-lined bazaar. Near this crossroad of cultures Emperor Theodosius the Great in 395 ran the line dividing the unwieldy Roman Empire administratively into East and West. Here, by the embanked Miljacka River, a pistol shot split the world when a Serbian student assassinated the heir to the Austro-Hungarian Empire, which had annexed lands once Serbian. Austria, backed by Germany, determined to crush Serbia. "Holy Russia" came to the aid of her Slavic Orthodox brother. And interlocking alliances swept Europe's nations into a war that claimed ten million lives.

Greece, entering that holocaust with the prospect of Turkish territory, at war's end occupied ancient Smyrna (today palm-shaded İzmir ringing its spacious Aegean harbor). Then, with defeated Turkey in revolt and the sultanate toppling, the Greeks saw their big chance. But their invasion deep into Asia Minor, hurled back, perished in the carnage of Smyrna and the mass exodus that ensued.

In Istanbul's Rum Patrikhanesi, a garden of peace amid the city's clamor and squalor, stands the eighteenth-century terra-cotta basilica of St. George and the modest residence and offices of the spiritual leader of the Orthodox faithful throughout the world. His All Holiness, Dimitrios, "by the Grace of God, Archbishop of Constantinople, New Rome, and Ecumenical Patriarch," rose from his desk and took my hand warmly in both of his.

The patriarch told me he sees as his role the promotion of understanding and harmony among "sister" Orthodox Churches. Many separated from Constantinople's fold when their nations broke free of the Turks.

More than 70 percent of the baptized Orthodox today dwell in Communist countries. Churches in exile abound. The national churches of Serbia, Bulgaria, Romania, and Russia are auto-cephalous (self-headed), with their own patriarchs. But the Ecumenical Patriarch is *primus inter pares*—first among equals—and his spiritual sway extends far beyond the confines of his church in Istanbul, which he heads as a Turkish citizen.

With a dwindling flock, stripped of the last vestige of civil authority, even forbidden to proselytize in his few Turkish parishes, why does he remain in a Muslim city? The Archbishop of Constantinople became head of the Byzantine Church because of his special position at the capital of the empire, he said. He is bound to this historic see.

On my way out I paused by the patriarchate's central gate, painted black and welded shut. Here a patriarch was hanged for treason when the War of Greek Independence broke out in 1821. As I stepped into the teeming streets where a priest is forbidden to wear his clerical garb, I thought back on the fallen glories of Byzantium's great church, still claiming universal dominion, still clinging in the City of Constantine.

God had punished the Greeks, Russians piously observed in 1453 when the Turks took Constantinople. For betraying their faith by submitting to Rome, He withdrew His protection, and their empire fell. Now Moscow moved from the periphery to the center of the Orthodox world, shining in the purity of her faith. "Two Romes have fallen. A third stands fast. A fourth there cannot be," ran the monkly prophecy.

Rising from medieval isolation in Russia's forested northern plains, Muscovy shook off the Mongol yoke that had crushed Kiev, overcame Novgorod and other fur-trading rivals, and pushed back Catholic Lithuanians and Poles. Ringed by enemies of her faith, xenophobic Moscow raised onion-domed churches and monasteries in forest clearings all the way to the inhospitable shores of the White Sea and fiercely clung to traditional rites.

Ivan the Great married Sophia Paleologos, niece of the last Byzantine emperor, and adopted the Byzantine double-headed eagle and the title of tsar, derived from Caesar. Holy Russia became one great religious house, ever purging herself. Military campaigns became crusades. The court banqueted to sacred readings. In homes the father took on the abbot's role, wielding absolute power over wife, child, servant, and serf. With the clanging of Moscow's five thousand church bells in their ears, visitors commented on fasts, church discipline, and seven-hour standing services "severe enough to turn children's hair gray."

Dogma and ritual from Byzantium fossilized in spiritual isolation and distrust of inquiry; so did the political and social structure rigidify, with sacred and temporal power vested in the tsar, supported by a subservient church. Inheriting the Byzantine conviction of her destiny to rule, and suspicious of the heretical and corrupt West, Russia grew to a giant with Orthodoxy in her veins, whether she worshiped at the shrines of the Mother of God or Marx. She knew no middle ground between autocracy and anarchy.

The tsars are gone; the Revolution of 1917 homogenized Russian society. But even the "new" Russian, embracing a Western ideology and Western technology, cannot escape his Byzantine roots. Ubiquitous party leaders' portraits are the icons of today. And the living iconostasis of officials at a review of armaments in Red Square is as precisely ordered as the ranks of saints flanking the image of Christ in Zagorsk's cathedral.

"There can be no change. It is a terrible thing. The program is the idol. If one link in the chain is broken, we will not be able to grasp the end." As he said this, shock showed on the face of the young Novosti Press agent with whom I would travel thousands of miles in the Soviet Union.

Involved was not the writ of God, but an itinerary prepared by bureaucrats. Yet the suggestion that it be altered to my objectives stirred the same visceral response that impelled thousands of Old Believers to choose death rather than change.

Since claiming the Byzantine birthright, Russia has looked possessively, obsessively south. In the 1770s she wrested from the Turks that ancient Byzantine frontier land, the Crimea. A treaty empowered her to build and protect a church in Istanbul. She interpreted this as a protectorate over the Balkan Orthodox, many of whom saw Holy Russia as a savior. Russian Pan-Slavism influenced Russian expansionism in the push toward the Mediterranean. "Economic and political motives figure as well," Soviet scholars told me in Moscow. "But yes, there *was* a Russian crusade to put the cross back on top of Hagia Sophia."

Like the Greeks, Catherine the Great had her own Great Idea— a restored Byzantine Empire in the Balkans, to be ruled from a reconquered Constantinople by her grandson Constantine. She even hired John Paul Jones, unemployed naval hero, to command a Russian flotilla fighting in that cause in the Black Sea. Ironically, Russia came within a hairbreadth of gaining Constantinople and the Straits in World War I. The Allies promised them to her upon Turkey's defeat. Then her revolution knocked Russia out of the war, scuttling that prospect.

Neither Britain nor France had wanted Russia in the Mediterranean. Six decades earlier both had supported Turkey against Russia in the Crimean War, which put Tennyson's stirring "into the valley of Death rode the six hundred" on every tongue.

While in the Crimea I sought Soviet permission to visit that valley where the Light Brigade, those cavalrymen who were unquestioningly but to do and die, had charged. But I was not allowed to go. Nor was I told the reason why.

"The Crimean War really began in Bethlehem," Yosef Uziely, then treasurer of Jerusalem, told me on the garden terrace of his home near the Israel Museum. The Ottomans, he said, had trouble keeping peace among Christian sects, who bloodied the shrines with their strife. In 1853 Russia's dispute with France over guardianship of Holy Land shrines came to a head. The Russians based their claims on the Byzantine establishment of these shrines; the French, on their reconquest by Latin crusaders.

Riot broke out in Bethlehem's Church of the Nativity. Several Orthodox monks were killed. Tsar Nicholas, accusing the Turkish police of complicity, reasserted his claim that he was protector of the sultan's Orthodox Christian subjects, invaded Turkey's Danubian provinces, ordered his ships to sea, and sank a Turkish fleet in port. The specter of Russia cutting the England-to-India lifeline soon brought Britain into the war, a war which ended seventeen months later with the fall of Sevastopol.

"Now it's Russian against Russian in Jerusalem," Uziely went on. "The Soviets against the émigré Russians. They've been battling in Israeli courts for years. At stake are millions of dollars of ecclesiastical properties in Israel."

In 1948 the new State of Israel, desperate for diplomatic recognition, acceded to the Soviet demand that all Russian religious holdings in Israel be turned over to its Orthodox Church in Moscow—despite their belonging to the Russian Orthodox Church Outside of Russia, now headquartered in New York City. The crowning irony: after the Six Day War in 1967, the Soviet Union severed relations with Israel.

It is the eve of Easter in Jerusalem—Easter by the Orthodox calendar. From early morning, pilgrims have filled the Church of the Holy Sepulchre for the ceremony of the holy fire, to me the most exalting ritual of the Eastern churches.

Squeezed against a parapet amid that press of humanity, I watch black-clad women kneel to spread oil on the Stone of Unction, said to be the slab on which the body of Jesus was anointed, and press their weeping faces against it.

The thump of maces and rhythmic clapping and chanting draw my eyes to phalanxes of the faithful slowly moving around Christ's tomb in the center of the rotunda. In the banners and gleaming vestments I see Byzantium pass in review: skull-capped Syrians, Armenians in pointed hoods, turbaned Copts of Alexandria, Greek Orthodox in cylindrical hats and robes of gold and crimson and black.

Thrice circling the tomb in solemn procession, the Greek Orthodox Patriarch of Jerusalem pauses at its entry. He steps inside. The clamor in the rotunda fades to silence. The church is dark, the tension electric.

Suddenly I see a lighted taper thrust from the tomb—the holy fire, symbolizing Christ rising from the dead. Flames leap from taper to taper until the darkness is punctured by a thousand fiery holes. Tower bells thunder, shaking the very walls. Cries rise in a multitude of throats as the splintered churches of Byzantium coalesce into a single mass of believers celebrating the Resurrection.

"He is risen!" Through faith in this miracle, Byzantium lives.

From *Balkan Ghosts*

BY ROBERT KAPLAN

∽

editor's note

As readers of my previous books know, I do not, as a general rule, include excerpts from books in *Collected Traveler* editions. I am not convinced that someone who reads an excerpt will always then read the book, and I believe that really outstanding books deserve to be read in full, the way the author intended. Occasionally, however, a piece that originally appeared in a periodical becomes a chapter in a book; or as with the piece below, the passage of time makes a text more significant, more importunate. Therefore I feel I should make an exception from time to time—it would be foolish to exclude a worthy essay simply for the sake of abiding by a self-imposed mandate.

This piece, by Robert Kaplan, is excerpted from *Balkan Ghosts,* an important and eye-opening book. The text is from the section of the book devoted to Greece, in the chapter entitled "Farewell to Salonika." While I encourage you to read *all* of *Balkan Ghosts*, I feel this essay can stand on its own in this anthology, and it is one of the few honest appraisals of, as Kaplan notes, "what Greece is, has been, and never was."

ROBERT KAPLAN has contributed to *The Atlantic Monthly* and *The New Republic,* among others, and his magazine articles of the 1980s and early 1990s were the first by an American to warn of the coming cataclysm in the Balkans. He is also the author of *The Arabists: The Romance of an American Elite* (The Free Press, 1993), *Soldiers of God* (Vintage, 2001), *Surrender or Starve* (Vintage, 2003), *Eastward to Tartary: Travels in the Balkans, the Middle East, and the Caucasus* (Random House, 2000, hardcover; Vintage, 2001, paperback), *The Ends of the Earth: From Togo to Turkmenistan, from Iran to Cambodia—A Journey to the Frontiers of Anarchy* (Peter Smith Publishers, 2001), and *Empire Wilderness: Travels into America's Future* (Random House, 1998, hardcover; Vintage, 1999, paperback), among others.

I lived in Greece for seven years and have visited it often before and since. I speak and read Greek, albeit badly. I met my wife in Greece, got married in Greece, and had a son born in Greece. I love Greece. But the Greece I love is a real country, warts and cruelties and all; not the make-believe land of the university classicists or of the travel posters.

Because I did not have a "travel experience" in Greece so much as I had a "living experience," my attitude toward Greece is more obsessive than my attitude concerning the rest of the Balkans. My living experience revealed Greece to me as a Balkan country. What made Greece particularly Balkan in the 1980s, when I lived there, was the politics. This is why I will dwell at length on Greece's modern political atmosphere: a subject about which little has been written, compared with all the books on Greek travel.

Before the end of the cold war, when the existence of the Warsaw Pact enforced an artificial separation between Greece and its northern neighbors, only Westerners like me, living in Greece, realized how Balkan Greece was. Those on the outside were determined to see Greece as a Mediterranean and Western country only: the facts be damned. As I began work on this book in 1989—when Macedonia was known only as the birthplace of Alexander the Great and not as the geopolitical problem it currently is—people advised me to leave Greece out of the story, since it "was not really part of the Balkans." I resisted. Events have borne me out. As the 1990s began, Greece was increasingly making the news in connection with border disputes in Macedonia and southern Albania. And Greece's political behavior in the region, despite a democratic tradition going back to antiquity, appeared no more reasonable than that of its neighbors to its north, whose democratic tradition was generally nonexistent.

The first time I arrived in Greece was by train from Yugoslavia. The second time was from Bulgaria, also by train. A third time was by bus from Albania. Each time, upon crossing the border into Greece, I became immediately conscious of a continuity: mountain ranges, folk costumes, musical rhythms, faces, and religions, all of which were deeply interwoven with those of the lands I had just come from. And just as everywhere else in the Balkans, where races and cultures collided and where the settlement pattern of national groups did not always conform with national boundaries, this intermingling was hotly denied.

"No Turks live in Greece," Greece's former deputy foreign minister, Ioannis Kapsis, once told me: "There are only some Greeks who happen to be Muslim and happen to speak Turkish to each other. Nor are there any Macedonians . . . ," Kapsis railed. He was unstoppable. In all the years I lived in Greece, from 1982 through 1989, I never once heard a Greek—outside of a few well-known politicians—bring up the question of the Parthenon (Elgin) Marbles and the British Museum's refusal to return them. And if that issue—which received so much publicity in the West—was brought up by a foreigner, I never heard native Greeks speak long or passionately about it. But hours of my life have been spent sitting quietly at a Greek table, hearing out paroxysms of rage on issues such as the Turks and Constantinople, the Serbs and Macedonia, and the persecuted Greek minority in Albania. When I arrived in Greece in 1990 from Macedonia and Bulgaria, I tried to explain the position of the Slavic Macedonians to a group of Greek friends. They fumed, practically in unison: "Just because those dirty Gypsies in Skopje filled your head with lies doesn't make it true!" To these Greeks, all Slavs who called themselves "Macedonian" were "dirty Gypsies."

That is why, when I arrived in Greece from Bulgaria in 1990, I did not think of myself as having left the Balkans, but as having entered the place that best summed up and explained the Balkans. The icon was a Greek invention. The Greek Orthodox Church was the mother of all Eastern Orthodox Churches. The Byzantine Empire was essentially a Greek empire. The Ottoman Turks ruled through Greeks—from the wealthy Phanar (Lighthouse) district of Constantinople—who were often the diplomats and local governors throughout the European part of the Turkish empire. *Constantinople* was a Greek word for an historically Greek city. Even the Turkish word for the place, Istanbul, was a corruption of the Greek phrase *eis teen polis* (in the city). The elite corps of Ottoman soldiery, the Janissaries, included many Greeks, who had been taken from their parents as young children and raised in the sultan's barracks. The Cyrillic alphabet, used in Bulgaria, Serbia, Macedonia, and Russia, emerged from the Greek alphabet when two monks, Cyril and Methodius, left Salonika in the ninth century A.D. to proselytize among the Slavs. The modern Greek race has been a compound of Greeks, Turks, Albanians, Romanians, assorted Slavs, and others, all of whom migrated south into the warm-water terminus of the Balkan Peninsula. The fact that few distinguishable minorities have survived in Greece is testimony to the assimilative drawing power of Greek culture. The peasants of Suli in western Greece, for example, and the Aegean islanders of Spetsai and Hydra, were originally of pure Albanian stock. "The Greece of the classical heritage and of the romantic philhellene has gone, and anyhow has always been irrelevant to the Greek situation," writes

Philip Sherrard, a translator of modern Greek poetry. "Greece . . . never had any Middle Ages, as we understand them, or any Renaissance, as we understand it, or an Age of Enlightenment. That elevation of the reason over the rest of life had not taken place."

Greece is Europe's last port of call, where the Balkans begin to be dissolved completely by the East. As such, approaching from the opposite direction, Greece is also where the oxygen of the West begins to diffuse the crushing and abstract logic of the Mesopotamian and Egyptian deserts. This, after all, was the ultimate achievement of Periclean Athens (and by extension, of the West): to breathe humanism—compassion for the individual—into the inhumanity of the East, which was at that time emblemized by the tyrannies of ancient Egypt, Persia, and Babylonia. At the National Archaeological Museum in Athens I saw this process at work, as the fierce and impersonal statues of the Early and Middle Bronze Ages, bearing the heavy influence of Pharaonic Egypt, gradually, feature by rounded feature, metamorphosed over two millennia into the uplifting beauty and idealism of classical Greek sculpture.

Classical Greece of the first millennium B.C. invented the West by humanizing the East. Greece accomplished this by concentrating its artistic and philosophical energies on the release of the human spirit, on the individual's struggle to find meaning in the world. Meanwhile, in Persia, for example, art existed to glorify an omnipotent ruler. But Greece was always part of the East, albeit on its western fringe. To see Greece in its true Oriental light is to recognize the magnitude of the ancient Greeks' achievement.

Moreover, understanding Greece's historic role as the ideological battleground between East and West lends a deeper insight into the process by which Western democracy and values, in our era, can influence the political systems of the third world. Greece is the eternal sieve, through which the assaults of the East on the West, and of the West on the East, must pass and immediately deposit their residue.

"Welcome back to the Orient," said Sotiris Papapoulitis, a leading member of Greece's conservative New Democracy Party, as he treated me to an expensive seafood lunch at a restaurant in the port city of Piraeus, adjacent to Athens. I had just arrived by bus from Thessaloníki. "But in the Orient," Papapoulitis cautioned me, "you must never confuse an open heart with an open mind."

Papapoulitis was referring to hmself. In the fall of 1990 he was engaged in an ultimately unsuccessful bid to be elected mayor of Piraeus. He was flamboyant, sophisticated, naïve, and narrowminded all at once. He was the kind of fellow who could quote from Descartes and believe a conspiracy theory, while wearing a tight shirt open to his navel. Papapoulitis knew this and relished the fact that his very personality, like the scene around us—yachts, blue sea, sunshine, mountains of seafood, inefficiency, and chaos—constituted the perfect synthesis of the Balkans, the Mediterranean, the European West, and the Levantine East.

"I hate the term *Greek*. It is a corruption of a Turkish word for dog or slave," Papapoulitis exclaimed for all the customers to hear. "Call me a *Hellene*. Call me a *Romios* even. But don't call me a *Greek*."

Hellene was what the ancient Greek called himself, and it has come to symbolize a Greek (or that part of the Greek psyche) whose roots are in the West. *Romios* literally means Roman and refers to a Greek of the Eastern Roman Empire (often referred to as Byzantium), whose roots are in the East. Patrick Leigh Fermor, a British travel writer with an unrivaled knowledge of the Greek language and culture, identified more than sixty characteristics and symbols that distinguish the Hellene mentality from the Romios mentality. Whereas the Hellene relies on principle and logic, the Romios relies on instinct; whereas the Hellene sees Greece as being part of Europe, the Romios sees Greece as lying outside Europe; whereas the Hellene is a man of enlightened disbelief, the Romios believes in the miracle-working properties of icons; whereas the Hellene follows a Western code of honor, the Romios evinces a lack of scruples for achieving personal ends; and so on . . . Obviously, as was the case with Papapoulitis and so many other Greeks I knew, both the Hellene and the Romios aspects of the Greek personality could exist side by side within the same person.

Fermor, like many philhellenes (foreign lovers of Greece), was keenly aware of Greece's Oriental aspect. A case in point: Lord Byron, the nineteenth-century Romantic poet and volunteer in the Greek War of Independence, detested scholars of classical Greece, whom he called "emasculated fogies" full of "antiquarian twaddle." Byron's philhellenic commitment was based on a true vision of the country, not on a myth. As for the squabbling Greek guerrilla fighters he encountered in the mosquito-infested swamps of western Greece in the 1820s, the English poet observed: "Their life is a struggle against truth; they are vicious in their defense." Nikos Kazantzakis, who was not a foreigner, also had no doubts about the true soul of Greece: "The modern Greek . . . when he begins to sing . . . breaks the crust of Greek logic; all at once the East, all darkness and mystery, rises up from deep within him."

To Greeks, the East—the realm of this darkness, mystery, sadness, and irrationality—includes specific memories and events that are central to the Byzantine and Ottoman legacy.

For Western tourists and admirers of Greece, the country's crowd symbol would have to be the Parthenon, erected by Pericles in the fifth century B.C.—the golden age of Athenian democracy, the

period of Greek history with which all of us in the West are familiar. In school we learned about how the Minoan and Mycenaean civilizations developed over several centuries into the Greek city-states,
among them Athens and Sparta, which fought wars against each
other and against the Persians, a people who at the time represented
the "barbarous East." We learned how Greek culture survived and
was spread through the conquests of a Greek Macedonian,
Alexander the Great. And we are generally aware of the scope and
grandeur of ancient Greek history: how the world of Homer's *Iliad*
and *Odyssey,* associated with Mycenaean culture of the second millennium B.C., is separated by nearly a thousand years from the world
of Socrates, Plato, and Aristotle. Greek history, as we in the West
have been taught it, is a long and inspiring saga. Unfortunately, this
great saga was just one element in Greece's past, and the past did not
end when the Dark Ages began. For what admirers of ancient Greece
consider the Dark Ages was, in truth, the beginning of another
period of Greek grandeur, that of Byzantium.

Thus, for the Greeks themselves, another building, far from the
Parthenon—indeed, standing outside the borders of present-day
Greece altogether—elicits far deeper surges of emotion and nostalgia.

The Greeks, like other Orthodox Christian peoples, are fixated
on their churches, which are not only places of worship but treasure
houses of their material culture that survived the awful centuries of
Ottoman rule. C. P. Cavafy, the greatest modern Greek poet,
described this feeling in his poem "In Church":

> . . . *when I enter a Greek church,*
> *the fragrance of its incenses,*
> *the voices of the liturgy and harmonies of sound,*
> *the orderly appearance of the priests,*
> *each moving to most solemn rhythm,*
> *all garbed in vestments most magnificent,*

recall to mind the glories of our race,
the greatness of our old Byzantine days.

And among Greek churches, one above all stands out: the Church of Hagia Sophia, or "Divine Wisdom," built in the middle of the sixth century A.D. by the Byzantine emperor Justinian and rising majestically—a flat, wide dome mounting a chorus of semi-domes and flaring buttresses, as though in an act of levitation—over the scummy waters of Seraglio Point in Constantinople (Istanbul). Even today, stripped of its gold and silver, with its frescoes faded and begrimed, there is arguably no building in all the world whose interior conjures up such a sense of boundless wealth and mystical power. I visited Hagia Sophia several times in the 1980s. Each time I instinctively knew that the political passions of modern Greece might be explained here—much more than at the Parthenon. Passing through the imperial door toward the main dome, I always felt as though I were inside a great indoor city of marble walls, galleries, and colonnades, and of mosaics, with vast, ambiguous spaces lurking in the peripheries. Hagia Sophia became the prototype for all Orthodox cathedrals, for St. Mark's Church in Venice, and for mosques throughout Turkey.

But Hagia Sophia is no longer a church. It is the Turkish "Museum of Aya Sofya." In place of bells, incense, and priests are massive round green plaques hung above the wall corners, that bear Arabic inscriptions, saying "Allah is Great." Although Greek tourists travel to Turkey to visit the "Museum of Aya Sofya," many come home unsettled by the experience, and the overwhelming majority of Greeks cannot bring themselves even to go. "The idea of going to our church in what for us was the greatest of Greek cities and seeing those Muslim signs, I cannot tell you how it would make me feel. It is something terrible," an Athenian friend once told me. Istanbul will forever be Constantinoupoli in Greek eyes, even if

"Constantine's city" no longer exists. Greeks cannot bring themselves to say the word *Istanbul*. Upon hearing it on the lips of a foreigner, they wince much as Israelis wince at the word *Palestine,* or many Arabs wince at the word *Israel*. His Holiness, Bartholomew, the Patriarch of the Greek Orthodox Church, sits not in Athens but in Constantinoupoli, in a wood-framed building amid narrow, dirty lanes. This is all that remains of Byzantium, a civilization and an empire created in A.D. 324, as the successor to Rome, and destroyed more than eleven hundred years later by an invading army of Ottoman Turks in 1453. During those eleven centuries the Byzantine Empire was a Greek empire, and Greece then was much more than the classical Mediterranean culture with which the West is familiar: it was a northerly cultural realm of unimaginable depth and texture, whose influence spread to medieval Muscovy.

But the Turks smashed it all. That is why Hagia Sophia expresses in stone and marble what Greeks cry out silently in their hearts: *We have lost so much, not one inch more, not Macedonia, not anything more will we lose!*

The pain of this loss was sharpened by the modern experience of war and exile. George Seferis, the Nobel Prize–winning Greek poet, writes in "The House Near the Sea":

> *The houses I had they took away from me. The times happened to be unpropitious: war, destruction, exile;*

The cause of Seferis's suffering was the Greek-Turkish War of 1922—the final event in the series of Balkan military struggles (beginning with the 1877 Russo-Turkish War in Bulgaria) that dominated news headlines from the last quarter of the nineteenth century through the first quarter of the twentieth, and set the boundaries of the Balkans more or less as they were in 1990, on the eve of the Yugoslav civil war.

Although the Ottoman Turks had ejected the Byzantine Greeks from Constantinople in the fifteenth century, large Greek communities survived in Istanbul and along the western shore of Asia Minor—particularly in the city of Smyrna—through the end of World War I. The dismemberment of the Ottoman Empire in the wake of World War I provided the Greeks (who had sided with the victorious Allies) an opportunity to regain this lost territory, where over a million ethnic Greeks still lived. But the Greeks wanted even more. For years the British prime minister and romantic philhellene David Lloyd George had encouraged them to believe that, whatever Greece did, the Western Allies would certainly support a Christian nation and the heir to ancient Greece against the Muslim Turks. This naïve trust, fortified by spreading anarchy in Turkey following the collapse of the sultanate, caused the Greeks to embark upon their *Megali Ithea,* the "Great Idea": the return of every inch of historic Greece to the motherland. Again, there was the same old Balkan revanchist syndrome, each nation claiming as its natural territory all the lands that it held at the time of its great historical expansion.

In 1921 the Greek army, against all military logic, advanced beyond the Greek-populated western coast of Asia Minor and deep into the mountainous Anatolian interior, only 150 miles from Ankara. This move made the army's supply lines so weak and disorganized as to be nonexistent. A reporter for the *Toronto Daily Star,* Ernest Hemingway, wrote that the Greek officers "did not know a god-damned thing," while the Greek troops came to battle in the ceremonial nineteenth-century uniform of "white ballet skirts and upturned shoes with pompoms on them."

At that point, in August 1922, the ruthless and charismatic young Turkish general Kemal Atatürk, who was in the midst of whipping together a new Turkish republic out of the anarchic morass of the Ottoman Empire, unleashed his forces. Hemingway wrote that the Turks advanced "steadily and lumpily." In only ten days Atatürk drove the Greek army back to the Aegean coast, where Greek troops deserted to offshore ships, leaving the Greek population of Smyrna exposed to fire and the Turkish soldiery. The Greek dead numbered 30,000. In the massive population exchange that followed, 400,000 Turks from Greek Thrace marched into Turkey, and 1,250,000 Greeks from Asia Minor went into exile in Greece— homeless, ill-clothed, and starving—increasing the population of Greece by 20 percent. The refugees overwhelmed Thessaloníki and more than tripled the size of Athens.

Concurrently, three thousand years of Greek civilization in Asia Minor came to an end. Smyrna became a Turkish city and was renamed İzmir. Greece was again small, insecure, reeling with poverty, utterly humiliated, and seething with hate. The dictatorial regimes of the 1920s and 1930s in Athens provided no stabilizing outlet for such emotions. Then came the horrors of the Nazi invasion and occupation, which left 8 percent of the population dead, a million homeless, and the countryside destroyed. Greek resistance against the Nazis was widespread, but the guerrilla movement it spawned was as divided as it was heroic. All of these divisions boiled over in the 1946–49 Greek Civil War, which saw even more casualties and destruction in Greece than had the war against the Nazis.

The United States backed the royalist Greek government in Athens, while the Soviet Union and its allies backed the Communist insurgents in the countryside. It was the first and last cold war counterinsurgency that the American-backed side won outright. However, the civil war in Greece was about much more than capitalism versus Communism.

Capitalism had never really existed in Greece, which in the mid-twentieth century was a poor Oriental society of refugees in which a small number of rapacious landowners and shipowners exploited everyone else, and where a middle class barely existed. The American-backed Greek government was characterized by corruption and pointless intrigue. Its supporters had only a vague notion of democracy and a free press, and they numbered more than a few former Nazi sympathizers. They were Western only in the sense that they aspired to be Western. The Greek Communists, meanwhile, had a completely different historical orientation—seeing Russia and the Kremlin not only as beacons of an ideology they supported but as a second motherland that, since the fall of Byzantium in 1453, had served as the protector of the Eastern Orthodox nations against the Turks. It may be no accident that the first proxy battle of the cold war, the archetypal East-West struggle, occurred on Greek soil.

In the learning centers of the West, however, the most recent two thousand years of Greek history were virtually ignored in favor of an idealized version of ancient Greece, a civilization that had already died before Jesus' birth. The West would not accept that Greece was more a child of Byzantium and Turkish despotism than of Periclean Athens. As a result, few Westerners could understand what began happening in Greece in the 1980s, an era when Greece's former prime minister and president, Constantine Karamanlis, described the country as a "vast lunatic asylum."

O, Greece!

BY HUGH LEONARD

editor's note

I took this piece to heart years before I first set foot in Greece. When I read it in 1983, I had already seen Chartres Cathedral from five miles away, just as Leonard describes, and I had already known it was an unforgettable sight. So when he included only one other site in the indelible image category, that of the Parthenon just after sunrise, I figured he was on to something. I dragged my husband out of our unairconditioned Athens hotel room (not difficult, even at 5:00 A.M.), and we hoofed it up the hill. I'm happy to say that yes, the view at that hour of the day is stunning, and it remains the most compelling reason to rise early that I've ever known.

HUGH LEONARD is the author of *A Wild People* (Thomas Dunne Books, 2002), *Da* (Methuen Publishing, London, 2003), and *Selected Plays of Hugh Leonard: Irish Drama Selections* (Catholic University of America Press, 1993), among others. He contributed this piece to *The Sophisticated Traveler* edition of *The New York Times Magazine*.

There are two sights the traveler in Europe never forgets. One is that first glimpse of Chartres Cathedral from five miles away, solitary and seeming to sail the wheat fields like a leviathan. The other is the Parthenon just after sunrise. Athens is slate gray with dusk and smog; high above it, pricked by first light, the columns soar, dwarfing even the Acropolis itself. No photograph can prepare the visitor for the actuality; it sandbags the senses. The heart is seized. And far off behind the temple and beyond Piraeus, the Aegean is molten silver.

I love Greece for many reasons: for its good manners, for the melancholy that masks its zest for life, for its climate and its islands, each one different from the next. But most of all I love it for the immediacy of the past. To arrive there is a homecoming; at once, and with a certainty as serene as it is absolute, the mystery is solved: this is where one began.

Athens, for all its size, yields its pleasures quickly. And you need no guide for the ninety-minute drive to Cape Sounion, no one to tell you where the land ends, that the sea has blues and violets that never knew an artist's palette, that Byron carved his name into the marble of the Temple of Poseidon. Elsewhere, however, it is good to travel with a Greek as mentor; inevitably, he will treat myth as history, time as an impertinence, and antiquity as last week.

On my own first visit to Greece, my guide was the venerable and gaunt Manos Katrakis, an actor who is to Greek theater as Olivier is to British. We drove on a January morning to the red-brown ruins of Mycenae, guarding an amphitheater of mountains, and passed through the Lion Gate across the threshold of the House of Atreus. "There," Katrakis declaimed, pointing to a nearby hilltop, "is where the sentinel saw Agamemnon returning from the Trojan Wars and ran to tell the adulterous Queen Clytemnestra that . . ." Caught by the rhetoric, I completed his sentence inelegantly: ". . . that the jig was up."

That afternoon we visited the magnificent theater at Epidaurus, to which countryfolk still come by donkey cart from a hundred miles away, often sleeping by the roadside. At Katrakis's bidding, I wheezed up to the topmost row (the theater can seat 14,000), and he proceeded to demonstrate the acoustics by reciting the prologue from *Prometheus*. Magically—for, as I have said, the month was January—people appeared as if out of the earth, stood, wondered, and applauded.

A word about the Greek character. Greece, whatever the maps or the rules of the Common Market may say, is not part of Europe. Least of all is it a part of Asia Minor: talk to an Athenian about "the war," and he will assume that you mean the final (1820–26) revolt against the Turks. Bring him further up to date, and he will shrug, mention Ohi Day (*ohi* means "no," and every year on October 28 the Greeks celebrate their "no" to Mussolini's demand in 1940 that the Greek-Albanian border be opened to Italian troops), and perhaps relate how an anonymous hero scaled the sheer cliffs of the Acropolis one night to replace the swastika of the occupying Nazis with the Greek flag. Greece, the visitor will discover, is a continent to itself.

Inevitably, there are niceties of behavior that should be observed. If a Greek is your host, for example, it is bad manners to drain a wineglass to the lees; it implies that he has been remiss by failing to top it up. Neither is it the done thing to wave goodbye with the palm of the hand forward—it is a gesture of rejection, and an accompanying smile only makes it worse.

The real difference between the Greeks and the Others goes deeper. Last summer in Thásos I had just left a vast open-air night-club when there was a power failure. Before candles could be brought, the tourists gleefully flocked out en masse without paying their tabs. Only the Greek customers remained. The New Yorker, the Londoner, and the Parisian will discover that even the most illiterate Greek villager still practices the two golden rules of Pericles: Moderation in All Things and Know Thyself.

I am a creature of habit. My hotel in Athens has always been the St. George Lycabettus, high up on a baby mountain and only a five-minute stroll downhill into the heart of the city. (For the uphill journey only a sherpa would disdain the services of a cab). And my restaurant in that city is unfailingly the Gerofinekas, an oasis of elegance at the end of what seems to be a tenement hallway. Outside Athens I rely on simple accommodations and local specialties or on the ubiquitous and ambrosial "village salad": tomatoes, cucumber, olives, and slices of feta cheese. And wine as light and simple as the meal. Gourmets may wince, but I have never eaten badly in a Greek taverna.

Every year the same impatience for the islands that has thus far robbed me of the glories of Delphi impels me across the Aegean. Islands are, like music, a matter of taste. Mykonos, for example, has always reminded me of Fire Island with windmills. Thíra, or Santorini, which may once have been Atlantis, is too stark; Límnos, although it boasts a superb hotel, is, alone among Greek islands, achingly dull.

The first of my islands was Skiathos, in the Sporades. It boasts one road, a small, lively town (the best taverna is Ilya's, which, let ailurophobes beware, has a garden infested by scores of lean, lap-addicted cats), and the finest beach in all Greece, a half-mile of flawless sand known as Koukounaries. The best hotel, the Skiathos Palace, is yards away. As in the case of many resort hotels, I use the word *best* in the relative sense. The rooms are a delight, the floors marble and cool to the naked foot; against this, the staff are surly, and lunch is a marvel of uninspired frugality.

Apart from the beaches, the only daytime diversion on Skiathos is the boat trip to Kastro, the remains of the island's former capital. The path upward is precipitous, and I remember sitting down, over-come by vertigo and unable to budge, while a local priest skipped by, goatlike in his peasant's boots, with a smiling salutation of "*Kalimera!*"

My second island was Crete, a world unto itself where, at Iráklion airport, the arriving visitor is confronted by the world's shortest conveyor belt. The piling of Pelion upon Ossa was as noth-ing compared to the chaos when a hundred or so suitcases, ruck-sacks, backpacks, and portmanteaus rise into a teetering mountain.

A visit—or if you like, a pilgrimage—should be paid to the grave of Nikos Kazantzakis, author of *Zorba the Greek,* on a hill-top overlooking Iráklion. A cab driver refused to allow me to leave Crete until I had seen the high, simple cross and the epitaph.

> *I expect nothing . . .*
> *I fear nothing . . .*
> *I am free.*

The ruins of Knossos, seat of the Minoan civilization, are a few miles away. These were excavated by Sir Arthur Evans as recently as 1909, and if his reconstructions and recopying of frescoes have caused fury among the purists, the impression of past grandeur disarms all others.

Crete is intimidating at first sight. The land itself, mountainous and sun-bleached, seems inhospitable; in the villages the faces are leathery and gaunt, the hands brown and toil-hardened. A very real tradition of kindness to strangers exists, however: a visitor in trouble instantly becomes not a tourist but a guest.

Actually, there is a sharp distinction to be made between traveler and tourist. The former will seek out the remotest inland villages, stay for a pittance in simple, white-scrubbed rooms, and allow the hours to creep by over cups of bitter Greek coffee. (It is Turkish, really, but nothing good, you are told, ever came out of *that* place). The latter will inevitably head for the resort town of Ágios Nikólaos.

The place is bustling; *syrtaki* music jangles the length of every street and alleyway; new high-rise blocks appear yearly. The town is probably unique in that it was ruined by television: a BBC series, *The Lotus Eaters,* exploited its picturesque charm and brought the tourists. Today it is good for souvenirs and restaurants (the best, overlooking the pebble beach, is the Faros) and not much else; for tranquility one takes the road for Elounda.

The drive—only seven miles—is best undertaken before nightfall: The Greeks have the custom of erecting guardrails along the straight stretches of road and leaving the hairpin turns unprotected. The journey is worth the consternation, however. For one thing, the Elounda Beach Hotel is a joy, with air-conditioned stone bungalows jutting over the sea. There is a pool, a sandy beach (rare for Crete), and "Cretan Night" every Tuesday, a lively cabaret with native foods, ouzo, and singing and dancing—as always in Greece, travelers are encouraged to join in. Only dinner is, as always in hotels, to be avoided. A mile away, the village of Elounda itself merits a shrug at first glance, but it has a bedraggled serenity. I remember a twilight supper at the water's edge: as the moon rose, we flicked pellets of bread over the quayside and watched the sea come alive in a scene worthy of a mini *Jaws*.

My favorite island now is Thásos, too far to the north to attract the cruise ships or tourists who use the Cyclades as so many steppingstones. It is ninety minutes from Kávala—a delight in itself—and drivers should know that in Greece one boards a ferry in reverse, with a stomach-turning glimpse of oil-slicked water on either side.

Most of Thásos is lush and mountainous; few European islands can surpass it for beauty or the redness of its sunsets. A good road encircles the island (the circuit is sixty miles), and one lingers at tiny, pine-shaded beaches such as Aliki or the sleepy port of Liminária, a paradise for the idler. The capital, Thásos (also called Limin), has a ruined theater and excavations; and as the sun goes down, there is the *volta*: residents and tourists alike parading on the quayside deriving untold mirth from the sight of one another.

Tavernas abound but can be noisy. Two rival establishments, next door to one another, have television sets mere inches apart and tuned to different channels. This, compounded by the bouzouki music from a nearby café, impelled us off toward the best restaurant on the island, at the port of Prinos Skala, forty minutes' drive away.

My preferred hotel is the Makyriammos Bungalows, just out of Thásos. The beach is idyllic to an unlikely degree, except when the day-trippers swarm in (at a price) by caïque and motor launch. The food is Greek and therefore good, and there is about the place an amiable dottiness. The bald headwaiter is Egyptian and frequently homesick; a young donkey is apt to stroll up, seize one's bottle of beer in his teeth, and guzzle the contents; and this must be the only hotel in Greece that regularly runs out of lemons and tomatoes.

Not long ago a friend asked me why I unfailingly return to the

Greek islands when there are so many other places to be seen and enjoyed. I could only answer that this is like approaching a man who is happily in love with a beautiful woman of intelligence, grace, and refinement and asking him why he does not go out on blind dates. Monogamy is beautiful.

Hugh Leonard's Greece

Athens

The St. George Lycabettus, on the slopes of Mount Lycabettus at 2 Kleomenous Street (210.72.90.711) has double rooms from about $175/night.

The Geronfinekas Restaurant, at 10 Pindarou Street (210.36.36.710), is open from 12:30 P.M. to 11:30 P.M. Reservations are strongly recommended.

Three Favored Isles

On Skiathos, the Skiathos Palace Hotel, Koukounaries is owned by Luxe Hotels (242.70.49.700; www.luxehotels.com) and prices run up to $180 for a double in high season.

On Crete, the Elounda Beach Hotel (284.10.41.4123; www.eloundabeach.gr) runs about $400/night for a double.

On Thásos, the Makyriammos Bungalows (259.30.22.101; makryamo@otenet.gr) has doubles for $90 off season and $150 and up in high.

Eating Around

"Allow me a cautionary word," Leonard says. "No surer way exists of managing to please no one than by attempting to please all, and 'international cuisine' invariably turns out to be anything but. The wise traveler will at sunset head for the nearest village; here, he will eat happily, cheaply and, on occasion, memorably.

"Menus exist only to be ignored. The diner-out is expected to enter the kitchen, peer at the uncooked kebabs, octopus, stuffed vine leaves, and meatballs, admire the freshly caught fish and lobsters, and pry into the simmering cooking pots. To end the meal, no sane person will sample either a raki (local moonshine) or Metaxa (Greek brandy) that is less than five-star."

Greek Drama

The theater at Epidaurus, about 120 miles from Athens, is open daily from 8 A.M. to 7 P.M. in summer; on weekends in July and August there are performances (in Greek) by the National Theater Company of Greece and visiting companies. (27.52.04.1248; www.culture.gr).

Bibliography

The Mediterranean: History, Natural History, and Personal Narratives

The Ancient Mediterranean, Michael Grant, Charles Scribner's Sons, 1969. In this scholarly work Grant reminds us that a huge proportion of the Western heritage, "almost in its entirety, came to us from the ancient Mediterranean— from Greece and from Rome and from Israel. This fact is given too little prominence today because so many other ancient cultures, some of them from much further afield, have now been discovered. Yet it still remains true that the Mediterranean was the region from which civilisation came our way."

The First Eden: The Mediterranean World and Man, Sir David Attenborough, William Collins Sons & Co., London, 1987. The four parts of this book deal with natural history, archaeology, history, and ecology, and it has very good coverage of Mediterranean plants and animals.

The Inner Sea: The Mediterranean and Its People, Robert Fox, Alfred A. Knopf, 1993.

The Mediterranean, Fernand Braudel, first published in France, 1949. English translation of second revised edition, HarperCollins, 1972. HarperCollins, 1992. Still the definitive classic.

Mediterranean, photography by Mimmo Jodice, essays by George Hersey and Predrag Matvejevic, Aperture, 1995.

Mediterranean: A Cultural Landscape, Predrag Matvejevic, translated by Michael Henry Heim, University of California Press, Berkeley, 1999. A beautiful, unusual book combining personal observations with history, maps, maritime details, people, and language.

Mediterranean: From Homer to Picasso, Xavier Girard, translated by Simon Pleasance and Fronza Woods, Assouline, 2001. This recent book is perhaps in a category by itself. Divided into five chapters—representations, narratives, figures, places, and arts—I've been waiting for a volume just like this, which is filled with color and black-and-white illustrations and photos. As stated in the prologue, "The Mediterranean," wrote Bernard Pingaud in the pages of *L'Arc* in 1959, "is nothing other than the image we make of it for ourselves. The unusual thing is that we all make an image of it for ourselves, and that it is still a magnet for all those who are lucky enough to discover it one day. Herein lies a secret. It is perhaps not the secret conjured up by the 'land where the orange tree blooms.' It is the secret of this image itself, the secret of a dream which paradoxically contrasts abundance and drought, merriness and poverty, moderation and excess, joy and tragedy. Who can say why we need the Midi? If the Mediterranean didn't exist, we would have to invent it."

The Mediterranean: Lands of the Olive Tree, Culture and Civilizations, Alain Cheneviere, Konecky and Konecky, New York, 1997. This is that rare coffee-table book that has both perceptive text and gorgeous photos.

The Mediterranean Shore: Travels in Lawrence Durrell Country, Paul Hogarth, Pavilion, London, 1988. This beautiful and unusual book has watercolors by Hogarth matched with text from many of Durrell's books—*Reflections on a Marine Venus, Bitter Lemons,* and *The Greek Islands* included—and also with poetry and a definitive statement about the Mediterranean not previously published.

Memory and the Mediterranean, Fernand Braudel, Alfred A. Knopf, 2001.

On the Shores of the Mediterranean, Eric Newby, Harvill Press, London, 1984. You have to travel with Eric and Wanda Newby to other places around the Mediterranean besides Greece—the former Yugoslavia, France, Turkey, Spain, Israel, North Africa, the Côte d'Azur, and Venice—but it's a pleasure every step of the way.

The Phoenicians, edited by Sabatino Moscati, Rizzoli, 1999. The Phoenician civilization remains mysterious, but this beautifully printed and fascinating paperback has informative essays by a number of scholars. I don't know about you, but the last time I spent much time delving into the Phoenicians was in junior high school, so this volume has been a welcome addition to Mediterranean literature.

The Pillars of Hercules: A Grand Tour of the Mediterranean, Paul Theroux, G. P. Putnam's Sons, 1995.

Playing Away: Roman Holidays and Other Mediterranean Encounters, Michael Mewshaw, Atheneum, 1988.

The Spirit of Mediterranean Places, Michel Butor, Marlboro Press, 1986. Essays on two Greek places—Thessaloníki and Delphi—are among the eight select places in this unique anthology.

The Sun at Midday: Tales of a Mediterranean Family, Gini Alhadeff, Pantheon, 1997. Though Alhadeff's life was and remains partly Italian, this is a full Mediterranean memoir, beautifully written and one of my most favorite books.

Mediterranean Architecture and Style

Mediterranean Color: Italy, France, Spain, Portugal, Morocco, Greece, Jeffrey Becom, Abbeville Press, 1990.

Mediterranean Lifestyle, Paco Assensio, photography by Pere Planells, Loft Publications; distributed in the United States by Watson-Guptill Publications, 2000.

Mediterranean Living, Lisa Lovatt-Smith, Whitney Library of Design, Watson-Guptill Publications, 1998.

Mediterranean Style, Catherine Haig, Abbeville Press, 1998; first published in Great Britain in 197 by Conran Octopus Ltd., London.

Mediterranean Vernacular: A Vanishing Architectural Tradition, V. I. Atroshenko and Milton Grundy, Rizzoli International Publications, 1991.

Villages in the Sun: Mediterranean Community Architecture, Myron Goldfinger, Rizzoli, 1993. Greek villages featured are on the islands of Mykonos, Serifos, Santorini, Skyros, and Sífnos.

Europe

The Civilization of Europe in the Renaissance, John Hale, Atheneum, 1994. I first picked up this book because the title was so similar to Jacob Burckhardt's *The Civilization of the Renaissance in Italy.* In the reviews on the back cover, the book was indeed compared not only to Burckhardt's classic but also to

Fernand Braudel's *The Mediterranean in the Time of Philip II*. I needed no further justification to purchase the book. Featuring more than one hundred black-and-white illustrations, this volume covers the period from about 1450 to 1620. Some of Hale's other works, which are ideal companion volumes to this one, include *Renaissance Europe, 1480–1520* (1971); *Renaissance War Studies* (1982); *War and Society in Renaissance Europe* (1985); and *Artists and Warfare in the Renaissance* (1990).

The Crusaders: Warriors of God, Georges Tate, Harry N. Abrams, 1996. The quotation on the inside front cover of this little paperback (small enough to pack easily in a handbag) is worth repeating: "In the long sequence of interaction and fusion between Orient and Occident out of which our civilization has grown, the crusades were a tragic and destructive episode. . . . There was so much courage and so little honor, so much devotion and so little understanding" (Steven Runciman, *A History of the Crusades*, vol. 3, 1954). A great number of titles have been published on the Crusades (including the one just named), the finest of which, in my opinion, is Karen Armstrong's (noted below); but as fond as I am of her book, and as fine as all the other tomes may be, I think this one—in the wonderful Discoveries series—may be the best for the traveler who wants a good, concise history that can be read rather quickly. All the Discoveries volumes I've read are great, and this one is no exception. The author was director of the Institut Français d'Archéologie du Proche-Orient from 1980 to 1990, and he is currently director of the Archaeological Mission of Northern Syria. He is also a specialist on the East from the third to the twelfth century. The book opens with a chapter on the Mediterranean world on the eve of the Crusades and concludes with Saladin's victory. The documents section of the book has a collection of excerpts on such topics as "Hospitalers and Templars," "Jihad and Holy War," "The Franks in Eastern Eyes," and "Lawrence of Arabia." Like other Discoveries books, this one is amply provided with color reproductions of artworks, maps, and black-and-white illustrations. For its size (192 pages) and price (about $12.95), this is also a very good value.

Europe: A History, Norman Davies, Oxford University Press, 1996. In the opening line to his preface, Davies states that "This book contains little that is original," but I would disagree. From the chapter titles ("Hellas," "Roma," "Origo," "Pestis," "Renatio," "Dynamo," etc.) to the manner in which ideas and material are presented, plus the useful appendixes and notes at the end of the book, this *is* an original work, highly recommended.

The Decisive Battles of the Western World and Their Influence Upon History, J.F.C. Fuller, Eyre & Spottiswoode, London; vol. 1, *From the Earliest Times to the Battle of Lepanto* (1954), vol. 2, *From the Defeat of the Spanish Armada to the Battle of Waterloo* (1955), and vol. 3, *From the American Civil War to the End of the Second World War* (1956). Though I know it is incorrect to place this trilogy under the heading "Europe," most of these decisive battles did take place in Europe, and truthfully I just haven't figured out yet how to categorize it. (Most likely I will create a separate heading for it, which it certainly deserves.) I came across this trilogy while I was reading a biography of Philip II by Sir Charles Petrie, in which Petrie referred to Fuller's account of the Battle of Lepanto as the single best one in print. By searching www.abebooks.com, I obtained the three-volume set from a book dealer in the U.K., not surprisingly, and I'm happy to report that it is a stunning publishing achievement. Major-General Fuller was apparently the "pioneer of mechanization in the British Army" and is "known all over the world as the most fearless and penetrating of military critics." Fuller notes in the preface that "Whether war is a necessary factor in the evolution of mankind may be disputed, but a fact which cannot be questioned is that, from the earliest records of man to the present age, war has been his dominant preoccupation. There has never been a period in human history altogether free from war, and seldom one of more than a generation which has not witnessed a major conflict: great wars flow and ebb almost as regularly as the tides." Not exactly uplifting, but he goes on to say, "Yet one thing is certain, and it is that the more we study the history of war, the more we shall be able to understand war itself, and, seeing that it is now the dominant factor, until we do understand it, how can we hope to regulate human affairs?" How, indeed. Greece figures in all three volumes, although significantly more in the first. No matter: this set is worth your most determined efforts to obtain.

Fifty Years of Europe: An Album, Jan Morris, Villard, 1997. At last count, I discovered I'd read all of Jan Morris's books except three. Hers are among the very first books I distinctly remember as being responsible for my developing wanderlust. When I saw this volume, I thought, who better to be a reader's companion on a tour of Europe on the brink of the twenty-first century? She's traveled to all of Europe's corners more than, I believe, any other contemporary writer. One of the most appealing aspects of this book is that she often includes multiple perspectives, relating her observations so the first time she visited a place as well as more recently. The final chapter, "Spasms of Unity: Six Attempts to Make a Whole of Europe, from the Holy Roman Empire to the European Union," is perhaps the best.

Great Sea Battles, Oliver Warner, George Weidenfeld & Nicholson Ltd, 1963; The Hamlyn Publishing Group Ltd., 1968. Naval historian Warner, who in his lifetime was referred to as 'the greatest living authority on marine art,' was also the author of a dozen or so volumes of naval history and biography. Featured with 48 pages of color illustrations and 350 black-and-white pictures are 26 naval battles, from Lepanto to Leyte Gulf in 1944, including Navarino Bay,

1827. Warner writes that Navarino was the last sea battle fought under sail, and "was not the least extraordinary in a long sequence. It took place in that classical area of great actions, the Morea, scarcely a hundred miles from the scene of Lepanto, in circumstances of complexity. It involved six nations [France, England, Russia, Turkey, Egypt, and Greece] and in itself it was a landmark in the struggle for the liberation of Greece."

History of the Present: Essays, Sketches, and Dispatches From Europe in the 1990s, Timothy Garton Ash, Random House, 1999. The bulk of this insightful book is made up of "analytical reportages" that were originally published in *The New York Review of Books.* Ash admits that the phrase "history of the present" is not his but rather was coined by American diplomat and historian George Kennan in a review of Ash's *The Uses of Adversity* in the 1980s. The phrase is the best description for what Ash has been trying to write for twenty years, combining the crafts of historian and journalist. I really like the way Ash has written this book, with a chronology for each piece and diarylike sketches inserted throughout that are drawn from Ash's own notebooks and recollections. It's an unusual way of reporting history, but an effective one.

Holy War: The Crusades and Their Impact on Today's World, Karen Armstrong, with a new preface, Anchor Books, 2002; originally published in hardcover in Great Britain by Macmillan, 1988. Though Greece was not a major participant in the Crusades, its Orthodox Christian, Muslim, and Jewish history makes a basic knowledge of the Crusades essential for a complete interpretation of Greece and the Greeks. Additionally, as Armstrong notes in her updated preface, "It is important for Western people to consider these contemporary holy wars in connection with the Crusades, because they remind us of our own input, involvement and responsibilities." I think this is the single most important book of our times, and I urge you to read it and to urge friends, family, and colleagues to do so as well. Armstrong concludes her preface by stating that the Crusades show religion at its very worst. "After writing *Holy War* I was so saddened by the conflict between the three Abraham traditions that I decided to embark on the research for my book *A History of God* [see my *Morocco* edition for details of this excellent work]. I wanted to demonstrate the strong and positive ideals and visions that Jews, Christians, and Muslims share in common. It is now over a millennium since Pope Urban II called the First Crusade in 1095, but the hatred and suspicion that this expedition unleashed still reverberates, never more so than on September 11, 2001, and during the terrible days that followed. It is tragic that our holy wars continue, but for that very reason we must strive for mutual understanding and for what in these pages I have called 'triple vision.'"

The Penguin Atlas of Ancient History (1967), *Medieval History* (1968), *Modern History—to 1815* (1973), and *Recent History—Europe Since 1815* (1982),

Colin McEvedy, Penguin Books. This is a brilliant idea: a chronological sequence of maps that illustrate political and military developments, which in turn illustrate history via geography. Each individual volume is remarkably fascinating, and the four volumes as a whole present an enlightening read. Maps appear on the right-hand pages while one page of explanatory text accompanies them on the left-hand pages. ~Also in the same series but compiled by different authors is *The Penguin Atlas of Diasporas,* (Gerard Chaliand and Jean-Pierre Rageau, 1995). This edition is equally fascinating—perhaps more so, as I've not seen another volume like it—and highlights Jewish, Armenian, Gypsy, Black, Chinese, Indian, Irish, Greek, Lebanese, Palestinian, Vietnamese, and Korean migrations. The year 1492 was a significant one in the history of diasporas, and among welcome places for the Jews and Muslims expelled from Spain were the Ottoman Empire (which included present-day Greece), Morocco, and the Netherlands (once it was free from Spain). All of these are essential for history novices and mavens alike.

Greece and the Greeks

Balkan Ghosts: A Journey Through History, Robert Kaplan, St. Martin's Press, 1993, hardcover; Vintage, 1994, paperback. This absolutely essential read highlights Yugoslavia (as it was in 1993), Romania, Bulgaria, and Greece; the Greece section alone is among the most insightful pieces ever written on Hellas. In the chapter entitled "Teach Me, Zorba. Teach Me to Dance!" Kaplan focuses on the films *Zorba the Greek* and *Never on Sunday,* as well as Durrell's *Prospero's Cell* (about Corfu) and *The Alexandria Quartet* and Miller's *The Colossus of Maroussi* and how they influenced the world's perception of Greece. What these books and movies all said, he observes, was essentially that there was a certain something about Greece that Spain, Italy, and other poor sun-drenched lands lacked. "The certain something that Greece had that other countries lacked—that was unique yet so familiar—was a faultlessly proportioned, atmospheric mix of East and West. The ululating quarter tones of bouzouki music, the raw material for Hadjidakis's theme song for *Never on Sunday,* are, in fact, siblings of Bulgarian and Serbian rhythms, and are close cousins of the Arab and Turkish music that, heard in its pure form, gives most Western listeners a headache. Yet run through a Mediterranean musical filter, these monotonous and orgasmic sounds of the Orient appeal perfectly to Western ears, especially when they are heard in the setting of a Cycladic island like Mykonos. . . . The Greek tourist myth depended on this fragile yet subtle recipe: of Greece being a summation of the Balkans, yet also being something apart; of Greece being only ninety minutes by plane from the tiresome and dangerous hatreds of the Middle East, yet also being millions of miles away."

The Classical Greek Reader, edited by Kenneth J. Atchity, Henry Holt, 1998. Atchity explains in the introduction that this book "seeks to present the widest possible perspective on the Greek classical period, from its roots in the Homeric epics to its echoes in the histories of Plutarch and romances of Heliodorus. Its purpose is to provide today's reader with direct access to the voices that shaped the classical Greek spirit." He includes not only the big names but also less familiar voices—women, doctors, storytellers, herbalists, and romance writers.

Classics: A Very Short Introduction, Mary Beard and John Henderson, Oxford University Press, 1995. I really had no idea what the point or purpose of this book would be when I picked it up, but a review on the back cover stated that the authors "could not be dull if they tried"; another reviewer said, "this little book should be in the hands of every student, and every tourist to the lands of the ancient world," so I decided it was worth a read. It was, and is, and at only 136 pages, it's hardly a lengthy investment of your time. Beard and Henderson begin their introduction in the British Museum and focus their attention on the Temple at Bassae, in the Peloponnese. They wisely remind us that we, as modern tourists of today, are both like and unlike early visitors to Greece. Among other things, we share a "set of problems about how we are to understand our visit, and how to deal with the sometimes awkward clash between the Greece that exists in our imagination and the Greece that exists on the ground. Even more important, perhaps, the experience of Greece is not something we discover for ourselves, entirely new; it is something that, at least in part, we inherit from those earlier travelers who experienced Greece before us." They also note that "We are *all* already *Classicists,* however much (or little) we think we know about the Greeks and Romans. We can never come to *Classics* as complete strangers. There is no other foreign culture that is so much a part of our history."

The Colossus of Maroussi, Henry Miller, New Directions, 1958; original copyright 1941. I was warned, before I read this book years ago, that I might lose my way occasionally or, at the least, not know exactly what Miller was trying to impart. I report, for those who have not yet read it, that this proved to be true; but conversely, Miller wrote some of the best passages about Greece here that have ever been penned. Before he ever landed in Greece, a girl named Betty Ryan, whom he knew in Paris, described the country for him, and he was mesmerized: "She is an artist of some sort because nobody has ever given me the ambiance of a place so thoroughly as she did Greece. Long afterwards I discovered that it was near Olympia that she had gone astray and I with her, but at the time it was just Greece to me, a world of light such as I had never dreamed of and never hoped to see." I found that this was best read with a glass of ouzo at hand.

Courtesans and Fishcakes, James Davidson, HarperCollins, 1999. This interesting and delightfully salacious book examines the ancient Greeks' attitudes toward sex and sexuality. It's very well written, nicely illustrated, and hard to put down.

Culture Shock! Greece: A Guide to the Customs and Etiquette, Sally Adamson Taylor, Graphic Arts Publishing, Portland, Oregon, 1990. Each Culture Shock! edition is authored by a different writer, and each is eminently enlightening. The Greece edition covers such topics as Greek cultural traditions; deforestation and other environmental problems; the Greek Orthodox Church; health and insurance; buying and renting property; food and drink; and language and education. The Culture Quiz at the end of the book is particularly helpful. Although some of the information is directed at people who plan to be in Greece for an extended stay, this is a really useful, basic guide that I consider *de rigueur* reading, even for a short visit.

Dinner with Persephone, Patricia Storace, Pantheon, 1996. The gorgeous cover of this book, featuring a beautiful just-cut pomegranate with a Greek key border around the edges, is reason enough to pick it up, and the contents live up to their attractive packaging. Storace, also a poet, weaves dozens of Greek literary references (Shakespeare too) throughout this rich memoir, described by writer Luc Sante as "seductive, many-layered, sweet and astringent, lucid and intoxicating." Storace has lived in and traveled around seemingly every corner of Greece, including many little-visited ones, which make for the best reading, in my opinion (though her profiles of Athens are excellent). I enjoyed every chapter, but I found myself most engrossed in "The Dream of Love After the Dance," about the Benaki family (the same family that founded the Athens museum) and in particular about Penelope Benaki, later to become Penelope Delta. The story of the family is a monumental saga, and a tragic one for Penelope, yet one senses that other wealthy and influential families who were contemporaries of the Benaki clan likely had, in essence, the very same story. At one point in the book, a friend reminds Storace what Emmanuel Roidis, a nineteenth-century Greek novelist, once wrote: "Every nation has its cross to bear: In England, for example, it's the weather. In Greece, it's the Greeks." This book is an essential read about the Greeks and Greece, and I feel certain it will earn the moniker of a classic.

Do's and Taboos Around the World, edited by Roger Axtell, John Wiley & Sons, 1985. Axtell, a former vice president of the Parker pen company, spent eighteen years living and traveling abroad; *The New Yorker* once referred to him as "an international Emily Post." I've long been a fan of this paperback, and Greece is referenced throughout, addressing such topics as greetings, gift giving, punctuality, women, and gestures. If you do a fair amount of traveling, this is a handy book to have; otherwise, you'll find all of these topics covered in a good guidebook.

Early Greece, Oswyn Murray, Harvard University Press, 2001. Murray, a renowned authority on the classics, examines the three centuries leading up to the Persian invasion of 480 B.C., in which Greece was transformed from a simple peasant society into a sophisticated civilization that dominated the shores of the Mediterranean from Spain to Syria and from the Crimea to Egypt. This is obviously a very specific historical period, and while Murray writes in an exceedingly accessible style, I recommend the book to dedicated readers only.

Eleni, Nicholas Gage, Random House, 1983. My husband read *Eleni* first. I could tell by looking at him, and watching him read, so engrossed that he couldn't hear me talking to him, that it was a good book. When he finished it, he didn't critique it but only said that I had to read it, and soon. But I was more than halfway through Rebecca West's *Black Lamb, Grey Falcon,* and when we crossed into Greece from the former Yugoslavia, I had just reached the portion of the book where the title is fully explained, and I wasn't about to abandon it. I think about ten days went by before I finally did finish West's epic (it remains on my short list of favorite books), and I started reading *Eleni* one evening at the campground where we were staying for a few days. When the sun went down, I reached for the flashlight. I don't know if I ate dinner or not; I'm sure I drank ouzo. And I don't remember when I fell asleep, only that when I awoke, the book was lying beside me and I picked it up again. If my husband spoke to me, I didn't hear him. We were near Metsovo, not very far from the village of Lia, in Epirus (which will be included in a volume I hope to compile on northern Greece), which is the center of this tale's drama, and I know that I put the book down to get out and explore, but I also remember that I couldn't wait to return to the book. It was by flashlight again, shaking with anger and fear, tears streaming down my cheeks, that I finished it. If you didn't know that Greece suffered a horrible civil war after World War II; if you want to read about one of the most amazing women of the twentieth century, Eleni Gatzoyiannis; or if you want to read a book that is one hundred percent unput-downable, rush out immediately and find this one. Then write Gage a letter and tell him his mother was a remarkable human being, and that he's remarkable too for having the courage to write this book.

Greece: An Illustrated History, Tom Stone, Hippocrene, 2000. Stone, who is also the author of *The Summer of My Greek Taverna* (a great read), has compiled a lively, 176-page history of Hellas that is positively the perfect book for those who yearn for a succinct yet thorough volume (Stone explains the confusing politics of contemporary Greece especially well). Featuring some black-and-white illustrations, this little hardcover (in Hippocrene's illustrated histories series) is slender and lightweight enough to pack in a handbag.

Greece: Land of Light, Nicholas Gage, photographs by Barry Brukoff, Bulfinch Press, 1998. Gage is a well-known chronicler of Greece and Greek Americans, but I suspect most readers do not recognize the name Barry Brukoff; though he is not Greek, he has visited Greece more than once a year for approximately the last twenty years. One of the reasons this book stands out among other Greek photography books is that the photos are not quite like others; as Brukoff states, "There are may who will readily point out that my view of Greece is idealistic. It does not show things as they really are. I can only say to them that there are many realities. I do not choose to focus my camera or my energy on those aspects of twentieth-century culture that have torn the fabric of the Greek tapestry I am attempting to record. It is still possible to go to Greece and find it the way it is seen herein, even in the most popular tourist spots. You may be required to rise at dawn, see those incredible sunrises, and wander the streets before the T-shirts and postcards are hung out for the tourists disembarking from their cruise ships. But it is still there for those who have eyes to see." My favorite photos in this wonderful book are two facing each other, one of the ancient city of Corinth and the other a view of the Parthenon from the temple of Olympian Zeus in Athens. Gage's text, too, is a perfect match for these unique photographs; no other author-photographer team could have crafted a better book.

The Greek Achievement: The Foundation of the Western World, Charles Freeman, Viking, 1999. I found myself stuck when trying to describe this book to a friend, and then I reread the author's preface and realized I could not summarize it better than he did in his first two sentences: "This book is an exploration of the culture and history of ancient Greece. It is written for the general reader in the strong belief that some appreciation of the achievements of ancient Greece is essential for any full understanding of the western tradition." If that description makes it sound like a textbook, rest assured that it's not. He covers not only sociology, economics, culture, religion, and the military but also art and architecture, drama and theater, olive trees, philosophy, mathematics, medicine, the origin of the Olympic Games, and Alexander the Great. With two black-and-white and one color insert.

The Greek File: Images from a Mythic Land, William Abranowicz, introduction by Edmund Keeley, Rizzoli, 2001. Only published a few years ago, this volume has quickly become one of my most treasured books. Readers may recognize the work of Abranowicz, who has taken many shots of Greece (and other places) in his role as a contributing photographer for *Condé Nast Traveler.* To my mind, this is a second-to-none collection of photos of Greece, which Abranowicz took over a period of ten years. The images, all black-and-white, reveal the essentials of everyday life and are simplicity defined: the face of an elderly widow; pistachio shells on a plate; a whitewashed, Aegean stairwell; an ancient olive tree; ouzo glasses on a table; a wall of family photographs; men of a village; water; grapes; fish; goats; donkeys; the sky; the sea. Keeley, author and renowned translator of many modern Greek poets, notes that Lawrence Durrell tells us the Greek journey is first of all one that offers the possibility of discovering oneself. "If that is so—and I am one who thinks it is—these photographs provide ample ground for the reader to begin that journey in a most illuminating if vicarious way, or in the case of the lucky ones who have experienced that discovery, to arouse their nostalgia for the journey already made. In either case, the gift of this collection should be gratefully acknowledged."

Greek Thought: A Guide to Classical Knowledge, edited by Jacques Brunschwig and Geoffrey E. R. Lloyd, Belknap Press, Harvard University Press, 2000; originally published in France in 1996 by Flammarion. This beautifully written and beautifully produced hardcover volume is divided into five chapters: philosophy, politics, the pursuit of knowledge, major figures, and currents of thought. It is decidedly not for the casual reader and includes four eight-page color inserts.

The Greek Way, Edith Hamilton, W. W. Norton, 1930. Though Hamilton wrote these lines for the preface to the 1942 edition, they ring as true today as they did then: "'Beyond the last peaks and all seas of the world' stands the serene republic of what Plato calls 'the fair and immortal children of the mind.' We need to seek that silent sanctuary to-day. In it there is one place distinguished even above the others for sanity and balance of thought—the literature of ancient Greece." This is an absolutely essential read for the curious traveler. Hamilton concludes by reminding us that we cannot recapture the Greek point of view, that the wheels of time never turn backward, and fortunately so. But if we "through our own intense realization of ourselves reach a unity with all men, seeing as deeply as the great tragic poets of old saw, that what is of any importance in us is what we share with all, then there will be a new distribution in the scales and the balance held so evenly in those great days of Greece may be ours as well. The goal which we see ourselves committed to struggle toward without method or any clear hope, can be attained in no other way: a world where no one shall be sacrificed against his will, where general expediency which is the mind of mankind, and the feeling for each human being which is the spirit and the heart of mankind, shall be reconciled."

The Greek World: Classical, Byzantine, and Modern, edited by Robert Browning, Thames & Hudson, 1985, hardcover; 2000, paperback. This is a favorite of mine for covering ancient Greece on up to the present day, and as such it's a unique volume. The text is excellent, and the book has more than 350 illustrations, seventy in color.

The Greeks and Greek Civilization, Jacob Burckhardt, edited by Oswyn Murray, translated by Sheila Stern, St. Martin's Griffin, 1998. Burckhardt, as many readers know, was one of the greatest historians of the nineteenth century, and this book began as a series of his lectures, presented between 1898 and 1902.

The book is divided into two sections, "The Greeks" and "Greek Civilization" and among the topics addressed are the Greeks and their mythology, the *polis,* and general characteristics of Greek life. The beautiful postscript—"The Intellectual Necessity of Studying Ancient History"—reminds us that "all human knowledge is accompanied by the history of the ancient world as music is by a base-chord heard again and again; the history, that is, of all those peoples whose life has flowed together into our own . . . we can never cut ourselves off from antiquity unless we intend to revert to barbarism. The barbarian and the creature of exclusively modern civilization both live without history."

Hellas: The Civilizations of Ancient Greece, Keith Branigan and Michael Vickers, McGraw-Hill, 1980. The authors describe this excellent book as "a celebration in word and picture," and I cannot better that phrase. Though it's out of print, I have seen this volume in a number of used bookstores, and it is well worth an effort to find. At the time the book was published, Branigan was professor and head of the department of archaeology at the University of Sheffield, England, his particular field of interest being prehistoric archaeology. Vickers was assistant keeper in the department of antiquities at the Ashmolean Museum, Oxford University, and responsible for the Greek collection there. The author of the foreword, John Boardman, you will find, is a well-known name in the world of Greek art, architecture, and archaeology. At this book's publication, Boardman was professor of classical archaeology at Oxford as well as keeper of the cast gallery at the Ashmolean. But don't let the impressive credentials of this team lead you to consider this book too academic: in only 217 pages and five chapters, the authors cover a remarkable amount of history in a brisk but thorough fashion. It is never dull, and this is the perfect book for readers who prefer to read history with illustrations and do not want a larger volume. One of my favorite parts, in the chapter entitled "Gods and Heroes," is the six-page summary of the Trojan War—two pages are devoted to, simply, "Troy: The Facts," followed by four pages of a step-by-step chronology of the war, each step illustrated by a piece of Greek vase painting depicting the scene described. Brilliant.

Inventing Paradise: The Greek Journey, 1937–47, Edmund Keeley, Farrar, Straus, and Giroux, 1999. This unusual book—which is personal memoir, literary criticism, and interpretive narrative all rolled into one—explores the friendship between George Seferis, George Katsimbalis (and other poets and writers from Greece's Generation of the 1930s), Henry Miller, and Lawrence Durrell. If that description seems a little hard to follow, the actual book is not. I seem to be drawn to books that are difficult to describe, and this is one of them, and it's quite intoxicating. Keeley served as director of both the creative writing and the Hellenic studies program at Princeton and has served twice as president of the Modern Greek Studies Association. He is also the noted translator of many modern Greek poets and is the ideal author of this wonderful volume. Keeley concludes that "*The Colossus of Maroussi, Prospero's Cell,* and *Reflections on a Marine Venus*—the first of these in particular—projected an image of Greece that was, however heightened by imaginative rhetoric, very contagious. Many English-speaking travelers in the postwar years—in fact, most subsequent English and American writers—who took the Greek journey, or who wanted to, were drawn there by the country Miller and Durrell had created and by the liberated sensibility they had caused it to project. And those who took the trouble to search out the work of their Greek companions—the poets Katsimbalis promoted, his friend Seferis first of all—discovered further riches that our two early voyagers were among the first to bring to light and celebrate."

A Literary Companion to Travel in Greece, edited by Richard Stoneman, J. Paul Getty Museum, Malibu, California, 1994; previous edition published by Penguin Books, 1984. This book, the author notes, "is the kind of book I would have liked to have had with me when I first visited Greece, a record of sensibility at large in Greek places rather than an account of historical data, which are available in many publications." I very much sympathize with him when he admits, "I have not read everything I might have, and I think a lifetime would not be long enough to do so." Stoneman has organized this anthology by regions, and six chapters are pertinent to this edition of *The Collected Traveler.*

Modern Greece: A Short History, C. M. Woodhouse, Faber and Faber, 1998. Originally published in 1968 as *The Story of Modern Greece,* this work was revised and published in 1977 and has since been revised and reprinted six times. While not for the casual visitor, it's also not dry and has been praised for being both very readable and very informative. Woodhouse himself, who has great affection for Greece, is acclaimed for his balance and insight.

Mythological Atlas of Greece, Pedro Olalla, Road Éditions, Athens, and with the assistance of The Alexander S. Onassis Public Benefit Foundation, 2001. This work, an original approach to Greek mythology through geography and ancient literary sources, is impressive. Pedro Olalla González de la Vega, a Spanish Hellenist from the northern Spanish city of Oviedo, is also a photographer, teacher, and translator. He was professor of modern Greek at the university in Oviedo, has published articles and essays on Greek culture, and for this enormous volume covered 100,000 kilometers traveling all over Greece, tracing the spoor of ancient myths, since 1995. This is the first book in which the geography of Greek mythology is marked accurately on detailed maps. As Olalla notes, it is "designed for journeys, leads us to mountains, rivers and landscapes, which in another age—when man was aware that 'everything is full of gods'—were treated as sacred." I'm not positive, but I don't think there's another book like this one in the universe. With gorgeous photographs and fifty-three maps, this is a volume you'll lose yourself in time and again.

The Olive Grove: Travels in Greece, Katherine Kizilos, Lonely Planet Journeys, 1997. "I did not know," Kizilos writes in the first chapter, "that, even in Athens, the colours of Greece are different, that the mountains are made of white rock and the buildings are marble and white cement and a shining blue sky spans it all. I did not know that the country, magically, was the colour of its flag. I knew nothing." Kizilos has written a book on Greece, to be sure, but she is the daughter of migrants who moved to Australia, so it is also a story of exile and return. For her father, Australia was a place of exile: it was "flat, without history," Kizilos recalls, "its people racist and ignorant. . . . Politically and culturally, Australia was still in the shadow of Britain, a country my father reviled because he believed it had betrayed the Greek Resistance and so had helped to engineer the Greek civil war, the cause of his exile and suffering. He also despised Australia's other wartime ally, the United States, because that great and powerful friend had sold napalm and bombers to the Greek royalists. In Australia the whole bloody mess was dead and obscure: no-one cared, no-one believed him, it didn't matter. He hated the place." For Kizilos it is a story of return, though she didn't land in Greece until she was seventeen, so it was a return for the family rather than for her as an individual. Besides trips to the "borderlands" (Istanbul and Thrace), Kizilos's journeys were all in Athens, the Aegean, and her family's village, Chrysambela, on the Peloponnese. This wonderful, poignant memoir deserves a wide audience.

The Peloponnesian War, Donald Kagan, Viking, 2003. This outstanding work, published to meet the needs of modern readers, is a new account—much smaller!—of Kagan's four-volume *History of the Peloponnesian War,* the leading scholarly work on the subject.

The Penguin Historical Atlas of Ancient Greece, Robert Morkot, Penguin, 1996. This is another volume in that wonderful Penguin historical atlas series. (Note to self: must find *all* volumes in the series—cannot carry on without them.) The text and more than sixty maps cover "Crete, Mycenae, and the Heroic Age"; "Dark Age to Athenian Ascendancy"; "The Persian Rival"; "Perikles to Philip"; and "Alexander and After."

Plutarch's Lives, translated by John Dryden, revised by Arthur Hugh Clough, 2 vols., Modern Library, 2001. Originally written at the beginning of the second century A.D., *Plutarch's Lives* is to Greek and Roman heroes what Vasari's *Lives of the Painters* is to the Italian Renaissance painters. The Dryden translation was published in 1683 and was revised in 1864 by the poet and scholar Arthur Hugh Clough. It's interesting to note, as James Atlas writes in the introduction, that "for a contemporary reader, one of the most notable features of the *Lives* is how closely they resemble our own. Plutarch's evocation of the texture of Greek and Roman life has an utterly familiar feel. The architecture of homes; the contrast between city and country; the rituals of meals; all this information is conveyed with a freshness that makes it seem as if we could be reading about the civic culture of twenty-first-century Rome—or of New York City." But the details of the lives portrayed, he notes, are not very accurate: "It has to be kept in mind that Plutarch was writing at a time when the world itself had yet to be mapped out. To say that his geography was shaky hardly covers the case." Scholarship in Plutarch's day was a "highly impressionable affair," and he himself stated that "my design is not to write Histories, but lives." As Atlas concludes, "The history of biography begins with Plutarch's discovery that men are defined by their most peculiar traits."

The Rise of the Greeks, Michael Grant, Phoenix Press, London, 1987. Grant, a prolific author on ancient Greece and Italy, presents the epoch between 1000 and 494 B.C., a period that he shows was one of the most creative in history. With a sixteen-page black-and-white insert.

Travelers' Tales: Greece, edited by Larry Habegger, Sean O'Reilly, and Brian Alexander, Travelers' Tales, San Francisco, 2000. I hope to meet the team who created this series one day because we seem to share similar ideas about travel. Each edition is a great mix of carefully chosen stories in the form of book excerpts and a few extracts from periodicals, as well as tales that have not been previously published. Among the writers whose work is excerpted in this edition are Paul Theroux, Robert Kaplan, Patricia Storace, Henry Miller, Nicholas Gage, Katherine Kizilos, Rolf Potts, and Don George.

Travelers to an Antique Land: The History and Literature of Travel to Greece, Robert Eisner, University of Michigan Press, 1991. Eisner notes in his prologue that there have been numerous directional calls to travel: the call of the north, of the jungle; to India, to the high Himalayas, to China and Japan, to Patagonia. Eisner's call, and my own, is of the south: "Whenever I look at a map of the Mediterranean, if only in a mind's-eye projection, I seem to see travelers streaming across the ages toward the shores of that inland sea, all of them clutching marbled notebooks of blue- or green-tinted paper (for writing in the glare of a mad-dog noon) in which they hope to record impressions of antique lands in lapidary prose to rival the reflections of their predecessors, whose bound works inspired them in the first place to go, and see, and write, and inspire others. This book describes an intellectual phenomenon and its artistic results—the history and literature of travel to that dry, rock-bound, sea girt, landmass of the imagination known sometimes as Hellas and usually as Greece." Eisner focuses solely on English visitors to Greece because their work has been the most substantial; he does not include women as they unfortunately have written more often about decidedly more exotic locales. Among the writers included are Patrick Leigh Fermor, Lawrence Durrell, William

Makepeace Thackeray, Edward Lear (whom Eisner refers to as "perhaps the finest writer of the century on Greece"), David Urquhart, Lord Byron, and Robert Pashley.

Vanishing Greece, photographs by Clay Perry, introduction by Patrick Leigh Fermor, text by Elizabeth Boleman-Herring, Conran Octopus, London, 1991. This photography book is a favorite of mine precisely because Perry, as he notes in the foreword, noticed that in Greece "something essential is changing. It is these changes, observed over 18 years, that have urged me to record as much as I could of this vanishing world." Included are individual chapters on the Peloponnese, the Aegean islands, and Crete. The photographs are memorable, and the text is excellent.

Who's Who in the Classical World, Oxford University Press, 2000. Distinguished Oxford is known for publishing "the world's most trusted reference books," and this volume is a superb example. In addition to the individual entries—which were written by more than 190 world experts in their subject—there are eight pages of maps and a six-page chronology.

Greek American History

Carved in Stone, Basil Douros, Five and Dot, 1999. Douros's wonderful work, which addresses the Greek diaspora as lived by his immigrant family in America, won seven literary awards in 1999 and 2000.

A Crowded Heart, Nicholas Papandreou, Picador, 1998. In a different vein, this is a memoir of Papandreou leaving California to return with his family to Greece, where his father pursued a career in politics.

Not Even My Name, Thea Halo, Picador, 2001. This heart-wrenching autobiographical tale describes the loss of Halo's home in the Pontic Mountains in Turkey, the 1921 forced march during which most of her family died, her parents' desperate attempt to save her by entrusting her to a family who changed her name and later sold her into marriage to a man three times her age, and her life in America as a young wife and mother. Halo is as remarkable a person as Eleni.

A Place for Us: A Triumphant Coming of Age in America, Nicholas Gage, Houghton Mifflin, 1989. I found this book while browsing the shelves at the Strand bookstore in New York, and as I had already read *Eleni,* I sensed it would be a must-read tale. It is, and I very much hope you will read it. I have admitted in previous books that I have the unfortunate talent of crying easily, not a trait you might expect from someone who used to be a news reporter in print, radio, and television; but I do, and just as when I read *Eleni,* tears poured down my cheeks several times while I was reading this book. Gage relates how, when his father was eighty-one years old and describing the scene into a tape recorder when he met the boat carrying his children, he too cried: "His tearful words of remembrance, our cries of greeting across the water, the murmurs of wonder at the sight of the statue who lifts her lamp beside the golden door—all those sounds are part of the chorus of the millions who entered this harbor seeking a place where they would be safe and free. First they came from northern Europe to settle a raw new nation, then from southern Europe, at the end of the nineteenth century and the beginning of the twentieth, seeking sanctuary from pogroms and famines, dictatorships, death camps and genocide. Entering this place, each uttered the same hymn of thanksgiving in his own tongue. Today that chorus has grown faint in our ears, for the old European immigrants have passed away, taking their memories with them. Their children have forgotten what it means not to be American. The new arrivals, fleeing from Asia, Latin America, and the Middle East, are still trying to find homes and jobs, to learn the language and send their children to school. They have not yet found a voice to tell their tale. . . . The particular calamities, heartaches, and triumphs in these pages are unique to my sisters and me, but our odyssey is as old as the nation: the arduous journey across the bridge that separates an old familiar world from a new and frightening one, to find a place for ourselves on the other side."

ΗΣΑΠ ΑΤΤΙΚΟ ΜΕΤΡΟ
ΟΑΣΑ ΑΤΤΙΚΟ
ΗΣΑΠ ΜΕΤΡΟ
ΟΑΣΑ

Μονή Οσίου Λουκά. Η Ανάσταση, ψηφιδωτό. 11ος αι.
Monastery of Osios Loukas. The Resurrection,
mosaic. 11th c.

Η ΑΝΑΣΤΑΣΙΣ

ΒΥΖΑΝΤΙΝΑ ΜΝΗΜΕΙΑ
BYZANTINE MONUMENTS

BME   132461

Παρακαλείσθε να κρατήσετε το απόκομμα του εισιτηρίου σας
μέχρι την έξοδό σας από το Μουσείο/Χώρο.
You are requested to preserve your ticket until you leave
the Museum/Site.

ΕΙΣΙΤΗΡΙΟ ΕΙΣΟΔΟΥ
ΕΥΡΩ **2** EURO
ENTRANCE TICKET

/3/2003   2   ΓΕΝΙΚΗ ΕΙΣΟΔΟΣ

ΜΟΥΣΕΙΟ ΜΠΕΝΑΚΗ   BENAKI MUSEUM
€ 12,00 ΕΥΡΩ

HELLAS

80
ΕΛΛΗΝΙΚΗ ΔΗΜΟΚΡΑΤΙΑ
1896
1996

Athens

"For Athens alone among her contemporaries is found when tested to be greater than her reputation."

—Pericles

The Secret Lives of Athens

BY PATRICIA STORACE

❧

editor's note

You will no doubt read disparaging comments about Athens. It may be hard to believe, but in a wonderful out-of-print book entitled *The Rulers of the Mediterranean* (Richard Harding Davis, Harper & Brothers, 1894), the author reported that Athens "is a pretty city, with the look of a water-color. The houses are a light yellow, and the shutters a watery green, and the tile roofs a delicate red, and the sky above a blue seldom shown to ordinary mortals, but reserved for the eyes of painters and poets, who have a sort of second sight, and so are always seeing it and using it for a background." A few adjectives you might come across include *sprawling, loud, smoggy, ugly,* and even *not worth your time.* Definitely ignore that last one, and also remember that many cities of the world share the first four. I am an unabashed fan of Athens. It will never be a gorgeous city like Venice, Paris, Florence, or Prague, and it should never be compared with them. But it's loaded with Mediterranean ease, spirit, and style.

This piece is among my favorite ever written about Athens, a city of profound seductions, where legends breathe and the real is ghostly, according to author Patricia Storace. In *Dinner with Persephone,* Storace observes that "Athens is a city that brims with people, but it can often seem like a city no one lives in; it has a haunted quality. All the unseen worlds of the past, classical, medieval, Ottoman (of which there are few reminders left, except in the language, because the Greeks so hate the evidence), surround you, above and beneath. The underworld is always present, the world of the dead. And the jumble of houses—the abandoned nineteenth-century mansions in odd corners, the tiny houses that were built at the turn of the century by villagers for refugees from Asia Minor in the 1920s, now overshadowed by large apartment buildings on either side like grown-ups holding the hands of a child about to cross the street—gives Athens the feeling that everyone here is both himself and his own ghost."

PATRICIA STORACE is the author of a book of poems, *Heredity* (Beacon Press, 1987), and *Dinner with Persephone* (Pantheon, 1996). She is the recipient of a poetry prize from the American Academy of Arts and

Letters and contributes frequently to the *New York Review of Books* and *Condé Nast Traveler,* where this piece first appeared.

A bysmal Athens," the novelist Nikos Kazantzakis called it in 1937, after literary obligations forced him to spend more time than he wanted to in the city. And in certain moods, I agree with him. "You are an Athenian and belong to a city which is the greatest and most famous in the world for its wisdom and strength," wrote Plato in the voice of Socrates in the fifth century B.C. And in certain moods, I agree with him.

Athens may be the most discussed city in Western history, and the voices idolizing and cursing it are as much a part of it as the cigarette-pack-shaped buildings that line it now, or the cascades of jasmine, hibiscus, bougainvillea, and gardenias pouring from the balconies of its banal apartment blocks, continuing the argument between beauty and destruction that is essentially Athenian. This city of marble and poured concrete still inspires passions, both of love and of hate.

Libanius of Antioch, the fourth-century philosopher, sounds almost tearful as he remembers his youthful ambition to study in Athens: "I think that I would have followed Odysseus's example and spurned even marriage with a goddess for a glimpse of the smoke of Athens."

On the other hand, another fourth-century provincial Greek wrote venomously, "May the accursed ship-captain perish who brought me here; Athens has no longer anything sublime except the country's famous names." A contemporary piece of verse asks accusingly, "Athens, daughter of the gods, where is your beauty . . . you drank hemlock along with Socrates." Another contemporary voice contributed to the debate in the 1980s. The novelist Kostas Taktsis wrote in his valedictory essay, "My Grandmother Athena":

"Many people say that, in the way it's degenerated, Athens is the foulest capital city in all the world. I don't know, and I don't care . . . for me it is special. She is the city in which my grandmother was born, lived, and finally died. It is necessary naturally to tell you that in many respects—exactly like Athens—she was a monster, and tortured me much of my childhood and adolescence, but what can I do; in my life, she was the only woman I ever loved."

This sequence of voices evokes a characteristic Athenian sensation, the feeling of being in an echo chamber, the disorientation of living in many worlds at once, in a place where everything that happens for the first time is also a repetition. Athens was, after all, a popular destination for Roman tourists well before the birth of Christ. In 79 B.C. Lucius Cicero remarked to a group of friends as they visited the sites of Athens, "There is no end to it in this city— wherever we walk, we set foot upon some history."

Athens is the city par excellence of the unconscious: it is part of the strange sleight of hand of this place that it is the modern buildings, reinforced against earthquakes, that seem impermanent, the ruins, both ancient and modern, that seem lasting. Here, where Europe ends and where Oedipus is supposed to be buried, there is a natural psychological crossroads. Athens has an uncanny power to draw to itself people who are themselves at crossroads, and to set choices before them. I had seen this effect myself in matters of personal archaeology, since I first visited, having grown up in the American South, which is so haunted by Greece. I left Greek Revival for the real thing. I lived in Athens last year, working on a book about Greece, and saw I was right about its habit of divination. Athens, where so much is underground, tells people their fortunes.

Athens has been a dream for as long as it has been a reality. One of the striking possessions of the Museum of the City of Athens is a set of fifteenth-, sixteenth-, and seventeenth-century engravings of imaginary views of Athens, fantasized as an Italian city and as a German one. It is also, of all cities in the world, the one most dominated by its own dream of itself. No other city I can think of is so uncompromisingly represented by one symbol. The vision of the Parthenon, part reconstruction, part ruin, rules Athens as no monument of Christianity has been able to do. How naïve we have been to accept so unquestioningly the formula that this building represents reason and philosophy—it has held our imaginations because it is as inexhaustible and ambiguous as a dream. No experience of Athens is symmetrical, no impression of it uncomplicatedly romantic or easily consistent.

It is a village and a metropolis, a place where middle-aged women in slippers and garishly flowered robes shuffle unconcernedly onto neighborhood streets, coffee in hand, to send their children off to school, and a place where shipowners' pampered mistresses impulsively dispatch helicopters to islands to bring friends to the city for an afternoon of shopping. Here, even in shabby-genteel buildings, the lobby stairs and floors are marble, as are the kitchen sinks—marble is more common than wood in southern Greece, and Ajax cleaning powder promotes itself through its claims to whiten marble.

At the heart of Athens is the building that generations of architects have considered the most perfectly conceived in the Western world; but the city is also the source of unrivaled kitsch, a kitsch so inventive that it becomes a kind of doppelgänger artistry. Only in Athens would a child be presented with a candle for the Orthodox Easter Saturday service in the shape of a hulking figure dressed in wrestling trunks, his massive wax forearms flexed, his chest labeled with a banner that identifies him as MACHO KING RANDY SAVAGE. The combination bridal and christening stores in every neighborhood (unthinkable for one to be detached from the other) display dresses that look like ruffled plaster casts, every inch stuccoed with lace and spangles, while even the traditional tall wedding candles, some as high as five feet, wear drapery of organdy and ribbons, perhaps to mask modestly the inevitable suggestion that they are votive offerings dedicated to securing extraordinary feats by the groom. And yet next to these bazaars of kitsch masterpieces may well be a store offering some of the abundantly exquisite jewelry in Athens; the surprising number of these stores was explained to me as the result of a point of etiquette, since it would be incorrect for an Athenian man to buy his wife and his mistress jewelry at the same address.

Athens is a city whose coarseness can make New York seem genteel, with Athenian voices at fever pitch even in agreement, and the unrivaled Athenian pushing and shoving carried on with great intensity by deceptively frail-looking old ladies, the mothers and grandmothers who make Sophie Portnoy of *Portnoy's Complaint* seem a rank amateur. And there is the searchlight frankness of Athenian questions and the running commentaries that make the city seem populated by amateur investigative journalists. Perusing the magazines at a kiosk, you feel someone's expert fingers examining the details of your sweater. "Sexy," the stranger says. "How much did you pay for it?" An army barracks housing the soldiers who guard Parliament and the presidential palace is set in one corner of the National Garden, and a pedestrian walking down the busy thoroughfare of Vassilíssis Sofías, or Queen Sofia Avenue, is often startled by the sudden resolution of trees and bushes into the shape of a soldier in camouflage, carrying a huge machine gun. "Ah, I like your earrings," I hear from between the iron railings one summer twilight on my way to a dinner party. This communiqué could only have come from the fierce-looking figure in combat boots on the other side of the fence, whose eyes never stopped scanning the street. The literal-minded might hear that whisper as a breach of discipline, but who could criticize the guard's power of observation, or feel less safe under the protection of a soldier with an appetite for life?

Brusque Athens is also, of course, a city whose elaborate network of courtesies is finer than silk, the Athenian streets a filament of wishes for good luck and health and long life, wishes more ardent and brave in their acknowledgment of the fragilities of the lives they would bless. And Greek courtesy has a fascination like no other. It is not a magnificent construction, a formal garden, like French courtesy, or a social contest following Marquess of Queensberry rules, like British courtesy; there is no stiff upper lip in Greek courtesy, but a volatile fusion of refinement and passion, a tough but breakable ceramic fired at high temperatures. A new baby makes a slow progress down the street in its mother's arms, halted by a series of neighbors and sometimes even passersby calling out, "May it live for you." After the credit card form is signed for the new radio or television set, the transaction doesn't end until the merchant wishes you *"Kaloríziko"*—"May it be well-rooted."

In the shops and restaurants of the Kolonáki quarter, still fashionable despite the current popularity of such suburbs as Kifissiá and Glyfada, distinguished old ladies with fine gold jewelry, lace gloves, and hair arranged in what can only be called coiffures speak a Greek gilded with *katharévousa,* the "purist Greek," with its intricate declensions and vocabulary drawn from ancient Greek, a kind of linguistic museum. Among these ladies it is not accent that is the mark of social finesse but grammatical elegance and nuance. These women brought obligatory dowries to their future husbands, and their bookshelves are lined with the complete works of Jules Verne, Dumas, and Victor Hugo, which they purchase in translation to give to their grandchildren. Athenian toy shops feature the dolls they prefer for their granddaughters, dolls dressed in turn-of-the-century costume. The nineteenth century came late to Greece because of its liberation by degrees from Turkey. When you overhear these women buying their cakes, choosing their letter paper, here in this city of enclaves of time as well as space, you are overhearing the last nineteenth-century Europeans.

Athens is the only place I know where buying a present is also like getting a present; gifts are wrapped with a flourish, and nearly always a small extra gift is tucked into the ribbon—a pretty ceramic rose, a tiny piece of jewelry. Even the slices of chocolate cake in the windows of Athenian pastry shops—open on Sunday morning to sell to the cityful of guests and relatives on their way to a four-hour weekend lunch—come tied with delicate gold cord, or perhaps a fresh rosebud topping each slice. You can be trampled, shoved, and roundly cursed on an Athens rush hour trolley, but when you reach home, battered and hostile, a perfect stranger in your building may knock at your door holding a three-course meal on her best china, wish you "*Kali orexi,*" the Greek *bon appetit,* and disappear.

One of the glories, and annoyances, of Athens is that it is the most personal of cities, a gossip, a busybody, an intimate friend, a lover from whom you have no secrets. During my first month on the shop-lined street named for the sculptor Praxiteles' girlfriend, I struggled to get used to the Athenian view that each life is a drama to which all Athenians have been admitted free of charge. The doorbell rang constantly. A neighboring housewife felt free to drop by at 7:30 A.M., to offer me coffee, look at my posters, and inform me, "By the way, Macedonia is Greek. I hope you realize that," before she began her Monday laundry. I, who was used to working quietly at home, found myself awash in visitors, a flood of people selling books and furniture door to door, asking for donations, advertising, surveying.

"Good afternoon," someone says, thrusting a leaflet into my hand. "Do you know the perfect method for contraception?" Never certain, I hesitated, and the visitor seized her advantage. "Ha, I can see you don't. But here it is on page one hundred eleven of volume three of this excellent medical encyclopedia, simply take a sponge and a fresh lemon . . ."

After a week of buying papers at the local *períptero,* the news kiosk, I am known. "So," asks the proprietor, "how much money do you have to live on while you're here?"

The Athenian telephone system, like Greece, is given to fatalism. A number correctly dialed frequently yields an unexpected conversation; wrong numbers first apologize, then ask you out for coffee. A talk show host concludes a program by sitting down to a real lunch with his guests and toasting the audience from a carafe of white wine. Signs in store windows insist, encourage, scold, and even develop into full-scale personal letters, poster-size. An impeccably chic dress store informs passersby of its vacation dates with a message of barely containable exuberance: "We are not staying here for August! We are not going to the café across the street! We are going to the sea!"

The style of Athens is one of direct, theatrical communication, and most of its problems are introduced in the first act—the *nefos,* the pollution cloud that settles on the city on windless days, the dust that compounds it ("Direct from the Sahara," say Athenians proudly, always sensitive to ancestry), the lawless traffic, the eccentric telephones, the electrical blackouts, the constant lightning strikes of taxi drivers, of farmers, of high school students, of everything but Athenian chatter, which never pauses, the disappearing sidewalks that expose a pedestrian to oncoming traffic. But if the irritations of Athens are immediately apparent, with the daily litanies of *"Ti na kanome, ti na kanome"* ("What can we do, what can we do"), this is also a city with an unmistakable charm—the spicy, herbal smells of Attica, most concentrated in the National Garden;

the oranges and figs that drop straight onto the city pavements from trees overhead; the way the entire city becomes an extended living room after dark, with Athenians strolling, shopping, eating at outdoor restaurants or by candlelight on their balconies overlooking the streets, balconies with an Acropolis view the most prized of all. Night in Athens is not night but another version of day. This city has always been ambitious for immortality, and it is as alive in the dark as it is in its pour of honey-colored light, driven to a divine sleeplessness relieved only by the siesta from three to five in the afternoon, hours during which a telephone call to a private house is a monumental gaffe.

The Parthenon is both a central motive for most visitors to Athens and a barrier beyond which they often will not pass to see the living city that cups it. But the Parthenon itself is only partly visible, although of course hundreds of visitors climb the marble steps every day to see a building that, though a human creation, has acquired the stature of a natural phenomenon, like the Grand Canyon or the Great Barrier Reef, rising above Athens like a man-made moon. It is only partly visible, not because it is literally obscured but because, like the rest of the city, it is not constructed just of marble or limestone or cement but of materials here just as substantial, of time and legend.

The history of the Parthenon, like the history of Athens itself, does not end when the conventional visitor's imagination of it does, with its construction under Pericles in the fifth century B.C. Its incarnations through time reflect with uncanny accuracy the panorama of Western politics and culture.

The visitor standing on the Acropolis often doesn't remember that Athena herself was evicted from the Parthenon when Theodosius II closed all the pagan temples in the Roman Empire with his edict of A.D. 435. The Parthenon, dedicated to the Virgin (*parthena*) Athena, was later converted into a Christian basilica, the temple of a new virgin, the Panayia Atheniotissa, the All Holy Virgin of Athens. A medieval Greek Orthodox bishop distinguished the Virgin Mary from Athena by referring to Athens's previous patroness as the pseudo-Parthena, the imposter Virgin. Masses were held where Athena had been dressed, at the culmination of the Panathenaic Festival, in the sacred gown woven for her by the girls of Athens.

During the schismatic struggle between the Roman and Constantinopolitan churches for domination, the Parthenon was reconsecrated after the Latin conquest as a Roman Catholic cathedral, known as Our Lady of Athens. Several hundred years later, in 1456, it underwent another identity change at the hands of the conquering Turks, who converted it into a mosque. An image rarely associated with the Acropolis is that of the black slaves living on its slopes during the Turkish period, brought over from Ethiopia by the Turks when the Acropolis functioned as a military garrison and the area around it was a largely Turkish village. Hans Christian Andersen recorded on his visit in 1841 that their descendants still lived in the neighborhood.

The Greek freedom fighters during their War of Independence (1821–29) against the Ottoman Empire fought hard battles against the Turks for the possession of the Acropolis; during the Ottoman occupation, Greeks were not allowed to enter it. On a moonlit evening in the fall of 1826, before a skirmish, the great memoirist of the Greek War of Independence, General Makriyannis, sang a song to his soldiers on the Acropolis, a song in which the sun narrates the pain of Greek men and women fighting to re-create their nation to an audience of the moon and the evening and morning stars.

Here, in 1854, another occupying army, made up jointly of French and English soldiers, was given a splendid banquet by the

Greek government. The *Illustrated London News* reported the occasion, accompanying it with an engraving showing the feast amid the ruins, tables set with white cloths in the Parthenon, soldiers in full dress, with sabers strapped to their waists, drinking wine while the drums of columns lay at their feet.

Standing on the Acropolis, Sigmund Freud gained an unexpected insight into his relationship with his father, which became the core of the famous paper "A Disturbance of Memory on the Acropolis." A lame Cole Porter probably managed the ascent partly by mule, partly with the help of Greek sailors from his borrowed yacht, the *Eros*. And the fashionable decorator Elsie de Wolfe, when she saw the Parthenon in the thirties, said jubilantly, "It's beige—my color!"

The Acropolis even has its Romeo and Juliet, in Michael Mimikos and Mary Weber. In 1893 Mary Weber, a German governess at the palace of King George I of Greece, fell in love with a Greek army surgeon who practiced in a military hospital built, with the labyrinthine coincidence of Athenian history, on the old property of General Makriyannis. The lovers met every afternoon on the nearby Acropolis, but in February the doctor abruptly missed their daily rendezvous for three days running. Mary Weber sent Mimikos letters, which went unanswered, and even tried to signal his house by waving her scarf in its direction. She sent him another note, brief and desperate, which read, "Tomorrow at noon, I will go to the Acropolis, and if you don't come, I will kill myself."

The next day, she waited for Mimikos to respond or to meet her himself, and when she knew he would not come, she leaped from the Acropolis to her death. Visiting foreign tourists found her body and helped transport it to the nearby hospital where Mimikos was a staff member. He arrived later the same afternoon, to discover Mary's letters, none of which had been forwarded to him while he was in bed with a fever at home. Mimikos was guided to a medical officer's room where he found Mary laid out for burial, holding violets and dressed like a bride, as is still the Greek custom when unmarried people die. "I swear to you I will follow," he is supposed to have said, and during the night he shot himself. The couple were buried separately, but on the night of the funerals, a group of the doctor's friends entered the cemetery and reburied Mimikos in Mary's grave. Generations of Athenians, with their still-pronounced taste for tragic romance, have commemorated them with poems, novels, and even a movie. "Mimikos and Mary were pure as angels," one poem reads, "and like angels, they fell from heaven."

Morbidity has a kind of glamour for Athenians. Around New Year's time the neighborhood stationery shops that are a fixture of every quarter of Athens are stacked with cheap matchbook-size page-a-day calendars filled with childish jokes, reminders of saint's days, recipes for *kataifi* (a death-dealing dessert of shredded wheat and honey), and doggerel verse promising varieties of eternal love beyond the grave, or asking for it.

The neighborhoods are studded with empty, once-grand neoclassical houses, with padlocked doors and overgrown gardens, their skull-like emptiness emphasized only by a stray cat or two skulking on the doorstep. Whenever I asked about the melancholy conditions of these houses, the explanations led back to the holy trinity of Greek motivation—family, money, government. There was an unresolved inherited struggle for the house on the corner; the family who owned the house on the hill no longer had the money to maintain a structure built on such a lavish scale. In some cases, I was told, when the government has forbidden the demolition of a fine neoclassical house, a family will try to force permission to erect a more profitable high-rise apartment building by letting the house deteriorate beyond repair. Many are said to be haunted, the sounds of sobbing or of parties from other eras issuing from them at night. There is the handsome house of the poet Sofia Laskaridou, in the neighborhood of Kalithea (120 Laskaridou Street), whose rejection of the poet Pericles Giannopoulos drove him to his dramatic suicide in 1900, when he rode naked on a white horse into the sea at the town of Skaramangas. Laskaridou is said to have rejected him out of pure caprice and to have mourned him for the rest of her life, a semirecluse until her death in 1963. In Kalithea, her ghost calls for him in her crumbling house.

This city is strangely haunted by its own present, as well as its past; behind the courtyards and surrounding the bland facades of the high-rises are the stories of modern Athens, a world rendered visible by events and personalities that visitors preoccupied by its classical past cannot see beneath its current camouflage.

Legends are alive here, but the immediate, the real, the daily, are ghostly. The visitors enjoying the shade and perfume of the National Garden are often unaware that it was a project representing in part the poignant ambition of nineteenth-century Athens to regain its stature as a European capital. Athens had been a Turkish village—the paradoxes of history are such that this ancient city became a new capital with none of the accoutrements necessary for a chief city of nineteenth-century Europe. The same visitors eating the grilled corn sold at the garden's entrance are even less likely to be conscious of the ghostly presence of the wounded and dead who lay on these grounds during the savage Greek civil war of 1946–49.

The non-Greek visitors climb the Acropolis, their heads full of images of Pericles but only rarely of the swastika-marked flag the Germans were so eager to raise on this site when they overran Athens in 1941. It is not only the darkness of much modern history that gives the present its disembodied quality here, but the fear of controversy, the habit of secrecy the Greeks learned under their various occupiers, and the bizarre, skewed Athenian sense of time. The past must have reached eternity in order to be dignified as the past; the more recent past simply isn't eternal enough. What will be remembered is what has acquired the status of legend, in the way that we remember Maria Callas costumed as Tosca, but we don't remember her at 61 Patission Street, a student wearing a Greek baptismal cross, learning about passion, betrayal, and courage—the things that would make her Tosca.

It is strange to realize how few familiar associations most visitors bring to modern Athens—visitors to Rome can request a song like "Arrivederci Roma," guests in Paris think of "La Vie en Rose," but who besides an Athenian knows "Athena, kai Pali Athena" ("Athens, Always Athens"), one of the cardinal songs of the Second World War period, part of the endless repertory of songs that are traded back and forth at dinner tables and *tavernas*? Athens is a city that has a second, separate existence in song, and its chameleon quality is traceable in these treasured fragments of air. In the decade between 1940 and 1950, the singer and composer Nikos Gounaris is singing in praise of "Beautiful Athens . . . with its modest girls, without painted lips," while only a short time later, in the 1970s, the city stars in a song as a prostitute who will sell herself for a glass of wine.

The splice between past and present in Rome or Paris is less violent than in Athens—a city that has been made, unmade, and remade throughout the centuries. Even in Plutarch's day, Athens had the reputation of being a city manipulated into existence; he describes the strategy of the ancient kings of Athens for persuading the Athenians to develop a primarily agrarian economy, instead of one based wholly on shipping trade. "It was they who had spread the legend about Athena, how when she and Poseidon were contesting the possession of the country, she produced the sacred olive tree on the Acropolis" and became the city's patron instead of the sea god.

Plutarch's anecdote is early evidence too of the Athenian appetite for rumor, still the ignition key for intellectual and political life in Athens, a city in which the evening's bons mots are rehearsed in the morning, before being launched into the orbit that inevitably brings them back to the speaker in some new version. Through this means I learned one evening on the telephone the glad tidings of my own marriage to a mildly detestable man I hardly knew. A speculation in the morning had metamorphosed into a contract in the evening.

Here is the summary of the sixteenth-century martyr Filothei, whose bones you can visit in their elaborate reliquary in the Metropolis Cathedral, from which her relics are always carried in procession on February 19, the anniversary of her martyrdom, by one of her descendants, members of the influential Benizelos family: "They cannot stand firm, these Athenians. They are a low-class people, good-for-nothing and dishonorable; indeed irresolute, faithless, shameless, abominable, desperate; their mouths always open in mockery and complaint, speaking a barbarous language, eager to blame, loving strife, cavilling, pusillanimous, gossiping, arrogant, lawless, guileful, snooping, eternally on the lookout for the disasters of others."

Athenians adore well-crafted verbal abuse—the Sunday evening reentry into the city from the seaside towns and country houses resounds with cries of "Drive on, masturbator" and threats to a rich variety of mothers. On the grounds of verbal relentlessness alone, Filothei might have been canonized. At any rate, it is amusing to be reminded that the city's most popular church for weddings, booked months in advance, is named for her.

Because it seems to consist only of the sights most important to visitors—the ancient Agora, the Acropolis, Syntagma Square,

Plaka, the marble Olympic Stadium, the temple of Olympian Zeus—Athens may look easily accessible at first glance. But it is in many ways a hidden city, its many vanished pasts alive in turns of phrase, in legends, in gestures, invisible to the uninitiated. As the British philhellene William Miller wrote in 1905, "There is little left to bridge over the chasm of centuries which separates the days of Pericles from those of Otho and his successor. . . . The traces of those intermediate ages must be sought in the manners and customs of the Athenians." This is a city that, after the fierce street-fighting between the Greeks and the Turks in 1827, was left with only sixty houses standing. It became the capital of modern Greece only by default, after Aegina and Nafplio, because of the Bavarian royal family's romantic Hellenism. It was, according to the nineteenth-century analyst of Greek life Edmond About, an archaeological choice, not a political one. "Athens is surely not on the great road of commerce," he wrote, but "Athens is named Athens," and in Greece, legend is a strong legislator.

The Athens we see, with its unplanned sprawl, is in part the aftermath of the upheavals of the 1922 debacle of the Asia Minor campaign, during which the government of Kemal Atatürk came to power in Turkey and the three-thousand-year-old Greek presence in Asia Minor was decisively ended. The entire Greek population of Turkey, with the exception of the inhabitants of Constantinople and western Thrace, poured back into Greece, doubling the population of Athens almost overnight. Athens's first high-rises were built to house the refugees, and one can still sense a refugee quality in the development of the city: the hastily built buildings, driven by considerations of need and profit alone, the insensitive use of land, a style of building extended by the later waves of emigrants from villages and islands, and by the custom of dowering Greek daughters with houses as a prerequisite for marriage, a custom that has not disappeared, although it is rarely referred to formally as dowry, since the practice is officially illegal. The chaotic growth of Athens is only beginning to be corrected through the efforts of such people as the late Antonis Tritsis, a visionary mayor of Athens, and by the current exemplary mayor of the Zoographou section of greater Athens, Fotini Sakellaridou. Tritsis fought to save the Plaka district from degenerating into a street-sex and souvenirs district, and developed a scheme to ban traffic from the center of Athens, a city whose narrow streets are more natural for pedestrians than cars.

A project developed under Tritsis but first conceived during the cultural ministry of Melina Mercouri in the 1980s is at last coming to fruition under the guidance of the brilliant architect Maria Patelarou. Through a complex design making use of overpasses and underground tunnels, the major archaeological sites of Athens will be united by pedestrian malls, free of traffic except for trams and horse-drawn cabs. This plan, so important to the future of Athens that it has survived under a series of ministers from opposing political parties, is scheduled to be completed in 1999, with the assistance of the European Union [it is almost fully complete as of this writing]. The plan will create in the city center an archaeological park, providing at last much-needed greenery, freedom of movement, and a sense of both repose and historical unity that the city's greatest sites deserve. The plan so radically reenvisions clogged, struggling, fragmented central Athens that it amounts to nothing less than a new vision of the city's life.

Athens is a city of neighborhoods, with the still-natural tendency of Greeks to form villagelike enclaves wherever they are, centered around a park or a hill, a view or an idea. Athens is essentially a city formed on the village pattern of clustering around a central *plateia,* or square. In and around the *plateia* are the neighborhood cafés, shops, and newsstands: the *plateia* is the backdrop for children's soccer games, newspaper-reading, pastry-eating, and people-watching. The central inner courtyard of an Athenian apartment building is a kind of feminine version of the *plateia*—if the men sitting at the cafés outdoors keep an eye on the community's public life, the women on the courtyard scrutinize its private life. In the elevator in my building, two women decoded my lingerie and the pattern of grapevines on the sheets hanging on the clothesline outside my apartment. The one with the poodle remarked, "There is a lot of black lace on her laundry line," and added, significantly, "and her lights go out very late. . . ."

Entire apartment buildings often house extended families, who wander in and out of each other's apartments, dandling each other's babies and stirring each other's pots of *stifado,* a beef stew with onions, wine, and cinnamon. A common and charming style of construction in all the city's quarters is a series of houses and gardens built on graduated levels of a hill, forming a kind of suspended cascade of residential gardens, momentarily separate worlds.

Among Athens's famous districts, there are Exarhia and Neapoli, the bohemian quarters, populated, as they were in the nineteenth century, by students, anarchists, the flocks of poets who still inhabit Athens, and the *philologika kafeneia* (literary cafés), where writers, critics, artists, and actors gather to sit over two-hour cups of coffee, 11 A.M. ouzos, and brilliant jokes. These were the neighborhoods of the turn-of-the-century *cantadori,* the bands of singers who would gather under the windows of their girls and serenade them, sometimes making the supreme gesture of cutting the strings of their guitars after the song, to give the music absolutely to the woman. The austere Greek fathers would call down the wrath of the police on the singers, afraid their daughters' reputations would be ruined.

There is, of course, Plaka, the oldest continuously inhabited village on the continent of Europe, settled since prehistoric times, with its unexpected grace of Cycladic Island houses in the Anafiotika quarter, built by settlers from the island of Anafi, a testament to the sheer unpredictability of Athens. There is Thissio, the area of the old Roman Agora, with its famous *House with the Caryatides,* painted by the definitive modern Greek painter Tsarouchis, in a canvas as familiar to Greeks as Edward Hopper's nocturnal coffee shop is to Americans. Thissio is the neighborhood for artists' ateliers, galleries, the distinguished frame shop Leonardo, said to practice its craft according to the aphorism of Tsarouchis (so celebrated for his aphorisms that in Greek they are simply called Tsarouchia) that "the frame is the pimp for the work of art."

The heroic center of anti-Nazi resistance, the leftist working-class neighborhood of Kesariani, with its streets named nostalgically after their towns in Asia Minor by the refugees who settled it, is a popular Sunday refreshment, the urban equivalent of a country outing, as is the monastery of the same name on Mount Hymettus just beyond it, where Athenians picnic, play soccer, and gather the olives the signs strictly forbid them to pick. The slopes of Hymettus were the setting well into the 1920s and 1930s for a *nyfopazaro,* a "bride bazaar," in which eligible young women would be strolled up and down the green paths by their parents, getting together afterward to discuss whose eyes met whose with the most significance. The Kesariani Monastery was such a cherished Athenian expedition that it was nicknamed Seriani—"stroll"—and found a place in a couplet about the three monasteries on the edge of Athens that all Athenians can repeat:

In Seriani, strolling—and in Pendeli—honey
and cold water that angels drink flows in Daphni.

An Athenian year moves to a different rhythm than those of other European cities, and it expresses itself with a different weather. At Christmas, possibly a better time to visit the city than the hot crowded summer, the streets are full of vendors selling gilded fruit, and the fruit-shop and jewelry-shop windows are full of pomegranates, real and jeweled, symbols of good luck in the coming year. The fruit are thrown against the thresholds on New Year's Eve and split open, symbolizing a fruitful year. You look through the glass windows to the bright fruit, the Christmas ornaments in the shape of pomegranates, the silver pomegranates in the jewelry window, half open to show their silver seeds, and realize— Persephone. In January come what are known as the "halcyon days," a mysterious cluster of days of warm, almost summery weather, slipped into the cold, damp Athens winter, days that in antiquity were supposed to have been granted for a princess to bear her child in gentle weather.

At Carnival time, temporary shops appear on street corners, filled with masks and costumes, and the women's magazines are full of hints about the right makeup for Cleopatra, Carmen, or Madonna. The rubber faces of current politicians and figures from the gossip pages hang in the windows too, as they did at the Carnival of 1875, reported by the *Illustrated London News,* when a "rollicking, popular humorist of the town, . . . reeling drunk . . . had put on the classic helmet of the princely Agamemnon, king of Mycenae, making a little fun of Dr. Schliemann's recent discoveries there."

At Easter, the racks of Easter candles in brilliant colors, wrapped with toys or charms of ships—the ship of Athena's festival, which later became a Christian symbol for the soul—appear on the sidewalks of neighborhoods like Pangrati, or along the streets of the handsome Mets quarter. And in summer the city moves out of doors. Tavernas are full at two in the morning with family parties, including young children, eating in gardens and savoring the cool night breezes. Some of the smaller streets are looped from house to house with grapevines that shield the street from the summer sun, and the *laiki agora,* the farmers' markets on the streets, are full of the magnificent Greek cherries, peaches, and melons, while competing vendors praise the perfumes and colors of their fruit with the chant "*Aromata kai chromata.*"

The colors of the seasons are different from the ones we know; New Year's is full of dark blues, glass good-luck charms, antidotes against the evil eye, and silver-wrapped heads of garlic to hang over your front door. The champagne and dancing are imported here; Greek New Year begins with wishes, threats, propitiations.

Easter, unlike Easters farther west, is not pastel but ruby red, the red that is repeated in the eggs that appear in flower arrangements and braided into sweet Easter breads. The feasts of the Church calendar give the progress of the year a medieval quality, with the medieval world's blurring of the secular and the sacred; on June 30 there is an annual celebration of the icon of the Church of the Holy Apostles, the patron saints specially honored by the Association of Used Goods Vendors. Every season in Athens has its panoply of presiding supernatural beings, its angels and mermaids, its ritual foods, its reinterpretation of the coexisting ancient and modern worlds. There is a McDonald's on a choice corner of central Syntagma Square, but in Pangrati a local fast-food takeout offers *pastitsio* (a Greek baked-pasta dish needing hours of preparation), braised okra, peppers, and tomatoes stuffed with rice pilaf, along with demibottles of wine. Fast food here is understood as fast food for the customer but not for the chef.

Athens is a demanding city, one that can be known only through some relationship to it, of instruction, of finding out its family jokes and secrets, of growing up. There is a neighborhood jogging track, one of the few in Athens, that I run on with a friend, T.; on one side of the track the joggers are framed by the Acropolis, on the other by the chapel of St. George on Lycabettus Hill. We swing back and forth, from one to the other, held, like the city, between the pincers of classicism and Christianity. For me, it is distracting to run in the presence of two such starkly contradictory metaphysics, but when I turn to look at T., I am reminded of how different it is to grow up in a place than it is to just live in it. For T., Athens is a place not only of symbols but of life, not just a memory but a fate. As I run, the shock of the Acropolis makes me blind to what T. might see: himself flying kites on Philopappus hill, being taken on the annual school trip to the Parthenon, meeting lovers. To me, these are places; to him, they are relationships.

The Greek poet Cavafy, acknowledged as one of the classic writers of the twentieth century, wrote a letter to a cousin describing his first visit to Athens in 1901: "I went to Athens—as to a Mecca—decided to like it and I kept my word . . . admiring with all the fervor—which is their due—the classical statues and columns; and I dwelt lovingly in the old churches in which I thought of the obscure generations that had there hoped and prayed for the third advent of our race; and was never shocked by the banality of the imitation French 'quartiers' for there too I saw . . . the interesting signs of an enduring people's new tendency. In all this, I assure you I was not activated by patriotism. I simply let myself be guided—as I like to do at times—by Sentiment and Illusion. They are not logical guides, I know. But . . . whoever despises them and exiles them from his life is either very strong or very rash."

I remembered his visit on an April morning walk, on Monday, the beginning of Megali Ebdomada, the Great Week of Easter, the central holiday of the Greek year. I passed stray roses growing in old cans of Mana olive oil, and the inevitable neighborhood religious-supplies store, its windows full of silver-plated icons and tin votive plaques stamped with houses, babies, and clasped hands over the raised script of the message I BEG YOU. The uglier buildings are covered with great swaths of the willing Athenian wisteria and lilac, like unattractive women with perfect jewelry. The grand buildings—like the house of the eccentric Duchesse de Plaisance, the French philhellene who was said to have kept her daughter's mummy preserved in her old room at home—all seem to be undergoing repairs at the same time. A giant delivery truck goes by; painted on its cab is a portrait of the Virgin Mary, whose face is framed with the word *Megalochari,* "great in grace." Between the railings of the National Garden, planted by Queen Amalia as the first queen of independent Greece before she and King Otho were sent back to Bavaria in 1862, a group of seven cats are intently giving themselves synchronized baths. Syntagma Square, once the site of the garden of the philosopher Theophrastus, is almost completely blocked off by subway construction; Athens vanishes even as it speaks to you, a city always in the process of disappearing and persisting. I choose another route for my errand, and as I wait for the traffic light to change, a bus speeds past, the destination lettered above its windshield reading METAMORPHOSIS.

The Living City: Quarters

Never trust your first impressions of Athens, which almost certainly will record chaotic traffic, blaring radios, compressed spaces filled with wildly conflicting styles of architecture and atmosphere, and the fact that Athenians simply do not feel sensations of claustrophobia. The whole city may appear to be suffering jet lag from having arrived too quickly and too unprepared in the twenty-first century.

Athens is a city that contradicts the proverb about familiarity and contempt: the charm of this city comes through familiarity. The way to enjoy Athens is not to visit here for five days, but to live here for five days.

For all its sprawl, Athens was conceived as a small city, and a city of neighborhoods, some so concentrated that they consist of only a street or two and flow almost imperceptibly into one another. If you dedicate time to a variety of the city's neighborhoods, you will experience Athens itself, not just great moments with its monuments.

Your first purchase should be a copy of the English-language *Athenscope* magazine, available at most newspaper kiosks. It is useful not only as a weekly guide to city happenings but as a comprehensive directory of restaurants, museums, and theaters, as well as the kaleidoscopic hours of opening and closing that these establishments keep.

Athens's equivalent of the Ritz Hotel is the **Grande Bretagne** (210.33.30.000; doubles from $350), on Syntagma Square, a favorite of Winston Churchill and visiting rock stars. Other recommended hotels are listed under the neighborhoods you'll find them in. In the original article, Storace recommended a few other hotels, restaurants, and shops than appear here. For this book, I only kept her recommendations if I could verify contact information, and as this piece was written ten years ago, it is inevitable that at least a few places may have closed (Greece being Greece, just because I was unable to confirm all information doesn't mean a particular place is no longer around—readers intent on knowing *all* of Storace's recommendations should look for a copy of the April 1994 issue of *Condé Nast Traveler* at the library or call (800) 777-0700 and inquire if back issues are still available).

Plaka and Monastiráki

Plaka, Athens's old town, and adjoining Monastiráki, the famous flea market quarter, are seductive places to explore. If you want to stay in Plaka, which has the greatest number of charming small hotels, the **Adonis Hotel,** with its pretty roof garden, is a good choice (210.32.49.737). The **Electra Palace** is famous for its swimming pool and views of the Parthenon (210.33.70.000; doubles from $115).

Plaka is rich in museums: From here you can visit the Roman Agora and its museum, an anthology of classical domestic life. The **Museum of Greek Folk Art** includes a magical room entirely covered with dreamlike images of ancient and modern Greek legends, painted by the great modern Greek folk artist Theophilus (17 Kydathinaion; 210.32.29.031). The **Kanellópoulos Museum,** at Theorios and Panos Streets, has fine Byzantine icons and impressive jewelry, and it's air-conditioned, an oasis on a hot summer day (210.32.12.313). The **Greek Popular Musical Instruments Museum,** on Aerides Square, infallibly enchants children (210.32.50.198).

There is good food in Plaka too, and the area is crammed with shops selling both tat and treasures. After you've explored Plaka and strolled through the flea market in Monastiráki, walk back to Metropolis Square for 6 P.M. vespers at the **Metropolis Cathedral,** where the singing is fine. Across the street from the cathedral, the peaceful **Kapnikarea Church,** redecorated by the Byzantine revivalist painter Fotis Condoglou, is a pleasant refuge.

Kendriki Agora (Central Market)

Near Monastiráki and Plaka, this is one of the most delightful and least-touristed neighborhoods for a morning's exploration. Here on Athinás Street and the squares and alleys off it, you will find copper and clay kitchenware, coffee services proclaiming the political party of your choice, herb shops with combinations for everything from sweet dreams to endless love (try **Dafnoula,** on Sofokleos Street), and shops that sell olive oil pressed from the fruit of their own groves.

Here too, in the enclosed meat market of the agora, are three inexpensive *tavernas* that serve the butchers, fishmongers, and truck drivers arriving during the night with meats and produce. These are the places to come to for *stifado* after the theater or a long night of dancing. They open at around 11 every night but Sunday and close in the morning.

Fokionos Negri

A good strategy is to combine a museum visit with a neighborhood meal and a browse. After a tour of the **National Archaeological Museum** (210.82.17.717; closed until June 2004), recover from the barrage of masterpieces over a long lunch at one of the tavernas along Fokionos Negri, a tree-lined plaza nearby. On Tuesday and Thursday, when stores reopen after 5 P.M., there is also amusing shopping. If you want to visit the museum every day, the modest **Hotel Museum,** often frequented by academics, is an option (Best Western; 210.36.05.611; doubles from $60).

Kolonáki

This cosmopolitan district has another good museum-and-frivolity combination. After a morning in the dream-world of the **Museum of Cycladic Art** (4 Neofitou Douka; 210.72.28.321), eat at **Kafeneío** (Loukianou 26; 210.72.37.277; entrées from $12). The Kolonáki area has a lavish hotel, the **St. George Lycabettus** (210.72.90.711; doubles from $175); and the cozy, tasteful **Athenian Inn** (210.72.38.097).

Kolonáki is full of tempting shops, and part of the pleasure of this quarter is in making your own discoveries.

Makriyanni

This residential district, named for a hero of the Greek War of Independence, sits just below the Acropolis. It is particularly convenient if you are here during the summer Athens Festival, whose dance, music, and theater performances take place in one of the world's most beautiful theaters, the marble odeon of Herodes Atticus, built in A.D. 161 by the great benefactor of Roman Athens. The **Hotel Herodion** is convenient to the theater and the Parthenon and is popular with festival performers (923.6832; doubles from $140).

These two residential neighborhoods are naturals to combine with a visit to the marble **Olympic Stadium,** where the first modern games were held, or to the **National Art Gallery,** with its fine collection of modern Greek art (210.72.35.857).

For admirers of Paris's Père Lachaise, Mets is home to one of the most distinctive European cemeteries, the **Proto Nekrotafio.** Here are the painters, tycoons, actresses, writers, and philhellenes whose lives are part of the legend of the modern Greek nation, such as the Nobel Prize–winning poet George Seferis, the pioneering nineteenth-century Greek feminist Kalliroee Parren, the philhellene historian George Finlay, and the American journalist George Polk.

Pangrati is one of the most pleasant districts for walking, with its handsome neoclassical houses and its colorful Arhimidous Street farmers' market on Friday from roughly 8 A.M. to 2 P.M. You can also find pretty clothes and handbags for less than you will pay in Kolonáki—and the best Easter candles in the city in their season.

The grandest hotel of this area is the **Athens Hilton,** known for its beautiful swimming pool (210.72.81.000; doubles from $400). The **Caravel** is a comfortable alternative (210.72.07.000; doubles from $375).

Kesariani

The eleventh-century monastery on Mount Hymettus, and the wildflower-lined trails and paths on the mountain, with their dramatic views of the city and the Saronic Gulf, offer a peaceful interlude rare in Athens. On Sunday morning families come here to stroll and picnic. Your best strategy is to arrange for a taxi to take you to the monastery, and have it wait to bring you down again to the center of the district. Kesariani, a neighborhood that features in a repertoire of Greek songs, retains traces of the mystique of Greek Asia Minor, a scent of close-knit village life, of social life extended onto the streets, and memories of the brightly painted doors and fertile gardens of a lost world. Plan your outing to Mount Hymettus in the morning and wander the streets of this haunting neighborhood.

Miscellany

The most daunting and frustrating prospect for visitors is the dreadful taxi system, in which drivers choose their own destinations; you are often unable to simply flag a taxi but must shout out the neighborhood you want, a method that is inefficient, not to mention traumatizing for the discreet, the shy, and anyone sensitive to rejection. In theory, an unoccupied cab is supposed to take you where you want to go, but . . . One possible solution is to make an arrangement with an individual driver to pick you up in the afternoon at a prearranged meeting place. Or ask your concierge for help.

Remember that dinners are late here; at 9 P.M. you will open the restaurant, which won't be fully alive until 11. Fortify yourself accordingly between 4 and 10.

A place often overlooked for gift items is the supermarket. Here you can buy Greek quince marmalade; the excellent Ion chocolate bars; Greek pasta such as *trahana,* mixed with yogurt and flour; and noodles made especially for pastitsio. You can also stock up on the ambrosial Greek fruit juices—two of the best brand names are Refresh and Life.

Classic Performance

Opera and theater buffs who are not intimidated by seeing a work in another language will relish a world of often-superb theatrical experiences. The trick is to choose a performance of a classic or a play you already know in your own language. One fine company near Plaka is **Embros** (2 Riga Palamidi, Agion Anargyron Square,

Psiri; 210.32.38.990), whose productions are mounted in an atmospheric old printing factory. Other names to look for: the brilliant Anna Kokkinou, who can play anything from a country grandfather to a green plant; Katia Dandoulaki, who even on an off night is a master class in elegance and wears jewelry better than any other actress alive; and the director Spiros Evangelatos, whose productions are always events here. You may also want to check with your hotel concierge, or with *Athenscope,* to see what's playing at the **Megaron Mousikis,** or Athens Concert Hall, recently completed and impeccably planned (89 Vassilíssis Sofías; 210.72.82.333), where a range of concerts take place, except in July and August, when everyone wants to hear music under the stars.

Athens (Look Closer)

BY ALAN BROWN

editor's note

You may not expect Athens to have one of the hottest nightlife scenes in all of Europe. As Patricia Storace notes in *Dinner with Persephone,* "the Greeks have made going to nightclubs a national art, a form of collective lovemaking, and one of the signals of enjoyment in their movies is the nightclub scene, with singing and dancing, and a table littered with bottles, glasses, fruit, and dancers. You go in search of *kefi,* of joyous abandonment." In this piece the author reveals an entirely other side to Athens, in its chic cafés, hip nightclubs, and less-touristed neighborhoods—all in the languid pace of Athenian time.

ALAN BROWN is a contributing editor at *Travel + Leisure,* where this piece first appeared. He writes frequently about Mediterranean destinations, and his work previously appeared in the *Southwest France* edition of *The Collected Traveler.*

There are thousands of squares in Athens, but when you say, 'Meet me in the square,' everyone knows you mean Kolonáki," says the Greek actor Antonis Fragakis, gesturing out from our marble-topped table in front of the Bibliothèque Café. It's dusk, and the fountain is lit. Across the square, above another café and behind a wall of plate glass, a row of svelte women on StairMasters huff and puff and survey the scene. All the tables at all the cafés on Kolonáki Square are occupied by unbearably fashionable people in chic (and very tight) clothes and designer sunglasses, cellular phones and cigarette packs set out next to their drinks, Armani and Versace shopping bags laid at their well-shod feet. In my Gap khakis and Converse sneakers, I feel seriously underdressed.

I first met Antonis in Manhattan, where he had moved to pursue his film and TV career after achieving celebrity in his native Athens. One Saturday in New York, over lunch following our yoga class, Antonis convinced me that, although I'd visited Athens, I'd never really *seen* it—not as I could with him as a guide. "People rush through Athens on their way to the islands," he said, "and take in nothing but the Acropolis." Antonis recited the words of a shepherd he'd encountered while lost in the mountains: "A foreigner and a blind man are the same. They don't see what's in front of them." And it's true—Athens has gotten a bad rap among travelers, for its traffic jams, overcrowded tourist sites, and seasonal air pollution. But there is another side to Athens, and those who focus only on the city's glorious past, Antonis says, are missing its seductive present: its sensual dry heat and sea light; its blue sky and bright flowers; the icy drinks, garlicky dips, and tangy cheeses served in cafés; the splashes of green and, everywhere, a citrusy smell; the startling hills that jut up heroically in the center of town.

So I booked my flight. What would *you* have done?

Kolonáki

Tumbling down the slopes of Lycabettus Hill in the center of Athens, Kolonáki's narrow, winding streets are lined with shops and restaurants. An aristocratic neighborhood since the nineteenth century, it reached the height of chic in the 1970s. Then, as other areas farther from the center blossomed, Kolonáki surrendered some of its status. "Too many people from outside now, a singles scene," sniffs Antonis, gazing out at the crowd from our café perch. Still, the modeling agencies and photographers remain, as does the prime minister, whose residence is just up the block.

Hilly Kolonáki is ideal for walking, shady and breezy even on hot days, and at once relaxing and lively. During the many afternoons we spend wandering the neighborhood, I never tire of looking up at the apartment buildings, their terraces dripping greenery; at the come-hither shop window displays (I didn't buy); at the actual oranges hanging from the trees; and at the Greeks enjoying life as only Mediterranean peoples do, talking for hours with good-looking friends and lounging about over cool drinks as if it were their birthright. *Oh, what we Americans miss,* I think.

On our third day in town Antonis takes me for lunch at Kafeneío, on Loukianou Street, where we sit at outdoor tables balanced on the steep hill. The angle of the wine in my glass makes me think I'm on a sinking ship. Kafeneío opened in the 1980s, during a Greek-retro craze, so it's designed to look like a traditional *kafeneion* (café). Real *kafeneia* tend not to welcome women, but here the tables are occupied mostly by well-tailored ladies who lunch, all sporting astonishingly severe, armorlike sunglasses.

"Once every village had a café like this," Antonis says. "The men gathered to drink ouzo, play backgammon, and argue politics. Every Greek is passionate about politics. 'If I were prime minister . . .' is probably the favorite line here."

Traditional *kafeneia* also don't serve meals, but we dine well on fava beans puréed with olive oil and garnished with green onions, and flaky spinach pie. Under our private orange tree, the breeze is dry and cool. I try to remember the last time I dined indoors (what an absurd notion). The hours pass. I am feeling very Greek.

Psiri

"We're at the beginning of the *vroom*," Antonis is telling me. "First came the small theater companies, then the artists, then the restaurants. In a decade this area will be ten times what Kolonáki is."

It is early afternoon, and of course we're sitting outside at a café. ("Now you see why Greece produced so many philosophers," Antonis says with a laugh. "In the old days, the men had slaves to do all the work, so they could sit around and think and talk all day.") We're sipping frappés—a concoction made with Nescafé, ice, and sugar—in the heart of Psiri, which Antonis predicts will soon be the SoHo of Athens. Yet as I look around, I see only faded buildings baking in the midday sun: small manufacturers; shops selling wholesale furniture, lamps, tools, fabric, motorcycle parts. One dimly lit shop repairs old gramophones, another deals only in metal wheels. I see no evidence of an artistic renaissance or of anything remotely fashionable, other than an occasional neoclassical facade in need of paint. And the streets are as dusty and deserted as the one in *High Noon* before the gunfight.

So I am dubious as we drink our frappés and eat our rich Greek yogurt and honey ("the best in the world," Antonis says). And I'm just as dubious when he leads me through the neighborhood to Psiri's meat and fish markets. On Euripídes Street, we peek into a dark cellar filled with freshly cut garlic bound into huge bouquets. An elderly man with a gleaming gold tooth slices through a green stem and hands it to me to smell. It's as thick as my thumb and oozing juice. "You work here, you breathe the garlic, it keeps you healthy," he tells us—although his wife sits chain-smoking as she works.

I am hot and very skeptical. "Just wait for the night," Antonis promises. "What's open now will be closed, and what's closed will be open."

That night we return to Psiri, and I hardly recognize it. It's as if one movie set has been struck and another constructed in its place. It's past midnight, and light and music and people are spilling out of cafés and into the streets. Antonis's friend Angelos, who owns a PR firm in town, takes us to Frourakhio, a huge multilevel restaurant housed in a former army barracks and onetime Communist Party headquarters. Staircases lead everywhere. It reminds me of an Escher print.

After much table-hopping and cheek-kissing, we sit down to eat in the central patio—sea bass from the Aegean, luscious mussels—while Antonis and Angelos hold court. Everyone here seems to know them, and as people and bottles of wine come and go, the conversation veers wildly from the architecture of the Parthenon to Cocteau to the historical Count Dracula. Back in New York, I'd been impressed by Antonis's erudition—he seemed to have an opinion on any topic. Now I see that this is a national trait: the Greeks are consummate conversationalists, delighting in their own verbosity.

Galaxídi

When Athenians want to escape the city, they don't necessarily go to the islands. Instead, Antonis suggests a tour of the ruins at Delphi and then a night in Galaxídi, a chic weekend retreat for the Kolonáki crowd, 125 miles from Athens on the Gulf of Corinth.

By the time we get started it's midafternoon on Saturday. With Angelos happily ensconced in the backseat with a pile of magazines, we drive northeast out of town, stopping to see Antonis's parents in the fashionable suburb of Kifissiá, where the old guard relocated when they fled Kolonáki in the 1970s and 1980s. Of course we're running too late to get into Delphi, but the drive is beautiful. We pass through stands of orange trees, willows, and eucalyptus, with Mount Parnassus always ahead of us.

Galaxídi is a fishing village on a quiet bay. Along the line of quayside restaurants and bars, I see the same well-heeled Athenians I saw in Kolonáki, with the same cell phones, but skimpier fashions. Despite their presence, Galaxídi is tranquil, offering nothing but long walks along the bay, beautiful mountain views, turquoise coves for swimming, and of course, cafés.

Past midnight, the music in the waterside bars grows louder and the patrons more boisterous. But we avoid what little scene there is by staying a few blocks away at an enchanting inn, the Ganimede Hotel, a nineteenth-century ship captain's house with a handful of simple rooms. It's owned by Brunello Perocco, an Italian who insists that, after thirty-one years here, he is "more Greek than the Greeks."

The Ganimede's greatest attraction, besides Bruno's hospitality, is an extravagant garden bursting with bougainvillea, roses, geraniums, flowering pomegranate, passion fruit, water lilies, olive trees, and the largest jasmine vine I have ever seen. It is here, the next morning, that Bruno serves an equally extravagant breakfast: eggs, cold cuts, cheeses, and whipped chickpeas; sun-dried-tomato rolls, lemon curd, and pound cake; an array of his own marmalades and chutneys; coffee and fresh juice. All this I must devour by myself, since my friends are still asleep. It's almost noon.

Gazi

If Psiri is newly hip, then nearby Gazi is on the verge. The physical heart of this Athens neighborhood is the former public gasworks, a sprawling, architecturally arresting building that's being transformed into a cultural center. Devoid of traffic and commerce at night, Gazi is dark, almost spooky. But galleries and theaters are opening up, and the actress-singer Irene Papas has founded an acting school here. There's a real buzz in Gazi, which you feel most at Mamacas, the hottest restaurant I visited all week.

Mamacas is edgy, but with a dreamlike atmosphere. At night the pistachio-colored neoclassical villa seems to float in the darkness, its tall windows thrown open, its tables spilling onto the sidewalk. Across the street a half-dozen more tables are placed at the edge of a leafy park, and the waiters—in crew cuts, T-shirts, and jeans— hustle back and forth, hoisting plates of Greek comfort food: *paximadia dakos,* a dark, chewy round of bread topped with olive oil, chopped tomatoes, olives, and feta; and *soutzoukakia,* herbed meatballs in tomato sauce.

A bright half-moon is shining above Mamacas when we arrive at eleven o'clock. The crowd is much artier and more relaxed than in Kolonáki. We're seated outside, underneath a French window, out of which the pretty blond hostess leans to talk to her friends at the table beside us. One is a young Bette Midler double with cropped blond hair, a skintight Harley-Davidson T-shirt, multiple earrings, and a lavishly tattooed arm. Everyone includes us in the conversation (switching between Greek and English for my benefit), and Bette buys us a bottle of credible Greek champagne. A Philippe Starck–designed silver-and-orange Aprilia motorcycle roars up, and a woman in a blue vinyl jacket and a tight mini jumps off. Someone turns up the jazz really loud, and the hostess brings us all sweet glasses of Visanto. Soon we're having a party.

Avenue of Poseidon

At the end of each summer workday, Athenians flee the city center for the nearby seaside, where their favorite clubs and restaurants set up warm-weather outposts in June. Late one night I find myself with Antonis and Angelos, speeding along Poseidornos (the Avenue of Poseidon), a road that stretches from Piraeus to Cape Sounion, site of the Temple of Poseidon. "The world's most historic coastline, traveled since thousands of years before Christ," Antonis tells me proudly. Tonight, though, this historic road is lined with rocking clubs.

We pull into Privilege, a branch of a trendy Athens nightspot. While space in the city center is at a premium, this place by the beach sprawls. Men with slicked-back hair and snazzy suits, and women in tight dresses and spiky heels, swarm across a football field–sized parking lot toward the glowing entrance. We join the crowd, passing a phalanx of white-suited bouncers, and enter— although *enter* implies an inside, and the arena-sized club is roofless, at the edge of the floodlit sea. To the left is a huge bar and dance floor; to the right, on a raised platform, is the restaurant, where waiters dressed like navy captains cruise between tables, pouring goblets of wine for cigar-smoking businessmen and their heavily accessorized dates. Everything is big, bright, and expensive-looking. It's Hollywood, it's Vegas—and it's midnight on a Tuesday.

Kesariani Hill

By my last evening I am totally exhausted. These past few days we've squeezed in some sightseeing: the Acropolis and the ancient Kerameikou Cemetery, the archaeology museum. But Antonis insists on one last excursion: a drive up Kesariani Hill for a view of the city. Even with traffic we're out of town in less than fifteen minutes, up in the hills amid a cool and breezy landscape lush with cypress trees and olive groves. My guide parks the car and leads me along a path past the ruins of a ninth-century church, its crumbling brickwork embedded with marble columns from ancient temples. And suddenly there it is: mountains receding in waves behind us, distant islands in front of us, and Athens—just as he'd described it over that fateful, postyoga lunch back in New York—flowing down to the sea like a river.

"You know, they're digging up all the streets down there for the new subway system," Antonis says. "But the problem is, every time you start digging in Athens, you find the old Athens underneath. You hit a statue or some ruins, and then you have to stop digging. It's the law." Overwhelmed by emotion—he's returning to New York tomorrow too—Antonis seems to be talking to himself. The past is a constant and powerful presence in the lives of today's Athenians, as I've come to realize during my week with Antonis. But Athens today is where they live—and what a vibrant city it is. Not just a jumping-off point but a fashionable destination in its own right. I never missed the islands during my week here. In fact, I never gave them a thought. Spring and fall are the best times to visit Athens—the days are warm, nights are cool, and the air quality is good. Currently there are three subway lines, with extensions in the works, which have improved traffic congestion and pollution.

Hotels

Andromeda Athens Hotel, *22 Timoleóntos Vassou; 643.7302; fax: 646.6361; doubles from about $300.* Stylish and luxurious boutique hotel on a quiet street near the American embassy, with a bar and restaurant.

Athenian Inn, *22 Haritos; 723.8097; fax: 724.2268; doubles from about $90.* A small, unadorned hotel in the heart of Kolonáki. The 28 rooms are simple yet comfortable, and breakfast is included.

Hilton Athens, *46 Vassilíssis Sofías Avenue; 728.1000; fax: 728.1111; doubles from $335.* Within walking distance of Kolonáki, it's well located and notable for its outdoor pool. Ask for a room facing the Acropolis.

Ganimede Hotel, *21 Gourgouris, Galaxídi; 265.41328; fax: 265.42160; doubles from about $43.*

Restaurants and Clubs

Kafeneío, *26 Loukianou; 722.9056; dinner for two about $35.*

Frourakhio, *6 Agion Anargyron; 321.5156; dinner for two $58.*

Mamacas, *41 Persefonis; 346.4984; dinner for two about $35.*

Privilege, *Poseidornos; no phone; also at 130 Pireós, 347.7388; dinner for two $145.*

Thalassinos, *36A Tsakalof; 361.4695; dinner for two about $58.* An excellent seafood restaurant on the upper floor of a stout neoclassical mansion in Kolonáki.

Aristeridexia, *3 Andronikou; 342.2606; dinner for two about $69.* Lively and modern, with an outstanding wine cellar and nouvelle Greek cuisine.

Diros, *10 Xenofóndos; 323.2292; dinner for two about $26.* So old-fashioned it's practically retro-chic, serving excellent traditional Greek food. Off Syntagma Square.

Strofi Taverna, *25 Rovertou Gkalli; 921.4130; dinner for two about $29.* A favorite of actors and dancers. Get a table on the roof for a view of the Acropolis.

Maritza, *Galaxídi; 265.41059; dinner for two about $29.* A casual restaurant with outdoor dining on the quay.

Liotrivi, *Galaxídi; 265.41781; dinner for two about $29.* The name means "olive press," and this atmospheric waterfront tavern has two giant ones on display, plus a wonderful view of the water and mountains. A good place to watch the sunset.

Parthenis, *20 Dimokritous; 363.3158.* Black, white, and beige fashions from the Greek designer of the same name.

Magia, *18 Haritos; 723.4572.* A wittily designed shop in Kolonáki that sells whimsical jewelry and clothes.

Martinos, *50 Pandrossou; 321.3110.* Four floors of fine antiques, ceramics, furniture, carpets, art, and jewelry in a building that's more than a century old.

Athens for the Gourmet Traveler

BY AGLAIA KREMEZI

editor's note

    The following two pieces detail two food lovers' walking tours through Athens. I decided to include both of them because they include different food shops and restaurants (only four are mentioned in both) and because, as with any good walking tour, one passes by a lot more than foodstuffs en route. So here are two great itineraries that will make you feel like a native.

    AGLAIA KREMEZI is the author of *The Foods of Greece* (Stewart, Tabori and Chang, 1993) and *The Foods of the Greek Islands: Cooking and Culture at the Crossroads of the Mediterranean* (Houghton Mifflin, 2000), among others. She lives in Athens and on the island of Kéa and contributed this piece to the British magazine *Food and Travel.*

My neighborhood is hell during the summer months. I happen to live right across from the Acropolis in Athens, and although I have a marvelous view, the noise and pollution from cars, buses, and flocks of tourists get even worse during the evenings, as both Athenians and foreigners come in droves for the popular performances at the ancient Herodes Atticus Theater. Living in the hub of things does, though, have a big advantage: a scenic fifteen-minute walk from my flat takes me to the central food market. With foodstuffs of all kinds readily available at good prices, along with a large variety of other products, traditional and modern, Athens's market is one of the last parts of the city to retains its original character; it's a joy to walk about it.

A short walk from the Agora—Athens's ancient marketplace and general meeting place for all and sundry (except women, who were banned back then)—through the narrow streets of Monastiráki, filled with kitschy "Greek arts" stores, brings you to the modern agora (all genders welcome). The triangle enclosed by the streets of Athinás, Evripidou, and Sophokleous is the core of the market, and although many stores and stalls have undergone serious renovation in recent years, the market retains its Eastern feeling. Whole slaughtered animals and cuts of meat hang unprotected in the corridors of the vast hall; elsewhere the aroma of oregano and other dried herbs sold by vendors at every corner intermingles with the briny smell of the seafood of all kinds and shapes laid out on the marble counters of the fish market. Walking down Evripidou Street, you detect the scent of cumin, cinnamon, and other spices, often mixed with sweet, intoxicating wafts of incense, also sold at spice shops. It is the smell you often notice when passing by the entrance to one of the many small churches that are scattered in the area, harmoniously coexisting with the cheap, seedy red-light hotels. At Elixir, one of the most interesting spice and herb shops, Perikles Koniaris will help you choose the herb mixture you need, from a myriad of dried aromatic Greek plants. The only thing Athens's central market is not particularly strong on is vegetables and fruits—despite the fact that seasonal vegetables and greens are key ingredients of every Greek meal. But thanks to the almost year-round growing season enjoyed by this area of Greece, touring farmers' markets appear once a week in every Athenian neighborhood, so everyone can choose the freshest seasonal produce. Two of the best are the farmers' market near the Acropolis, which takes place every Friday, and the huge Saturday market of Neos Kosmos, behind the Intercontinental Hotel.

The intermingled smells of cheese and salt cod, and especially the tangy scent of olives (much more enticing as an olfactory experience than it sounds), will guide you to my favourite taverna, Diporto, on the corner of Sokratous and Theatrou Streets, right in the heart of the market. At street level the now-closed shop offered the the most spectacular selection of olives. A somewhat smaller selection can be found across the street. Wooden and plastic vats hold about twenty different kinds of green, black, purple, small, large, and medium-sized olives, as well as pickled vegetables, capers, and brined grape leaves. Diporto, in the basement, has no sign, but everybody knows that it is one of the very last remaining authentic places in the city. An entire wall of the taverna is lined with barrels filled with retsina, and many of the patrons—people working in and around the market—come here just to share a carafe of the house wine during their lunch break. The rest of the clientele—a mixture of artists, yuppies, and food lovers—come for the delicious simple dishes that Mitsos, the owner and cook, prepares each day using the freshest seasonal ingredients from the market. Thick lemony chickpea soup, stewed potatoes with celery and carrots, with or without pieces of succulent veal, grilled sardines or small mackerel scented with dried oregano and savory, a salad of steamed wild greens or tender, thinly shredded cabbage, dressed with lemon and fruity extra-virgin olive oil. There are only a few tables, but such is the demand for the food that people are more than happy to share. This enforced communality has been known to produce somewhat unexpected outcomes: late afternoons are quite often known to erupt into bouts of spontaneous singing and dancing. (Lunch here costs about 15 euros.)

Stoa Athanaton, a taverna right above the meat market, offers musical entertainment of a more formalized nature. A faithful crowd of traveling salesmen, blue-collar workers, office clerks, and music lovers is attracted not just by the desire to quench its collective thirst on ouzo but also by the live performances at 3:30 P.M. every day of *rembétika.* Hugely popular in the 1930s and 1950s, *rembétika* is possibly best defined as the Greek answer to Portuguese fado or American blues—but it sounds like neither. It began as the music of the urban underclasses, and the lyrics are heavily laced with tales of life's hardships—and the drugs needed to cope with them. (About 5 euros for ouzo or other drinks.)

Those with a sugar craving to satisfy should seek out the traditional patisseries and bakeries. **Krinos** is an old Athenian institution, where light and crunchy *loukoumadhes* (dough puffs) are fried before your eyes and served piping hot doused with honey syrup and sprinkled with cinnamon. For more elaborate sweet-toothed satisfaction, there is the **Agapitos** patisserie, the outlet of a well-known Thessaloníki firm that brings to Athens the famous *trigona* (crunchy phyllo triangles stuffed with thick buffalo milk cream) and many other wonderful Oriental sweets. One block away **Aristokratikon** makes excellent pear-shaped almond cookies scented with rose or orange-blossom water.

Across from Agapitos is another of the city's institutions, **Ariston,** the place where three generations of Athenians (I used to come here with my mother) have stopped for *tyropita* (cheese pie) when shopping in downtown Athens. My favorite is the unusual, half-circle-shaped *kourou* (with a thick biscuitlike crust) made at Ariston. *Tyropita* and spanakopita (spinach pie, with or without cheese) are Greeks' favorite street foods. Bakeries at every corner have their own versions. Most flavorful is the *horiátiki pita* (country pie) wrapped in thick olive oil phyllo pastry and baked in large pans. Pieces are cut and sold individually at most bakeries.

Not altogether unsurprisingly, there is a plentiful supply of restaurants that advertise as their main attraction a good view of the Acropolis (and no matter how many times you've been to Athens, the magnificence of this sight remains undiminished). While the food at **Strofi,** my neighborhood taverna, is fine, it's not exceptional—what is, though, is its roof terrace. On warmer nights you can dine up here while admiring the breathtaking vision of the Acropolis in changing colored lights during the "sound and light" sessions (about 24 euros). For diners of a more sophisticated bent, there's sophisticated **Symposio,** on Erechthiou, a side street across from the ancient theater. Symposio is a nice restaurant in a turn-of-the-century house. The dining room has a glass-covered patio that extends into the garden. In summer, the tables are set al fresco, under the palm trees (about 45 euros).

Following the restoration of Plaka, town planners turned their attention to the old neighborhoods of Thission, Psiri, and Gazi and changed them completely. In Thiseio the multitude of bars, coffee shops, and clubs at Herakleidon Street are the most popular meeting points for young Athenians. On sunny days you can enjoy a frappé (ice-cold foamy instant coffee) sitting at a pavement table, as the locals do. Psiri, the area southwest of the central market, once a working-class neighborhood, had declined sharply and housed small workshops and warehouses in dilapidated buildings. Now every house is either a restaurant or a bar, and the narrow streets are pedestrianized, which makes it ideal for a fun stroll late on a

Sunday afternoon, when most places have live music and the neighborhood is full of life.

Athens does not have much in the way of a restaurant tradition, and as is so often the case, the best food was always enjoyed in homes. You will often find wonderful foods in humble downtown tavernas, while many of the much-praised, expensive Athenian restaurants may disappoint. But things may be changing. Some young, talented chefs have started to leave behind mediocre imitations of French and northern Italian cooking to create dishes based on the foods of their mothers and grandmothers. Urban Greeks have finally begun to appreciate their rich regional culinary tradition, a trend possibly inspired by seeing what expatriate Greeks have achieved in restaurants like London's Real Greek and New York's Molyvos, Periyali, and Milos.

Funky **Kitrino Podilato** (Yellow Bicycle) is a good place for dinner. It is the most interesting of the upscale restaurants that sprang up around Gazi, the restored gasworks factory. French-trained chef Yannis Baxevanis—who works at a resort hotel in Crete during the summer—has been heavily influenced by traditional Cretan cooking. He uses various seasonal wild greens to create fragrant raw salads, which he also wraps around slices of smoked salmon, dressing them with a brilliant orange vinaigrette. He also uses greens in his homemade pasta sauces or combines them with meat and poultry. Although some of his creations may sound a bit strange, like the spring lamb with figs, sour cream, honey, orange peel, and foamy coffee sauce, the resulting dishes are usually well balanced. His desserts are excellent, especially his orange-cream millefeuille with fresh mint leaves (about 50–60 euros).

The most memorable food in Athens, though, is not in Athens at all but in Piraeus, a twenty-minute drive away. Lefteris Lazarou, the most creative Greek chef, has not chosen to move his successful **Varoulko** to one of the fashionable, newly restored neighborhoods of Athens. Lazarou started Varoulko in 1987, bringing a breath of fresh air to the stale landscape of Athenian restaurants. He specializes in fish and seafood, ingeniously combining few fresh seasonal ingredients of excellent quality to create dishes with clear layered tastes, inspired by the Greek and Mediterranean tradition. Varoulko has no written menu, and while the chef's signature starter of sautéed calamari curls in pesto sauce served over crispy potato matchsticks is usually available, he tends to create different *mezéthes* and main courses each evening using the freshest fish and seafood. His fried monkfish liver in sweet and sour sauce is unbelievable, and so is the day's fish carpaccio, which he simply dresses with lemon and ground pepper. If available, try the delicate cockles with Muscat wine, garlic, and parsley, or the cuttlefish with green beans in garlic, wine, and tomato sauce. The beer and rosemary steamed mussels with lentil and green fava salad is another dish I love. I will never forget the tiny piece of orange caramelized octopus he once served me in a shot glass, or a creamy but light sea urchin soup. Whatever dishes you happen to try, dining at Varoulko is always an exhilarating experience (50–60 euros).

The move toward creativity in Greek cooking may not be a hurried process, but the signs are positive. Perhaps come the 2004 Summer Olympic Games, Athens's chefs may be challenging the rest of the world's restaurateuring Olympiads to look to their laurels.

Restaurants and Food Stores

Agapitos, 7 Voulis Street; 32.58.110

Aristokratikon, 9 Karagiorgi Servias Street; 32.20.546

Ariston, 10, Voulis Street; 32.27.626

Diporto, Sokratous and Theatrou Streets; 321.1463; lunch only

Elixir, 41 Evripidou Street; 32.15.141

Kitrino Podilato, Iera Odos and 116 Kerameikou Streets; 346.58.30); dinner only

Krinos, 87 Eolou Street; 321.68.52

Stoa Athanaton, 19 Sophokleous Street; 32.14.362; late afternoon and evening

Strofi, 25 Rovertou Gkalli Street; 921.41.30; dinner only

Symposio, 46 Erechthiou Street; 922.53.21; dinner only

Varoulko, 14 Deligiorgi Street; Piraeus 411.20.43; dinner only

Additional Restaurants

To Ouzadiko, 25–29 Karneadou Street; 729.5484. Interesting *mezéthes* at the small, always-packed meeting place of the Athenian in crowd. Lunch and dinner, about 15 euros.

Cellier Le Bistrot, 10 Panepistimiou Avenue; 363.8525. International and Greek dishes with many Greek wines by the glass. Lunch and dinner, about 32 euros.

Kafeneio, 26 Loukianou Street; 722.9056. Homey Greek foods in a retro atmosphere. Lunch and dinner, about 15 euros.

Votanikos, 34–36 Kastorias Street, Gazi; 348.000. In Athinais, a restored factory, which also houses a museum, cinema, music hall, conference room, and gift shop. Lunch and dinner, about 26 euros.

Margaro, 126 Hatzikyriakou Street; Piraeus; 451.4226. Excellent fried shrimp and red mullet. Lunch and dinner, about 21 euros.

Greek Soul

BY DIANE KOCHILAS

∾

DIANE KOCHILAS is the author of *The Glorious Foods of Greece: Traditional Recipes from the Islands, Cities, and Villages* (2001) and *Meze: Small Plates to Savor and Share from the Mediterranean Table* (2003), both published by William Morrow. She is chef-owner of Villa Thanassi, a country restaurant with its own kitchen garden, which she runs with her husband, Vassilis Stenos, on the island of Ikaria. Kochilas also operates The Glorious Greek Kitchen Cooking School and organizes culinary trips and walking tours in Athens and in other parts of Greece. She divides her time between New York, Ikaria, and Athens, where she is the city's best-known restaurant critic and food journalist. Her weekly columns appear in *Ta Nea* (The News), Greece's largest newspaper. Kochilas contributes frequently to *The New York Times, Saveur,* and *Gourmet,* where this piece first appeared.

Something has happened in Greece's chaotic cement jungle of a capital. Until about ten years ago, regional foods rarely made their way to Athens. But the city has suddenly transformed itself from a provincial city into a sophisticated European metropolis where all the country's regions—and all their foods—happily converge.

I think of this as I enter Manolis Androulakis's shop, **Mesogaia,** on the edge of the Plaka, a quaint, labyrinthine neighborhood carved into the foothills of the Acropolis. Androulakis is coddling a few heads of basket-shaped, cave-aged *graviéra* cheese that have just arrived from his native Crete. The subtle scent of sheep's-milk cheese mingles with the sweet, incenselike aromas of dried Greek sage and herbal mountain tea. "Everything starts from the earth," says Androulakis, who gave up his career as a geophysicist to indulge his passion for food. He tilts a basket of tawny barley rusks, another Cretan specialty, toward me to sample.

"I grew up in a family that would spend the better part of Sunday afternoon driving to a certain cheesemaker's, so I was taught early to seek out the best ingredients," he tells me. Surrounding him are a food lover's Greek treasures, discovered on his travels all over the country: hand-cut flat strands of pasta from the island of Tínos; thin rounds of pregrilled phyllo, made by immigrants from the Caucasus; jars of ruby-red cherries, amber strips of bitter-orange rind in syrup, and other spoon sweets glistening like stained glass; golden thyme honey from Kythera and lavender honey from the Máni; and wild greens in brine, such as Santorini caper leaves and the delicate buds of Mount Pelion pistachios.

A few years ago it would have been impossible to find such a cornucopia here. Now, however, urban Greeks have rediscovered the flavors of the countryside they left behind a generation ago.

Not far from Androulakis's place, Nikos Barlas and his mother, Ainie Pandia, arrange towering jars of pine honey and royal jelly (the nectar of queen bees) from their home island of Ikaria. As she stands in their two-by-four-foot shop, called **Gnision Esti** (It Is Original), Pandia can expound in one breath on everything from the depth of flavor in a sun-dried tomato paste from Milos (which she insists you taste) to the healthfulness of the Lenten *trahana,* a pebble-shaped pasta from Lesbos speckled with vegetables, to her years as a TV reporter. Her son is shy by comparison—but he is a passionate beekeeper, and once he gets started on the subject, he too can chat endlessly.

The shopkeepers of Athens are not alone—chefs have gotten in on the act too. Until recently, dining out in the city was almost totally limited to the traditional tavernas. Today new upscale restaurants serving modern food that takes its cue from the provinces have enlivened a once cliché-ridden cuisine.

A short walk from Gnision Esti, Takis and Stella Perdika preside over **To Ouzadiko,** a small *ouzeria* in Kolonáki, Athens's ritzy residential area. Takis has amassed a collection of more than 250 varieties of ouzo and *tsipouro* (Greece's answer to grappa), and Stella has assembled some of the finest traditional *mezéthes* in town, little dishes mostly from her native Thessaloníki.

On the other side of Athens's center, in a recently gentrified area known as Kerameikou, very close to the ancient Athenian cemetery (one of the city's major archaeological sites), chef Yiannis Baxevanis has created a cuisine that is both blindly Greek and clearly contemporary—drawing on wild mountain greens such as nettles, *mâche,* chicories, and lemon balm, as well as other regional and seasonal products. The restaurant, called **Kitrino Podilato** (Yellow Bicycle), occupies a sprawling former industrial space that has been transformed into one of the chicest, most modern restaurants in town.

Greeks are traditionalists at heart, though, and they haven't completely forfeited their old favorites. Athens is still dotted with specialty food shops that have been run by the same families for decades, and the tavernas, serving familiar dishes in a no-nonsense atmosphere, are as vibrant as ever.

Avoid the tourist traps in the Plaka and head for **Tou Xynou,** a taverna that has been in the Xynos family for a century. In winter, the murals in the dining rooms transport you to the Athens of another era, and in summer, amid the jasmine vines and lush trees, you feel as though you're in a Greek island village. The moussaka is a standard-bearer, the cabbage dolmas (stuffed grape leaves) are plump and succulent, and the deep-fried potato halves are not to be missed.

Fish tavernas abound in Piraeus, Athens's nearby twin city and port. Most of them, though picturesque and right on the water, serve up a predictable menu of typical *mezéthes* and grilled fish. It's worth sacrificing the view for something better. The place I like best is **Thalassinos,** in the residential area of Tzitzifies, about a ten-minute taxi ride from the city center. In a decidedly low-key venue, diners sit outdoors in summer or indoors amid a collection of maritime paraphernalia and modern Greek paintings. Yiorgos Loukas and his wife, Dina, offer a catch that comes exclusively from Greek waters, and their range of *mezéthes* is both unusual and delicious. I love their various versions of *saghanáki*—here, usually shrimp or mussels cooked with wine and herbs or with cheese in an individual skillet. The fritters of greens and seafood are also excellent, and the grilled fish and boiled vegetable salad is a simply perfect Greek classic. In a break with tradition, Thalassinos is famous among Athenians for its decidedly modern warm chocolate soufflé.

For early risers with a sense of adventure, a good option is a traditional breakfast among the sorts who spend their days hawking fish, meat, and just about everything else. Head to the extremely busy **Kendriki Agora,** or Central Market, a fascinating if rough-hewn area. The stalls are still quiet in the dawn hours, but you can sate your appetite in one of two ways: with a workingman's breakfast—maybe some hearty chickpea soup, or fried fresh picarel or sardines and boiled greens—or with the breakfast of champion night owls, who are ending their day as the sun comes up and hoping to mitigate the effects of their overindulgence with a piping hot bowl of *patsas,* or tripe soup.

For the former, head to **Diporto,** a small old *mageirion* (working-class restaurant) on Theatrou Street, just on the other side of Athinás Street and across the way from a corner shop that sells almost nothing but olives. Barba Mitsos, the cook, started his career here a few decades ago as a busboy, only to finally buy the place himself. Diporto attracts a real cross-section of the city, from local neighborhood kooks to yuppies and artsy types. If bean soup and boiled greens are not your ideal breakfast, you can certainly venture in at noontime.

If it's tripe you're after, though, gravitate toward the market in the wee hours. Its seedy but safe alleyways are home to three other *mageiria*. My favorite is called **To Monastiri**, or The Monastery, which sounds like someone's idea of a joke, given the, well, unrefined environment. As in all *mageiria,* the kitchen is open, so you just head to the front of the restaurant, peer into the pots, and choose from a daily selection of about twenty dishes, including not only tripe soup but also the likes of stewed peas with dill; lamb and orzo casserole; and pork and greens with *avgolémono* (tangy egg and lemon sauce).

While you're in the area, stop in at the quaint **Stoa tou Vangeli**, on Evripidou Street. *Stoa* refers to a kind of portico, or long cavernous entranceway, and that's exactly where this *mageirion* is situated. As you walk in, you hear the chirping of a wall full of birds lined up in their cages. At one table there will surely be a few old men, stationed there since early morning, passing their shiny copper carafe of retsina back and forth. But urban professionals also come here, for the home cooking and unselfconscious kitsch. If you savor but one dish here, make sure it is the *anginares a la polita,* a classic stew of artichokes, potatoes, and carrots in *avgolémono*.

A walk down Evripidou Street is a treat in itself. This is Athens's spice row. Once you cross Athinás Street, you'll pass, on the right, a few basement shops whose aroma will greet you before you reach the doorway. It's garlic, tons of it, being tied up in those familiar ornamental braids and readied for distribution all over the city.

You might want to stop in at **Elixir**, where Panos Koniaris, a third-generation spice merchant, sells the best Greek herbs in the city. He speaks English and is a formidable source of information. Here you will be able to choose from a half-dozen Greek oreganos, foraged from mountain slopes and salt-sprayed islands both. And you can learn about Cretan *dictamo,* the "lovers' herb." It's not by chance that the place looks like an old apothecary, its dried herbs stocked in lovely deep wooden drawers—herbs play a considerable role in the country's folk medicine.

Practically next door is **Miran,** not a spice vendor but a seller of something equally pungent: *pastoúrma,* a kind of charcuterie of air-dried beef seasoned with a thick coat of pepper, fenugreek, and other spices. You can buy a few slices and have a hotel room picnic with some good bread and Greek cheeses—feta, *kasséri,* and some less familiar ones like *manouri* (semisoft and mild) and *kopanisti* (fiery and spreadable)—which you'll be able to procure easily by backtracking a little on Evripidou, to the other side of Athínas Street. There you'll encounter two of the best cheesemongers in Athens: **Vassílis Ziogos** and **Laskaris Brothers.**

Street food should be part of the eating experience of every visitor to Athens, which means seeking out a rich, cheesy *tyropita* or a temptingly tangy souvlaki. My favorite *tyropita* can be found at a nondescript old-time bakery on Sarri Street (about a ten-minute walk from Evripidou), in Psiri, an area once filled with leather crafters and metalsmiths but now overtaken by bars, cafés, and faux-rustic *meze* restaurants (none very good). The *tyropita* is baked by **Efstathios Tzovas,** and though his sardonic humor will be lost on non–Greek speakers, his doughy feta-filled pies surmount all language barriers. Psiri is a fun place to stroll, looking through small shops for copperware and other trinkets.

Fans of hand-held foods will also find bliss at **Thanasis,** on Mitropoleos Street, home of dripping souvlaki and gyro—skewered and grilled or sliced and roasted meat wrapped in pita. A veritable Athenian landmark, it was opened in the early nineteenth century by an Armenian who arrived via Turkey. (In fact, souvlaki and gyro first came to Greece with Armenian refugees.) You can either sit at one of the sidewalk tables to enjoy a whole platter of thinly sliced lamb or pork, grilled tomatoes, onions, parsley, and *tzatziki* (yogurt, cucumber, and garlic sauce) with warm toasted pita, or order to go and eat on the run.

The best souvlaki, however, can be had at a seatless hole-in-the-wall known as **Tou Hasapi,** on Apollonos Street, at the beginning of the Plaka, just off Voulis Street. The butcher shop across the street (*hasapi* means "butcher") supplies the meat for the garlicky, spicy, and well-sauced souvlaki.

Another good snack is a vegetable or cheese pie from always-packed **Ariston,** on Voulis Street, near Syntagma. Ariston hasn't changed much since it first opened in 1906, the brainchild of an accomplished phyllo maker named Anastasios Lombotesis, who had emigrated from the island of Zákinthos to seek his fortune. He made it, and big, thanks largely to his first recipe: to this day, Ariston's crisp cheese pie with its characteristic elliptical shape, homemade pastry, and simple filling of feta and *myzíthra* is the cornerstone of his heirs' continued success.

What would a Greek city be without baklava? Without Greek coffee, a thin layer of froth afloat on the steaming brew, sipped slowly from a small demitasse? Without frappé, the turbopowered indigenous iced-coffee creation? (Frappé is made by shaking instant-coffee granules with sugar and ice, then adding cold water and a touch of evaporated milk.) And finally, what would any of that be without great venues to people-watch or just read the paper?

The finest baklava in town is at **Caravan.** The flagship shop, on Voukourestiou Street, is my favorite. You can't sit here, but you can buy kilos of a huge variety of jewel-size bites. There are the traditional diamonds and squares packed with walnuts and/or almonds, as well as little phyllo crowns—finger-size shirred cylinders called *saraglidakia*—filled with pistachios, with dried apricots, with prunes, and more. Sheep's-milk butter perfumes every piece. My own weaknesses are the chocolaty coils and the chocolate phyllo squares (known as *sokolatenio* baklava).

Athens is a café society, and the cream of the crop sips at **Da Capo,** on Kolonáki Square. The best time to come here is in the morning, around eight o'clock, when the city's newspaper editors, government ministers, and other power brokers gather to sip a frappé or a not-so-Greek cappuccino. The attraction at this time of the day is as much the atmosphere as the breakfast special, a chocolate-filled *tsoureki* (the briochelike Greek Easter bread). If you get here much past 8:45, it's likely to be sold out.

I often find refuge at **Desiree,** on Dimokritou Street, off Kolonáki Square. Just about the last 1950s pastry parlor left in Athens, it's the place to see dowagers gossiping over dainty pastries and good Greek coffee. It's also the place to sample classic *koulourakia* and *voutimata*, lightly sweetened cookies and dunking biscuits, respectively.

Another pleasant spot for coffee—or ouzo or a light snack—is **Oraia Ellas** (Beautiful Greece), the café at the Center for Greek Folk Art, on Pandrossou Street. And the shops here—offering a whole range of household antiques, from island-made plates to kneading troughs and wooden bread stamps, as well as some table linens and other textiles—encourage browsing for hours.

The charms of Athens have revealed themselves to me slowly. For as long as this city has been my adopted home, it has seemed at once daunting and welcoming. So it is the hunt for its little secrets that I've embraced, the stripping away of layers to find the heart. That odyssey has kept Athens alive and ever fascinating for me. It will for you too.

A Food Lover's Athens Address Book

When calling Athens from elsewhere in Greece, dial 01 before the numbers below.

Food Shops

Elixir, *Herbs,* 41 Evripidou Street, 321.5141

Gnision Esti, *Regional food products,* 2 Christou Lada Street, 324.4784

Laskaris Brothers, *Cheese,* 19 Evripidou Street, 321.6194

Mesogaia, *Regional food products,* 52 Nikis Street, 322.9146

Miran, *Air-dried beef,* 45 Evripidou Street, 321.7187

Vassílis Ziogos, *Cheese,* 25 Evripidou Street, 325.0781

Restaurants

Diporto, Mageirion, Theatrou and Sokratous Streets, 321.1463

Kitrino Podilato, *Contemporary Greek fare,* 116–118 Kerameikou, 346.5830

To Ouzadiko, *Ouzo and* mezéthes *bar,* 25–29 Karneadou, 729.5484

Stoa tou Vangeli, Mageirion, 63 Evripidou Street, 325.1513

Thalassinos, *Fish taverna,* Irakleous and Lisikratous Streets, 940.4518

To Monastiri, Mageirion, 4 Philopimenos Street

Tou Xynou, *Traditional taverna; closed weekends,* Angelou Gerontou, 322.1065

Ariston, *Cheese and vegetable pies,* 10 Voulis Street, 322.7626

Efstathios Tzovas's Bread Bakery, Tyropita, 13 Sarri Street, 321.4035

Thanasis, *Souvlaki and gyro,* 69 Mitropoleos Street, 324.4705

Tou Hasapi, *Souvlaki,* Apollonos Street, near Voulis Street

Coffee and Sweets

Caravan, *Baklava and* sokolatenio *baklava,* Voukourestiou Street, 364.1540

Da Capo, Tsoureki, Kolonáki Square, 821.0030

Desirée, Koulourakia *and* voutimata, Dimokritou Street, 363.2333

Oraia Ellas, *Spoon sweets,* Center for Greek Folk Art, 36 Pandrossou Street, 321.3842

Bibliography

L'Acropole d'Athenes: Photographies 1839–1959, Haris Yiakoumis, published simultaneously in 2000 in Athens by Potamos and in Paris by Picard. In my lifetime the Acropolis has always been at least partially obscured by scaffolding. It is a necessary evil, I realize, but it makes taking a decent photograph very difficult. One somewhat satisfying alternative is to take a look at (or better yet, buy) Yiakoumis's coffee table book. It's a lush collection of photos taken before the days of repairs and restoration, showing the site as it once was: a temple atop a hill, almost floating above the city of Athens. The text is in Greek, French, and English (the Greek text gets an entire page to itself, where the French and English translations usually share a facing page, so you get a sense of missing out on some of the details and explanations), but the point is to admire the illustrations. It's especially striking to compare the Athens of the photos—which was essentially a large village—to the Athens of today, which is undoubtedly a city in the modern sense of the word.

Athens Guide, Athinorama Guides, Desmi Publications, Athens. This is the only guidebook I recommend in this entire book because it's only available in Greece. It's distributed by the Hellenic Distribution Agency and is sold at newsstands and bookshops. I wouldn't single it out if it weren't such an excellent source of information: history; eating out; nightlife; shows and music; children; art; accommodation; beaches; leisure; gastronomy; services; shopping; excursions; Olympic Games; maps (including a pull-out of the main archaeological walk); a glossy bookmark; practical information; and color photographs throughout. If I were you, purchasing this is the second task I would set out to do upon arriving in Athens—the first would be to get a copy of the updated museums and monuments schedule from the tourist office, as I mentioned earlier.

The Parthenon, Mary Beard, Harvard University Press, 2003. On the page following the table of contents, Beard shares an exchange that I'm still trying to fathom: "*Reporter:* 'Did you visit the Parthenon during your trip to Greece?' *Shaquille O'Neal* (U.S. basketball star): 'I can't really remember the names of the clubs we went to.'" Happily, besides disclosing this shocking reality, Beard shares many more reports of those who actually *did* get to the Parthenon: "Against all the odds—the inescapable sun, the crowds of people, the surly guards blowing their whistles at any deviants who try to stray from the prescribed route around the site and, for more than a decade now, the barrage of scaffolding—the Parthenon seems to work for almost everyone, almost every time." Beard sets out, with this handsome little hardcover, to think "harder about how we can make sense of the ancient Parthenon and the culture in which it was created. But at the same time I shall constantly be keeping an eye on its later history, after antiquity and up to the present day. The Parthenon is, after all, as much a modern icon as an ancient ruin. If we wish to understand its significance in the ancient world, we need also to understand what has happened to it over the last two millennia, and how we have come to invest in it so much of our own cultural energy." At 209 pages, this is the most accessible—while also being informative—volume on the history and controversy over the Parthenon.

The Parthenon Frieze, Jenifer Neils, Cambridge University Press, 2001. As this excellent book was already mentioned and its author quoted from, I won't sing its praises excessively here; but it's worth repeating that Neils has created a unique masterpiece with this project, as she has included a companion CD-ROM and a double-sided, five-panel, fold-out sheet featuring complete views of the four walls of the Parthenon frieze. The CD-ROM viewer allows you to click on the view you'd like to see—north, south, east, or west—and you may tour the length of the selected wall using the arrow keys. There are also line drawing views on the disc, allowing you to see what the frieze might have looked like in its original, undamaged state by laying a line drawing over the frieze images that then completes the missing portions of the frieze. This work is scholarly and is intended for readers especially interested in the Parthenon, but Neils writes in a very engaging and accessible manner, and I encourage anyone interested in art and architecture history in general to seek it out at a good bookstore or your local library.

Preserving the World's Great Cities, Anthony Tung, Clarkson Potter, 2001. "The Destruction and Renewal of the Historic Metropolis" is the subtitle of this landmark book. One of the twenty-two cities Tung identified for studying "how architectural preservation worked and failed in some of the most artistically and historically significant places around the globe" is Athens, profiled in the chapter entitled "The City of the Gods Besieged." Tung opens the chapter by stating that "perhaps in no other place in the world is the urban conflict of old versus new as conspicuous as it is in Athens. . . . Amid a broad sea of somewhat shabby low-rise urban sprawl, stretching for miles in all directions, rises a massive and time-honored promontory, one of the singular rock outcroppings on the planet: the Athenian Acropolis, a site of unsurpassed artistic and architectural brilliance." *Acro* and *polis* combine, as Tung informs us, to mean "upper city," and this upper city has become "more than a local matter." Tung concludes this fascinating chapter by noting that "one can only hope that someday this unsurpassed sculptural and architectural achievement will once more be seen, comprehended, and felt by future generations and that the surviving artistic components of the Parthenon will eventually stand together in the particular sunlight of the city that gave them birth."

Αθήνα, Εθνικό Αρχαιολογικό Μουσείο. Η τοιχογραφία
της Άνοιξης από το Ακρωτήρι της Θήρας. 1500 π.Χ.
Athens National Archaeological Museum. The Spring fresco
from Akrotiri on Thera. 1500 BC.

ΑΚΡΩΤΗΡΙ ΘΗΡΑΣ
AKROTIRI THERA

ΑΘ 219409

Παρακαλείσθε να κρατήσετε το απόκομμα του εισιτηρίου σας
μέχρι την έξοδό σας από το Μουσείο Χώρο.
You are requested to preserve your ticket until you leave
the Museum/Site.

ΕΙΣΙΤΗΡΙΟ ΕΙΣΟΔΟΥ
ΕΥΡΩ **5** EURO
ENTRANCE TICKET

ΕΛΛΗΝΙΚΗ
ΔΗΜΟΚΡΑΤΙΑ

Α.Σ. ΚΑΛΩΝ ΤΕΧΝΩΝ 1837 – 1987

HELLAS
26

THE PREHISTORIC CITY OF AKROTIRI ON THERA

The Aegean Islands

"What Robert Liddell wrote in Aegean Greece in 1954 remains true: "To some of us who most love the Aegean, it is like a type or foretaste of Paradise. In the mountains and dry streams of these wind-shaken islands our home-sickness for 'that imperial palace whence we came' is soothed, we almost forget that we are exiles, and we recognize places where we have never been before. Here, more frequently than anywhere else, come those unsought and unseekable moments of penetrating bliss, of Wordsworthian joy and quiet, when 'we see into the life of things.' As dismissive as one would like to be of such Lake Poets prose, the feeling of having returned to the home of pastoral Romance—where love, nature, and wisdom are eternally conjoined—overwhelms the traveler as soon as he climbs a cicada-loud hillside. Noise, pollution, and all the excesses of tourism fall out of sight and out of mind. One seems to be sitting in a cleft in the otherwise smooth sphere of reality. The time and trouble of getting here have been all worthwhile."
—Robert Eisner, TRAVELERS IN AN ANTIQUE LAND

Islands of Revelation

BY PATRICIA STORACE

~⌒~

editor's note

Elizabeth Boleman-Herring, in *Vanishing Greece,* observed that both for the Greeks and for foreign visitors, "the Aegean islands conjure up images of summer, sandy beaches, simplicity and, most vividly, of the sea. Thrown like vulnerable, bright dice into the dark water these islands, and their Greek inhabitants, have always depended upon the sea: what it brought to their shores, and what it took away." This and the following three pieces focus on clusters of Aegean islands or designated island groups, such as the Dodecánese, while the last three pieces in this section are devoted to individual islands.

PATRICIA STORACE, introduced on page 192, contributed this piece to *Condé Nast Traveler.* Superb photographs by William Abranowicz, who captured uncommon views of Kárpathos, Naxos, Santorini, Sími, and Tínos, accompanied the article.

It is a given that no photograph can be as beautiful as the truth of the Greek landscape. Where is the scent of the wild thyme and rosemary that follows you indoors in the form of the incense burned in churches? The taste of the salty sea urchin caviar that makes the Aegean itself momentarily edible? Or the applause for a singer being celebrated with basket after basket of carnations rained on his head, or drachmas being torn into shreds and flung at her feet because her artistry transcends possession? If it is hard to convey the sensual experience of the Greek world, it is equally hard to capture on film a people who are old masters of the grand gesture. And a photograph of Greece has a built-in disadvantage—it reminds you that you are not in Greece.

It may seem a strange comparison, but Greece is as hard to photograph as babies are. In both cases, reality outdoes the camera, and in both cases, the photographer's problem is to translate not just what he sees but what he can't see, or can only glimpse—not only the real but the inexplicable, not only the present but the eternal. Every day I lived there I was presented with a metaphysical conundrum: it is not possible, I would think, that such beauty exists. Then I would think: but it does exist. In a way, extreme beauty is ordinary in Greece—in order to bring the place to life, it is more important to show the miraculous than the beautiful.

Fred Astaire says of Cyd Charisse in the movie *The Bandwagon,* "She came at me in sections." Greece, especially island Greece, comes at you in archetypes, which resort hotels and pizza parlors and kitschy souvenir shops may coexist with but seem powerless to destroy. It is a world suffused with the divine, whose mythological population remains as present and accounted for as its current inhabitants. Pan-like flocks of goats fix you with topaz-colored stares as you pass, as if daring you to recognize them in their camouflage. It is a fact that I have met Circe herself, a great poet and hostess, who seems surrounded by a permanent collection of guests drinking her ouzo and eating her homegrown pistachios. Some visitors who have previously experienced this delicious amnesia alert friends to come and retrieve them by hydrofoil if they have not surfaced after a week.

It is not possible to emerge onto the beach from a swim without at some point thinking of Aphrodite—or on Patmos, the island of Revelation, without thinking of baptismal waters, of Christ. The improbable situation of Santorini—that Lazarus among islands, hovering over its volcanically created abyss—recalls icons of the Virgin Mary supporting ships between her two hands just above voracious seas.

Indeed, gods and goddesses do still arise from the Greek seas, assisted by cranes and cables after discovery by a passing diver. The seas are full of gods, as is the soil, where dreams send people to dig for miraculous icons or to build churches on divinely chosen sites. This is earth that has been held sacred for as far as memory extends; the divine is all-encompassing here, the gods are very close, as are ancient ways of honoring them. In island chapels you often see hammered-tin votive plaques, with images of joined wreaths that are an important symbol in the Orthodox wedding ritual, or of houses, donkeys, parts of the body—a frieze of human longing and thanksgiving. I once stopped at an inland chapel on Corfu on Easter morning and saw its threshold strewn with bay laurel leaves, an ancient tribute to athletes, here dedicated to one who prevailed in a match with death. Even the lovely island lullabies, the *nanouris-mata,* join the divine and the human in tender intimacy, with pleas that the Virgin will hold the sleeping child on her knees along with her own Son, or that the two children will play together in the garden of Paradise for the duration of the nap.

It is not surprising that a strong sense of the magical and the miraculous persists on these life-sustaining outcroppings seemingly snatched from the sea, with their seafoam-colored cottages. They seem to exist by supernatural fiat alone, and always by precarious arrangement with a moody sea. The sea often turns up as a character in her own right in Greek fairy tales. In one particular favorite, she seizes a man she has wanted for a long time who risked going close to the waves, but she is forced to restore him from her depths thanks to three magic phrases spoken by someone who loves him. In an island song I particularly love, the singer tries to charm the sea into becoming rose water to give her husband a sweet journey home. When you wander through an island market and pause at a basket of silvery fish, you are seeing another set of fairy-tale characters: fish that guide, that save, that supply an infinite abundance of food. It is always moving to approach an island harbor on a ferry laboring through a dark sea—before the houses become more distinct, they look like votive candles set in rows on the altarlike hills to ask mercy of the sea.

The island floats before you like a mirage, with its honeycomb networks of white stairs and terraces, which seem to lead straight into the stars if you climb them at night after dinner at a harbor taverna. These stairs also function as an informal method of census taking. The traffic on the stairs eventually reveals who has just arrived home, what strangers are staying at Kyria S.'s guest house, what child is taking a spontaneous vacation from school, what boy is meeting which girl. I have probably accepted and declined more staircase dinner engagements than I ever have telephone ones. Men set up impromptu *kafeneia,* with cups and card tables on sharply inclined side streets, speculating and editorializing about the significance of the meetings they observe. Messages pass up and down the stairs, heavy luggage is borne up and down by donkeys, which turn out to be models of super-efficiency.

"Greece will never die," ran a song popular during the Second World War. The sentiment is true to Greece's most cherished ambition, to its aesthetic, perhaps even to its achievement. If the characteristic American aesthetic is "Make it new," Greece's is "Make it get up out of its grave—make it live forever." It is rare to see a group of photographs of Greece in which the photographer's eye isn't mysteriously turned toward the permanent rather than the fleeting, to images that predate the very invention of his instrument. Greece's great holiday, of course, is Easter, the celebration not of birth but of eternal life. Its most cherished images are its icons, painted again and again from the same models, according to strictly prescribed rules. It is a stunning experience to realize that the eerie familiarity of the faces you see on your daily circuit is the result of your having seen them on icons and in the Greco-Roman grave portraits painted on the shrouds at al Fayyum. They are alive. And it is that, above all, which accounts, I think, for our unending fascination with the place. Greece has always recognized the reality of tragedy, even embraced it—but it has also made death seem an illusion. And as long as people have made journeys or dreamed of them, a place where journeys don't end has been their most longed-for destination.

Secrets of the Aegean

BY BRUCE STUTZ

∾

BRUCE STUTZ contributed this piece on the Sporades—where he discovered that rare vestiges of the natural Mediterranean still exist—to the December 2002 issue of *Condé Nast Traveler*. He is also the author of *Natural Lives, Modern Times: People and Places of the Delaware River* (Crown, 1992), and is the editor-in-chief of *Natural History*.

By the time I catch sight of the little sun-drenched cove, I've put all one hundred cubic centimeters of the rented scooter's engine to the test. For the last two hours I've been riding over rutted roads, spinning and bucking for a bruising ten miles under a speckless Aegean sky. The pebbled beach lies a steep hundred yards below, down a goat path. Not a soul on it, and so just the setting I've come to these islands to find. The Sporades hold some of the last remnants of real nature in the Mediterranean. Some—bare rock and scrub—

remain uninhabited. On larger islands, sheep and goats graze in rocky pastures, and montane forests run into steep gorges. Villages provide tastes of indigenous feasts, and tavernas provide sounds of *rembétika,* the folk blues that brings grown Greeks to tears.

As I begin to walk, I wonder if the hundred-degree heat is getting to me: the fragrance of the Aleppo pines, the fantastic shapes of man-size prickly pear cactuses, and the rattling of cicadas make the silent beach below seem like a mirage. Waves lap the bases of great blocks of limestone. All this place is missing, I think, is FedEx packages washing in on the surf.

Bleary-eyed, giddy, and sweaty, I drop into the water. When I come out, I squint up toward the pitched forests from which I've come. A falcon soars. I imagine a wood-shingled taverna clinging to the rock ledge, offering shade and a cold beer. But exhausted, I shamble over to one of the sea-carved rocks and nestle into a shaded niche. The last thing I recall before dozing off is marveling at the rock's gleaming crystalline underside. I awake to find that the taverna is real.

So it seems to be on the Sporades Islands: otherworldly landscapes coexist with magical realities. Skyros is my first stop—at 81 square miles, slightly bigger than Aruba, it's the largest of the Sporades. From the air it looks like a bristly hide left to dry under the Aegean sun. The landing strip—*airport* would be too grand a term—is stranded on a sun-scoured plain. The drive toward Skyros Town passes scrub-covered hills, but then the brilliant little town appears—white cubes that cascade toward the sea from a high spire of rock, in whose shadow stands the wall of an ancient fortress. I have to enter on foot from the east, a steep climb up stone stairs that wind through high grasses where goats graze, overlooking the sea. I enter a maze of narrow, labyrinthine flagstone streets where voices can be heard but no one can be seen. Then I round a corner into a street full of cafés and kiosks, and a town square where children play and old men drink *tsipouro* (an industrial-strength ouzo) over the clack of backgammon dice.

Sophocles called Skyros "the stony, windswept home of valiant men." Dionysius, the traveler, called it "goat trodden." The local historian's guidebook says that the island's several freshwater springs inspired an ancient cult of nymph worshipers; that Skyros was the home and death place of Theseus; that to outwit the fate that marked Achilles for death in the Trojan War, his mother, Thetis, brought her son to Skyros, where he lived disguised as a girl in the court of Lycomedes. Overlooking forested mountains, rough pastures, and the embracing sea from the town's summit, I find it easy to imagine a mythical Skyros, a rock citadel anchored in a more ancient Aegean.

Islands always provide intriguing natural histories, and on Skyros, typical of the Aegean archipelago, the land is far older than the sea that surrounds it. Had I driven to the highest point on Skyros thirteen million years ago, I would have looked out on a land of forested plains and tall mountain peaks. Some four million years ago this great basin, known as Aegeis and stretching to Africa, began to flood. The Aegean Islands are the peaks of Aegeis's drowned mountains.

Skyros has a character as homespun as the three-hundred-year-old hand-embroidered linens preserved in the little Faltaits Museum of local crafts. Red, blue, and gold threads, still vibrant, animate ships, horses and peacocks, serpents and birds, and brides and bridegrooms perched on a fruited tree of life. Anastasia Faltaits, whose father-in-law began the collections, serves me coffee in her parlor. "This is an island," she tells me, "that keeps its own traditions." The limestone floor and stucco walls hold the cool of the evening well through the heat of the day.

There is only one main road, which winds north past the airport, then uphill, where I stop a few times to take in the views through the pines to the sea, then down again. I pass small beaches where bathers have set up umbrellas and campers have clean little bivouacs. But I'm after something more singular, and just past one beach I pull over. I take out my snorkeling gear, then traipse through some dense brush and down a gray spine of bonelike rocks that borders a narrow creek wash. It leads to an uninhabited cove where the cool waters are full of small fish and the rocks are mottled with sea urchins, which, if you know how, will serve up a sweet snack.

Refreshed, I decide to hazard the unpaved roads into the mountains. I drive on gravel for a while, then clay, on my way up Mount Dekatria until, at a thousand feet, I'm seeing a scene that probably hasn't changed for a few hundred years. Goats graze under olive trees. A Skyrian pony, as ancient a breed of horse as exists today, stands on a hill colored with dianthus, heather, and flame-orange thistles. A lone white chapel sits on a hillside, or in the cool of a shaded ravine.

Back in Skyros, the head of Skyros Travel, Lefteris Trakos, eyes the dust-covered Hyundai he rented me. I assure him that the undercarriage and gears are fine. As we lunch on sea urchins and a local lobster weighing a couple of pounds, I tell him how much I like the embroidery at the museum, so he introduces me to Amersa Panagiotou, who just happens to be taking a swim at the beach. "Come to my house," she says, "for dinner."

A cherubic woman who lives along a lane of small farms in the village of Kalamitsa, Amersa is one of the last to practice the Skyrian art of fine embroidery. She follows the exacting patterns I saw in the museum, and her walls are filled with her framed work—exquisite primitives of sailing ships, of birds and horses, of pantalooned children. She speaks no English, but my phrase book is rife with terms expressing astonishment and appreciation. *Oreio!* Beautiful. I chide her for having her shop so out of the way. She shows me that she does now have a website, although the only computer she has use of is one in town. This is a great step for a woman who says that her parents didn't have a phone until 1999.

Skyros once expected a tourist boom, but it never came. In order to reach Alónnisos, 60 miles north, I had to take the ferry west to Evia, drive 120 miles to Ágios Konstantinos, and then take a ferry to Skopelos and another to Alónnisos—an all-day affair that, aside from the sight of some frolicking dolphins, had little to offer. But as the crowds on the ferries thinned after each successive island, Alónnisos appeared like the end of the line that it was. Just beyond lay the uninhabited Sporades, islands and waters that form a marine national park, the protectorate of the Mediterranean monk seal, one of the rarest sea mammals on earth.

Homer wrote in the *Odyssey:*

> Once ashore, [the Sea God] lies down to sleep under the arching caves, and around him is a throng of seals, the brood of the lovely child of Ocean; they too have come up through the gray waters, and they too lie down to sleep, smelling rankly of the deep brine below. . . . First he will pass along all the seals and count them; then, having viewed them and made his reckoning, he will lie down among them all like a shepherd among his flock of sheep.

These days, uninhabited places, even small ones like the outer Sporades, hold a poignant dignity that comes from the successful but lonely defiance of the crowded world around them. They hold no harbors, no permanent dwellings. They are ancient rock affected only by wind and sea. In among their coves and sea caves, the last pods of the Sea God's seals hold out.

"The best way to kill one," offers Pliny the Elder in his *Natural History,* "is to shatter its skull." So despite these creatures' love of sea and sun, which put them under the protection of both Poseidon and Apollo (*phoke,* the Greek word for seal, comes from Phokos, the son of Poseidon), plenty of them were brutally dispatched over the millennia. They were killed for their lush gray-black coats and for their oil, and most recently, they were slaughtered by fishermen who considered a fish-eating animal weighing up to eight hundred pounds a too-efficient competitor. Pods of monk seals once ranged from the Black and Adriatic seas through the Mediterranean to the West African coast. Now extinction threatens, with a colony of a hundred or so living off Mauritania and perhaps the same number in the Sporades, and a few fragile colonies of no more than twenty scattered around the globe.

The fate of the seals was what first interested me in these islands. Here, in the midst of the overdeveloped Mediterranean, a place remains undisturbed enough to harbor the last of these reclusive animals. In many years of travel, I've found that where the nature of a place is preserved, the culture too maintains its integrity. Alónnisos is on the frontier. The islands to its east remain uninhabited. In 1992 the Greek government created the Northern Sporades National Marine Park, the largest protected area in the Mediterranean basin. The entire 850 square miles is off limits to development, and fishing and boating are restricted. If it was good enough for the seals, it was good enough for me.

The morning haze lifts after we leave Alónnisos's little harbor of Patitiri, and soon the two-masted wooden *Mikros Kosmos* (*Small World*) is motoring through whitecaps. "In all the time I spend out around these islands," says Chris Browne, the schooner's naturalist, "I see seals only three or four times a year." And at this time of year, either pregnant or with young pups along, the seals are even more secretive. Disturbed during this period, they have been known to reject a pup or lose a pregnancy. Pipéri, where the seals congregate in caves along the craggy coastal cliffs, is off limits to anyone but the park patrol. Scientists monitor the pods with remote-controlled infrared cameras.

Soon the whole cloistered archipelago spreads out before us. Psathura, the one volcanic outlier, seems to float under a light haze. Likouza, like the silhouette of a supine pregnant woman, takes the foreground. On unforested Gioúra, wild goats with cruciform black tail markings thrive on low-growing myrtle and heaths. Here in the subterranean maze of the Cyclops Cave, archaeologists found ten-thousand-year-old bonefish hooks and stone knives. Skandzoúra, forested with cedar, is the breeding ground for the rare Audouin's gull.

We drift into an inlet and anchor just off an outcrop on tiny Kyra Panagiá. We disembark to climb a steep, rocky, and ancient monk's path through sage, heather, and resinous rock roses. Above us is an eighteenth-century monastery built on the site of a ninth-century monastery—making this a path traveled for more than a thousand years. At the summit we look out over the other islands in the park. An Eleonora's falcon, having traveled from Madagascar to summer in the Mediterranean, soars above the monastery, veers, flares its tail feathers, then dives seaward like a pitched shard of the island's reddish-brown sandstone.

In the small blue-domed Chapel of Mary burning tapers illuminate the brass of the hanging lamps and the gold in the paintings of saints. The Church still owns these islands. The monasteries are outposts that extend the Church's holy realm beyond its center on Mount Athos on the mainland, visible from Skyros and other islands of the Sporades.

As we head back toward Alónnisos, I'm thinking, Why not? Why not give it all up and live just this close to the sea, just this far from the familiar, "the world forgetting, by the world forgot."

Exercise some defiance. Chris did it. Grew tired of a London broker's life and moved here, where he now leads tours. In winter, he has these landscapes and seascapes all to himself. Greek isles have always inspired such thoughts. The Sporades still do. "When I tell Greeks who visit from Athens that I live here on Alónnisos," Chris says, "for them it's as if I've died and gone to heaven."

Sadly, the marine park's research station at Gérakas Bay stands abandoned and defunct. And the paved road to reach it now serves truckers and sightseers. Locals on the Sporades will tell you that there are three kinds of roads: paved, few of which exist, all marked at their blind curves by little white memorial boxes; gravel, which may or may not connect to the paved roads; and dirt, which even goats stay clear of. When you show the locals a map, they just shake their heads and give you an incredulous look.

Confident, however, after my ventures on Skyros, I veer onto a road that begins as gravel but eventually narrows to a car's width, pitches steeply, and makes barely navigable switchbacks. I plow through vegetation in first gear until I dead-end in a pile of fallen rock. The car is hot and sprouting branches from its bumpers and wheels, but the view of Peristéra, the long, narrow, all-but-uninhabited sister island to Alónnisos, is an idiot's delight. The beaches below seem no closer, however. The gods must be amused. I maneuver back and stay on the paved road, a harrowing enough course to the coast. Once again the reward is a lone rocky spot where the snorkeling is fine and the quiet unsurpassable.

Near dusk I hike a trail from the port of Patitiri to Palio Horio, or Old Alónnisos. Night comes quickly in the shadows of the overhanging trees, and the trail is longer than I thought. After a while I hear footsteps and laughter: a couple walking down the hill—she holding her shoes in her hand, he a bottle of wine—come out of the darkness, pass, and vanish. Another twenty minutes, and the town materializes as scattered incandescent lights.

It's nearly ten o'clock, and Old Alónnisos is just coming to life. Taverna patios jut invitingly into view from the narrow, terraced alleyways. I take a table at one, and the owner recommends the moussaka. It is, she tells me, just coming into moussaka season— meaning enough tourists are showing up to make the cooking process worthwhile. As I drink my wine, music drifts from somewhere up the hill. Couples, families, and children pass by. The moussaka arrives in its small stoneware tureen, the dense cheese still percolating. At the first taste I predict that this will be a good season for moussaka.

I head up the hill for coffee and find a crowd in front of the Kastro Taverna, where Nikos, who I size up to be at least six foot six, sits on a stool playing the bouzouki. Dressed in black pants and a balloon-sleeved black shirt, with a Steven Seagal–style ponytail, he's playing *rembétika*. The old men and women sing along, the young join in the choruses. When I talk to Nikos later, I discover that during the winter he is a neighbor of mine, living not far from me in Brooklyn. He drives a cab and plays gigs at Greek festivals and weddings, but since his father's death a couple of years ago, he returns here each spring to reopen his family's restaurant. "Give me a call," he says. "I'll be back in New York in September."

Although anchored close to one another, each island in the Sporades shapes its own *mikros kosmos*. Insular Skyros, with its one town and scattered settlements, has a monastic ambience; Alónnisos, with its lively little port of Patitiri and its Palio Horio overlooking the uninhabited islands beyond, seems more connected to the sea. On Skopelos, the elements collaborate to create dramatic scenic turns and unforgettable characters. Thankfully, I have Dick Caldwell to serve as tummler.

A retired professor and a tour guide, raconteur, and translator of classics, Caldwell has been a summer fixture on Skopelos for thirty years. Without him I might have missed meeting Dimitris "Jimmy" Papastergiou at his beachfront taverna, Dichta (Fishing Net), in the little horseshoe cove of Panormos. To regulars, the place is better known as Jimmy's Parakalo—*parakalo* being Greek for "can I help you," "please," "excuse me," and "don't mention it." Jimmy, a tall man with a gap-toothed smile, brings the word even more color and connotations. It's a hearty greeting, a deftly inflected *voilà* when dinner is served, a *shazam!* when a plate crashes.

Jimmy, it seems, lost his lease on his place in the main town of Skopelos due to the revelries he provoked. Out here he can provoke as he pleases. After sausage and peppers and pastitsio and more wine, Jimmy sets a magnum of Metaxa brandy on the table—a bottle with a tap at the bottom and a flame at the top. He retreats to the kitchen, and then—*"parakalo!"*—he's back with a red accordion and his fifteen-year-old spike-haired son, George, who has a bouzouki.

They let loose on a rousing tune, and we clap and drink, Jimmy mixing white wine and Coke (his poor man's cognac recipe), and Dick and I tapping the Metaxa. Diners join in clapping. Then Jimmy puts down his accordion, struts center, poses akimbo, and begins to dance—toe, heel, toe, heel—loose and lithe. George works up a sweat, and Jimmy wraps his arm around my shoulder and leads me through the simple steps—simple, that is, to do one at a time, difficult to combine. He releases me and—*"parakalo!"*— I'm on my own, Zorba-like, arms outstretched, fingers snapping.

The fact that Jimmy's son is playing these folk songs, Dick notes, is a hopeful sign. And Skopelos, he adds, is "a bastion of *rembétika*," an urban music that grew up in hashish bars at the turn of the twentieth century and that shares with American blues a focus on the alienated life. Its heyday came in the years following Greece's failed invasion of Turkey in 1921 and the exile of some two million Greeks from Turkey in 1922. The exiles combined their songs of loss—of home, of love, of work—with songs of political protest. By the 1930s, *rembétika* was banned. It went through a revival and modernization during and after the war, then nearly died out until its themes attracted the rebellious spirit of the late 1960s.

One of the musicians who came to Skopelos and to *rembétika* in those days is Kostas Kalafatis. When he first began playing, they'd start at ten P.M. on the balcony of a taverna and play until eight the next morning. We go to see his group at a little outdoor stage, where amplified instruments ring clear in the humid evening air. The first interruption comes when a light rain begins and everyone moves under the terrace's roof. The second comes when the police arrive to charge the band with playing outside in a residential area. It is a familiar scene. Even now *rembetis* are harassed, but the musicians simply unplug their instruments and begin an acoustic session with an intimacy rare anywhere these days.

Nights in Skopelos give me a fresh appreciation of the island's nature during my day's rides. Knowing, by now, that I will hit the dusty forest trails, I rent a motorbike, put some food and water under the seat, and head out. The main road veers south from Skopelos Town and follows the contour of the western coast, past solitary beaches, fishing villages, little resorts. But I want to test the bike inland.

More than any of the Sporades, Skopelos has an interior that is primeval. Barely a quarter of a mile from the coast, I'm in pine forest, with occasional untended groves of olive trees. I aim uphill, heading for Avgeri, the island's central two-thousand-foot peak. I pass abandoned cottages, forested chasms. Though I kick up clouds of dust, the forest is damp, holding a perpetual dew. I'm lost and perfectly content to be so. I park in a solitary olive grove for lunch. This could be the grove I passed an hour ago, who knows? There's no direction home. But, worst comes to worst, if dusk threatens, I'll head west toward the sun and the coast road. Despite all the beautiful coves along the sea, this forest seems to me the very soul of Skopelos—not made for tourists, but the hidden source of the island's serenity.

The scene is not so serene on Skiathos. For me it is the last island of the Sporades, but for most tourists it's the first and the only. By mid-July, you're more likely to hear West Londonese than Greek in the main port. Papadiamandis Street becomes a midway crammed with cafés and souvenir shops. The restaurants and tavernas along the waterfront are so close, you can't tell which one you're sitting in. On the docks you can walk a quarter of a mile by stepping from boat to boat.

While each island on my trip has grown a little less itself, Skiathos appears to have been transformed utterly. I can escape the crowds on the old winding backstreets, where a church, a quiet taverna, or an antiques shop might provide refuge, but I decide to just get out of town. And whereas in Skyros, Alónnisos, or Skopelos that meant traveling half a mile or so, the name-brand resorts and beachfront condominium complexes around Skiathos stretch for miles. For the first time even the map of the island is accurate, a sure sign that something has gone awry.

Determined, however, that there is an island here somewhere, I head out, looking for the worst roads. But much of the interior has been logged. I wind around treeless cliffsides, red and raw with eroding sandstone. At a high point I look down at the red-tile roofs of the crowded town. Am I far enough? I catch sight of a sign in English: PANORAMA PIZZA. I turn north, aiming for the most distant coast.

The sun is baking the dust with kilnlike intensity, and the motorbike is scorching hot, but I hold on until a gravel road leads me to a shady oasis. On one side stands the little church of the prophet Elias, on the other a wood-framed taverna, where I order cooling yogurt with honey, nuts, and fruit. The patio is cantilevered above the cliffside, overlooking the sea and the distant islands. The trees all around bear small red plums and ripe figs. I know the heart of the island is nearby.

Refreshed and hopeful, I continue north toward the *kastro*, the citadel where the islanders, under attack by pirates in the twelfth century, fled and built a hidden town of stone whose remains lie scattered on a dramatic outcropping above the sea. I ride past sheep and goats that in the heat stand as still as stuffed specimens. Thirsty, I cup water from a hillside spring and then climb a plum tree to shake down a dozen ripe fruits that I eat in the tree's shade. A mile on I can take the bike no farther. I begin to walk, and soon I see it, the miragelike little cove that I've come to find. And not another soul on its pebbled beach.

The Far Shores of Greece

The scenic qualities of the Sporades Islands are such that concerns over where to stay are of less importance than those over what to see. The most remote spot on any island is no more than a morning's drive from the main town. That said, I advise novice visitors to find lodgings in the main town. You can then venture out by day and return for dinner to a choice of handy, lively tavernas.

Although the water is still cool in late May and early June, the wildflowers are in bloom, flocks of birds migrate through, and you'll be welcomed as befits the first visitors after a long winter (when islanders remain insulated from the outside world). Skyros, in particular, celebrates spring with an Easter-season masque that predates Christian times. Tourists flock in and prices go up from mid-July through early September, but even in high season a double room in a good island hotel is likely to be less than $125 per night. Skiathos has more sophisticated accommodations, but island lodgings are usually alike: clean and comfortable, most with private baths, some with AC. Since towns rise up steep hillsides overlooking the sea, ask about balconies with views. As for food, a typical dinner, with wine, might cost about $20.

Motorbikes maneuver better than cars on the narrow roads, have room for food and water under the seat, and cost about $12 a day, plus a dollar or two for a mandatory helmet. To climb into the mountains, rent one with 90 cc's or better.

The only way to island-hop from Skyros, which has the main airport, is to catch the ferry to Evia, then take a bus or a hired car ($110) a couple of hours north, across the mainland, to Ágios Konstantinos. From there, ferries and jet-ferries run pretty regularly.

With a series of arrests in the summer of 2002, the risk from Greece's so-called November 17 terrorist group appears to be minimized; the U.S. State Department reports "no specific threats against private American citizens traveling in Greece." The nearest American consulate is at the **U.S. Embassy** in Athens, at 91 Vassilíssis Sofías Avenue (210.72.12.951; usembassy.gr). Skiathos has a large police presence; perhaps its crowded streets offer asylum to petty thieves, although I never ran into any. The nearest office of the **National Tourism Police** is on Evia, but the emergency number (171) can be dialed from anywhere in Greece.

Prices, quoted for the month of May, could increase by as much as 20 percent during high season.

Alónnisos

The new GPS-compatible map is quite accurate and is available in tourist shops in Patitiri ($8). *Alonissos on Foot,* by Bente Keller and Elias Tsoukanas, is a detailed guide to beaches and hikes ($12).

Albedo Tours runs the *Mikros Kosmos* schooner, which alternates excursions to Kyra Panagiá and Skandzoúra (4240.65804; info@albedotravel.com). Chris Browne leads tours to island monasteries that include lunch and time to swim and snorkel. His hikes will get you into the landscape to view farms, forests, wildflowers, and birds (alonissoswalks.co.uk; about $40 per person).

The rooms in the Haravgi Hotel, in Patitiri, are small but pleasant, and there's a flowered terrace where breakfast is served overlooking the harbor (4240.65090; doubles, about $25). But I advise staying right in Old Alónnisos town. Konstantina Studio is just below the town center (4240.65900; doubles, about $80). Alónnisos also has rural villas that often have exquisite views of the sea. VG Travel Club has one villa that sleeps three to six for about $75 to $110 a night (210.8047244; vacation-sporades.com).

Incessant motorbikes ruin alfresco dining in Patitiri, so head up into the old town, where the taverna scene remains lively until late and vehicles are banned. I had a very fine moussaka, with appetizers, wine, and coffee, at Bubulinya (entrées, $15–$20). For an evening drink and jazz beneath the stars, stroll to the top of Alónnisos and join the young crowd at Azzurro, or buy some terrific traditional Greek pastries at Xariati.

Skiathos

The island has infinite lodgings, from small hotels to resort spas. The Bourtzi, like its sister hotel, the Pothos, is centrally located on a small, quiet street. Both—like many in Skiathos—cater to English and German charters, so book in advance (4270.21304; fax: .23243; doubles, about $60).

The many tourists make dining relatively expensive—from $25 to $60 per person, with wine—unless you stick to the cafés and tavernas that line the winding side streets. Briki, on Trion Ierarchon

Square, is hard to find but worth it for the excellent Greek coffee, ices, and a papaya yogurt shake served in a carved-out papaya shell.

Skopelos

If you decide to stay on just one island, choose Skopelos. It has plenty to explore, fine beaches, steep central mountains, dense forests, and a lively town life. And from here, it's just a short ferry ride east to Alónnisos and the marine park, or west to bustling Skiathos.

The British colonial **Prince Stafilos Hotel** is worth booking ahead. In a quiet compound with trumpet vines and roses, it's only a ten-minute walk along the quay into town. It also has a pool and an extremely helpful staff (4240.22775; fax: .22825; doubles, about $175).

Perivoli is less casual and more expensive than most restaurants in Skopelos Town, but it has a vine-covered terrace and a good wine list and takes care in its nouvelle presentations (4240.23.758; entrées, $18–$25). Along the waterfront, try **Molos** for meat dishes (entrées, $8–$15). On a small balcony not far from Perivoli stands **Greca's Creperie**. Greca will hold forth on art and politics, if you inquire, and her crepes make for satisfying late-evening dining ($5–$12).

Dick Caldwell does tours of Skopelos, mostly in conjunction with larger tours of the Aegean from Turkey to Albania. A classics professor emeritus from the University of Southern California, Caldwell is a walking encyclopedia of Aegean myth, history, and culture—and of good hotels, local wines, and restaurants (www.greecetravel.com/sporadestours).

Fishing and pleasure boats come to Agnóndas, which is crowded with beachfront apartments and tavernas. **Korali** has fine fish and salads (4240.22407; entrées, $15–$20).

To see the more remote east coast beaches of Glysteri, Vathias, or Limonari, catch a boat from the harbor in Panormos. Pack a lunch; they pick you up at the end of the day. In Panormos, stop at Dimitris "Jimmy" Papastergiou's **Dichta,** better known as Jimmy's Parakalo, a little covered patio on the right as you pull into town. You don't need any special introduction to get Jimmy's full attention. I promise you a joyous evening (dinner with wine, about $15).

Skyros

In Skyros Town my spacious room at the **Hotel Paliopyrgos** had a balcony with views of the sea, the sunrise, and the islands beyond. A fine breakfast of hard-boiled eggs, bread, jam, dense local yogurt with honey, and Greek coffee is served on the vine-shaded terrace overlooking the sea (2220.91.014; doubles, about $40–$60).

Skyros Travel and Tourism can help with anything. Accommodations? The owner, Lefteris Trakos, happens to own **Pegasus,** a little motel on Ahironis Beach (2220.91.600; fax: .92.123; doubles, about $32–$52). Something more upscale? The **Hotel Dioni** is a hideaway of apartments sturdily constructed in accord with Skyrian tradition (called *sfas*): white stucco walls, dark wood beams, and tile floors (2220.092.199 or .399; sportivo.gr/dh; doubles, about $73). Cars? Yes, about $40 per day. Motorbikes? Yes, those too. I rented a Hyundai, which led Trakos to warn me that going off the main road can be treacherous—for the car (2220.092.199 or .399; skyrostravel@hol.gr).

Sleepy Syros Town perks up at night. At **Orexis** (Appetite), I sat on the patio under a large mulberry tree, drank a nice juicy house wine from a chilled metal cup, and dined on marinated octopus, olives, *tzatziki,* french fries dusted with Skyrian cheese, and a rack of goat ribs that was mildly gamy and intense with citrus sauce (2220.91311; entrées, $12–$20).

If you can find a copy of the 1983 *The Gates of the Wind,* you've struck gold. Michael Carroll lovingly describes his time living on and exploring the Sporades (try Amazon.co.uk or, for excerpts, users. otenet.gr/~skopelos/books/carroll.htm). Most of the best reading—and this is not to say great—is on the Web. For **Skyros,** skyrosnet.gr/ uk/index_uk.htm will give you a little more information on touring the island. Much better resources are available on **Alónnisos** and the marine park: www.monachus.org is devoted to the monk seal, whose scientific name is monachus; greekisland.co.uk has pages on Alónnisos and the Sporades put together by Brits, who seem to make up the main tourist market for the Sporades (besides the Greeks themselves); www.alonissos.gr/en, the island's official site, is short on description but good for details such as phone numbers and ferry schedules. **Skopelos**'s official site has everything from history to hotels and maps (skopelosweb.gr). Matt Barrett has an honest, helpful site (greecetravel.com/skopelos). He works in conjunction with Mimi Rekkas, who is most easily found by typing her name into your search engine—not via her wildly long URL. For more about *rembétika* music, visit home.earthlink.net/~lkritikos/index1.html or go to acousticguitar.com and search for *bouzouki* for a history of this distinctive instrument. For **Skiathos,** use its official site, n-skiathos.gr, or skiathosinfo.com.

Culture—Zorba Is Everywhere

From their crafts to their music, the Sporades Islands harbor the real thing in the Aegean

Some of the best *rembétika* can be heard on **Skopelos,** when Kostas Kalafatis and his group play at **Mpampalo** (pronounced *ba-ba-lo*), a terrace bar just past the Hotel Denise. Also check posted handbills for special *rembétika* concerts. The **Photographic Center** runs exhibitions throughout the summer (4240.24121). If you're looking for local crafts, **Nick Rodios** represents the third generation practicing a ceramic tradition. The ceramics, which are sold in the shop just up the street from the waterfront, are made from Skopelos clay and have been singed by heat to give them color (no paints are used) and to imbue them with a silken sheen. From traditional oil lamps to animal sculptures, the ceramics all bear refined curves. You can watch Rodios work, shaping and firing his ceramics, across the street (from $25). **Potoki** has a good collection of fine jewelry, as well as worry beads with tiger-eye stones that sell for $80.

On **Skyros,** the **Manos Faltaits Museum** displays crafts, costumes and masks like the fearsome goat-faced masks for the island's unique Easter celebration, and hand-woven silks and linens with distinctive embroideries. The website has good information on the history and nature of Skyros (2220.91232; users.otenet.gr/~faltaits). The shop sells only painted replicas of the embroideries, so visit **Amersa Panagiotou,** in Kalamitsa. The sign on the road is as modest as the proprietress, whose exquisite one-of-a-kind silks and embroideries range from $400 to $1,200 (2220.92.827; inskyros.gr/amersa.htm).

On **Alónnisos,** tours of the marine park can be booked in Patitiri, the commercial center, which also has an office of the **Hellenic Society for the Study and Protection of the Monk Seal.** Volunteers answer questions and show a video of the history of monk seal protection (mom.gr).

On **Skiathos,** the main street, Papadiamandi, is like a midway of trinket sellers, but there are a few shops worth a visit. **Phaedra** sells some fine and interesting jewelry from local makers. **Markos Botsaris's Archipelagos** displays modern Greek paintings, sculptures, and ceramics, along with antiques and jewelry, in an elegant two-story house (4270.22163).

The Isles That Launched a Thousand Trips

BY G. Y. DRYANSKY

༈

G. Y. DRYANSKY is European Editor at *Condé Nast Traveler*, where this piece first appeared in the July 2002 issue. Over the years he has written about a multitude of Mediterranean destinations, including the two Aegean gems featured in this piece: Santorini and Mykonos.

Time was—I'm thinking of the 1960s—when Greece had not yet come to define a dream destination. Hotels were scarce. Fishermen who welcomed travelers into their primitive homes were often offended when you offered to pay them. Two islands, though, were already on their way to putting themselves on the map for more prescient travelers: Mykonos and Santorini.

These islands became the smart venues for a bright blue summer in Greece, so much so that they now lose much of their identity in high summer, when crowds invade. But the secret of their persistent appeal has to do with the strong roots that make both unique. You could argue that each began creating its current image four thousand years ago.

I went to Santorini and Mykonos in May. I probably should have waited until the end of September, when the water is warmest, the winds are favorable, and the crowds have gone, but May does reveal the islands' essential natures.

I'd never been to Mykonos. And so while on Santorini, I asked for a heads-up on it. I should have realized that this was like asking a Yankees fan about the Red Sox. My friend Yannis Tseklenis, an Athenian designer with a home on Santorini, told me, more or less with tongue in cheek, that "Mykonos began as a bordello for its neighbor, the holy island of Delos, and it's been like that ever since."

Shortly after I arrived on Mykonos, the young, conservative mayor, Christos Veronis, invited me to his office. It was a Sunday morning, and he went out of his way to show me charts with all his plans for zoning laws and road improvements. But when I asked what mattered most for the future of Mykonos, he said: "This is a very free island."

Such were my starting points toward understanding a reputation that began in antiquity.

Call me Pegasus: I landed on Mykonos in a Eurocopter Colibri, a shiny new metal bird, flying low over the arid, faintly undulating landscape and the white cubic houses that inspired Le Corbusier. They had an unexciting sameness to them, relieved only by occasional windmills and pigeon coops with laced facades, and by the interposition of little red-roofed churches. Where were the glitzy villas? They were just bigger cubes.

The helicopter, I had figured, was the right etiquette to make an entrance on Mykonos. Such is the drill in St. Tropez and Monte Carlo. As it turned out, the one public helipad was at my hotel, the Santa Marina, which was the first grand resort on the island. The Santa Marina is gated, with views of the indigo sea, a big swimming pool, a private beach (albeit pebbled, unlike Mykonos's great sand beaches), a sauna, a gym, and a fairly good restaurant run by a congenial Italian. If you stay there, you might be tempted to forget about the rest of Mykonos. In May the room rates drop to as low as $90 for two. I've never seen value like that before, but the Santa Marina is still struggling to become a hot place to stay. It's the *enfant chéri* of shipping magnate Elias Papageorgiou, who spared no expense in creating it. But the Santa Marina, I quickly learned, is not quite Mykonos.

From their yachts or from a few villas, celebrities regularly pop up in the town of Mykonos. They help the island's reputation, but Mykonos, unlike St. Tropez, is not a venue for gawkers looking for the famous. Instead, the famous, it seems, come to rub shoulders with the anonymous. There are no VIP rooms in the clubs, and name designers like Thierry Mugler and Jean-Paul Gaultier are often seen hanging out in the streets into which the club crowd overflows.

Everyone on the island seems familiar with the Barbra Streisand story. "Do you know who I am?" she once asked a baker in the town of Mykonos, who was looking at his overhead TV instead of serving her. "Yes, but I'm watching a football game," he answered. The designer Valentino, a living benchmark for glitz who likes to arrive on his yacht, the *TM Blue* (*TM* for "too much"), can't get taxis to wait while he makes the rounds of the clubs.

You need something other than fame to get noticed on Mykonos. Something even more precious: you need to be young and good-looking. It's the gay community, where class lines blur most easily, that has made these criteria prevail. And social life here emanates from the gays, for whom Mykonos is the island of choice for "fun, sun, and bun."

A good measure of my briefing on the local mores came from my designated pathfinder, Edward Prendergast, a good-looking young guy who spends seven months a year selling at the Lalaounis jewelry shop and the other five partying in Brazil. Boutiques close around midnight, after which Edward steps out into the better part of his waking day.

Would I, being neither gay, young, nor lovely, find Mykonos of interest? Could I survive a night in the clubs?

A round of bars at eleven put dinner at midnight, still early by Mykonos standards. Then Edward and I went clubbing until four, when the only after-hours disco, Cavo Paradiso at Paradise Beach, opens—for those who like to dance until the sun rises from the sea.

Up a flight of narrow steps, in Little Venice, where the houses abut the very edge of the port, hefty Evangelina served us scotch and fruit punch in her bar called Diva. A local personality for years, Evangelina was the bouncer at Pierros, the island's first and foremost club. Her special habit is picking up tables with her teeth. Mykonos's seasonal society, I was beginning to learn, is a nomenclature of established figures. Andreas Koutsoukos, who owns Pierros, is one such person. At the Montparnasse we were served by Jodie Duncan, originally from West Palm Beach, who's been living with Nikos Hristodoulakis and sharing the bar with him for years. The Montparnasse is not a dance club but a place you go to drink and chat with Nikos and Jodie, and where an American, Phyllis Pastore, has been singing season after season. When Phyllis sings, the place is packed—year after year, with the same people.

Yes, the same people keep returning, Edward said, but nobody comes looking for the hottest, latest, newest, most keenly designed place to go. Guys want the very same beach chair on Paradise or Super Paradise beach. So, on an island reputed to be hot, there's this cool undercurrent of conservatism.

Of course, if you ask Geraldine Kenway, you'll find out soon enough that Mykonos has changed enormously since she first arrived in 1963. We met Geraldine near her house in the labyrinth of lanes that form the locus of Mykonos nightlife. I had been waiting to hear that I'd come late to Mykonos, and Geraldine confirmed it. She remembered the island when the yachts and the once-a-day, seven-hour ferries from Athens had no suitable harbor, and it seemed that the whole island would come out to watch the fishing boats pick you up and drop you at the foot of town.

Those were the days when Aristotle Onassis brought Jackie to the Greek islands. He had been colluding with Elsa Maxwell to make Greece fashionable for cruise ships and yachts. (Back in the Roaring Twenties, Maxwell, a public relations genius with a flair for starting fashions, had done much to create the summer season on the Côte d'Azur.)

Mykonos had great potential. It is the closest inhabited island to Delos, and Delos is one of the world's outstanding archaeological sites. As early as the 1920s upper-class Athenians and the sophisticated yacht and cruise boat people were doing the site and afterward visiting nearby Mykonos, with its cute waterfront town. The airplane arrived in 1971 in the form of nine-passenger Islanders, and soon after there were Skyvans, flying boxes that accommodated eighteen. Then the runway was extended, bringing package tours. But people whom Elsa would be proud to accompany still come to the island. Last summer George Bush senior arrived on the yacht of one of Greece's richest men, John Latsis.

Geraldine is nostalgic about long nights of conversation at the Seven Sins, the one bar the suave seasonal people used to frequent. The Seven Sins—which the chaste colonels of the Greek junta that ruled in the 1960s had renamed the Seven Seas—is no more. But the celebrities brought creative people with them, and among the creative people were many gays. More and more gays followed, and the dance music came with them.

Geraldine pointed out that the north wind energized people on Mykonos and encouraged them to stay up late. After dinner at Katrin's, with its conservative French cuisine, which passes for the best food on Mykonos, I gave the north wind its shot.

Young men were dancing cheek to cheek or with tongues inter-
twined at Pierros, which is just a room with a bar. The beat was
techno, the mood surprisingly mellow, very Apollonian. Inside the
club and in the street, beer appeared to be the drug of choice.

The other clubs were much like Pierros. The music seemed
almost identical. I'd expected thronged, blasting warehouses, the
disco equivalent of Saturday night in hell. The clubs, though, were
all as small as bars, clustered so close that the crowd from one spills
into the crowd from another, and the street scene and the club scene
blend in a most convivial way.

Even at three A.M. on Matoyianni Street, nobody looked worn
out or drugged out. Edward and I had passed through the Anchor
Bar, Caprice, the Mykonos Bar, and places whose names I forget,
and wound up where we'd started, at Pierros—which was packed.
You could still get a quick meal, an ice cream, or a bagel at innu-
merable little food shops.

We had an hour before Cavo Paradiso opened on the beach. In
a few hours, though, I had to catch the ferry to Delos with Tassos
Stamoulis, Edward's boss, who was anxious to prove that vacation-
ing on Mykonos offered more than house music. I opted for sleep
and closed the windows of my suite at the Santa Marina to the
north wind.

"Delos enjoys the greatest concentration of light in the
Mediterranean," Tassos assured me as, blinking but unbleary-eyed,
I boarded the ferry with him for the half-hour trip. "This exceptional amount of light," he said, "has been scientifically verified by
the Institute of Doxiadis in Athens." No wonder the ancients
believed that Apollo, the sun god, was born on tiny Delos, which
grew, over many centuries before Christ, from a sanctuary into one
of the most important trading centers of the world. The Cyclades

Islands are named for the circle they form around what had been mighty little Delos.

Ruins never warm my heart, but as Tassos and I picked our way through the marble and granite, overrun by a full spectrum of wild-flowers (the island has seven hundred varieties), the story of Delos and its influence on Mykonos fascinated me. We were privileged to hear it from Chadjidakis Panayotis, curator of the Delos and Mykonos museums, who lives alone on Delos, in one room that once sheltered a shepherd.

"From the seventh to the second century B.C., Delos was a free city," Panayotis said, "and that was the golden era of the island's tradition of cosmopolitanism and hospitality." Among the ruins, he pointed out the remains of an Egyptian temple and a synagogue. After Delos was sacked by the fleet of Mithradates, king of Pontus, in 88 B.C., numerous Delians fled to Mykonos, taking their traditions with them. Even the cooking utensils common on the island until the last century were of the same design as those found on Delos.

That morning, when I took the ferry from Mykonos, the little market in the port was full of fishermen with their new catch and farmers with an array of fresh greens, newly dug beets, and zucchini whose flowers had not yet opened. I recalled that while I was having my first drink of the night before at the Veranda Bar, the Mykonians who lived on the floor below were in their boat preparing to go fishing.

The Mykonians have their own established rounds. In late fall they will hold their traditional *chirosfagia,* or pig-killing feast, even though each family no longer depends on one pig a year for meat, and the pigeons that were once another source of protein are now pets. The church feasts, or *panegyri,* go on in each parish as always. Andreas Koutsoukos, who has made a fortune at Pierros, still fishes and sells his catch in the market.

I remembered something Edward had said: "The Mykonians are not tolerant because the gays spend money. The gays come here to spend their money because the Mykonians are tolerant." There is no question but that the Mykonians have cashed in on a virtue in tune with our times. Those who rent rooms to Americans can afford first-class vacations in Thailand these days.

I came to understand that a symbiosis has developed on Mykonos between the seasonal people and the local people—two ways of life that touch without either colliding or coalescing. As the crowds get bigger and coarser, as they do everywhere now, the relationship seems all the more special. And no doubt fragile.

The black-sand beaches of Santorini can't compare with the sands of Mykonos, and the nightlife is nothing exceptional. What you find on Santorini is a very special, paradoxical equanimity, whose roots reach back to times of great adversity and calamity.

Carpe diem, or rather *carpe noctem,* might work as a motto for the clubbers on Mykonos. On Santorini, your impulse is not to seize but to accept. Yet the imperative is just as strong. The island's aficionados, who come to warm themselves under the sun, are there to chill out inside—beside some of the world's purest deep water, on a startling landscape of cliffs that form a seamless whole, with dazzling white dwellings carved into them.

But if nature has always been glorious here, it has not always been benevolent. Every year the Santorinians enjoy a feast day as jolly as a great Irish wake, to commemorate one of the most calamitous days in the long history of their island: July 9, 1956.

That morning Giorgios Arkiros, a man now in his eighties, left his house in the village of Mesaconia to tend his tomato fields. Very early he felt the earth tremble, but he kept on hoeing. At dusk, when he returned home, Arkiros, who had never been anywhere but

Santorini, found himself on another planet. Mesaconia was a pile of rubble. An earthquake with a force of 7.8 on the Richter scale had struck.

The disaster of 1956 destroyed a vast number of houses and brought a plague of poverty; Santorini in the late 1950s and 1960s was as poor and primitive as Greece got.

But that earthquake was a wink of nature compared with the quake-inspired volcanic eruption that happened around 1500 B.C., when a huge piece of the island, some 32 square miles, sank into the sea, and waves 600 feet high struck as far away as Crete. Is Santorini the lost Atlantis? The best guess of scholars these days is that Santorini was a prosperous tributary island of the Minoan civilization of Crete. In 1967 the archaeologist Spyridon Marinatos dug into the hillside at Akrotiri and bared to the world just how prosperous and refined was the community destroyed by natural disaster.

The ruins of ancient Thera, the ninth-century B.C. city created by the Spartan king Thiras, which the Germans uncovered on Santorini in the 1890s, are impressive enough. But Akrotiri, sometimes called "the Pompeii of the Aegean," is breathtaking. With just 3 percent of the site uncovered, you can walk through streets with whole houses as high as three stories, containing stacks of exquisite pottery and whose walls are decorated with delicate, brilliantly colored frescoes. The people of Akrotiri remain a mystery. No skeletons have been found, nor anything of value except for one small golden bull. Apparently the citizens, having had some kind of warning, left before the volcanic eruption buried the town. And went where? Maybe only to be buried themselves under layers of pumice 1,300 feet below the sea, in the lagoonlike caldera that forms a horseshoe on the western side of the island.

The sparkling towns of Oia and Fira, which rim the caldera, bear witness to the prosperity that the discovery at Akrotiri brought. Tourism now nourishes the island. But modern Santorinians, who trace their roots to the Spartans, shy away from defining themselves as professionals of hospitality. Less open to being cosmopolitan than the Mykonians, they are also more apt to allow you to slip a little into their way of life.

At the best tavernas local people are all around you. The owners don't serve food geared to please an international clientele. They'll introduce you to dishes hard to find elsewhere: fava, the local yellow pea puree; tomato fritters, which are the poor Santorinian's meatball; along with the freshest seafood. I am thinking in particular of Katina's, in the tiny port of Amoudi, where Costas Pagonis and his friends catch the fish and spiny lobsters that his wife, Katina, prepares. They will serve you wine from a local grape called the *assyrtiko*, whose traces they claim exist in the ruins of Akrotiri—the oldest wine grape still planted in the world. If you're lucky, you'll have a good bottle vinified by Paris Sigalas, a math teacher who has improved his family's vineyard with the latest enological techniques.

Many Santorini families extended their roots to Odessa through the wine trade. Manos Psychas, a sea captain, was born in Odessa, but when his job as captain of Queen Frederika's royal yacht brought him to Santorini, he decided to renew his ties with his family's island. The Psychases' house had been downed in the earthquake of '56, but in 1969 Manos paid $3,000 for a piece of cliff with some cave dwellings and stables in Oia. Out of this was born Perivolas, one of the most pleasant places I know for a serene vacation. After Manos and his wife died, their son, Costis, who'd designed the expansion, continued to run it, and it's he or his sister, Maria Irini, who'll greet you at Perivolas, where the rooms are suavely comfortable, the service kindly, and the view of the caldera as good as a sea view gets.

I don't believe in ghosts, but I believe that the spirit of an elegant and determined woman still prevails in another place where I like to stay on Santorini, the Zannos Melathron, far from the crowds, in the hillside village of Pyrgos. Eroulia Zannos was the daughter of a shipper who built this neoclassic manor for her as a wedding present in 1886. Her daughter, Manya Tsividis, rebuilt the house after the 1956 earthquake. After her death in 1981, it fell into disrepair until her grandson-in-law, Evangelos Fytros, who made his fortune in tourist hotels in the new village of Kamari, recently restored it, transforming it into a small inn. The frescoes Manya had ordered are bright and lovely again, and the furniture reflects a certain Greek provincialism, authentic and charming.

The lanes of Pyrgos are inaccessible to cars. There are, so far, no souvenir shops in the village. As you change to go to dinner on the terrace, donkeys being led back from the vegetable fields pass the windows of your room.

What did I do on this last trip to Santorini? I swam, ate well, saw two museums and two ruins that are worth the trip from anywhere in the world. And I unwound.

The day before I left I visited Panaghia Episcope, a tiny hillside church not to be missed. Inside and out it is a Byzantine jewel, even though its best icons have been stolen.

I arrived on a hot day, while Maria Argyrou, the keeper, was in the yard cleaning *cardamidis,* wild greens that she'd gathered. When I came out of the church, she offered me what the Greeks call a sweet spoon—a spoonful of taffy in cold water. There I sat, under an old carob tree in the middle of the yard, enjoying the refreshment. I was on one of the world's most celebrated islands, and we know how celebrity can change a place for the worse. But what I felt then was a privileged, simple serenity. I count that among today's greatest luxuries.

On Mykonos—as on Santorini—the "hottest" rarely means the newest. The favorite places to go are frequented by those who visit year after year and give the island its communal feeling. The **Santa Marina** resort is both a wealthy owner's plaything and the guests' joy. Its Italian restaurant, **Daniele's,** is the island's most upscale (2890.23220; www.santamarinahotel.com; doubles, about $243–$369; entrées, $18–$32). The **Dorion** has seaside luxury (2890.28270, fax .28269; doubles, about $197–$222). Simple but up to date, the **Hotel Apollonia Bay** is near a scenic harbor and beach (2890.27890; apollonia_bay@hotmail.com; doubles, about $157–$190). Above Mykonos Town, the **Semeli** is small and luxurious (2890.27466; semeliht@otenet.gr; doubles, about $225).

With its great seaside location and Greek music, **Sea Satin** is a popular taverna among Athenians (2890.24676; entrées, $13–$18). One of the oldest restaurants in town, **Katrin's** serves decent French-style Greek food (2890.22169; entrées, $18–$40). The Italian **Interni** has a modern design and a private patio (2890.26333; entrées, $13–$40). **Philippi** has long been a meeting place for Athenians and Mykonians, but the bar scene is better than the food (2890.22295; entrées, $10–$18). **Basoulas** is a new taverna on the road to Ano Mera, with hip decor, local specialties, and friendly service (2890.71513; entrées, $6–$13). For seafood, **Daphne's** has the ambience of Ano Mera square (2890.72222; entrées, $16–$27). For simple fare at reasonable prices ($15–$20 for a meal), try the beach tavernas at Fokos and Agios Sostis (near Ftelia).

Fun clubs include **Space** in Mykonos town and **Cavo Paradiso** on Paradise Beach. Among the bars in Mykonos town, **Astra** is popular with Athenians, **Celebrities** is open year round, and **Caprice** has a great location on the sea. **Pierros,** however, is still number one.

Visit **www.greekislands.com/mykonos** for up-to-date information.

Among hotels, both **Perivolas** (2860.71308; www.perivolas.gr; doubles, about $320–$407) and **Zannos Melathron** (2860.28220; zannos.gr; doubles, about $287–$340) are recommended. Rooms at the **Tsitouras Collection** are either the ultimate in chic or over the top—you decide. What it certainly has is great sea views from an urbanized cliff (2860.23747; www.tsitouras.gr; doubles, about $497–$500).

As this issue went to press, **La Maltese,** bidding to be the most upscale restaurant on Santorini, was due to open in Imerovigli with a French chef and a pan-Mediterranean menu (2860.28080; entrées, $24–$37). In Fira, **Koukoumavlos** maintains world-class creative cooking (2860.23807; entrées, $13–$18). Among tavernas, **Dimitris** is an authentic waterfront spot in Ammoudi, with great fish and country food (2860.82532; entrées, $5–$9), and **Finikia,** in Oia, has quite a sophisticated kitchen (2860.71373; entrées, $8–$18).

Santonet.gr is reasonably thorough.

Fire and Light

BY CASKIE STINNETT

༜

editor's note

Santorini being the extraordinary island it is, I feel it is worthy of being featured twice in this anthology. Here is one of the best pieces written about the island that I've ever read.

CASKIE STINNETT, former editor of both *Holiday* and *Travel +
Leisure*, contributed a great number of wonderful travel pieces to a great
number of national and international publications before he passed away.
He was also the author of *One Man's Island: Reflections on Maine Life from
Slightly Offshore* (Down East Books, 1984).

If the rarity of Greece lies in the singular purity of its landscapes,
as Lawrence Durrell insists, then Santorini must be among the
two or three most purely and resonantly Greek of the ancient sites.
Like Delphi and the Acropolis of Athens, Santorini's historic memories echo on and on through the centuries as if they were no more
than passing years.

The place itself—bare rock and blueness rearing from the surface of the Aegean Sea—is the possessor of a sly innocence. For on
this tiny island, this rock anchored in the quiet sea, occurred the
most violent and terrifying explosion that is believed ever to have
taken place on this planet. The Santorini explosion was many times
greater than that of Krakatoa in Indonesia in 1883, which reverberated around the world and created a wave more than 50 feet high,
destroying towns hundreds of miles away. It was the Santorini eruption in 1450 B.C. that brought an end to the Minoan civilization on
the island of Crete and at the same time caused nearly two-thirds of
Santorini itself to disappear into the sea.

The force that is buried in the rocky cliff occasionally reasserts
itself—the village at the top of the towering rock was last destroyed
by an earthquake in 1956—but Santorini is now a quiet place, sleeping in the Aegean sunlight, its stillness broken only by the footsteps
of tourists moving about the narrow streets of Thira, its principal
village. (The island has undergone several name changes, from
Kallisti to Thira, after Dorian Thiras, founder of the town of Thira
in the ninth century B.C., to Santorini, based upon St. Irene of
Thessaloniki, and most recently, back to the official name of

Thira.) Here and there a few plumes of sulphurous vapor bubble through the surface of the sea, and some rock ledges still smolder, but vulcanologists say that Santorini's strength is spent, and it is no longer a threat to the people who live there or those who come by ship to see one of the most ravishingly beautiful sights in the world.

I once arose at dawn to watch from the terrace of the Atlantis Hotel the first escaping beams of sunlight as they moved across the sea. The hotel stood on the very edge of the cliff where the island broke away, and the terrace commanded a view that was dizzying. Only an iron railing protected the visitor from a drop of 600 feet to the sea. When the reflected light of the sun began to lift the shadows from the island, I could see the winding footpath up and down which the little burros tediously made their way, bringing goods and supplies and baggage and even the tourists themselves to the summit. But in the early morning light, everything looked strange, more clean than it could possibly be, more pristine, more brilliant.

I have always thought that the boisterous, clamorous character of the Neapolitan was due to the fact that embedded in the subconscious mind was the knowledge that he or she walked constantly above the banked fires of Vesuvius, and I wondered if the people of Santorini had acquired any characteristics from an inner awareness of the volcano's ability to make more mischief in the future. Never mind. In the rising sun the great white church came into view, first its pinnacle, then its round dome and then its stairways of stone, the tiny balconies, the walled walkways. In a few moments it was gleaming white; only its windows and doors remained dark.

Delphi is regarded by most scholars and travelers as the most sacred and grand of the ancient sites of Greece, but I don't wholly agree. I have been to Delphi, and I was moved by the sight of that long sweep of olive groves leading to the sea, the bare rocks, the symbolism of the Delphic ruins, but I still feel that the splendor of Santorini exceeds anything in Greece and ranks very high among all of the natural wonders of the world.

I can't say how many times I have visited Santorini, but it has been often, and many times I have cruised from Piraeus on an Epirotiki ship just because the line's vessels almost always put in there. On my earlier visits I went from the quayside to the village of Thira astride one of the tiny burros, whose owners meet all cruise ships, but when a chairlift was recently installed I gave up the burros because I had come to believe they were cruelly treated by their owners. The tiny animals were raced up the steep incline, speeded by whips, in order to get back quickly for another payload, and I never saw them permitted to rest or to drink or to eat. One day I saw an abandoned burro, totally exhausted, standing beside the trail, its sides heaving convulsively, and I am sure it was left there to die by an owner who felt it had no further value to him. I never patronized the burros after that.

The heart of Santorini—the modern heart—is the village of Thira on the summit, with its narrow, winding streets that often lead nowhere, its confusing layers of levels, its stone steps, its balconies, its courtyards and that terrifying cliffside that falls away to the sea. Here are the shops that sell trinkets and clothes to the tourists and provisions to the natives. The nearest large town, where natives must go when they need something not stocked by Thira's shops, is Heraklion, on Crete, 70 miles away. One doesn't regard casually a trip of that distance in a small boat.

Cruise ships calling on Santorini must bring their passengers to the island by lighters, since there are no docking facilities for large craft, and even then the ships often have to sail idly about in the waters surrounding Santorini until departure time, because the sea here is too deep for effective anchoring. It is a rugged island spawned by a rugged birth and it possesses rugged traditions. The entire island consists of only 29 square miles and has a population of about 12,000 people. Not all of these people live in Thira, since there are dwellings scattered all over the island, but the major part of the population is concentrated here.

But one always comes back to the island's violent catastrophe because even today—nearly 3,500 years after the event—there are reminders everywhere of what happened. Some scholars insist the evidence exists that Santorini was the legendary continent of Atlantis, one of the earth's earliest and richest civilizations, and that it was destroyed when it fell into the sea following the eruption. Whatever happened, one thing is fairly certain: The explosion occurred very close to 1450 B.C., at a time when the population was about 35,000 people.

Serious excavation of the buried city of Akrotiri began in 1967 under the direction of Professor Spyridon Marinatos, and the findings—ancient vases, Hellenistic sculpture and Byzantine works of art—are richer by far than those discovered in the ruins of Knossos on Crete. Archaeologists are convinced that there was sufficient warning of imminent disaster for the island's population to leave before the explosion; skeletons and bones of dogs were found, but none of human beings. A museum is being built at the site but it is not yet open to the public. Some of the priceless frescoes found in the buried city have been placed in the National Archaeological Museum in Athens and can be seen there.

Once, many years ago, I was chatting at the excavation site with Professor Marinatos while workmen beneath us were shoveling dirt from what appeared to be a stone wall. Suddenly a signal was given from the pit and Marinatos excused himself and jumped down beside the workmen. After a moment he beckoned for me to join him. With a soft brush he began very gently to sweep the dust of centuries from some object that finally lay revealed as an entire vase, and I realized that we—Professor Marinatos and I—were gazing at something no human eye had seen for 3,500 years. It was a strange and thrilling sensation.

Visitors seem to have limited time on Santorini (there's that cruise ship circling the island waiting for the passengers to return) and I think that is unfortunate. No one sits for long in the cafes of Thira, although the view from most of them is breathtaking. Once I stayed behind, and when the last of the burros took the last of the passengers down the spiral trail to the quay, Santorini became a different place. The hurrying ceased abruptly. Shopkeepers brought inside goods displayed on the sidewalks; some sat on steps drinking coffee and talking. Some of the larger cafes closed. Only a handful of strangers, mostly guests of the Atlantis Hotel, wandered about the streets, taking photographs of the village as it normally looks.

And then, suddenly, it was night on Santorini. There were no dazzling lights, no neon, only soft lights in the windows of houses. From the terrace of the Atlantis, as I gazed across the dark sea, there were only stars reflected in the water. The cool sky alone was filled with light. The village was quiet and seemed to have buried itself in the folds of darkness like secrets.

It was then I felt that of all the encircling islands, Santorini was the priceless jewel in the necklace called the Cyclades—and of all the rare places in that country, the repository and guardian of what is singularly, sacredly Greek.

Endless Blue

BY RON HALL

~~

RON HALL may not be a household name, but he's well known in mine. In the August 1988 issue of *Condé Nast Traveler,* a publication that has featured Hall's work for many years, he contributed an epic piece titled "Odyssey Now," in which he searched for the perfect Greek island and evaluated fifty of them. He observed that islands may be dramatically transformed, seemingly overnight: "First they become more and more internationalized, until the character that attracted discriminating visitors in the first place is lost. Then nondiscriminating visitors take over and the process of decline is accelerated." Hall defined something that I have come to realize more and more often ever since: that what I'm looking for is an island that hasn't happened yet. "The trick," as Hall noted, "is to catch the period in an island's development between its getting basic facilities and the arrival of mass tour operators." My feeling is that you can take me to what may be described as the most beautiful spot on the planet, but if I can't get fresh local food, local (alcoholic) libations, indoor plumbing, a café or its equivalent, and a simple, clean bed, it's not my idea of heaven, only a beautiful, natural place that probably shouldn't receive visitors anyway. Hall's article proved to be my bible the first time I was visiting Greek islands, and even though it is now fifteen years old, it's worth searching the archives to read. He has since done a bit of updating, notably in a piece entitled "Island Fever" (Patricia Storace, *Condé Nast Traveler,* 1991, and also still worth tracking down) and this one, compiled in 1999, which focuses on the Dodecanese Islands.

E ven by the usual sun-drenched standards of the Dodecanese Islands of Greece, the summer of 1998 was exceptional. There had, it is true, been a brief shower of rain on June 10, just before my arrival at the Dodecanesian capital of Rhodes, but days, then weeks, then months, went by that were not only free of rain but free from cloud of any sort. As I subsequently traveled around the smaller Dodecanese Islands, I checked off in my diary forty-five consecutive days when there wasn't even so much as a wisp of mist on the mountaintops, nor a streak of stratus to pattern the sunset. For fourteen or more hours a day, every day, the sky was a permanent, relentless, total blue.

That, of course, is the evidence of just one visit, but Rhodes's reputation as the "sun capital of Europe" goes back much farther in time. When, according to Greek mythology, Zeus was sharing out Greek islands to the lesser immortals, it was Helios, the sun god, who took a fancy to Rhodes and made it his personal domain. The Rhodians were proud of being the islanders of the sun god, and when they wished to celebrate their deliverance from a siege, they built an enormous bronze statue of Helios. Sadly, the statue was soon felled by an earthquake, but not before it had become famous as the Colossus of Rhodes and was proclaimed one of the Seven Wonders of the World.

Later in its exotic history Rhodes became ruinously enmeshed in the Crusades, and then, for four centuries, fell under Turkish domination before becoming a bargaining chip in the carve-up of Mediterranean territories that followed the First World War. Perversely, instead of being made part of Greece, the Dodecanese were confirmed as belonging to Italy, even though their language, religion, and culture were unquestionably Greek. (Not until 1947 were the islands at last allowed to join their mother country.)

In 1922, when the dictator Mussolini took control of Italy, he saw rich imperial possibilities in his sunny colony of Rhodes—not only as a naval base but as a holiday playground. Sun worship (in the modern sense) was at the time enjoying its first great vogue around the rivieras of the Mediterranean, but the Italians believed that Rhodes had the potential to outshine them all, both for the brilliance of its sea and sky and for its ancient heritage.

Mussolini started to divert huge sums of Italian taxpayers' money into developing Rhodes as a tourist mecca. Water resources were secured, roads and bridges built, public transportation and electric lighting introduced. The waterfront of Rhodes New Town was laid out as a handsome tree-lined boulevard backed by grandiose public buildings in the heavy, arcaded style then much favored by European dictators.

Behind the beach near the island's northern tip, it acquired a large and posh hotel, the Grande Albergo delle Rose, also fashioned in arcaded "Mussolini style." It was much enjoyed by the writer Lawrence Durrell, but not, it seems, by the Greeks, who—perhaps because of the hotel's dubious political provenance—allowed it to fall into disrepair during the post–World War II decades. Only now, after twenty-five years of closure, is it at last being brought back to life, scheduled to reopen next month as the Playboy Casino, with luxury hotel suites—not a role that some romantics might have wished for it, but an improvement on the dereliction that had gone before. (Another Mussolini-period hotel, a large hunting lodge in Italian Alpine style, high in Rhodes's mountains, has been left to rot; for it there is no rescuer in sight.)

The biggest part of Mussolini's munificence, however, went into renovating the miles of picturesque fortifications surrounding Rhodes Old Town and restoring the Grand Master's Palace, the cardboard-cutout Crusader castle that crowns the medieval skyline. The palace, needless to say, was earmarked as Mussolini's personal summer residence, so no expense was spared in doing it up. Its upper levels were rebuilt and fringed with fancy Oriental crenellations; the interior walls were lined with a priceless jumble of classical and Byzantine antiquities; and the floors throughout were paved in a way that only a dictator could command—with a breathtaking expanse of genuine Roman and Hellenistic mosaics, purloined from ancient sites on the nearby island of Kos. The irony was that having lavished all of this money, Mussolini never even got to see his fairy-tale castle. Work on the restoration began in 1937 and wasn't completed until 1940, by which time Mussolini, and the world, were engaged in other things.

Today Rhodes as a Greek holiday destination gets rather a mixed press, and it can't be denied that in recent years tourism has fostered some hideous excrescences. The once-pristine beach of the island's main seaside resort, Faliráki, for instance, has become a bizarre jungle of builders' cranes used for overwater bungee-jumping. Farther down the coast the exquisite fifteenth-century village of Lindos, sandwiched between a golden beach and an ancient acropolis, has become barely habitable in summer because of the crush of day-trippers blocking its narrow streets and the nightly cacophony of discos and rock bars.

But steer clear of the tourist black spots, and Rhodes still has wonderful things to offer. The island's mountain villages, rich in folk culture, are—thanks to Mussolini's road builders—easily accessible to anyone with a rented jeep. Rhodes Old Town, with its towers, minarets, and maze of tiny streets, is one of the two most complete medieval walled cities in Europe (the other being Dubrovnik) and is an inexhaustible source of interest and enjoyment. Even Rhodes New Town is a place of some style. Its "Mussolini" buildings may not be exactly what most people are looking for when choosing a Greek island, but they have architectural quality as well as a niche in history.

The most lasting effect of Rhodes's brush with fascism, however, was that postwar Greece inherited the foundations of a flourishing tourist industry. By the mid-1930s, Rhodes was already receiving 20,000 visitors a year, a figure that would get an enormous boost with the postwar arrival of cheap air travel. But the profligate spending by Mussolini's henchmen had resulted in Italy's failing to make a penny's profit, either before or after the war, from its lavish investment in Rhodes's summer sunshine.

I have come this far without having said exactly what the Dodecanese are—not quite such a straightforward matter as might be thought. In Greek *Dodecanese* means, simply, "twelve islands" and is the name that for most of this century has been applied to the cluster of islands in the southeastern corner of the Aegean Sea that have shared, with Rhodes, a common political destiny. The confusion arises because no two guidebooks can agree on which islands to include, or even whether twelve is the right number in the first place. (The cover of the Cadogan guide lists fifteen islands, that of the Rough Guide no fewer than eighteen.) Greek official-dom, however, is more or less settled on fourteen: Patmos, Lipsos, Leros, Kalymnos, Kos, Rhodes, Kastellórizon, Nísiros, Tílos, Sími, Khalkē, Kasos, Kárpathos, and Astipálaia, which for my money is quite enough to be going on with.

Geographically, the Dodecanese are as far to the east as Greece goes. The islands are scattered at roughly 10-to-15-mile intervals along the deep serrations of the Turkish coast, in some places barely swimming distance from the mainland. Despite the immemorial enmity between Greek and Turk, there was, during the long years of the Ottoman Empire, a considerable degree of sym-biosis. In return for the islanders' maritime expertise, the Turks rewarded them with valuable trading concessions.

Nowhere benefited more from these than Sími, an arid but beau-tiful island just to the north of Rhodes.

The roots of Sími's wealth go back to the sixteenth century, when Süleyman the Magnificent, no less, was planning his great assault on the Crusader knights in Rhodes. The Simiotes, guessing (correctly) that their protectors would be defeated, approached

Süleyman and offered to surrender without further ado, provided they could go about their affairs unmolested. Their delegation was accompanied by women carrying gifts of sponges (much in demand for the royal harem) and loaves of island bread. Süleyman was charmed and issued a *firman* (a royal decree) giving Sími virtual autonomy in return for a nominal annual tax and a continuing supply of sponges. The Simiotes were also given "sole rights to fish for sponges in all seas of the Ottoman Empire," while another valuable concession gave Sími's much-vaunted shipbuilders access to mainland timber, which was vital in view of the island's already fast-depleted forests. (Nowadays Sími is virtually a treeless rock.)

On these two lucrative products—sponges and boats—Sími quietly prospered until, by the second half of the nineteenth century, it had become one of the richest small islands in the entire Mediterranean. At peak, some 20,000 people lived in Chorio, the island's hill town, overlooking the steep-sided, fjordlike harbor, Gialos. A broad flight of five hundred stone steps stretched up from the harborside warehouses toward Chorio, and on either side of this, tier upon tier of grand neoclassical houses were built, clinging limpetlike to the steep limestone rock. The steps became known as the Kali Strata (Beautiful Street), and indeed there was—and is— nowhere in Greece to equal the harmony of its buildings. Each house was topped by a pediment, tastefully highlighted in blue, or dark red, or ocher. Even the smaller, older white cube houses, higher up the island, often had their facades rebuilt to incorporate fashionable neoclassical flourishes.

But then, abruptly, at the beginning of this century, the island's fortunes went into reverse. Ottoman rule was drawing to a close, and with it Sími's privileged supply of shipbuilding timber. The sponge industry was also in trouble. In an attempt to meet ever-growing demand, traditional free-diving methods had been abandoned in favor of air pumps and diving suits, resulting, inevitably, in disastrous overfishing of the sponge beds and an epidemic of a little-understood sickness called "the bends." As the death toll mounted, the Simiotes rebelled against their dangerous calling. They continued to market sponges and to maintain sponge-fishing boats, but actual divers were increasingly recruited from the neighboring islands of Kalymnos and Khalkē. Those Símiotes who wished to continue diving emigrated en masse to Tarpon Springs, Florida, where an expatriate Greek sponge-diving community was (and is) thriving.

World War II brought further calamities, as control of the Dodecanese switched fitfully between the Italians, the Germans, and the British. The blowing up of an ammunition dump by departing Germans reduced most of Chorio to rubble, and Allied incendiary bombs left gaping holes in the Kali Strata. By the end of the war Sími was a ghost island, its population reduced to a little over two thousand and its mercantile fleet wiped out.

Sími's recovery began fortuitously. In the mid-1970s, tensions between Greece and Turkey over the invasion of Cyprus meant that Rhodes's day-trip boats could no longer visit the Turkish mainland, so they switched instead to forgotten Sími. This daily injection of tourist money put life back into the island. Scores of houses were restored, and for once the Greek government had the foresight to list the town as a national monument and ensure preservation of its architectural style. The rebirth of Sími had begun.

Fashions in Greek islands change only slowly, but over the past two decades it has been intriguing to watch Sími's steady rise from an obscure day-trip destination to a major Aegean showpiece. Some Sími devotees even believe that the island is destined to join the superleague of top Mediterranean resorts, to be spoken of in the same breath as Portofino, Capri, Ibiza, St. Tropez, Positano, and the like. That is probably pitching it a bit high, but certainly each time I go there I am surprised not only at how the visiting yachts are getting bigger and glossier but at the many other symptoms of growing sophistication.

In just two years since my last visit, the island had acquired an arts festival, a newspaper, a fitness center, a smart designer restaurant (named Milopetra), a hydrofoil (to add to the ferryboat and the high-speed catamaran that the community already owned), a traffic cop, a fashion boutique, a classical music school, an ambulance (though not yet a hospital!), a cell phone mast (yes, Sími's goatherds can sometimes be seen checking in on their mobiles), and a "wine restaurant" (Hellenikon) with a specialized cellar of Greek wine.

This last item is such an apparent oxymoron that it requires a word of explanation. Although Greeks are often credited with having invented wine, their present-day attempts at winemaking are, to say the least, undistinguished. However, small producers of well-made organic wine do exist in Greece—if you have the time to şeek them out. A Sími trader, Nikos Psarros, having made a modest fortune selling sponges to Rhodes day-trippers, set out to do just that: he embarked on an obsessive hunt through Greece to assemble what he believes is the nation's most important collection of small producers' regional wines.

I spent an hour with Nikos in his air-conditioned, light-controlled Sími cellar, where he holds stocks of 140 different Greek wines for his restaurant next door. I enjoyed tasting a selection of them, though I have to admit that wrestling with the names of obscure Greek grape varieties, all sounding vaguely alike—*xinomavro, mavrodaphne, moschofilero, assyrtiko, agiorgitiko, liatiko*—proved to be too intellectually demanding for a Greek island holiday, and I escaped, as soon as I decently could, back to my regular bar and usual tipple of factory-made retsina.

The one problem with Sími is the influx of trippers from Rhodes, who mostly arrive in the late morning and leave by midafternoon. Longer-term visitors usually slip away to the next bay or the upper town for lunch.

Rhodes and Sími apart, the other most popular Dodecanese destinations are Patmos and Kos—two islands of vastly differing temperament.

Patmos is the gentlest and most restrained of all the Greek Islands. Its massive hilltop monastery, dedicated to Saint John the Divine (for it was on Patmos that he had his revelation of the Apocalypse), dominates the island and sets its tone. A white hill town of fine sea captains' mansions is wrapped tightly around the monastery. Many of the larger houses are now owned by well-to-do expatriates, who are usually in residence only a few weeks a year. As a result, the town, though exceptionally beautiful, often has a rather forlorn and underpopulated air, lacking the vitality and incident of normal Greek street life.

Kos has completely the opposite problem. Its main town, built around a harborside Crusader castle, has been given over to tourism to such a degree that entire streets are devoted to nothing but bars, discos, and fast-food joints, and other streets sell nothing but tourist trash.

There is, however, another side to Kos. In 1933 the town was leveled by an earthquake that exposed the remains of an ancient Roman city that turned out to be far more extensive than had previously been realized. Also, a few miles inland is the evocative ancient site of the Asklepieion, the hospital-cum-sanctuary built where Hippocrates (he of the Hippocratic oath) practiced medicine. No other island in the Dodecanese, not even Rhodes, can match Kos for archaeological interest. It is an essential antidote to the tourist nightmare.

If any one single thing differentiates the Dodecanese from other Greek Island groups, it is that for much of their history they have been relatively well off—especially when compared with the islands of the central Aegean, which, until tourism came to their rescue, knew long periods of grinding, if picturesque, poverty. Social customs in the Dodecanese tend to be not just colorful folklore, but devices for keeping fortunes intact and the population at a sustainable level.

At the root of most customs is the Dodecanese system of marriage and inheritance, found in its most extreme form on the large and dramatic island of Kárpathos, and particularly in its deeply conservative northern hill town of Olympos—one of the last places in Greece where women still wear island costume to go about their daily business. Instead of the eldest son inheriting the family fortune, as happens in most European countries, in Olympos everything is concentrated on the eldest daughter. She is known as the *kanakara* (variously translated as "the cherished one" or "the spoiled one"), and she is brought up from childhood in the knowledge that as soon as she marries, the family home, complete with all of its heirlooms, will immediately become hers.

Just in case anyone has any doubt about the family's pecuniary worth, the *kanakara* wears over her traditional dress, on festive occasions, a *kolaïna*—a broad necklace weighed down with large, heavy gold pieces and coins. At regular intervals in her life yet more gold is added to the *kolaïna* until, by the time of marriage, it is almost too ponderous to wear. The father's wealth, usually far less considerable than that on the maternal side, is also left undivided and intact, to be inherited by the eldest son, with not a penny going to the younger siblings.

This rigid form of primogeniture guards against the dilution of landholdings and resources. But it also means that anyone other than the firstborn finds it virtually impossible to marry within the village, and many choose to emigrate rather than be reduced to working as laborers in their elder brothers' fields. As a result of all the emigration, the Karpathiot communities in cities such as Pittsburgh, Washington, and Baltimore are often larger and more bound by tradition than in Kárpathos itself. (Patmos is another Dodecanese island known for exporting people to the United States in large numbers, while "Kassies," as Australians call the people of Kastellórizon, form a surprising chunk of the present-day populations of Sydney and Melbourne.)

This traffic in people, it should be said, isn't all one-way. The money and gifts sent home by émigrés or brought home at retirement (for it remains the dream of every Greek islander to return to his birthplace later in life) adds much to the wealth of Dodecanese villages and is still an important component of Greece's foreign earnings.

One of the most engaging things about Greek island life is the way festivals and festivities include the entire village; and if you are lucky with your choice of island, even tourists get roped in. I had been in Kárpathos only three days when I was asked to attend a wedding taking place that very weekend in the old-fashioned hill town of Menetes. It was, I was told, the island's wedding of the year: a young and dashing local lawyer marrying a high-ranking *kanakara* named Kea.

Long before the actual ceremony, the preliminaries began in the bridal home. The main room into which I was ushered was furnished, down to the last detail, in traditional Dodecanese manner, the richly decorated walls crowded with photographs, keepsakes, embroidery, icons, Oriental rugs, and racks full of porcelain. Along one side of the room was the *soufas*—a raised and elaborately carved wooden platform, piled with cushions, where the bride in all her finery had been put on display, like some exotic new arrival at a zoo. The guests inspected her and her gold-laden *kolaïna* with evident approval before taking their seats around the edge of the room, men on one side, women on the other.

The singing, accompanied by a lute and a lira, was extraordinary. Elderly members of the family took turns with the *mandinadhes*—improvised couplets commenting on the event in a gently satirical manner. Throughout the Dodecanese, *mandinadhes* are a favorite musical form—infectiously enjoyable, even if you don't understand a word of the dialect. With their subtly varied repetitions and shifting harmonies, they had, for me, the same mesmeric effect as improvised blues.

Processions through narrow lanes of the village came next, each accompanied by yet more lira-and-lute combos: first the groom and his retinue making a long climb to the bride's house, and then the bride and groom together, now with an entourage of several hundred people, making the last short ascent to the church and, at last, the wedding ceremony itself.

That evening, as the entire village turned out to eat, drink, and dance, I got into conversation with a member of the bride's family and learned something that brought a new dimension to the proceedings. The bride, it turned out, was not, as I had blithely assumed, a village girl but had been born in Washington, D.C., into an émigré Karpathiot family and had never broken free from her roots. Now here she was, adjusting to life in a claustrophobic little mountain village, bound by tradition and by the narrow confines of Greek island life. I would have felt worried for her but for the fact that she looked so radiantly happy and at home. And for the knowledge that the Dodecanesians have—as Süleyman and Mussolini found out—the quality of adaptability.

The Island Finder
From civilized Patmos to remote Kastelorizo, Ron Hall rates the islands' main features.

Patmos
A highly civilized island dominated by an 11th-century fortified monastery and an imposing hill town of prosperous mansions. The

best beach, Psilli Amos, is difficult to reach other than by sea, but this at least protects it from overcrowding.

Lipsi
A pleasant little island that relies mostly on day-trippers from Patmos. It is now developing a low-key tourist business of its own, though its resources are still too limited for more than a short stay.

Astipalaia
Rapidly evolving as a tourist destination. However, its remote location, between the Cyclades and the Dodecanese, guards against its being overrun. A huge Venetian castle crowns the island, surrounded by a white-cube hill town recently restored by colonizing French and Germans.

Leros
The fine harbor at Lakki was chosen by Mussolini as a naval base, and fashionable Italian architects were sent to build the garrison town. The result is a textbook example of Art Deco and International Modern, wonderful in its way but hilariously out of place on a Greek island. This, plus the presence of a large mental hospital, creates rather a negative image for tourism, even though most of the island is pleasantly traditional.

Kos
The raucous nightlife of Kos town—and the even noisier satellite resort of Kardamena—has most visitors reaching for their earplugs. But it is a large island, and there are many escapes: to the ancient classical sites or the excellent beaches in the southwest.

Nissyros
A dormant volcano rising steeply from the sea, with picturesque villages perched on the edge of the caldera. It's usually visited as a day-

trip from Kos, but the quaint waterfront of Mandraki justifies an overnight stay.

Karpathos

The south is fringed by small beach resorts used by tour operators but is far from spoiled. The rough jeep track northward through the mountains becomes increasingly dramatic and culminates in the village of Olympos, where island customs are preserved as nowhere else in Greece.

Kassos

The tiny harbor town is charmingly old-fashioned, but the hill villages have lost much of their character. There are good walks through the island's stark interior.

Kalymnos

The tourist resorts on the west of the island are bland and boring, but the capital, Pothia, is the opposite—a vibrant working town that originally prospered on sponge fishing but is now a buzz of varied waterfront activities.

Tilos

It has lonely (but stony) beaches, fine mountain walks, and an amusing café life, but it is under-resourced for a long stay.

Halki

A miniature Sími-style island popular with Brits. The highlight is the walk up Tarpon Springs Boulevard (named for the expat Halki community in Florida) to the old Crusader castle, spectacularly sited on a high ridge.

Sími

Has the most beautiful harbor town in Greece, with tier upon tier of neoclassical houses stacked around a steep-sided bay. It first became popular as a day-trip from Rhodes but now attracts an increasingly sophisticated long-stay clientele.

Rhodes
A large and mountainous island with a superbly restored medieval walled city and a busy cruise-boat terminal. Down the island, the 15th-century village of Lindos is exquisitely sited but heavily touristed.

Kastelorizo
A remote and rarely visited gem of the Dodecanese that achieved fleeting fame as the location of the 1991 Oscar-winning movie *Mediterraneo*. Its large neoclassical harbor town was once the equal of Sími's, but war damage is still heavily in evidence. Although the residents mostly decamped to Australia in the postwar years, enough of them have now returned to create a strange yet appealing ambience, half Greek, half Antipodean.

Seeing Chios
Through Greek Eyes

BY DAVID PLANTE

∽

editor's note

I know I said previously that I was reluctant to name a favorite Greek island, and I do feel that you should read as much as you can about the Aegean islands and decide for yourself what suits you; but I also admit that

Chios is my most favorite. To this day I have not met a single other person who has been there, and that may be reason enough for you to add it to your itinerary. The *ch* is pronounced gutturally, similar to the Hebrew *ch* as in *chai*, and it is not, by any stretch of the imagination, to be confused with Ios. Additionally, as *Boston Globe* staff writer Richard Carpenter opined in 1992, "Chios has no chaos. There are no souvlaki stands sprouting from every corner of this green and sunny Greek island. Nor is there an oversupply of shops where Day-Glo T-shirts and plastic Parthenons are hawked with vigor." I had a difficult time deciding if I even wanted to include this piece, loath as I am to one day find a horde of North Americans in one of my favorite villages, Pirgi, or at my favorite beach, Mavra Volia. But ultimately I think that's selfish, and pompous, which I'm really not. Go to Chios, and see for yourself what I mean.

DAVID PLANTE contributed this piece to the travel section of *The New York Times,* where it appeared in 1983. He is the author of *The Age of Terror* (St. Martin's Press, 1999), *Man of My Dreams* (Chronicle Books, 1996), and *Annunciation* (Ticknor & Fields, 1994), among others. Plante travels often to Greece, and is a professor in the writing division at Columbia University's School of the Arts.

*P*rovincial is an unfortunate term, if by *provincial* is meant a place so removed from the big centers of culture it has no culture. In fact, where in the big centers the native culture can thin out and hardly hold itself against the expanding population and, given the many tourists, become crude, it is in the small, withdrawn places where a more subtle culture can be found, more subtle in its consistencies and more subtle in its variations. I am less curious to know the world of a person from Athens than, say, a person from the port town of the Greek island of Chios.

It is an overnight boat trip to Chios from Piraeus. By plane it is 30 minutes. I prefer boats, but I flew to have more time on the island. I went with two friends, a brother and sister who are Athenians. We were met at Chios's small, seaside airport by another friend, who is a Chian.

My Athenian friends told me it is a custom in Chios to feed a traveler the moment he arrives. Our Chian friend said he had to stop for a moment in Hora. In the islands this simply means "town" and is, appropriately, the name of many Greek island port towns. Then he drove us along the coast to his family house, and we travelers, who had eaten breakfast in Athens two hours earlier, were shown immediately into the dining room.

There was a big nineteenth-century carved sideboard and other pieces of large carved furniture, and a round table, covered with a bright white linen cloth, set with white plates and white linen napkins. Crowding the center and spaces between the settings were a huge brioche, a vanilla and chocolate marbleized cake on a cut-glass cake stand, and an oval glass plate heaped with sweet biscuits. As we sat, in came an enormous glass dish of—my Athenian friends exclaimed—"*loukoumadhes!*" Our host had stopped in Chios town to get them fresh. A Chian specialty, they are like doughnuts but larger, puffier, crisper, and we ate them dripping with honey and sprinkled with cinnamon. Our host said, "I thought you'd like them for your elevenses," an English expression that was not out of keeping on the island.

Through the shutters of one window in the dining room, lines of bright sunlight beamed diagonally across the table. The shutter was drawn back from another window, and I saw, out in the garden, a palm tree. A smell came in of sea and lemon blossoms.

What my Athenian companions and I were shown on the island by our friend is open for any traveler to see; but what we saw was given the context of our host's stories. For example, from the terrace of the house we looked out, beyond the palms and lemon trees, onto the strait, its waves glinting, and beyond the strait was the coast of Turkey. If we looked closely, we were told, we might see houses, roads, cars. To learn, even as personal stories, the history of a place is of course to learn of its present. Because of the closeness of Turkey, I was, on Chios, constantly aware of everything as an object of the island's complicated history and therefore its present.

After our fortifying *loukoumadhes,* we went back into Hora to look around. It is a busy town with narrow streets and shops under the second-floor balconies with latticed windows. Facing the main square, behind an iron fence, is a disused mosque, its minaret still standing, though at a slight angle. It is rare to see a minaret in Greece. We stopped in a workshop, filled with floating sawdust and the sounds of mallets hitting chisels, in which the heavy Chian furniture, carved with birds and flowers, continues to be made.

In the afternoon, our host drove us all over the island. He had to pull over to the side of a mountain road to stop and let a truck pass. In the cab of the truck were two dark black-haired men. Tucked under the windshield wiper, as in the buttonhole of a lapel, was a wilted rose. The truck was covered in fine dust. I thought: this too is an object of a complicated history.

We went to Néa Moní, an eleventh-century Byzantine monastery, high in the mountains above Hora, but with a view of the town and the sea. When he was a child, our host told us, he would be taken to Néa Moní by his parents. In what was a deeply holy place to them, they didn't speak above whispers. They could not enter the main church, they were told by a monk, until it had been swept out by a nun, and this meant sweeping out the mosaic stones that had fallen during the night from the arches and domes inlaid with some of the most delicate mosaics in the Byzantine Empire. Now about 50 percent of the mosaics have been secured and cleaned. Kept with other relics of the past in glass cases, I noted, were heaped baskets of mosaic stones, the gold shining among the blue and purple.

As I studied the mosaics, I also examined the trappings and was drawn to an icon of the Virgin covered in gold leaf, leaving only her badly cracked face visible. It is a miraculous icon, and I was interested to see, amid gold chains, rings, earrings, hung all over the icon, some Turkish coins suspended from thin chains like medals.

In a side chapel of the monastery was a huge old glass case, its shelves sagging, in which were stacked the bones of the victims of the massacre of Chios by the Turks in 1822.

By the door of the church, next to an old nun asleep on a chair, was a big clock, its pendulum swinging silently. It occurred to me that either it or my watch was off by hours. My host said the clock, made in Smyrna, as the Greeks call İzmir, was set to Byzantine time.

The uneven, worn stone floors of the church and chapels were strewn with laurel leaves.

We drove on into the mountains, where men walking along the roads wore fringed cloths tied about their heads in what I thought was a distinctly Middle Eastern manner. In a town called Pyrgi the house fronts were decorated in gray and white geometrical patterns, a custom unknown in any other part of the island, much less Greece. Then we went farther into the mountains to Mesta, the medieval fortress town.

As if he were deliberately bringing us from the past closer to the present, our host took us the following day to a part of the island developed in the nineteenth century. It is called Kambos, along the sea to the south of Chios Town, where, among orange, lemon, and tangerine groves, the rich Chians built their summer villas. Enormous, many falling apart, they combine elements of Ottoman and Genoese architecture. So, for example, you see, over an Italianate arched street entrance of massive double doors, the latticed bay where the women sat and sewed and looked down at the street at people passing. You see great marble Italianate staircases inset with Ottoman carvings.

Chios has always been rich. In the Middle Ages it was rich from its exportation of mastic, a resin collected from the mastic trees that grow all over the southern part of the island, to be chewed as gum or to flavor puddings. Then Chios exported what were considered the sweetest oranges in the known world. With such great exports, it is not surprising that most of the Greek shipowners and sailors are Chians. Shipping is the modern source of income for the island, and it is this wealth that not only gives the island its sense of independence but adds a distinct level to the culture of a remote island. For if I, on the edge of Turkey, felt references everywhere to the East, I also felt strong references back to the West, to England especially, where so many of the new generation of Chian shipowners were born, and live, and have become Anglicized.

In Hora there is a beautiful, neoclassical library—one of the best libraries, I was told, in Greece—the top floor of which is devoted to the collection of the pictures of the Argenti family. Most of the paintings, including the impressive ones painted by an artist named du Bois, appear to be of nineteenth-century English ladies and gentlemen, sometimes with pastoral English landscapes in the background. On one wall of the gallery is a huge genealogy of the family, which traces its ancestry five generations back. All the known ancestors are depicted in miniature paintings set into a wide wooden panel. They are connected by lines, starting on the top row. The men and women are dressed in what must have been grand Chian costumes and which are entirely Eastern—the men in high, conical black hats, a little like the hats worn today by Greek priests, but swelling out at the top. The connecting lines all converge on the miniature of a solitary figure, the descendant of them all, wearing a college blazer and tie, and looking totally Western.

Under all these interconnecting cultures is the culture of classical Greece. There is a stone in an olive grove, not far from a seaside restaurant, where Homer, I was told, stood to declaim his epic. I have not mentioned the Archaeological Museum. I must, however, mention this: Chios is noted for its sweets, and before we left, our host took us to a shop on the seafront of Hora where we bought *glyka koutaliou,* preserves to be eaten with a spoon: small green bitter oranges in syrup, soft pistachios, figs, rose petals, all in syrup, and *masticha,* the sweet made from mastic resin, which, an almost intractable white paste, you pull out with a spoon and plunge into a glass of iced water before you eat it. Civilizations are made of such small things.

Off Course in Crete

BY JOHN KRICH

editor's note

Elizabeth Boleman-Herring, who has lived in Greece for more than thirty years, wrote in *Vanishing Greece* that "on Crete, and throughout all of Greece, what is most Greek is no longer to be found where the beach awning has been raised, and the 'Wine Tasting Evening' is touted. Faced for so many centuries with invaders, the Greeks have learned to leave for the plunderer what he seeks, and to retreat with the real valuables. And if the Greek can be richly paid for the things left behind, things he feels, for the most part, to be worthless, so much the better. The Cretan beaches he will cede to Athenian developers and Cretan businessmen—for a price—but his daughters are rarely offered in marriage to the 'foreigners' (from Athens and Munich alike), his village real estate is largely not for sale, and the 'Cretan glance' he reserves for other Cretans. In this way only can the Cretan obey the legendary laws of Cretan hospitality, extending a hand to the stranger in utmost generosity, and still preserve, in the other hand, for Nikos's grandchildren, and great-grandchildren, the precious, blood-spattered rock that is Crete." Crete may be wildly popular; it is with good reason, I say: the island is home to Knossos, the Samaria Gorge, a fabulous Relais & Chateaux property, great beaches, and outstanding cuisine. But here's the thing of it: Crete is a big island, and if you happen to be there when there are crowds, it's a simple matter to head for the hills, so to speak, and find a quiet, gorgeous corner of Aegean paradise.

JOHN KRICH writes for the *Asian Wall Street Journal* and is the author of *Music in Every Room: Around the World in a Bad Mood* (Atlantic Monthly Press, 1988), *Why Is This Country Dancing?* (Simon & Schuster, 1993, hardcover; Cooper Square Press, 2003, paperback), and *El Beisbol: The Pleasures and Passions of the Latin American Game* (Ivan R. Dee, 2002), among others. He wrote this piece for the former *European Travel & Life*.

Every journey places us within a labyrinth. We make our reservations based on wrong assumptions and misguided guidebooks, plan itineraries as though we know where each step will lead—only to fight our way home along an impromptu route fraught with dead ends and disappointments, rooms with a view that turn out to face blind alleys, corners we can't see around until we've gone too far. No matter how innocent our intentions, each foreign exploration sends us groping through a fun house of cross-cultural mirrors. This is especially true on the isle of the labyrinth—from the Greek word *labrys,* for double-edged ax. There's a double-edged quality to any exploration of Crete, the place where Europe as we know it began and where Europe as we recognize it whites out in a Saharan sun. On the home turf of the dreaded Minotaur, some of the continent's most touristed zones are but a bucking bull's lunge from its wildest reaches. And the unpaved roads of Crete, better suited to donkeys than to the battalions of rented Suzuki jeeps, all lead to the sea and a thousand village lairs' shrouded silence.

"Crete's mystery is extremely deep," wrote Nikos Kazantzakis, always a proud, if heretical, navigator through his native labyrinth. "Whoever sets foot on this island senses a mysterious force branching warmly and beneficently through his veins, senses his soul begin to grow." I only wish my first inklings of his island had been so soul-stirring. My fascination with Crete began with flush toilets. I must have been in the fifth grade, or whatever grade it is when schoolchildren get to pick a pet country to map out in crayons, then proudly unveil in a report before the whole class. I can still recall my pastel drawings, thick and smudgy within a blue manila folder, of the tapered clay-red columns of Knossos, a reconstruction of palace life that was half Sir Arthur Evans, half Walt Disney. My Crete was a realm where kids like me rode dolphins to school as though they were surfboards, and where, yes, the modern plumbing that did such miraculous things with water pressure on the tenth floor of a Manhattan apartment building was supposedly first installed. I envisioned the whole Minoan civilization set before cascades of flushing. Before I dug into my first moussaka or sniffed at my first quivering slab of feta cheese, I knew that Homer had made reference to "a land called Crete, in the midst of the wine-dark sea, a fair, rich land begirt with water, and therein are many men, past counting and ninety cities." Padded with all the mythology I could pluck from the *Encyclopaedia Britannica,* my report probably contained few of the facts that have shaped the island's recent destiny: that Crete is one-sixteenth of the entire landmass of sunny Greece, one-fifth uninhabited, and three-fourths mountainous, with over six hundred miles of coastline.

Iráklion is the kind of town that crushes boyhood dreams. The dominant architecture is flapjack stacks of concrete. Viewed from the appropriately lofty grave of Kazantzakis—a main attraction within the old city walls, marked by an un-Orthodox cross made of two stripped tree branches and providing locals with a free view of the soccer stadium below—the whole place looks like some haze-strafed Middle Eastern citadel in the grip of unplanned growth or civil war. Spinning out from the cafés and pistachio carts of shaded Eleftherias Square, Iráklion's avenues are dusty, drab, and seemingly random. At night there's a certain amount of forced gaiety in the open-air eateries grouped around the town's single, dwarfed Venetian fountain. Farmers flood into this working port to sell their produce, tourists to book passage elsewhere.

I almost don't mind that I'm booked into a hotel several miles out along a growing beachfront strip. Here I get minigolf, mosquitoes, and mostly sun-starved Aryan types. By the end of my first night I've had enough of the Crete toward which most tourists are steered: hastily erected stucco bungalows, hot sands crisscrossed with walkways and cabanas, rows of souvenir stands, discos, and outdoor *Zorba the Greek* tavernas featuring identical menus and piped-in bouzouki music.

"It's better with an explanation," plead the guides who lurk at the entrance to the Knossos palace. What better statement could one make about a labyrinth? For the meaning of these stones, I prefer to consult Kazantzakis: "Here in Crete the monstrous immovable statues of Egypt or Assyria became small and graceful, with bodies that moved, mouths that smiled; the features and stature of God took on the features and stature of man. A new, original humanity full of agility, grace, and oriental luxury lived and played in the Cretan soil."

To plant myself in that soil, I'm willing to forgo a late-afternoon swim and risk taking off at dusk. I persist even after the rude discovery that the brakes on my rental car have a tendency to lock. Slowing to squeeze past a truck on the narrow coastal road, I go into a 360-degree spin. I'm more embarrassed than shaken—what's the word for "junker" in Greek?—but the trucker, a huge fellow with muttonchop sideburns, leaps from his cab and won't let me go until he's reached through my window and, in a split second, taken my pulse. The gesture seems characteristic somehow. On one level, the Cretans take things with a certain placidity and resignation; on the other, they move quickly when given any excuse to be drawn into the moment, seeking whatever sparks can be generated by that dull old rubbing of man's intrepid will against life's quotidian traps.

With my heart rate, but not my brakes, passing inspection, I head toward my chosen destination: Fodele. This is a small village, some 15 miles away, that's been designated, belatedly and on the basis of scanty evidence, the birthplace of the painter El Greco. From long experience, I know that I'll find little there. So why do I persist? My first evening pass through the Cretan labyrinth yields several lessons. For starters, I recognize that on this island, maps are worthless. The distance is always shorter than it looks in miles and longer in minutes than calculated. That's because every highway, even the new three-lane wonder that speeds commerce up and down the north coast, winds, twists, and plummets over far too much topography. Around the first big bend outside the city, I'm treated to hints of what Crete is all about: rugged ravines, sweeping vistas reminiscent of the American West, New Mexican unforested high country, stubby and unconquered mountain peaks that look like melted soft chocolate frozen yogurt, the minty whistling presence of olive orchards, goats and donkeys camouflaged amid the wild scrub and black rocks, caves like the hollow eye sockets of departed spirits, angry terrain falling into placid bays, an odd vastness that belies the fact that you're on an island, belies all finiteness.

In Fodele, El Greco's supposed shack-of-birth is up a rock trail I don't dare attempt on my brakes. But I get my first view of whitewashed staircases that look hewn from the sides of the ravine, punctuated with flowers planted in rusted cans. I count the widows, swathed in the all-black outfits that seem such a perverse denial of Crete's hedonist climate, knitting in cane chairs that face inward toward their houses, emerging into the sweet evening air but never daring to look like they enjoy it, like they enjoy anything. The men in high boots and curled moustaches play cards at the *kafeneion*, ready to be charming or charmed but always waiting for the intruder to make the first move. Lesson two: there are few tourists out here and no real tourist sites that can compete with the simple observation of this rich pattern of being, of people proudly making do in these hills. But when do they do anything but sit and stare?

On the way back I spy the lights of Agia Pelagia, the genuine beach town closest to the capital. From afar, it looks like I'm headed down to a mini–Monte Carlo or at least Portofino. But I find a single perfect cove that's lined with the sort of simple restaurants that rent rooms over the kitchen. Just pick one, any one, and a curly-haired lad will bear swordfish and retsina with little trace of resentment. You don't even have to put your shoes on for supper. Maybe this is what Kazantzakis meant about the playfulness, maybe this is a tiny remnant of the Minoan legacy. For the Greek way, and the Cretan way, is always easy, yields to romance and informality at the slightest pressure. Aside from the ubiquitous thumping canned music, I feel like Agia Pelagia could be some distant undiscovered island outpost. Lesson three: anyone who says that Crete has gone the way of Coney Island must lack a road map or imagination or both.

Still, Crete is a place that makes you work to mine its treasures, which are hidden behind place names that sound unappealing to an English ear. Rethymnon, Sfakion, Palaiokhora. After changing cars—I'm not reassured by the rental agency's claim that my brakes will quit acting spastic after the first 20 miles—I head for the Lasithion Plateau, a wagon-train encampment of villages gathered in one high green valley. At one of the surprisingly few tavernas, a dollar in drachmas buys me a plateload of daffodil-yellow stuffed zucchini blossoms. Crammed with half-baked kernels of rice, bits of fresh tomatoes, and oregano, they taste like some Platonic essence of the earth. Except for main drags draped with tablecloths and hand-loomed rugs for sale, the towns themselves are remarkably unaffected by foreign traffic.

My destination for the night is Ágios Nikólaos, the town most emblematic of the new Crete. From afar, the quaint town sparkles like a recent discovery of the jet set. But you'll find no jet set à la Bianca Jagger, just the one-week charter set à la "Manchester Holidaymakers Limited." "Ag Nik," as it's pronounced in cockney, has no other business now but catering to teenage working-class Apollonians. Discos have replaced net-repairers, and the fleet here goes mostly on day cruises to Spinalónga, an offshore island.

There are only two ways out of this package tour syndrome. There's the quest for authenticity and the retreat into luxury—and you know which is easier. The coast around "Ag Nik" is becoming known as the Cretan Riviera, its views and drives reminiscent of the Amalfi Coast. Along a precipitous stretch near the uninspiring town of Elounda, the coastal slopes have been claimed by several resort complexes, their new cabanas almost outdoing the towns in whiteness. I've been recommended to the Elounda Mare, the newest of these spas, and the most tasteful. A Cretan-born architect has designed a hillside of individual bungalows inspired by the rounded stucco of indigenous villages. It's lovely to sleep on a bed that's built into an alcove, enveloped in the hearthlike roundness. Purple bougainvillea overhangs each room's wooden gate. This Crete is not for soul-testing but for collapsing in high style, with water-skiing, ballooning, and all-you-can-eat lobster feeds accompanied by Beatles tunes. Here any old credit card guarantees you the right to be a peasant with your own one-man swimming pool.

It's easy to see why most travelers stay in the beach towns and take day excursions into the hills. But a glimpse at native Crete is probably better achieved if you dare to arrange things the other way around. Unless you spend the night in simple rooms over the taverna and see what village life looks like once the tourists have departed, then you have to make do with places like Kritsá. Billed as "the authentic Cretan village," this lovely hill town, built on switchbacks, has been reduced to a handicrafts mall. One sight of this signpost in the labyrinth makes me head south, where the coast is supposed to be less "discovered." I'm feeling more hopeful of escape when I pass Gourniá, and then Mírtos, first of numerous beach towns where there's just a taverna or two along the waterfront and you get to know the restaurateurs on a first-name basis.

Asking directions for the eighth time, I run into Darron, about as lost a soul as I could have ordered. At first I think this fair-haired young Brit in shorts and backpack must be a mirage, plodding down the one street of a dusty farm town. It turns out he's been hitching about quite contentedly for days in this steaming cauldron. He's about to recline under a favorite olive tree when he realizes that I'm heading straight toward Mátala, a beach resort in the vicinity of the small town where he's spent his Cretan holiday picking okra and potatoes. I offer him a ride. Together we squint over maps. Main highways are indistinguishable from feeder roads. Sometimes the potholes are an indication of heavy traffic, while the newly paved surfaces lead to nowhere. Yet the emergency of being this far off course forces me to distinguish between the white clumps of Cretan villages as I haven't done before. In the devil-may-care company of Darron, I feel like I'm really traveling at last.

I don't know who's more shaken by the sight of Mátala, Darron or I. I leave him at one of the tavernas that now line the cove that became world-famous for its hillside of caves turned into a hippie colony. Today the caves are fenced off, the beach is crowded, and the young people who stay here prefer motorcycles to mantras. Darron says he prefers to sleep in a field near a beach called Komos. The next morning I'll see why. Komos Beach is as vast and unclaimed as Mátala is runty and overrun. Crete seems to provide the former and the latter in paired sets.

I ponder my next move only after a morning's skinny-dip in the "Libyan Sea." (Why is it a better swim because it's the "Libyan Sea" and not just warm ocean water?) I head for the hills, heeding my guidebook's tip to make way toward Rethymnon through the Amari Valley because "this area features large in almost everything written about Crete—and especially in tales of wartime resistance—yet is hardly explored by modern visitors." I should know by now: history is a fine thing, but unfortunately, history can sometimes be invisible. I skirt the edges of an immense ravine at sunset. One more surprise for the day, and a treat. Rethymnon has the bad rap of being a mere supply center, a middle-of-the-island provincial capital. But Crete has been open to so many influences that nothing about it can be called provincial. In the early evening, I stroll by slatted brown Turkish over-hangs, Ottoman minarets, Venetian arches. Rethymnon's harbor retains a remarkable amount of charm, considering that it's become one immense cafeteria. The high-toned seafood joints offer candlelit dining right inside of the old Venetian fort. On a warm evening, the whole population joins the tourists in a vast promenade. It's here, finally, that I come upon an eating establishment named Labyrinth Pizza. Unlike fair Theseus, I dare not enter. Instead, I plunge back into Rethymnon's back alleys and confront the monster of real Cretan music. To mandolins and zithers, a merry old fellow with a bushy moustache wails his guts out. Crete's song sounds more effu-sive than I would have expected, and even more Arabian. In Rethymnon, one feels truly on the frayed edges of Europe.

Farther east, separated by more little coves than the most invet-erate beachcombers could ever explore, is the charmer of Canea.

This town is the hub of Crete's most prosperous area and the jumping-off point for all-day hikes down the Samaria Gorge, a ritual in mass exertion, which I decide to forgo. Canea is a good deal smaller than Rethymnon and more thoroughly Venetian. The place was occupied by Venice for over four hundred years, and the old sections, draped with laundry, lack only the canals to complete their colonial illusion. At night the former Turkish fortress makes its presence felt. Proof that the Turks failed is close by: today's younger generation of Cretans, eager to be part of a unified Europe, clog the waterfront watering holes. Canea's night scene is rather gentrified for Greece, featuring clubs with names like Oblomov, Nota Bene, and Bla Bla Bla. And some bars that look exclusive on the outside can be rowdy on the inside, catering to U.S. sailors stationed at the naval base in Souda. Still, it's refreshing to see how much Canea is appreciated by its own inhabitants. Some young people are renovating old Venetian palazzi and turning them into fine hotels like the Casa Delfino.

In Canea there's even a hardy, and most proud, expatriate community. Over a lunch of *bourekia*—cheese pies dotted with sesame seeds—in a neighborhood tavern, I make the acquaintance of a retired Greek American professor, Mike Daskalakis. "All my life my father told me about a magical place where oranges grow at the base of snowcapped mountains. I never believed him until I saw it for myself." Daskalakis declares, "Crete is the villages," explaining that even the most sophisticated-looking natives of Canea return to tend olive plots on the weekends. But he admits that they transport their oil in Toyota trucks instead of more traditional means.

I spend my final day dutifully following the path suggested to me by two part-time natives, Sam Abrams, an English literature teacher and poet, and his wife, Barbara. As so often happens, the last and most offhand traveler's tip proves the best. Past Kíssamos, at the far western end of Crete, giant beaches loom. Off-road vehicles are required to get to the best ones. This part of the island shows all the foreboding wildness of Cape Hatteras. But a sign within the city limits of Canea leads down a recommended road to Therisso, birthplace of the Greek freedom fighter Eleuthérios Venizélos. And it turns out to be my favorite dead-end road of the many dead ends in the labyrinth. This 14-mile wonder leads through an increasingly narrow ravine that may not be as spectacular as Samaria but is considerably less crowded. The farther I go, the more I'm hemmed in: by odd and terrifying rock formations, by ravine walls deeply veined with silver- and bronze-colored layers, by beauty. Everywhere there's something mossy or minty. Either I'm at the center of Crete's mystery now, or I've entered a Bartók rhapsody—accompanied by goat bells and olive leaves hissing in the wind. Usually I'm not such a nature boy, but I can't help stopping every hundred yards or so on the road to Therisso, first to snap photos, then to gawk, or simply to breathe as I haven't for quite some time.

For the last word on such matters, I refer back to Kazantzakis: "There is a kind of flame in Crete—let us call it 'soul'—something more powerful than either life or death. There is pride, obstinacy, valor, and together with these something else inexpressible and imponderable, something which makes you rejoice that you are a human being, and at the same time tremble." I feel that I've come to the labyrinth's last door, its most terrifying turn. What's the prize on the other side? The perfect beach? The comforts of lithe maidens who aren't part of a package tour junket? The courage of the *palikares,* those grizzled high-country patriots, gods of billy-goat stubbornness in human form? A hint of ancient cultures buried below? Or the recognition that the only way out of Crete's conundrum is to quit looking for a way out? There's much more to escaping Crete's labyrinth than just catching the morning ferry out.

Nísiros

BY ANNE MEREWOOD

ভ্

editor's note

I wanted to include a piece in this section about an island that, just perhaps, very few readers would know. I have a few candidates in my files that meet this criterion, but I chose this one, about Nísiros, an island near Kos and Rhodes, that I've never visited. After reading this piece, I would very much like to go and plan to, in fact, just as soon as I score tickets to the Athens Festival. I would be grateful to hear from any readers who have had the good fortune, like the author, to visit this decidedly untrendy island.

ANNE MEREWOOD contributed this piece to *Islands*.

Eight years later, and she was still here, a wizened yet ageless woman with gray-streaked black hair that escaped in strands from a tight bun on the back of her head. Sitting behind a huge desk in a small, high-ceilinged travel office, she was talking in a patient mixture of English and Greek to a confused couple from Germany.

"Today Friday." She consulted her spidery notes. "No, today Saturday. Yes, *Sábbato*. Boat go tonight, *apópse*. Nine o'clock. Rhodes. Understand?"

They shook their heads. She took a blank piece of paper from her heavy metal desk and scrawled the number nine. "Ferryboat. *Samstag*. To Rhodes. Nine. Okay?"

They consulted, doubtful, and reluctantly left the cool, dark room for the harsh sunlight, clutching their number nine. I could sympathize. Getting off the island of Nísiros was not easy; a missed ferry might result in a delay of several days.

Meanwhile the woman behind the desk, her brown eyes surrounded by wrinkles, had been scrutinizing the three of us—a couple with a small child.

"I'm sure you don't remember," I began, in hesitant Greek, "but eight years ago . . ." I stopped. How could she possibly recall that back then, in her capacity as Olympic Airways representative, she had located a wayward rucksack (which had traveled solo from London to Madrid), retrieved it, flown it via Athens to Kos, and somehow shipped it to Nísiros on a fishing boat. To me, luggageless and traveling with a friend and her five-year-old to a small dot in an undeniably inefficient nation, those efforts smacked of heroism.

She offered a crooked, yellowed grin of recognition. "You came before," she said, looking at me. She pointed at my Greek-born husband and added, "But not him. Not him either," indicating my three-year-old American-born son. "But there was a little girl," she said. "I remember."

Together, the four of us strolled outside into a bright stone courtyard bursting with red geraniums and running with scrawny kittens.

"I was writing a book about unspoiled Greek islands. I wrote about Nísiros," I reminded her.

She nodded, amused. "Some things have changed a little since then."

Perhaps, but later, when we left her to re-explore the town's narrow "baby streets" (as my son, Gregory, put it), I was relieved to find that a decade of change amounted to little more than two new hotels, four or five moped rental outfits, and a gas station, usually closed.

My husband, Makis, was looking around anxiously too, but for other reasons. While some Greek islands have immediate appeal— sparkling white port towns tumbling down steep hillsides toward enticing beaches—Nísiros, a 16-square-mile volcanic rock in the Greek Dodecanese chain, is an acquired taste. As he surveyed the dusty, workaday harbor and the lack of obvious sandy spots, I knew he was wondering why we had come here at all.

Mandráki, the island's only real town, is not tumbling down a hillside but is, at first sight, tumbling down. A gray, dilapidated ocean wall punctuated by crumbling, sea-rooted dwellings and a few hopeful tavernas create an unappealing seafront—and with good reason: for centuries the waters of the Aegean were rife with marauding pirates, and nobody wanted to tempt them ashore.

The real town deliberately turns its back on the sea, its true focus the tangle of streets laid out in complex patterns to foil the pirates. So narrow you can touch both sides at once, the alleyways weave and twist like the lines of a Greek dance, with white-edged flagstones, blinding white walls, and pastel-painted balconies decked with strings of garlic.

As we walked by, older men and women sitting on doorsteps tapped their sticks and nodded greetings. A teenager wobbled past on a rickety bike, garlic wrapped about his neck, a bread basket on the handlebars. A group of children whirled about Gregory like blowing leaves, then skittered away down an alley.

We stopped in briefly at a couple of tiny cavelike *pantopoleion* (selling everything) stores, holes-in-the-wall with no exterior display, their floor-to-ceiling shelves crammed with a variety of canned food, toys, sunscreens, shoes, chocolate, tissues, cookware, rice, and plastic buckets—all covered in a thick layer of dust.

Outside we paused for a frappé—iced instant coffee, frothing with lots of milk and even more sugar—beneath the plane trees of the small main square and found ourselves between two tables of fishermen. On one side a toothless group was complaining about government pensions; on the other side a faction sporting handlebar moustaches teased them gently and argued among themselves about the next day's outing. Our waitress, a skinny and dusty-legged eight-year-old wearing her mother's apron, took an immediate fancy to my son and dragged him off to the kitchen.

"What do you do in winter?" I asked her when she returned.

She shrugged shyly. "*Pame mesa, thia*"—"We go inside, aunt."

I swallowed both my apparent age and my instant acceptance with equal grace.

After paying our bill and extracting our son, we headed for the pension Drosia, where my previous traveling companion (a bohemian single mother) and I (a strapped-for-cash new graduate) had rented a large three-bedded room for $3 from Mama Anna. We relished its location on a tiny square with a huge white-walled well and a constant crowd of women washing clothes, sewing, and gossiping. We felt privileged that the shared bathroom overlooked (and in retrospect, probably emptied into) the sea, which beat against the foundations.

I was pleasantly surprised to find the wave-battered pension still standing, let alone functioning. But after peering through the heavy shutters at worn wooden floorboards, spartan iron bedsteads, and a multitude of bursting backpacks, I'd seen enough. My husband raised his eyebrows. Realizing with some chagrin that I might have changed more than the island had, I shook my head and directed my family toward the White Beach Hotel.

The White Beach, a crag-climbing structure hanging 100 feet above the Aegean, is as classy as it gets on Nísiros, yet the small, simple rooms with balconies go for just $17 a night and represent a tainted glory for Tony Karpathios, a native of the island who spent many years working in New York and saving his money to build the place.

"It was his dream," said Tony's wife, Georgia, who already spends several months a year with their teenage children in her native Thessaloníki and appears to be considering a more permanent absence. She showed us the empty marble dining room, the roof garden, and the grand, echoing lobby. "It looks wonderful," she said. "Oh yes, everything *looks* wonderful. But there are no tourists. The island is too small for this hotel."

Although Tony Karpathios meets every ferry with his green minivan and hopeful eyes, the White Beach remains one inconvenient mile out of Mandráki.

In my new role as responsible parent, accountable this time for my own child rather than someone else's, I had determined back home in Boston not to use a moped this trip. ("Surely there are rental cars by now," I had said.) Alas, Nísiros had no rental cars, only two taxis and a lone bus that ran but twice a day. Makis and I were soon casting meaningful sidelong glances at infant-toting island families riding Kawasakis.

Inevitably, we approached a moped rental store. I shamelessly delegated my parental responsibility to a fourteen-year-old in a leather vest: "What about him?" I asked, indicating my wide-eyed toddler and envisaging future arguments over tricycle helmets.

The teenager grinned. "He'll be okay. The policeman is a good guy. He doesn't give tickets."

It wasn't quite what I had meant, but Makis and I rented a Vespa, wedged Gregory between us, and held on to him for dear life. Eight years roared away, as I looked around and wondered where to go. That was easily answered. There is only one real sight to see outside of town. So one warm, breezy evening we took the island's only road up the only mountain to find it.

Zigzagging crazily up the steep, painstakingly terraced slopes, some abandoned, some still heavily farmed, we were overwhelmed by the scent of figs and almonds, distracted by magnificent Aegean views, and ambushed by countless potholes. We rounded a bend and skidded to a heart-stopping halt just short of a flock of goats.

"Look!" cried my unperturbed, pitifully urban son. "It's a zoo!"

We wound our way through the goats, negotiated a stubborn cow, and puttered on toward the peak, which proved illusory, because Nísiros has no real summit. Just as we thought we'd arrived, a narrow rim suddenly and shockingly gave way to a vast, flat-bottomed volcanic crater cradling miles of the most fertile farmland in the Aegean. Among the cattle, wheat fields, and circular threshing floors of this sunken plateau lay five inner craters, all hot and yellow with sulfurous steam.

The road dropped through a series of nasty curves, crossed the fertile flatlands, and ended beside a deserted café and the biggest inner crater, almost 400 yards wide and 25 yards deep. A narrow path descended into the hot, soft-floored, smelly basin, where smoldering mounded fumaroles—tiny, sulfur-edged holes—hissed and vented stinking, boiling steam like a colony of crazy kettles.

According to Greek myth, Nísiros was created during the great war between the gods and the giants. As the giant Polybates fled the battle in defeat, Poseidon flung a chunk of Kos at him, pinning him beneath the rock, where he has fumed, groaned, sighed, and occasionally erupted ever since.

The volcano's modern history is almost as mythical. Eruptions were reported in 1871, 1873, 1888, 1933 (accompanied by a 6.6 earthquake), and 1968. Yet in three different books, the volcano is listed variously as "active," "dormant," and "extinct." I smelled the giant's foul breath and listened to his angry whisper. Nísiros did not seem extinct to me.

Extinction does, however, threaten the island's two mountain villages, Nikiá and Emborios, which cling patiently and hopelessly to the edge of an abyss.

In the 1400s Nísiros—about 200 miles southeast of Athens and just 10 miles from Turkey—lay on crucial east-west shipping routes and supported 12,000 inhabitants. For centuries, safe from pirates and convenient to the fields, these two settlements were busy towns.

By 1910 the island's population was down to 5,000; today residents number only 900. Spectacularly located Nikiá is fading away, and Emborios has all but evaporated, leaving nothing but a view and twenty-three souls who inhabit the few maintained homes amid an eerie network of ruined, empty streets.

We guzzled warm, gassy lemonade at Emborios's café, where a rickety two-tabled balcony hangs precariously over the silent volcano. The young woman who served us played with her frilled and beribboned baby on the floor. The only other patron, an old man, shifted his stick and nodded companionably.

"I have seven brothers," he volunteered. "They are in America, Australia, Athens, Rhodes, and Mándraki."

After the volcano we felt duty bound to take a look at Mándraki's fifteenth-century monastery, now devoid of monks but mentioned in every local guide. A textbook Greek island bell tower in white and turquoise greeted us at the top of 180 hot stone steps. Beside it hung a row of shawls, several ankle-length, elastic-waisted skirts, and a sign for immodest tourists: "Visitors are pleased to be propably and adequately dressed."

The incense-scented inner sanctuary, carved into a cliffside cave, was heavy with ornate silver icons and strings of tiny brass "favors" depicting babies, fishing boats, hearts, legs, and other body parts that represented hopeful prayers and grateful thanks from pilgrims and local worshipers.

Gregory's attention, inevitably, was drawn to the collection of candles, set in a tray of sand. We lit one for Gregory, one for Mommy, one for Daddy, and were proceeding inexorably toward the ranks of other relatives when the custodian, a squat old woman in a shapeless black dress, came to our aid.

She poured warm oil from a swinging dish into two plastic bottles, wrapped them in aluminum foil, and handed them to Gregory. "One for you, one for your grandmother," she said. Then she dipped her finger into the dish, made a cross on his forehead, and said, "God bless you."

Gregory looked at me in wonder. I needed a fast explanation: now was hardly the time for me to expound on Orthodox Christian doctrine.

"It's special oil to make you feel good and happy," I said.

Instantaneously his features broke into a saintly grin. "Mommy, it works!"

The custodian was gratified, and Mommy grasped the oil's potential at once. (At difficult moments the little plastic bottle, carried proudly back to Boston, is retrieved, the oil applied, and instant happiness is assured.)

Descending back to the streets, Gregory beaming beatifically beside us, we stopped at a travel office advertising weekly round-the-island boat trips.

Could we sign up for the next day?

The young woman shook her head dolefully. "We need twenty people to run the tour."

"Well, there are three of us here—how many more do you have?

She consulted her book. "Two."

After that we stopped trying to sightsee. Like everyone else, we accepted that the easier you took life on Nísiros, the more you enjoyed it. Each morning after watching Mr. Karpathios clear up the night's accumulated seaweed, we descended 100 feet to the fine marbled mix of black-and-white volcanic sand that made up the misnamed "White Beach" below our hotel.

Other visitors did the same. We soon came to know them, a

handful of northern European, like-minded Nísiros-lovers, some of whom had returned year after year to enjoy that rare, unspoiled Greek-island essence.

As we chatted with them, mostly comparing notes on other untainted spots, Gregory and his new friend, Maximillian, patronized the small, hotel-run snack bar, where two Nisirian teenagers whittled away the Karpathioses' meager profits by lavishing free ice creams on anyone cute, blond, and under five.

We began breakfasting with our new friends in Páli, a cheerful fishing village and the last of the island's four settlements. Savoring our yogurt and honey, we would watch as the fishermen brought home their catch. One morning it included two lobster, an inflated puffer fish, six squid—and a four-foot guitar fish, an ugly, unappetizing gray monster with a flat head.

Landing a fish this size was obviously not an ordinary event. Within minutes wives, children, taverna cooks, and fishing boat owners gathered, followed by the village priest in floor-length black gown and pillbox hat, who arrived smoking a cigarette on the back of a three-wheeler pickup truck. An accomplished nine-year-old cycled up with a machete and an enormous carving knife, which he sharpened with terrifying ease on a stone. As we ate, the group heaved the fish onto a slab, wedged open the enormous jaws with a stick, and sawed off the head.

I stole a glance at Gregory, whose lone brush with death was a fast-distracted glimpse of a "sleeping" bird and whose last vacation was in Disney World. He was staring at the scene, mesmerized. At home our family outlaws toy guns and Saturday morning cartoons, but this was different, an unavoidable encounter with the facts of life.

I seized his hand. "Let's watch," I said.

Headed by a migrant Nisirian who, we were told, spends his winters on Australian fishing boats, the group sliced open the beast, removing heavy internal organs and long loops of entrails. Red blood gushed over the quay and drained into the harbor.

"Poor fish," said Gregory. "Why they do that?"

I chewed my lip. "They need fish to eat."

"These people hungry?"

"They would be, if they didn't catch fish."

He nodded, satisfied. "I eat fish too." It was stark and simple. He never mentioned it again.

Perhaps inspired by the morning's catch, the same group of men brought their music to Páli that evening. Gathered around a rough table, they unpacked a bouzouki, a small mandolinlike *lyra,* and a mini-bouzouki called a *baglamas,* before launching into a wailing series of *mandinadhes,* balladlike songs with words often improvised on the spot. Noticing my bulging belly, they dedicated one to me, "the woman who will soon give birth."

Gregory, who had exhausted the village's supply of stale bread, feeding it chunk by chunk to the bubbling fish in the darkening harbor waters, was now training as a waiter, clearing plates, empty or not, from all tables and rushing them to the kitchen. As the music switched to a *hasapikos* and took flight, he ditched his dishes and grabbed his father.

"Dance, Daddy, dance!"

Soon everyone was dancing. Chairs flew and ouzo flowed, while tables of foreign diners cheered and bought drinks for the impromptu band, who toasted us in return. Gregory was possessed—staring, dancing, and singing for more than two hours.

I watched him, marveling at the transformation the island had worked. It was almost midnight—yet where was that overtired, terrible two-year-old we'd dragged around Disney World a few months earlier? Come to think of it, where was his overextended, irritable mother? My husband watched and smiled, the quiet observer as usual in our boisterous little family. He said nothing. But now he knew why we had come to Nísiros.

Bibliography

The Greek Islands, Lawrence Durrell, Viking, 1978. This outstanding paperback volume is the definitive book to read on all the Greek islands, not only those in the Aegean. In his preface Durrell lays out his premise. Today's tourists, he says, have access to a great number of guides and reference books, particularly about Greece, so he never intended to compete in this field but wanted to answer two questions: "What would you have been glad to know when you were on the spot? What would you feel sorry to have missed while you were there?" And this he does admirably. I will personally be forever in debt to Durrell for this book because had he not written it, I would never have been inspired to go to Chios. You see, it was August, and though my husband and I very much wanted to see Mykonos and Santorini, we knew only fools would show up in the most crowded month with no reservations—*that* was a scenario we were trying to avoid. So while we were enjoying Sífnos, figuring out where to go next, I spent one afternoon poring over this book, and when I read about the unusual plant called *masticha,* which I had never heard of at that time, and that "the prevailing odour of dust and lemons and rock-honey is what you will most probably bring with you out of Chios," I concluded that the island had our names written all over it. You will have noticed by now that I quote often from this wonderful book, and it's because I just can't help it. In addition to individual chapters on the various island groups, Durrell provides an indispensable nine-page directory of the flora, fauna, and festivals of the Greek islands. There *are* good guidebooks to the islands, but there is not a single other book quite like this one. Do not even *think* about setting foot on any Greek island without reading this book.

Ill Met By Moonlight, W. Stanley Moss, Burford Books, 1950. In 1944 Moss and Patrick Leigh Fermor hatched a plan that, on the surface, seemed like the stuff of a not-entirely-believable Hollywood movie: kidnap Nazi General Karl Kreipe, commander of the Sevastopol Division in Crete, hike across the island,

and deliver him to British-occupied Egypt. Believe it or not, they really did it, and what a dramatic story it is. The book was first published in 1950, and Moss wrote then that he did not attempt to bring the story up to date or to rewrite any part of it, "for to do so would be to lose the spirit of light-heartedness and twenty-two-year-old exuberance (almost bumptiousness) with which it was written. . . . Rewritten diaries, carefully edited and bolstered with after-thought, rarely present a reflection of things and people as they really were; and therfore I have chosen that this book shall remain an almost direct tran-scription of a diary which I kept in 1944." It was fortunate for Moss and Leigh Fermor that their *sortie* was performed on Crete, as "the speed with which they [the Cretans] can travel, the loads which they can carry, and their ability to find, follow, and remember old trails or goat-tracks are comparable to the skill of North American Indians." On the other hand, Moss notes that in many Balkan countries the standard measure of distance is the length of time it takes to smoke a cigarette. "You are told that a village is ten cigarettes away. This method of calculation, especially when offered by a non-smoker, is guaranteed to be at least one hundred percent in error, and more than once I have known what was supposed to be a two-hour journey last from breakfast till dinner." This paperback edition is one volume in Burford's Classics of War series, with which I was unfamiliar until I picked up this edition. (Interested readers may contact Burford Books, 32 Morris Avenue, Springfield, New Jersey 07081; (973) 258-0960; www.burfordbooks.com and request a complete list of titles in the series, which features reprints of the most memorable and vivid books on war.) A related book—but one which I haven't yet read—is *The Cretan Runner: The Story of the German Occupation* (Penguin, 1999) by Giorgo Psychoundakis, who played a major role in the kidnapping of Kreipe. Patrick Leigh Fermor translated the book, and Xan Fielding, another Brit who spent much time on Crete as a secret agent, edited it. I'm anxious to read this book and am grateful that a colleague brought it to my attention, but I recently become positively obsessed with reading it when I read this short excerpt, "At the going down of the sun, and in the morning. We will remember them."

Reflections on a Marine Venus, Lawrence Durrell, E.P. Dutton, 1960. "A com-panion to the landscape of Rhodes" is the subtitle of this book, another excel-lent volume by the prolific Durrell. Writer Robert Kaplan, in a travel piece he wrote for the travel section of *The New York Times* in 1989, noted that *Reflections* "became the first book of postwar Mediterranean travel, and the opening note in a chorus of books, songs, movies and travel-poster images from which the Greek tourist boom of the 1960s would emerge." This may be Durrell's best-known work, and I knew I would love it after reading the very first paragraph, in which he wrote, "Somewhere among the note-books of Gideon I once found a list of diseases as yet unclassified by medical science, and among these there occurred the word *islomania,* which was described as a rare but by no means unknown affliction of spirit. There are people, Gideon used to say, by way of explanation, who find islands somehow irresistible. The mere knowledge that they are on an island, a little world surrounded by the sea, fills them with an indescribable intoxication." Durrell admitted that he was definitely sick with this disease, and I am too; and though I love all islands, no matter where they are, the first ones that come to my mind when I hear the word *islomania* are unquestionably those of the Aegean. "In Rhodes," Durrell writes, "the days drop as softly as fruit from trees." I don't know about you, but that inviting line pulls me in hook, line, and sinker. I didn't read this until I was already on the island, and I was already having an immensely interesting and fun time, so that when I finished it, I didn't want to leave. Ever.

The Summer of My Greek Taverna, Tom Stone, Simon and Schuster, 2002. Stone went to Greece one summer to write a novel—and stayed twenty-two years. How great is that for part of one's life story? The taverna that Stone ended up cooking for is on the island of Patmos, though the experience isn't without a dose of disappointment and deception. Stone shares some of the recipes made famous at the taverna, including an unlikely one for retsina chicken that I'm actually anxious to try. This is a great escapist read that, once begun, must be finished, as soon as possible (it won't take long).

Villa Ariadne, Dilys Powell, Hodder & Stoughton, London, 1973, hardcover; Trafalgar Square, 2001, paperback. The Villa Ariadne, on Crete, was the home Sir Arthur Evans built when he was excavating Knossos, and later it was also home to decades of classicists, including a young archaeologist who was Dilys Powell's husband. During World War II the villa was requisitioned by the Nazis and was the scene of the famous kidnapping of the same General Kriepe mentioned above. After the war, Powell wrote this book to recreate the world of the classicists at an exciting moment in archaeological history, and to tell the stories of those who worked for the Greek resistance. It is an unbeatable read, even if you don't plan on going to Crete.

The Peloponnese

"To all intents and purposes, the Peloponnese is an island, and an island-microcosm of everything most Greek. The country is cinched tight at the narrow Isthmus of Corinth and has been sliced in two, since 1893, by the Corinth Canal. Beneath the Corinthian Gulf, which severs it from mainland Greece, and washed on the east, west and south by the Aegean, Ionian and Cretan Seas, the Peloponnese, or 'Island of Pelops,' billows out like a ragged dirndl skirt—spangled with fertile valleys, patterned with sun-bleached mountains and scalloped with sandy bays."
        —Elizabeth Boleman-Herring, VANISHING GREECE

Drawn by Wolfensberger   NAUPLIA. THE FORTRESS OF PALAMEDI (1834)   *Engraved by M. Starling*

The Peloponnese

BY CATHARINE REYNOLDS

∽

Utter the adjective *Peloponnesian,* and most of us—trained Pavlov-style to answer our college boards the Kaplan way—will retort, "Thucydides." Yet to limit our interest in and knowledge of the Peloponnese to the great struggle that consumed Greece at the end of the fifth century B.C. would be to neglect an area that Henry Miller conjectures "affects everyone . . . like a soft, quick stab to the heart."

The Peloponnesian peninsula extends clawlike off southern mainland Greece. Its 8,277 square miles are a veritable baklava, sandwiching artifacts of successive civilizations—the Neolithic, Mycenaean, Classical Greek, Roman, Byzantine, Frankish, Venetian, Turkish, and modern Greek—within its honeyed layers. Epidaurus, Mycenae, and Olympia have long been the goals of classicists, but books and exhibitions have recently raised our consciousness of the broader heritage of the Peloponnese. The Metropolitan Museum of Art's dazzling show on Byzantium in 1997 inspired me to spend ten days on a circle tour of the peninsula, investigating the great Byzantine strongholds and at the same time revisiting the classical sites.

Most accommodation in the Peloponnese is geared for bus-borne groups, who overrun the ancient ruins each summer, so we were thrilled when friends told us of **Kándia House,** an oasis in the midst of the overdevelopment of the Argolid Peninsula, the easternmost pincer of the Peloponnesian claw.

Kándia, situated southeast of Nafplion, is a handsome beach house with ten spacious whitewashed suites arcing around the pool. The raised octagonal dining room provides panoramas of the neighboring beach and the Gulf of Argolis. Service is thoughtful to a fault, right down to the fresh-from-the-oven lemon-honey cake at breakfast.

Kándia proved ideal for exploring the Argolid. Our first stop was Corinth, the strategic linchpin, located on the three-mile-wide isthmus that connects the peninsula to the mainland. The modern port of Corinth, which is little more than a grid of concrete anonymity designed to resist the earthquakes that periodically devastate the area, belies the city's reputation as the ancient world's capital of sin. Saint Paul's epistles, written during his eighteen months there as a tent-maker, enshrine Corinthians' wicked ways.

Ancient Corinth, now little more than a village centered on the sixth-century B.C. Doric Temple of Apollo, is situated southwest of the modern city. After visiting the museum, we wandered, following Greek Nobel laureate Odysseus Elytis's advice to drink "the sun of Corinth, reading the marble ruins."

Acrocorinth, site of the acropolis and the Temple of Aphrodite—which was tended by the elite of Corinth's corps of prostitutes—soars nearly two thousand feet above the city. On our next trip we vowed to stay a night at the super-simple rooms above the café at Acrocorinth, if only to take in the scene tourist-free, at dawn's light.

On the way back to Kándia, we paused at the fortified Monastery of Agnoundos, with its church of the Koimisis tis Theotokou enclosed in a pretty courtyard. A few black-clad nuns tend the flowers and ensure that those who come to see the fourteenth-century Byzantine frescoes dress modestly.

Another day we ventured to Epidaurus, sacred to Asclepius, the Greek god of healing. This shrine, which reached its zenith in the fourth century B.C., was both a place of pilgrimage and a spa. The priests there recognized the therapeutic value of entertainment and accordingly built a 14,000-seat theater. Admirably preserved, it each year hosts a summer season of classical drama. The nearby museum enriched our understanding of the magic-medicine practiced there in classical times and provided us with an excellent plan for exploring the rest of the evocative site.

We visited the "huge walled citadel" of Mycenae, seat of the House of Atreus, whose blood-soaked history Homer, Aeschylus, and Sophocles have kept alive. Using Homer as his guide, Heinrich Schliemann, nineteenth-century uncoverer of Troy, also opened up Mycenae's *tholos,* or beehive, tombs, revealing a cache of glorious goldwork, including the death mask he mistakenly thought to be Agamemnon's. The Lion Gate, named for the two sleek lionesses that frame its pediment, illustrates the artful tactics of this civilization fifteen centuries before Christ.

Situation, scale, and history render a visit to Mycenae at once haunting and exhausting. I blessed my over-the-ankle boots as I scaled the polished Cyclopean stones—and then recuperated in the parking lot with supersweet orange juice squeezed from fruit grown on the surrounding plain.

The port of Nafplio charmed us with its gay pastel-washed, balconied houses and its gardens burgeoning with bougainvillea and hibiscus, all huddled under the seventeenth- and eighteenth-century Venetian citadel. We meandered the sleepy pedestrian streets of what was the first capital of independent Greece, stopping for frappés, the country's delectable iced coffee, in atmospheric Syntagma Square after visiting the intriguing small museum, with its near-intact suit of Mycenaean armor. Afterward, we lunched along the port to celebrate a purchase at **Preludio,** a local jeweler that makes pieces inspired by both Mycenaean discoveries and elegant Byzantine work—at prices noticeably more attractive than those asked by Athens's famed goldsmiths.

The hotelkeepers of modern Sparta uphold the tradition of privation characteristic of that city when it dominated the peninsula, lending new meaning to the adjective *spartan.* Bathroom lighting at the grimly functional **Lida** can only be described as Stygian, cleaning could best be termed approximate, and breakfast, prepackaged.

The only reason to stay in Sparta is five miles distant: Mistra, which knew a brief but brilliant two centuries as a beacon of civilization and scholarship as the Byzantine world based in Constantinople was disintegrating. Founded by the Frankish prince of Achaea in the thirteenth century, the fortress was ceded to the Byzantines, who in the century before 1453 created there the most magnificent ensemble of Byzantine architecture that has come down to us.

We parked at the entrance to the upper town and, armed with water, spent the morning rambling down through the crumbling medieval city spread across a spur of Mount Taygetus. As we had driven up the road, we'd been delighted by the sumptuous ruffled domes of the restored Hodegetria and the Evangelístria poking up among the remains of aristocratic dwellings, but nothing had prepared us for the solemn, collected faces in the frescoes decorating the churches' walls.

The romance of the place, with its seven churches, castle, and palaces, is irresistible and was summed up for us when a group of German students entered the Periouleplos Church and broke into spontaneous alleluias, their voices echoing descants heavenward. We were especially delighted to have seen this sober cruciform building in the morning, because we might have missed the subdued melancholy of the Nativity, with its recumbent Virgin sheltered in a rocky landscape, once the sun passed overhead.

The view over the fertile plain to the mauve foothills of Mount Parnon from the arcades at both the Pantanassa Convent and the Metropolis Cathedral was equally enthralling—and encouraged our imaginations to people Mistra's streets with the bejeweled late-Byzantine despots. **Marmara,** the terraced restaurant just outside the walls of the stronghold, shared that same view. There we feasted on excellent stuffed tomatoes and peppers, nutmeg-spiced pastitsio (pasta layered with ground meat), and honey-soaked pastries before hitching a ride back to the parking lot.

Our appetite for Byzantine frescoes sharpened, we detoured to Geráki, a sleepy village that might be forgotten but for its thirteenth- and fourteenth-century fresco-walled chapels. These are too small to be kept open, so we addressed ourselves to the café on the square, asking for the *klidhi* (key) for the *ekklesia* (church) from the *phylakas* (caretaker), who led us on a motorbike toward Ágios Dimítrios, where, among olive and almond groves, we visited five of the chapels. The naïve frescoes mesmerized us. Our favorite church was the Evangelístria, sited amid cypresses, with its barrel vault and enchanting stylized angels surrounding the Pantocrator on a too-high dome.

Monemvasía, to the southeast, is altogether more austere. Its name, meaning "single entrance" (*moni emvasis*), explains some of the fascination of this medieval town, linked to the southeastern pincer of the Peloponnese by a narrow causeway. From the mainland, the rock—known as "the Gibraltar of Greece"—appears deserted. Only from the causeway does the extent of the seaward-facing town unfold. After negotiating the vaulted chicane, we found ourselves on the main street—little more than an alley—today lined with shops.

Astride the trade routes between the western Mediterranean and the Levant, Monemvasía was fortified in 1248. Franks, Byzantines, the Papacy, Venetians, and Turks—almost all of whom had to take the town by siege—have in turn ruled here. At one stage the town's population exceeded 30,000, and the sweet white wine, known in English as malmsey and shipped from local ports, was prized throughout Europe; but by the end of the nineteenth century Monemvasía was nearly deserted. Lately the tumbledown houses of its mercantile and seafaring grandees have begun to be restored under strict architectural and historical supervision. We concluded that the nicest of the several hotels was the **Goulás,** with its handful of pretty rooms, one of them with a flower-decked private terrace overlooking the sea.

We filled two days wandering the lanes, swimming off the rocks, and climbing to the citadel, nearly a thousand feet above sea level. The Church of Ágia Sophía crowns the rock, offering entrancing vistas and some fine Byzantine lowrelief capitals decorated with whimsical animals, including two billing doves.

On the red-checked tablecloths at **To Kanoni** we ate some of the best food we were to enjoy in the Peloponnese: sassy *tzatziki* (yogurt, cucumber, and garlic dip), succulent *gigántes* (fat white beans) in tomato sauce, spanokopita (spinach in phyllo), and carefully grilled sole, followed by sugar-dusted fritters. A bottle of Cava Boutari '92 capped our pleasure. All of this provided a happy change from the delicious if steady diet of *horiátiki* (Greek salad), pastitsio, moussaka, figs, and thick Greek yogurt sparked with herb-scented local honey.

We lunched the next day on the seafront at Gythium and visited Marathonisi, the offshore island where Homer tells us Paris and Helen spent the first delirious night of their journey from Sparta to Troy "lost in love." Its lush greenery was the last we were to see for several days as we launched ourselves into the stony fastnesses of the Máni, the Peloponnese's least hospitable reach, renowned for its vendettas and tower houses, known to us thanks to Patrick Leigh Fermor's beautifully crafted book named after the region.

We based ourselves at **Tsitsiris castle,** a converted tower house at Stavri, deep in the Inner Máni. The rooms were as stark in style as the surrounding landscape but comfortably appointed. Váthia, with its Manhattan skyline superimposed on the harsh peaks marching down to the sea, captivated us, as did the fishing port of Geroliménas.

We also traipsed across stone fields amid stunted trees, searching out neglected Byzantine churches. When a caretaker could be found, the interiors often revealed weathered frescoes that, if not sophisticated, demonstrate the liveliness of local faith around the twelfth century.

We forayed north toward Kalamata, the port that gave its name to fat, brine-cured black olives, watching the land grow more fertile with each mile. At Pirgos Lefktrou we purchased superb organic olive oil at **Bläuel,** pressed on the premises by delightful Austrians Fritz and Burgi Bläuel, who then directed us to lunch at **Taverna Lela** in Kardamili. Fried mullet served under the trees was the perfect complement to the view of the Ionian Sea.

The following day we set out up the coast for Olympia, stopping at the Palace of Nestor near Chora. This important Bronze Age palace dates from the same period as Mycenae, but its magnificent setting five hundred feet above Navarino Bay makes it much more inviting, in spite of the tin roof that protects the excavation from the elements. Though we cannot prove that the Nestor Homer described as "the man of winning words" was associated with it, all evidence suggests that he and his descendants governed "Pylos' holy realm" from the throne room. The jewels and Linear B tablets excavated here are at the National Archaeological Museum in Athens, but Chora's small modern museum houses the pottery and the remains of the bold frescoes that brightened the walls.

We followed the coast to Tholó and then headed inland for Phigalia en route to Bassae. The road was occasionally rocky and consistently vertiginous, reminding us how pleased we were to have rented a sturdy mid-sized car and invested in good maps. We spelled each other at the wheel, the better to admire the scenery safely and practice deciphering the Greek-alphabet signs on these less-traveled tracks.

Spectacular views rewarded the risk. The country grew steadily more desolate as we approached Bassae, site of the most isolated temple in Greece. The fifth-century gray limestone Doric building that Ictinus terraced into Mount Kotilion was built to honor Apollo Epikourios for having shielded the local population from pestilence. The structure—among the ancient world's best preserved—is shrouded in surreal sheeting. Even stripped of the splendid Phigalian marbles depicting the battle of the Greeks and the Amazons that enlivened the frieze of its cella, this long temple, perched on a crag dotted with asphodel and campanulas, does great honor to its architect.

To the northwest, in the valley of the Alpheus, Olympia is probably the most visited spot in the Peloponnese. Myth has it that Heracles, son of Zeus, after laboring to cleanse the Augean Stables by diverting the Alpheus, erected a temple in his father's honor in the Altis, the sacred grove, on the side of Mount Krónion and inaugurated quadrennial athletic competitions to honor him.

Settled into the comfortable, modern forty-two-room **Hotel Europa,** we spent an evening boning up on Olympia's past and enjoying dinner near the bar beyond the glistening swimming pool with the backdrop of Arcadia's hills.

Early in the morning, before buses could disgorge the multitudes, we went to explore the attractively landscaped ancient site, circling through the remains of the Palestra and crawling over what had been the workshop where Phidias sculpted the great ivory cult statue of Zeus cloaked in gold that was considered one of the Seven Wonders of the Ancient World.

Lines from "Ozymandias" tripped off our tongues as we sniffed the resin-laden air and gazed at the columns of the Temple to Zeus cast down on the south side of the stylobate, looking like nothing so much as a toppled stack of giant Oreos. Not far away grew the olive tree that provided the winning athletes' wreaths. Generations of tourists have loped—as we did—through the vaulted tunnel leading out into the stadium, identifying, if just for a moment, with the great who competed there.

The central hall of the museum across the road contains pieced-together elements of the east and west pediments of Zeus' temple, illustrating the Pelops myth and the battle of the Centaurs and the Lapiths, along with the metopes recounting Heracles' labors. Other rooms exhibit the Praxiteles *Hermes,* as well as Paeonius' resplendent *Niké.*

Deliciously sated, we wended our way back to Athens, to consolidate our new appreciation of the Greek world with visits to the

Byzantine Museum and the National Archaeological Museum. The latter houses precious items excavated at most of the Classical Peloponnesian sites. We goggled at the sculptures and the dazzling displays of Mycenaean gold jewelry—baubles and bracelets as wearable today as when they might have graced "white-armed Helen."

Hotels

Kándia House, Irion, 21100 Kándia, Argolis, 752.94060; fax: 752.94480

Goulás Hotel, 23070 Monemvasía, Laconia, 732.61223; fax: 732.61707

Hotel Europa, Drouva 3, 27065 Olympia, Elia, 624.22650; fax: 624.23166

Hotel Lida, Atreidon 1, 23100 Sparta, Laconia, Tel. 731.23601; fax: 731.24493

Tsitsiris Castle, 23071 Stavri, Laconia, 733.56297; fax: 168.58962

Restaurants and Shops

Marmara, at the foot of Mistra, Laconia, no telephone number.

Preludio, 2 Vas. Constantinou, Syntagma Square, Nafplio, Argolis, 752.25277

Bläuel Greek Organic Products, Pirgos Lefktrou, 24024 Kalamata, Messenia, 721.77711; fax: 721.77590

Taverna Lela, Kardamili, Messenia, 721.73140

To Kanoni, within the fortress at Monemvasía, Laconia, 732.61387; fax: 732.61169

Hidden Riches in a Harsh Setting

BY SHERRY MARKER

∾

editor's note

Here is a pair of articles focusing on two different corners of the southern Peloponnese.

SHERRY MARKER has been traveling to, and writing about, Greece for more than twenty-five years. She contributes frequently to the travel section of *The New York Times,* where this piece first appeared.

There's no place in Greece where the wind is hotter in summer or harsher in winter than the Máni Peninsula, the 19-mile spur of Mount Taygetus that stretches to Cape Matapan at the southernmost tip of the Peloponnesus. Where else in Greece are there mountains as utterly devoid of vegetation as the grim, gray range known as Kakavouna (Evil Mountains)? And where else would you be grateful to crouch in the shade of a prickly pear and call a village crowded if you encountered a clutch of goats?

I've made a number of trips to southern Greece during the last twenty years and have to admit that the Máni is an acquired taste. Still, the point of traveling there is not to mortify the flesh, but to feast the eyes. First, there are the Máni's eerie towers: two, three, and four stories tall, clustered in villages and built of the local gray limestone with finely corbeled marble windows and walls. Some say that the idea for the tower houses was brought back to Greece by Maniote mercenaries who served in Italy in the sixteenth century and saw Tuscan hilltowns like San Gimignano, but many think that nothing here depends on foreign influence.

Scattered over the mountain slopes, hidden in gullies and perched on hilltops are the Máni's other architectural wonders: tiny chapels, some dating to the ninth century, when Christianity finally made inroads into these isolated mountains. No one church here is as splendid as the churches at nearby Mistra, but there are few experiences more startling than stumbling upon one of these chapels, whose exterior walls are ornamented with elaborate cloisonné brickwork and marble architectural ornament of entwined flowers and whimsical beasts. Inside, crumbling walls are decorated with rich fresco cycles: warrior saints on white chargers, John the Baptist holding his head on a salver, scenes of the damned roasting in hell and the blessed frolicking in Heaven.

The tower villages and the chapels, along with the terraced mountains, where now the only grain that grows is wild, are clues that the Máni—now home to no more than 5,000—was once thickly populated. When the English traveler Colonel William Leake visited in 1806, some 30,000 people lived in 130 flourishing tower villages. Leake also noted that the 30,000 inhabitants possessed 10,000 guns: blood feuds were a way of life in the Máni, where the men fought all day and rebuilt their towers by night. (Sometimes they took a break to practice piracy on unwary ships that ventured too close to the shore.) Not surprisingly, the Máni's principal artistic legacy is the dirges that women sang over their fallen men.

In this century, both feuds and farming stopped as almost everyone moved away in search of jobs. If anything draws people back, it's likely to be the development of tourism; already a sprinkling of hotels has appeared along sandy beaches and three hotels have opened in restored towers farther inland. Right now the Máni offers visitors the creature comforts of its incipient tourist industry in a setting essentially removed from tourist Greece.

The port town of Gythium is a good jumping-off spot for the Máni—and, like almost every town in Greece, this is a place with a glorious past. Helen and Paris eloped to Gythium from nearby Sparta. According to legend, the lovers spent their "honeymoon night" on Kranae (now called Marathonisi), a pine-clad islet in Gythium's harbor, linked to the mainland by a narrow quay. Before sailing off with Helen to Troy, Paris erected a statue to the Aphrodite of Erotic Love; when Menelaus reclaimed Helen after the fall of Troy, he destroyed Paris's shrine and rather smugly erected statues of Themis (Justice) and Praxidica (Retribution).

No trace of either shrine remains, although Gythium has a well-preserved Roman theater, and the nineteenth-century Tsanetakis Tower on Marathonisi has recently been restored (actually overly restored, with an unfortunate stuccoed exterior) as an ethnological museum. A string of seafood restaurants, along the harbor, offers the chance to try such Greek menu items as fish roe salad and fried squid before heading across the peninsula toward Areopolis.

As you might expect of a town named for the god of war, Areopolis is a harsh place. Even at high noon, a thicket of tall towers keeps the sun off Areopolis's narrow streets except in the small *plateia* (square) in front of the church of Ágii Taxiarchi. Just beyond Ágii Taxiarchi (itself named for warrior saints) is the seven-room Kapetanakos Tower Hotel. Like the tower hotels at Stavri and Váthia, the Kapetanakos Tower has stoned-paved floors decorated with multicolored rag rugs and several rooms with sleeping lofts.

The hotel's interior staircase is a concession to modern visitors; the original inhabitants made their way from floor to floor by ladder, retreating to the top floor during sieges. The tower's windows are absurdly small—not much bigger than gunslits, which is just what they were designed to be. When I stayed here in May, the shutters rattled on their hinges as the wind howled all night.

In the morning, I headed on a day trip from Areopolis along the Gulf of Itilo into Outer Máni, which is north of the Máni proper, to revisit a number of Maniote churches, many of which are grouped handily beside the main road. The eleventh-century Church of the Transfiguration (Metamorphosis) in Nomitsi and the ninth-century St. Nicholas (Ágios Nikólaos) outside the village of Platsa both have fanciful architectural decoration, and St. Nicholas incorporates classical blocks in its facade. Directly across the road from St. Nicholas is the quarry where the ancient blocks came from. A few miles away, the Demangelio Museum of the Máni in Thalames has a good collection of old prints and a mélange of wooden agricultural implements, matchboxes, spindle whorls, and *yatagans,* the deadly Maniote scimitar.

Kardamili, about 12 miles north of Thalames, is one of the appealing villages in Outer Máni. The town, which sprawls along the coast of the Gulf of Messenia, is surrounded by lush olive groves. Kardamili has some good fish restaurants and is a pleasant spot to stop for lunch and toast local resident Patrick Leigh Fermor, the Anglo-Irish Second World War hero and author of *Mani.*

Inner Máni begins south of Areopolis; this is where the finest tower villages and chapels straddle hilltops and hide in valleys in the bleak landscape. It's also where the Máni's one real tourist attraction is: the caves of Dirou, with rosy red, amber, and cream-colored stalagmites as thick as temple columns and multicolored stalactites as slender as needles. In the summer Dirou is popular with Greeks. When I last visited, the crowds were considerable and I had to wait an hour to get a seat in one of the flotilla of little boats that glide through some 6,000 feet of the caves. When I showed up in May, my initial smugness at being the only visitor faded when the boatman explained that we wouldn't head out until he had enough customers to make the trip worthwhile. Once again I waited about an hour.

Although tours are conducted in Greek, the boatmen translated the nicknames of caverns such as the Cathedral and the Red Room for the benefit of a couple who didn't know the language. As we floated some 650 feet underground over the black water that reaches a depth of nearly 100 feet, I remembered that the caves were rumored to be the home of giant eels and asked the boatman if he'd seen any. "Lots," he said, and waved his leg to give me an idea of the eels' girth. Dirou is one of the earliest inhabited spots in Greece: pottery, obsidian blades, and wall paintings from the Late Paleolithic and Neolithic eras (25,000 to 5,000 B.C.) have been found here.

There are almost two dozen chapels south of Dirou, many far out on the great bulge of Cavo Grosso, topped by a slender projection that looks like the handle of a frying pan (and is called just that in Greek: Tigani). Unlike the chapels conveniently strung out along the road from Areopolis to Kardamili, many of these chapels seem to have been built in remote spots chosen to test the devotion (and stamina) of the faithful—and to reward them with beautiful views. Stands of cypresses are often a sign of a church, and there are occasional inconspicuous hand-lettered roadside signs pointing the way to churches. (Unfortunately for those who do not know the language, almost as many signs urge you not to throw garbage on the road.)

Even though I can read the signs, finding a new church usually involves getting lost and asking for the *palaia ekklesia* (old church). More than once I've been led to a church that not only wasn't the one I was looking for but was one I had never heard of. That is how I first stumbled on the chapels of St. Michael at Glezou and Charouda, St. Barbara at Erimos, and St. Peter at Triandafilia. Saints Barbara at Erimos and Michael at Charouda both have elaborate brickwork and ancient marble blocks in their walls, and St. Michael stands in a walled courtyard shaded by what local residents say is the largest olive tree in the Máni. Like many Maniote chapels, St. Michael's is usually locked, but it's often possible to scout out the villager who has *ta klidhia* (the keys). If not, try not to resent the locked doors; in recent years vandalism has taken an increasing toll on these churches, as antiques dealers hack off bits of frescoes and architectural ornaments.

That's what happened at one of my favorite churches, St. Michael at Ano Boulari, now usually locked, and still worth a visit for its lovely setting. A dirt road runs steeply uphill through the towers of Ano Boulari until it lurches to a stop outside a ruined chapel that encloses yet another chapel. From here St. Michael's is invisible, its slate roof and belltower perhaps 50 feet behind the ruined chapel. Ano Boulari has another wonderful church: St. Panteleimon, which is reached by a dirt track from the bridge by the village's modern church. This primitive chapel is well worth the scramble for its frescoes with strange frontal saints who look more Middle Eastern than Greek. Monks fleeing troubles in Asia Minor built this church in the tenth century.

If I had to choose my favorite Maniote church, it might well be the beguiling Episkopi, which is reached by turning off the road to Stavri to Ágios Giorgos. That's the easy part: then comes a prickly descent on foot along the path that takes off between two well-restored towers, passes a modern house, and plunges down between scrub oak, thistles and the inevitable prickly pears. After ten minutes of feeling increasingly lost and resentful, just as I began to think I'd taken the wrong path, I saw Episkopi's red-tiled roof and looked out on a landscape that seemed to be taken from a Pompeiian wall painting. On a distant slope above the sea, cattle grazed outside a farm near the ruined walls of the church of Vlacherna. The low building that looks like a ruined sheep shed on the western hill is yet another church, St. Procopius, whose fresco of red crosses dates from the ninth-century Iconoclastic period, when figured decorations were banned from churches.

All around, hidden in the hills, are yet more chapels, and the startling tower villages of Kita, Nomia, and Váthia. The Greek National Tourist Organization has converted virtually the entire village of Váthia into a tower hotel with some fifteen rooms. In summer, the hotel is often full, but out of season, it's not unusual to be the only guest. After spending a night here with nothing but the unnerving roar of the wind and the haunting cries of owls to keep me company, I wasn't at all surprised to learn that the ancient Greeks thought that an entrance to the Underworld was just down the road, at the tip of Cape Matapan.

A Corner of Greece

Hotels

For information on the hotels mentioned in this piece, it is best to contact the Greek National Tourist Office and ask for any contact information the staff can provide—addresses, phone numbers, e-mail addresses, or websites—for the local tourist offices in the Máni.

Restaurants

The Máni is not a gastronomic delight; early travelers report being offered plates of prickly pears.

There are some small restaurants on the main square in Areopolis, and by the harbor at Limeni, the port of Areopolis, and Geroliménas, the port south of Areopolis, as well as in Gythium and Kardamili. Expect to pay $10 or so for a simple lunch, perhaps twice that for dinner. You can usually get good seafood in Gythium and Kardamili, although even here the squid is usually frozen.

Most restaurants are supplied by one or more local fishermen, so what's on the menu depends on the luck of the catch of the day.

Transport

The best way to get around the Máni is by car and on foot. Both Avis and Hertz have rental offices in the Peloponnese at Patras, as well as in Athens.

If you have a fluid schedule, you can also get to most villages (but not most days) by bus.

A Playground, Once a Battlefield

BY SHERRY MARKER

～

There is not much Greek countryside I'd call lush, yet that's just the word for Messenia, the southwest corner of the Peloponnese. Messenia's sybaritic pleasures include juicy Kalamata olives and succulent figs and melon, as well as the Peloponnese's best sand beaches, many flanked by the small hotels and restaurants favored by savvy German and Italian travelers. One restaurant, the Klimataria in the village of Methone, serves what may well be the best food in the Peloponnese, in a garden shaded by a grape arbor, just steps from Methone's medieval fortress.

I'd never take even those few steps if I began a trip to Messenia with a meal at the Klimataria, where the *mezéthes* (hors d'oeuvres) include fluffy croquettes of zucchini, tomato, cheese, and cucumber, spicy octopus salad, fried cheese, onion pie, and a zesty *tzatziki* (yogurt, cucumber, and garlic dip) that makes you realize just how insipid most restaurant *tzatziki* is. I'd certainly never bestir myself to visit Messenia's other sites, which include the Mycenaean palace of Nestor at Pylos from the thirteenth century B.C., the Hellenistic city of Messene from the fourth century B.C., and Korone, the companion fortress to Methone. Messenia, a six-hour drive southwest of Athens, has good roads, and distances between the sites are short. So it's perfectly possible to see all these sites in two vigorous or three leisurely days by car, but it usually takes longer by local bus.

When I first visited Messenia some thirty years ago, few of its seaside hamlets had even one hotel. Now they have become mini-resorts that cater a bit too wholeheartedly to tourists for my tastes. For some time now I have stayed in the harbor town of Pylos, which retains its character with arcaded shops and cafés surrounding the main square, or *plateia*.

Twice Pylos has been the scene of a crucial naval battle: in 425 B.C. during the Peloponnesian War, when the Athenians defeated the Spartans here, and then in 1827 during the Greek War of Independence, when the combined naval forces of England, France, and Russia essentially eradicated the Turkish fleet. The boat captains who offer tours of the harbor cheerfully point out the submerged wrecks of several Turkish ships.

From the town of Pylos, it's an 11-mile drive north to the Palace of Nestor, which Homer says was at "sandy Pylos." Nestor's palace straddles a low ridge called Ano Englianos, with a view back to the deep blues of the Pylos harbor, beyond hills shimmering with the silver leaves of some of the tallest olive trees in Greece. The main palace area is covered with an unabashedly ugly metal roof that protects the site from the elements; it also helps visitors envision the dimensions of the original 163-by-104-foot, two-story building from its low remains.

Unlike the compact palaces at Mycenae and Tiryns, Nestor's palace sprawls like a country villa across its unfortified site. Visiting here, it's easy to imagine the day Homer describes when young Telemachus arrived seeking news of his absentee father Odysseus, still not home from the Trojan War. Telemachus, accustomed to his father's more provincial island home in Ithaca, must have been dazzled by the palace's frescoed walls showing griffins and lions, fragments of which are now in the Archaeological Museum at Chora, about a mile from the palace. Even though many archaeologists question the accuracy of these heavily restored frescoes (re-created, some would say), I always stop at the museum to see them and to admire the delicate gold cups and jewelry and the enormous pottery jars.

When Telemachus came here, probably he and Nestor, the irredeemably loquacious old King of Pylos, would have sat in the Megaron (Throne Room), toasting each other with cups of the local wine beside the raised round hearth. In fact, so many cups have been found in the palace—2,853 in one room alone—that archaeologists have speculated that the cups were smashed after each toast.

While Nestor talked and Telemachus listened, the business of the palace would have gone on: in the archives just to the left of the main entrance, scribes writing on unbaked clay tablets updated palace inventories, listing the hundreds of jars of herb-scented olive oil and kraters of honeyed wine, some of which are still visible in the palace storehouses. When the palace burned to the ground around 1200 B.C. (no one knows why), the intense heat baked the tablets, which lay buried until April 4, 1939. That's when the American archaeologist Carl Blegen began to excavate here on the suspicion that Nestor's palace might be in the neighborhood.

Incredibly, Blegen's first excavation trench hit the palace archives, unearthing hundreds of tablets written in the unknown script dubbed Linear B. It was not until 1952 that Michael Ventris, a brilliant young English architect, deciphered the tablets, demonstrating that they were the earliest known form of written Greek. Some words, like those for *oil* and *wine,* are almost identical in today's Greek.

From Nestor's palace, I like to head away from the sea, deeper into the Messenian hills, to the fourth century B.C. site of Messene at the foot of Mount Ithome. Even though I know why I'm heading toward Messene and what I'm going to see, the countryside is so startlingly lush that I usually find myself daydreaming, until I come around a bend in the road and see Messene's gray limestone defense walls, several stretches still standing more than 15 feet tall, running for more than five and a half miles along a ridge above the remains of the ancient city.

Most travelers to Greece soon become familiar with the experience of arriving at a famous temple, or fortress, or entire city, and trying to conjure up ancient glories from ankle-high remains. Even Nestor's Pylos, were it not for Homer and the Linear B tablets, would be very hard to imagine. Not so at Messene, where you can clamber about in several of the defense circuit's thirty original square or semicircular watchtowers and stride through the monumental 17-foot-wide Arcadian Gate, with its 65-foot interior courtyard.

As to the ancient city itself, the Asclepeion (shrine to the healing deity Asclepius) with its 235-by-219-foot central courtyard, is so enormous that excavators originally thought this one shrine must be the entire marketplace and civic center. There is plenty more to be unearthed at Messene: in fact, when I was last there, excavators were using a bulldozer to hoist the topsoil off a seemingly endless colonnade flanking the partially excavated stadium.

The day was hot, and I envied the plump jade-green frogs lounging in a basin, which was fed by the spring that watered ancient Messene and still supplies the modern village of Mavromati. Fortunately, Mavromati's one restaurant, the Ithome, where I headed for some salad and souvlaki, is just across from the spring, and has a superb shaded view over the site.

After lunch I headed off to take in another, even better view. Thanks to a new dirt track, it is arguably possible to creep and lurch almost all the way up Mount Ithome by car, then scramble up the last few yards. From the summit, with its deserted sixteenth-century whitewashed stone Monastery of Vourkano, there is an astonishing 360-degree view of all Messenia, dotted with villages amid olive groves, and of Taygetus, the jagged range that separates Messenia from Laconia, the district to the east.

The scene atop Mount Ithome is so peaceful, with small lemon- and lime-colored butterflies fluttering about the blue blossoms of spiky thistles, that it's easy to forget the centuries of warfare for the rich land below. The Laconian Spartans were Messenia's greatest enemies, and Messene itself was founded and fortified in 369 B.C. in one of a series of attempts to protect Messenia from Spartan attacks.

The contrast between today's picturesque ruins and yesterday's bloody battlegrounds is particularly stark at the two medieval fortresses once known as Venice's "twin eyes of empire," Korone, on the Gulf of Messenia, and Methone, on the Ionian sea. During the centuries that Venice contested the Franks and Turks for control of the Mediterranean Sea routes, Methone and Korone were vital outposts in an empire that stretched from Venice itself to Constantinople, the Holy Land, and the spice routes to the east.

It's somewhat unnerving to look at Methone's picture-postcard island fort, the miniature octagonal Bourtzi, and realize that this is where the last of the 5,000 Venetian defenders were slaughtered by the Turks in 1500. And it's no less disquieting to stroll Korone's summit, with its fragrant rosebushes tended by the nuns who live in the small convent here, and contemplate the thanksgiving service held in 1685, when the Venetians got their revenge and slaughtered the 1,500 Turkish defenders in one August afternoon.

In those days, the towns of Methone and Korone crouched inside their fortifications. Now a small village, Korone, its narrow streets crowded with tile-roofed houses that have delicate wrought-iron balconies, spills down the steep hill that is girdled by the fortress walls. At the foot of the hill, tavernas and cafés line the harbor where merchant ships once anchored and fishing boats now bob. Today's inhabitants of Korone, perhaps following an ancestral instinct to confuse potential invaders, have fiendishly reversed several road signs, so that arrows point down to the fortress and up to the harbor.

Unlike Korone, whose steep hill is a natural fortress, the castle of Methone stretches the length of a 1,000-foot-long low peninsula. Not surprisingly, Methone has a complex system of walls within walls, some linked by underground passages, many crowned by crenellated walls and turrets, all designed to make this very vulnerable knoll invulnerable.

Inside Methone, carved lions of St. Mark watch over the ruins of a Turkish bath and mosque. There are even a few concrete pillboxes left from the Italian and German occupation during World War II, when Methone's strategic location overlooking the sea routes across the Mediterranean made it worth fighting for again.

This is a bleak spot, with none of the charms of Korone's rose garden, convent and harbor. Still, the views out over the sea, both from the fortress and from the fine sand beach, especially at sunset, are tremendous. And for me, sunset is a sure sign that it's time to head to the Klimataria restaurant, for some of the lightly resinated rosé wine that people have been drinking in Messenia at least since Telemachus and Nestor toasted each other.

A Monument of Byzantium

BY FERGUS M. BORDEWICH

༄

editor's note

Mistra, though it is hardly off the beaten path on the Peloponnese, is one of my most favorite places in all of Greece. If you climb the path upward early in the day you will be rewarded with next to no fellow visitors and exceptional peace and quiet, perfect for viewing the church interiors and contemplating this symbolic spot in Byzantine history.

FERGUS M. BORDEWICH lived in Greece when he contributed this piece to the travel section of *The New York Times*. He is also the author of *My Mother's Ghost* (Doubleday, 2000), *Killing the White Man's Indian* (Anchor, 1997), and *Cathay: A Journey in Search of Old China* (iUniverse, 2001), among others.

The green crag of Mistra rears up like an altar into the vast natural cathedral of the Taygetus Massif. At its crest, like a grim offering, the black walls of the Frankish citadel hang in brutal silhouette against the snow-crusted backdrop beyond. Below, amid a cascade of ruined vaults, arches, turreted walls, chapels, homes, and palaces, lie perhaps the most spectacular surviving monuments to the last flourish of medieval Byzantium.

Mistra is empty of people today, except for a handful of lonely monks and nuns, solitary figures swathed in black, who hobble feebly among the broken walls and dwell in the few still active monasteries. Between the thirteenth and fifteenth centuries, however, as many as 50,000 people lived here, in lofty houses that clung like talons to the crag's rocky slope. Their rulers held sway over the entire Peloponnese, mimicking the pomp of the imperial court at Constantinople. Their philosophers taught the works of ancient

Greece to the scholars of the Florentine Renaissance. Their artists bathed the city's churches in some of the finest frescoes ever painted by Byzantine hands.

The frescoes embody a wide range of styles and sensibilities and offer an unparalleled view into the obscure and pious Byzantine cosmos. The whole span of Orthodox belief is written in them, in evocative visual texts that blended compassion and dogma, gentleness and ferocity, gloom and hope into a skein of didactic theology and intense emotion. The best of them, the most delicate and ethereal, reveal a brilliant vision of a world at climax. "It was a time," wrote the British historian Steven Runciman, "when men were beginning to foresee the end of the Empire and foretell the end of the world, with Anti-Christ and Armageddon close ahead."

Mistra may be reached by car or public bus from the modern city of Sparta, eight miles away. However, the sprawling ruins may only be visited on foot, by cobbled paths that twist around the upward sprawl of shattered homes and bastions toward the citadel. Empty though it may be, the site is far too dramatic, far too Greek in the idiosyncrasy of its landscape, to succumb to solemnity. The air is almost narcotic with the smell of countless violet, scarlet, white, blue, pink, and lavender flowers that burst everywhere from the ruined walls. Lizards scamper over the stones, and yellow butterflies dance where bishops once walked. The spring breeze whistles gaily through the arched windows of the palace once inhabited by the Despots of the Morea, as the city's rulers were known. Far below, on the hazy valley floor, a silvery carpet of olive groves stretches as far as the eye can see across the orange earth.

Mistra is not very old, by Greek standards. The citadel was built in 1249 by the Frankish freebooter William de Villehardouin who, according to the medieval *Chronicle of the Morea,* "found a remarkable hill, a fragment of a mountain," and "called it Myzithras because they shouted it thus." The bastion soon became a stronghold of the resurgent Byzantines, and later a fiefdom of the imperial families who ruled from Constantinople. A city gradually spread out under the citadel, as the inhabitants of the valley climbed closer to its walls for security.

Indeed, it was really the violence and instability of the age that brought forth the glory of Mistra, as it was now known, on such an inhospitable peak. Turkish, Catalan, and Frankish marauders prowled the coasts and valleys. In a single year, the bubonic plague killed a third of Constantinople's population, and probably as many in the Peloponneses. The imperial throne itself was insecure, and politics little more than the rivalry of private tyrannies.

Nevertheless, behind its serrated battlements, the new city prospered. Its despots were simultaneously soldiers and men of culture and patronized scholars like George Gemistos Plethon, the early Renaissance Platonist, with as much ease as they led their armies over the Peloponnesian hills.

The shell of the Despots' palace stands on a shoulder of the slope, forming two sides of what must once have been the city's central square. During the Turkish era the already ruined complex was known fancifully as the "Palace of Menelaus," the legendary Spartan king and the husband of Helen of Troy, though it was in fact built mostly in the late fourteenth century. Across the square, the homes of the city's lords and burghers rose steeply in huddled ranks. The secular city is no more than a fading shadow of its past. But in its churches a glow of its one-time glory can still be seen.

Although only four of the churches—there are about a dozen in all—still possess extensive frescoes, nearly every one is a modest symphony of tiled domes, rhythmic colonnades and arches, and elegant red brickwork that lends a humble gaiety to the mass of their yellow stone walls. Many of the churches were built according to the classical Byzantine plan of a cross inscribed within a square and surmounted by a steep central dome with smaller domes at the four corners. Unusual in the Byzantine world, however, several others were constructed as basilicas with three naves. Nearly all the churches have benefited from rehabilitation that has restored them to their original appearance without damaging the time-worn ambiance that gives the entire site so much of its charm.

The Byzantines conceived the church building as a single huge icon, revealing in its recesses all the mysteries of the Christian faith. The building's dome was heaven, from which the fierce, brooding or compassionate face of Christ Pantocrator—"Ruler of All"—gazed down upon what He had created. Painted images of the Twelve Apostles supported the dome, and the apse was the cave of Bethlehem, in which the worshiper would find the images of the Madonna and Child. The altar was the table of the Last Supper, and the ciborium above it the Holy Sepulcher.

Most of the great Mistra frescoes are built around the cycles of Christ's life and miracles, the life of Mary, and stories from the lives of saints. Icons, to the Byzantines, were not mere paintings. They represented a mystical union between God and color.

Traditionally, a painter would take up his brush only after deep prayer and meditation, on the name day of the saint he intended to portray, thereby infusing the pigment, he believed, with the holy one's pure spirit. The simple worshiper was surrounded not just by paint but by an overwhelming swarm of living presences.

Perhaps the finest of all the Mistra churches is the Perivleptos, which stands off from the rest of the ruins in a copse of pines, wedged against a cleft in the rock. The damp cave that it shelters was once probably a shrine to pagan gods and still lends the chapel's raw stone entryway a vaguely primeval air. Scarcely more than twenty paces in breadth, the Perivleptos has an intimate, private quality and, but for its lavish frescoes, is decorated only with a few simple columns and a gray-and-white marble floor. From the walls, rank upon rank of warrior saints, sword or spear in hand, their flesh glazed with a weird greenish tint, stare out with melancholy eyes from the shadows. Above them angels reel through the sky, saints weep, prophets thunder, Lazarus rises from the grave, Christ is born and transfigured.

Several of the most important frescoes—the Ascension, the Dormition of the Virgin, the Nativity, and the Last Supper, among others—were apparently painted by a single brilliant though unknown artist. In his painting of the Ascension, even the trees and strange stylized rocks seem to swarm upward with a ferocious energy. The modeling of the apostles who stand shading their eyes from the blinding vision before them welds, as do so many of the best works at Mistra, vestiges of the classical humanism that never died out in Byzantine art, to the spiritual loftiness of the Orthodox faith. They are without a doubt men who crouch transfixed, paralyzed in Christ's splendorous light, yet their bodies seem at the same time somehow weightless, more spirit than flesh—their hands seem too delicate ever to have gripped a tool, their ankles too fragile to have ever walked the earth.

The same painter's version of the Nativity is generally considered one of the masterpieces of Byzantine art. The three kings appear through a sort of hole in the red rock, while angels clamber solemnly over olive-green hills. Behind them, the sky is an impossibly rich, almost violent blue while, below, the Virgin, wrapped in blue and curled gracefully in a cave, exudes a strange, magnetic gravity, as if she were swollen with ominous knowledge of the fate that lay in store for the tiny Child beside her.

After the Perivleptos, probably the best frescoes are to be found in the Hodegetria, the largest of the surviving churches. It was once the center of an influential monastery and stands poised dramatically against the northern battlements, its domes and vaults undulating like a miniature landscape of red hills and valleys framed against the green slopes.

Unfortunately, many of the most important frescoes are partly obscured by an arcaded recess on the second story and are difficult to see from below. A dramatic exception, however, is the extraordinary Madonna that fills the small dome of the western wing: an awesome, luminous figure of inexpressible softness, dressed in a red robe and looming with a half-worshipful, half-sheltering gesture over the figure of her son.

The more easily visible walls are dominated by battalions of angels, martyrs, and saints. In startling contrast to the gentle, ethereal images of the Perivleptos, many of these are lean and fearsome figures, ruthless warriors of the spirit whose swirling beards, muscular hands, and glaring eyes must have sent shivers down the spine of many a guilt-ridden penitent with the blood of a neighbor or the theft of his lord's cattle on his mind.

The oldest of the Mistra churches is the late-thirteenth-century Metropolis, formerly the seat of the city's bishop. Its frescoes, although they have a certain rough force, are modest by comparison to the brilliant panels of the Perivleptos and the Hodegetria. A small museum attached to the Metropolis offers an interesting collection of icons, pottery, fragments of frescoes, and architectural details.

The latest of the great churches, the Pantanassa, was built in the 1420s, hardly a generation before the collapse of the empire. Once it was probably hidden among the dense press of the city's houses, but the classical rhythms of its arched facade and multidomed roof, punctuated abruptly by a lofty belltower, stand out now in stark and dignified solitude against the green hillside. From a tidy row of whitewashed cells next to the church, aged nuns carry on ever more feebly the elaborate rites of the Byzantine faith.

But by the time the Pantanassa was built, the Turks were at the gates of Constantinople and the end of the empire was in sight.

The creative force of Byzantine art was spent. The quaintly charming though artistically insignificant religious paintings that fill the church's huge *ikonostasis* illustrate with melancholy clarity how the four centuries of Turkish occupation inexorably sterilized the Byzantine esthetic: in these eighteenth- or nineteenth-century pictures the saints have been reduced to stiff, primitive figures, the once-tumultuous landscapes to crude sketches, and the compositions to bland convention.

In 1453 Constantinople fell to the Turks. In May 1460, fatally entangled in his own intrigues and ringed by enemies, the last of the Despots handed Mistra over to the Turkish sultan and disappeared into oblivion. The great princes and patrons, the connoisseurs who could afford to ensure that their faith was endowed with art, all were swept away. The great secular painters fled to Serbia, Bulgaria, and Italy. Painting was left in the hands of the monks, and the last vestiges of the classical tradition hardened into a rigid orthodoxy.

Turkish occupation sapped the cultural life that had made Mistra famous. There was no room in the Islamic domain for a neo-pagan like Plethon, the Platonist scholar, who had died in 1450, or his followers. The Greek Renaissance was aborted. The stump of a slender minaret poking up from the ruined belltower of a one-time chapel bears silent, poignant witness to what must have been a traumatic time for the citizens of what the *Chronicle of the Morea* called the "God-guarded country of Myzithra." The armageddon the Byzantines feared had come at last.

Cut off from the West except for two brief periods of Venetian rule, Mistra eventually adjusted to its new and unsung place in the backwaters of the Turkish empire. Greeks buried the double-headed eagle of Byzantium in their folk embroidery, while the empire's name passed pathetically into the languages of the West as a synonym for something shadowy, impenetrable, and treacherous. Later Europeans who climbed through Mistra's sleepy, decaying lanes mistook it more than once for the site of ancient Sparta, which actually lay on a hillock some miles away. The city endured until the mid-nineteenth century, when the rulers of liberated Greece finally called the Greeks down from the ruins of their Byzantine past to the clean, uninspired grid of the new town they had laid out on the valley floor.

Visiting Sparta and Mistra

Basics

The modern city of Sparta is about 180 miles southwest of Athens, a four-hour trip by car or bus. Visitors should allow at least half a day to see nearby Mistra. While the cobbled paths are not difficult to negotiate, they are in some places fairly steep and occasionally unpaved. The Perivleptos is built into the side of the mountain and its frescoes are best seen in the morning. An English-language guidebook by Manolis Chatzidakis, *Mystras: The Medieval City and the Castle,* is widely available in Athens for about $3.

Accommodations

A wide range of hotel accommodations may be found in Sparta. Among the better hotels are the **Lida** (double about $23, single $19, 0731.23601); **Menelaion** (double $17, single $12, including breakfast; 0731.22161); **Dioscuri** (double $14, single $11; 0731.28484), and the **Apollo** (double $12, single $9; 0731.22491).

Sparta Today

The outdoor cafés in the central square and on Greeks of New York Street—named in honor of the many immigrants Sparta has sent to New York—offer a spectacular view of Mount Taygetus, where the ancient rulers of Sparta put out the crippled and deformed to die.

Very little is left of ancient Sparta. Its extent is barely suggested by a vague litter of stone walls that may be seen in an olive orchard somewhat north of the modern town. The regional museum contains a few interesting relics, including votive offerings, Mycenean pottery, mosaics from a Roman villa, and a marble bust of the Spartan king Leonidas. It is open from 9 A.M. to 4 P.M. weekdays except Tuesday, and 10 A.M. to 3 P.M. Sundays and holidays. The admission price is less than $1.

Side Trips

Monemvasía, about 50 miles to the southwest, was the port of the Mistra Despotate. It consists today of a dense clutter of Byzantine and Venetian homes and churches jammed behind fortress walls at the base of a 600-foot-high cliff that rises to form an island just a few hundred feet off the coast.

Greece at Its Most Greek

BY PHYLLIS ROSE

editor's note

I had not visited Nafplio, capital of Greece from 1829 to 1834, until recently, and I can't even guess at why I had not stopped there previously. The drive there passed through orchards and orchards of orange trees, as far as my eyes could see, and I found the city charming and interesting once I arrived. (And by the way, when I was last there, the Xenia and Xenia Palace hotels were still closed and didn't look like they'd be open anytime soon. But no matter: make a reservation at the lovely little Byron Hotel—see *Good Things, Favorite Places* for contact information—and you'll be in good hands and in a convenient location for walking to just about everything.)

PHYLLIS ROSE is the author of *The Year of Reading Proust* (Scribner, 1997) and *Parallel Lives: Five Victorian Marriages* (Alfred A. Knopf, 1983) and is the editor of *The Norton Book of Women's Lives* (W.W. Norton, 1993), among others. She contributed this piece to the "The Sophisticated Traveler" section of *The New York Times Magazine*.

I believe that a traveler in a new place should buy something, preferably through bargaining. Buy something, make a friend, get information. It's the human contact, not the acquisition, that counts. Consequently, and not to satisfy any low material desires, I was bargaining for a hand-woven cotton tablecloth in Nafplio.

Even in Greece, even in Nafplio (or Nauplion, as it is also called), even in a souvenir shop where hardly anything sells for more than $40, we had all entered this new May week in a state of anxiety about Wall Street. The store owner, while spiritedly taking part in our negotiation, was keeping an eye on the television above the counter. CNN was about to report on how the American stock market, seven hours behind us, had opened. The previous week had been disastrous, and this was either a real crash, if the market opened low, or yet another hard ride, if it rallied.

When your grins bin sniff, Mr. Roussos, the shopowner, said with a conspiratorial twinkle that suggested I should understand his allusion and appreciate his savvy.

Pardon me?

What they say: When your Mr. Grinsbin sniff, the rest of world go to hospital.

When Greenspan sneezes, the rest of the world gets pneumonia, and Nafplio's tourist business gets even worse than it is. The armies of tourists from various nations in bus-size battalions of eighty have left the field here. This is a blessing for the independent traveler, if hard on local businessmen.

Nafplio is the prettiest and most lovable city I've seen in Greece. The setting of the red-roofed Old Town, on the Bay of Argolis, backed by the rocky heights of Acronauplia and even higher Palamidi, is spectacular. For centuries Venetians and Turks took turns ruling Nafplio, leaving behind palpable layers of elegance and exoticism. At one end of the immense, marble-paved piazza, Constitution Square, is an arcaded brick building constructed by the Venetians in the eighteenth century (now the Archaeological Museum); at the other end is a converted Turkish mosque. Bougainvillea grows through the wrought-iron balconies of many neoclassical mansions and spills overhead on narrow streets. In the evenings, tavernas put out tables and chairs in these alleys, so you can eat and drink beneath the stars and flowers.

Here, in 1821, Greeks won independence by storming the fortress at the top of Palamidi, taking it from the Turks after a siege of more than a year. Nafplio became a center for philhellenic political activity. The first Greek parliament was here, and for six years, until 1834, this was the capital of Greece. I have an easy time here imagining I'm in the freedom-seeking, passionate, semibarbaric, Western, Eastern, silk-and-velvet, early-nineteenth-century Greece that Byron fought for.

I am thinking of the famous painting of Byron in what he called his Albanian outfit, a red-and-yellow-striped silk bandana around his forehead. That morning my husband, Laurent, and I saw many costumes of even greater splendor at the Folk Art Museum (formally the Peloponnesian Folklore Foundation), dresses to make Christian Lacroix frantic with envy, embroidered velvets on top of silks, silks on velvet, gold-embroidered vests, silver-embroidered waistbands, coin necklaces, metal breastplates, life-size mannequins swathed, wrapped, and decorated as vividly and imaginatively as ever I've seen outside the Costume Institute at the Metropolitan Museum of Art. The Folklore Foundation specializes in weaving, embroidery, clothing, and jewelry, making it—along with the Nafplio Archaeological Museum, with its fantastically patterned Mycenaean pottery—a design inspiration. For me, it helped people the city with fantasy figures in colorful clothes uniting to throw off the yoke of oppression.

After my negotiation for the tablecloth was completed, Mr. Roussos and I advanced quickly from matters of world economy to where to eat, swim, stroll, and sleep in Nafplio. For strolling, he recommended the walk along the base of Acronauplia to the beach of Karathona. For swimming, he recommended the Arvanitia beach. For sleeping, he recommended the Pension Marianna. Quiet as the grave.

We, however, were staying at the Xenia Palace hotel, according to my information the only luxury hotel in town, set sensationally atop the Acronauplia, looking over the roofs of the Old Town to the bay and distant mountains of the Argolid. An elevator, I'd read, takes you down from the hotel through the heart of the rock and deposits you in the center of town. That sounded great.

When I made the reservation, I imagined a grand old converted structure, like the San Domenico in Taormina. But our arrival was unpromising, even disconcerting. First, few people seemed able to tell us how to find the hotel. When our Athenian driver, Kristos, finally found the right road and a hotel that said "Xenia," it looked derelict and was in fact closed. The Xenia Palace was farther up the mountain, a modern building aging badly. A thick cable blocked us from pulling up to it. We had to leave the car about 100 yards from the entrance—no porters or bellboys in sight—and walk through an empty, graceless lobby to the front desk.

Greeks usually care about the quality of hospitality. A cordial reception has been valued since Homeric times. We'd gotten used to better welcomes. I was so unnerved by our reception that I demanded to know if there was any good reason we could not drive to the front door. At first the man at reception avoided the question, but finally he admitted there were "structural problems." No more than five cars could be in front of the hotel at any one time without danger of road collapse. They weren't taking any chances.

I don't want to dwell on the strangeness of the Xenia Palace, where we and our traveling companions, Ron and Joanne, seemed to be the only guests. Joanne and I both took a Wildean dislike to the avocado-colored bathroom fixtures ("Either this wallpaper goes or I do," was Oscar Wilde's dying quip) and especially the sinks, which looked like urinals. The lighting in the rooms was too dim for reading. The elevator down to town deposited us at the end of a tunnel, on the ceiling of which were stuck what seemed to be Styrofoam blocks painted green (to deaden screams?); the walls looked like high school lockers and shelves had been ripped off them.

This creepy, until recently government-run hotel, with its spectacular placement and views all squandered, is the town's biggest problem. As I was too dumb to understand immediately, no more than five cars at the front door means no buses, and no buses means no tour groups, and no tour groups means few guests. Add the avocado bathroom fixtures and the urinal-sinks, and you have a real disaster, a supposedly high-end hotel that appeals to no one. With the luxury-class Xenia Palace empty, the first-class Xenia down the hill closed, and the other first-class hotel, the Amfitrion, also closed, it was no wonder Nafplio seemed light on tourists. Groups visiting Mycenae and Epidaurus, who might use Nafplio as a base, stay at the Amalia, miles out of town, or in Tolo, farther down the coast.

This situation won't last long. The Xenia Palace, the Xenia, and the Amfitrion have all been bought by the hotel group that owns the world-class Elounda Beach Hotel in Crete. They and the town are ripe for renovation. So if you like the authenticity and charm of semiabandoned places, go to Nafplio quickly.

You are likely to find unexpected pleasures. For example, the Komboloï Museum, around the corner from the Folk Art Museum.

The Greeks have quickly picked up the connection between museums and museum shops, and the Komboloï Museum looked like a bead store. One man was at work stringing beads under a sign that said "Workshop." A younger man stood behind the counter.

Can you tell me what komboloï would be in English? I asked him.

He waved his hand around the store in reply.

Beads? I said.

Not beads. Special beads. Beads for this, he said.

He picked up a strand of amber beads loosely strung on a red silk thread and started pushing them to one side. Worry beads!

Where's the museum? I asked.

He pointed up some narrow stairs and to a sign asking the equivalent of $1.50 for admission. Stairs and price seemed steep, but we were intrigued: what would a worry-bead museum consist of?

It was an extensive collection of prayer beads—Buddhist, Hindu, Muslim, Catholic—with an explanation of how they evolved one from the other: Muslim traders brought prayer beads from Asia and adapted them to Islam; in the late twelfth century Crusaders brought them back from Constantinople to Catholic Europe, where they metamorphosed into rosary beads. Buddhist strands have 108 beads; Muslim beads track the 99 identities of Allah, usually with 33 beads for three prayers each, and rosaries most often consist of 5 groups of 10 small beads with larger beads separating them. From these prayer beads, the strictly secular Greek worry beads evolved, having no specified number of beads to a strand, chosen for aesthetic considerations like feel and look, a combination toy and meditation device. We didn't see many in use in present-day Nafplio, but they proved popular presents for harried Americans upon our return to the United States.

In the afternoon we took the walk Mr. Roussos had recommended. Just beyond the pier where fishing boats tie up, the walk under Palamidi starts. A wide, flat, stone-paved pathway heads around the other side of the rocky peninsula, between cliff and water. We passed a seaside taverna, an abandoned swim club, and the entrance to the nearly one thousand steps that lead up to the fortress, from which there are spectacular Santorini-like views of an immense sea, distant land, and dwellings far below. Quickly we were beyond any buildings, walking between red cliffs and blue water. Birds, roosting in the cliff face, flew over our heads, and their song filled the air. An old woman, her hair in a gray bun, gathered herbs growing from the rocks. We exchanged a *kalispera* ("good evening"). At any point we could have walked out onto rocks and gone for a swim. Farther along, men were fishing and others swimming at what must have been Karathona Beach.

Returning, we stopped to watch the sunset at one of the dozens of cafés lining the waterfront and looked across the Bay of Argolis toward hazy blue mountains massed in receding rows. A tiny island in the bay, close to the port, bears the picturesque remains of a fortress. It's called Bourtzi and is festooned now with bougainvillea. (Funny how charming military installations can look with the passage of time; they seem to age better than hotels.) Boats leave every half-hour for Bourtzi—the trip takes five minutes—and you can witness the sunset from there. But we preferred the café.

We sat shaded by market umbrellas big and high enough to seem like ceilings, and birds flew underneath them. We sipped our Scotch-and-sodas and observed neighbors who were talking on cell phones and handling paperwork as they consumed enormous pastries and coffees in what for them was midafternoon. Again, the comparison that presented itself to me was with Santorini, where we had recently been. It is a fact universally acknowledged that the sunset seen from Oia in Santorini is the most beautiful sunset in the world. But the sunset seen from a waterfront café in Nafplio seemed to me every bit as beautiful and vastly less attended.

Greeks eat late, nine P.M. at the earliest. So we had time to investigate the restaurants Mr. Roussos had suggested. We had no trouble finding the Omorpho Tavernaki, two streets back from the waterfront, in a relatively empty part of town. People, all Greek, were eating and talking vivaciously at tables set up in the street. Basilis, another place Mr. Roussos recommended, was more of a challenge because it's on a street with many tavernas whose customers were eating outside. It was hard to tell where one taverna ended and another began. My husband and I performed the restaurant-scouter stroll, eyeing menus, checking out ambience, glancing into people's plates as they ate, all the while trying to look as if we were on some other mission entirely. Unfortunately, my husband turned on his heel and, pretending not to look at anything, walked straight into me. The waiters could not keep from laughing. Thus we made up our minds where to dine.

We waited in the middle of Constitution Square for our friends to rejoin us. They had gone to the island of Hydra for the day. The square has white marble paving, and many children were trying to ride bikes on the slippery surface. They fell and were brave or cried and were comforted. It seemed strange and a pleasure to watch people living their everyday lives. In Athens's Syntagma Square, you see fake folk dancing. In the Piazza Navona in Rome, there's nary a native in sight. Local people come to this square in the evening with their kids. Waiting, we watched them and also indulged in the peculiarly satisfying task of deciphering a non-Roman alphabet. From

ΕΝΝΙΚΗ ΤΡΑΒΕΖΑ we made out ETHNIK TRAPEZE and from there it was a short but exhilarating step to National Bank. This building's architectural style is one you don't often encounter: neo-Mycenaean. Yet there is a fully functioning A.T.M. just inside the door, which opens to the same card that opens the door of our Citizens Bank in Connecticut.

Ron and Joanne, wearing white cotton shirts they'd acquired on Hydra, joined us soon, and we had a terrific dinner at Omorpho. There was no table free when we arrived, but that was not a problem: they put another table and four chairs on the street for us. We ate croquettes of a green vegetable resembling spinach, stuffed zucchini, grilled local sausages, and veal chops. We ate, as is normal in Greece, exactly as much as we wanted, got our food quickly, and were waited on efficiently and with no pretension. We drank two bottles of Nimea, an excellent red wine that comes from vineyards we had passed on our way to Nafplio. The bill was $37, service included. We had a sticker-shock moment of a novel sort. Anyway, we were feeling flush because the stock market had rallied.

My husband and I were heading from Nafplio to Olympia, a three-hour drive, but Ron and Joanne had decided to go right on to Delphi. Kristos found a Nafplio cabby who would take them there in a comfortable car at a reasonable price. So we left separately the next day, Laurent and I in a yellow Athens cab, Joanne and Ron in a red Nafplio one.

When Telemachus, in search of Odysseus, arrived at a new castle, he would usually be given dinner before he was expected to impart his lineage and his purpose in traveling. We stopped for gas a mile or so outside of town. The gas station owner, while filling the tank, said to Kristos, I know who you are. You are driving one of the two American couples who were staying at the Xenia Palace. Are you the ones headed to Delphi or to Olympia?

So our herald revealed our identity and destination.

Getting There, Staying There

Nafplio is a three- or four-hour drive south of Athens. We wanted to tour the Peloponnese by car but were worried about driving in Greece, which is nerve-racking at best. **Taxis** are a good alternative. The cost is about $260 a day, and four people can fit in one cab, which is often a Mercedes. Kristos Exarhopoulou, the cab driver who took us to Nafplio, Olympia, and Delphi, proved to be an excellent driver, a tactful and intelligent companion, and a resourceful representative; his telephone number is 197.68557.

There are pleasant, though not luxurious, places to stay in Nafplio. Perhaps the most highly recommended is the **Byron Hotel,** 2 Platonos Street (752.22351; fax: .26338), in the heart of the Old Town; there are eighteen rooms, with showers, air conditioning, and excellent views; prices range from about $50 to $60; breakfast costs about $2.75; no restaurant.

Also in the Old Town, near Constitution Square, is the **Ilion Hotel,** 6 Kapodistriou Street (752.25114; fax: .24497), which has ten uniquely decorated suites; all have baths and air conditioning; prices range from about $55 to $110, including breakfast; no restaurant. The **King Othon Hotel,** 4 Farmakopoulou (tel. and fax: 752.27595), is inexpensive and the rooms somewhat cramped and basic, but the neoclassical building is recently restored, and the hallways and exterior are beautiful. There are eleven rooms, and a double, with bath and air conditioning, costs from about $50 to $60, including breakfast; no restaurant. Farther up on the Acronauplia, and a little outside of the central (and perhaps noisy) heart of the Old Town, is the **Marianna Pension,** 9 Potamianou Street (752.24256; fax: 752.21783), recommended by Mr. Roussos; all fourteen rooms have bathrooms and air conditioning; a double is about $45, including breakfast. The **Xenia Palace,** where we had a less than ideal stay, is under new ownership and scheduled for renovation.

"Give us this day our daily squid" was Joanne's assessment of Greek food. Among other wonderful fried fish specialties, I especially liked the whitebait, tiny and consumed by the dozen. Squeeze on lemon, and by a miracle of timing, they stay crisp until you've reached the last mouthful, only then becoming sodden and inedible. Greek salads are also predictably good, as are olives, feta, and stuffed grape leaves. Forget about butter when you're in Greece. They don't understand it.

The Napflio restaurants that we checked out all had menus similar to that of the Omorpho Tavernaki, 1 Kostonopoulou Street (752.25944), where we had a meal that included stuffed zucchini, grilled local sausage, and veal chops; the prices were extremely reasonable, often less than $10 a person.

One last thing: eat yogurt and honey for breakfast. Greek yogurt tastes more like sour cream than it does like our yogurt, and with Greek honey, it's the food of the gods.

Bibliography

Mani: Travels in the Southern Peloponnese, Patrick Leigh Fermor, John Murray, London, 1958. As you can see from this rather nonexistent bibliography, next to no books have been published that focus exclusively on the Peloponnese. But even if there were many more, *Mani* would still tower above all the others and would be *the* book to read. To precisely define the Máni, Leigh Fermor explains that "on the map the southern part of the Peloponnese looks like a misshapen tooth fresh torn from its gum with three peninsulas jutting southward in jagged and carious roots. The central prong is formed by the Taygetus mountains, which, from their northern foothills in the heart of the Moorea to their storm-beaten southern point, Cape Matapan, are roughly a hundred miles long. About half their length—seventy-five miles on their western and forty-five on their eastern flank and measuring fifty miles across—projects tapering into the sea. This is the Mani." This masterpiece—along with Leigh Fermor's companion volume, *Roumeli,* about Northern Greece, which I will cover in a separate volume—ranks among the pantheon of legendary travel books. It is, in fact, much more a work of history and anthropology than a travelogue, and though Leigh Fermor felt it was worthwhile to observe and record some of the less famous aspects in this corner of Greece before they faded away forever, much of the landscape, traditions, and superstitions delved into here are virtually unchanged. He explains further that *Mani* is directed at the least frequented areas, often the hardest of access and the least inviting to most travelers. *Mani* is, in a way, the opposite of a guide book, "for many of the best-known parts of ancient Greece, many of the world's marvels, will be, perforce and most unwillingly—unless their link with some aspect of modern Greek life is especially compelling—left out. There are two thoughts which make this exclusion seem less unjust. Firstly, the famous shrines and temples of antiquity usually occupy so much space in books on Greece that all subsequent history is ignored; and secondly, hundreds of deft pens are forever at work on them, while in this century, scarcely a word has been written on the remote and barren but astonishing region of the Mani." Leigh Fermor mentions another book, *The Morea* by Robert Liddell (Jonathan Cape, London, 1958), that includes an "admirable chapter" on the Máni. I haven't yet tracked down this volume, and while I'm sure it is worthy, I would say to travelers that *Mani* is an indispensable read.

The Greek Table

"*I believe Greek cooking is, foremost, the product of great ingenuity. Every day the Greek cook manages to create a new dish from the same few, humble, seasonal ingredients. . . . Greek food is not sophisticated or refined. It is simple and down to earth, tied to and making the most of the seasonal produce of each region.*"

—Aglaia Kremezi, THE FOODS OF GREECE

"*Feasting and fasting, richness and frugality, especially among traditional and religious Greeks, is still the pattern of gastronomic life; food cannot truly be valued unless, at some other time, it has been denied.*"

—Rosemary Barron, FLAVORS OF GREECE

The Original Extra Virgins:
The Olive Oils of Greece

BY ARI WEINZWEIG

~∾~

editor's note

In an article entitled "Olive Oil: Elixir of the Gods" (*National Geographic,* September 1999), writer Erla Zwingle noted that not every olive-growing country produces enough oil to satisfy local and export demand, Italy foremost. So there is a very good chance that a bottle of Italian oil may contain Greek or Spanish oil, too. Though international trade standards now require labels to fully state their contents, the Greeks and the Spanish feel their oils deserve to be better known (I agree), believing their oils are "hidden in the shadow of the image of Italian oil," according to Zwingle. "The Italians were first to capture the foreign market—73 percent of the European olive oil the U.S. imports comes from Italy—and they continue to dominate at least with their reputation for high-quality oil. The others chafe. 'You know what we say?' a Greek asked me. 'Italian oil is like water.'" On my last visit to Greece I bought a variety of oils to bring home, a few of which I've been able to find here, including the wonderful Terra Medi (the house olive oil at New York City's Molyvos restaurant), and each one was delicious. I like Italian olive oils, too, but they don't have anything on their Greek cousins, as the writer of this piece attests.

ARI WEINZWEIG is the founder and "guiding taste bud" of Zingerman's, the famous food emporium in Ann Arbor, Michigan. (The editors of *Saveur* have called it "a food lover's paradise.") He is also the author of *Zingerman's Guide to Good Eating* (Houghton Mifflin, 2003), a great book that chef Mario Batali refers to as "the New Testament for the religion of the palate." If you don't already know about Zingerman's, you should, and if you do already know about it and love it as much as I do, do yourself the great favor of subscribing to *Zingerman's News,* the quarterly newsletter that Ari's been writing since the store opened in 1982 (and where this piece originally appeared). Though the Zingerman's mail-order catalog is also a great read, the newsletter is even more so and has developed a cult-like following among food writers and food lovers of all stripes across the United States. Zingerman's has several excellent Greek olive oils, available both in the store and by mail. Many of you undoubtedly receive as many mail-order catalogs as I do; the arrival of the Zingerman's catalog—and the newsletter—is a special event worth celebrating. To add your name to the mailing list and/or to subscribe to the newsletter, contact Zingerman's at 422 Detroit Street, Ann Arbor MI 48104; 888-636-8162; fax: 734-477-6988; www.zingermans.com.

Hey, all you olive oil lovers, here's a strange scenario for you. Statistics show that Greece is the largest single producer of extra-virgin oil in the world ("the Saudi Arabia of extra-virgin," so to speak). And Greeks have the highest per capita consumption of olive oil in the world. Yet amazingly, extra-virgin olive oil has only recently appeared in Greek supermarkets.

How can this have happened? Is it a European episode for the X-Files: "Extra Virgin Olive Oil Reappears After Abduction by Aliens"?

Don't panic. It's actually not as strange as it might seem. The answer is to be found, not in the files at FBI headquarters or in some Interpol office, but in the recent history and current countryside of Greece.

Of all the members of the European Economic Community, Greece is probably the most recently urbanized. So although Athens itself is enormous—its population is multiplying at an almost astronomical rate—nearly every Athenian still has relatives in the countryside. The same is true for folks in Greece's other major metropolitan areas. And as a result, when most Greeks want olive oil, they tend to just take a trip to their ancestral village, not to the supermarkets. Meaning that up until the last ten years or so, the only people who shopped supermarkets for olive oil were either foreigners or ultra-cosmopolitan, upper-class Greeks, neither of whom have traditionally been big olive oil buyers. So supermarkets sans olive oil were pretty much the Greek norm up until the 1990s.

The story starts in ancient Greek mythology. Legend has it that Athena and Poseidon were competing to gain "ownership" of Greece's principal city. Zeus, a good leader amongst the gods, determined that whoever gave the greatest gift to humankind would have the city named for them. Poseidon did well, presenting the people of ancient Greece with their first horses. But Athena outdid him: she showed up with an olive tree. You probably have already guessed that the city in question is Athens. Later, the myths tells us, Aristalos, the son of Apollo, taught mankind how to crush the fruit of their new gift to make olive oil, an integral part of Greek life ever since.

Everywhere you look in Greek life and history, you find olive trees, olives, and oil. Olives have been cultivated since 3500 B.C., originally by the Minoans on Crete, later almost everywhere else as well. Ancient Greeks marked sacred spots with olive oil. Priests still bless babies with it at christenings. Olive oil was revered as an aphrodisiac. (Try it for yourself and see what you think. I can't show you any scientific studies to back up that theory, but what have you got to lose?) Olive oil was the principal cleansing substance for Greeks. It was also awarded as *the* prize in ancient athletic competitions, the original Olympic games. Winners of various events won Athenian amphorae (four-foot-high clay jugs) filled with oil. The biggest winner? The equestrian champion took home 140 amphorae of oil, well over a year's supply for even the most eager eaters. Up until the time of the Ottoman conquest in the fifteenth century, olive oil was the only fat used in Greece. An Ottoman-authorized survey in Thrace reported that "Turks ate butter, the Jews ate sesame oil, and the Greeks olive oil." In the middle of the eighteenth century there were more than two thousand oil presses on the island of Crete alone!

While Greece has certainly seen much modernization, olive oil has retained its primary role in Greek culture. It's even in the language: the color *ladi* (the word for "oil") is one of the standard spectrum of colors in the Greek equivalent of Crayola crayons or J. Crew catalogs. On the underside of life, to this day Greek men are taught never to relieve themselves under an olive tree—it's a sure way to bring on the evil eye. Even modern Greek bureaucracy recognizes the power of olive oil: Greek civil servants are entitled to an annual "olive leave"—a special pass to skip out of the office, head back to the ancestral village, and help pick olives during the harvest.

And, as I mentioned above, Greece is the largest producer of extra-virgin olive oil in the world. Total olive oil production is about 100,000 tons a year, from 90 million trees.

Freeing Your Inner Olive Oil

In twenty years of learning about food, I don't think I've encountered many foods more completely integrated into the culture and cuisine of a country than olive oil is in Greece. Perhaps you could compare it to corn for Native Americans, or rice in China.

When it comes right down to it, Greek people have, in essence, an intimate relationship with their oil. Olive oil is so much a part of Greek eating and Greek life that they have, for all practical purposes, "internalized" it. One of the researchers who accompanied Dr. Ancel Keys in his pioneering Seven Countries Study of the relationship between diet and heart disease said, "Many Greeks consume olive oil as they consume oxygen, without paying particular attention to it." They rarely seem to realize how much of it they really eat; nor are they aware of how much they would miss it if they had to go without it. In the same way that the mere mention of chicken soup and chopped liver evoke lovely memories of Jewish tradition and culture, so too does olive oil elicit visions of warm village vistas and caring cousins in the countryside. In Greece olive oil is about eating, not intellectualizing.

The somewhat ironic outcome of all of this is that, for the most part, Greeks can't really tell you what they like or don't like in oil. They don't think about it. They just eat it. What I've learned is that, quite simply, Greeks almost always just "like what they know." They select from a "wine list" of one: the oil they grew up with is the way oil ought to be. Period. No discussion. Try other oils? Why bother? The local oil is an object of enormous pride.

Chris Veneris, one of Crete's leading cooks, told me quite simply, "I can tell you only one thing about olive oil. That is, that Cretan olive oil is the best." Later, though, he confessed to me with a wink, a smile, and a shrug of the shoulders, "If you don't give your house a compliment, the roof will fall on your head." In other words, what else could he do but express his support for his native oil? I have the distinct feeling that I'd hear the same thing said about the local *ladi* in every other part of the country.

Cooperative in the Countryside

The communal approach to life in the Greek countryside has pretty much eliminated the sort of single-estate olive oils that we, at Zingerman's, actively investigate and then import from Italy or Spain. Instead, almost all the oil is produced cooperatively in the villages. Now, this is not necessarily a negative, but for decades the standard Greek practice has been for the local village coops to sell their oil to bigger regional coops, who in turn sell it to even bigger coops, where it is blended again. In the interest of economics, the best oils are anonymously blended in with lesser oils. Good for business, bad for flavor: all this blending betrays the unique character, flavor, and aroma that would be found in the best small-production oils.

Of late though, there is a move toward recognition and differentiation. People are waking up to the possibilities and opportunities available. Most likely this will come in the form of "single village oils"—few farms have the size to make single-estate oils like we get from Italy and Spain. There is also a growing interest in organic production.

Eating Olive Oil in Greece

As I mentioned, Greeks, as a people, are the world's largest per capita consumers of olive oil. The average Hellene eats about 20 liters a year. On Crete, the star of the Seven Countries Study for its long-lived residents, the average islander eats over 40 liters of olive oil each year.

From simple to sensational, nearly every major component of Greek cooking relies on olive oil for its flavor and character. They put olive oil on everything: bread, wild greens, fish, salads, soups. It starts with simple stuff, like *papara:* bread, brushed with lots of olive oil, sprinkled with some sea salt and dried oregano. Along with cured olives, *papara* was the staple food of the countryside up until the last few decades. "This is what we grew up with," Aglaia Kremezi, a friend and food writer in Athens, told me.

To the Home of Feta

BY DIANE KOCHILAS

$\sim$

editor's note

Feta may be the most recognized item in Greece's culinary pantry—you'll encounter it often no matter where you travel in the country. In an interesting piece in the July 2001 issue of *Gourmet*, Steve Jenkins (author of

Cheese Primer) reported that some Greek feta nowadays is made in Sardinia, due to the huge worldwide demand, and then is sent to Greece, where it is shipped around the world. I don't always buy Greek feta, often preferring Bulgarian, but it is never better than when I'm eating it in Greece. One of my most favorite *mezéthes*—the way I have had it served to me in Greece— is a large slice of good bread with a slice of feta on top, sprinkled with dried oregano, and a generous bath of good olive oil drizzled over the whole thing. You need a knife and fork to eat it unless you are prepared for quite a messy nibble; or you could make mini versions using small slices of a baguette.

DIANE KOCHILAS, introduced previously, writes frequently for *Saveur,* where this piece first appeared. She is also the author of a number of cookbooks, including *The Glorious Foods of Greece* (Morrow, 2001, and winner of the prestigious Jane Grigson Award for Excellence in Scholarship by the International Association of Culinary Professionals), *Meze: Small Plates to Savor and Share from the Mediterranean Table* (William Morrow, 2003), *The Food and Wines of Greece* (1990 hardcover, 1993 paperback), and *The Greek Vegetarian* (1996), both published by St. Martin's Press.

Everything is damp at Takis Langas's cheese factory on the cool mountain plateau of Mandinía, deep in the Peloponnese—one of about eight hundred small, family-run, traditional-style cheese concerns left in the country. The strange, thick, sweet-and-sour smell of fermenting milk permeates the place. Hoses carrying milk and whey snake across the wet cement floors. Salt cracks beneath your feet as you walk around. Balls of *myzíthra*—an air-dried whey cheese made with feta residuals—dangle like Christmas ornaments from the rafters. There are barrels everywhere—empty ones piled in pyramids outside, new ones being washed out with whey, barrels filled with feta at various stages of maturity, barrels deconstructed into tired staves destined for the wood-burning oven that Langas lights once a week to cook his famed roast pork "for the boys."

Feta, the definitive Greek cheese, salty and sourish and earthy, is descended from the soft, tart goat's-milk cheeses that have been known in the Balkans, and especially in Greece and Bulgaria, forever. The Greek word *feta* means "slice"—the form in which the cheese is customarily served. It is not an old name; it was probably coined by a market-savvy cheesemonger or producer around the turn of the century.

Greek law decrees that feta must be made from at least 70 percent ewe's milk and up to 30 percent goat's milk. Each animal produces one to three kilos of milk per day; it takes at least four kilos to make a kilo of cheese. The more goat's milk in the mix, the firmer the cheese will be. (Bulgarian feta is traditionally made with about the same ratio of ewe's milk to goat's milk, but cow's milk is sometimes added today because the country faces an overall milk shortage.)

Feta of one kind or another is made in many European countries and in North America. Bulgarian feta can be excellent—though it is quite sour and tangy because of the local yeast used as a starter. There are also good ones from Sardinia (a Greek-style, barrel-aged version), where many of the cheesemakers are expatriate Greeks, and from France—a wonderful, creamy feta made, ironically, in Roquefort. The Danes, the Dutch, and the Germans make generally dismal versions of feta, mostly from cow's milk; these are typically chalky, and squeaky in the mouth. American and Canadian feta is usually sold at half the price of the rest—and with good reason. Non-Greek European feta is about to become a thing of the past, though—at least by that name. According to a recent European Economic Community ruling, after July 21, 2001, no member nation will be able to sell white brine cheese—either inside the European Community or anywhere else—as feta. Names like "white cheese" and "white brine cheese" (or their equivalents in the local language) are suggested alternatives—though the marketing departments of the major European cheese producers will doubtless come up with more evocative terminology.

According to Eric Moschalaidis, the president of Krinos Foods, the largest importer of Greek food products in America, feta is the fastest-growing specialty cheese in the United States. It was first imported to this country in the 1930s, but for years it was sold only in ethnic markets. Exports from Greece stopped during World War II and the ensuing Greek Civil War. During the latter conflict, says John Moscahlaidis—Eric's father—who founded Krinos Foods in 1956, many Greek cheesemakers moved to Sardinia "because that's where they found sheep." A few entrepreneurs even tried producing fetalike cheeses in the United States—one marketed under the very weird name Cream-O-Gal. The elder Moscahlaidis credits the award-winning 1964 film *Zorba the Greek* and the marriage of Jacqueline Kennedy to Aristotle Onassis with spurring American interest in Greek foods—feta included. The many Greek-owned coffee shops and diners along the eastern seaboard helped too. Today, with the American mania for all things Mediterranean, it's only natural that the cheese (which, incidentally, is lower in fat than most other firm cheeses) should be more popular than ever.

The Langas factory turns out about 250 tons of handmade feta each year, between December and the end of June. Production is supervised by a wiry Ionian named Gerasimos Theodoratos, who learned the cheesemaker's craft from his father and grandfather on his native island of Cephalonia—long famous for its cheeses—then made feta in the United States, Canada, and Sardinia for decades before returning to Greece.

It is noon when I arrive at the factory, and the day's production cycle is well under way. The four tons or so of ewe's and goat's milk that Langas buys daily from some sixty-three local shepherds arrived, as usual, at around 8:30 A.M. It has already been checked for contamination, skimmed slightly—about 15 percent of the fat is removed to help give the final product a firmer texture—pasteurized at about 150°F, and cooled by being pumped through a contraption resembling a radiator. It now resides in the three enormous vats in the center of the feta room.

You can't tell by looking—the vats' contents seem deceptively still—but the rennet and starter necessary to make the curds set have already been added, and the milk is now in the midst of ferocious fermentation. Every few minutes Theodoratos runs his arm, and then a thermometer, through each vat. The temperature has to remain constant, somewhere between 95°F and 100°F, depending on the weather and on the final texture desired. "It's a delicate balance," he says. "One degree off, and you've ruined the cheese." At one point he adds salt—big crystals of it, scooped up with a slotted cup and rinsed in a barrel of water. "I can't tell you how much I add," says Theodoratos. "I just know by looking." Takis Langas, who is watching, interrupts. "It's about four kilos per vat," he assures me.

It takes about forty-five minutes for the milk to be transformed into the curds, or *pasta*—a sweet, warm, soft substance, thick and white like yogurt and about as tenuously solid as Jell-O, bathed in deep yellow whey. The next step in the feta-making process is to cut the pasta. To do this, Theodoratos takes a long stainless-steel paddlelike frame, outfitted with rows of wire evenly spaced about an inch apart, and runs it horizontally, then vertically, through each vat, forming a grid. "If you want very firm cheese," he explains, "you coagulate the milk at a slightly higher temperature and cut the curds very small. If you want soft feta, you do the opposite—lower temperature, bigger curds." Next, the cheesemaker stirs the curds with a long wooden oar docked with several large holes. Finally, he runs his hands through them, breaking up the mass from the bottom of the vat; this is literally handmade cheese.

Feta is relatively easy to produce. It doesn't require long and careful aging; and because it has no rind, it doesn't need to be methodically rinsed like Camembert or Brie. In fact, it is made pretty much the same way whether in a huge factory or in a smaller operation like Langas's: set the milk with starter, drain and salt the cheese, place it in molds to drain further, and then leave it to mature in brine. One obvious difference, besides scale, is that the larger manufacturers are automated. At the ultramodern Epirus cheese-making factory in the Epirus region, for instance—where annual feta production is about 3,000 tons—1,000 liters of milk are processed every four minutes on a production line. There are minor differences in technique too, depending on whether the feta is to be packed in barrels or in tins. Tinned feta is a recent invention; the first country to produce and export it may have been Romania, in the early 1960s. Feta packed this way tends to be firmer and a little saltier than its barrel-aged counterpart. To aficionados like myself, the barrel-aged version is unquestionably superior.

As Theodoratos's feta sets, he weighs down the thickened curds in each vat with the round slotted molds in which the cheese will eventually be shaped—placing as many as will fit on the surface of each vat, then pumping out the golden green whey. Next, he fills the molds with the pasta, patting down and distributing the curds evenly so that all the molds are filled to exactly the same height. "If the pasta is too soft," he explains, "it won't drain properly." He salts the molds. In about an hour, he will flip them, salt them again, and cut each mass into three triangular wedges. The curds are flipped and salted by hand three times over the course of the day. By the next morning the cheese will be solid enough to be placed in a barrel for the first time, in five salted layers.

After three to five days in the barrel, the cheese is removed, washed down with brine, and placed in other barrels whose interiors have been steam-sterilized, then rubbed with soft whey cheese to insulate the feta from the taste of wood. Each one holds 50 kilos (over 100 pounds) of cheese. The feta now rests for anywhere from two weeks to forty days, to ferment, mature, and exude its own brine. Finally, it is refrigerated for a minimum of two months (by law). Then it can be sold—to be eaten in slices, crumbled into salads, used as a filling for savory pastries, even cooked into sauces.

"Isn't it an amazing thing?" Theodoratos asks me as I'm leaving. "A few hours ago all this was just milk."

Paximadia: Food for Sailors, Travelers, and Poor Islanders

BY AGLAIA KREMEZI

editor's note

Sooner or later during your travels in Greece you'll encounter *paximadia,* barley biscuits that are especially known on Crete. (Crete is, in fact, sometimes known as Paximadi because of the similarity of its contours to the rugged, rocky shape of the bread.) Though they are not a culinary item I necessarily swoon over, I do like to bring home a few packages—they're great in soups, and after I tried the Cretan Seafood Salad at Molyvos in New York, I tried to recreate it at home (an assortment of seafood is piled on top of an olive oil-soaked *paximadi*), and it was delicious and refreshing (and healthful too).

AGLAIA KREMEZI, introduced on page 230, is the author of several Greek cookbooks and contributes frequently to a wide range of European and American periodicals.

The staple food of the common people is a biscuit made of barley from which only the very outer husk has been discarded. They bake it two or three times a year. It is so black that when I showed a piece to one of our monks in Naxos, he sincerely told me that in France it would be bread to give to the dogs, but he doubted that even the dogs would eat it. Nevertheless, here the small children eat it from early morning on with great appetite, and they seem to be thriving. But it would cause hemorrhaging and death to those unaccustomed to it," writes François Richard, who visited the island of Santorini in the seventeenth century. "With this biscuit, which many soak in water before lunch, they eat their vegetables, their usual meal, because they only rarely taste meat, with the exception of the rich, who buy it once a year in order to secure that they will not go without it."

Theveno, who visited Santorini a few years later, describes somewhat finer biscuits: "Their bread, which they call *schises*, is a kind of biscuit made with half wheat and half barley flour, black like tar, and so rough that one cannot swallow it; they only fire the oven twice a year . . . maybe they do it because they don't have wood to burn and have to import it from Nio."

Paximadi (plural *paximadia*) was and still is the Greek word for this barley biscuit (rusk or hardtack), although in recent years the word came to mean all kinds of twice-baked bread. Many believe that the word *paximadi* comes from Paxamus, a cook and author who probably lived in Rome in the first century. As Andrew Dalby points out, from this Greek word came the Arabic *bashmat* or *baqsimat*, the Turkish *beksemad*, the Serbo-Croatian *peksimet*, the Romanian *pesmet*, and the Venetian *pasimata*.

Barley, cultivated in the Mediterranean from the beginnings of civilization, was for many centuries the basic food of the regional populations. It was roasted so that some of its husk could be rubbed off, then ground and mixed with water, spices, and maybe honey, to be made into a gruel, or it was kneaded with water, shaped into cakes, and then baked. The barley cakes were called *maza,* and according to the laws of Solon, *maza* was the everyday food of Athenians in Classical times, while the more refined breads, made of wheat or a combination of barley and wheat, could be baked on only festive days. "When we come to our regular daily food, we require that our barley cake (*maza*) be white, yet take pains that the broth which goes with it be black, and stain the fine color of the cake with the dye," writes Alexis. *Maza* was probably a kind of heavy unleavened flat bread, unlike *paximadi,* which is first baked as a leavened bread. The way *maza* was eaten, though—dipped in a more or less rich broth—was very similar to the way *paximadi* is consumed to this day.

Since barley contains less gluten than wheat, the bread made with it is heavy, darker in color, and dries faster. So it is not surprising that it was baked again in order to be preserved. "But the flavor is good, with an unmistakably earthy tang—anyone who has ever eaten a good barley or Scotch broth will recognize the taste and the aroma," writes Elizabeth David. She advises modern bakers to add a small amount of barley to their usual wheat flour when making bread, a widespread tradition in most Mediterranean countries.

C. S. Sonnini, who visited Greece and Turkey in the last years of the eighteenth century, writes that in Kímolos (then called Argentiere) and other islands of the Aegean, people baked only barley bread. He is one of the very few who agree with David on its taste: "Having lived there for a long time, I did not find this bread disagreeable, but thought it tasty and appetizing." Sonnini also claims that all over the Orient barley bread was the usual food, and the Jews used it a lot in their diet.

Either baked in the form of a loaf, or shaped like a large doughnut, the bread destined to be made into *paximadia* is sliced—vertically in the case of the loaf and horizontally in the case of the doughnut—and left to dry for many hours in a low oven. *Dipyros artos* (twice-baked bread) was the ancient word, and both the Italian *biscotto* as well as the French and English *biscuit*, derive their names from the description of the technique in Latin (*bis-coto*).

During Byzantine times, *paximadi* "was probably the food that the future Emperor Justin II, uncle of Justinian, carried in his knapsack, the food that kept him alive on his long walk from Illyria to Constantinople; it was certainly food for soldiers and for frugal priests as well," writes Dalby.

In the mid-eighteenth century, Nicolas-Ernest Kleeman writes that after the fall of the Byzantine Empire the Turks served biscuits to the army during their sea and land expeditions.

European travelers of the seventeenth and eighteenth centuries also carried with them biscuits during their long journeys over sea and land, but their biscuits were probably made with white wheat flour, much more refined than the rough *paximadia* of the poor inhabitants of the Orient. During his wanderings on camelback, through the vast Ottoman Empire—or the Levant, as the eastern Mediterranean region was often called—Carlier de Pinon thought the Arab camel drivers were extremely grateful when offered a taste of the European biscuits. He describes with contempt the Arab flatbreads prepared fresh each time the caravan stopped and baked using camel's dung as fuel. My impression is that Europeans misjudged the big gestures with which Arabs politely thanked them. I have no doubt that the locals definitely preferred their fresh breads to the dried European biscuits, especially as they often rolled their warm pitas over stuffings of fresh cheese and dates, as documented by Sauveboef.

From the Islands to the City

An old man from Mykonos told me that not so long ago merchant ships preferred his island as a stopover because sailors loved to stock up on *paximadia* from the local bakeries, made with a combination of barley and wheat flour. Similar biscuits are still baked in most islands of the Aegean, and the ones from Crete are the most popular throughout Greece. One can get Cretan *paximadia* in specialty shops around the Central Market of Athens, as well as in grocery stores and recently even at some supermarkets. Although the people belonging to the generation that traditionally fed on this kind of dried bread have either died or switched to more refined foods, a new generation of consumers have tasted *paximadia* during their summer vacations in the islands and loved them. Once back in the city they looked for them in their local bakeries, so now in most Athenian neighborhoods one can find darker or lighter *paximadia,* baked using mixtures containing more or less barley flour in addition to the wheat flour, making lighter and crunchier biscuits that need no soaking.

Paximadia were not just eaten as an accompaniment to cheese, olives, or dried fish and meats, but were used as the main ingredient of cooked dishes. Villamont describes a soup made with "black biscuits," water, and salt, which was prepared by a Genoan, during his voyage from Cyprus to Jerusalem. Similar soups, with the addition of vegetables, herbs, pulses, or even a little meat or fish, can be found in the peasant cooking of Greece, Italy, Spain, and other Mediterranean countries. In the island of Santorini people make a kind of sweetmeat, pounding together in a mortar the very black local *paximadia* with sultanas and shaping the thick dough into walnut-size balls, which they often roll in toasted sesame seeds.

Briefly dipped in water drizzled with olive oil and sprinkled with coarse sea salt and oregano, *paximadi* becomes a delicious snack called *riganada* in the Peloponnese. In the island of Kéa, I recently tasted soaked *paximadia* with *kopanistí*—the local sharp fermented soft cheese—and chopped tomatoes, an excellent combination. Food writer Çolman Andrews mentions a very similar dish served in Triora, the back country above Sanremo. There the medium-brown biscuits are baked with buckwheat, not barley flour, and are usually soaked in a combination of water and vinegar.

In the Calabrian bakeries and grocery stores on Arthur Avenue in New York's Bronx, one finds barley biscuits very similar to the ones from Crete. Their taste complements fantastically the spicy *caccio cavallo* cheese of southern Italy, which is covered with crushed dried *peperoncini* (hot chiles). In a similar way one couldn't find a more perfect combination than *paximadi* and the hard sharp *anthotyro* of Crete.

When, in the 1950s, Ansel Keys and his colleagues studied the eating habits, the state of health, and the life expectancy of various peoples in seven countries, they decided that the inhabitants of Crete were faring best of all. *Paximadia,* in those days, were the staple food of the Cretans. But when their traditional eating habits became the model for the now-famed Mediterranean Diet, the barley biscuits were translated into "whole wheat bread" for the unaccustomed and refined northern Europeans and Americans. Barley flour has now completely disappeared from the shelves of the supermarkets, and one can only find it if one goes to a health food shop or to a wholesale distributor of animal fodder.

Aglaia Kremezi's Barley and Wheat Cretan Paximadia

From a Cretan recipe; makes 16 large (4½-inch) biscuits

2 tablespoons honey
1⅓ cup warm water, or more if needed
2 tablespoons dried yeast
1 tablespoon coarse sea salt
1 tablespoon green aniseeds

2–2½ cups unbleached all-purpose wheat flour
2 cups whole barley flour
½ cup olive oil
½ cup sweet red wine such as mavrodaphne or port
½ cup dry red wine
Olive oil to brush the dough and the baking sheets

In a 4-cup mixing bowl, dilute the honey in ⅓ cup warm water. Add the yeast, stir, and let proof for 10 minutes.

In a mortar beat together the salt and the aniseeds to get a coarse powder. In a large bowl stir together the wheat and barley flours and the aniseed-salt powder. Make a well in the center, and pour in the olive oil, the sweet and dry wines, the yeast mixture, and ½ cup warm water. Draw the flour toward the center, mixing it with the liquids to form a rather sticky dough. Knead patiently, adding a little more warm water or flour to obtain a smooth dough.

(Alternatively, work this dough in a food processor, equipped with a dough hook. Add all ingredients to the processor's bowl, and process for 1½–2 minutes, at high speed. Scrape the bowl with the spatula, let rest for 5–10 minutes, and process another 1–2 minutes.)

Turn the dough onto a lightly floured board, and continue kneading, folding, pushing, turning, and folding for another 2–3 minutes. You must end up with a soft, very slightly sticky dough. Form a ball, oil it all over with a few drops of olive oil, place it in a 3-quart bowl, cover with plastic film, and let it rise in a draft-free place for about 1½ hours, until it has doubled in size.

Cut the dough in half, and divide each half into quarters. Form each piece into a 1-inch-thick cord, then shape each cord into a small circle with overlapping ends (like a large doughnut).

Place them on lightly oiled baking sheets, spaced 1½ inches apart. Cover with plastic film and let rise for 1½–2 hours.

Preheat the oven to 400°F.

When you place the bread circles in the oven, reduce the temperature to 375°F. Bake for 30–40 minutes, until the breads are light golden on top and sound hollow when tapped.

Let them cool for 5–10 minutes. Turn the oven down to its lowest setting (175°F). Using a very good bread knife, slice the circles in half horizontally. Place the halves on the oven rack and leave for 1½–2 hours, until they are completely dry. Let cool and keep in tins in a dry place.

The *paximadia* will keep for up to 6 months.

Greek Tavernas: Outside Athens, the Catch of the Day

BY AGLAIA KREMEZI

editor's note

In *The Foods of Greece,* published originally in 1993, Aglaia Kremezi noted that "what most Greeks of my age and younger have known as 'Greek' food is the 'neither Eastern nor European' dishes that Nicholas Tselementes promoted—food that cannot compete with French or Italian cooking. To a certain extent, it is understandable why Greek and Mediterranean cooking is not very 'fashionable' in Athens. Dozens of Chinese, Thai, German, Indian, and other ethnic restaurants, together with a lot of French and Italian ones, have opened lately. Recently we also got our first McDonald's and Wendy's; both have been extremely successful. Alas, as of now, we have hardly any restaurants that serve good-quality Greek dishes in a pleasant atmosphere." Though I think Kremezi would still agree with this statement in general terms, I think she would also agree that the situation has improved somewhat in the last ten years.

It's revealing to note, as Andy Harris relates in *Taste of the Aegean*, the three events that irrevocably changed the eating habits of Athens: "The sack of Smyrna in 1922 and the exchange of populations between Turkey and Greece, bringing 1½ million refugees into the country; the opening of the first fast-food outlet, called the Royale, in 1969; and Greece's entrance into the EEC in 1981. The sophistication of the refugees, who were settled in areas of Piraeus like Drapetzona or new suburbs like Nea Ionia, Nea Smyrni, and Kesariani, brought new Eastern influences into mainstream life. The cosmopolitan café lifestyle of the rich and *tekés* (hashish dens) of the poor refugees slowly infiltrated into the mainstream through their *rembétika* music and Turkish names for the food they liked to eat like *fasolia piaz* and *yaourtlou*." Perhaps inevitably, after Greece joined the Common Market, new products began to flood the shops, and these were often cheaper than local foodstuffs. "The slow homogenization into the western European style has only really just begun," Harris concluded.

All of this noted, Athens does now have some wonderful restaurants whose chefs are turning out exciting dishes true to local ingredients and traditions. Most of these places are recommended in guidebooks, and you may learn of others from the front desk staff at your hotel. This piece, however, focuses on a few excellent places you may not discover on your own: tavernas that specialize in the catch of the day that are *outside* Athens.

AGLAIA KREMEZI contributed this piece to *Gourmet*. In addition to her cookbooks and food writing, Aglaia is also a consultant to the Greek restaurant Molyvos in New York City.

A thenians have always loved fish. And on weekends or over any of Greece's numerous holidays, the inhabitants of this country's vast and densely populated capital city waste no time abandoning their homes and heading for the sea. Implicit in their journeys are scheduled stops at some of the region's fish tavernas (none more than an hour's drive from downtown), where the catch of the day is washed down with ouzos amid sun and salty air.

There's a ritual Greeks follow when dining in a fish taverna. The most knowledgeable person in the party gets up from the table and goes back to the kitchen to choose the fish for the meal. The owner or headwaiter of the establishment opens one refrigerator drawer after another, digging into the crushed ice and taking out fish of various sizes until the customer finds something to his liking.

"Be suspicious when you find a taverna's fridge full of all kinds of fish," my father, a self-proclaimed expert, used to say. "This means most of it is imported." In Greece, "imported" refers to fish that has come from the sea off the coast of North Africa, which, unlike our increasingly fish-bereft waters, is still rich in seafood. But North African fish is much less flavorful than that which is locally caught, in part because it has traveled so far to reach its destination. Owners of seaside tavernas in Greece often try to pass off the large, cheap, Moroccan *barboúnia* (red mullet) as local, and unsuspecting customers—especially tourists—end up paying dearly for something that tastes nothing like *barboúnia* from the Aegean.

For it is freshness, more than anything else, that is responsible for the incredible taste of even the most humble fish of Greece. Good tavernas, those with loyal clienteles, carry only the freshest catch; often they won't even bother to open if their providers haven't managed to snag anything acceptable.

Once selected, the fish is weighed in front of the customer before being scaled and gutted. Preparation is minimal: the fish is either grilled over a charcoal fire; fried in olive oil; or made into *kakaviá*, the simple fish soup of the islands. Small fish are always served whole, with the head on; large specimens occasionally are sliced into steaks but are never filleted.

While the fish is being cooked, the waiter brings out *mezéthes* (starters), salads, and drinks. The marinated or grilled octopus, *taramosaláta* (fish-roe spread), *melitzanosaláta* (eggplant spread), fried or grilled squid, and fresh and boiled vegetable salads that are the standard first courses in most tavernas are often so delicious and satisfying that it's easy to forget the most important dish is yet to come. But even those who think they can't eat another mouthful find, when the steaming fish arrives with its *ladolémono* (lemon, olive oil, and oregano vinaigrette), that they indeed have room for more. In any case, "fish is like fruit," as we Greeks say—so light and healthful you can enjoy it even when you're full.

North of Athens, beyond the moneyed suburbs of Kifissiá and Ekáli, the scenic mountain road through Diónissos turns south and leads down the eastern coast of Attica. My favorite fish taverna, **Kavoúri,** is in the town of Paralia Marathónas, the coastal annex of the ancient village of Marathón. With light-blue-cloth–covered tables set right on the sheltered, sunny beach, Kavoúri offers only dishes that Mina Kákari, its owner and supervising chef, would like to eat herself. "I don't like *tzatziki*," she says bluntly of the popular yogurt, cucumber, and garlic mixture, "so we never make it." Freshly marinated *gávros* (anchovies) with chopped garlic, parsley, and extra-virgin olive oil are her specialty. In addition to the usual *mezéthes,* she serves (in season) succulent whole squid stuffed with feta and grilled over a charcoal fire. Her mixed salad has the rich taste of the area's renowned vegetables: tomatoes, arugula, bell peppers, cucumbers, and carrots, among others. The fish, from off the nearby coast of Evia, is grilled to juicy perfection. And lobster is boiled and served with a simple lemon vinaigrette. Mina makes her special *kakaviá,* prepared using only tomatoes and potatoes, for customers who order it in advance. Dessert, the traditional semolina *halvá*, with nuts and raisins, arrives free of charge. Two to three nights before and a couple of nights after each full moon in summer, Mina turns the electricity off and guests enjoy romantic candlelit dinners by the light of the moon emerging from the sea. In winter, the cozy, stone-walled dining room is warmed by an open fireplace.

Farther down the eastern coast, in Rafína, is **Ioakim,** a small, traditional taverna situated right at the port from which ferries leave for Andros, Tínos, and other islands. Owner Eleni Anastassiádi is carrying on the business her father began here among the fishmongers' stands more than forty years ago. In her tiny, immaculate kitchen, amid the noise of cars and ferries, Eleni fries *marídhes* (tiny picarel), concocts a delicious *fáva* (yellow split-pea mash), and bakes fresh anchovies with garlic, oregano, and olive oil. She grills *sargós* (white bream) and other fish, achieving stellar results, and offers a lovely bean salad and other simple, home-cooked dishes at very reasonable prices.

To get to Lávrion, farther south, one can either follow the western coast road, through Várkiza and Anávissos, or drive through the villages of Mesógea (the inland), all of which were once surrounded by the vineyards that used to produce most of the resinated wine consumed in Greece. Today the region is becoming increasingly built up, and as Lávrion is close to the site of the new Athens airport, the town's port is being extended to accommodate more ferries to and from the islands—a situation that is sure to change the landscape even more. But wine is still produced here, and some of the local wineries open their doors to visitors and even host tastings—a nice way to break up a trip to the coast.

The port for Markópoulo, the largest of the inland villages, is Pórto Ráfti, also called Limani Mesogéas. Once an idyllic enclave with a few villas hidden behind tall trees, Pórto Ráfti is now crowded with blocks of weekend and summer apartments. But the port itself, where small cargo boats and ferries dock, hasn't changed much. **To Limani,** favored by the town's few permanent inhabitants, spreads its plastic-cloth-covered tables right onto the pier. Overlooking the busy end of the round gulf and the modern high-rise apartment buildings that at night are lit up like Christmas trees, the humble restaurant (its sole design element, a line strung with drying octopi) is owned by Maria Karadima. Among her specialties are grilled octopus, stewed squid in tomato sauce, and *gávro skordáto* (anchovies baked with garlic and olive oil).

Located near the far end of Avláki, the second beach of Pórto Ráfti, is **Bibikos,** the gathering spot for those with weekend homes in the area. Regulars refer to it as "Kyrá [Mrs.] Maria," for the owner's mother, who is chief cook. In addition to the usual *mezéthes* and fish, Maria serves *karabidópsicha* (fried prawns) and spaghetti with lobster, a dish that's become a standard at sophisticated tavernas all over. Maria's sweets—baklava, *galatomboúreko* (milk pie), and *karidópita* (walnut cake)—garner much-deserved praise.

Yánnis Veletakos's Lávrion taverna is perhaps the best-kept secret of fish-loving Athenians. The small town, with its lovely neoclassical buildings and fascinating ruins of ancient silver mines, went through a period of steep decline when the zinc and lead mines that thrived at the turn of the century closed down in 1978. Yánnis, like everybody else, had worked in the mines for years. During his free time he would go fishing with his friends, selling the catch to supplement his income. When the mines closed, he started **Yannis,** which he opens only if he or his friends have had a successful enough catch. Situated on the ground floor of a rather ugly new building near the church of Agía Paraskevi, the taverna is without a sign, but any Lavriot will be happy to point it out to you.

In summer Yánnis sets his tables on the street and people dine overlooking the port. Usually caught by longline rather than in a net, his fish (charcoal-grilled) always prove a memorable gastronomic experience. His boiled lobster, dressed with a sauce of black pepper, mustard, oregano, lemon, and olive oil, also is a delight, as are the fried *marídes*.

Fish tavernas large and small are scattered on both sides of the road that winds along the shore at Cape Sounion, on the tip of the Attican peninsula on either side of the magnificent ruins of the ancient Temple of Poseidon. Bearing such names as Zorba and Syrtaki (a so-called "Greek" dance beloved by tourists), these restaurants offer more or less the same mediocre dishes, and their grilled fish—even when fresh—tends to be overcooked and dry. But some are well situated, with tables by the sea, and they attract tourists and Athenians who stop in to enjoy a meal or a few *mezéthes* while admiring the view and the brilliant sunsets.

Up the western side of the peninsula, almost to Athens, in the suburb of Kavoúri, is the elegant **Gárbi,** with a bilevel wooden deck sheltered by white-and-blue-striped canopies and overlooking the sea. Angelika Gárbi, the beautiful young owner, is following in the footsteps of her late father, who in 1924 was the first to open a fish taverna in the nearby resort town of Vouliagméni. Gárbi offers her sophisticated clientele interesting warm and cold *mezéthes,* among them a lightly smoked *melitzanosaláta* that is one of the best I've ever tasted. People stop in here to enjoy her small dishes with an ouzo and watch the evening colors over the water. The menu features such retro offerings as shrimp cocktail with ketchup-flavored mayonnaise and fish *athinaiki,* combining pieces of fish with peas, diced potatoes and carrots, and pickled cucumber, all mixed with mayonnaise.

In Piraeus, Greece's principal seaport, is **Kollias,** a relatively new and already extremely successful taverna situated in the middle of Taboúria, a crowded working-class neighborhood. With a lovely roof garden for summer dining, Kollias offers such rare treats as sea urchins from Crete and *porphyra* (a mollusk) from the Dodecanese Islands. It was there that I first tasted fried whole squid with its ink, which I loved. I also was impressed by the octopus stew, made with red wine, onions, garlic, and tomatoes. The fish here is consistently cooked to perfection, and the wine list is impressive—which, unfortunately, is not the case at most tavernas.

Also in Piraeus, **Margaro,** a small establishment located next to the gate of Hatzikyriákou, the Greek naval academy, is a fun place to go. From its concrete terrace studded with tiny, brown-paper-covered tables, you can look through the academy's gate to the busy entrance of the port. In addition to a salad, Margaro offers three dishes: *barboúnia, lithrínia* (red bream), and *karavídes* (prawns), all fried and all served with the heads on. Visitors to this white-on-white establishment are given a fork but no knife, so be prepared to use your fingers. Still, the food is fabulous, and the prices couldn't be better. It's no wonder the place is busy from noon to midnight. Reservations aren't accepted, but if you arrive between six and eight (for an early dinner by Greek standards), chances are you'll get a table.

Tavernas

As some tavernas are open only on weekends in the off season (late October through mid-April), it's a good idea to call before going.

Bibikos, 118 Leoforos Avlakiou, Pórto Ráfti, 02.99.71.292

Gárbi, 21 Iliou and Selinis, Kavoúri, 01.89.63.480

Ioakim (at the port of Rafína), 02.94.23.421

Kavoúri, Paralia Marathónas (south of the church), 02.94.55.243

Kollias, 3 Plastira (Dramas) and Kalokairinou Streets, Taboúria, Piraeus, 01.46.29.620, dinner only; closed on Sundays

Margaro, 126 Leoforos Hatzikyriákou, Piraeus, 01.45.14.226; closed on Sundays

To Limani (at the port of Pórto Ráfti—Limani Mesogéas), 02.99.71.791

Yannis (near Agía Paraskevi), Laurium, 02.92.23.167

Ouzo Bars of Athens

BY CYNTHIA HACINLI

~~

editor's note

I've enjoyed eating in some of Athens's restaurants, but I have probably had more memorable meals at the city's ouzo bars, most of which I found with the help of this article.

CYNTHIA HACINLI is restaurant critic and wine-and-food editor at *Washingtonian,* and has contributed to *GQ, Travel + Leisure, National Geographic Traveler, The New York Times,* and *Saveur,* where this piece first appeared. Hacinli is also the author of *Down Eats: The Essential Maine Restaurant Guide* (Tilbury House) and is co-author, with her husband, of *Romantic Days and Nights in Washington, D.C.* (Globe Pequot Press). She has been featured on the Food Network's *Food Fantasies* series and has traveled often in Greece.

The denim-shirted journalist at the next table has a system. He taps on his PowerBook, catapults what looks like a french fry into his mouth, then quaffs clear liquid from a glass as a look of pure bliss ignites his face. Of course, because this is Athens, it's not a french fry, but a sliver-thin fish called *marídhes,* whitebait to Americans, deep-fried and eaten whole—head, eyes, tail, everything. And the drink isn't water but ouzo, the fiery, anise-flavored national spirit. Solo dining is a rare thing in this land of olives and honey, where food and the company you keep while eating is all and the working lunch is unheard of. But elections loom this weekend, and a man's gotta do what a man's gotta do.

I watch this scene play out from my sun-streaked corner at Apotsos, one of the oldest *ouzeríes* (pronounced oo-zer-EEZ), or ouzo bars, in Athens—a dimly lit, cavernous hall of a place, with vintage ads on the walls, ceiling fans, and waiters in black pants and white shirts.

When you think *ouzerí,* think tapas bar. A place to drink, with food attached. Not full meals, but bits of savory this and piquant that—the Greek appetizers called *mezéthes,* which marry so well with ouzo, beer, and wine. The difference is that, while Spaniards tapas-hop as a prelude to dinner, Greeks are content to sit down in one place, nibble on an ample round of *mezéthes,* and call it a meal.

Ouzeríes are very much the thing now. They serve some of the most exuberant and sophisticated food in Athens—which is decidedly not a restaurant city. There's even talk of "ouzo culture," the Greek equivalent of café society. Modern-day Zeuses and Athenas of media, politics, commerce, movies, and music mix with Athenian yuppies at lunchtimes that stretch into the waning afternoon. They gather in family groups for dinner late into the night. *Ouzeríes* are magnets for women, who feel more comfortable in these civilized confines than they do in certain Zorba-style tavernas or the old-style coffeehouses that can be bastions of maleness.

Once upon a time *ouzeríes,* which originated as workingmen's hangouts in northern Greece—the birthplace of ouzo—served small helpings of simple fare: sliced sausages and feta cheese, olives, maybe a heap of fried peppers, rough bread.

Now that the *mezéthes* have become more elaborate, the breads are apt to be sesame-studded French, and some *ouzeríes* serve portions generous enough to be mistaken for main courses were they not offered on dessert plates. The menus have changed too. Along with the traditional flavoring trio of lemon, oregano, and olive oil, you'll find dill, cloves, cinnamon, even hot chiles—all staples of Greek regional cuisine, not previously common in these urban *ouzeríes*. A few have even started experimenting with what can only be called Greek nouvelle cuisine.

I discovered *ouzeríes* myself on a trip to Athens several years ago. My most recent stay in the city, late last year, was all too fleeting, just four days long—but I did find time for an *ouzerí* crawl, revisiting my favorite places: the classic I think of as the Carnegie Deli of *ouzeríes,* the ones in the most intriguing neighborhoods, and the ones with the most provocative food.

"No names, no names," says Lileta Apotsos, the carefully coiffed owner of Apotsos, ever protective of her customers' privacy. (The elections have the place humming with politicos from parliament and diplomats from the embassies of nearby Syntagma Square.)

Apotsos's grandfather opened a grocery store a block from here in 1900, supplying the royal palace and the city's aristocratic houses with everything from the salamis of Lefkas to marmalade from London. The place evolved almost accidentally: one day a glass of water was proffered to a general waiting for his order; the next day it was a glass of ouzo. Since it is anathema to Greeks to drink without eating, bits of *regga* (smoked herring) were soon passed around. The custom grew, and by the time Apotsos's father took over in 1942, the grocery had become an *ouzerí*.

Since then, Apotsos has been a no-frills purist's haunt, known for its authentically Greek *mezéthes*. Perhaps the finest foil to ouzo is *saghanáki* (fried cheese), made here with salty, stretchy sheep's-milk *kefalotyri*. Then there's the purée of yellow split peas and olive oil known as *fáva,* as common in Greece as baked beans once were in America. (This dish is not to be confused either with fava beans or with *gigántes*—large fava-shaped white beans cooked lazily in tomato sauce with vegetables and herbs.)

At Apotsos you'll also find such specialties as deep-fried veal meatballs and fiercely livery feta-stuffed veal spleen, which tastes a lot better than you might expect. On the menu too are spicy marinated sausage from Volos, in the north, for instance, and *kopanistí*—a cheese spread made here from feta and other pungent cheeses from the Cycladic Islands.

"These are the Greek dishes, not Turkish ones," says Apotsos, with not a little disdain. Cuisine can be as quick a flashpoint as politics around here. Nearly four hundred years of Ottoman rule over Greece (ending in 1827) had a strong impact on the national kitchen, and some of what passes for Greek food is really Turkish in origin, or from another one-time Ottoman possession in the Balkans or the Near East. Such dishes as *imam bayildí* (onion-stuffed baked eggplant), *taramosaláta* (the gutsy, salty carp roe spread), lamb souvlaki, and kebabs all probably developed in various parts of the once-vast Turkish empire.

The concept of *mezéthes*, however (despite the fact that the word derives from the Turkish), dates back in Greece at least to Plato, who described a preprandial array of radishes and olives, beans and cheese. There is even mention in ancient texts of sweet cheese pies, perhaps forerunners of *tyrópitakia*, the feta-phyllo squares that are the quintessential Greek appetizer.

Athens is not an easy town to love at first sight. A cacophonous, traffic-filled dustbowl, it virtually defines urban sprawl. But the city begins to reveal its charms as you walk its neighborhoods, especially venerable labyrinths such as Plaka and Monastiráki, in the shadow of the Acropolis, and Kolonáki, which is SoHo and Madison Avenue rolled into one.

Tonight I'm dining at Kafeneio, an *ouzerí* almost formal enough to be a restaurant, jammed into one of Kolonáki's tortuous streets. "*Stin igia mas* (to our health)," says Costas Tsamis, the bartender, pushing a small bottle of Barbayiánnis, the champagne of ouzos, in my direction. It was at Kafeneio that I first learned the secret of drinking ouzo. Too many people gulp it the way they would tequila— and come up gasping. Ouzo is meant to be tempered with food— sipped, for instance, between morsels of smoky grilled octopus.

It's about nine now. Large families and vogueish couples in black are settling into the handsome dining room with its gleaming olive-wood bar hung with peppers and *matia,* enamel charms to ward off the evil eye.

The food at Kafeneio is more creative than at most *ouzeríes.* Owner Elli Theodorou, a serious woman in a chic suit, has a way of crossing traditional Greek elements with up-to-the-minute culinary ideas. (Often at these places the force behind the cuisine is the owner, who perfects the recipes that the staff then cooks.) One specialty of the place, for instance, is a silky potato gratin, enhanced with lemon juice and olive oil. Crunchy marinated raw zucchini salad is a signature dish, in which the squash, a Greek mainstay, is cut into shreds, then tossed with string beans, bits of mushroom, and a veritable avalanche of dill. Classic zucchini fritters take on a special luxuriance here: shredded zucchini, mashed potato, and cheese are cloaked in a tempura batter. Lamb-stuffed lettuce leaves with velvety *avgolémono* (egg-lemon) sauce is a riff on stuffed grape leaves. More traditional fare is served, too: the deep-fried *marídhes,* brought to the table still sizzling, are superb. And if leek pie happens to be on the menu tonight, I will, in the words of Socrates, be "nearest to the Gods."

Friday I go over to Plaka, for lunch at To Gerani, minutes from the site of the ancient Agora—the marketplace where the Epicureans and Stoics once expounded their philosophies. Greek and Roman ruins are everywhere. Given the neighborhood's weighty past, it is fitting that many of the habitués of To Gerani are leather-sandaled professors and their students, who thrust and parry for hours on the vined terraces. The women in the open kitchen don't speak English, so it's point-and-pantomime. A colossal tray of small plates comes my way. There is a traditional octopus stew and fried eggplant wedges, as well as *tzatziki*, the Balkan dip of garlic, cucumber, and yogurt, and, of course, dolmades. But what always brings me back are the flambés—sausages or *regga* splashed with an intense orange-scented ouzo and set aflame.

It's girls' night out at Gyali Kafenes, an *ouzerí* back in Kolonáki, with several groups of matrons in suede pants and serious jewelry in evidence. I am sitting at one of the tables under a eucalyptus tree. A smartly turned-out older couple next to me share puffy, blistered *saganáki*. Meanwhile Amanda Kanas—who owns the place with Antonio Efstragiatis, formerly a singer of some note—holds court.

Gyali Kafenes is a blend of old and new. There are stark pewlike wood benches against the walls, antiques, copper accents, and bistro-close marble tables. But Kanas's culinary vision is modern. The food here is spicier than in most Athens *ouzeríes*. (Efstragiatis is from Thessaloníki, in the north, where hot peppers are held in high esteem.) Seafood dominates the menu. Mussels are grilled, deep-fried in a corn-flour crust, or baked with wine, feta, and hot and sweet peppers in a tomato sauce. Shrimp and squid are prepared *saghanáki*-style. Another staple, *gávros* (a type of sardine), is marinated in vinegar, olive oil, parsley, and garlic, then roasted or grilled. I am always happily amazed, too, by the sausage-shaped Cypriot *skeftalies*—ground lamb and pork with acres of onion, parsley, and breadcrumbs—served on pita bread that's been dipped in oil and blistered on the fire. Kanas also does a little more with dessert than is typical at *ouzeríes*. One treat is quinces, glazed in a brew of red wine, cloves, and sugar—like a more aromatic version of baked apples.

The sun is high on Sunday, my last day in Athens. A slow saunter through touristy Monastiráki to the inner reaches of Avyssinia Square—a down-at-the-heels wedge of junk shops that is also a bohemian's playground—has become for me a ritual of Athens leave-taking.

Ketty Touros, the queenly proprietor of the *ouzerí* named after the square, chose this locale "because it had challenge." Awash in blues, greens, and saffron, with chintz-lined walls and a Florentine-style ceiling, Avyssinia is an exotic, eclectic jewel box of a place.

The food is eclectic too. Touros lived in London for eleven years and traveled the Continent, and alongside her Macedonian special-ties—like a tart, fibrous cabbage salad and mussels in their own hot chile-scented juice—are peppery sheep's brains in black butter sauce, and smoked pork with prunes and escargots. But it's the egg-plant with fresh tomatoes and melted cheeses that I find comfort-ing on this last day.

Like many *ouzeríes,* Avyssinia takes on a different feel at differ-ent times. During the week its tables are filled with ladies who lunch and models blowing smoke rings. On weekends the customers mul-tiply, and tables sprawl across the square. The mood is rollicking, with rich boys from Kolonáki on their Harleys and Sunday revelers added to the mix, as a dashing accordionist provides background music.

According to Touros, the musician just started coming one day. The hordes followed. Now he gets paid.

Ouzo—As Fine as Silk?

In every wine-producing corner of the Mediterranean, spirits are distilled from wine grape residuals—seeds, pits, skins, and the like. The French call such liquors *marc;* the Italians call them *grappa.* The Greek equivalent of grappa is *tsipouro.* Many Mediterranean lands also produce anise-flavored alcohols—*arak* in Lebanon, *pastis* in France, *anís* (dry or sweet) in Spain, *sambuca* (sweet, and also flavored with elderberry) in Italy, and so on. Ouzo, virtually the national tipple of Greece, began as something of a combination of the two, with a twist.

According to the early twentieth-century philologist Achilles Tzartzanos—Diane Kochilas recounts the story in her *The Food and Wine of Greece* (St. Martin's Press)—both the product and its name were born sometime between 1878 and 1881 in the town of Tirnavos, in Thessaloníki, in northeastern Greece. Tirnavos was noted for two things: its fiery liquors and the quality of its silks. According to Tzartzanos, three local aficionados of strong drink decided to try to improve the town's best raki, an anise-scented grape-residual spirit distilled three times for smoothness. To this raki, they added mastic, an incenselike gum from Chios (and the heart of another clear Greek liquor, *masticha*), and various other flavorings. The result, declared one of their number (who happened to be a textile merchant), was "as good as USO Massalias"—the name given to silk bound for market in Marseille, the optimum quality. "USO" became "ouzo."

It might be noted in passing, incidentally, that this sounds suspiciously like folk etymology—and that Tzartzanos was a resident of Tirnavos, so may have had a vested interest in promoting the town as ouzo's birthplace. But whatever the origins of ouzo, there is no question that it quickly gained popularity throughout Greece. Today it is not necessarily made with grape-residual spirits, and the law allows some latitude regarding flavorings (though anise is essential). Because of improved distillation methods, it is no longer necessary to distill the spirits three times, either—though several brands, including Ouzo No. 12 and Metaxa, are distilled twice.

Though ouzo has always been consumed with food, it may at first have been swallowed straight, undiluted. Some native fans of the drink might still take it straight, or with water on the side—but the favored way to drink ouzo today is with a splash of water, which turns it cloudy.

Ouzo No. 12, a worldwide best-seller readily available in the United States, is a good introduction to ouzo. Its flavor is complex, with hints of anise, star anise, mastic, fennel, nutmeg, coriander, and other spices. Others have fewer ingredients. One brand, Barbayiánnis, highly prized by the Greeks, has an almost floral bouquet, with a rich, refined finish. (It is not yet available in the United States but will be soon.) Among other popular commercial brands are Metáxa, Boutari, Sans Rival, Achaia Clauss, Tsantalis, Olympic, Cambas, Keo, and Ouzo 7. Many of these can be found in the United States, at prices ranging from $8 to $14.

At least one century-old custom celebrating the spirit survives in Tirnavos. It occurs on Shrove Monday, when the townspeople drink ouzo from giant, gaudily painted phallic vessels—a paean to the ancient fertility gods. Surprisingly, this practice is apparently sanctioned by the Greek Orthodox Church.

The Guide

Dinner with drinks, tax, and tip:

Expensive—Over $25

Moderate—$15–$25

Inexpensive—Under $15

Where to Stay

The Greek word for hotel is xenodochion *("container for strangers")—which may help explain why this city's hostelries can be so indifferent. Here are some exceptions.*

Andromeda, *Timoleónlos Vassou 22, 643.7302; fax: 646.6361.*
Rates: $280–$420. Near the American Embassy, this is one of the
rare boutique hotels in Athens. Its thirty rooms have designer
furnishings and fax outlets.

Grande Bretagne, *Syntagma Square, 800-223-6800 or, in Greece,*
331.4444; fax: 322.2261. Rates: $295–$345. The GB may be a bit
dated, but it's still one of Europe's genuine grand hotels—huge
(385 rooms) and luxurious.

St. George Lycabettus, *Kleomenous 2, 800-448-8355 or, in Greece,*
729.0711; fax: 729.0439. Rates: $120–$240. In fashionable
Kolonáki, with 165 nicely appointed but not exactly deluxe
contemporary-style rooms.

Where to Eat

For something beside ouzerí *fare, Athens has countless tavernas,*
restaurants, and patisseries with good food at ridiculously low
prices. Here are a few.

Dekaokto, *Suedias 51, 723.5561. Dinner: Expensive.* There are
about a dozen tables, all with white linens, and a few booths at
this romantic, candlelit second-floor restaurant in Kolonáki. The
food is well prepared and interesting. Try grilled fish or assorted
mezéthes.

Ellinikon, *Kolonáki Square 20, 360.1858. Light meals:*
Inexpensive. This large, elegant Kolonáki patisserie-café serves
classics like moussaka and pastitsio. The display cases are filled
with the shop's famous chocolate-and-pistachio Baton Select
cookies, as well as other specialties.

Lalagis, *Spefsippou 23, 723.3885. Takeout pastries: Inexpensive.* A
tiny shop in Kolonáki with Greek and European sweets.

Taverna Dimokritos, *Dimokritou 23, 361.3588. Dinner: Moderate.* A local favorite in Kolonáki, with classic Greek dishes like cuttlefish in wine sauce, lamb tongue in lemon sauce, and grilled lamb chops, tiny and done to perfection. Stylish crowd.

Thanasis, *Mitropoleos 69, 324.4705. Dinner: Inexpensive.* In Monastiráki, this chaotic, brightly lit restaurant may have all the atmosphere of a lunchroom, but it's one of the city's best souvlaki places. There is able waiter service amid the chaos.

Vlassis, *Armatolon Klefton 20, 642.5337. Dinner: Moderate.* This large taverna-cum-restaurant in Neapoli is a favorite with artists and academics. Classic Greek food like grilled lamb with greens and a *mezéthes* sampler tray are brought right to the table.

Ouzeríes

Apotsos, *Panepistimiou 10, near Syntagma Square, 324.7605. Lunch only: Inexpensive.*

Avyssinia, *Avyssinia Square, Monastiráki, 321.7047. Lunch: Inexpensive.* Dinner served only during the warm months.

Gyali Kafenes, *Plutárkhou 18, Kolonáki, 722.5846. Dinner: Moderate.* Closed July and August.

To Gerani, *Tripodon 14, Plaka, 324.7605. Lunch and dinner: Inexpensive.*

Kafeneío, *Loukianou 26, Kolonáki, 723.7277. Dinner: Moderate.* Sophisticated ambiance.

What to Do

Central Market. Just off Athinás Street. A must for food lovers— olives, cheeses, grains, honey, fish, and lots of local color. Open every day from dawn to 1 P.M.

Kolonáki Square. Great people-watching at the cafés on the northeast side of the square. Pull up a chair at our favorite, Kolonáki Tops, for a fabulous frappé.

National Archaeological Museum, *Patission 44.* Open Tuesday–Sunday, 8 A.M.–7 P.M.; Monday 12:30–7 P.M. Cooking pots and other vessels and utensils, including items from Santorini, discovered perfectly preserved under a blanket of solidified lava from the cataclysmic volcanic eruption of 1450 B.C.

Simple as Pie

BY ANYA VON BREMZEN

editor's note

The local food on Crete, as Diane Kochilas notes in *The Glorious Foods of Greece,* mirrors the island's rich past, which included influences from the Romans, Byzantines, Moors, and Venetians. "But mostly the Cretan table reflects the island's own natural abundance. Crete is one of the most fertile places in Greece—with which it was reunited in 1913—and its flora is among the richest in the Mediterranean. Over half of the indigenous plants in Europe are found here. It is no accident that Cretans are fiercely independent people; they have always been able to sustain themselves exceptionally well on what the island—and nature—so generously provides." Here is a piece profiling six Cretan tavernas, all authentic places where the food is uncomplicated and the pace is slow.

ANYA VON BREMZEN is a contributing editor at *Travel + Leisure,* where this piece first appeared. She also contributes regularly to *Food &*

Wine, and is the author of *The Greatest Dishes!: Around the World in 80 Recipes* (HarperCollins, 2004) and *Fiesta! A Celebration of Latin Hospitality* (Doubleday, 1997). She is also co-author, with John Welchman, of *Please to the Table: The Russian Cookbook* (Workman, 1990) and *Terrific Pacific* (Workman, 1995), and is the recipient of two James Beard Awards. Her work has been included in previous editions of *The Collected Traveler.*

I arrived in Crete at the height of wine-making season. The fall, then at its ripest stage, brought finger-size squash, ambrosial peaches, a profusion of *horta* (greens), and riots of apples and quince. "Don't drive," locals warned. "The roads are slippery with grape juice that leaks from the trucks." But who could pass up roads slick with wine? So my friends and I packed into a car with my food-obsessed acquaintance Giorgos, taking him up on his promise to show us the island's best rustic tavernas. For a week we peeked in at Minoan sites, gazed at faded Byzantine frescoes, and feasted on the Mediterranean's loveliest and most lyrical food.

A word of warning: Crete has its share of microwaved moussakas, nasty schnitzels, and limp fish-and-chips (often spelled "ships" or "sheeps," both things very Greek). To get away from all that, dodge the touristy beach restaurants—or better yet, go slightly inland—and explore the world of authentic Cretan tavernas.

Arkhánes

Giorgos insisted we begin our taverna tour in Arkhánes, a bustling village that has been a viticultural center since Minoan times—archaeologists working nearby have unearthed four-thousand-year-old clay wine-storing *pithoi,* smaller versions of which are still in use today. We had come to Arkhánes for dinner at **O Aristos.** Simply furnished with long wooden tables, family-owned, and serving homemade wine and just a few daily specials, it's a village taverna like any other. (If a place is too cute, beware of the food.) And like many Cretan taverna meals, ours began with *dakos,* a brown barley rusk slathered with dense gold-green olive oil and foamy tomato pulp. "Our shepherds eat *dakos* in the pastures," said the owner, Grigori Konstantakis, his hands purple from days spent crushing grapes, as he brought out warm cheese pies, tiny stuffed grape leaves, and thick herb-flecked *tzatziki* (yogurt dip).

But our real reason for choosing Aristos was Grigori's famous boiled rooster. It owes its remarkable flavor and succulence to a diet of wheat and wild herbs, and came accompanied by a rice pilaf soupy and plump with rooster broth. "Cretans serve roosters at weddings as a symbol of happiness," said Grigori's wife, Kaiti.

Courtesy of our neighbors—twelve winemakers in tattered striped shirts—we ended with shots of raki, a grape liquor so fiery and coarse we nearly choked. It seemed to go down more smoothly for the striped shirts: they sang *mandinadhes,* or two-line poems, about vultures, eagles, and freedom, then taught us their dance. Eleven steps to the right, two to the left. You move your feet very slowly and stomp sparingly.

"Let's leave before the bill argument starts," Giorgos pleaded. "They'll each want to treat, and sometimes these disputes end up in shooting."

Iráklion

"Escape the urban blight of Iráklion," my guidebook read. But we were in no hurry to flee Crete's gritty and strangely beguiling port capital. We rambled around its oregano-scented market, then enjoyed *bougátsa,* the heavenly warm cheese custard enclosed in thin sheets of phyllo, and iced coffee frappé on the clamorous Venizélos Square. "Nescafé has become the Greek national drink," Giorgos sighed.

Annoyingly hidden in a warren of cacophonous side streets in central Iráklion, **Empolo** is the only place in town that delivers genuine Cretan cuisine. More restaurant than taverna—decorated like a traditional house—it excels at rich peasant soups, omelettes, and *macaronia,* thin pasta cooked in potent goat broth and scattered with a ricottalike cheese called *anthotyro.* After a sour-milk soup with pork and boiled wheat, we tried *zigouri vrasto,* a long-simmered garlicky goat brew well known as a hangover cure to anyone with a fondness for raki.

Crete is a botanist's Eden; besides the standard dandelion greens, more than 2,500 species of *horta* are used by the local cooks. Tonight's selection was tender two-week-old cabbage shoots, boiled (as always) and enlivened by splashes of lemon and olive oil. It's the insistent use of greens, grains, and olive oil that makes Cretan cuisine—according to scientific studies—the most healthful in the world.

Vrakhási

Pites—pies—are the pride of Cretan gastronomy. Pies with *myzithra* (a soft and tangy whey cheese), drizzled with honey. Pies with *horta* or meat. Small pies, grand pies, pies fried, baked, thin as a pancake, or twisted into a rope and curled like a snail.

We discovered a veritable shrine to *pites* under an old mulberry tree at **Taverna Platanos** in Vrakhási, a somnolent whitewashed village with two Byzantine churches and an Ottoman fountain. Eleni Soulavaki, the owner, brought us platters of *pites,* stuffed with *myzíthra;* fennel, spinach, and Swiss chard; and cumin-scented lamb. When we asked what else she'd cooked that day, she returned with bowls of lovely zucchini blossoms filled with minted potatoes and rice; an autumnal mélange of squash, broad beans, greens, and snails cooked in olive oil; and three stews, all magnificent—especially the sweet-sour, cinnamon-spiked *stifado* with beef and pearl onions.

After lunch Giorgos delivered his snail lecture: "Cretans gather them at night after a good rain, then feed them broken-up uncooked spaghetti to fatten and sweeten them. Cretans don't like skinny snails." Meanwhile, Eleni's small, sturdy granddaughter tried out her new fountain pen on our white trousers, then disappeared—with my camera lens cap—not to be spotted again.

Mátala

Sure, Mátala's beaches and caves were "discovered" years ago—Cat Stevens and Bob Dylan were celebrity cave dwellers. But after a visit to the nearby Minoan ruins of Phaestos, Mátala isn't a bad place for a swim and a lazy lunch.

Judging from the scary photos of kitschy Greek food displayed near the entrance, you'd never know that **Minos Palace** is the finest taverna in town—not until you settle on the upstairs terrace, ouzo in hand, and order a cool, crisp salad of shredded romaine, tomatoes, olives, and feta; and the fried zucchini and eggplant, greaseless and light as a whisper. While most Greek fish tavernas overcook seafood, here the fried shrimp and the grilled *ksifias* (the famous swordfish from the south coast) arrived juicy, sweet, and impeccably fresh. And the *htopodi* (octopus) was the best I've tasted in Greece: charred, tender, bathed in a lemon–olive oil emulsion.

For many Cretan taverna owners, the restaurant is just a seasonal social diversion. The proprietors of Minos Palace—two brothers-in-law, both named Mihalis—make a real living tending their grapevines and olive groves. One Mihalis, the one who proposed to my friend Maria, was even running for local office—and has since won. And to think that Maria could have been the First Lady of Mátala!

Khaniá

With an intimate, fragrant harbor that is as pretty as Portofino's and nearly as hopping as Hong Kong's, Khaniá is the jewel of Crete.

As befits a taverna with serious culinary credentials, **Karnagio** is slightly removed from the tourist action, tucked away in the harbor's eastern corner with only a partial view of the sea.

No matter. Everyone's here under the vine-draped trellis: curly-haired Circes-in-training—lipstick the color of figs—and their beach-bum lovers, town matrons, businessmen, grandmas in black, plus a few international types. (The waiters here speak passable English.)

We chose from an encyclopedic selection of *mezéthes* (appetizers), then enjoyed perfect fried vegetables, grilled baby lamb chops, and a mean cuttlefish stew with olives and fennel. My friend especially loved the *boureki*: custardy layers of minted zucchini and *myzithra* cheese, baked under a cap of sesame-sprinkled phyllo. "This really puts moussaka to shame," she raved. Even the after-dinner giveaways (honey-drenched mini-baklava; smoother-than-usual raki) were pretty superb.

We stayed on in Khaniá for our last meal—at **Anaplous,** in a four-hundred-year-old Venetian-style house that had been bombed during World War II and only partially restored. Here we dined on a patio surrounded by operatically illuminated crumbling walls (as if we hadn't seen enough ruins already). The wine was presented in decorative carafes, and the faux-rustic menu completed the designer vision of Crete. A taverna this wasn't.

Anaplous opened in 1992 as a vegetarian restaurant, but now its main attraction is meat, such as lamb on the bone slowly cooked with wine and wild thyme (a recipe from Sfakia, a place famous for cheese pies and vendettas), and other riffs on highland preparations for meat baked in the earth, in clay, or on stones. The *pites* here are lovely pizzalike crackles of dough smothered with fresh cheese and topped with smoked sausage or air-cured beef. And the *dakos* could pass for an upmarket bruschetta. Dessert was a vast plate of thick yogurt mosaicked with every conceivable nut, seed, and dried fruit. Now, *that* was like eating the countryside.

Back home, I decided to test Giorgos's recipe. I collected a bowl-ful of garden snails and tried to feed them raw pasta.

They didn't survive, I'm sorry to say.

The Facts

Few waiters or proprietors at Cretan tavernas speak fluent English, and few of these restaurants have printed menus. For extra help with ordering, ask your hotel to inquire about the daily specials—or persuade your waiter to give you a peek at the pots in the kitchen. The food is well worth the challenge.

O Aristos, *Kato Arkhánes; 81.751.243; lunch for two about $15.* A twenty-minute drive from Iráklion, and a good lunch stop after a visit to Knossos, Crete's premier Minoan site. Call ahead to order the rooster.

Empolo, *7 Manou Miliara, Iráklion; 81.284.244; dinner for two about $17.*

Taverna Platanos, *Vrakhási; 841.31488; lunch for two about $16.* About 13 miles from the resort town of Ágios Nikólaos, on the northeastern coast.

Minos Palace, *Mátala; 892.45066; lunch for two about $20.* Close to Phaestos, Crete's second-most-extensive Minoan site.

Karnagio, *8 Katechaki Square, Khaniá; 821.53366; dinner for two about $26.*

Anaplous, *Sifaka and E. Melxisedek, Khaniá; 821.41320; dinner for two about $26.*

Prices do not include drinks, tax, or tip.

Originally published in *Travel + Leisure*, September 1999. © 1999 American Express Publishing Corporation. All rights reserved. Reprinted with permission of the author.

Wine of the Gods

BY GERALD ASHER

editor's note

I believe that food and vines that grow together, go together, so it's not accidental that the foods unique to Greece taste so good with the grapes grown on the same land. Not surprisingly, Greece produces more white wines (that match splendidly with all those seafood dishes) than red (that match equally well with more robust dishes). White grape varieties include *assyrtiko, moschofilero, robolla,* and *roditis,* while there are two main red varietals to recognize: *agiorgitiko* and *xinomavro.* I urge you to try them all (as well as retsina!) at tavernas, in restaurants, or bought from a store. I think you'll find them to be just the right accompaniment to the food you're eating.

This piece has long been a favorite of mine, and I have long been fond of the author's writings on wine because he frequently takes readers off on various tangents but always returns to some simple, elemental point about wine and, more important, about life.

GERALD ASHER has been writing about wine for *Gourmet* for many years and is also the author of *The Pleasures of Wine* (2002) and *Vineyard Tales* (1996), both published by Chronicle Books, among others.

I'd picked out a small island with direct flights from Athens for a quiet week in the Aegean, imagining, I suppose, that it would be inaccessible to everyone in the world except me. Needless to say, the beaches were crowded by day, and by night the narrow whitewashed alleys of the island's one small town throbbed with disco.

I rose late each morning, lunched under a canvas awning behind the minuscule cathedral, and spent my afternoons with the *Herald Tribune* under a tree in a public square the size of a suburban patio. With the evening star the first of the Day-Glo tank tops would appear, the little square would fill with suntanned limbs, and the *plinka-plonk* of bouzouki would begin drifting from the bars and cafés. Later the music would get louder, the dancing more frantic. As the crowd got tipsier, girls would occasionally shriek with excitement and the young men would get boisterous.

An Athenian friend of a friend, a woman who kept a house on the island, told me over dinner, on my third or fourth evening, of a few remote beaches in coves difficult to reach by land. Local fishing boats called in on them, but none had a jetty or quay to receive the harbor craft I saw listing out of port every morning, crammed with tourists and tape players. She gave me directions to one I could reach on foot in at most three quarters of an hour. "There's even a bar of sorts," she said.

Next morning, with book and beach mat, I climbed a high ridge a mile or so behind the town, passed a herd of goats making what they could of the scrubby pasture on the far side, and then followed a barely visible track as it twisted down through coarse grass and rushes toward the sea. The ridge, curving behind me, extended down into the water, isolating a beach of fine sand. It was deserted except for a fisherman beating his catch of octopus on a rock, slapping them down, rubbing them against the rough surface, and dashing a crock of seawater over them from time to time. I had no urge to take a closer look, and settled at a distance to read and to sun myself.

A collection of flotsam was arranged against the side of the hill to give shade. Rickety posts sunk into the sand supported a canopy of reeds over a few wooden chairs and tables, bleached and partly rotted by sun and sea spray. It was the bar, and after a while I went over and sat down at one of the tables. By then the octopus beater had left, and I could hear nothing but the ripple of tranquil water. A small sail grazed the horizon, far away where sea and sky melded together in a blue haze.

A boy brought me some wine, pale golden and mildly resinated. Without my asking he also brought a few olives and a hunk of dense, slightly sour bread. A ray of sunlight, piercing the reeds overhead, was shattered by the wineglass. It was hot, I was drowsy. The distant sail was now at hand, and once close enough, a man jumped down to swim and wade ashore. It could have been Dionysus himself, stepping from his raft, or Noah, released from his ark and relishing again the feel of sand between his toes. Noah and his vineyard seem remote from us now, and Dionysus, smiling languidly in the shade of a vine-sprouting mast—as he once had arrived in the Aegean, guided by dolphins—is a total stranger; yet both still influence our lives in ways we scarcely recognize and rarely understand.

I sipped my wine and broke the bread, thinking how essential they had been to life around that sea. Most of us have a special feeling for bread—even when it's stale, we shrink from throwing it out; and though we make a show of not taking wine too seriously and joke about its little rituals, we pour it and drink it with particular attention. Without thinking, we receive guests with an offering of bread and wine—though these days one might be disguised as cheese crackers and the other as a glass of Lillet—regardless of whether we or they are either hungry or thirsty. And we do it because the role of bread and wine in our lives is older than history. The Eucharist itself is rooted in a far more ancient belief that to eat bread and drink wine was to partake of the body of the corn god and the blood of the vine god. "The drinking of wine in the rites of a vine-god like Dionysus," wrote Sir James Frazer in *The Golden Bough,* "is not an act of revelry, it is a solemn sacrament."

Sacrament or not, breaking bread and drinking wine, one with another, is the most basic act of community. Is it Athenaeus, the third-century Greek writer, who suggests that civilization began when men came together to eat food rather than fight over who would possess it? Certainly it is he who describes, though quoting an earlier author, the custom of first consecrating the dish to be eaten, following which "each man was permitted to drink a little [wine] from a bowl, and the one offering it [to another] would say 'Good dinner to you!'" We rarely pass a loving cup now, but is our ritual of saying grace, of raising a glass to each other, or wishing the company *bon appétit* so very different?

When describing how an early king and his companions had received a group of traveling strangers, Athenaeus says that "wine seems to possess a power which draws to friendship by lightly warming and fusing the soul. Hence they did not even ask their guests too soon who they were, but postponed that until later, as though they honored the mere act of hospitality, and not the individual and the personal in us."

As Greeks, they would have respected strangers who could well have been gods. Gods. We are entertained, even amused, by the ancients and their mythological gods; but the Greeks used their myths to come to terms with truth and paradox too profound and too disturbing to be considered, let alone revealed, in any other way. They were able to grasp the meaning of their world better than we do ours.

Wine, in any case, was at the center of their mythology and of their universe as a metaphor for Dionysus and for the duality of being. It was a symbol of renewal, of the cycle of death and rebirth. The god's myth, expressed in his cult through music and sometimes frenzied dance, combined calm and uproar, horror and ecstasy, as well as both the light and dark sides of human nature. At times it allowed and even encouraged sexual license and wild abandon.

But if wine could bring violence, it also brought ineffable joy. Dionysus, born of a god and a mortal mother, drew heaven and earth together. Wine was man's portion of the divine, promising him life at its most intense. In the words of Walter Otto, author of the classic study *Dionysus: Myth and Cult,* celebrants of the

Dionysiac rites were "thrust out of everything secure, everything settled, out of every haven of thought and feeling, and . . . flung into the primeval cosmic turmoil in which life, surrounded and intoxicated with death, undergoes eternal change and renewal." Wine, in short, was seen by the ancients as nothing less than the paradox, the mystery, and the miracle of life itself.

It meant life to them in a literal sense too. The vine finds sustenance where there appears to be none, as do the ivy and the pine tree, both plants also sacred to Dionysus. (The ivy was worn as a garland, while pine resin often scented the Greeks' wine and still does.) In the Dionysus myth and its enactment in the cult, celebrants strike barren rock with the *thrysus,* a rod of ivy-wood tipped with a pine cone, and cause streams of water and springs of wine to gush forth. Dionysus, after all, is god of water, of moisture in general, not just of wine: his annual festivals began with his epiphany in the mountains where rains were heaviest. According to Plutarch, he would appear in midwinter on Parnassus as a newborn child in a cradle, and it was there that the women went to find him. In spring, with new growth visible everywhere, his festivals reached a climax when he reemerged from the sea as a young man, pulled ashore, at Athens and Smyrna, in a boat mounted on wheels.

In this century, before forklifts and containerized cargo ships, French dockworkers each drank two and three liters of red wine a day. They didn't drink it to forget their troubles, still less for the bouquet and flavor. They drank it because a liter of wine, with roughly seven hundred calories, replaced not only lost moisture but also the energy they burned in hard physical labor. In our automated, fossil-fueled, calorie-conscious age we forget that most people once struggled to obtain the calories needed to fire their bodies. Wine, as much as bread, was an important, a vital, food to the ancient Greek.

Furthermore, it protected and healed him as effectively as it nourished him. The ancient Greek might have been ignorant of the bacterium and the bacillus, but he knew from experience how effective wine could be as an antiseptic. Hippocrates—our physicians still make an oath to him when they qualify to practice—had little but wine to rely on for most of his remedies. Recently, we have again been reminded of benefits—obvious to the ancients—inherent in the moderate daily consumption of wine.

So potently did wine bind sustenance and healing to religion that the highly charged act of offering it was only further heightened by its association with economic power. In the sixth century B.C., when trade had overtaken marauding and mutual raiding as the chief source of revenues of the Greek city-states, wine was the principal commodity. It brought to ancient Greece the accumulation of wealth that made possible the surge in the arts and the sciences known to us as the Classical age.

It's no wonder, then, that wine, or rather its more easily depicted symbols—the vine and the cup—should have figured so prominently in the arts and artifacts of that age; nor should we be surprised that it continued and continues to do so. A fine wine cup, substituting for what it would normally contain, became an object of such esteem that its possession lent enormous prestige. It is not by chance that to those we wish to honor, we present a silver cup: for millennia it has been the traditional reward of victors. A bold two-handled version in the British Museum, wrought in Anatolia nearly four thousand years ago, could be the prototype for every such prize given since.

But as one might expect, given the duality of Dionysus, there was a dark side to wine's sixth-century success. As commercial vineyards expanded and flourished, subsistence farmers and their families were dispossessed to make room for them. Migrating to the towns—as in all times since—they yearned angrily for what they had lost. In desperation they sought comfort from their nature god and lent Dionysus's cult a new and violently rebellious aspect. The ascendant landed aristocracy, fearful, instigated or at least willingly acquiesced in the tyrannies that sprang up in the Greek world at that time in response to this social ferment.

Dionysus the healer and nourisher, provider of relief and comfort, revealed himself as a god of personal liberty too. Or that, at least, is the way the oppressed perceived him. It was an attribute so potent that Nietzsche, two and a half thousand years later, borrowed their mythic vocabulary in making Dionysus his symbol of the inner force that encourages each of us to respond to the world, freely, in his or her own way. Nietzsche contrasted Dionysus to Apollo, the god who imposed conformity, regulation, and order. Apollo, all cold perfection, moves, as a respected historical geographer wrote recently, "only among the best people"; but Dionysus, ever exhilarating, ever outrageous, ever for the individual, ever for life, offered liberty to all without distinction. Isn't it clear why authority everywhere demeaned Dionysus, presented him as a god of foolish, drunken revelry, and either subverted his cult in order to tame it or ruthlessly repressed it as obscene?

A particularly egregious episode in second-century B.C. Rome— another period of farm dispossession—began a decline that marked the end of the Republic and the imposition of imperial rule on free citizens. A harlot was rewarded handsomely for giving unsupported evidence of rites allegedly so vile that the government was able to justify not only a ban on the cult but the execution of many thousands of its political opponents. The consuls made speeches filled with innuendo about hidden "conspirators," talked of treachery, and offered rewards to those who would name names. To our ears, more than two thousand years later, their words form the depressingly familiar litany of a repressive regime. Especially chilling are those warning the citizenry against sheltering or assisting intended victims in any way, or even sympathizing with them.

"I have thought it right to give you this warning," a consul told the assembled Romans, "so that no superstitious fear may agitate your minds when you see us suppressing the Bacchanalia and breaking up these criminal gatherings."

The Jews meanwhile used wine for the sacrament of blessing God's name, but did not see it as a metaphor for Him—their monotheistic religion had need of neither metaphors for God nor of gods as metaphors. Yet they too set bread and wine apart from other foods. While the obligatory blessing over bread extends to all other food to be eaten with it at the same meal (because bread is humanity's mainstay), the blessing over wine is more than a form of grace because the family table, to a strictly observant Jew, is an altar at which wine is fundamental to the fulfillment of his religious obligations. It is at his table, silver wine cup in hand, that he welcomes the Sabbath into his house, greets every festival, and sanctifies the celebration of all family occasions.

Such a controlled and formal role for wine seems at first far removed from the Greeks' perception of it. But a closer look at the major festival of Passover, celebrated, like Easter (and like the Great Dionysia), at the first full moon after the spring equinox, reveals what once can only have been an allusion to birth and to life's origins in the sea—the Seder, the Passover meal, begins, for most Jews, with a hard-cooked egg served in a pool of salt water. There are also references to nature itself in the bitter green herbs that must be present—they are the kind of salad herbs once usually picked wild.

In a study of food in the Bible published by the *Annales* school of historians in Paris, Jean Soler points out that this festival, commemorating the exodus from Egypt and the birth of the Jewish nation, probably began as a feast of renewal in which participants ate foods that recalled their most distant origins. "The bitter herbs," he says, "must be understood . . . as the opposite of vegetables produced by agriculture." Roast rather than boiled meat is eaten, he explains, because boiling implies an ability to make pots to cook in, a skill acquired late.

Passover, interestingly enough, is the only Jewish festival at which those present are *obliged* to drink wine copiously—at least four cups each. And like the Dionysiac rites, one might add, it is a festival that celebrates liberty: "We were Pharaoh's slaves in Egypt," runs one verse of the Haggadah, the story of the exodus read at every Seder, "but now we are free."

It was at just such a Seder, celebrating birth, freedom, and life's renewal, that Jesus pointed to the wine and said, "This is my blood." His disciples would have understood, surely, the Judaic significance of those words—Jews believe blood is life, is sacred, and belongs to God alone. But how would those words have reverberated, as they later did, in the ears of a Greco-Roman world with its own perception of wine and life and divinity, a world in which our division of the religious from the secular would have seemed artificial?

It was a world in which the early church, taking account of customs and rituals that were the very fabric of the communities it sought to convert, had to find ways to adapt and adopt, sometimes to avoid generating popular discontent—the singing of stirring Christian hymns springs from the joyous music and chanting that had accompanied pre-Christian rites: the church drew the line, however, at dancing—and sometimes to comfort those anxious not to offend their old gods in accepting the new. If, for example, the devotees of Venus (protector of marriage and therefore, by extension, of the married home) wanted to continue to offer and eat fish in her honor—Venus, like Dionysus, arose from the sea—why then, the church would make it Christian to do so on Friday, a day still dedicated to Venus in Latin-rooted languages. At a more modest level, every village adopted a saint to merge with the local god or goddess who formerly had given his or her protection to the community, its flocks, and its fields. From Cyprus to Northumberland those patron saints endure in place-names to this day.

In the ancient religious rites, wine—humanity's portion of the divine—had brought the celebrants into the presence of the god. Even when Christian, much of the Greco-Roman world continued to think of wine that way. Ramsay MacMullen describes, in his book *Christianizing the Roman Empire,* A.D. *100–400,* the many adherents to the new Christian creed who took wine to the tombs of the martyrs on saints' days and, to the great concern of Ambrose and Augustine, drank there till evening, believing that without wine their supplications would not, could not, be heard. But for them, spiritual descendants, at least, of the men who had drunk from Athenaeus' common bowl and of those who had accepted wine from the hands of kings, wine was already a metaphor for god—for life itself—so the doctrine of Holy Communion through wine become sacred, as the blood of God needed no impossible new leap of faith.

I woke from a light sleep to find the man from the boat standing almost beside me under the canopy of reeds. He had dried himself on a coarse cotton cloth dangling from a string in the sun and was stepping into a pair of old pants he must have left at the bar. He was obviously at ease there but looked around as if choosing a place to sit. I invited him, with a gesture of my open hand, to join me and share my bottle. Another glass appeared for him, and when I had filled it, he raised it to me.

"*Yia sou,*" he said, smiling.

"*L'chayim,*" I replied. To life.

A Traveler's Finest Hour

BY THOMAS SWICK

ربی

editor's note

To be precise, the word for the ubiquitous sesame-studded rings that typically suffice for breakfast is *kouloures,* while *koulourakia* are more like cookies and are always sweet, often made with butter. Both are good coffee companions, and I am a huge fan of both, but I have never had the honored experience, as this writer did, of being mistaken for a vendor of either.

THOMAS SWICK is travel editor at the *South Florida Sun-Sentinel*. He contributed this piece to the travel section of *The New York Times* in 1988.

Every tourist, it has been said, wants to be taken for a traveler, but the real achievement is to be mistaken for a native. To be looked on as a native, however fleetingly, is one of the most sublime pleasures travel can offer. It is a sign that often your worst fear—of standing out, appearing different—is unwarranted. It suggests that, having passed beyond the role of outside observer, you can, with your newly found cover, begin to participate in the life of the people.

Evelyn Waugh, who in all the countries he traveled through was surely never taken for anything but an Englishman, nevertheless expressed great admiration for the more chameleonic members of the human race. "Everywhere he went," he wrote of his Armenian guide in Abyssinia, "he seemed to be welcome; everywhere he not only adapted, but completely transformed, his manners to the environment."

A few times in my life I have had the pleasure of successfully masquerading as a native. This has been facilitated by long stints abroad, which, by the way, can have the reverse effect of getting you mistaken for a foreigner when you return home.

Yet contrary to what most people might assume, to appear the native does not demand a lengthy stay or even language fluency. It can happen, with no warning, to the two-week tourist. What American's day is not made when, taking his morning walk through London, he is stopped by a troop of Japanese and asked the way to Buckingham Palace? It is an event that can make a traveler feel at home and in command, even when one is desperately far from being either. In this respect it can sometimes be a welcome anodyne to the minor irritations of life abroad.

My most rewarding encounter of this sort occurred in Greece. I had arrived in Athens and soon found it to be one of the few cities in the world that I have ever been anxious to leave. In the mornings I would stroll the streets, passing modern apartment buildings with balconies from which housewives, unfurling their tablecloths, would pelt me with breakfast crumbs. Downtown, later in the day, insistent young men would accompany me, telling of uncles in Newark and great bargains on medallions one block up. Food—the mute traveler's daily trial—came through my pointing to a large upright column of pitted meat to which a taciturn, mustachioed man took a saber, before stuffing the shavings into a folded, doughy discus. The drippings from these sandwiches permanently discolored my shoes. After a few weeks I decided to leave and went to the municipal bus terminal. There are basically two forms of mechanical transportation in Greece, buses and boats. (The topography makes the going too rugged for trains.) My plan was to escape the capital by traveling north to Arta, a small city with a legendary bridge.

As the day of my departure was a Friday, the station was besieged. Lumbering blue buses, weighted down by rooftop baggage, inched into and out of their bays, dispelling crowds of clamorous travelers and dousing them with noxious fumes. There was loud discussion and dramatic confusion. I learned that the bus to Arta would be delayed at least an hour and went outside for a breath of air. Finding a spot near one of the main entrances, I leaned against a stone wall to watch the procession of travelers. It was here that my masquerade began.

For out of the crowd a young boy broke in my direction, walking undisturbed and carrying a tray on his shoulder. He was tall and looked somewhat poorly fed in his loose-fitting undershirt. He had longish black hair that fell in waves; he could not have been older than fourteen. The tray was a thin wooden board piled perilously high with *koulourakia,* the crusty bread rings smothered with sesame seeds that are hawked throughout the city. I had first sighted them in large wicker baskets outside the entrance to the Olympic Gardens. On my first try I found them to be unsatisfyingly dry and tasteless.

The boy came up next to me and placed the tray atop the stone wall against which I was leaning. He then pulled out from under the first a second tray and began loading it with more *koulourakia*. He did this with a certain urgency of movement. When he had piled half of the supply onto the second tray, he indicated to me that I should sell as many of the remaining *koulourakia* as I could. None of his words were understood by me, though his request was obvious. Luckily, I knew from eating them that they sold for four drachmas apiece. Having thus quickly doubled the size of his concern, the boy started off in a purposeful gait toward the station, little aware of the inappropriateness of his appointment.

It is astonishing the attention one gets in Greece when standing by a tray of *koulourakia*. A fair number of people began drifting over for a pre-journey snack, and I made my transactions deftly, if wordlessly. Most of my customers were able to fish in their pockets for the appropriate number of drachmas; when they couldn't, I gave from my own. Business prospered. I grew in confidence, humming pseudo-Greek melodies and increasing my range of southern gesture. For attractive young women I picked out especially well-baked rings. I loosened the top buttons of my shirt.

As the supply dwindled, I began to feel a kinship with other vendors worldwide. I thought of the men selling chestnuts on the sidewalks of New York, and those with soft pretzels, infinitely superior to these cracknels, in Philadelphia. I remember hoping that a group of American tourists would appear, and I could send them away reeling in awe at the English proficiency of Greek sidewalk merchants.

Better than that, however, was a matronly woman who approached with a little boy in tow. She wore a look of impatience and waved a 100-drachma note. It was much more than I could make change for. The boy, oblivious to the realities of commerce, picked up a *koulouraki* and started nibbling. I motioned to the mother that I did not have change, increasing my variety of gestures.

She grew irritated and acted rashly, shaking and fulminating at me in her incomprehensible tongue. The boy continued nibbling.

At last I explained, in unruffled English: "I don't have change. I don't work here. I don't speak Greek. I am not a *koulouraki* vendor by profession. In other words, ma'am, you picked the wrong vendor."

Her reaction showed less surprise than active annoyance. She tore the *koulouraki* out of her son's mouth, slammed it back onto the pile—nearly crashing them all to the ground—and stalked away, pulling a baffled, wide-eyed boy along with her.

I, meanwhile, basked in a sort of afterglow. The event had provided one of the finest, most remedial sensations for the tourist: for I, so often foiled by the unintelligible utterances of the native vendors, had become a vendor and foiled a native. A sweet reversal.

When my partner reappeared, I turned over to him a few remaining *koulourakia* as well as a handsome profit.

Bibliography

Cookbooks

As with so many other cuisines, it seems to me that one cannot separate Greek cooking from Greek history. Keith Famie, of *Keith Famie's Adventures* on the Food Network, noted in his book *You Haven't Really Been There Until You've Eaten the Food* (Clarkson Potter, 2003) that "Food is not only the quickest way to learn about a place but also the only way to get a true feel for a community's sensory history." And Paula Wolfert, one of the world's foremost authorities on Mediterranean cuisine, has noted that "Recipes represent the way people live, their relation to their heritage and their land." Really good cookbooks—ones that offer tried and true, authentic recipes, as well as detailed commentary on the food traditions of the country or region and the history behind the recipes and the ingredients unique to the cuisine—are just as essential to travel as guidebooks. I read these cookbooks the way other people read novels; therefore the authors have to be more than just good cooks, and the books have to be more than just a collection of recipes. All of the authors and books listed below fit the bill, and because they are *all* my favorites, I feature them alphabetically as opposed to any order of preference. I use each of them at different times throughout the year, and I couldn't envision my kitchen without a single one. The Mediterranean cookbooks are in some ways the most interesting, because as Claudia Roden notes in *Mediterranean Cookery,* "Looking for the imprint of the past in the Mediterranean can be fascinating and helps to explain why a dish on one side of the sea is like another on the other side. But it is even more exciting to discover the extraordinary regional diversity of the area. For here unity does not mean uniformity. Obviously a Berber village clinging to a rock has a different way of interpreting a stew from a city like Granada. The Mediterranean has many faces: eastern and western, Christian and Muslim, one intimate with the sea, one with the desert, one which knows the mountains and one which looks beyond the olive trees at northern Europe, one which is rooted to the land, another which glitters with ancient grandeur. And regional cooking reflects them all." I do not provide lengthy descriptions of these titles as I think it is sufficient to state that they are nearly all definitive and stand quite apart from the multitude of cookbooks crowding bookstore shelves. I have also included a few titles that aren't strictly cookbooks but are equally as interesting and relevant nonetheless.

Mediterranean Cookbooks and Food

A Book of Mediterranean Food, Elizabeth David, Penguin, 1988. In her introduction David shares an observation by Marcel Boulestin that it is not really an exaggeration "to say that peace and happiness begin, geographically, where garlic is used in cooking." She herself notes that "from Gibraltar to the Bosphorus, down the Rhone Valley, through the great seaports of Marseilles, Barcelona, and Genoa, across to Tunis and Alexandria, embracing all the Mediterranean islands, Corsica, Sicily, Sardinia, Crete, the Cyclades, Cyprus (where the Byzantine influence begins to be felt), to the mainland of Greece and the much disputed territories of Syria, the Lebanon, Constantinople, and Smyrna, stretches the influence of Mediterranean cooking, conditioned naturally by variations in climate and soil and the relative industry or indolence of the inhabitants."

Cod: A Biography of the Fish That Changed the World, Mark Kurlansky, Walker Publishing Company, 1997. The first single-subject book I read about a culinary ingredient was *Peppers: A Story of Hot Pursuits* (by Amal Naj, Alfred A. Knopf, 1992), and I discovered I was crazy for this type of book. So years later, when I discovered *Cod,* I knew I would love it, and indeed I did. I couldn't stop talking about it, in fact, just as I couldn't stop talking about all the wonderful things I learned about peppers. The fascinating story of cod criss-crosses the globe from Newfoundland and New England to the Basque coast of Spain, Brazil, West Africa, and Scandinavia, but the Mediterranean is never very far from the thread. Kurlansky notes that "from the Middle Ages to the present, the most demanding cod market has always been the Mediterranean. These countries experienced a huge population growth in the nineteenth century. Fresh or dried salt cod is a ubiquitous Mediterranean staple (except in the Muslim countries), making an appearance in such dishes as *bacalao a la vizcaína* (País Vasco), *sonhos de bacalhau* (Portugal), salted cod croquettes (Italy), *brandade de morue* (France), and *taramosaláta* (Greece), among others." Kurlansky provides recipes for each.

The Essential Mediterranean: How Regional Cooks Transform Key Ingredients into the World's Favorite Cuisines, Nancy Harmon Jenkins, William Morrow, 2003. Jenkins continues her lifelong exploration of Mediterranean food that began with *The Mediterranean Diet Cookbook* (below), and in this book she introduces (or expands upon) a handful of core ingredients (salt; olives and olive oil; wheat, pasta, and couscous; wine; chickpeas, lentils, and fava beans; peppers and tomatoes; and cheese and yogurt) and foodways (the family pig; the sea) that are fundamental to all of the Mediterranean's diverse cuisines. I found her chapter on the sea especially interesting (and the recipes are good too!). I had long thought, because of the images of dolphins (especially at Knossos), other fish, and waves painted on walls and carved into pottery and sculpture, that the Mediterranean was once brimming with sea creatures—it was only in recent years that the sea life was depleted because it was overfished; but Jenkins informs us that the Mediterranean, "although it always surprises people to hear this, is not and never has been a rich sea, especially when compared with an ocean as prodigal of fishy wealth as the North Atlantic once was. Of the 1,255 species recorded for the Northeast Atlantic and the Mediterranean, fewer than half are actually present in the Mediterranean. The reasons for this dearth have to do primarily with geography and climate, although in the last half-century the human hand has weighted heavily on the sea's fragile ecosystem. Despite its poverty of resources, though, the Mediterranean has always carried a great, at times almost a sacred, significance for the people around its shores. . . . And that significance continues, a tightly braided cord that marries past and present. I love the story I've been told of Greek fishermen who, to this day, are prepared for a mermaid rising from the waves who demands, '*Zi o Megalexandros?*' (Does Alexander the Great still live?") To which the wise fisherman replies, '*O Megalexandros zi ke vasilevi*' (Great Alexander not only lives, but he still reigns!) Poor in resources, the sea is rich in cultural significance, the very emblem of Mediterranean civilization."

The Feast of the Olive, Maggie Blyth Klein, Aris Books (Addison-Wesley), 1983. A wonderfully written book with a number of Greek references and recipes.

The Flavors of Olive Oil: A Tasting Guide and Cookbook, Deborah Krasner, Simon and Schuster, 2002. This book, the winner of a 2003 James Beard Award in the category of "Best Book: Single Subject," is my favorite on the subject of olive oil. Much as I also enjoy the other olive oil titles I recommend here, Krasner simply provides even more useful and interesting information in this volume, *and* tasting notes and recommended producers (ten from Greece are included), as well as an excellent list of retail resources and producers that sell direct to consumers. Krasner is also a kitchen designer but is first and foremost a cook, so most of the book (152 pages) is devoted to recipes, even some for desserts.

From Tapas to Meze: First Courses from the Mediterranean Shores of Spain, France, Italy, Greece, Turkey, the Middle East, and North Africa, Joanna

Weir, Crown, 1994. Weir trained with Madeleine Kamman and cooked at Chez Panisse with Alice Waters, and her recipes are a unique and delicious collection of tapas, entrées, antipasti, *primi piatti,* and *mezéthes.* I've made many of these recipes, and they are great for a celebratory party or a light, healthful meal with family and friends.

Mediterranean: The Beautiful Cookbook, recipes and food text by Joyce Goldstein, regional text by Ayla Algar, Collins (produced by Welden Owen), 1994. I admit to having had a certain prejudice against this series when it was first introduced (I thought the books were just pretty coffee table volumes not meant for serious cooks), and I still feel that not every volume in the series is successful; this one, however, is on my short list of favorites. "Greece and the Balkans" is a good overview of the cultural history of Greece, and Greek recipes are featured throughout the book.

Mediterranean Cookery, Claudia Roden, Alfred A. Knopf, 1987. Long a favorite volume of mine, this was one of the early Mediterranean cookbooks to appear at a time when there were few others on the subject. I remain particularly fond of it because Roden includes many recipes for popular street foods and common dishes that regular people eat and that travelers will encounter often, as opposed to fancier restaurant dishes. Also, I learned a great tip from Roden: when the weather doesn't permit you to light your outdoor grill, and you don't want to permeate your house or apartment with the smell of roasting red peppers on the stovetop, put them in a baking dish, uncovered, and roast them in a 400-degree oven. Trust me: they come out just as delicious as those cooked over a flame.

Mediterranean Cooking, Paula Wolfert, HarperCollins, 1994. Greece is rarely mentioned in this volume and there are no Greek recipes, but it's an outstanding book. And Wolfert shares some of the timeless wisdom of Fernand Braudel: "In the sixteenth century, a native of the Mediterranean, wherever he might come from, would never feel out of place in any part of the sea. To later colonial settlers their journey simply meant finding in a new place the same trees and plants, the same food on the table that they had known in their homeland; it meant living under the same sky, watching the same familiar seasons."

The Mediterranean Diet Cookbook: A Delicious Alternative for Lifelong Health, Nancy Harmon Jenkins, Bantam Books, 1994. I have simply not devoted the time to find out if this was the very first book published on the Mediterranean Diet, but it is safe to say it was the groundbreaking book on the subject. It's worth emphasizing the credentials of the two doctors—both born and raised in Greece—who contributed the introduction: Antonia Trichopoulou M.D. is professor of nutrition and biochemistry at the Athens School of Public Health and director of the World Health Organization Collaborating Center for Nutrition Education in Europe; Dimitrios Trichopoulos M.D. is Vincent L. Gregory Professor of Cancer Prevention and Epidemiology, Harvard School of Public

Health. In other words, the Mediterranean Diet is not a flash-in-the-pan gimmick! As they point out, one way we know that people in a particular area of the world have a healthier diet than our Western one is through epidemiology, the study of disease patterns: "Studies of migrants have shown that whatever the disease pattern in their country of origin, they tend to acquire, sooner or later, the disease pattern of their host country, even when they remain relatively isolated within ethnic communities. For instance, the frequency of cancer of the large intestine is much lower in Japan than in the United States but rises to American levels within 20 years among Japanese immigrants to this country." They also note that "nobody knows for sure what the ideal diet *is,* but there are good reasons to believe that the Mediterranean diet may come closer to it than any other realistic diet." If you would like to learn how to incorporate it into your life and start cooking some delicious, healthful meals, this book is the one to turn to first. I am considering including the chapter entitled "Making the Change" in all of my future books, but until that time I will simply share the major components of a Mediterranean Diet and lifestyle that Jenkins outlines in her excellent book:

- Start off by structuring mealtimes.
- Switch from whatever fats you now use to olive oil, preferably extra virgin.
- Get out of the butter habit.
- Add bread in abundance to the meal.
- Begin or end each meal with a salad.
- Add both more vegetables and different vegetables to the menu.
- Cut down on the amount of meat consumed. (In fairness, I think this element needs some clarification. Colman Andrews, in the chapter entitled "The Myth of the Mediterranean Diet" in his wonderful book *Flavors of the Riviera,* notes that this moderation was imposed in many parts of the Mediterranean "by insufficiency, and by the dietary laws of the Catholic church—which mandated periods of fasting and of abstinence from meat and other animal products. It was not elected as a secular moral or nutritional choice." Andrews adds that Leland Allbaugh, in a 1953 study undertaken on Crete, reported that "While fish, meat, and dairy products provided only seven percent of the energy in the Cretan diet, some 72 percent of the families he surveyed identified meat as their favorite food, and that Cretans overall listed meat as the element they most desired more of to improve the way they ate.")
- Substitute wine in moderation for other alcoholic beverages.
- Don't fuss with dessert. (On this point I personally digress from the diet when company is coming, as I am a fairly accomplished baker and really enjoy making a fuss with dessert. But most of the time I make fruit desserts, which are not quite the same as much more sugary confections.)
- Think about the quality of the food you buy and seek out the best.

A Mediterranean Feast: The Story of the Birth of the Celebrated Cuisines of the Mediterranean, From the Merchants of Venice to the Barbary Corsairs, Clifford A. Wright, William Morrow, 1999. If you want to read only one book on Mediterranean cuisine, this outstanding and exhaustively researched book is the one. Wright reveals that "I wrote this book in an attempt to extend one man's—Fernand Braudel's—vision, love, and scholarship, and I augmented it with my own research and love of Mediterranean food, in the hope of providing a guide to the Mediterranean that has not been attempted before. The weaving of history and gastronomy in *A Mediterranean Feast* was meant to reveal the culinary structure of the Mediterranean—its rugged contours, oppressive reality and blue delight—through the eyes of geographers, travelers, historians, and cooks, what Braudel means by 'total history.' Braudel's writings were an attempt to seek out the 'constant' of Mediterranean history, the structures and recurrent patterns of everyday life that provide the reference grid. For myself, and this book, the constant is the food of the Mediterranean, its cuisine and recipes."

Mediterranean: Food of the Sun: A Culinary Tour of Sun-Drenched Shores with Evocative Dishes from Southern Europe, Jacqueline Clark and Joanna Farrow, Lorenz Books, 2001. Though a few of the recipes in this volume are common, a great number of them do not appear in other Mediterranean cookbooks, and the ones I've tried have been really delicious.

The Mediterranean Kitchen, Joyce Goldstein, William Morrow, 1989. A unique feature of this wonderful book is that Goldstein indicates how, by changing only an ingredient or two, a recipe can go from being Italian, say, to Greek, Portuguese, or Moroccan. This illustrates the core ingredients that all countries in the region share and also allows for more mileage out of nearly every recipe.

Mediterranean Light, Martha Rose Shulman, Bantam, 1989. I've enjoyed cooking from this book over the years, though some recipes have proved less successful than others. It's especially good for people who, for health reasons other than weight loss, are on a restrictive diet and are looking for a healthy diet to maintain for life.

The Mediterranean Pantry: Creating and Using Condiments and Seasonings, Aglaia Kremezi, Artisan, 1994. Though the title doesn't convey it, the majority of the recipes for these condiments and seasonings are Greek, though a number of these staples are good to have on hand for many Mediterranean recipes.

Mediterranean Street Food: Stories, Soups, Snacks, Sandwiches, Barbecues, Sweets, and More, From Europe, North Africa, and the Middle East, Anissa Helou, HarperCollins, 2002. I was so happy when this book was published because though some street foods are included in a number of Mediterranean cookbooks, they have not really been given the pride of place they deserve, as they are so much a part of the Mediterranean lifestyle. Helou presents a great variety of recipes for soups; snacks, salads, and dips; pizzas, breads, and savory pastries; sandwiches; barbecues; one-pot meals; sweets and desserts; and drinks. Of those I have tried, all have been great. Most of these recipes are perfect for cocktail parties or hors d'oeuvres, even light lunches and dinners. Halou grew up in Beirut, then moved to London and later to Paris, where, "even if the city is not by the sea, it is the capital of a Mediterranean country with a culture and a way of life, at least in the south, that are closer to mine . . . as for eating in the street, I was back in business. Whether it was time for breakfast, lunch, or dinner, there was always an ambulant vendor, a hole in the wall, or a café opening onto the street providing fun and tasty specialties to eat."

Mostly Mediterranean: More Than 200 Recipes from France, Spain, Greece, Morocco, and Sicily, Paula Wolfert, Penguin, 1988. Only thirteen Greek recipes are included in this collection, but the book is a winner nonetheless.

Olives, Anchovies, and Capers: The Secret Ingredients of the Mediterranean Table, Georgeanne Brennan, Chronicle Books, 2001. As Brennan notes, some of the Mediterranean's most humble snacks and dishes deliver a sense of gustatory well-being completely out of proportion to their simplicity because "the traditional uses of three preserved ingredients, olives, anchovies, and capers, give the food an endless variation of character and depth." In addition to recipes (a few I particularly liked are Anchovies and Lemon on Black Olive Bread, Anchovy Stuffed Eggs, and Pan-Seared Salmon with Capers and Green Peppercorns), Brennan provides information on the cultivation and preservation of olives and capers (and a good brine recipe for salt-curing olives) and the fishing for and preservation of anchovies.

Olives: The Life and Love of a Noble Fruit, Mort Rosenblum, North Point Press, 1996. "An olive, to many, is no more than a humble lump at the bottom of a martini," notes Rosenblum, "yet a closer look reveals a portrait in miniature of the richest parts of our world. Olives have oiled the wheels of civilization since Jericho built walls and ancient Greece was the morning news. From the first Egyptians, they have symbolized everything happy and holy in the Mediterranean. But it is simpler than all that. Next time the sun is bright and the tomatoes are ripe, take a hunk of bread, sprinkle it with fresh thyme, and think about where to dunk it. I rest my case." Two chapters—"The Lesbos Groves" and "The Big Kalamata"—focus on singular Greek olives.

Salt: A World History, Mark Kurlansky, Walker & Co., 2002. Here's another fascinating volume from Kurlansky, this time the single subject being something humans and animals cannot survive without. Early on Kurlansky reminds us that "salt is so common, so easy to obtain, and so inexpensive that we have forgotten that from the beginning of civilization until about 100 years ago, salt was one of the most sought-after commodities in human history." (Note that the low cost of salt does not apply to today's designer salts, such as *fleur de sel,* which is handmade and somewhat labor intensive, and is "traditional in a world increasingly hungry for a sense of artisans.") One thing I love about books like this is the wealth of trivia one discovers: Kurlansky leaves no stone unturned, and you feel like you've just read a long version of *Ripley's Believe It or Not.* I usually walk around for weeks asking, "Did you know . . . ?" questions to anyone who will listen, then I reel off all the amazing things there are to know about cod or salt. For example, did you know that salt makes ice cream freeze, removes rust, seals cracks, cleans bamboo furniture, kills poison ivy, and treats dyspepsia, sprains, sore throats, and earaches? (Readers interested in more of the myriad uses for salt should get a copy of the nifty *Solve It with Salt: 110 Surprising and Ingenious Household Uses for Table Salt,* Patty Moosbrugger, Three Rivers Press, 1998.) Besides its practical uses, salt is believed by Muslims and Jews to ward off the evil eye, and bringing bread and salt to a new home is a Jewish tradition dating back to the Middle Ages. "In Christianity, salt is associated not only with longevity and permanence but, by extension, with truth and wisdom. The Catholic Church dispenses not only holy water but holy salt, *Sal Sapientia,* the Salt of Wisdom." As the title indicates, this is worldwide story, but it's very much a Mediterranean story, too. Kurlansky writes that "The entire coast of the Mediterranean was studded with saltworks, some small local operations, others big commercial enterprises such as the ones in Constantinople and the Crimea. The ancient Mediterranean saltworks that had been started by the Phoenicians, like power itself, passed from Romans to Byzantines to Muslims. The saltworks that the Romans had praised remained the most valued. Egyptian salt from Alexandria was highly appreciated, especially their *fleur de sel,* the light crystals skimmed off the surface of the water. Salt from Egypt, Trapani, Cyprus, and Crete all had great standing because they had been mentioned by Pliny in Roman times." Finally, as in *Cod,* Kurlansky warns of what can happen to a seemingly endless resource due to greed and short-sightedness. The lovely French coastal village of Collioure, where artists such as Matisse spent many happy days, once had eight hundred anchovy fishermen; now it has none. I was humbled when I learned that the La Baleine sea salt I've been buying for years is owned by Morton's; and I was surprised to learn that most of the salt mined today is destined for de-icing roads in cold-weather places around the world.

Secrets of Saffron: The Vagabond Life of the World's Most Seductive Spice, Pat Willard, Beacon Press, 2001. As a nut for single-subject food books, I was thrilled to discover this wonderful and fascinating little book on saffron. Willard has uncovered a wealth of facts and figures. One that most impressed me was that Nuremberg, in the mid-1400s, was the main marketplace for goods coming into central Europe from the Mediterranean. I guess I hadn't considered it before, but the city is situated at the crossroads of the major trade routes and is surrounded by a superior network of rivers and bridges. In 1358 the city passed the Safranschou law, which was "to govern the inspection and quality of saffron. On any given day, there were at least seven different varieties of imported saffron for sale in the city's market—French, Spanish, Sicilian, Cretan, Austrian, Greek, and Turkish—all with their own subtle differences in taste and potency." I never knew before I read this book that saffron also once thrived in England (Norfolk, Suffolk, and in the coastal area of Essex), Switzerland (in Basel), and Lancaster County, Pennsylvania (a small amount still does, actually, but it makes it as far as the Reading Terminal Market in Philadelphia). Sadly, when Willard visited the town of Consuegra, in La Mancha, there was only one saffron farmer; this in an area that was "once brimming with saffron." I loved this book so much I read it in one day (it's only 216 pages), and I think my most favorite part appears in the next-to-last chapter, when Willard finally finds the answer to the question that has haunted her since her trip to Consuegra: Why has she had such an absorbing obsession with saffron? She discovers "at last, what this tiny flower has always embodied and through the ages shared with the world—that so little is needed to turn life into a sumptuous feast." This is a beautifully written book. Willard includes a handful of recipes as well as tips on buying, storing, cooking with, and growing saffron (also on how to use it as a dye).

The Sephardic Kitchen: The Healthful Food and Rich Culture of the Mediterranean Jews, Rabbi Robert Sternberg, HarperCollins, 1996. Greece is included in this collection of recipes, which are adapted from ancient Spanish and Portuguese sources and from the Sephardic kitchens of Italy, southeast France, Morocco, Algeria, Tunisia, and the countries and cities of the former Ottoman Empire (Turkey, Albania, parts of Romania, Egypt, Lebanon, Syria, and Jerusalem).

Zingerman's Guide to Good Vinegar and *Zingerman's Guide to Good Olive Oil*, both by Ari Weinzweig, Zingerman's/Dancing Sandwich Enterprises, 1996. Of the wonderful Zingerman's you already know if you read "The Original Extra Virgins" on page 383." Here is a duo of little paperback books—well, nicely produced pamphlets, really—in the Zingerman's Guides to Good Eating series that are seriously addictive and positively must-haves in your kitchen. Truly, there have been a multitude of articles written about olive oil and vinegar, and books, too; I've read nearly all of them, and rarely do they address all the questions consumers have about these two Mediterranean comestibles. The olive oil guide offers answers to such questions as "What is extra-virgin anyway?" "Why does one olive oil sell for $10 and another for $30?" "How long can you store olive oil?" and—my favorite—"How come my Italian grandmother didn't use extra-virgin olive oil?" Ari's answer is, "Though it will come as a surprise to many (and certainly no offense is intended), most of the Italians who immigrated to this country didn't use very good olive oil after they arrived. Most of them were poor, and even in Italy at the turn of the century the best extra virgin olive oils were costly. In poorer households, which didn't have their own olive trees, it was common to use refined oils that were not particularly good. They were affordable, though, and these were the oils most immigrants could afford to bring with them to North America. Even those Italians who used the best extra virgin oils in Italy couldn't find them in this country. Olive trees don't grow on the Lower East Side or in Brooklyn. The only place in this country in which olive trees grow is California, and most growers there planted olive trees to produce table olives, not oil." In addition to some wonderful recipes, Weinzweig includes two pages of cool olive oil trivia. (Did you know that 95 percent of the world's olive trees are grown in the countries of the Mediterranean? And that it takes about eleven pounds of olives to produce a liter of olive oil?) The vinegar guide addresses questions like "Can you really taste the difference?" "What's wrong with the stuff in the supermarket?" and "What can you learn from the label?" Also provided is a list of ten things to do with vinegar (besides washing windows).

Best Seasonal Cookbooks

Beginning with this edition, I am including a list of cookbooks whose authors feel that ingredients used in their proper seasons are of paramount importance. One could say, of course, that *all* Mediterranean cookbooks—from any country on its shores—focus on seasonality, and they do. But I feel it's important to single out the volumes below and applaud their authors for championing seasonal foods. (Remember: our supermarkets make it easy to forget that foods do still have seasons in which they grow and thrive and are harvested. Just because they sell asparagus and plastic tomatoes in January doesn't mean they're in season—they're only inferior, tasteless, and flown in from somewhere else.) Seasonality is an essential cuisine guideline that every Greek cook respects.

The Art of Seasonal Cooking, Perla Myers, Simon and Schuster, 1991. Myers, also the author of *The Seasonal Kitchen* (1973), which I've not seen, asks, "What has happened to the simple concept of seasonal dishes? What has happened to real cooking?" I ask this as well, and some of the most memorable dishes I've ever made have been from this outstanding book.

Chez Panisse Fruit, Chez Panisse Vegetables (both HarperCollins), and all of the Chez Panisse family of cookbooks (these include the *Chez Panisse Cookbook* and *Chez Panisse Menu Cookbook* published by Random House), all by Alice

Waters except for *Chez Panisse Desserts* (by Lindsay Shere and sadly out of print). I mentioned in my *Southwest France* edition that I have, over the years, not found the Chez Panisse books very user-friendly. Though I often began with a great desire to love and cherish each Chez Panisse book, I ended up admiring the text and finding it inspiring but felt compelled to try only a few of the recipes. Upon reflection, however, I decided that Alice Waters is too much a champion of fresh, seasonal cuisine in America to omit her from these pages, and plus I think she is a swell human being. Writing about *Chez Panisse Fruit* in *The Art of Eating*, contributor James MacGuire notes that "Waters's writing may be low-key, but her ardor is undiminished. The introduction describes the way she begins writing a book. 'I throw open the window,' she says, 'start to flail my arms, and scream: "Pay attention to what you're eating!" And then I calm down a little and try to explain why this matters so much to me.' Readers are warned of 'extremely noxious agricultural chemicals' sprayed on commercial strawberries and are reassured that she buys strawberries harvested by 'well-paid unionized workers' (shades of Cesar Chavez and the 1960s). Waters, as much as anyone, has made American chefs pay attention to high-quality, small-scale organic growers. Those growers remain a tiny minority, and this book is part of her effort, slowly increasing in success, to persuade everyday cooks to do the same." (As an aside, I have read elsewhere about those noxious chemicals sprayed on strawberries, and in a list I cut out of a magazine highlighting organic foods that are worth the money, strawberries were at the top as one item in particular that should never be purchased unless they are certified organic.) The *Fruit* and *Vegetables* books are beautifully produced with artwork that is suitable for framing. The other Chez Panisse titles are not quite as attractive, though they are all of high quality, but I believe the definitive Chez Panisse book hasn't yet been published.

Cooking with Daniel Boulud, Random House, 1993. Readers unfamiliar with this book may be wondering why a work by a famous restaurant chef appears here, but readers who *do* know this book are familiar with the Seasonal Markets Lists found at the end of the book. There are also *great* recipes interspersed between these seasonal food lists; in fact, this is an extremely outstanding cookbook with incredible recipes, and I think it belongs in the category of culinary classics.

The Greens Cook Book, Deborah Madison, Bantam, 1987. There were, and still are, vegetarian cookbooks, and then there is *Greens,* head and shoulders above the rest. Many of the recipes require a long list of ingredients, many are time-consuming and are definitely not for weeknight cooking; but all are true to every season of the year and produce delicious results.

"The food and gastronomy of Greece," writes Andrew Dalby in *Siren Feasts,* "are part of the background to the history of the country, a history that demands the attention of all who are interested in the sources of their own civilisation. Greek gastronomy is also the direct ancestor of the much better known food culture of Rome. Thus it stands at the origin of much in modern European food and cuisine."

The Flavors of Greece: The Best of Classic and Modern Greek Culinary Traditions in More Than 250 Recipes, Rosemary Barron, William Morrow, 1991. "It is almost impossible for me," Barron writes, "to think of Greece without thinking of the colors, sights, aromas, and, above all, the flavors of Greek cooking. So many of my happy memories of the country are linked with food enjoyed in the company of good Greek friends or of new food experiences associated with out-of-the-way or exotically beautiful places—high in the mountains, by the glistening blue Aegean Sea, or in medieval ports, picturesque villages, or the heart of cosmopolitan Athens." I have a soft spot in my heart for this book as it was the first Greek cookbook I ever had, a gift from my friend Bill B. Author Barron founded the Kandra Kitchen cooking school on Crete and Santorini in 1981 and has been teaching for more than twenty-five years. As a result, she is very thorough in her directions, and though this book has no photographs, it is nonetheless an authoritative volume. She notes that her recipes "are the result of tasting and more tasting, until I was satisfied I had reproduced an authentic Greek flavor. Most of the recipes have been adapted,to a greater or lesser degree to suit our kitchens and tastes. Where I have used a recipe exactly as it was given me, or stressed a technique or ingredient in the way it was stressed to me, I have said so and credited the cook who passed the recipe on to me. These were usually the recipes of the chefs, who understood my need for a concise explanation. However, even they tended to answer the question 'Why?' with the response, 'Because that is the way it has always been done.'" Chapters are organized by types of food (appetizers and first courses; soups; light meals; meats; pilafs and pastas; breads, etc.), and Barron also provides a section featuring menus for different occasions. This is a really good book to cook from—both novices and more accomplished cooks will find it rewarding—and to gain a good introduction to the basics of Greek cuisine. Barron's parting comments are especially appealing to me: "I hope my recipes will pay some tribute to the wonderful spirit of friendliness that has engulfed me, and warms any visitor, in Greece; that they will revive happy memories in those who have already traveled to Greece or her islands and in the Greeks who now live abroad. Perhaps too they will persuade others to visit that beautiful and hospitable country and experience the delights of Greek food for themselves."

The Food and Wine of Greece, Diane Kochilas, St. Martin's Press, 1990. In this, Kochilas's first book on Greek cuisine, she reminds us that when most of us think of Greek food, what first comes to mind are those clichéd dishes served up in Greek diners across the United States: "Deadpan moussaka, cloying baklava preserved in, not merely flavored with, syrup; and skewers of grilled meat carved of anything but the tenderest spring lamb." Though Kochilas compiled this book more than ten years ago, and though she champions the new restaurant scene in Athens (and even helped develop the menu for at least one), it is still generally true that "the indigenous food of Greece—the rich warm stews, the myriad vegetable dishes, the sweets made possible by only the most skilled of hands—are rarely tasted beyond its boundaries and seldom sampled in any restaurant, even in Greece. Greek cuisine is country cookery at its best, home-based, dependent on the seasons, and often passed on in nothing more than a calligraphic hand in a ragged notebook from grandmother to mother to daughter." This volume is not the *magnum opus* her more recent book (below) is, but it is a very good, overall introduction to the culture and way of life of Greece through its food. And despite her truthful statement that the trio of crisp cucumber, pickled octopus, and pearly ouzo—a perfect blend of flavor and texture—is "irreproducible outside of summertime Greece," it is very much worth the effort to try and reproduce it in your kitchen. Trust me.

The Food of Greece: Cooking, Folkways, and Travel in the Mainland and Islands of Greece, Vilma Liacouras Chantiles, Fireside, 1992. Though this paperback is not as authoritative as the books by Aglaia Kremezi and Diane Kochilas, it is an authentic volume—the author, a Greek American, did not visit Greece until she was an adult, but she made up for lost time by thoroughly immersing herself in the subject. There are no photographs, only a few illustrations, but the recipes I've tried have all been easy to follow and have turned out fine. Most of the recipes are for dishes that are common in tavernas, so many readers will already be familiar with them. I appreciate this book more for the author's personal notes and food commentary, and she is spot on when she writes that "Greek foods integrate qualities of the land, people, history and culture. Particularly when tasting fresh, delicious meals outdoors, I have felt Greek culture and nature pervading my spirit. Whether sampling foods rich and Thessalian, or frugal and Spartan, whether sitting by the quiet sea near the jagged, awesome coast by day, or reveling in a friendly, noisy tavern at evening, I have felt food become an elemental experience. I have sensed the meaning of the proverb '*Ola kala kai to meli glyko*' (All's well and the honey is sweet)."

The Foods of Greece, Aglaia Kremezi, Stewart, Tabori and Chang, 1993. The large size of this book (approximately nine inches by twelve) and the gorgeous color photographs make it perhaps the best book to browse to begin learning about the cuisine of Greece and the specialties of each region. That the book was published over a decade ago is irrelevant—Kremezi is one of the world's top authorities on Greek cooking, and this volume remains definitive on the subject. She notes in the preface that by the end of the 1990s, just as the world was applauding the benefits of the Mediterranean Diet, Greeks were running away from it: "It was not until the end of the 1960s that Greece stopped being one of the underdeveloped countries and joined Europe as an equal partner. No longer a poor relation, Greece became more prosperous, and its people felt that they had to remove any vestiges of a difficult past. So the old, handmade copper pots and pans, the wooden troughs in which bread was kneaded, and the lovely, hand-woven curtains and blankets were sold to traveling merchants for a song, replaced by plastic tablecloths and aluminum kitchenware. With the passing of these traditional utensils and furnishings we also lost many of our old eating habits, our culinary heritage. Greece has never had great chefs to record its cooking traditions. My mother's generation, which came of age before World War II, and especially women who have lived in the countryside most of their lives, are the last remaining link with a rich culinary past. In remote villages—and especially on the islands, where traditions are more important—one can still find the crude and tasty peasant cooking of our great grandmothers. But one has to search hard for it. In the tavernas, in the holiday resorts, hardly anyone cooks dishes typical of the region. Souvlaki, hamburgers, veal or pork chops, spaghetti, and pizza are everywhere in Greece, often served with badly cooked moussaka." In my experience there are many more classic (and delicious) Greek dishes on taverna and restaurant menus these days, and indeed Kremezi happily notes that things seem to be changing: "People are growing tired of sophisticated 'foreign' foods and processed ingredients, and they are feeling a need to go back to the source. . . . Now Americans—who introduced us to a lot of meat and processed foods—are turning to our food traditions. Cookbook authors, journalists, and chefs from all over the Western world are looking at old Greek recipes. I don't think it unrealistically optimistic to foresee the day when young Greek chefs start using almost-forgotten recipes to create the next chapter of our age-old cooking." Kremezi presents individual chapters on appetizers, salads, and egg dishes; fish and seafood; meatless meals and vegetable dishes; meat; breads, biscuits, phyllo, and pasta; and desserts and sweets. I have a few favorite recipes in this book (notably the Smoked Trout in Dill and Scallion Marinade; Artichoke, Carrot, and Fresh Fava Bean Stew; and Honey Cookies), but I personally prefer the introductory chapters entitled "Edesmata: The Foods of Greece" (on the foods of the ancient Greeks and other influences), "The Elements of Greek Food" (which reviews the key ingredients—olives, vinegar, yogurt, cheese, tomatoes, onions, garlic, wild greens, currants and raisins, chili peppers, vine leaves, capers, almonds and walnuts, herbs, spices, and wines and spirits), and "Gods and Saints at the Table" (which details fairs and festivals throughout the calendar year).

The Foods of the Greek Islands: Cooking and Culture at the Crossroads of the Mediterranean, Aglaia Kremezi, Houghton Mifflin, 2000. At the close of her preface to *The Foods of Greece,* Kremezi wrote, "I know that I have not found all the recipes worth writing about, so my search continues." Happily, this different but no less carefully researched book appeared seven years later. Kremezi divides this book into chapters featuring *mezéthes;* pitas and pies; fish and seafood; meat; beans, rice, bulgar, and pasta; salads, vegetables and potatoes; bread, and island desserts. As she notes in the foreword, "This book is not an encyclopedia of Greek island cooking but a very personal selection from thousands of recipes that I have collected over the years. Besides relying on personal preference, I have chosen dishes that can be successfully cooked away from the islands and outside Greece. Some islands are better represented than others, and I have undoubtedly missed some foods worth recording. Each village on each island has many different versions of the same dish, often using diverse ingredients; and Greece has about 170 inhabited islands in all." Readers who live in the New York metropolitan area may know that Kremezi is also a consultant to New York City restaurant Molyvos, and a number of the recipes in this volume are for dishes found on the Molyvos menu. (For the record, I feel Molyvos is not only New York's premier Greek restaurant but one of New York's best restaurants in *any* category.) The gorgeous photos in this book are seductive enough, but as I was working on this manuscript, I tried some different recipes from those I had previously made, and I was reminded that there are so many gems here—Blue Cheese and Tomato Spread, Fava Skordalia, Feta Cheese Pancakes, Tomato Patties from Santorini, and Baked Quinces in Spiced Sweet Wine Syrup are just a few of my favorites. Many of these recipes have been passed from generation to generation by word of mouth. This book holds the additional distinction of being the first extensively researched cookbook in English to record the cooking of the Greek islands.

The Glorious Foods of Greece: Traditional Recipes from the Islands, Cities, and Villages, Diane Kochilas, William Morrow, 2001. This is the definitive Greek cookbook that devotees of Greek cuisine (like me) were waiting for, even if we didn't quite realize it, for years. It is much, much more than a book of collected recipes, many of which Kochilas has recorded for the first time. It does not feature any photographs, but Kochilas organized the book by regions of Greece, as opposed to types of food, so readers become familiar with the traditions and dishes unique to each. Kochilas, a Greek American originally from New York, moved to Athens in the early 1990s. She notes that "One of the great lessons I learned during my research and writing is that there is really no such thing as a 'comprehensive' book." But I can't even begin to imagine what might be missing from this most impressive work, which took her eight years to write and research. The gorgeous cover alone should make you want to pick it up off the shelf, but I would not describe it as the best choice for beginner cooks unless they are truly enthusiastic and dedicated. Still, it is a wonderful, and essential, book to read, even if all you have in your refrigerator/freezer is an eye mask and a bottle of vodka, like my friend Andrea R. In addition to the rest of Greece, individual chapters include the Peloponnese, the islands of the northeastern Aegean, the Cyclades, the Dodecanese, Crete, and Athens.

Greek Generations: A Medley of Ethnic Recipes, Folklore, and Village Traditions, Susie Atsaides, Noble House, Baltimore, 2003. I found this (gigantic) book at Kitchen Arts and Letters in New York and fell in love with it—less for its recipes, truthfully (and there are more than four hundred of them), than for all the other interesting stuff that's documented in it. I like books like this because they are created and compiled as a labor of love and are authentic archives of a community. In this case, the community includes village kitchens, ovens, and olive orchards in Greece. The recipes, cultural details, ancestral superstitions, and stories have been passed down from mother to daughter for generations. This hardcover compendium is a great joy to read, even if you never make a single recipe. Atsaides, who hails from the Greek community of Baltimore, now lives on Rhodes and maintains a good website, www.faliraki-info.com, which is devoted to the history of Rhodes and also includes accommodation information, travel tips, recipes, and a good section on Greek traditions and village superstitions. This book is a major accomplishment.

The Greek Vegetarian, Diane Kochilas, St. Martin's Press, 1996.

Meze: Small Bites, Big Flavors from the Greek Table, Rosemary Barron, Chronicle Books, 2002. I was so happy when this book was published because for some years I have felt that the wonderful tradition of *mezéthes,* which I enthused about in the *Practical Information* section, deserved wider recognition, and there is not, to my knowledge, another book devoted solely to them. It seems to have taken a number of years for the Spanish tapas tradition to take hold in North America, and I suspect it will take some time for us to adopt the *meze* tradition too, but we are off to a good start with Rosemary Barron's book. Barron informs us that her interest in the Greek food past began when she took part in archaeological digs on Crete in the 1960s: "I can still remember being amazed that I was eating, quite naturally, and in the same manner, foods of which we were uncovering evidence of thousands of years earlier: wild greens, grains, fish, game, wines, olives, and olive oil." This food connection with the ancients, however, caused her to wonder: "Does the *meze* table have any relevance for our modern lifestyle, and is it hard work? To the first, I would answer emphatically 'yes' and to the second, a resounding 'no!' *Mezes* are very well-suited to the way we live now and, for the most part, take no longer to prepare than a casserole. Above all, the Greek *meze* table shows us how to slow down; how to enjoy flavor, texture, and diversity; how to make the most of simple preparations and seasonal goodness. Best of all, *mezes* are supremely sociable; this is food to share with other people in an atmosphere of friendship and community." Barron divides the book up into chapters featuring the *meze* pantry, *mezedakia* (small *mezéthes*), cold plates, greens and salads, hot plates and savory pies, and grilled *mezéthes*. She also provides a glossary of key ingredients and a short list of resources. This is a good menu-planning book for light and healthful everyday meals, cocktail parties, and other festive events.

Meze: Small Plates to Savor and Share From the Mediterranean Table, Diane Kochilas, William Morrow, 2003. Kochilas's first paragraph of this wonderful book speaks volumes about Greek life and is worth repeating here: "When I moved to Greece ten years ago I had to switch gears from the frenzied pace of New York City to the more relaxed rhythms of the Mediterranean. I moved to Athens, a chaotic, bustling city whose charms take some time to uncover. One of the things I loved from the very start though was something I used to joke about, granted, with a little bit of New York sarcasm—that in the middle of every afternoon, throngs of people of working age, men and women alike from every walk of life, were crowded around small tables all over the city, clinking glasses, sharing plates, talking loudly in that lively, excessive way Greeks have when discussing . . . everything. They were doing what people in this part of the world have been doing for literally thousands of years—partaking in the trinity of food, drink and dialogue (not always in that order), relaxing and socializing over a glass or two of wine or beer or ouzo and some savory tidbits of food. I was witnessing meze culture firsthand. It seemed much more civilized than 'doing' lunch New York style." In this volume Kochilas has divided the chapters by specific types of *mezéthes,* such dips, spreads, and relishes; small egg dishes; from meatballs to kebabs; and finger foods and fried treats. I have tried a few of the recipes, and they were big hits with my family and friends. There are two pages of *meze* ingredient sources at the back of the book.

Modern Greek: 170 Contemporary Recipes from the Mediterranean, Andy Harris, Chronicle Books, 2002. There is no glut of Greek cookbooks, as you'll discover if you spend any time in the cookbook section of bookstores. Nearly all of those that exist concentrate on the more classic Greek dishes, so *Modern*

Greek is a welcome addition to the current selection. Recipes for the familiar *tzatziki, taramosaláta,* dolmades, and pastitsio are included, but there are many less familiar dishes and even new takes on favorites like moussaka (here made with zucchini instead of eggplants and potatoes). Harris was the former editor in chief of the now-defunct *Williams-Sonoma Taste,* a magazine I was quite fond of, and I was sorry that it was only published for a little more than a year. Harris has been going to Greece since the age of three and is also the author of *A Taste of the Aegean* (below). I have made a few of the recipes for *mezéthes* and pasta, and they were quite delicious and great for parties. But I admit it was the photo of one of my most favorite treats in the world, the submarine, that won me over and earned this book a place in my kitchen.

Siren Feasts: A History of Food and Gastronomy in Greece, Andrew Dalby, Routledge, 1996. The first line of Dalby's preface reads, "This is the book that I wanted to have beside me when I began to study the social history of Greece," the kind of line that immediately grabs my attention. Happily, it isn't the only line worth reading in this engrossing book, the first scholarly social history of food and gastronomy in Greece. Dalby draws upon classical texts, the archaeology of prehistoric sites, art, and literature and illustrates how an understanding of the food and gastronomy of ancient Greece provides a useful background to reading Greek comedy and lyric poetry. As Dalby notes, "The food and entertainment of the classical Aegean are rich fields for research, endlessly fascinating in themselves, indispensable background for all who study the ancient world, important to anthropologists and to students of later Mediterranean history." There are no recipes in this volume, as it is not a cookbook; rather, it's an excellent source for travelers who want to learn more about the history of Greek cuisine.

A Taste of the Aegean: Greek Cooking and Culture, Andy Harris, Abbeville Press, 1992. As the title indicates, this book (which I believe is out of print) is a collection of recipes from all the islands in the Aegean Sea. But it is not, as the author states, "merely a cookery book full of recipes, it is also an exploration into the ways in which the Greeks live and eat." As other food writers have informed us, Greek cuisine in general has been under attack by Greeks themselves. This book is "a celebration of what remains—a continuity of inheritance that shows that life still must go on." Harris notes that though the influence of the Ottoman Empire is indelibly stamped on Greece's culinary subconscious, and though many people claim the basis of present-day Greek cuisine is wholly influenced by the Turks and the influx of refugees from Asia Minor in 1922, this is only partly true on the mainland and on the larger islands like Crete and Rhodes: "In the traditional cooking methods of the smaller islands of the Aegean and areas like the Máni not subjected to Turkish rule, there is a cuisine more directly linked to an ancient past." Individual chapters focus on specific islands; fishing in the Aegean; mountains, lakes, and plains; and Athens. (I love the full-page photo of Brettos, one of the few remaining ouzo and liqueur distilleries, in Plaka—see *Good Things, Special Places* for more details.) Though I have made some of the recipes, to me the real value of this book is the related text. As it is one of a kind, this volume is worth a search.

Of Related Interest

Cheese Primer, Steven Jenkins, Workman Publishing, 1996. Jenkins—the first American to be awarded France's Chevalier du Taste-Fromage—created and/or revitalized the cheese counters at such New York food emporiums as Dean and DeLuca and Fairway. In addition to presenting the cheeses of thirteen other regions of the world, he explains how cheese is made, the basics of butterfat, and the seasons that are best for making and eating cheese. (Yes, most cheeses have a season, which is determined by pasturage—vegetation that cows, goats, and sheep have been eating at the time of milking.) For travelers, Jenkins provides the names of cheeses—many never exported—to try. This is the most comprehensive book on cheese I've ever seen. Only eight pages are devoted to the cheeses of the Balkan countries, but the information on Greek cheese is more than you'll find just about anywhere else.

The Joy of Coffee: The Essential Guide to Buying, Brewing, and Enjoying, Corby Kummer, Chapters Publishing (Houghton Mifflin), 1995. A comment I hear often from people who visit France, Spain, and Italy is that the coffee is so much better there. In my opinion it's not the coffee that's better but the quality of the dairy products added. Coffee, after all, doesn't grow in the Mediterranean, and roasters and vendors can buy excellent beans as easily as anybody else around the world. Though this book is devoted almost exclusively to types of coffee not readily available in Greece (except at Italian *caffès*), Kummer does cover Greek (or Turkish) coffee in one chapter. There are other coffee books on the shelves, but I find this to be the best volume on coffee ever published. Kummer, a well-known food journalist and the author of *The Pleasures of Slow Food,* covers coffee plantations, cupping, roasting, grinding, storing (the best place, if you drink it every day, is not in the freezer, as many people mistakenly believe), and brewing, plus separate chapters on espresso, caffeine versus decaf, and a country-by-country guide. There are also recipes for baked goods that pair particularly well with coffee. (I've made almost all of them and can vouch that they are especially yummy.)

Refreshingly, Greece is not a nation obsessed with culinary stars and celebrity chefs. As Andy Harris notes in *A Taste of the Aegean,* "There is no battle between rival chefs fighting the Michelin star wars with guileful adaptations of old recipes, but there are plenty of cooks who continue to make dishes in exactly the same way as their ancestors." In fact, there are only two Michelin-starred chefs in the entire country. Vilma Liacouras Chantiles notes in *The Food of Greece* that "Experience leads me to believe that, with few exceptions, the finest food in Athens is prepared and served in private homes." As a result, few dining-out guides are available, either in Greece or abroad. Your best bet is to consult the guidebook(s) you trust, read the articles in this section, and keep up with travel periodicals—many of the Greek food authorities featured here are also cookbook authors and contribute pieces about Greek restaurants to travel magazines and newspapers. A word about guides that rate eating establishments in general: understand that they are all subjective, and that one should not be a slave to them. Ed Behr, in an interesting article about Italy in his fall 1999 newsletter *The Art of Eating,* noted that the two most influential food guidebooks in Italy are *Espresso* and *Gambero Rosso Ristoranti d'Italia,* while the Michelin Guide is most effective at filling tables at establishments awarded the most stars. The Slow Food guides are also used by those looking for more traditional places, but Behr found that the Italian guides are widely seen as corrupt, whereas Michelin is seen as having too obvious a French bias. Wine and food industry friends of Behr told him they rarely or never follow the guidebooks because they don't agree with them; rather, they follow leads from people whose palates they trust. "There's no perfect way," Behr concluded, and I couldn't agree more. I typically follow the opinions of rather picky critics with exacting standards—I am not a fan of the popular single-city Zagat survey guides, for example, because they are compiled not by critics but by the general restaurant-going population, the majority of whom do not cook, read cookbooks, or travel and wouldn't know an authentic Greek dish if it hit them on the head. Behr has written that Zagat "has all the defects of democracy," and William Grimes, restaurant critic of *The New York Times,* has written about "the self-levitating phenomenon that I think of as the Zagat Effect, in which a restaurant, once it has achieved a top rating, continues to do so year after year, regardless of the quality of the food. Diners flock to it, Zagat guide in hand (either literally or metaphorically) and, convinced that they are eating at a top-flight establishment, cannot bring themselves to believe otherwise." Once I have determined that I trust a food or wine writer, I will happily follow his or her leads, knowing that I will always eat and drink well, occasionally fabulously. It's true that places that appear repeatedly in numerous guides may sometimes slip in quality; but if you set out with an optimistic, not-too-beholden attitude, I think you'll agree with these critics' opinions and have some very excellent meals indeed (and hopefully discover some good places on your own that I hope you'll share with me!).

About Wine in General

Great Wine Made Simple: Straight Talk From a Master Sommelier, Andrea Immer, Broadway Books, 2000. In 1997 Immer, one of only nine women in the world to qualify as a master sommelier, was named Best Sommelier in America. Though no Greek wines are included in this edition, it's a good volume for wine novices and mavens alike. A great companion volume is Immer's *Great Tastes Made Simple* (Broadway Books, 2002). In this book she concentrates on matching food and wine and provides recipes and explanations for why certain wines pair so well with certain types of food. Chapters cover peak-fresh food, earthy flavors, smoky and meaty, acidic accents, sweet, spicy, and hot, cheese, desserts, and classic matches. She also provides some mail-order sources if you have trouble finding some of the specialty food items she recommends, and if you would like to receive her monthly *Great Tastes* newsletter, join her Buying Guide tasting panel, or share your food and wine experiences, log onto her website, www.greatwinemadesimple.com. Most important, Immer reminds us in her introduction that "Good food, plain or fancy, can be a died-and-gone-to-heaven experience," and she asks, "Can wine make food even better? It stands to reason, because we know that the Europeans, justly famous for their eating and drinking lifestyle, have been enjoying wine with their meals—daily, not just on special occasions—for millennia. And we're talking lunch *and* dinner. I think every food lover and wine drinker yearns for a shot at those frequent flavor and pleasure possibilities. I also think that most of us feel stymied by one or more of these obvious hurdles: wine confusion, cost concerns, and, most frustrating of all, the rules." Immer rightly points out that drinking wine with meals represents a conscious choice on the part of the diner to spend more than he or she would on an alternative beverage, such as beer, milk, soda, iced tea, water, whatever. And though many diners (myself included) have decided that the extra expense is worth it, "still, the cost consideration is a real incentive for anyone to want to increase his or her odds of pairing success, and I've found that is true regardless of budget. Working in luxury hotels and restaurants, I've waited on my share of moneyed moguls, tycoons, and trust-fund types. They want good deals, too, *especially* if they're trying something new to them, as is so often the case with wine. It's universal: everyone wants to feel he or she is getting his or her money's worth." Which is where Immer's *Wine Buying Guide for*

Everyone (Broadway, 2004) comes in. For this refreshingly honest little guide (it's approximately the same shape as the Zagat guides), Immer surveyed wine professionals and ordinary consumers to identify the most popular and available wines on the market. The result is a compilation of more than four hundred top wines that are available around the country in stores and restaurants. No vintage bottles are listed; these are current, ready-to-drink wines. An Immer insight: "Ninety-five percent of the quality wines on the market are meant to be consumed within one to three years of the harvest (the vintage date on the label), while they are young, fresh, and in good condition. Most wines do not get better with age, so why wait?" I didn't see a copy of this until this manuscript was due, and in my quick read I did not see any Greek wines recommended (must let Immer know!) but it is still an excellent book to consult. I am an especially big fan of Immer's observation that American wine publications lack "someone with a little authoritative perspective validating the average person's taste and budget." It seems to me that American vintners have collectively decided to ignore the concept of everyday wine and concentrate instead on wines that begin to be priced at $15 to $20 a bottle. They clearly don't understand (or don't care to) that in order to create a nation of wine drinkers, the industry must continually raise new generations of wine drinkers. I mean no disrespect to American vintners, in any particular state; but this is an important concept to touch upon and is essential to understanding much of the culture in Greece and elsewhere. Creating pricey boutique wines is an exciting, creative challenge for vintners, but in wine-drinking countries, consumers drink wine every day, at least with one meal and more often with two. Wines, therefore, must be priced accordingly. Readers who have visited Greece (or Italy, France, Spain, or Portugal) may have noticed that the vast majority of wines available for sale—whether at a supermarket or a small specialty shop—are priced under $10, many under $5. At bars, a glass of wine is priced between $1 to $4 dollars, and even at many restaurants a good bottle of wine costs only about $10. People who live amid vineyards simply take a plastic jug to a vintner and have it filled with the local red or white. When my brother and sister-in-law visited Provence, they enjoyed a red wine one evening at an inn where they were staying; when they asked about it, the *patron* told them it was from the vineyard down the road, so the next day they set out to buy a few bottles. The price? Three bucks a bottle. To this day, they maintain it was among the best table wines they've ever had. While it's possible to find a few American wines under $10 a bottle, I personally have found them undrinkable. (They give me a headache before I've finished one glass.) Dear readers, if you have found a favorite everyday American wine under $10, please write and let me know about it;

and if, like me, you haven't, be vocal and let the vintners of our nation know that we will support their efforts in making quality, inexpensive wines we can drink every day. Finally, read Immer's book for some great affordable wine recommendations!

Jancis Robinson's Wine Course, BBC Books, London, 1995. This is the book that really, truly helped me to understand wine.

The Oxford Companion to Wine, edited by Jancis Robinson, A. Dinsmoor Webb, and Richard E. Smart, Getty Center for Education in the Arts, 1999. About a dozen pages in this essential volume are devoted to Greece.

Pairing Wine and Food: A Handbook for All Cuisines, Linda Johnson-Bell, Burford Books, 1999. Though other wine books touch upon food pairing, I have found this rather little-known paperback to be the best guide. I'm a big fan of Immer's *Great Wine Made Simple* (above), which includes a wealth of recipes; but when I need some food-pairing inspiration, I most often turn to this volume.

The Pleasures of Wine, Gerald Asher, Chronicle Books, 2002. Asher, who has been wine editor at *Gourmet* for more than thirty years, writes warmly and wonderfully about wine (as he does in "Wine of the Gods" on page 427) and leaves readers with the notion that wine is much more than a beverage. As he notes in the introduction to this splendid collection, "Wine, the thread that binds these essays together, is actually a prism. Through it we see the world—and ourselves—in a different light. If we pay attention, it gives us the measure of Spain's economy and tells us where the money that allowed Chile's first families to establish their prestigious nineteenth-century wine estates around Santiago came from. Just by tasting the wines we can grasp the difference between classical, rank-conscious Bordeaux and voluptuous, democratic Burgundy. We can read California history in the evolution of its wines, and take the pulse of the organic farming movement by noticing how grape growing is changing." I love this book, as well as Asher's anthology (below), simply for itself—I enjoy reading about wine, even if the wine being featured is one I've never even sipped. But I especially love this for the nuggets of wisdom Asher sprinkles throughout, wisdom that emphasizes his enthusiasm for life and the people and things in it. He reminds us that novelist Iris Murdoch once said that the purpose of wine is to stimulate the flow of talk. "She urged against fine wine in favor of an indefinite supply of something cheaper. I take her point—the spirit of hospitality is better served by a pint of Beaujolais than an ounce of some rarity. But she may have missed an equally important truth: Within reason, the better the wine—and the food—the better the conversation." He concludes with a recollection of a scene from *Zorba the Greek* (one of my most favorite books, and a good movie too): "Zorba and the narrator

are sitting on a beach late at night—drinking wine, talking, and warming themselves by a brazier on which they're roasting chestnuts. The narrator is marveling at how uncomplicated happiness really is. A glass of wine, he thinks to
himself, the warmth of the coals, the sound of the sea. That's all. But enough
to make a man happy, if his heart is simple enough to recognize what he has
and to seize it."

Vineyard Tales: Reflections on Wine, Gerald Asher, Chronicle Books, 1996. The
first essay in this anthology features malmsey, the ancient Cretan wine "that
had made Venice rich and England happy."

The Wine Bible, Karen MacNeil, Workman Publishing, 2001. Though I think it
is by now obvious, I love books that have "bible" in the title, so I was eager for
this book's publication. Author MacNeil is director of the wine program at the
Culinary Institute of America in Napa Valley, California, and has written
about wine for a number of periodicals, including *The New York Times, Food
& Wine, Saveur,* and *Wine Spectator.* This accomplishment may indeed represent, as vintner Robert Mondavi attests, "the most complete wine book
ever." In addition to devoting nineteen pages to Greek wines (including contact information for visiting some wineries), MacNeil covers the rest of the
wine-growing world and also provides individual glossaries of wine terms for
Greece, Spain, France, Italy, Portugal, Germany, Austria, and Hungary; the
1855 classification of Bordeaux chart; and a thorough bibliography. This is an
outstanding book, profusely illustrated, and packed with history, recommended labels, and even some tips for visitors.

Wine People, Stephen Brook, Vendome Press, 2001. I saw this lovely book one
day while I was browsing at one of my most favorite bookstores, Rizzoli, on
Fifty-seventh Street in Manhattan. I was surprised that I had not previously
heard of it and was immediately smitten by its premise: a collection of forty
portraits of individuals involved in all aspects of wine production and consumption. The profiles are not limited to proprietors and producers but also
include merchants and traders, writers, a collector, an auctioneer, and a sommelier. Brook is a contributing editor for *Decanter* and is the author of a number of other wine books. He reminds us that "Wine is more than a business; it
is a culture that binds together the aristocrat and the peasant, the producer
wedded to his soil and the sharp-eyed city merchant, the cautious grower and
the extravagant consumer. It is a major source of conviviality. A raised glass
can bring down, if only temporarily, national boundaries. Wine unites continuity and flux. It remains essentially the same product enjoyed on the slopes of
the Caucasus mountains and around the Mediterranean shores four thousand
years ago and yet it is constantly evolving, steadily improving in overall quality and gradually shifting in style to meet the supposed tastes and expectations
of consumers. That is what makes wine so fascinating a subject." Brook has

aimed for diversity in this collection, though he admits that it proved impossible to include individuals from every single wine-growing region of the world. Representatives from Chile, South Africa, and Argentina are absent not because of some implied judgment on the quality of wines from those regions, Brook explains, but because the central focus of the book remains European, rightly so, he feels. Though there are no wine profiles from Greece. While this is a worthy read for wine enthusiasts, it would also make a superb gift—with bottles of wine from the producers mentioned—for a major birthday, wedding, or any major cause for celebration.

The World Atlas of Wine, Hugh Johnson and Jancis Robinson, Mitchell Beazley, London, 2001. When this book was published, I bought it as a birthday gift for my brother-in-law, Gordon. It wasn't long after, however, that I wished I'd bought a copy for myself, as it is truly an absolute must-have volume. The previous four editions were authored only by Johnson and were amazingly authoritative and excellent. But the addition of Robinson gives readers a dream team of brilliant wine writers, and the book is now nothing less than astonishing. Only two pages are devoted to Greece, and the authors note that "Of all the wine-producing countries that have been radically transformed since the last edition of this Atlas (and there are many), it is perhaps Greece that is the most exciting. Modern Greek wine's reputation is built not on imported international grapes—although these are certainly grown—but on indigenous grapes which may well be able to trace their lineage back to Ancient Greece, the cradle of modern wine culture as we know it." I believe that even readers who are not interested in wine but love maps and geography will find this an engrossing volume. (After a few months I could hold out no longer and finally bought a copy for myself. I have since pored over it, getting lost in it again and again, and I think you will too.)

Greek Wines and Spirits

Greek Wines: A Comprehensive Guide, Geoff Adams, Winemaster Publishing, 2002. A confession: I do not own this book and I have never seen it. I mention it here, however, because Greek cookbook author and food writer Aglaia Kremezi recommended it to me. I asked her if she knew of a good book on Greek wines, since I was unable to find one anywhere, and this is the (only) title she suggested. It's published in the United Kingdom, so it may be a little difficult to find here in North America, though specialty bookstores, such as Kitchen Arts and Letters, may have one in stock or may be able to obtain a copy. This volume was recently published, so it is probably a good read for anyone wanting a single volume devoted to the fruit of the vine in Greece.

The 130 Best Greek Wines (Only the Best), Axon Publications, 2002. Like Geoff Adams's book, this one is published in the U.K. and may not be readily available. I tend to steer clear of books with titles like this one, as I am not interested in the "hit parade" of anything, be it wine, hotels, restaurants, whatever. But as there are virtually no volumes (yet) to be found on Greek wines, this one might be worth perusing for some (hopefully) worthy recommendations.

Other Greek Wine Resources

~Athenee Importers is America's largest and oldest firm devoted to importing and distributing Greek wines. The company was founded in 1975 by Tony and Giota Englisis; following Tony's unfortunate death in 1999, Andrea, the couple's daughter, now comanages the business. Athenee may now be the only wine-importing company in America that is owned and managed by two women. It prides itself on representing producers who are at the forefront of the Greek wine revolution. If you're having trouble finding Greek wines where you live, contact Athenee: P.O. Box 2039, Hempstead NY 11551; 516-505-4800; fax: -4876; www.atheneeimporters.com.

~eRobertParker.com is the website of wine guru Robert Parker, and as one might expect, the·site is excellent. Though anyone may log onto the site and generally browse around, the site is actually a subscription service; but I think subscribers will tell you that for wine nuts, it is well worth the money ($99 a year). The *Wine Advocate* today has approximately 40,000 subscribers in about thirty-eight countries, and impressively, it is also translated in French. On March 29, 1999, President Jacques Chirac bestowed upon Parker the honor of Chevalier dans l'Ordre de la Legion d'Honneur. There are a number of Greek wines in the site's database (again, you need to join to search for them). The folks at Greekwinemakers.com learned that the site's chief programmer is Jim Vradelis, a wine-loving Greek American!

~*Food & Wine* (June 2003) included an article about Greek wines by Richard Nalley that included his picks for the top ten bottles, which were: 2001 Antonopoulos Adoli Ghis; 2001 Chateau Carras Malagouzia; 2002 Gai'a Notios; 2001 Domaine Spiropoulos Meliasto; 2000 Estate Averoff Ktima Averoff; 2000 Karydas Naoussa; 1999 Papaïoannou Estate Nemea; 2000 Tsantali Xinomavro; 1999 Cooperative of Samos Nectar; and 1997 Boutari Grande Reserve Naoussa. I've tried only three (and can report they were great), and Athenee imports five. Nalley noted that many producers are using indigenous Greek grapes, such as Naoussa's *xinomavro* and Nemea's *agiorgitiko,* both red; native white varieties include *malagouzia* and *assyrtiko.* Nalley added that the new generation of internationally trained Greek winemakers is "turning out some truly gorgeous wines. Their top offerings aren't cheap, but their prices haven't yet caught up with their remarkable achievements."

~Greekwinemakers.com (www.greekwinemakers.com) is a Web-based consultancy designed to "help fill the void created by the absence of a generic export promotions program for the Greek wine industry." The organization connects Greek producers with consumers, the wine trade, and the wine media, but of most importance to you and me, it's a comprehensive source of information about Greek wine. The site has profiles of Greek winemakers; information about wine history, regions, appellations, and unique grape varieties; forums; photographs; a wine locator database; and a wine reviews section, where amateurs and professionals alike can share descriptions of wines they've tasted. The site's editor, Nick Cobb, recently shared the story of a reader who reports on his experiences as a consumer in America's heartland from time to time. This particular reader's retail adventures indicate to Nick that Greek wines have a long way to go in the States, and he posted a plea to the site's browsers: "On behalf of Greece's winemakers, I ask one thing of you. If you can't find Greek wine at your local store, ask the manager why not. If the manager tells you, 'I really don't know much about Greek wine,' you can send them to greekwinemakers.com. If the response is, 'There is no market for it,' please send me a phone number or e-mail address. I'll take it from there."

~Nestor Imports is another leading importer dedicated to Greek wines and spirits. Aristides and Kathy Spiliotopoulos founded the company in 1984, and over the years, according to Greekwinemakers.com, Kathy in particular has been "indefatigable in her efforts to organize support for Greek wine and cuisine in America." Contact Nestor for information on retailers and distributors that carry its brands: Nestor Imports, 225 Broadway, Suite 2911, New York NY 10007; 800-775-8857 or 212-267-1133; fax: -2233; www.nestorimports.com.

~Vina Mediterranean, founded by Sotiris Bafitis, is another importer of quality Greek wines. Bafitis's story is also a rather unusual one: he landed in the States in 1986 and began working as a waiter in Washington, D.C., at restaurants where the wine was taken as seriously as the food. Bafitis then gravitated to wine retail and realized that quality Greek wine suffered from poor exposure in the U.S. market. During this time he had a chance encounter with Pierre Rovani, who was then working at a local liquor store and is now a co-reviewer for Robert Parker's *Wine Advocate*. Rovani apparently did not have a good word to say, then, about Greek wines, but Bafitis was determined to prove him wrong. It wasn't easy, but as Greekwinemakers.com reported, "Today Rovani is one of a handful of elite reviewers in the field who devote energy to Greek wine." In 1999 Bafitis put together a plan and financial backing to begin Vina Mediterranean. Stelios Boutaris, marketing director of Naoussa's prestigious Kir-Yianni estate, was the first to agree to give Bafitis a try. Boutaris stated that "It was a huge leap of faith to commit to an importer who had no track record," but added that "It is very important to us to have access to mainstream outlets as well as the Greek American market—maybe more important." Bafitis, at this writing, now represents eleven producers and distributes in at least ten states. Contact information: Vina Mediterranean, 6243-B Fallard Drive, Upper Marlboro MD 20772; 301-599-8380; fax: -8382; www.vinamediterranean.com.

Good Things,
Favorite Places

"You sit, like so many before and so many will do after you, quite still and silent over your drink, watching the dusk fall, veil on magical veil, over the blue gulf which itself will soon be turned to lead and then to silver under the visiting moon. You will have heard stories by now of people who came for an afternoon and stayed for a lifetime, or who came for a week and stayed a century and a half; and you realize the danger of your position. . . . 'Yes,' you find yourself saying, 'I will stay one more day, just one more. . . .'"
—Lawrence Durrell, THE GREEK ISLANDS

ΕΒΡΑΤΚΟ ΜΟΥΣΕΙΟ ΕΛΛΑΔΟΣ · THE JEWISH MUSEUM OF GREECE ·

ΠΡΟΔΡΟΜΟΣ ΗΝΩΜΕΝΩΝ ΕΘΝΩΝ

ΔΕΛΦΟΙ ΑΜΦΙΚΤΙΟΝΙΕΣ

90
ΕΛΛΗΝΙΚΗ ΔΗΜΟΚΡΑΤΙΑ

ΗΕLLAS

ATHENS
BENAKI
MUSEUM
ΑΘΗΝΑ
ΜΟΥΣΕΙΟ
ΜΠΕΝΑΚΗ

Drawn by Wolfensberger.

Engraved by S. Fisher.

Napoli di Romania, Greece (Nauplia 1700)

MUSEUM
OF CYCLADIC
ART

K A T I K I E S

Weavers of Crete
Preserve an Old Art

BY CARYL STERN

～

editor's note

The art of embroidery is not unique to Crete, but it has flourished here as nowhere else in Greece. Like weavings elsewhere, it began not as an art but as a necessity, gracing clothing, towels, bedcovers, cushions, and other household items. But the colors and designs are exuberant, fanciful, and bright, making old and new items popular with visitors and collectors. I found three woolen tote bags on Crete that I had made into pillows—I knew that, over time, if I used the bags for their original purpose, they would be difficult to clean and that I would probably stuff too many things in them and rip the braided handles. So I simply collected old socks and T-shirts for stuffing, asked a local tailor to sew up the open side, and *opa!* I had a collection of unique pillows. If you, unlike me, are talented in the arts of needlepoint or cross-stitch, you may want to try and duplicate some Cretan (and other Greek) patterns. A magazine that is now defunct, *Sphere,* originally based in Santa Barbara, California, devoted its April 1978 issue to Greece and featured four pages of design motifs and instructions (for the Cretan stitch, Cretan feather stitch, cross-stitch, block shading, stem stitch, and chain stitch), and they appear to be relatively easy to accomplish, even for me.

CARYL STERN is a New York-based actress and writer. She contributed this piece to the travel section of *The New York Times* in November 1983.

In the Cretan village of Daratso, past an arbor heavy with clusters of purple grapes, lies the courtyard of Veta Chatziagelaki, filled with flowers and bright sunshine and summer silence. A stranger can choose between intruding upon the silence with a shout and turning tail for the short drive back to Chania, the island's cultural capital. If you are serious about your mission, you shout.

Veta Chatziagelaki is a weaver. She is a wife and mother as well, a black-haired, bright-eyed woman who takes a hand in running the family farm while keeping the children in line. But at least four hours of each day she spends bent over her room-sized, hand-operated loom, making fine cotton tablecloths and curtains. The designs she uses are traditional, handed down from one generation to the next, for weaving is an ancient skill among the women of Crete. Most of her customers are local people, but she welcomes travelers too.

If you want to bring home some samples of world-famous Cretan weavings, you can haunt tourist shops in the big cities, though the prices are often high, and machine-made goods lurk on every corner. But there are ways to increase the odds on getting reasonably priced goods and to build some adventure into the process. There are experts to consult, clues to look for—and workshops off the beaten path to explore.

Cretan handwoven textiles come in two basic varieties. So-called "fine" weaving, like that produced by Chatziagelaki, is made with thin threads of cotton or silk tightly woven; it is a slow, painstaking process. Among the best products for a traveler are decorative pieces known as towels, which are used in Greek homes as table runners or are draped over a chair or couch. The other kind of weaving, known as carpet weaving, is generally made with heavier yarns and ranges from rugs to wall hangings and pillow covers.

Weaving has long been part of the nation's life—Greeks of the Classical era thought any covering other than wool was less than respectable. Yet the twentieth century has seen something of a decline in this and other types of traditional handicrafts. The government in Athens has been trying to reverse the trend—setting up schools, encouraging weavers to form cooperatives for the marketing of their products. The program enables women to earn money on their own and achieve greater independence; it is also aimed at slowing down the movement of rural women toward the big cities.

For centuries the Venetians and the Turks took turns ruling Chania, and they left their architectural marks on this charming port. Venice raised a mighty city wall and ramparts, and the Ottomans put up the mosque that is a focal point of the harbor promenade.

A search for weavings in Chania might well start in the mosque, which is shared today by the national tourist organization and a branch office of HOMMEH, an acronym in Greek for the Hellenic Organization of Small and Medium-Sized Industries and Handicrafts, a government unit. The staff has filled its space with a display of handicrafts by local artisans, including weavers. Similar facilities exist in the cities of Rethymnon and Iráklion, the Cretan capital, and there's a HOMMEH showroom in Athens at 9 Mitropoleos Street, near Syntagma Square.

If you see a sample you like—the prices are indicated—the staff will give you a card identifying its source, either a store or a private workshop. If you see a type of weaving that appeals, they will give you a list of approved weavers in the area who produce it. And they can also offer advice about other sources of woven goods—monasteries, for example, or special exhibits, or the handful of Cretan villages whose main streets each morning turn into a rainbow of wall-to-wall weavings hung up for sale.

The HOMMEH staff cannot guarantee the quality of a particular rug or curtain, but if you place an order with one of the weavers on their list and leave a record of the transaction with the local staff, they will act as intermediary in case there is a delay in delivery. HOMMEH also vouches for the skill and integrity of the women they recommend, and that's worth a lot if you're not sure about your ability to distinguish good weaving from bad, or wool from acrylic. You're on your own, however, when it comes to price.

In the Double Ax, a tiny store at 67 Potie Street, a sign firmly announces: "Fixed Prices." Bargaining is a hallmark of Greek shopping, and a bold visitor can expect to whittle a price down by at least 10 percent, often more. That's not true, though, at many of the stores and workshops approved by HOMMEH. Agapé, the clerk at the Double Ax, shakes her head angrily as a local Greek woman leaves the store having tried, unsuccessfully, to bargain. Of all people, Agapé says in her limited English, a woman from Chania should understand how much work goes into the weaving. Still, the prices demanded by the weavers who supply the store are remarkably low by American standards. A handwoven cotton dress with vibrantly colored embroidered bodice, for example, is in the $50 range; similar blouses are around $30. If you see Cretan dresses and blouses in tourist shops for $8 or $9, you can be pretty sure they are factory made.

Down near the harbor, at 61 Zampeliou Street, is a shop called Roka, and Veatriki Manousakis's loom sits just inside the entrance. She spends most of her day seated there, working, chatting with neighbors. The interior of the store is cool, quiet, spacious, and during the summer months, presided over by a vivacious London schoolteacher, Susan Mitchell. Rugs, pillow covers, and wall hangings are the specialties, and many of the designs are geometric and traditional, with strongly contrasting colors. (She generally uses natural dyes, no longer the rule in modern Crete.) Reversible wool rugs in red and black, reminiscent of American Indian work, four feet by two and a half feet, range in price from $20 to $35. There is also a wide variety of rugs and loop rugs.

While you shop in the store that her son set up for her five years ago, Manousakis will provide an accompaniment on the loom: the squeak of wood on wood, the pause as the shuttle is tossed from one side to the other, then the double crash signaling that another thread has been added to the fabric—more inventory in the making.

You can get a closer glimpse of the Greek way of life by tracking down one or two of the workshops recommended by HOM-MEH. At Veta Chatziagelaki's home in Daratso, for example, you may arrive as she's returning from picking figs along the road and be offered some of the luscious fruit along with a glass of cool water. Most of the weavers speak little English, so it's wise to have a few Greek phrases ready and to bring along a Greek-English dictionary, though sign language and good will certainly help.

At 32 Ipirou Street, several blocks beyond the shopping center, Arayroula Kavroulaki produces some of Chania's most elegant curtains and "towels." Finding your way to her door can be an adventure—the Greek alphabet is used for street signs in Greece, so it's best to have addresses written down in Greek in case you need to ask for help along the way. But eventually, at the end of a narrow, dusty, down-at-the-heels road, you'll spot the modern house at No. 32.

Kavroulaki will show you her huge loom on the second floor and demonstrate how she works on a seven-foot-wide fabric, moving back and forth across the seat of the loom. In the first-floor parlor, hung with her intricate creations, she has a homemade catalog filled with color photos. A curtain, big enough to cover a bed, with a rich, many-colored garland of flowers, may cost $350. Smaller, less intricate items are proportionately less expensive. A small tablecloth, for example, in tan and white with matching napkins, costs about $40.

Because weaving is so much a part of traditional life in Crete, it can be found wherever you turn. HOMMEH, the workshop weavers, or the tourist office can guide you to special exhibits, schools, or convents where local weavings are for sale. At the Holy Convent of St. John, for example, a few miles outside Chania, there is a small selection of tablecloths and inexpensive aprons made by the sisters. Assuming that you are properly dressed (men are expected to wear slacks; slacks are forbidden for women), you can visit until 8 P.M. in winter and all day in summer except between 1:30 and 4:30. The byways and low white buildings of the convent are set in a lush landscape of orange trees and flowering plants; the scent of jasmine prevails.

The town of Kritsa is set on a hillside a few twisting miles from the port town of Ágios Nikólaos. Once safely arrived, leave your car in the parking lot at the foot of the town—there is no room for it in the center.

Rugs and tablecloths hang in front of the dozens of shops along Kritsa's main street; looms are part of the furniture. Maria E. Tavla, the cheerful, round-faced proprietor of one of the stores, admitted to having worked the loom for forty-six of her fifty-eight years. Her rule of thumb for shoppers: "Little design, little price; big design, big price." The hundreds of rugs and bolts of hand-woven fabric in her shop, she said, are produced by twenty local women who work in their own homes.

Across the island, up another winding mountain road, sits another town of weavers. Anogia too has attracted tourists with its street of shops hung with multicolored fabrics. In fact, some charge that tourism has spoiled the place, lowering the level of craftsmanship, ruining the old ways of life. Yet shepherds in high leather boots still stride past steps where women draw thread from their hand-held spindles. Young women still sit by the front windows, weaving the linens that will make up their dowries.

Outside one of the shops, Anastasios Nikólaos Xilouris, a shepherd of great dignity sits in the sun, watching the passing parade; in the doorway, his wife Ourania urges a visitor to enter. "*Ela. Ela,*" she calls softly, musically. "Come in. Come in." You can hear those words at weaving workshops and stores all over Crete. It is not so much a summons as an invitation.

Good Things, Favorite Places

Granted, it's quite personal, but this is my list—in no particular order, and subject to change on any day of the week—of some favorite things to see, do, and buy in southern Greece. I am mindful that singling out "bests" and "favorites" inevitably means that something I very much like will be forgotten. Which is why I emphasize that this is by no means a definitive list; rather, these are some wonderful things that I am happy to share with you here in the hope that you might also enjoy them, and that you will reciprocate by sharing your discoveries with me.

A word about shopping: I am not much into acquiring things, so as a general rule shopping is not one of my favorite pastimes; but I do enjoy buying gifts for other people, especially when I'm traveling. To borrow a quote from a great little book called *The Fearless Shopper: How to Get the Best Deals on the Planet* (by Kathy Borrus, Travelers Tales, 2000), shopping is "about exploring culture and preserving memory—the sights, sounds, smells, tastes, tempo, and touch of a place." Most of what I purchase, therefore—even for myself—falls into the culinary category, because for me, food and drink are inextricably linked to a place. Food and drink can be extended, of course, to tabletop items such as pottery, for which I have a particular weakness. Though a beautifully set table can never mask inferior ingredients or carelessly prepared food, to me a delicious meal is even better when it is served in vessels, on dishes, and with utensils unique to its origins. Every time I open the little glass jar of sun-dried cherry tomatoes from Santorini, a bottle of Greek olive oil, or the container of *masticha* in my pantry, I am instantly transported back to the shops where I bought them, and I remember as if it were yesterday all the delicious meals I had in Greece; each time I serve olives in two small, deep blue ceramic bowls, I think of the island of Sífnos, where I bought them; and when I set my table with the unique terracotta vases and candleholders I bought on Cyprus, there is no doubt that, for an evening, my family and friends and I are all in the Aegean islands. To quote again from Kathy Borrus, "I am surrounded—not by things but history and culture and memory." Even the simplest neighborhood shops in Greece sell beautifully packaged items of yummy stuff that in North America is either hard to find or expensive, or both.

A word about stores: business hours being what they are in Greece, you might want to adopt my motto "When in doubt, buy it now." I learned years ago that the likelihood of my being able to retrace my steps back to a particular merchant *when it was open* was slim. If you spy a delicious treat or savory in the window of a bakery or at an open-air market, or some jewelry, a painting, a bottle of ouzo in the shape of a bouzouki, or a Greek vase, or *anything* that has your name all over it, stop then and there and get it—one has regrets in life only for the roads not taken, or in this case the objects not purchased!

In North America
Before you arrive in Greece, there are a few good things you should know about:

~Matt Barrett's website, www.greecetravel.com. I don't know Matt, but I wish I did, and hope to one day meet him. He epitomizes the kind of traveler I hope every *Collected Traveler* reader is or will be, someone who is completely infatuated with a place (in his case, Greece) and wants to learn everything about it, and becomes consumed by it, and travels there as often as he or she can. Matt's infatuation led him to create and maintain one of the very few outstanding travel-related websites I've ever seen. You simply cannot set your first or your tenth foot in Greece without browsing Matt's site. It is uncommonly helpful, illuminating, interesting (just try and log off in less than thirty minutes), fun, and authoritative. Very few guidebook writers know Greece as well as or better than Matt. If it wouldn't have turned this book into an encyclopedia, I would have asked Matt for permission to devote a section to the entire contents of his website. 'Nuff said. Log on and go wild.

~Total yogurt. If you don't try Total until you return from Greece, it won't be the end of the world, but if you can find it at a local supermarket or specialty shop before you leave, that would be better. As you know by now, Greek yogurt is the best in the world, and Total, a Greek brand recently introduced in North America, is the closest type you'll find to it. I won't fool you—Total is *not* as good as yogurt in Greece, but it's close, and it's the only brand I've ever tried, including organic, that doesn't leave an unpleasant aftertaste in my mouth. Total, produced by Fage, the largest Greek dairy company, is available in whole milk and zero percent milk varieties and is also available with honey in a two-part package. (This last was included on *Saveur*'s 2002 list of top one hundred food finds.) To find out where you can purchase Total, contact Fage USA at 718-204-5323; fax: -1842; www.fage.gr.

~*The Rape of Europa,* a painting by Titian, at the Isabella Stewart Gardner Museum, Boston. Though there are other paintings with Greek mythological themes in other museums in North

America, this Titian masterpiece is easily my favorite, and I'm not the only one who admires it: Thomas Hoving, in *Greatest Works of Art of Western Civilization,* admitted that "If I were to select the single most exciting painting in the West, I might choose Titian's 'Rape of Europa.' Painted for Philip II, King of Spain, the grandiose picture illustrates the legend of Jupiter appearing in the guise of a white bull to seize and make love to Europa. It is both a pagan celebration and a morality play painted with the richest colors, lines, and glazes ever applied to canvas." In *Eye of the Beholder: Masterpieces From the Isabella Stewart Gardner Museum* (Beacon Press, 2003), the editors note that "Europa's rape will literally give rise to Europe. From her union with Jupiter, Minos will be born, and the most ancient of European civilizations on the island of Crete. Her brother Cadmus, the inventor of writing, will search for her, and found the great ancient city of Thebes. The painting records no less than the birth of civilization." There are only a dozen or so canvases that have literally made me gasp when I first saw them (Renoir's *Luncheon of the Boating Party* at the Phillips Collection, Van Gogh's *Almond Tree in Bloom* at the Norton Simon, to name a few), and this *Europa* is one of them. The Gardner Museum, by the way, has a number of Greek and Roman pieces in its superb collection, but if you live far from Boston and cannot visit it, *Eye of the Beholder,* published in celebration of the museum's one hundredth anniversary, is the next best thing.

~The north pediment, east courtyard, and east entrance of the Philadelphia Museum of Art. Readers who have visited this outstanding museum know that the building is not only famous for a scene in the film *Rocky* but for its pediment sculptures that evoke ancient Greek myths and techniques. The north pediment features Zeus in the center, and flanking him on either side are Demeter, Triptolemus, Ariadne, Theseus slaying the Minotaur, Python, Aphrodite, Eros, Hippomenes, Adonis, Nous, and Eos. The terracotta figures are glazed and painted in bright colors, the way they would have been in ancient Greece, and the whole thing—the sculptures, columns, painted detail, and symmetry—is just beautiful. And the museum is not, of course, the only North American expression of Greek architecture or ideology: think of all the buildings, public and residential, constructed in the style known as Greek Revival. Nicholas Gage, in *A Place For Us,* describes his new home in Massachusetts in 1949: "The huge gleaming granite building with a Doric portico supported by white columns, which father said was the civic auditorium, seemed to me a replica of the Parthenon. Main Street was lined with imposing white marble structures: the courthouse, churches, and office buildings, all demonstrating the influence of classical Greece on Worcester's settlers." Think, too, of all of the place names, including Philadelphia (one in Pennsylvania, another in Mississippi), Phoenix, Annapolis, Memphis, Demopolis (Alabama), Smyrna (one in Georgia, another in Tennessee), Sparta (Wisconsin), Troy (Alabama, New Hampshire, New York, and Michigan), and Ithaca (New York) to name just a few. Look around where you live and you may be surprised at how many references there are to Greece.

~Greek food festivals. In North America, we have sizable Greek communities in such large cities as Toronto, San Francisco, Chicago, Baltimore, Minneapolis, and New York as well as in dozens of smaller towns and suburbs (after all, there are, according to the Council of Hellenes Abroad, seventeen million Greeks worldwide; and according to Mark Mazower in *The Balkans,* by 1912, 250,000 Greeks emigrated to the United States, nearly ten percent of the population and the largest proportion from any European state after 1900). Community centers and Greek Orthodox churches in these communities all have annual fairs and festivals that often double as fundraisers, and they're great fun. Typically, the food doesn't rise above taverna fare, but you will often taste some outstanding samples. There may be folk dancing and singing, though no bingo—the Greek Orthodox church frowns on gambling—and a festive atmosphere prevails. In an article about Greek food festivals in southwestern Pennsylvania that appeared in the fall of 2003, a reporter noted that "The church has been the center of Greek-American cultural life, and its festival is the apex of community participation." Spending a few hours at a Greek festival is immersion of the very best kind, so keep your eyes open for one near you.

~Greek seasoning from Penzeys. "Merchants of Quality Spices" is the Penzeys motto, an affirmation with which I agree. I order all of my dried herbs and spices from Penzeys because I have found that it offers an extensive range of international herbs and spices in a variety of quantities, so that I can buy only a few ounces of Greek oregano, for example, or a much larger quantity of Indian Tellicherry peppercorns. Penzeys Greek seasoning contains salt, garlic, lemon peel, pepper, oregano, and marjoram, and it's perfect for making gyros, marinating chicken or lamb cubes (destined for the grill, broiler, or frying pan), or salad dressing, or sprinkled on a Greek salad. Penzeys operates retail stores in more than a dozen U.S. cities, but you should add your name to its mailing list because its catalog is a great resource. Contact information: Penzeys, 19300 West Janacek Court, P.O. Box 924, Brookfield WI 53008; 800-741-7787 or 262-785-7676; fax: -7678; www.penzeys.com.

Anywhere in Greece

~Retsina. Andrew Dalby, in *Siren Feasts,* informs us that "The Greek enthusiasm for retsina was not shared by medieval travellers to Greece from abroad: many modern travellers agree. Even where pine resin is not used, fresh pine wood is allowed to add its flavour to must in parts of modern Greece, as it was in medieval Attica. Retsina is now made chiefly in central and southern Greece and some of the Aegean islands; in Attica even a fizzy retsina can be found." Karen MacNeil, in *Wine Bible*, notes that "Few visitors to Greece escape without falling in love with or learning to abhor retsina, the pungent, pine-resin-flavored wine, the drinking of which is virtually a baptismal right in Greek tavernas." I fall into the first category: I genuinely like retsina and find it the perfect match with a number of Greek dishes. So saying, I'm not implying that it doesn't take a *little* getting used to—my husband insists it tastes like turpentine—but I think if you give it a fair try, you'll agree with me that it does complement many simple dishes, such as Greek salad, fried calamari, feta, olives, and phyllo casseroles. Though I have not yet conducted exhaustive research on the subject, I believe retsina is also one of the few wines, perhaps *the* only one, that is almost exclusively ordered by the bottle and not by the glass. You'll discover this yourself if you try and order a glass at a bar or taverna—retsina is so inexpensive (seriously, a lot of it costs at most the equivalent of a dollar a bottle, topping off at perhaps six dollars) that it is most often sold by the bottle. Bars charge barely more than stores do, so even if you request an entire bottle and you find you don't like it, you won't have spent much in the endeavor.

~Spending time talking with all the shopkeepers I met, in every part of Greece. In true eastern fashion, making a purchase in Greece is generally not a task done in a hurry. Even though I cherish the material objects I have bought in Greece (including a blue-and-white ceramic bowl in Sparta; a Peloponnesian weaving and a limited edition print, both purchased in Napflio; reproductions of artwork in the National Archaeological Museum; and deep-blue glazed pottery on Sífnos), it's the conversations I've had with vendors and shopkeepers that remain in my mind and mean the most to me. Especially on my most recent visit, it was actually rather remarkable how much time my friends and I spent in each store we stepped into, and not because we were necessarily looking at the wares. *Everyone* we met was genuinely interested in learning where we were from and how we were enjoying Greece, and *everyone* expressed great sympathy and solidarity regarding the September 11th tragedy. Talking with the locals in this way is of course how one also learns about great places to eat and visit. On several occasions, my friends and I showed some shopkeepers our various guidebooks and asked for their opinions on the restaurants, tavernas, and bars—it was interesting to hear what they had to say, and we were never given bad advice. Greeks everywhere want visitors to love their country as they do, and take pride in recommending the best.

~*Komboloï,* worry beads that you'll see *everywhere* in Greece. Men, mostly of older generations, never go anywhere without their *komboloï,* and it would seem they have a *lot* to worry about, as they run their fingers through the beads all day long. They are not to be confused with rosary beads, though they were originally a form of rosary.

~Wooden bread stamps. Though I am a baker, I do not bake bread. There are so many wonderful artisanal bread bakers in and around New York City that I have no incentive to learn how to do it. (The only reason I started baking desserts in the first place is that no one else did—I could never understand why someone would go to some trouble to prepare dinner, but then buy a frozen pie from the supermarket for dessert.) *Psomi* (bread) in Greece holds the same importance as it does in France. According to *World Food: Greece,* it is "not merely the staff of life, it is life, and birth, and death, and all that transpires in between. It marks the seasons and the ages. There is a bread for your name day. There is a bread for Easter. There is a bread for Christmas, for fast days, feast days, birthdays and days of remembrance. There is oven bread, pan bread, and pot bread. Wheat, barley, and corn bread. Bread in a hundred shapes. Holy bread, profane bread, sweet bread, sour bread." I like buying bread stamps for friends who *do* love to bake bread, but some of the Greek stamps are so elaborate and beautiful that I like buying them as souvenirs of a culinary item so significant to Greeks. Plus, they make great designs on cookies.

~Ouzo. In *The Greek Islands*, Lawrence Durrell aptly noted "From now on, all day long you will wander about in a delightful daze, drinking in the light. Evening will find you once more seated at your little café—you will already have adopted one—drinking ouzo." My husband fell into the most delightful pattern of drinking ouzo every evening for about four weeks, and I do mean *every* evening. Ouzo is the traditional aperitif of Greece, and like its fennel-infused cousins, *pastis* in France and raki in Turkey, it is served with a pitcher of iced or very cold water—you add the amount of water you prefer to the glass of ouzo. (The Italian fennel drink *sambuca*, by contrast, is an after-dinner drink that is drunk straight up, never mixed with water.) The great thing of it is that ouzo is very affordable, so you really can buy it every day, even at cafés and tavernas. It is a most refreshing drink on a hot day.

~Greek salad. Drs. Antonia Trichopoulou and Dimitrios Trichopoulos, in *The Mediterranean Diet Cookbook*, write that the Mediterranean Diet is "frequently, and rightly, associated in the minds of many Americans with that lively salad made from fresh vegetables, olive oil, and feta cheese, known in this country as *Greek salad*. Usually prepared with tomatoes, cucumbers, onions, and olives, the original Greek salad is different from its American variant; in the Greek version, vegetables are fresher and tastier, olive oil is much more abundant, and the serving is much larger. A Greek fresh vegetable salad can also be made from just greens, herbs, olive oil, and lemon juice; again, feta cheese, made from goat's or sheep's milk, is frequently added." The doctors underscore a truth common to all Mediterranean cuisine that is so often ignored or misunderstood in North America: the simpler the dish, the more essential it remains that the ingredients be of superb quality, and that includes herbs, spices, olive oil, and vinegar. I have eaten more Greek salads in Greece than I can possibly count, including one in late February—and even though the waiter offered his apologies for it being off season for tomatoes, it was uncommonly delicious, including the tomatoes, which were not as good as they would have been in July but were a thousand times better than any February tomato in the States. My favorite version of Greek salad has a single large slice of feta sprinkled generously with oregano placed atop the tomatoes, onions, and olives—not cut into cubes or crumbled.

~The habit that proprietors of simple tavernas in the country have of watering the outdoor "floor" (dirt) before the lunch and dinner hours begin. I mostly saw this in the Peloponnese, but I think it is common in any part of Greece that is particularly dry and dusty in the summer months. After seeing this repeatedly, I finally asked a gentleman who was quite adept with his watering hose why this was being done, and he told me it was to make the taverna seem more appealing—it is so hot and dry in Greece in the summer that when you pull a chair back to sit down at an outdoor taverna, dust often consumes your feet and is thick in the air. No one wants to eat in a dusty atmosphere, so why not water the dirt? It's all about curb appeal.

~Quince. Surely some of my readers are familiar with the quince, but I would not be surprised to learn that a good number aren't. The quince is a very popular fruit in Greece, not least because it is known as the fruit of Aphrodite, the goddess of love. Its Latin name, *Cydonia oblonga,* derives from a superior variety of quince found in Cydonia, now Chania, a city on Crete. It probably was not an apple that Eve offered Adam but a quince, as apple trees do not thrive in the arid climate of the Near East, probable location of the Garden of Eden. My introduction to the quince came when I was living for some years in California, where they grow well, and about the same time as I discovered them in a Berkeley produce market, an article about them appeared in *Gourmet* (October 1988) by the late Leon Lianides, proprietor of a beloved New York restaurant, the Coach House, that closed in 1993 after a forty-four-year run. Lianides wrote that "When I came to the United States, I soon discovered that the quince was not as well known here and that those who were familiar with it thought of it as destined only for preserves and jellies. They were unaware of the fruit's savory applications. In Greece and other Mediterranean countries the quince is as likely to be found paired with game or lamb in a stew as with sugar or honey in a dessert. Its dry, firm flesh holds up well under lengthy, slow cooking, keeping its shape long after a potato or an apple would have softened and crumbled." Lianides shared a few quince recipes in this piece, including one for a quince tart, that I have made almost every year at Thanksgiving—it's a departure from pumpkin pie but is completely in keeping with the harvest theme, as the quince is a fall fruit. It is one of my most favorite pie recipes, and though I originally wanted to reprint it here, my editor warned me that we just did not have the space; but the article can be found by searching the *Gourmet* archives online or at a library, and I encourage you to seek it out if you're interested in making the tart. (The other recipes include quince compote with calvados cream—also very yummy—and beef stew with quinces.) Additionally, *Saveur* featured a piece on quinces (September/October 1996) with other good recipes, including quinces in red wine, quinces in honey, and quince pancakes. If you just don't want to bother cooking them, quinces also have the wonderful quality of smelling delicious, and if you put them in a bowl on your kitchen counter, they will gently perfume the room for a few days in the fall.

~Goats, large herds of them, and the sound of goat bells in the distance. I have a ridiculous number of photos of goats. I just love how they stop traffic, especially on small roads on the Peloponnese, each one slowly meandering across the tarmac. There have been times when I never saw the shepherd, but often a man and his son were herding the goats. My most memorable goat occasion was on a gorgeous day in August. My husband and I were in our Talbot, and an American couple we had met a week prior, Chris and Sarah, were in their rental car. We had visited the Temple of Bassae that morning and were making our way to the eastern coast, south of Napflio. The "road" we were traversing was unpaved and filled with a number of large rocks; it was therefore slow going, and we were concerned about our well-worn tires. We reached the top of a steep hill and began our descent, only to come upon dozens and dozens of goats (I think about a hundred), which forced us to come to a complete halt. Sarah and I didn't mind stopping, as it provided us with an excellent picture-taking opportunity, but the men were a bit impatient after some time, as they had visions of the beach on their minds. Finally, after about twenty minutes, we were able to slowly move the cars down the hill, but at the bottom we came across more goats as well as their keepers: a mustachioed man and his young son, who, naturally, provided another photo op. I know that many people count sheep when they have trouble falling asleep, but I count goats, and it is always this scene that I reenact in my head when I begin counting.

~Ex-votos, devotional renderings that convey thanks for miracles, are found all over Greece, hanging outside houses, in churches, and from racks in shops. I'm particularly fond of the tin ex-votos featuring a hand, sometimes with the arm too. I'm not sure what the significance of the hand is, but it's a common design for door knockers.

~Greek costumes. I like looking at old books about Greece that include illustrations of men and women in a great number of different costumes. I was surprised, years ago, to discover there was such a diverse range of daily and festive attire. You can see outstanding examples of these sometimes-dazzling outfits in Athens at the Benaki and Jewish Museums.

~The special thematic collection of Athens 2004 Summer Olympic stamps published by the Hellenic Post. The set comes in a hardcover blue cloth folder and includes one sheet of eight stamps and a first day cover envelope. The stamps are designed by the artist A. Fassianos, who stated, "I believe that these small pieces of paper will become the Apostles of the spirit of modern Greece." The set is great for collectors but is also a wonderful souvenir for visitors— I intend to have mine framed—and it (and some other assortments) may be purchased at any Hellenic Post office.

~The Greek gesture for "follow me" or "come this way." After you become accustomed to the gestures for "no" and "yes" (and that rude one of holding up an outstretched hand, which of course you will not do), you may then notice the gesture of waving one's hand back and forth behind the body. It may look a bit funny, and in fact when it was first extended to me and my husband, we assumed it meant "Wait there," or "I'll be right back." A few seconds later we learned that it meant "Follow me." One of the most common scenes where this gesture is employed is a busy street corner or intersection, where a teacher or parent is signaling to a line of children or a single child that it's okay to cross.

~George, the Famous Taxi Driver of Greece. As I mentioned in the Taxis entry in *Practical Information,* George Kokkotos (that's him pictured on the introductory pages to this section) is no ordinary taxi driver. He is most definitely the *most* famous taxi driver in Greece, and he is also the *best* taxi driver in Greece. My friend Arlene, famous for keeping a daily journal on her many travels, made the following entry about George: "As we approach Greece, I look forward with great anticipation to meeting George, the most famous taxi driver in all of Greece. Lord knows how Barrie finds out about such people . . . oh yeah, the website of Matt Barrett.

George is meeting us at the airport . . . stay tuned for the George report." Later: "Well, George lived up to his reputation and then some." Honestly, dear reader, it is impossible for me to say enough good things about him; I end up going on and on, sounding like a broken record and an unbelievable one at that. George has lived in New York, speaks English very well, doesn't smoke, and is passionate about Greece—he speaks knowledgeably about ancient history as well as current politics and economics, and he of course knows how long it takes to cut through Athens traffic and will deliver you on time for your ferry, airplane, bus, or train connection. George drives visitors all over Greece, north and south, and also arranges special excursions, around Athens for example, or to the Parthenon, or to museums, restaurants, beaches, even shopping trips. (He has saved many visitors money by doing the bargaining.) Additionally, he is happy to help Greek Americans find their ancestral towns and villages and has witnessed many happy family reunions. As much as I adore George, his son Dennis, who works with him, is equally as wonderful (handsome too), and he reserves his Mercedes limousine for groups of up to seven. Another charming fellow, Christos, serves as the webmaster for the company, but he also fills in as an excellent driver when necessary. (He's also very good at teaching visitors words and phrases in Greek.) As much as I enthuse, I can't beat what George himself says: "I can promise you that if you take a journey with me, whether it is a half-day trip in Athens or a week-long excursion around the country, you will come back with an understanding of Greece that you will treasure and you will have perhaps the best vacation of your life. You will eat the best food and be treated like a guest of my country, and when we say good-bye at the airport, you will be saying good-bye to a friend you will always remember and hope to see again." Contact information: 210.96.37.030; mobile: 093.22.05.887; fax: 210.96.37.029; greektaxi@aol.com; www.greecetravel.com/taxi.

Athens

~*Akrokerama,* the terracotta elements that appear along the rooflines of neoclassical houses, mostly, are everywhere in Athens (and on a few islands too), and I adore them. I am crazy for them and have taken entirely too many photographs of rooftops filled with rows of *akrokerama.* I even bought some cheap copies in the Plaka. I'm not sure what I'm going to do with them, but I have it in my head to paint my living room a burnt sienna color and display my collection on the fireplace mantle. I'll let you know what my husband, the churl, says.

~The Kolonáki (Little Column) neighborhood, "named for the column once standing alone on the edge of town but now in a busy square close to the city center," according to Edmund Keeley in *Inventing Paradise.* Keeley notes that Kolonáki used to be considered the ritziest (and most conservative) part of Athens, until too much traffic and pollution began to tarnish its image. But it always had a bohemian fringe around the slope of Lycabettus Hill, where writers and artists could still find relatively cheap lodgings. Very recently, apparently, according to Keeley, "Some Athenians on the rise who chose to live in the distant suburbs where the air is cleaner and the parking easy have begun to come back into Kolonáki because they miss the sidewalk cafés and restaurants, however upgraded, where the talk about politics and films and trips to the islands still has some wit in it, and where the boutiques that have taken over the ground-floor apartments on street after street are as classy as any in Europe. But Kolonáki still has its village aura. The pharmacist will know your recurring ailments and sometimes give you unsolicited advice, the small bookstore around the corner will help to shape your taste in local literature, the taverna up on the hill will know your preference for barreled wine and a grilled porgy." Much as I enjoy walking around Kolonáki and soaking it up, I also enjoy *looking* at it—sitting as it does on Lycabettus Hill—from the Parthenon, for example, or from any other spot in the city where you can see it.

~Street vendors in Athens with their carts of roasted corn, nuts, and coconut logs. I had never tried roasted corn before I first visited Athens (though it is prepared this way in other parts of the Balkans, too) and it's delicious. If you're walking around the city and you need a little snack to tide you over until the Greek lunch hour, the corn, warmed nuts, and yummy coconut logs are great sustenance.

~The three glories of neoclassical architecture: the Academy (1859–85), the University (1839–64), and the National Library (1887–1903), all on Panepistimiou. I am a nut for architecture—classic, modern, secular, sacred, whatever—and when I saw these three magnificent buildings, I nearly flipped. (My zoom lens had a serious workout that morning.) All three buildings were designed by a team of Danish brothers (named Hansen) and a German architect (named Ziller) and date from the time Greece won its independence from the Turks and the world powers assigned a Bavarian king—Otto, son of King Ludwig of Bavaria—to Greece. Patricia Storace, in *Dinner with Persephone,* writes that Otto, who "had envisioned Munich as the 'Athens of the North,' reimagined Athens as—Athens. She adds that when Constantine created the Eastern Roman Empire in Constantinople, Athens began to lose all but its symbolic significance, and even under the Ottomans, Athens was never as significant as Constantinople and Thessaloníki. "Otto and his Bavarian architects set out to rebuild [Athens]—few houses were left standing after the years of the War of Independence, so they had a remarkably blank canvas, in a dilapidated Turkish town with hardly an important public building. They set about to reinvent the city, and although there are those who claim they fatally misunderstood the site, and turned Athens into the Munich of the

Mediterranean, the domestic scale of the neoclassicism they inspired is endearing."

~To Ouzádiko, Kolonáki. This may be the most perfect ouzo place, at least to my mind: it's cozy, a little dark, and filled with bottles and bottles and bottles of ouzo, lining the walls and on shelves—if you thought ouzo came in only a few varieties, stop in here for a reality check. Additionally, there are positively no tourists here (or there weren't when my friend Amy and I came for lunch). The menu is entirely in Greek, but thankfully our waitress knew enough English to describe a few dishes, which we promptly ordered: eggplant salad, mixed green salad with endive, tomatoes, arugula, and walnuts (delicious and unusual), and zucchini fritters. Though these dishes sound plain, they were absolutely loaded with depth of flavor and were delicious. I neglected to record the brand of ouzo we selected, but it was, naturally, quite good. There are only about fifteen tables at To Ouzadiko, which seem to fill up fast, but people come and go all the time, some simply for an ouzo or a coffee, others for a complete meal. Our waitress told us the *ouzería* was open seven days a week, from 8:00 A.M. to 12:00 midnight, but I would not recommend counting on that schedule. Note that it's not exactly obvious where To Ouzadiko is located: the street address is Karneadou 25–29 (210.72.95.484), but looking for this address will put you in front of a rather unattractive shopping complex called an International Center. This is your clue that you're at the right spot, but you have to walk into the Center toward the back; To Ouzadiko is in the far corner at street level.

~The Athens Metro. Readers who've visited Paris and were impressed by the Louvre Metro stop will be astonished at the Syntagma Square Metro station. As the quotable Matt Barrett says, "The Athens metro has to be the most beautiful system in the world." Even if you have no reason to ride the Metro, you should not miss visiting the Syntagma stop—it's a veritable museum, including glass cases displaying the stratified excavation with artifacts from various periods of Athenian civilization, pre-historic, classical Greek, Roman, and Byzantine. In separate glass display cases are beautiful amphora, columns, and artefacts that were uncovered while the station was being dug, and wonderful photographs of Athens, dating from about a hundred years ago, are also enlarged and displayed. The Metro currently displays no advertising or graffiti(!), and Matt Barrett, and I, hope it stays this way.

~National Archaeological Museum, Exarhia. The incomparable Arkheologiko Mouseio is justifiably famous and deserves all its accolades. It is so outstanding, with the most beautiful and extensive collection of ancient Greek art in the world, that I can add nothing except to say that you must go and don't rush through it. (I spent two full days in it and bought a comprehensive catalog of its collections, but I still feel I could return ten thousand times.) As I write this, however, the museum has been closed for extensive renovations and is not due to open until April 2004; so if you will be in Athens before that time, I sympathize with your inevitable disappointment. Your consolation, though, is that there are other outstanding (if smaller) museums in Athens, and it would be a mistake to ignore them. An art and culture writer, Louise Levathes, in a piece she penned for the travel section of *The New York Times* in 1992, observed that "With persistent myopia, visitors have been drawn to classical Greece, oblivious to other periods in the country's rich cultural history." The Greeks themselves, however, as Levathes noted, have always taken a great interest in preserving the full spectrum of their heritage, and a few private collectors have given Athens some specialized museums that are among the best in the world. (I used to work at the American Association of Museums in Washington, D.C., so I know a little about what distinguishes an excellent museum from a mediocre one.) Among these specialty collections are the Benaki Museum (see entry on page 498); and the Byzantine Museum, which is absolutely, positively a must if you plan on visiting even one Byzantine church; the George Lampakis antiquities and photographs section includes a collection of over three thousand icons, one of the largest in the world; Vassilíssis Sofías 210.72.11.027. The Museum of Cycladic Art (see entry on page 505) is another, while the Vorres Museum is an exquisite museum of traditional Greek arts and crafts, collected by Greek-Canadian businessman/art critic/biographer Ian Vorres. Aiming to recreate the total Greek experience in art and artifact in his home, Vorres created a living monument of all that is Greek; and years ago he was quoted as saying, "If you retain the Greek in everything you use, you will keep Greece in your soul and in your heart." Of the four museums, the Vorres receives the least number of visitors, which is a shame; though it's outside Athens, in Paiania, it's only nine miles northeast of the city (190-02 Paiania, Attica, 210.66.42.520).

~St. George Lycabettus Hotel. This wonderful boutique hotel has been perched on Lycabettus Hill for a number of years, but only since its major recent renovation did it really become a destination hotel in Athens. I admit that I landed here somewhat by accident, as the Grande Bretagne (see page 508) was closed for *its* major pre-Olympics renovation. But I had some clippings in my files about the St. George, and it seemed a worthy substitute. In fact, I'm happy to report that the hotel is not a substitute: it's a quality place to stay in every respect. Its efficient, friendly staff all deserve praise for their efforts during my stay: I was with two friends, you see, and the three of us kept the heads of the front desk staff spinning and the bellboys hopping. I'm not entirely sure if we amused them or con-fused them, but they rose to every challenge we presented to them, which ranged from making a room change, storing luggage and shopping bags, arranging different wake-up calls, making restaurant reservations, calling taxis, handling a frantic call from the room maid, and answering questions, questions, questions. Seemingly everyone took it all in stride. The hotel's many other attributes are worth noting: the corridors are tastefully decorated with traditional weavings and artwork, the rooms are quite nice (I had both a single and triple), the box of pistachio nuts every day is a wonderful touch, and the lobby bar, rooftop pool, and restaurant are all great places to install oneself. But it's the staff that I remember the most. Contact information: Kleomenous 2, 106-75 Athens; 210.72.90.711; fax: 210.72.90.439; www.sglycabettus.gr.

~Frame, a lounge, bar, and restaurant on the lower level of the St. George Lycabettus Hotel. Frame is one of the hippest, most interesting, best establishments of any kind that I've frequented. It's a bit hard to describe, as one part of the downstairs room is given over to a bar that is filled with the sort of shaggy, mod chairs (including one hanging from a chain) that Americans were used to seeing about thirty years ago. Then there is the zinc bar itself, always crowded. The other half of the room is set with tables and serves as the restaurant portion of the joint. My friends and I first had a late-night drink in the bar, and on another night we returned for a late-night dinner. Even the dishware at Frame is unique: oversize plates in the shape of flowers and triangles. Among the dishes we tried were cream of pumpkin soup with croutons and sliced almonds; mixed greens with Parmigiano-Reggiano, sun-dried tomatoes, and capers; and a pasta with seasonal vegetables and ginger essence. Did I mention the mini-rolls filled with sun-dried tomatoes and the feta cheese spread to go with them? I began the meal with low expectations, due to the happening bar scene, but I ended by really enjoying every dish as well as the attentive service.

~The Jewish Museum of Greece, on the edge of the Plaka. The Jewish Museum of Greece is considered to be one of the four most important European Jewish museums and was ranked by *The New*

York Times as among the twelve best museums in Greece. I, too, feel the museum is among the best I've visited anywyhere. Its permanent collection includes over seven thousand objects of rare art, and a major goal of the staff is to emphasize to visitors, regardless of their faith, the common roots of Jews and Christians. Founded in 1977, the museum reflects the life, customs, rites and traditions of Greek Judaism. The artifacts are divided into different thematic entities, and I was very impressed with how thorough the explanatory cards were at each exhibit (the large cards are laminated and are printed in several languages), important because the unique traditions of Greek Judaism are not widely known outside of Greece. Among the most memorable objects in the collection are the reconstruction of the interior of the synagogue of Patras, on the far western coast of the Peloponnese; the beautiful cylindrical wooden cases (Tikim) for the Sefer Torah (Book of the Pentateuch), which belong to the Greek Romaniote tradition; the traditional costumes, covering the period from the mid-eighteenth century to the mid-twentieth, highlighting the dress code of the Romaniote and Sephardic Jews and a past that is gone forever; and the moving exhibits dedicated to the Shoah, including the original letter from the head of the Greek Orthodox Church, Archbishop Damaskinos, in 1943, officially demanding the German occupation authorities to stop the persecution of the Greek Jews (Damaskinos was the only head of a European church to make such a request). The museum is not large and, as it's literally steps away from the beginning of the Plaka, a visit can easily be added to a day's itinerary in the neighborhood. Contact information: Nikis Street 39, 210.32.25.582; www.jewishmuseum.gr.

~To Kafeneío. On my last visit to Athens, I left almost no meals to chance and knew exactly where I wanted to eat lunch and dinner most every day. Therefore I did not stumble upon any great finds, but I sure did dine well at places that I read about, one of which was this simple place in Kolonáki. With only about twenty tables, To Kafeneío is not large, but it is warm and inviting, with pale golden walls, dark brown furniture, and framed illustrations and old views of Athens. My friends and I selected a few dishes immediately— leeks baked with cheese, spinach pie, meatballs with tomato sauce and rice, and octopus—but we wanted a few recommendations from our waiter, who enthusiastically informed us we had "to trust people who are older and fatter." That is how we ended up with a delicious, memorable, chopped salad that was so good he shared the recipe with me, and I in turn will share it with you here because I've since made it at home and it is easy and healthful. Mix together in a bowl the following ingredients, chopped—not minced—into small pieces: green scallions, green beans, artichokes, zucchini, and mushrooms. (The beans and artichokes may be either canned or frozen, but don't buy artichokes in a marinade.) Toss the ingredients with sunflower oil (I've also used olive oil), white wine vinegar, salt, and pepper, two to three hours in advance of when you want to eat it. It doesn't have to be refrigerated, but if you decide you want to put it in the fridge, allow it to return to room temperature before you eat it. As far as the quantity goes, base it on the number of people you're serving—in my experience, one package of regular mushrooms combined with an equal amount of the other ingredients serves four to six people, depending on what else is on the plate. (This is not an after-the-meal salad but is served together with other dishes.)

~Benaki Museum. The Benaki has become my favorite museum in Athens, perhaps in all of Greece, and it is not to be missed. Antonis Benakis (1873–1954) was the son of a wealthy Greek family from Alexandria. At a young age, before his family resettled in Athens in 1919, he began collecting Coptic textiles and works of Islamic culture. Once in Athens, he continued his interest in fabrics and collected Greek peasant dresses, bridal gowns, and court costumes, but also branched out to include a veritable treasure trove of all aspects of Greek culture from its beginnings to the twentieth century. The ground floor of this beautiful building (it was once the Benaki family home) has Neolithic items as well as Cycladic and Mycenean art, Byzantine icons and paintings; the first floor includes embroidery, ceramics, and household items from a number of Aegean islands and the Greek communities of Smyrna, Constantinople, and the Pontos, as well as ecclesiastical goldwork and silverwork. The second floor features an assortment of items relating to daily life in the Hellenic world, including dance, music, and song; and the third floor is devoted to paintings and paraphernalia relating to the Greek War of Independence and to notable Greeks in the literary arts. Among my most favorite items are the Byzantine jewelry; marble door frames from a mansion on Ios (typical examples of the decorative stone carving that adorned ecclesiastical and secular buildings in the Cyclades, with spiraling vine branches of Renaissance origin); a rare type of Cretan armchair with only one arm; the multicolored *sperveri,* a tent from Rhodes that was meant to isolate the sleeping platform from the lower sitting area and hide the bridal bed from prying eyes (this is the best preserved and most spectacular of the few comparable surviving examples from the Dodecanese); *View of Constantinople,* a tinted engraving by Konstantionos P. Kaldis, 1851; the magnificent wood-carved and painted reception rooms from a mansion in Kozáni (Macedonia), mid-eighteenth century; the *In Thee Rejoiceth . . .* icon by Theodoros Poulakis, from the second half of the seventeenth century; the map of Parte del Grecia and Crete, dating from the late seventeenth or early eighteenth century and annotated in Italian (this beautiful, portable painted map, painted in egg tempera on wood, is believed to be associated with Venice's efforts to repossess the territories annexed by the Ottoman Turks—it is also possible the map comes directly from the map cycle in the Guardaroba

Medicea in the Palazzo Vecchio in Florence—the cherub holding up a crown over a shield is the Medici coat of arms, which appears atop the cartouche in the lower left corner; happily, the Benaki bookstore sells good-quality copies of the map, which my friend Arlene and I bought and had framed); the entire third floor, but especially *Lord Byron Taking the Oath at Missolonghi,* a painting by Ludovico Lipparini, 1850; *The Liberation of Greece,* thirty-two hand-colored lithographs by Peter von Hess (1792–1871), a distinguished painter of battle scenes (not only are these views beautiful, but murals were produced from them in 1841 that decorated the royal garden in the palace at Munich; the murals were destroyed by bombing during World War II, so these original drawings and lithographs are the only memories of the murals); the photograph of the Greek military corps parading before the Arc de Triomphe during the celebrations of the Allies in Paris on July 14, 1919; and the diploma of the Nobel Prize for Literature awarded to George Seferis in 1963. The Benaki's bookstore and gift shop is very good, with a nice selection of carefully chosen items, including a selection of CD recordings of *rembétika,* jewelry, books on the museum's collections (including the excellent annual journal, published in Greek and English, with in-depth essays on specific items), weavings, and sturdy tote bags. Additionally, the café on the rooftop terrace is one of the most pleasant places to relax, reflect, or have a Nescafé or a nosh—and the witty murals on the walls, by Antonis Kiriakoulis, ensure that the café is decidedly not like any other in Athens! Contact information: Koumbari 1, at the corner of Vassilíssis Sofías; 210.36.71.000; www.benaki.gr.

~Plaka, or *the* Plaka, neighborhood. I've seen it in print both ways, and heard it referred to both ways, so whatever you're comfortable with seems to work. It doesn't take a rocket scientist to know that Plaka is touristy, crowded almost all the time, and filled with mediocre restaurants and shops; but I like it, and I think if you walk around the winding streets with the right attitude, you'll like it too. The name *plaka* is believed to derive from "flat place," to distinguish it from the northern slope of the Acropolis that towers above it. Plaka is known as a neighborhood or district but is often considered part of neighboring Anafiotika or Monastiráki. What I like about Plaka is that you can see ancient Greek and Roman ruins side by side with Byzantine churches and midnineteenth-century structures. Plus, it's *fun,* fun to meander slowly, fun to sit down for something to drink or eat, fun to people-watch, fun to bargain.

~To Kafeneío, Plaka. There *are* a few good places to satisfy a hungry stomach in Plaka, and this is one of them. You may quickly notice that a great number of establishments have the name To Kafeneíon, or something very similar, and this is because the name simply means "the café." On my last visit I stopped in here twice because it was so good and the host was so nice. It's a bit dark inside but has great character, and the menus are made of thin boards of wood and are quite beautiful. There is a fireplace and about twenty tables in all, and a soaring wooden-beam ceiling. The building was a private house in 1854 and was a piano bar from the 1950s to the late 1970s. Happily, someone had the bright idea to make the transition to a café with a good reputation, and now it is open every day from 10:00 to 1:00 A.M. My friends and I enjoyed in particular a marinated octopus dish, fried cheese, veal and pork meatballs baked with spices and feta, an admirable *tzatziki,* a dry and refreshing white wine, and a better-than-average Greek salad. Note that you have to walk in a bit off the street itself to find the entrance to this great place—if the weather is warm, tables will be set up outside in front, so you may see them before you see the official entrance. The bathrooms, by the way, are reached by opening the door to the left of the fireplace, and once you are outside, descend the stairs to the bathrooms below. Contact information: corner of Tripodon and Epiharmou; 210.32.46.916.

~The Old Tavern of Psara's, Plaka. This is another very good restaurant in Plaka that was recommended by the very wonderful Laura at Byzantino (see the entry just below). Sure, there are a few tourists here, even though it's not the kind of place one stumbles upon because it's tucked away a bit; but this is mostly a place for locals. Ask for Aleko or Kosta, and you'll be in good hands. My friends and I enjoyed an excellent dinner here, and it would have been great even without the live music. (Only the locals could sing along.) Most memorable was a hot mushroom appetizer and our seafood main course. If a guy approaches your table and offers to take a Polaroid photo of you, beware: that picture will cost you approximately $20. (By the way, in case you're wondering why I haven't mentioned Daphne's— arguably the most famous restaurant in Greece—it's because I couldn't secure a reservation, and it was February. I very much regret that I have not yet been to Daphne's, and I will not make the same mistake twice: in advance of my arrival in Athens, I will call for a reservation, and I recommend that you do so, too.)

~Byzantino, Plaka. You will most likely have read of Byzantino in some guidebooks, and if you have browsed the section of Matt Barrett's website devoted to Plaka, you will *definitely* have learned of it. The shop specializes in gorgeous handcrafted reproductions of ancient Hellenic jewelry. Matt's wife, a jewelry designer, visits Byzantino whenever she is in Athens and buys a variety of pieces and stones from the shop because she thinks it is one of the few jewelry shops in all of Greece that offers authentic high-quality designs at good-value prices. Byzantino was founded by two friends, Kostas and Giorgos, in 1987, and they have an exuberant partner, Laura, a gemologist and an American of both Greek and Italian heritage. She is also one of the kindest, most interesting, warm, funny, and smart women I've ever had the pleasure of meeting (plus, she's really pretty). Laura is an amazing authority on jewelry of all types, but especially Byzantine designs and history. It was Laura who informed me that the popular Greek key design does not signify good luck, good health, or long life, but that the Greek circular design signifies a never-ending circle, or eternity. If you're interested in buying any jewelry in Greece, for yourself or for gifts, I recommend you start by visiting Byzantino, and hopefully, Laura will be there, and you'll be well on your way to understanding and appreciating more about Greek jewelry than you ever thought possible. (The Byzantino website, www.byzantino.com, also has an excellent history of Greek jewelry.) Byzantino designs are stunning, and if you question their authenticity, just view the jewelry in the Benaki Museum and question no longer. When I used the phrase "good value" previously, I meant it, but I do not want to mislead you: quality and workmanship like this are never inexpensive; even I did not realize this at first, accustomed as I am to buying all my jewelry in New York's Diamond District, where bargaining is accepted but the quality is not at all the same. I would venture that no jewelry anywhere in North America is equivalent to what Byzantino crafts, so though the staff is able to extend good prices, you should not compare Byzantino pieces with any you know from home. As Laura says, jewelry is not an item anyone "needs," so you should make a purchase because you absolutely love it, because you'll wear it (and not hide it away in a drawer), and because it represents a good value to *you*. My friend Amy bought a matching ring, necklace, and bracelet here, for a fair price, and when we were back in New York, she wore at least one piece every day, and still does. Laura is very honest about what does and does not look appealing on a person, so if you're trying some pieces on, rest assured you will be given a critical but constructive review. Byzantino has two storefronts in Plaka, one devoted to more modern designs, on the same street, but Laura is most often found at Adrianou Street 120, 3010.32.46.605; fax: 3010.32.47.079; www.byzantino.com; also, by now I believe there is a third shop in Monastiráki.

~Erofili, Plaka. This little jewelry shop had a window display that really stood apart from the multitude of others, and that's why I walked in, and I'm so glad I did because the owner, a nice attractive Greek woman who speaks English well (she has family in New York) was a joy to talk to—and she stocks a select range of quality jewelry, ceramics, and other gift items. I bought some silver earrings by a designer with the last name of Koukas, whose work I really liked, and a friend parted with her money for a gorgeous silver and mother of pearl bracelet she had her eye on. It seemed to me that this shop, located at Vironos 8, was a cut above most others in Plaka.

~Brettos (or Vrettos) distillery, Plaka. Hats off once again to Matt Barrett, who wrote so enthusiastically of this little distillery/bar that I added it to my Plaka itinerary. But part of what makes my memory of this amazing place so special is that my visit was accidental. I was walking around Plaka with two friends, and at some point that afternoon we were planning on tracking down Brettos, the oldest distillery in Athens, but we weren't quite ready for the experience, when all of a sudden, there it was and there we were, and so we walked in. I have never, ever had more fun at any like establishment in my life, and I can't wait to return. Michel Brettos makes, on the premises, his own ouzo (hands down the best) and several varieties of brandy, as well as a variety of liqueurs, including a delicious cherry version. Brettos himself is an unassuming, sweet man, proud of his establishment, which is filled to the ceiling with bottles on two walls and with casks on another. When we walked in, we were instantly approached by a Greek American woman, Connie, who regularly holds court at Brettos. Connie was on her fifth or sixth glass of brandy, and she happily welcomed us into the Brettos fold. You see—and this is a good tip for anyone planning on living in Athens for a time—Brettos is a great place to meet people on Sundays, because many expatriates head there after church. In fact, Connie claims that the church is really *the* place to meet people (I think the same could be said for any house of worship). I can't confirm that, but I *can* confirm that if you come to Brettos and Connie is there, you will meet everyone in the entire place; if Connie isn't there, you'll still probably meet almost everyone because it's just that kind of place. One could simply come here to make a quick purchase, but it's awfully difficult not to sit down for a spell and try some house ouzo. My friends and I sat down for quite a while, and then we bought as many bottles as we could carry, including several gift boxes that had an assortment of small bottles. We were sorry to leave, but we had so many more stops to make. Many hours later, we happened to walk by Brettos again, and we spotted Connie, her husband, and good friend just leaving. . . . Brettos is infectious: don't miss it!

~Da Capo, Kolonáki. Facing *plateia Kolonakiou* (Kolonáki Square), where Tsakalof Street enters the square, Da Capo is an Italian-style café (its printed napkins state the address, appropriately, as being on *piazza Kolonáki*), with authentic espresso drinks and delicious Italian specialties like *panettone.* Ordinarily when I travel, I only frequent places offering local food and drink. But coffee being what it is in Greece, sometimes one just has to have something other than a Nescafé, and Da Capo more than satisfies. It is quite crowded in the mornings, by Greeks young and old, so it's obvious that the Italian way with coffee appeals not only to us North Americans.

~Museum of Cycladic Art, also known as the Nicholas P. Goulandris Foundation. This wonderful museum was founded by shipowner Goulandris and his wife, Dolly. They began collecting Cycladic art in the 1960s because, as Dolly has been quoted as saying, "it has such a modern feeling and was so immediate, accessible." I suppose that is why I, and so many others, are drawn to these white marble figures as well: they look like they were carved yesterday, or at least by Brancusi or Modigliani. Though the National Archaeological Museum has its own very excellent collection of Cycladic art, the Goulandris collection is recognized as one of the most important in the world. The museum itself is in a rather nondescript building, but one quickly forgets about the structure as the collection of sculpture, terracotta and bronze vessels, and coins draws one in immediately. The accompanying maps and documentation are very good, and the bookstore carries some excellent volumes not only on Cycladic art but also on other Greek art forms and on Athens. There is a street-level café that is open to the sky. Contact information: Neofýtou Doúka 4 (just off Vassilíssis Sofías), 210.72.28.321.

~The Acropolis. Sometimes the most obvious sites are those I *almost* forget to mention, and while you certainly don't need to be told that the Acopolis is amazing, I would add that it is more spectacular than you may imagine. As I noted previously, go early in the morning if you can, and spend the extra money (about $50) for a guide. What I have found about guidebooks is that in order to retain everything—history, architecture, names, dates—you have to read a number of books as one may focus more on architectural details while another specializes in history and politics. The first time I visited the Acropolis, I brought a canvas bag stuffed with a bunch of books and I intended to stay up there all day if I had to to read everything. I did stay up there nearly the whole day, but I don't recommend this approach to anyone. Read something before you visit, hire a guide, and retire to a café or taverna and read some more. Finally, I thought it was interesting to read in *The Rulers of the Mediterranean,* of 1894, that the author, even then, observed of the Elgin Marbles, ". . . how do the marbles look under the soot-stained windows or the gray of London fog? Like the few Lord Elgin did not want, and that stand out like ivory in their proper height against the soft sky that knows and loves them? When the people of

Great Britain have returned the Elgin marbles to Greece, and the Rock of Gibraltar to Spain, and the Koh-i-noor diamond to India, and Egypt to the Egyptians, they will be a proud and haughty people, and will be able to hold their heads as high as any one."

~Kallisti restaurant, Neapoli Exarcheion. Kallisti (the word for *beautiful*) is one of a new breed of Athens restaurants, offering less traditional dishes but still highlighting traditional Greek and Mediterranean ingredients. But it's unique in that it's in a house— you literally walk through different rooms, as if you were invited into someone's home, and you may be seated in a room with other tables or have an entire little room all to yourselves. The evening my friends and I were at Kallisti, the host brought us a small plate with rye toasts, soft white cheese drizzled with olive oil, smoked pork slices, tiny olives, and small glasses of raki, a wonderful start to our meal. We did not find every dish after that to be flawless, but every dish we ordered was quite good and creatively presented. The staff is very enthusiastic about the restaurant, and their enthusiasm is infectious. The artwork, by various artists and in varying styles and different in each room, is at least as interesting as the food. Kallisti is a great place to go for contemporary food and to avoid the tourist hordes. Contact information: Asklipiou 137, 210.64.53.179.

~Moní Kesariani, Mount Hymettus. The Kesariani Monastery, on the slopes of beautiful Mount Hymettus, about three miles from Athens, is a remarkably unaltered Byzantine monastery dating from the Middle Ages. Because it is in such an excellent state of preservation, visitors are able to clearly identify its different parts, including the kitchen, bathhouse and fountain, the monks' cells, and refectory. Kesariani is in a lovely green setting with cypress trees all around and flowering plants. If you need a break from the noise and traffic of Athens, spend a few hours up here. The drive up the hill is pretty, and there are a few simple places to have something to drink or eat.

~Daphni Monastery, seven miles from Athens. Daphni, considered the most important Byzantine monument in or around Athens, is the most beautiful Byzantine monument of any kind that I've ever seen, in Greece or in Turkey. The name *daphni* dates from an earlier time, as the site was once occupied by a temple dedicated to Apollo, one of whose symbols was the laurel or *daphni*. This temple was destroyed by the Goths in 395, and the monastery as we know it was reconstructed in the ninth century. Some historians have speculated that this reconstruction was linked to the Monastery of Daphni in Constantinople, which perhaps better explains its name. Daphni is not in as peaceful or beautiful a setting as Kesariani (above), but it is positively the one monastery to see if you only have time for one (though Athens itself has the very lovely Ágios Theodori and Ágios Elefthérios). Note, however, that Daphni was closed for some repairs after the 1999 earthquake in Athens, so be sure to check the museums and monuments sheet, from the Greek National Tourist Office, for updated information before you set out.

~Grande Bretagne Hotel, Syntagma. My fondness for the Grande Bretagne, the most famous and prestigious hotel in all of Greece, began with a call from nature. My husband and I had spent a few hours in and around Syntagma, and I needed to find a bathroom. The hotel was right there, so I walked in to see if there were public restrooms on the lobby level. I was quite presentable, but any staff member would undoubtedly have known I was not a guest, and it is precisely this scenario by which I initially measure a hotel's worth. I didn't see any restrooms, so I walked up to an employee and inquired where they were, removing any possible doubt about my guest status, and the employee graciously walked me to the bathroom. As I passed back through the lobby, the employee asked me if I was enjoying Athens and wanted to know what I had seen so far and if was planning on traveling to other parts of Greece, and he seemed genuinely interested in my responses. Now *that* is the way the staff at every hotel, one star or five, should treat everyone who walks through its doors (and believe me, it isn't common; I have been made to feel most unwelcome at some places, and I wasn't searching for the women's room; these are the places I call snooty and not worth the money). Due to this simple but nice experience, not only did the Grande Bretagne have me as guest, but I have told many friends and colleagues to stay at the hotel on their travels to Athens. I'm sorry that I was unable to stay there on my last visit, but the hotel was in the final stages of a magnificent renovation. Dating from 1862, the Grande Bretagne is now a member of the Luxury Collection line of the Starwood Hotels and Resorts group, and among its newest features are a spa with an indoor pool; a fitness center; a rooftop swimming pool with a sun deck and pool bar (talk about a view!); a butler service; a ballroom; and a presidential suite with Greek architectural masterpieces. More than its amenities, I like the Grande Bretagne most for its historical link with the city of Athens: it earned its nickname "the Royal Box of Athens" because it has hosted Greek regents; Kennedys, Rockefellers, and Rothschilds; Greek prime minister Constantine Karamanlis; and Agatha Christie, Henry Miller, Winston Churchill, Aristotle Onassis, and Maria Callas. In unhappier times, the hotel was headquarters for the Germans, and at the start of the Greek Civil War, the British made it their headquarters. In the century and a half since the hotel opened, Syntagma and Athens have changed much. I like knowing that the stately Grande Bretagne, the beautiful, well-preserved dowager of Athens, stands as if unmarked by time. Even if you choose not to stay here, do walk in to admire this architectural gem—you'll be made to feel welcome. Contact information: Syntagma Square, 105-63 Athens; 210.33.30.000; fax: 210.33.30.200; www.grandebretagne.gr.

~Piraeus. I am often drawn to neighborhoods or cities that are decidedly gritty, downmarket, or reportedly "not worth your time." So it was natural that I would want to see Piraeus beyond the port area, and as I expected, there's a lot more of interest here than meets the eye. In the years before the birth of Christ, Piraeus had superb public buildings, agoras, sanctuaries, a theater, and of course a great harbor. It became known as the "Emporium of Greece" as well as the "London of Antiquity." Many visitors do not realize that from 1318 onward Piraeus was referred to on maps as Porto Leone, a name derived from the marble statue of a lion that was placed in the harbor. This statue was stolen by the Italian Francesco Morosini in 1688 during his campaign against Athens. He carried it off to Venice, where today it is on display in the Arsenale. (Attempts to secure its return have apparently been unsuccessful.) Also little known is the event that did the most to destroy much of the character of Piraeus: on April 6, 1941 (the day Germany declared war on Greece), an order was given for some ships to leave the harbor to make room for others, but due to misjudgments by both Greek and British authorities, who were both responsible for unloading military equipment, some of the ships that should have been the first to leave the harbor stayed behind. At 3:20 A.M. one of those ships, the *Clan Fraser,* which was filled with 250 tons of explosives, blew up. The following day Piraeus as it had been known was completely unrecognizable. The damage in the port was estimated at 325 million prewar drachmas, with 13,282 dead; more than 10,000 of them died from starvation. Obviously, a city that was repaired and rebuilt beginning in the 1940s is not going to retain the quality it once had. But the Hellenic Maritime Museum is excellent (visitor information is included in guidebooks); it's fun to walk around the bustling streets and poke into shops; the restaurant, the only Michelin two-star in all of Greece is here; and Piraeus is easily reached from Athens by an electric railway.

The Aegean Islands

~The tradition, especially on the islands of Mykonos and Sífnos, of painting a pattern, on the surface of the towns' narrow lanes, that follow the shape of each stone, outlining the stones, so to speak, with bright white paint. I never tire of casting my eyes on these walkways and marveling at how perfectly whitewashed they are. I have taken boatloads of photographs of whitewashed stones on Sífnos, too many, according to my husband. I had them framed, and years later I still find the photos beautiful and appealing.

~The island of Chios, all of it, but especially Pirgi, Néa Moní, and the beach of Mavra Volia, with its lava black, flat, smooth stones. Many readers may already be familiar with a famous reference to Chios: Delacroix's *Massacre at Chios,* a large canvas he painted in 1824 that now hangs in the Louvre, commemorating the nearly 30,000 islanders who were massacred by the army of Kara Ali in 1822. Though that horrible episode is more complex than Delacroix depicted it (the Chians, in fact, had a longstanding good relationship with the Ottomans and were reluctant to join the fight against the Turks), Chios is better known in modern times for pleasant pursuits. The village of Pirgi is noted for the *xysta* designs on most of its buildings (*xysta* is similar to Italian *sgraffito*: alternate layers of gray and white plaster are applied to the facades and scraped into dazling geometric patterns). In Pirgi I particularly enjoyed participating in the evening *volta* and greeting all the mostly widowed women sitting on their stoops. I would say *kalispera,* and they would reply, in unison, *parakalo.* Food writer Aglaia Kremezi, in a brochure piece she wrote for the Oldways "Magic of the North Aegean" symposium (held on Chios) in 1999, suggested that "If you want to savor the essence of Chios you need to spend a day walking or cycling in the maze of streets surrounding the sumptuous estates of Kambos." Kambos, as Kremezi notes, was throbbing with life for five centuries, "inhabited by wealthy Genoans and Greek gentry who enjoyed a way of life that was unique in the Middle East." Readers intent on visiting Chios should read Kremezi's article entitled "The Wild Islands of Greece" (*Gourmet,* April 2000), filled with excellent suggestions for unique accommodations, great places to eat, historical sites to see, and a few recipes, including one for the most delicious pumpkin and fennel pastries.

~Sitting at a table in the main square of Pirgi, Chios, in the late summer when nearly the whole village is filled with Greek Americans, enjoying a submarine. Lawrence Durrell, in *The Greek Islands,* wrote that "of the 'submarine'—that absurdity invented by the cafés to thrill its youngest customers—I have written elsewhere. It consists of a spoonful of mastic confiture plunged into a glass of cold water. The name in Greek means 'an underwater thing' and you see a very ancient Greek expression on children's faces as they suck the white jam from the spoon." I am a *huge* fan of submarines, even if I am the oldest person enjoying one. I'm also a fan of all the products made from mastic, which include chewing gym, a liqueur, hard crystals that look like rock candy used for cooking or breath mints, and a finely ground substance to be rolled with tobacco. (This last I've never tried, as I don't smoke.) Oldways founder K. Dun Gifford, in a lecture he prepared for the Oldways symposium on Chios, reported that mastic is also used as an agent in ice creams, and as an aphrodisiac in southern Morocco and Mauritania, and that it has a variety of nonfood uses: in frankincense, textile finishing, perfumes, toothpaste, and restoring paintings. The ancients believed mastic to be good for brightening teeth and tightening gums, strengthening blood, drying up coughs and colds, aiding digestion, and healing wounds. Modern medical and health authorities confirm most of these judgments and have established some of the reasons: mastic absorbs cholesterol (reducing heart disease); it is an antibacterial (reduces dental disease); it stimulates secretion of saliva and gastric acids (aids digestion); and it has anticancer properties. Mastic plants are native only to Chios, and according to Gifford, for centuries "powerful Mediterranean civilizations have tried to transplant the mastic tree to their homelands, to escape the monopoly prices charged by the Chian producers. Despite these determined efforts, however, Chios has always remained the only producer of mastic. The tree will not grow and produce anywhere else." Mastic is neither a spice nor an herb but rather is the resin of the mastic tree, otherwise known as the *Pistachia lentiscus var. Chia*, an evergreen related to the pistachio plant, that thrives on Chios. (Again according to Gifford, the mastic tree has cousins in the Mediterranean basin—*Pistachia lentiscus, Pistachia atlantica Desf.*, and *Pistachia terebinthus*, among others—but these cousins are not sources of mastic.) Mastic was known in antiquity and is a fairly common ingredient in Greek and near Eastern recipes. (I once made an outstanding rice pudding from a recipe in Claudia Roden's *Mediterranean Cookery* that included mastic.) It has a subtle taste, and you don't need much of it to flavor a dish. More often I chew mastic crystals to rid my mouth of garlic and other strong flavors, and I have not found a better breath freshener. (You do have to chew the crystals, which start out hard and crunchy and then become soft and chewy, for at least an hour.) I have read that mastic crystals were popular breath fresheners in the harem in Topkapi Palace in Istanbul. You can find mastic in shops specializing in foodstuffs from the Levant—a few New York stores that fill mail orders are Şahadi Importing Company (718-624-4550) and Kalustyan's (212-685-3451)—and though it may cost anywhere from $60 to $100 a pound, a little bit goes a long way—the small plastic container I buy from Yaranush in White Plains, New York, costs $4.50. Food writer Suzanne Hamlin, in a piece she wrote about mastic for *The New York Times* (October 14, 1998), noted that she began using "a half teaspoon or so of mastic as a flavoring in standard bread and cookie recipes, all of which, so far, have been masticated happily by all comers."

~Sitting at a table in *any* Greek square on *any* Aegean island, for as Katherine Kizilos notes in *The Olive Grove,* "to be in a Greek square on a summer evening was, in itself, a cause for celebration, and the setting matched my perception that now my journey had begun, and that the world was full of unexpected possibilities."

~*Krokalia,* the decorative mosaic of pebbles used in patios and around pools, mostly in the Dodecanese Islands. The pebbles, mostly black and white, are oval and flat and are placed on their sides into the cement. (There are some good pictures of *krokalia* in *Greek Style,* a book recommended below.) I have seen patios just like these in Andalucia, notably in Seville, and just as I did for *akro-kerama,* I took dozens of photos of these patios, as I intend to reproduce one in my nonexistent backyard.

~Crete. The best part about visiting Crete is traveling around it, as due to its size, it is different from north to south and east to west. Richard Stoneman, in *A Literary Companion to Travel in Greece,* noted of the island that it "is a world in itself, differing in important aspects of history, character, and culture from other parts of Greece." As Elizabeth Boleman-Herring reminds us in *Vanishing Greece,* "It was on Crete, the rocky wall that separates Europe from Africa—that linked Europe *to* Africa and Asia—that our first recognizably 'Western' graffiti were elegantly painted. The southernmost sector of Greece became the foundation of the pyramid, the firm pediment upon which we all, as Mycenaean and Periclean Greeks, as Romans, Byzantines, and Latins, as Europeans, Americans, and Moderns of all cultures and creeds, have built. Europe's most ancient road was laid at Knossos, and it survives to this day—a path we have all taken. We are all, in a very real sense, Cretans." I believe that part of what makes Crete a bit different is its geographic position, lying as it does in an isolating position in the Mediterranean, between Greece and Egypt. I have not been *everywhere* on the island, but did manage to see quite a bit of it, and among my favorites on the island are the site of Knossos (especially the frescoes of 'The Ladies in Blue,' 'The Bullfight,' and 'The Cup-Bearers'; and a word of advice: go early in the day or in the late afternoon or there will be so many other tourists you'll wish you'd never come) and the towns of Chania and Mátala. (I know Mátala is on that list of places that "aren't what they used to be," but I was there in October and it was *great*; besides, I *had* to go there no matter what because, being the enormous fan of Joni Mitchell that I am, I was determined to hang out "beneath the Matala moon," as she sings in "Carey" on her perfect album, *Blue*.)

~Samaria Gorge, Crete. Though the Gorge—the longest in Europe, now designated a National Park—has received a great deal of publicity and a great many walkers traverse its route, it remains one of the greatest hikes I've ever experienced. Buses from Chania, Kissamos, and Rethymnon depart early in the morning for the village of Omalós, where the trail begins. But you can also spend the night in Omalós, which is what I did. Either way, the trail begins in a forest and heads downhill, allowing one to see Crete's flora and, occasionally, fauna. Near the end of the trail is a section called Sideróportes (iron gates), the most photographed portion of the hike, where walls rise up nearly 1,000 feet on either side of a narrow passage. Eighteen kilometers and about five or six hours later, one reaches the end of the trail, which simply gives way to a lovely umbrella-lined sand beach, with a few welcoming cafés and tavernas. This stretch of beach is actually known as new Ágios Rouméli, the old original town having been washed away, literally, in 1954. A bus picks up all the hikers at approximately 2:00 P.M. (I believe there is one other, a few hours later) and makes the return trip to Omalós. It is one of the world's greatest rambles.

~Sponges from the waters around Kalymnos especially but also Sími. About a dozen years or so ago I discovered how wonderful sponges are for washing my face and removing eye makeup. You'll find sponges for sale all over Athens and on the islands, and they come in large and small sizes and are sold individually or in packages. Ordinarily I do not support an activity that kills a living species; but after reading about the sponge divers and the sponge trade in Lawrence Durrell's *The Greek Islands,* I concluded that I wanted to support the men who do this rather dangerous work for a living, and I am hopeful that the islanders will continue to work toward a balance of sponge bed growth and profit to maintain an ancient tradition. For as Durrell noted, "The sponge has almost as long and eventful a history as the Mediterranean itself. Even within the time-span of our own civilization, this useful little animal was a commonplace household adjunct in Greece and Rome. The servants in the *Odyssey* swabbed tables with it, while it was in great demand with artisans, who used it to apply paint, and with soldiers who had no drinking vessels to hand. In the Middle Ages, burned sponge was reputed to cure various illnesses. Together with olive oil it has been used from time immemorial as a contraceptive pessary by the oldest professionals—who, oblivious of the fact that they figure in the pages of Athenaeus, still flourish in the Athens Plaka today—using roughly the same sort of slang, in which the word *sponge* finds many a picturesque use. Another out-of-the-way use for it was as a pad worn inside classical armour—one can see why." Durrell informs us that some five thousand species of sponge exist, of every color under the sun, but the richest and most common variety is harvested in the eastern Mediterranean. Dried sponges last a very, very long time; to refresh them, you simply put some baking soda in a bowl or a jar with lukewarm water and soak them for twenty to thirty minutes. Rinse them and squeeze them out, and they smell good as new.

~The island of Rhodes (Rhodos in Greek). About a dozen years ago or so author Robert Kaplan wrote a profile of Rhodes for *The New York Times*, in which he stated that the island epitomized "not only the best but also the Worst aspects of tourist development. The northwest point of the 542-square-mile island is today one of those placeless places: an esthetic disaster zone of luxury, concrete eyesores and marble lobbies that are veritable museums of bad interior decorating; with Muzak and paperback shops where the works of Jackie Collins abound and those of Durrell or other literary admirers of Greece nearly impossible to find. But four decades have proved long enough to spoil only a part of the island, and only a part of Rhodes town at that. With a bit of cunning, Rhodes can still offer what it gave Durell after the hardships of war—the tranquil, meditative rediscovery of self." I think he has hit the nail on the head with this description. My husband and I experienced both crowds and quiet corners on Rhodes and concluded that it is a lovely island with an extremely interesting history. It is also one of the larger Aegean islands and therefore is a popular port of call for many arrivals and departures, so you may find yourself there as the result of a ferry itinerary. Relax, and remember that the island boasts the distinction of being the sunniest place in all of Greece.

~Dovecotes. I first noticed beautiful whitewashed dovecotes on the island of Sífnos, where I took dozens of photographs of them. But I have since read that the Venetians are said to have brought doves to Tínos, which, after the Venetians departed in the eighteenth century, quickly became home to about a thousand dovecotes, and that is reportedly a conservative number. I saw some books at the Cycladic Museum in Athens devoted to the dovecotes of Tínos, so they must be something special. Greek writer Angeliki Kharitonidou has noted that "What is certain is that on Tínos, the simple birds' house became a superb example of vernacular architecture. In the cornfields, and in the vegetable-gardens of the river valleys, the craftsmen built elegant rectangular two-story buildings with a flat roof and an upper roof surmounted by abstract three-dimensional compositions made of thin slabs of unworked schist. The small windows through which the birds came and went formed the basis for the superb decoration that adorned the walls." I had long thought, and still do think, that the dovecotes looked rather eastern, yet according to Kharitonidou the patterns represent "the countless shapes and motifs beloved by the sensitive craftsmen."

~Santorini, which gets my vote for most dramatic Greek island, in any season of the year. If you can at all arrange it, go to Santorini in either late April, May, June, September, or October; in the off season the island really does mostly shut down, and at the height of high season, I imagine it's rather unbearably crowded. (I've never been then, but I understand the island can be overwhelmed by tourists in July and August.) That said, if high season is the only time you're able to go, then simply go: I still think you will find it to be a remarkable island. I especially enjoyed visiting Akrotiri, the ongoing archaeological dig discovered by Spyridon Marinatos in 1967, and the new (only three or four years old) Museum of Prehistoric Thíra. I jotted in my notebook that the excavations at Akrotiri did not confirm Marinatos's theory concerning the demise of Minoan civilization, but the excellent preservation of the city's buildings, the impressive wall paintings, and the wealth and variety of movable finds have enhanced the site as a center for interdisciplinary research in Aegean archeology. The excavation has also contributed to Santorini's own development as a leading center of tourism in Greece. The wall paintings (frescoes) displayed at the museum are alone worth the price of admission, and one of them was moved here from the National Archaeological Museum in Athens.

~Melina's Tavern, Santorini. I am so happy I met Viola Katris in the Athens airport en route to Santorini. Viola, originally from

Australia, owns and operates Melina's Tavern with her Greek husband. They opened the restaurant in 1996, beginning literally with a shovel, a wheelbarrow, and their bare hands, and they both take much pride in the entire operation. If you read the *Bon Appetit* special collector's edition "Islands of the Mediterranean" (May 2002), you may remember reading about Melina's: the editors recommended the beachfront taverna and included a great color photograph of it in a piece entitled "Rustic Charmers," and elsewhere in the issue they shared a recipe for one of the house specialties, grilled eggplant salad with garlic. The word *beachfront* is entirely apropos here, as the water really does lap at your feet if you're sitting at the edge. Melina's is within walking distance of Akrotiri (just leave the site and turn left and follow the road to the water; you'll see Melina's to your right), so for a perfect day in paradise, I recommend a visit to Akrotiri in the morning, lunch at Melina's, and then a visit to the excellent Museum of Prehistoric Thíra. I leave the choice of where to have a sundowner to you.

~The postcards at Kisiris gift shop, Fira, Santorini. Most of the items that Kisiris offers to visitors are rather pedestrian (though it has a good assortment of *komboloï* keychains), but its selection of bright, unique postcards is terrific, and to my knowledge, these hand-painted cards are not sold elsewhere. Each card is of course one of a kind, and many sport fish and sea creatures. The cards would certainly be welcome by their recipients if sent by mail, but I had a different idea: when I got home, I punched a hole in one corner of each card and threaded a ribbon through it and then wrapped the ribbon around an accompanying gift. Whatever you decide to do with them, buy a bunch—you'll be glad you did.

~Katikies, Oia, Santorini. Ah, Katikies. My thesaurus does not have enough superlatives to describe it, but I'll try a few: stunningly beautiful, to die for, like you read about. Katikies is a fantasy come true and is the most amazing place I've ever stayed. Honestly. By proclaiming that, I don't mean to imply that I will never stay at a comparable establishment in the future—I probably will, and look forward to it—but even knowing that takes nothing away from this unique property. Katikies is built into the side of a cliff in Oia (pronounced *EE*-ah), and its name is derived from the local dialect word for countryside accommodations or "residences"—during the annual grape harvest, the farmers would stay in simple, makeshift residences for the duration of the harvest, approximately twenty days at the end of August or beginning of September. Transportation years ago on the island was quite primitive and time consuming, and these residences—*katikies*—were temporary homes away from home. If you reserve one of the twenty-three rooms in advance, you too may experience one of the most memorable homes away from your home in your life. The hotel staff believe *katikies* also stands for hospitality, and they think of it as a word that reminds us of the past and inspires the future. The hotel's logo is taken from a traditional wooden chair design in Greece, not unique to Santorini, and appears on the towels and room keys. (These keys, by the way, hang from a strand of beautiful turquoise *komboloï* beads that happily can be purchased at the reception desk—one of the coolest souvenirs I've ever purchased.) Each guest room at Katikies is different; some are meant for two while others accommodate three or four people. In addition to the seven standard double rooms, there are also junior, senior, and superior suites, plus a honeymoon suite and the Katikies suite. (I've seen all the rooms, and believe me, the "standard" rooms are anything but standard, and the suites will make you want to move in.) *Travel + Leisure* writer Richard Alleman wrote about Katikies that it is "a fantasy of free form stairs, bridges, walks and cave houses that duplicate on a small scale the surreal lay out of Oia itself." The rooms are simply but tastefully furnished, with framed black-and-white and color illustrations on the walls, a mini wine cellar, an individual CD player, and traditional furniture. The property also includes three restaurants (the dinner I had one night—pasta with prawns and tomato sauce, Greek salad, goblets of white Santorini wine, and yogurt and honey—is one of the best I've ever had anywhere), two pools, and a sunbathing deck, and shuttle service is provided to and from the beach and to the airport or port. Katikies is a member of the Small Luxury Hotels of the World group, but don't let the word *luxury* give you the impression that this is either luxurious or stuffy: Katikies is luxurious in a sensual, even sexy way, and it's classy but very informal, never stuffy. For me, it epitomizes the perfect blend of informality and style that I seek in accommodations, but what places it in a special category is its singular location and architectural character, making it a destination in itself. (While I can't wait to visit Santorini again, I have an even greater desire to stay at Katikies.) One of my favorite books, *Hotel Gems of Mediterranean Europe* (by Luc Quisenaerts, D-Publications, 2003), includes Katikies in its selection of unforgettable Mediterranean properties. (The selection also includes two other wonderful Santorini properties, Tsitouras Collection and Zannos Melathron; Katikies only has twenty-three rooms, after all, and in the interest of recommending comparable alternatives, these two are worth considering.) Before September 11 about 70 percent of the guests at Katikies were North American, while currently the percentage hovers between 40 and 50. Count yourself in that group, but remember to reserve ahead: by December 2002, nearly every room was booked for June, July, and August 2003. Contact information: Katikies, 84-702 Oia, Santorini; 228.60.71.401; fax: 228.60.71.129; www.katikies.com.

The Peloponnese
~Driving around the Peloponnese, anywhere. I suppose because the GNTO discourages visitors from driving and because there are corners of the Peloponnese that simply are not very populated, I

have rarely, even in high season, been in a traffic jam on the Peloponnese. It is a joy to drive around and pass through small towns and stop for lunch in unassuming little places—the names of which I have long forgotten—without a tourist in sight.

~The roadside stand, somewhere between Kardamili and Mistra, where an elderly man and his son sold honey, wooden walking sticks, and goat bells. My friend Sarah and I bought some honey and two goat bells; my bell, heavy and brass, remains one of my prized possessions, and my daughter loves ringing it. Upon learning that we were from the States, the elderly man exclaimed, "*Amerika!*" and clasped our hands and kissed our cheeks. It was a moment I'll never forget.

~Olympia. Nikos Kazantzakis, in *Travels in Greece,* noted of Olympia that "In all Greece there is no landscape more inspiring, none that so gently and perseveringly invites peace and reconciliation." I agree that the site of Olympia, as well as the surrounding area, is beautiful, and seeing this moving spot is well worth the journey to the far western corner of the Peloponnese. A few years ago, writer Frederic Raphael wrote an in-depth piece about Olympia and the history of the Olympic games that unfortunately I was unable to include here in full. However, as it is such a good piece, my editor agreed to feature a short excerpt:

"Can any visitor to Greece not feel drawn to Olympia? After the Parthenon and Delphi, few places are as famous, fewer so remote. The permanent site of the most famous Games in the ancient world, from which the Baron Pierre de Coubertin got the idea for the first modern Olympics in 1896, lies in what was a fairly inaccessible valley ten miles inland from the north-west coast of the Peloponnese. We first drove to it, in the early 1960s, across furrowed roads, from Megalopolis and Bassae (whose Doric temple is probably the most perfect on the mainland, equalled only by Segesta in Sicily). In those days, you could take rooms adjacent to the sacred enclosure and wander in at any time. Today, officious fences and regular opening hours block off such casual familiarity. However, good roads to now take you quickly to Olympia either south, along the coast, from Patras or across the (alas and hurrah!) much modernised Peloponnese. Once there, you may wonder what gave travellers from all over the ancient world the urge, and nerve, to converge on it, once every four years, for more than a millenium. The Games were the main attraction, but—especially after 430 B.C.—by no means the only one. For centuries, a temple—whose stumpy foundations remain—housed Pheidias' great statue of Zeus, which was soon enlisted as one of the Seven Wonders of the Ancient World. Very little visible trace survives: you can only see it depicted, in miniature, on Elian coins of the period. The sole evidence of the great sculptor's years of secret toil is a drinking cup inscribed "I belong to Pheidias." The latter's studio is tucked away, below the training ground, behind the 'Priests' House.'

Today's Olympia is more like a one-horse town than the Mecca of athletes or aesthetes. There is no shortage of decent tavernas, but the Olympic precinct, and the museum, are the only cultural calls worth making. You can stroll down to the site, but don't fail to take your imagination with you. Excavation and restoration have been going on for almost centuries, but as you walk through the gate you need a gang of mental extras to recreate the thronging excitement of the ancient festival and you have to put roofs and apply color to what is, today, more like a three-dimensional, monochrome ground plan . . . Olympia was once rich, not to say jammed, with monuments but earthquakes, floods, robbers and Christian zealots effaced most of them. Part of Olympia's charm lay in its shaded seclusion. Inexhaustible wells guaranteed that visitors rarely went thirsty, even in the Greek summer when the Games were held (the local melons are accordingly juicy)." [FREDERIC RAPHAEL lives in France but has had a second home in Greece for many years. Copyright © 2000 by Frederic Raphael. Reprinted with permission of the author.]

~Nafplio, especially walking up the 999 steps (or is it 857? every guidebook states a different number; whatever it is, it's a lot) to the Palamidi fortress—the last built by the Venetians in Greece—and the views all around; walking along Bouboulinas; the jewelry stores of Morphes (vas. Konstantinou 4) and Camara (vas. Konstantinou 10, www.camaraworkshop.com; the couple that owns this little shop was featured in a book titled *Ethnography of European Traditional Cultures: Arts, Techniques and Heritage,* published by the Institute of Cultural Studies of Europe and the Mediterranean, 1998, and they were the only jewelers included); the Peloponnesian Folklore Museum (Sofrani 13; not only is this museum excellent, but the gift shop is filled with interesting, authentic, and unique items); the Old Mansion taverna (Siokou 7) and Savouras taverna, specializing in seafood (Bouboulinas 71).

~Camping Olympia—a well maintained campground with a swimming pool—where my husband and I had the great pleasure of meeting Chris and Sarah K., who agreed to travel around the Peloponnese with us for ten days and who, happily, are among our best friends today.

~The Lion Gate and Beehive Tomb at Mycenae, and the town of Kardamili.

~Byron Hotel, Nafplio. The Byron is recommended in a number of guidebooks, with good reason, but rather than repeat what all the other travel writers say, I will add a few remarks they didn't. The staff at the hotel is exceptionally helpful and welcoming, and they patiently answer many questions and offer suggestions for places to eat. (Plus, they have a collection of menus from restaurants and tavernas around town at the front desk for visitors to peruse.) Though the Byron is within the Old Town and is therefore very convenient, it is set back just enough from one of the main streets that guests never have to worry about noise. Not only is the building itself beautifully renovated, but each room is traditionally decorated with taste and quality. Breakfast, which is served at 8:00 (a problem only if you have to be up earlier, in which case you may have to forage in town for coffee and a *kouloura*), is very nice, complete with honey, a basket of fresh breads, cheese, a pot of coffee or tea, and fresh-squeezed orange juice. Even if the Xenia Palace reopens as the luxury property it's supposed to be, I will continue to recommend the Byron to anyone going to Nafplio, and I will never stay anywhere else. The Byron is a far greater value and is among the loveliest, most charming places I've ever stayed. Contact information: Platonos 2, Plateia Ágiou Spiridona 2110, Nafplio; 307.52.22.351; fax: 307.52.26.338; www.byronhotel.gr.

Companion Reading

Drama

Norman Cantor, in his recent book *Antiquity: The Civilization of the Ancient World* (HarperCollins, 2003), notes that Greek tragedies deal with one of three major themes: "The struggle of individual conscience and sensibility against the needs of the community and the power of the state; arrogance (*hubris*) that blinds the strong and self-righteous individual to possible misfortune and defeat; and endless series of bloody revenges triggered by mad acts rising from anger and sexual drive. In the hands of the dramatists, Aeschylus, Sophocles, and Euripides, they remain works of unsurpassed psychological grandeur." There are many, many books of Greek dramas and tragedies, too many to recommend here. If you'd like to reread a few or tackle some for the first time, visit a good bookstore or your local library and select an anthology or individual volumes that meet your reading expectations. Look for titles published by colleges and universities (the Ivy League schools all have classics departments, as do a handful of other schools in North

America) and by prolific translators, such as Bernard Knox, Robert Fagles, and David Grene.

Fiction

Little Infamies, Panos Karnezis, Farrar, Straus and Giroux, 2003.
The Magus, John Fowles, Little, Brown, 1965.
Middlesex: A Novel, Jeffrey Eugenides, Picador, 2003.
Nike: A Romance, Nicholas Flokos, Mariner Books, 1998.

Individual Authors

Elia Kazan

Readers may be more familiar with director Kazan's films, including *A Streetcar Named Desire, Death of a Salesman*, and *Cat on a Hot Tin Roof*, but his epic novels are quite good too.
America America, Stein and Day, 1974.
The Anatolian, Random House, 1984.
The Arrangement, Scarborough House, 1967.
Beyond the Aegean: A Novel, Alfred A. Knopf, 1994. The cover photo is of refugees fleeing the burning city of Smyrna, 1922.

Nikos Kazantzakis

At the Palaces of Knossos: A Novel, Ohio University Press, 1988.
The Last Temptation of Christ, Simon and Schuster, 1960.
Report to Greco, Simon and Schuster, 1975.
Zorba the Greek, Simon and Schuster, 1953.

Mary Renault

The Bull From the Sea, Pantheon, 1962, hardcover; Vintage, 1975, paperback.
The Charioteer, Random House, 1973, hardcover; Vintage, 2003, paperback.
Fire From Heaven, Pantheon, 1969, hardcover; Vintage, 2002, paperback.
The Friendly Young Ladies, Random House, 1987, hardcover; Vintage, 2003, paperback.
The King Must Die, Pantheon, 1958, hardcover; Vintage, 1988, paperback.
The Last of the Wine, Pantheon, 1956, hardcover; Vintage, 1975, paperback.
The Mask of Apollo, Vintage, 2003, paperback.
The Nature of Alexander, 1975, hardcover and 1976, paperback, both Pantheon.
The Persian Boy, Pantheon, 1972, hardcover; Vintage, 1988, paperback.
The Praise Singer, John Murray, 1979, hardcover; Vintage, 2003, paperback.

Vassílis Vassilikos

And Dreams Are Dreams, translated by Mary Kitroeff, Seven Stories Press, 1996.
The Few Things I Know About Glafkos Thrassakis, translated by Karen Emmerich, Seven Stories Press, 2002.
Z, Ballantine, 1969, paperback; Four Walls Eight Windows, 1999, hardcover.

Poetry

Modern Greek literature has a rich tradition where poetry is concerned, which is only to be expected from the nation that gave the world the epic form. Greece has produced two Nobel laureates in the field of literature, both poets: George Seferis in 1963, and Odysseus Elytis in 1979. Sadly, their work is largely out of print, but with a little effort many of their volumes can be found. A useful website, for those who are serious about reading the works of poets of the eighteenth, nineteenth, and early twentieth centuries, is www1.fhw.gr/chronos/12/en/1833_1897/civilization.come. This comprehensive site includes poets of the Heptanesian School, the First Athenian School, and the New Athenian School. (The only poets with which I am familiar are a few from this last group, notably Georgios Drossinis and Kostis Palamas.) Again, as with Greek drama, look for anthologies or translated works by David A. Campbell, Edmund Keeley, and Bernard Knox. I cannot, however, fail to mention two wonderful anthologies:

A Garden of Greek Verse, J. Paul Getty Museum, 2000. A beautifully illustrated, slender hardcover volume with ancient Greek verse and inspired translations. Slender enough to bring along.

Greece in Poetry, edited by Simoni Zafiropoulos, Harry N. Abrams, 1993. With gorgeous reproductions of paintings, drawings, photographs, and other works of art, this is one of the loveliest and most beautifully printed books I've ever seen. Among the ancient and contemporary poets featured are Aeschylus, Aristophanes, Lord Byron, Constantine Cavafy, Lawrence Durrell, Odysseus Elytis, Robert Graves, Homer, Kazantzakis, Keats, James Merrill, Ovid, Pindar, Sappho, Shelley, and Oscar Wilde. This is a must-have volume.

Individual Poets

Bacchylides

Complete Poems, Bacchylides, translated by Robert Fagles, Yale University Press, 1998.

Olga Broumas

Beginning With O, Yale University Press, 1977.
Black Holes/Black Stockings, Wesleyan University Press, 1985.

Ithaca: Little Summer in Winter, Radiolarian Press, 1996.

Perpetua, Copper Canyon Press, 1989.

Rave: Poems 1975–1999, Consortium, 1999.

Sappho's Gymnasium, Copper Canyon Press, 1994.

Constantine P. Cavafy (or Kavafy)

C. P. Cavafy, translated by W. H. Auden, Harcourt, Brace and World, 1961.

Essential Cavafy, translated by Edmund Keeley, Ecco, 1996.

Odysseus Elytis

The Collected Poems of Odysseus Elytis, translated by Jeffrey Carson and Nikko Sarris, John Hopkins University Press, 1997.

Eros, Eros, Eros, translated by Olga Broumas, Copper Canyon Press, 1998.

The Sovereign Sun: Selected Poems, translated by Kimon Fiar, Temple University Press, 1974.

Yannis Ritsos

Exile and Return: Selected Poems 1967–1974, translated by Edmund Keeley, Ecco, 1987.

Yannis Ritsos, translated by Edmund Keeley, Princeton University Press, 1991.

Sappho

If Not, Winter: Fragments of Sappho, translated by Anne Carson, Alfred A. Knopf, 2002. This beautifully produced book features the English translation opposite pages of the ancient Greek.

The Love Songs of Sappho, translated by Paul Roche, Prometheus Books, 1999.

George Seferis

A Poet's Journal: Days of 1945–1951, translated by Athan Anagnostopoulos, Replica Books, 2001.

George Seferis, translated by Edmund Keeley, Princeton University Press, 1995.

Three Secret Poems, translated by Walter Kaiser, Harvard University Press, 1969.

Design and Decorating

Greek Style, Suzanne Slesin, Stafford Cliff, and Daniel Rozensztroch, photographs by Gilles de Chabaneix, Clarkson Potter, 1988. This edition was the fifth to be published in the highly acclaimed, groundbreaking Style Library. It's a must-have resource for the architectural, design, and decorating details that are uniquely Greek. More than seven hundred beautiful color photos illustrate a variety of images of Greece and interiors of private homes and villas, both traditional and modern. A helpful eight-page Greek lexicon at the back has a list of the music, art, architecture, and food traditions of the country.

Other Good Things

~*Ancient Greece Knowledge Cards,* British Museum, Pomegranate. This nifty deck of cards draws on the vast resources of the British Museum, which are legendary. Each of the forty-eight cards has a color photograph of an antiquity that relates to a particular topic, addressed in a concise essay on the reverse.

~"Antiquity's Enduring Power," by Benedict Nightingale, *The New York Times,* August 12, 2001. For more than twenty years Nightingale and his wife have been traveling to Greece, and he has penned nearly as many articles about Greece for the travel section of the *Times.* In this one he outlines many of the amazing sites they've visited and the unforgettable experiences they've had in Greece, and he informs readers that they aren't finished yet. "What's the continuing appeal?" he asks. "For me, there are three main attractions, three reasons I keep returning to Greece. First, it's a place where one can stretch that underused muscle, the imagination. For ancient Greeks, a tree might be a dryad and a spring a water nymph. The sacred and miraculous were everywhere. . . . Second, serendipity. You can be driving through a dull modern city or a flinty landscape, and suddenly the place pulsates with history. . . . Third, texture, by which I mean horizontal richness: layer on layer of history." Nightingale also shares a short list of his favorite offbeat destinations, and among those in southern Greece are Néa Moní, on Chios; Mistra, on the Peloponnese; the views on the Cycladic island of Naxos; and Ermoúpolis, the port town of Syros in the Aegean. He wisely declines to name his favorite island, stating, "That changes. Ten years ago I would have said Patmos, whose great monastery dominates the landscape like its sinister counterpart in Umberto Eco's *Name of the Rose,* or the much larger, more diverse Chios. But after a brief affair with Siros, my wife and I seem to have plighted our troth to Naxos, which is supposed to have been Byron's favorite island . . . ask me ten, twenty years from now which part of Greece has my heart—and who knows what I'll answer."

~*The Greek Way,* Edith Hamilton, W.W. Norton, 1942. I know I referenced this book previously, in the *Kiosque—Points of View* section, but I am including it here for a different reason: to highlight a nugget of worthy wisdom that may be the best expression of the Greek character ever written: "To rejoice in life, to find the world beautiful and delightful to live in, was a mark of the Greek spirit which distinguished it from all that had gone before. It is a vital distinction. The joy of life is written upon everything the Greeks left behind and they who leave it out of account fail to reckon with something that is of first importance in understanding how the Greek achievement came to pass in the world of antiquity." I strive to remember this every day.

~*A Krater Full of Good Cheer,* Stavroula Kourakou-Dragona, translated by William Phelps, Lucy Braggiotti Editions, Athens, 2001. What a wonderful idea for a book—a history of Greek drinking vessels, amply illustrated, by a noted Greek oenologist. Kourakou-Dragona earned her doctorate in chemistry and studied oenology in France, and for twenty years she was director of the Institute of Wine, a Ministry of Agriculture foundation for technological research. She represented Greece at the Intergovernmental Organization of the Vine and Wine, based in Paris, from 1960 to 1979, and she is an international expert on the vine and wine in ancient Greek texts. This unique book, which I bought at the archaeology museum in Nafplio, is great fun to read and is filled with interesting facts and trivia. "The Greeks," Kourakou-Dragona writes, "were always sociable beings; they sought out friendly company, good conversation, singing, witty stories and the good life generally. For these reasons they did not like to eat and drink alone. They therefore began to organize banquets, which during the historical period grew into formal institutions with their own rules and etiquette. The social basis of the banquet, which the Greeks called a *symposion*, was associating with equals. The grouping was not based on blood ties or social dependency, but on equality and friendship. Thus the *symposion* which, as the word indicates, means drinking together, became an event where wine and good company were thoroughly enjoyed."

~*The Wisdom of Ancient Greece,* compiled by Jacques Lacarrière, Abbeville, 1996. This slender hardcover, one edition in Abbeville's *The Wisdom of* series, is a beautiful little book, great for gift giving or keeping for yourself. Words of Greek wisdom are paired with color photographs (also taken by Lacarrière) taken throughout Greece, making for an irresistible, inspiring volume.

additional credits

Practical Information: Victor Walker, *Collins Independent Travellers Guide: Mainland Greece,* 1988.

The Kiosque: Lawrence Durrell, *The Greek Islands,* Viking, 1978.

The Aegean Islands: Robert Eisner, *Travelers in an Antique Land: The History and Literature of Travel to Greece,* University of Michigan Press, 1991.

The Peloponnese: Elizabeth Boleman-Herring, *Vanishing Greece,* Conran Octopus, London, 1991.

The Greek Table: Aglaia Kremezi, *The Foods of Greece,* Stewart, Tabori & Chang, 1993. Rosemary Barron, *The Flavors of Greece,* William Morrow, 1991.

Good Things, Favorite Places: Lawrence Durrell, *The Greek Islands,* Viking, 1978.